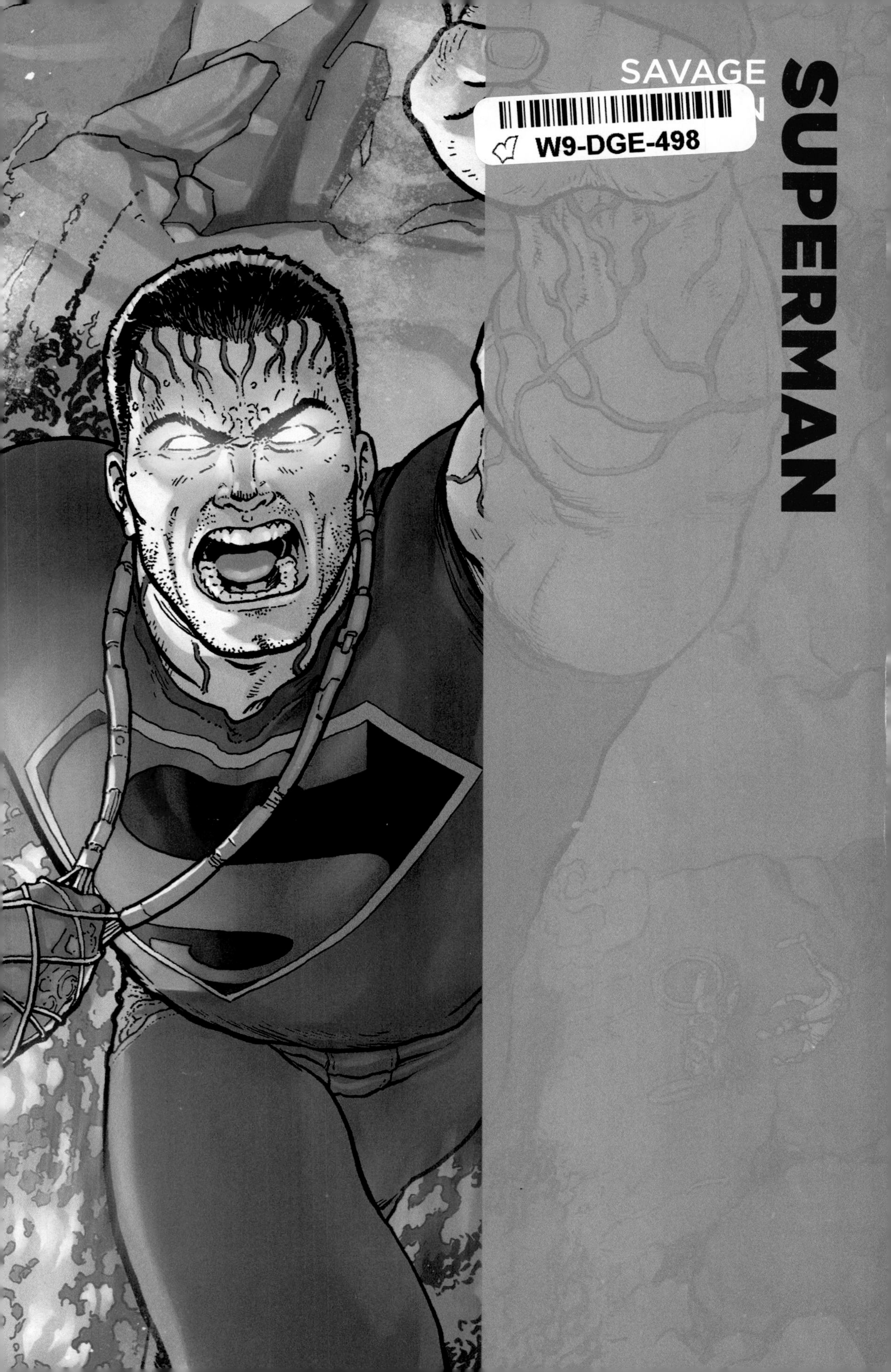
SAVAGE
N
W9-DGE-498
SUPERMAN

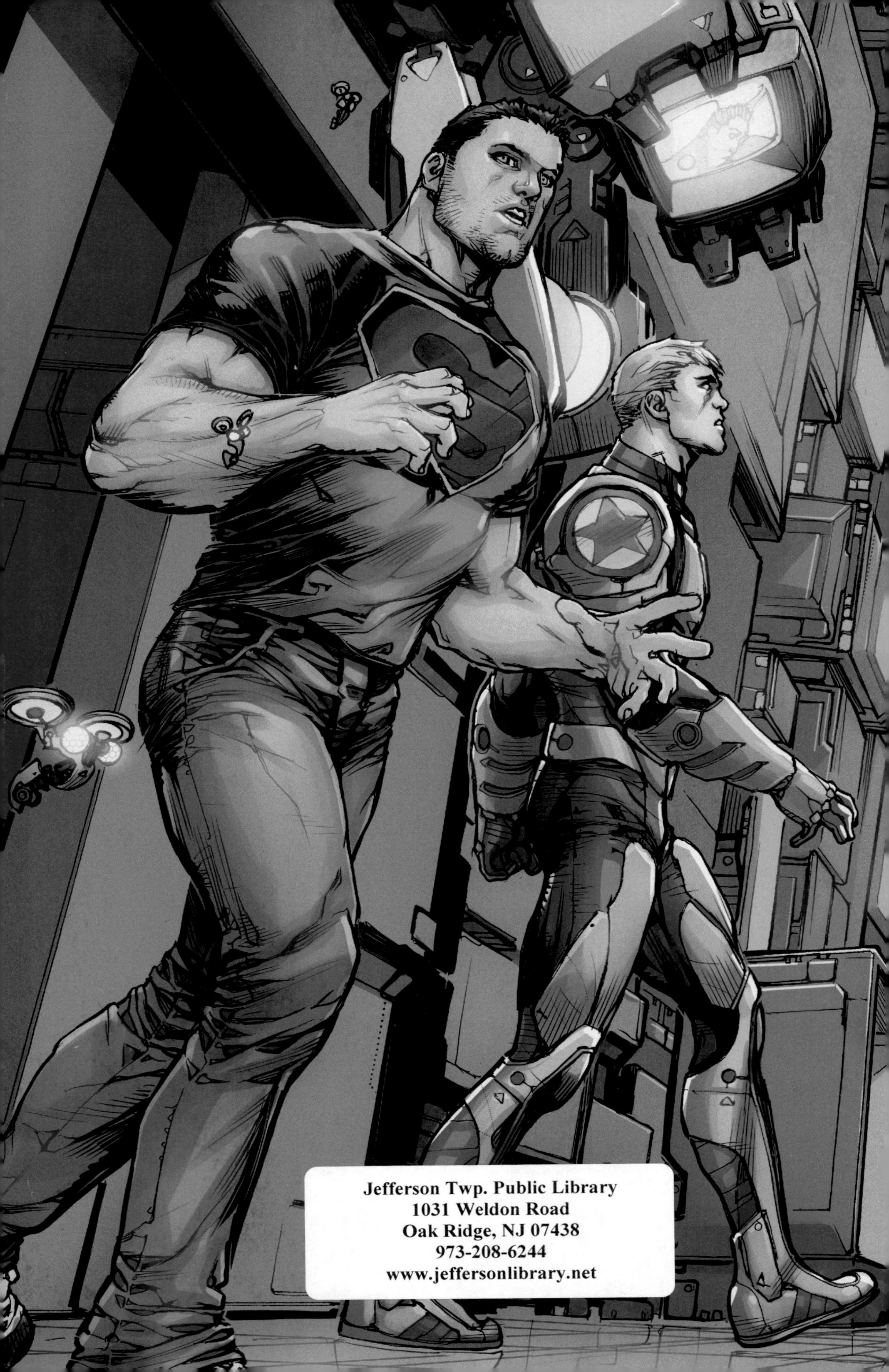

SAVAGE DAWN

WRITTEN BY
AARON KUDER GREG PAK
PETER J. TOMASI GENE LUEN YANG

LAYOUT ART BY
AARON KUDER

PENCILS BY
JON BOGDANOVE VICENTE CIFUENTES
JAVI FERNANDEZ AARON KUDER
JACK HERBERT DAN JURGENS DOUG MAHNKE
DAVID MESSINA BEN OLIVER HOWARD PORTER
BRUNO REDONDO CLIFF RICHARDS
RAFA SANDOVAL ARDIAN SYAF
PATRICK ZIRCHER

INKS BY
JUAN ALBARRAN JON BOGDANOVE
GAETANO CARLUCCI VICENTE CIFUENTES
JAVI FERNANDEZ JONATHAN GLAPION
SCOTT HANNA JACK HERBERT DON HO
SANDRA HOPE AARON KUDER
HOWARD PORTER DOUG MAHNKE
JAIME MENDOZA JEROME K. MOORE
BEN OLIVER CLIFF RICHARDS
BILL SIENKIEWICZ ARDIAN SYAF
JORDI TARRAGONA PATRICK ZIRCHER

COLORS BY
BLOND HI-FI LEE LOUGHRIDGE
TOMEU MOREY TRISH MULVIHILL
BEN OLIVER ARIF PRIANTO
WIL QUINTANA

LETTERS BY
A LARGER WORLD STUDIOS
ROB LEIGH STEVE WANDS

COLLECTION COVER ART BY
AARON KUDER TOMEU MOREY

SUPERMAN CREATED BY
JERRY SIEGEL
AND **JOE SHUSTER**
BY SPECIAL ARRANGEMENT WITH THE JERRY SIEGEL FAMILY

WONDER WOMAN CREATED BY
WILLIAM MOULTON MARSTON

SUPERMAN

DAVID WOHL Editor – Original Content
ANDREW MARINO Assistant Editor – Original Series
EDDIE BERGANZA Group Editor – Original Series
JEB WOODARD Group Editor – Collected Editions
SUZANNAH ROWNTREE Editor – Collected Edition
STEVE COOK Design Director – Books
DAMIAN RYLAND Publication Design

BOB HARRAS Senior VP – Editor-in-Chief, DC Comics

DIANE NELSON President
DAN DiDIO Publisher
JIM LEE Publisher
GEOFF JOHNS President & Chief Creative Officer
AMIT DESAI Executive VP – Business & Marketing Strategy,
Direct to Consumer & Global Franchise Management
SAM ADES Senior VP – Direct to Consumer
BOBBIE CHASE VP – Talent Development
MARK CHIARELLO Senior VP – Art, Design & Collected Editions
JOHN CUNN!NGHAM Senior VP – Sales & Trade Marketing
ANNE DePIES Senior VP – Business Strategy, Finance & Administration
DON FALLETTI VP – Manufacturing Operations
LAWRENCE GANEM VP – Editorial Administration & Talent Relations
ALISON GILL Senior VP – Manufacturing & Operations
HANK KANALZ Senior VP – Editorial Strategy & Administration
JAY KOGAN VP – Legal Affairs
THOMAS LOFTUS VP – Business Affairs
JACK MAHAN VP – Business Affairs
NICK J. NAPOLITANO VP – Manufacturing Administration
EDDIE SCANNELL VP – Consumer Marketing
COURTNEY SIMMONS Senior VP – Publicity & Communications
JIM (SKI) SOKOLOWSKI VP – Comic Book Specialty Sales & Trade Marketing
NANCY SPEARS VP – Mass, Book, Digital Sales & Trade Marketing

SUPERMAN: SAVAGE DAWN

DC Comics, 2900 West Alameda Ave., Burbank, CA 91505
Printed by LSC Communications, Owensville, MO, USA. 6/30/17. First Printing.
ISBN: 978-1-4012-7125-1

Library of Congress Cataloging-in-Publication Data is available.

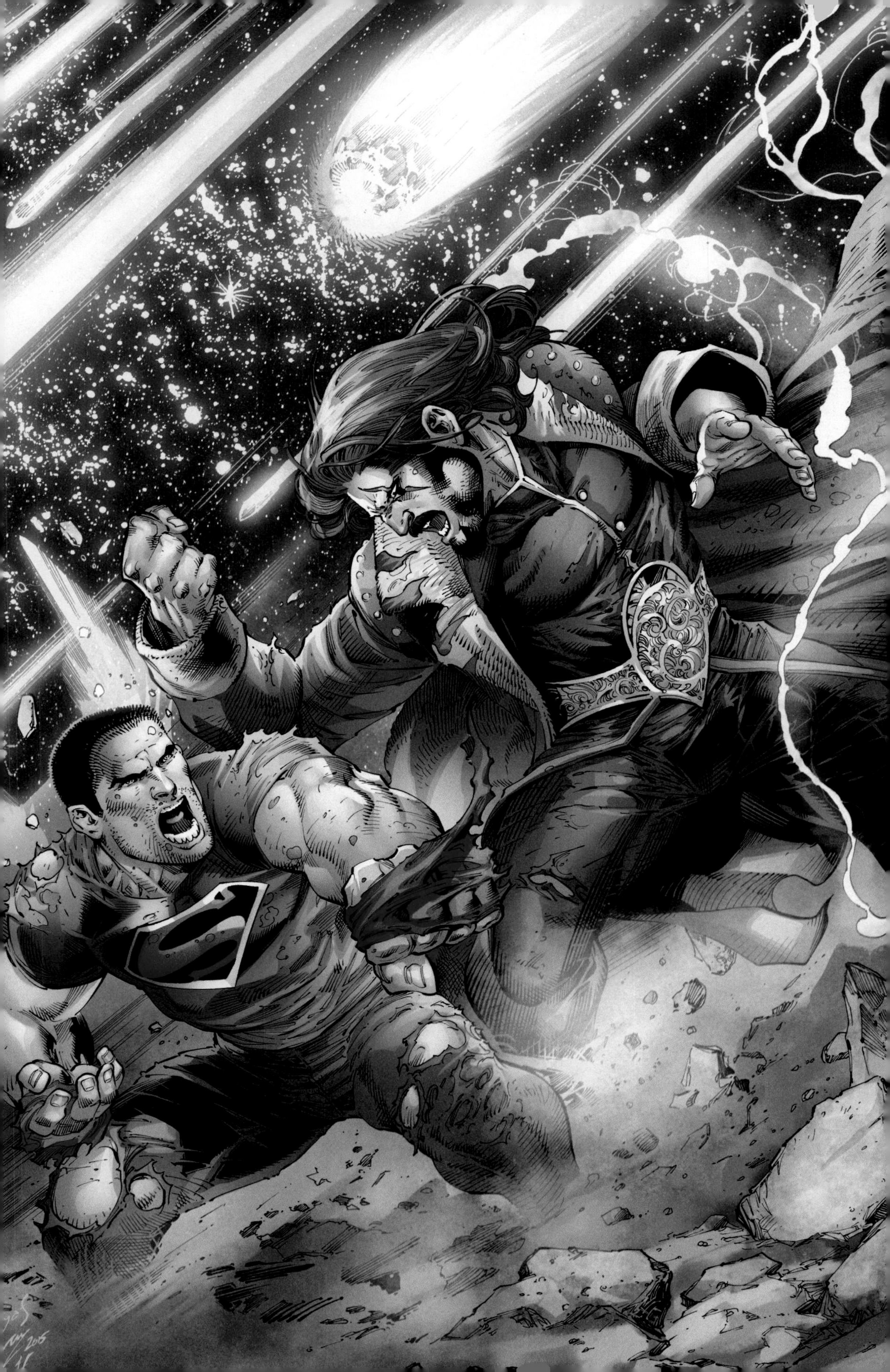

SAVAGE DAWN

GREG PAK GENE LUEN YANG PETER J. TOMASI AARON KUDER writers DAN JURGENS RAFA SANDOVAL BEN OLIVER pencillers BILL SIENKIEWICZ BEN OLIVER inkers TRISH MULVIHILL LEE LOUGHRIDGE TOMEU MOREY BEN OLIVER colorists A LARGER WORLD STUDIOS letterer ARDIAN SYAF VICENTE CIFUENTES ULISES ARREOLA cover

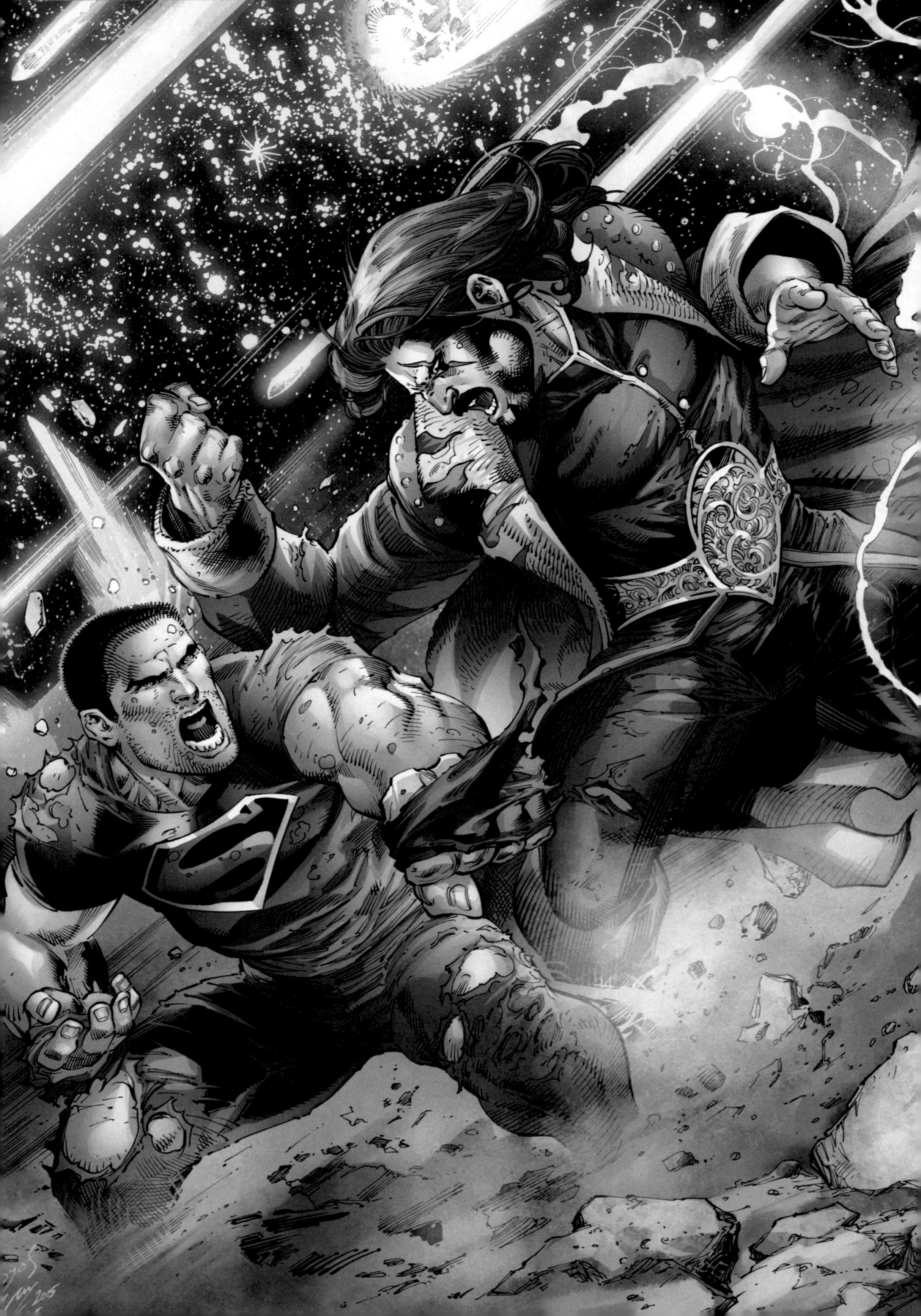

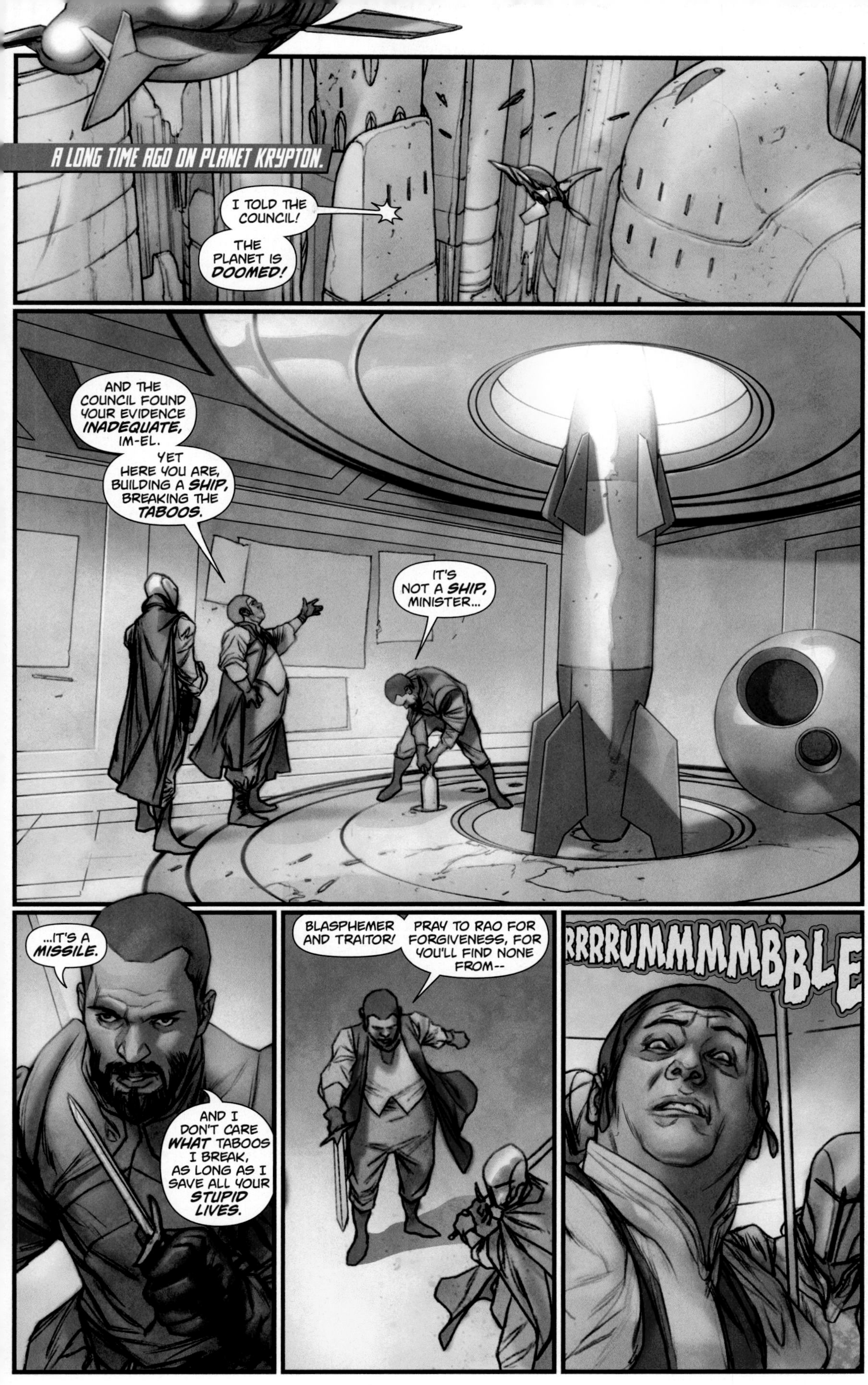

A LONG TIME AGO ON PLANET KRYPTON.
I TOLD THE COUNCIL!
THE PLANET IS DOOMED!
AND THE COUNCIL FOUND YOUR EVIDENCE INADEQUATE, IM-EL.
YET HERE YOU ARE, BUILDING A SHIP, BREAKING THE TABOOS.
IT'S NOT A SHIP, MINISTER...
...IT'S A MISSILE.
AND I DON'T CARE WHAT TABOOS I BREAK, AS LONG AS I SAVE ALL YOUR STUPID LIVES.
BLASPHEMER AND TRAITOR!
PRAY TO RAO FOR FORGIVENESS, FOR YOU'LL FIND NONE FROM--
RRRRUMMMMMBBLE

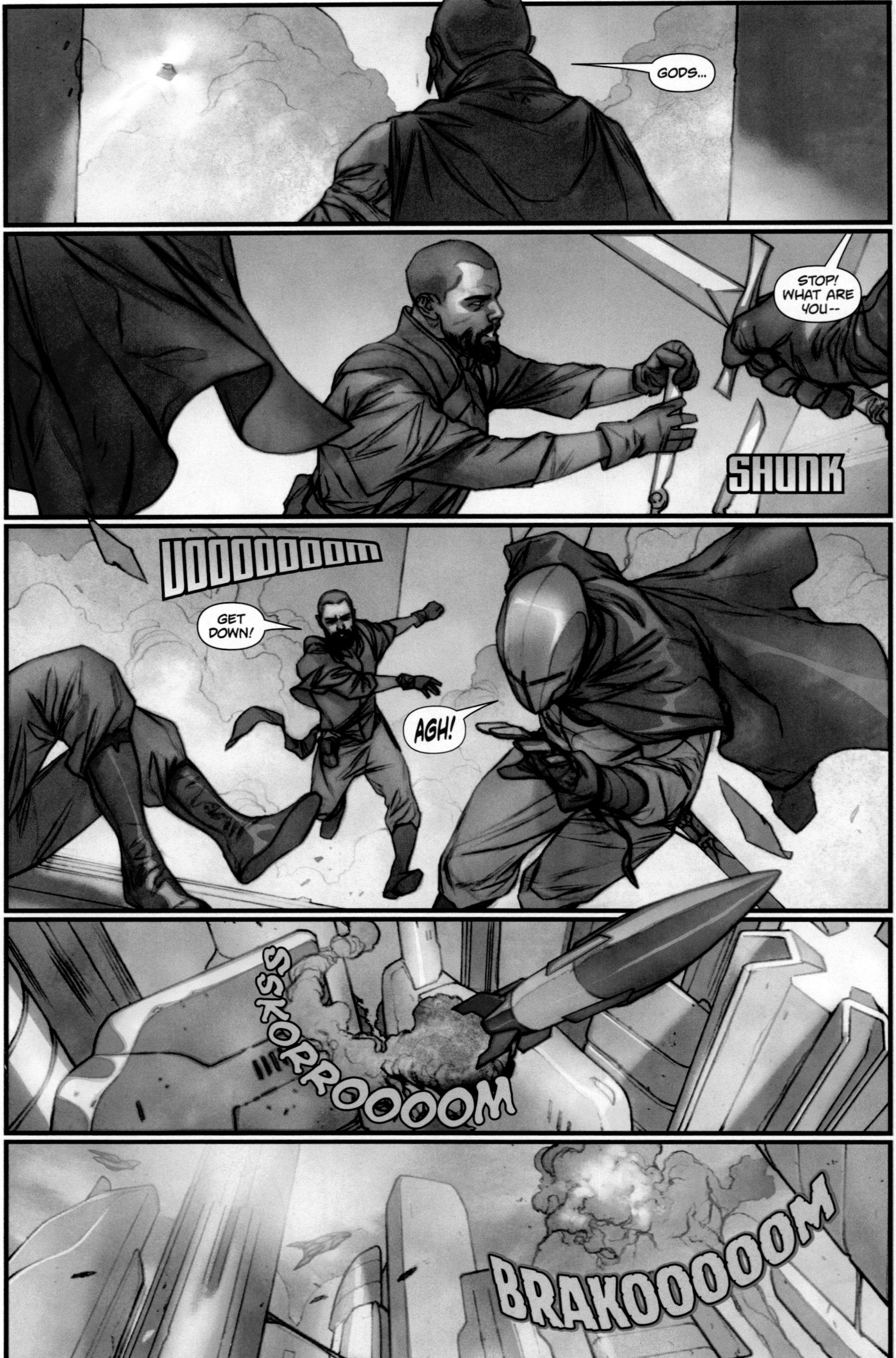
GODS...
STOP! WHAT ARE YOU--
SHUNK
VOOOOOOOOM
GET DOWN!
AGH!
SSKORROOOOM
BRAKOOOOOOM

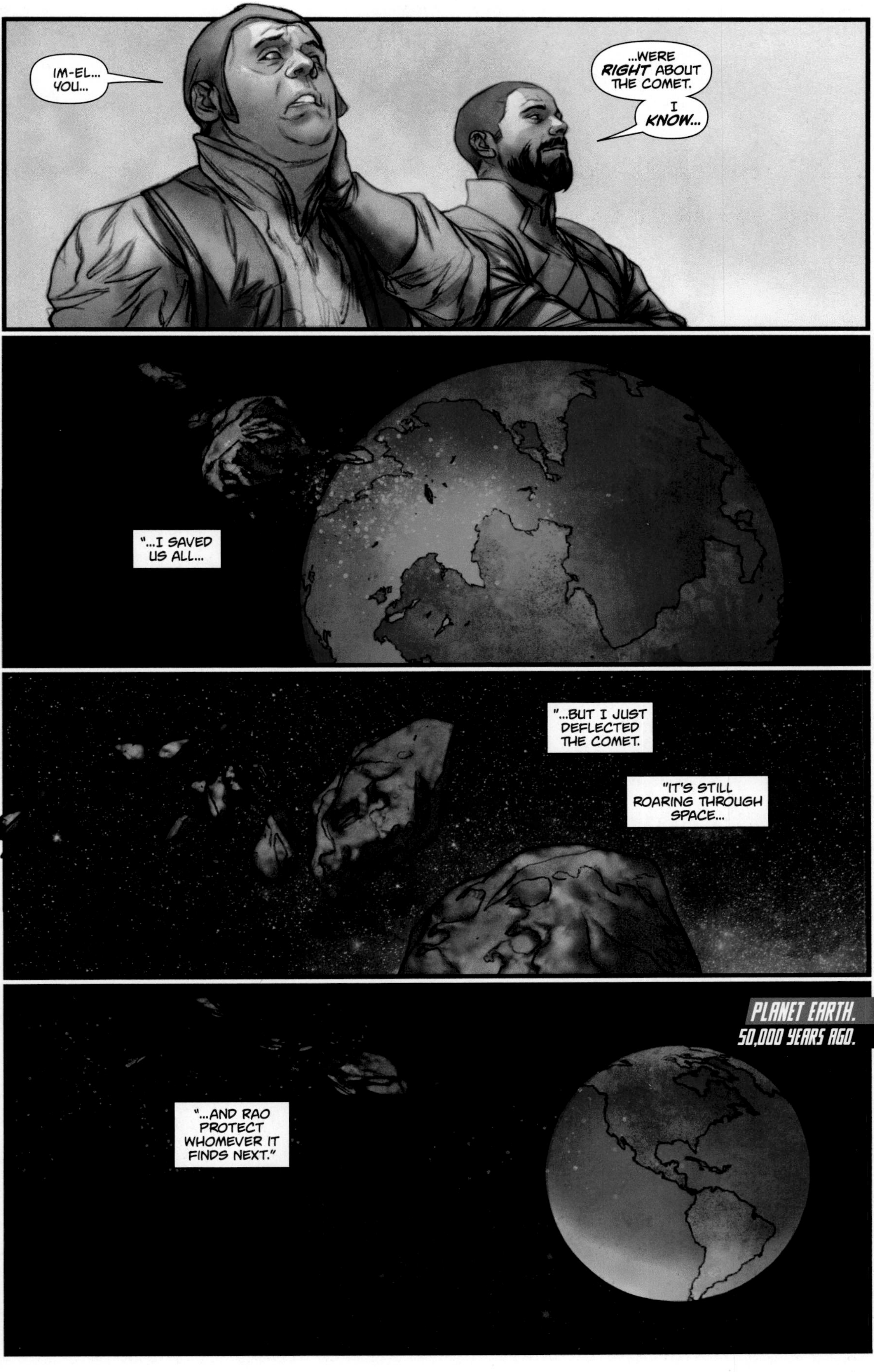
IM-EL... YOU...
...WERE RIGHT ABOUT THE COMET.
I KNOW...
"...I SAVED US ALL...
"...BUT I JUST DEFLECTED THE COMET.
"IT'S STILL ROARING THROUGH SPACE...
PLANET EARTH.
50,000 YEARS AGO.
"...AND RAO PROTECT WHOMEVER IT FINDS NEXT."

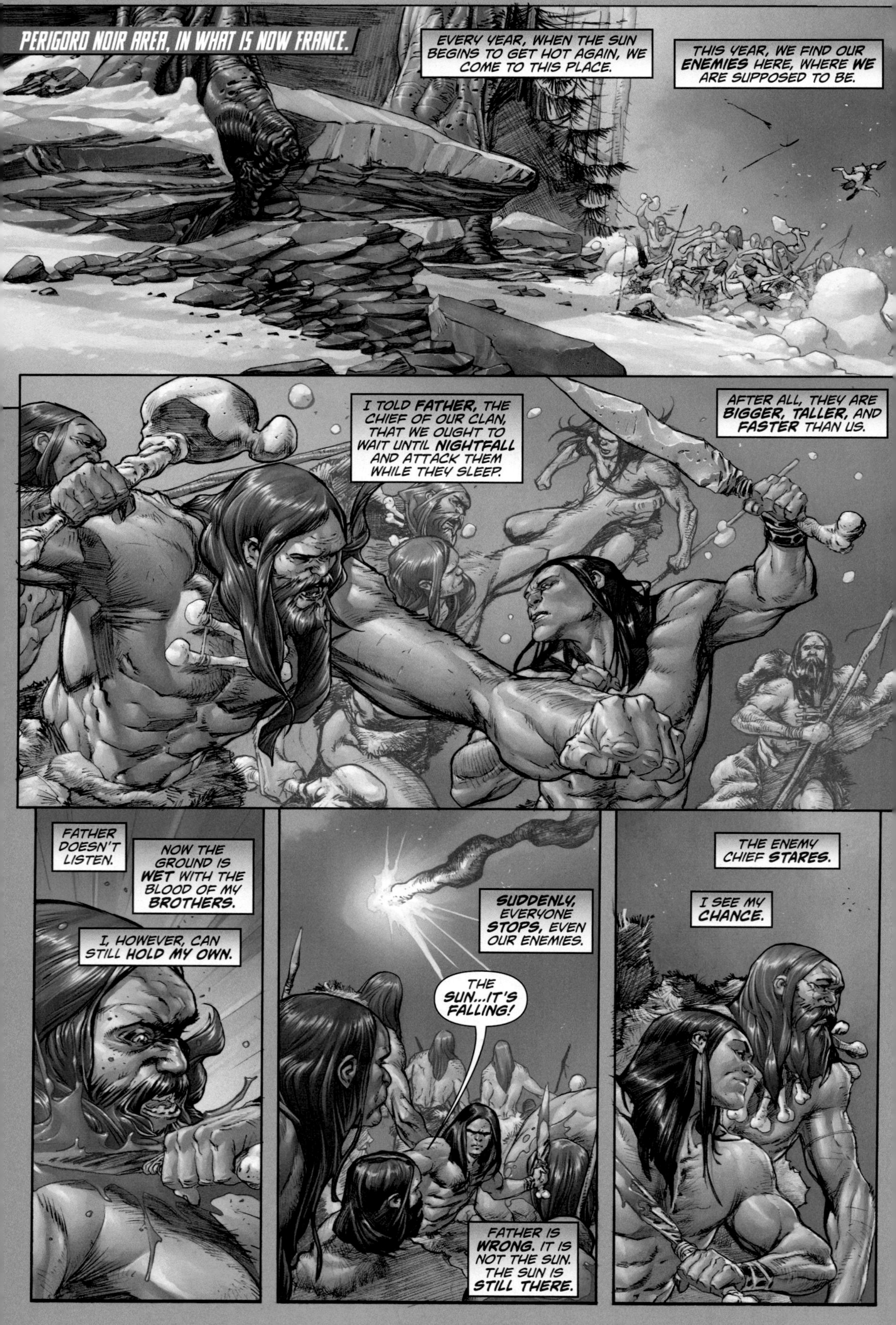
PERIGORD NOIR AREA, IN WHAT IS NOW FRANCE.
EVERY YEAR, WHEN THE SUN BEGINS TO GET HOT AGAIN, WE COME TO THIS PLACE.
THIS YEAR, WE FIND OUR ENEMIES HERE, WHERE WE ARE SUPPOSED TO BE.
I TOLD FATHER, THE CHIEF OF OUR CLAN, THAT WE OUGHT TO WAIT UNTIL NIGHTFALL AND ATTACK THEM WHILE THEY SLEEP.
AFTER ALL, THEY ARE BIGGER, TALLER, AND FASTER THAN US.
FATHER DOESN'T LISTEN.
NOW THE GROUND IS WET WITH THE BLOOD OF MY BROTHERS.
I, HOWEVER, CAN STILL HOLD MY OWN.
SUDDENLY, EVERYONE STOPS, EVEN OUR ENEMIES.
THE SUN...IT'S FALLING!
FATHER IS WRONG. IT IS NOT THE SUN. THE SUN IS STILL THERE.
THE ENEMY CHIEF STARES.
I SEE MY CHANCE.

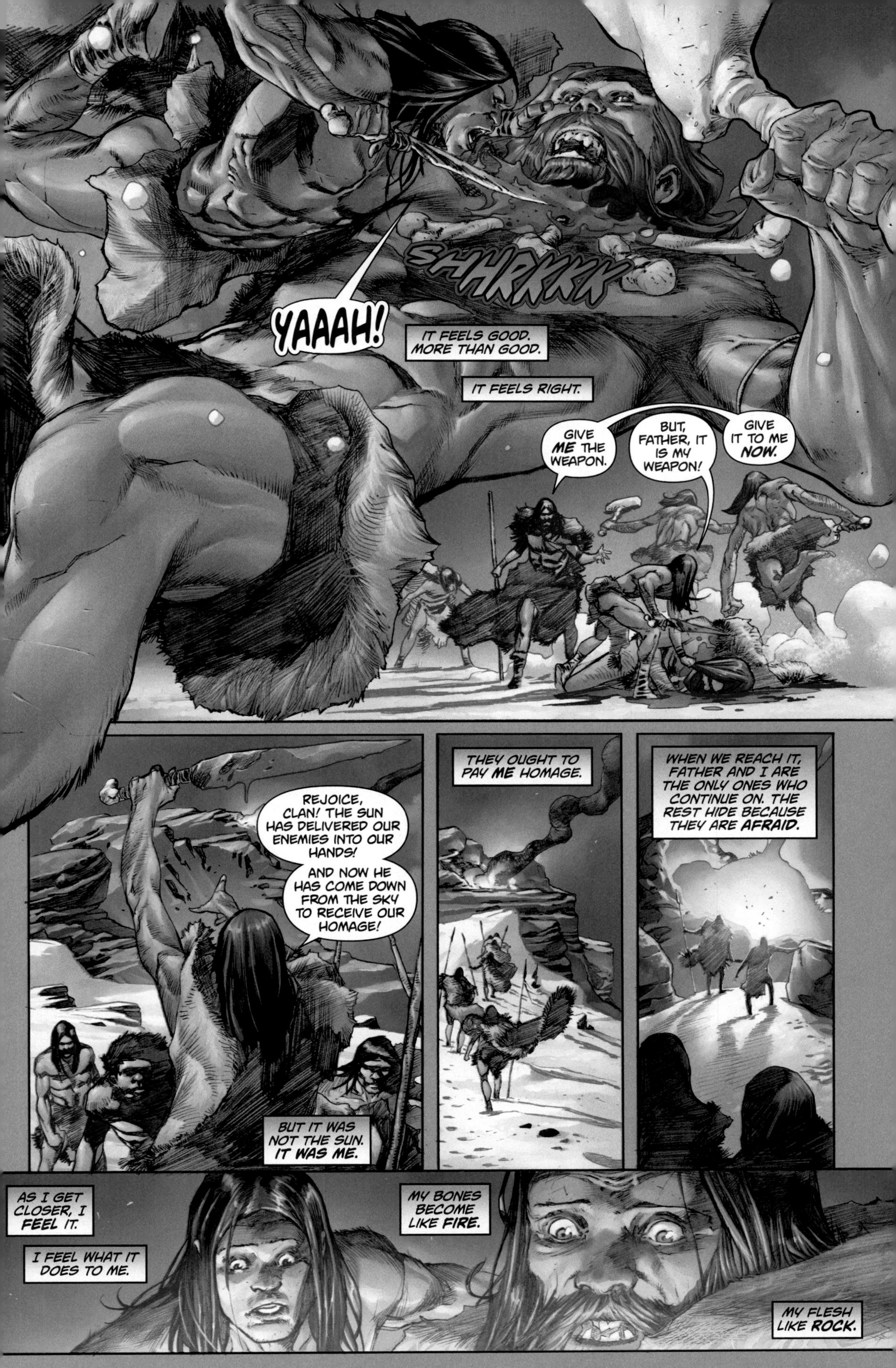
SHHRKKK
YAAAH!
IT FEELS GOOD. MORE THAN GOOD.
IT FEELS RIGHT.
GIVE ME THE WEAPON.
BUT, FATHER, IT IS MY WEAPON!
GIVE IT TO ME NOW.
REJOICE, CLAN! THE SUN HAS DELIVERED OUR ENEMIES INTO OUR HANDS!
AND NOW HE HAS COME DOWN FROM THE SKY TO RECEIVE OUR HOMAGE!
BUT IT WAS NOT THE SUN. IT WAS ME.
THEY OUGHT TO PAY ME HOMAGE.
WHEN WE REACH IT, FATHER AND I ARE THE ONLY ONES WHO CONTINUE ON. THE REST HIDE BECAUSE THEY ARE AFRAID.
AS I GET CLOSER, I FEEL IT.
I FEEL WHAT IT DOES TO ME.
MY BONES BECOME LIKE FIRE.
MY FLESH LIKE ROCK.

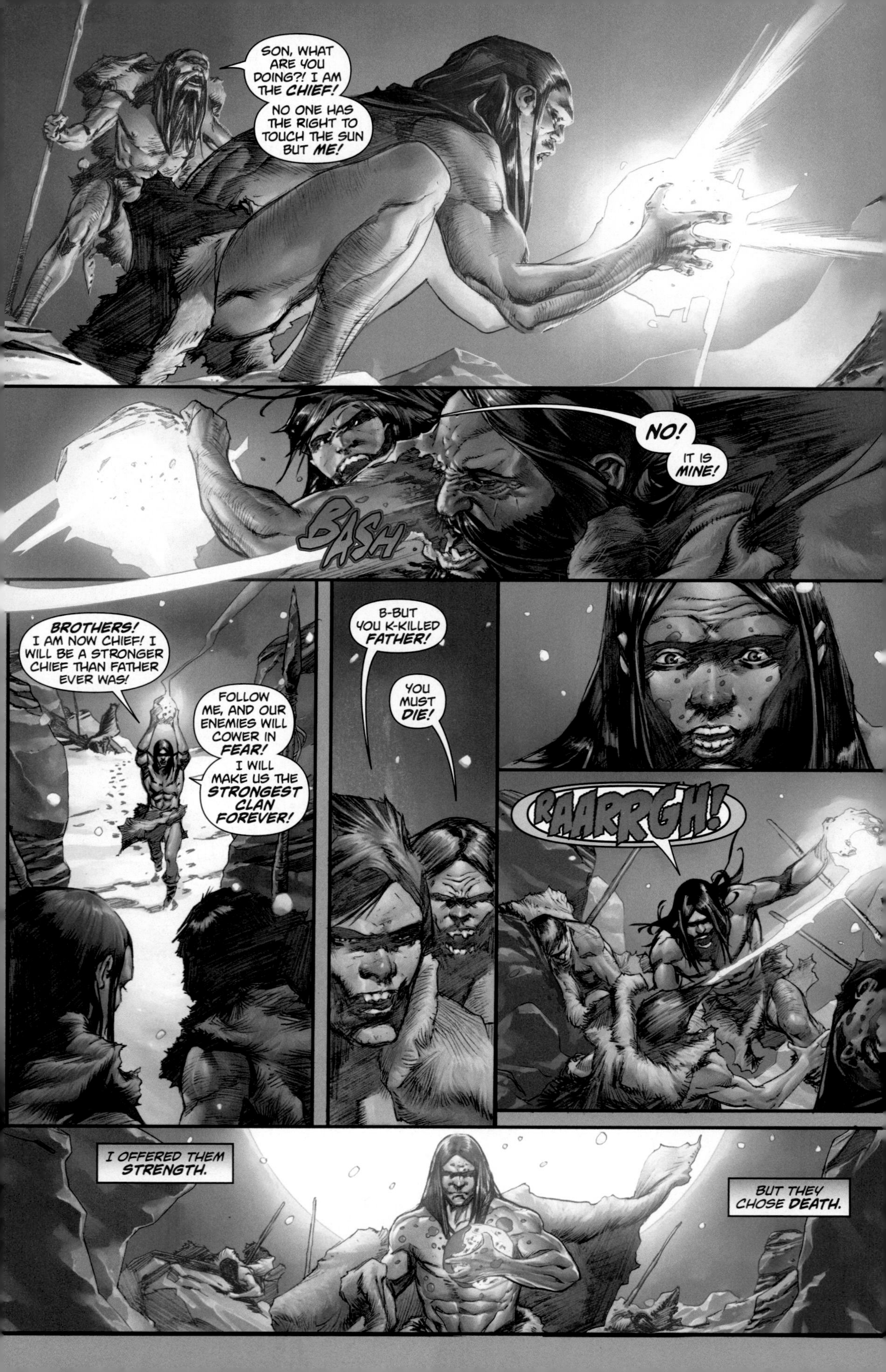

SON, WHAT ARE YOU DOING?! I AM THE CHIEF!
NO ONE HAS THE RIGHT TO TOUCH THE SUN BUT ME!
NO!
IT IS MINE!
BASH
BROTHERS! I AM NOW CHIEF! I WILL BE A STRONGER CHIEF THAN FATHER EVER WAS!
FOLLOW ME, AND OUR ENEMIES WILL COWER IN FEAR!
I WILL MAKE US THE STRONGEST CLAN FOREVER!
B-BUT YOU K-KILLED FATHER!
YOU MUST DIE!
RAARRGH!
I OFFERED THEM STRENGTH.
BUT THEY CHOSE DEATH.

BIP BIP BOOP BIP

HEE!

SO HERE'S MY NEW LIFE.

THE WHOLE WORLD KNOWS I'M *CLARK KENT* AND I'VE LOST MOST OF MY *POWERS*...

SKRAKOOOM

UFF!

...BUT WHEN A HIGH-TECH ROBOT STEALS A HIGH-TECH GIZMO FROM A HIGH-TECH LAB...

...AND I'M THE GUY ON THE STREET WHO FINDS OUT ABOUT IT FIRST...

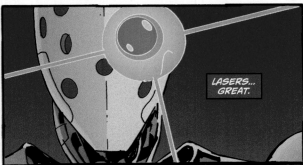

LASERS... GREAT.

MAY NOT HAVE MY POWERS, BUT...

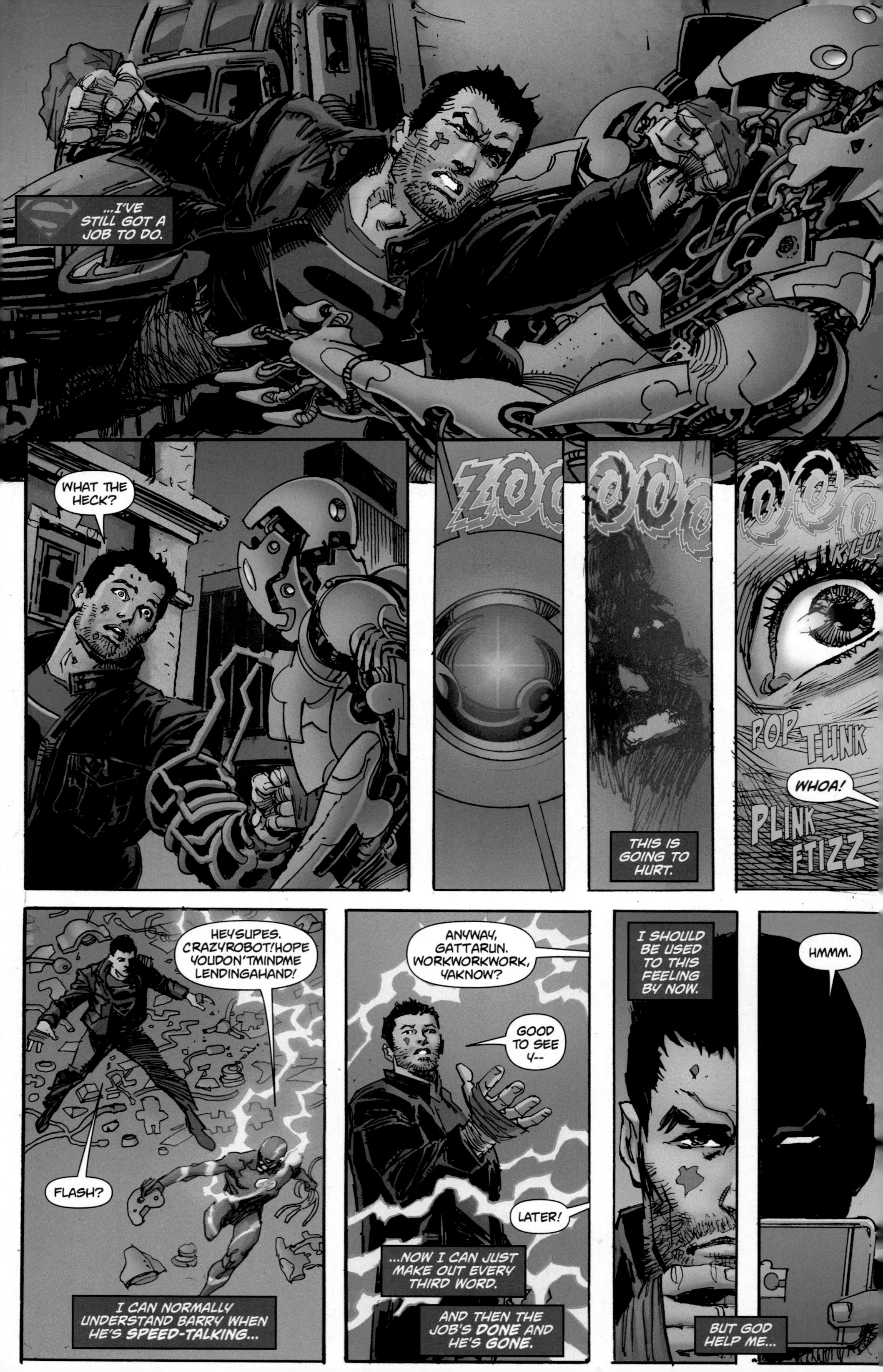
...I'VE STILL GOT A JOB TO DO.
WHAT THE HECK?
ZOOOOOOOOO
THIS IS GOING TO HURT.
KLU
POP TUNK
WHOA!
PLINK FTIZZ
HEYSUPES. CRAZYROBOT!HOPE YOUDON'TMINDME LENDINGAHAND!
FLASH?
I CAN NORMALLY UNDERSTAND BARRY WHEN HE'S SPEED-TALKING...
ANYWAY, GATTARUN. WORKWORKWORK, YAKNOW?
GOOD TO SEE Y--
LATER!
...NOW I CAN JUST MAKE OUT EVERY THIRD WORD.
AND THEN THE JOB'S DONE AND HE'S GONE.
I SHOULD BE USED TO THIS FEELING BY NOW.
HMMM.
BUT GOD HELP ME...

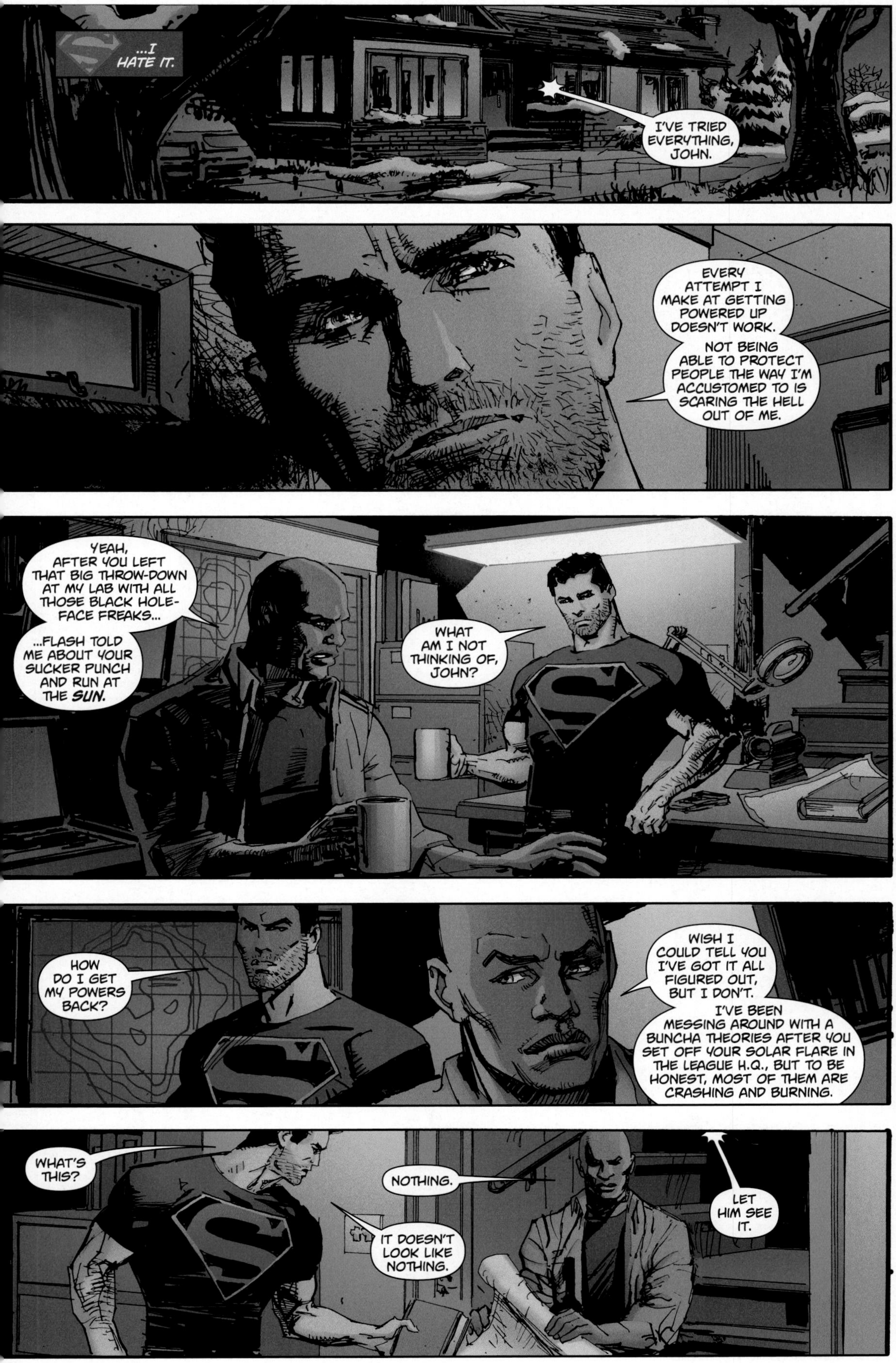
...I HATE IT.
I'VE TRIED EVERYTHING, JOHN.
EVERY ATTEMPT I MAKE AT GETTING POWERED UP DOESN'T WORK.
NOT BEING ABLE TO PROTECT PEOPLE THE WAY I'M ACCUSTOMED TO IS SCARING THE HELL OUT OF ME.
YEAH, AFTER YOU LEFT THAT BIG THROW-DOWN AT MY LAB WITH ALL THOSE BLACK HOLE-FACE FREAKS...
...FLASH TOLD ME ABOUT YOUR SUCKER PUNCH AND RUN AT THE SUN.
WHAT AM I NOT THINKING OF, JOHN?
HOW DO I GET MY POWERS BACK?
WISH I COULD TELL YOU I'VE GOT IT ALL FIGURED OUT, BUT I DON'T.
I'VE BEEN MESSING AROUND WITH A BUNCHA THEORIES AFTER YOU SET OFF YOUR SOLAR FLARE IN THE LEAGUE H.Q., BUT TO BE HONEST, MOST OF THEM ARE CRASHING AND BURNING.
WHAT'S THIS?
NOTHING.
IT DOESN'T LOOK LIKE NOTHING.
LET HIM SEE IT.

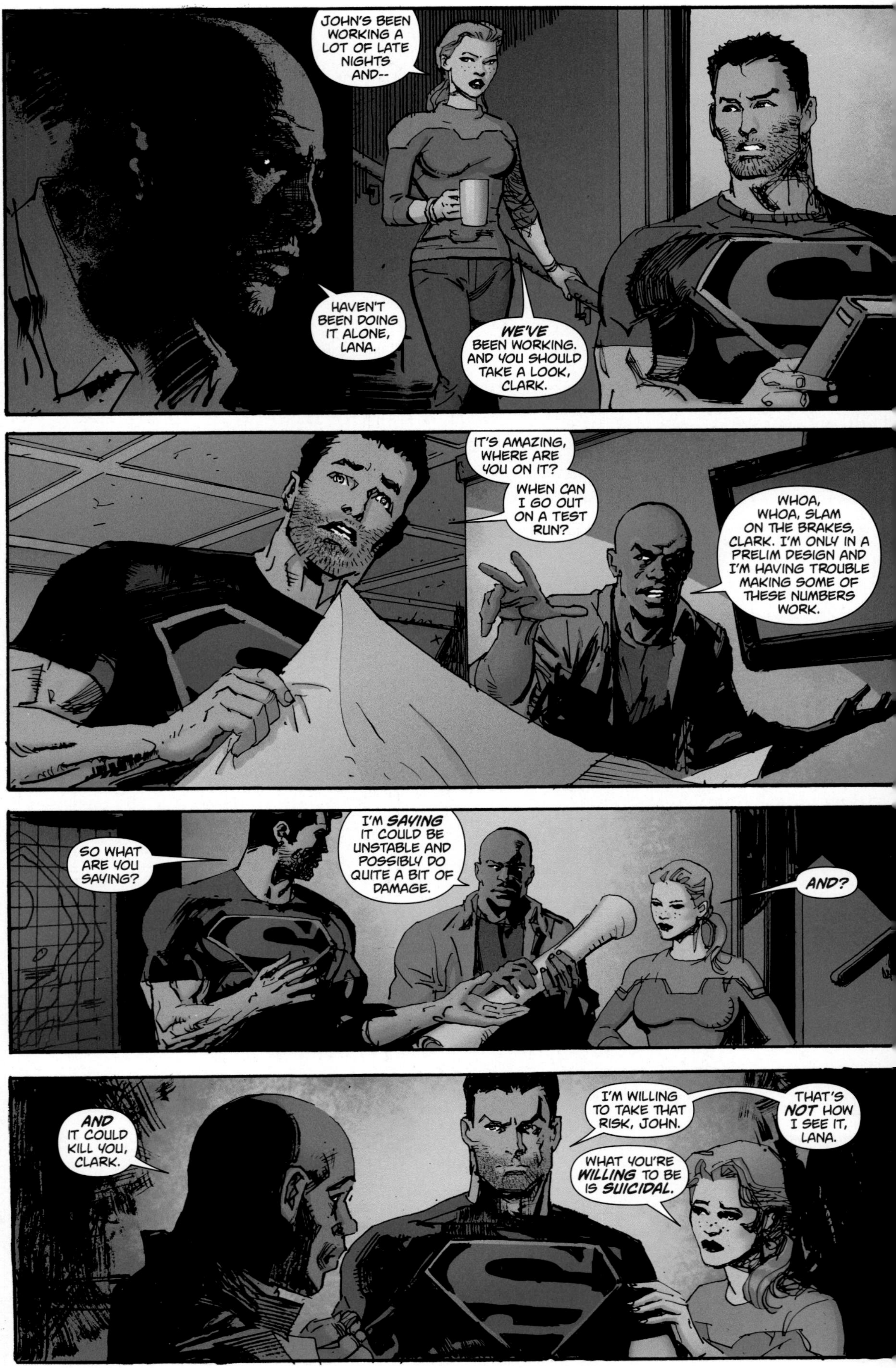
JOHN'S BEEN WORKING A LOT OF LATE NIGHTS AND--
HAVEN'T BEEN DOING IT ALONE, LANA.
WE'VE BEEN WORKING. AND YOU SHOULD TAKE A LOOK, CLARK.
IT'S AMAZING, WHERE ARE YOU ON IT?
WHEN CAN I GO OUT ON A TEST RUN?
WHOA, WHOA, SLAM ON THE BRAKES, CLARK. I'M ONLY IN A PRELIM DESIGN AND I'M HAVING TROUBLE MAKING SOME OF THESE NUMBERS WORK.
SO WHAT ARE YOU SAYING?
I'M SAYING IT COULD BE UNSTABLE AND POSSIBLY DO QUITE A BIT OF DAMAGE.
AND?
AND IT COULD KILL YOU, CLARK.
I'M WILLING TO TAKE THAT RISK, JOHN.
THAT'S NOT HOW I SEE IT, LANA.
WHAT YOU'RE WILLING TO BE IS SUICIDAL.

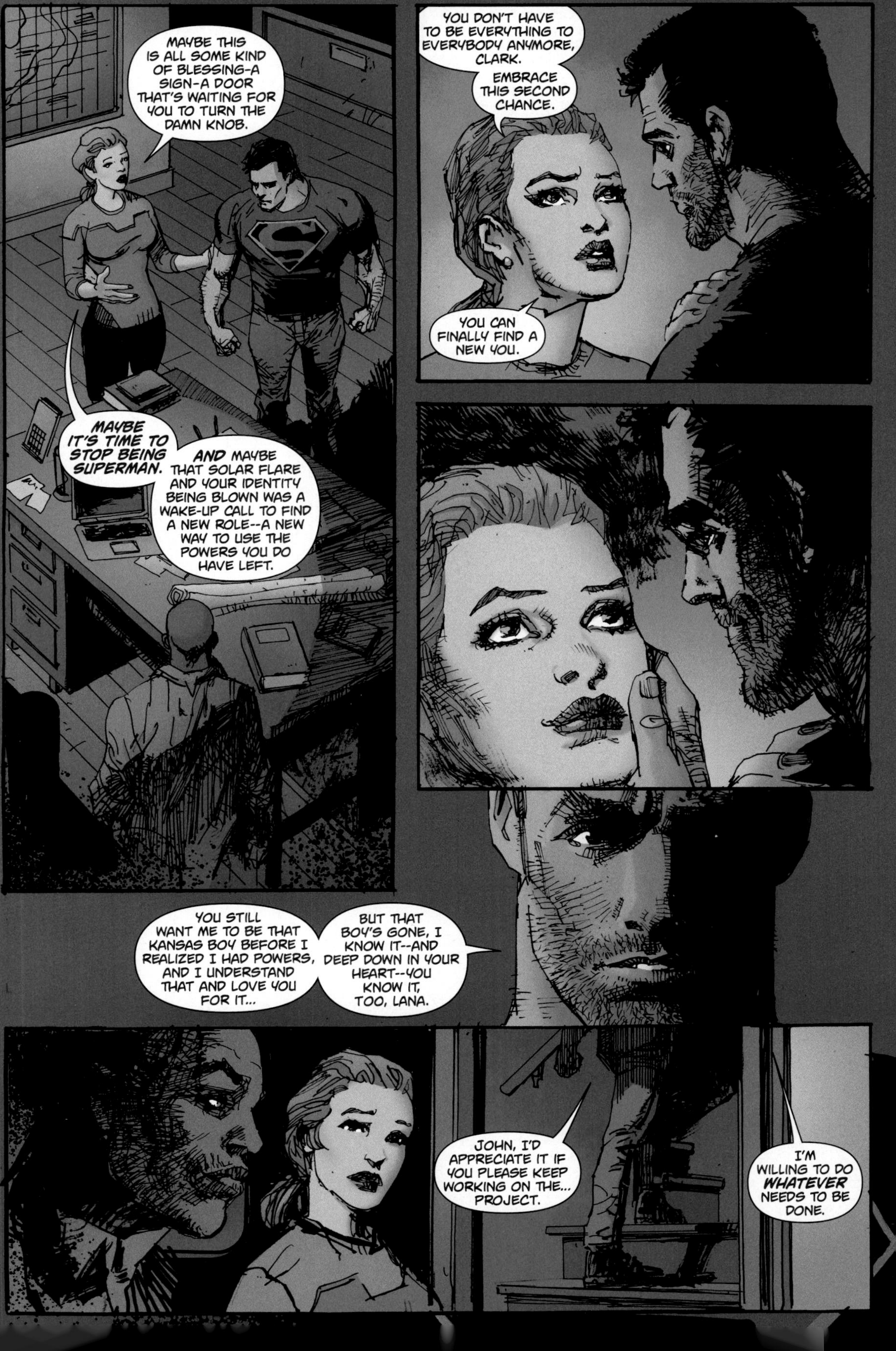
MAYBE THIS IS ALL SOME KIND OF BLESSING-A SIGN-A DOOR THAT'S WAITING FOR YOU TO TURN THE DAMN KNOB.
MAYBE IT'S TIME TO STOP BEING SUPERMAN.
AND MAYBE THAT SOLAR FLARE AND YOUR IDENTITY BEING BLOWN WAS A WAKE-UP CALL TO FIND A NEW ROLE--A NEW WAY TO USE THE POWERS YOU DO HAVE LEFT.
YOU DON'T HAVE TO BE EVERYTHING TO EVERYBODY ANYMORE, CLARK.
EMBRACE THIS SECOND CHANCE.
YOU CAN FINALLY FIND A NEW YOU.
YOU STILL WANT ME TO BE THAT KANSAS BOY BEFORE I REALIZED I HAD POWERS, AND I UNDERSTAND THAT AND LOVE YOU FOR IT...
BUT THAT BOY'S GONE, I KNOW IT--AND DEEP DOWN IN YOUR HEART--YOU KNOW IT, TOO, LANA.
JOHN, I'D APPRECIATE IT IF YOU PLEASE KEEP WORKING ON THE... PROJECT.
I'M WILLING TO DO WHATEVER NEEDS TO BE DONE.

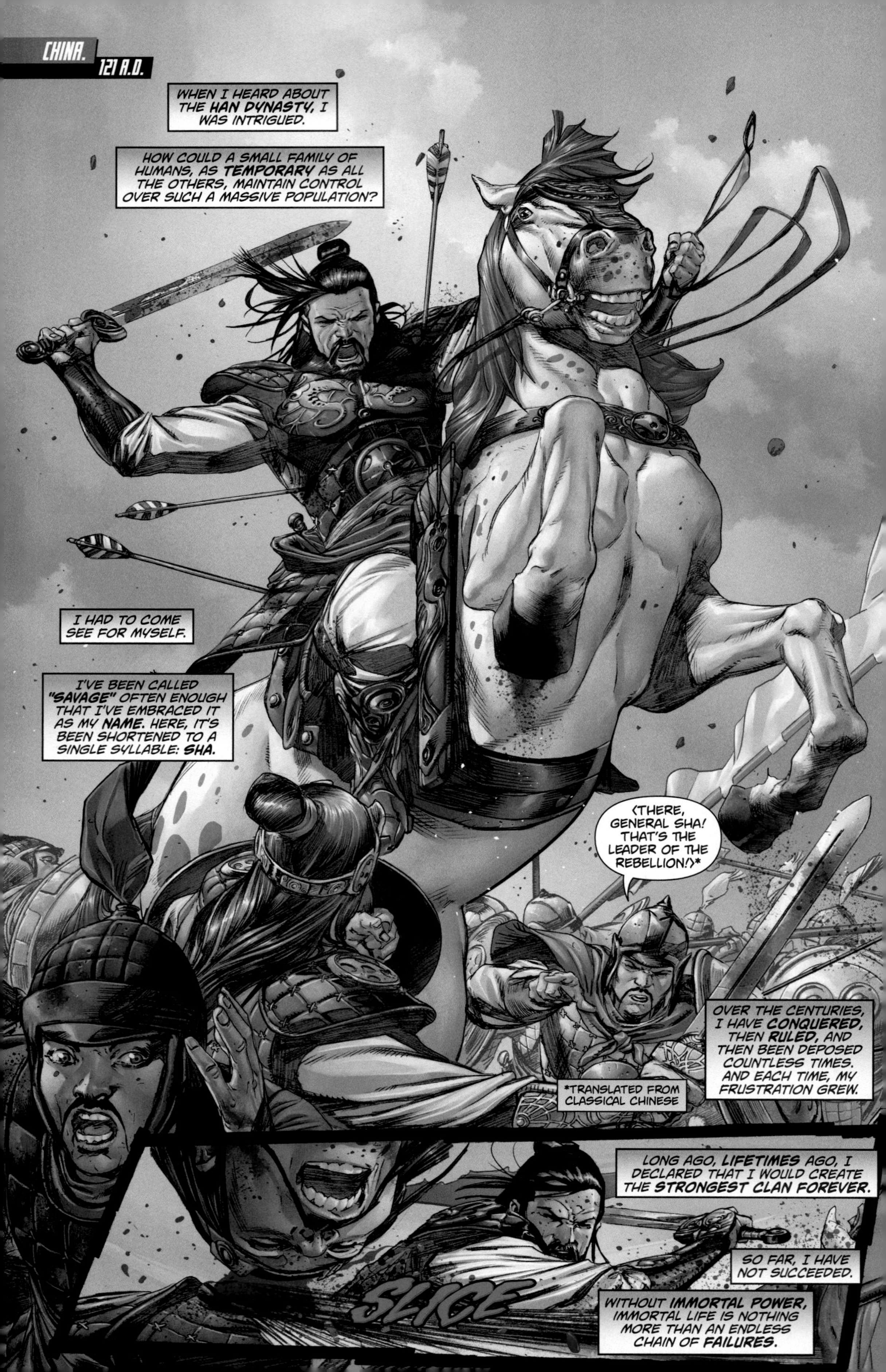
CHINA.
121 A.D.
WHEN I HEARD ABOUT THE HAN DYNASTY, I WAS INTRIGUED.
HOW COULD A SMALL FAMILY OF HUMANS, AS TEMPORARY AS ALL THE OTHERS, MAINTAIN CONTROL OVER SUCH A MASSIVE POPULATION?
I HAD TO COME SEE FOR MYSELF.
I'VE BEEN CALLED "SAVAGE" OFTEN ENOUGH THAT I'VE EMBRACED IT AS MY NAME. HERE, IT'S BEEN SHORTENED TO A SINGLE SYLLABLE: SHA.
⟨THERE, GENERAL SHA! THAT'S THE LEADER OF THE REBELLION!⟩*
OVER THE CENTURIES, I HAVE CONQUERED, THEN RULED, AND THEN BEEN DEPOSED COUNTLESS TIMES. AND EACH TIME, MY FRUSTRATION GREW.
*TRANSLATED FROM CLASSICAL CHINESE
LONG AGO, LIFETIMES AGO, I DECLARED THAT I WOULD CREATE THE STRONGEST CLAN FOREVER.
SO FAR, I HAVE NOT SUCCEEDED.
SLICE
WITHOUT IMMORTAL POWER, IMMORTAL LIFE IS NOTHING MORE THAN AN ENDLESS CHAIN OF FAILURES.

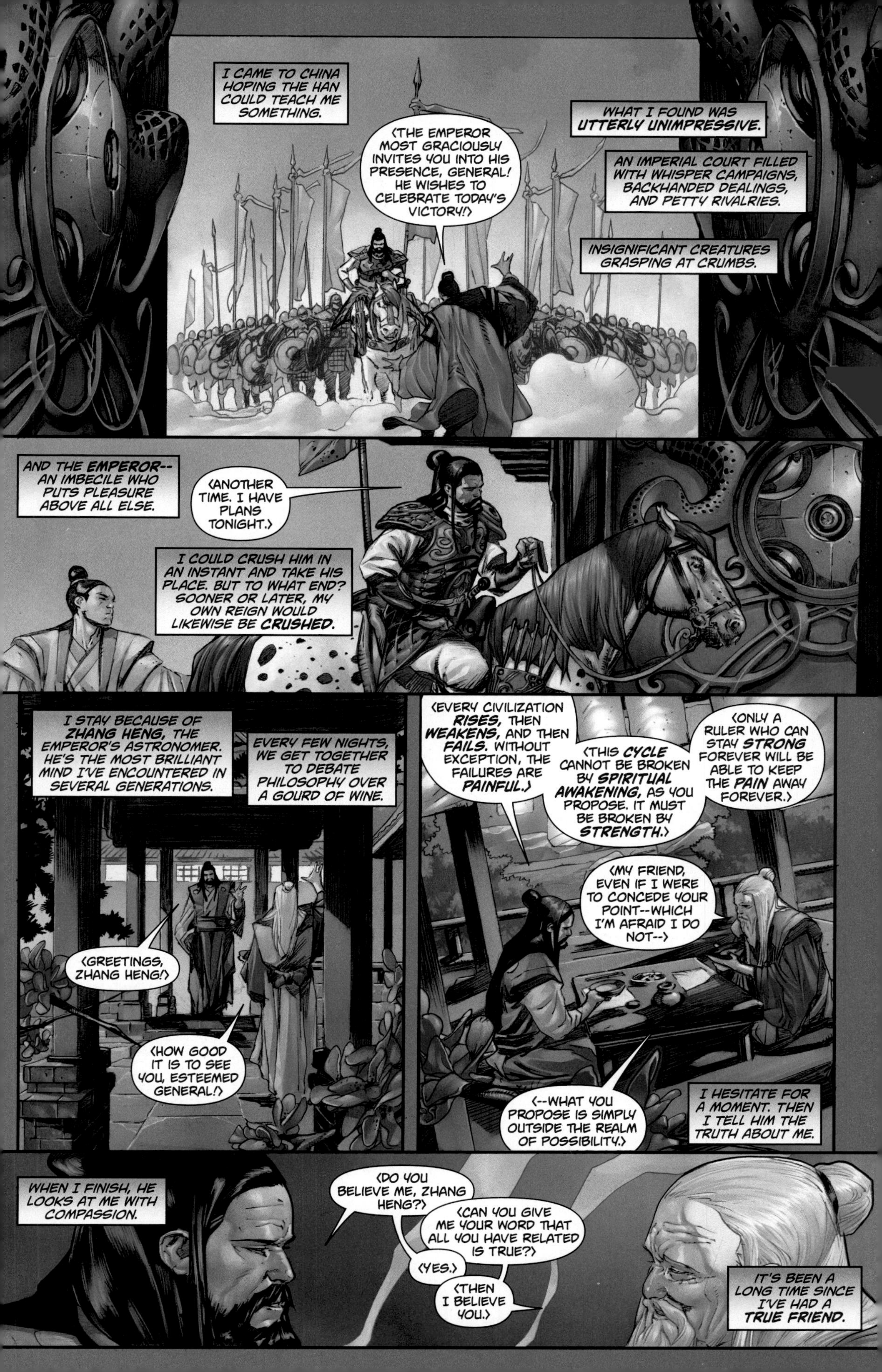
I CAME TO CHINA HOPING THE HAN COULD TEACH ME SOMETHING.
<THE EMPEROR MOST GRACIOUSLY INVITES YOU INTO HIS PRESENCE, GENERAL! HE WISHES TO CELEBRATE TODAY'S VICTORY!>
WHAT I FOUND WAS UTTERLY UNIMPRESSIVE.
AN IMPERIAL COURT FILLED WITH WHISPER CAMPAIGNS, BACKHANDED DEALINGS, AND PETTY RIVALRIES.
INSIGNIFICANT CREATURES GRASPING AT CRUMBS.
AND THE EMPEROR-- AN IMBECILE WHO PUTS PLEASURE ABOVE ALL ELSE.
<ANOTHER TIME. I HAVE PLANS TONIGHT.>
I COULD CRUSH HIM IN AN INSTANT AND TAKE HIS PLACE. BUT TO WHAT END? SOONER OR LATER, MY OWN REIGN WOULD LIKEWISE BE CRUSHED.
I STAY BECAUSE OF ZHANG HENG, THE EMPEROR'S ASTRONOMER. HE'S THE MOST BRILLIANT MIND I'VE ENCOUNTERED IN SEVERAL GENERATIONS.
EVERY FEW NIGHTS, WE GET TOGETHER TO DEBATE PHILOSOPHY OVER A GOURD OF WINE.
<GREETINGS, ZHANG HENG!>
<HOW GOOD IT IS TO SEE YOU, ESTEEMED GENERAL!>
<EVERY CIVILIZATION RISES, THEN WEAKENS, AND THEN FAILS. WITHOUT EXCEPTION, THE FAILURES ARE PAINFUL.>
<THIS CYCLE CANNOT BE BROKEN BY SPIRITUAL AWAKENING, AS YOU PROPOSE. IT MUST BE BROKEN BY STRENGTH.>
<ONLY A RULER WHO CAN STAY STRONG FOREVER WILL BE ABLE TO KEEP THE PAIN AWAY FOREVER.>
<MY FRIEND, EVEN IF I WERE TO CONCEDE YOUR POINT--WHICH I'M AFRAID I DO NOT-->
<--WHAT YOU PROPOSE IS SIMPLY OUTSIDE THE REALM OF POSSIBILITY.>
I HESITATE FOR A MOMENT. THEN I TELL HIM THE TRUTH ABOUT ME.
WHEN I FINISH, HE LOOKS AT ME WITH COMPASSION.
<DO YOU BELIEVE ME, ZHANG HENG?>
<CAN YOU GIVE ME YOUR WORD THAT ALL YOU HAVE RELATED IS TRUE?>
<YES.>
<THEN I BELIEVE YOU.>
IT'S BEEN A LONG TIME SINCE I'VE HAD A TRUE FRIEND.

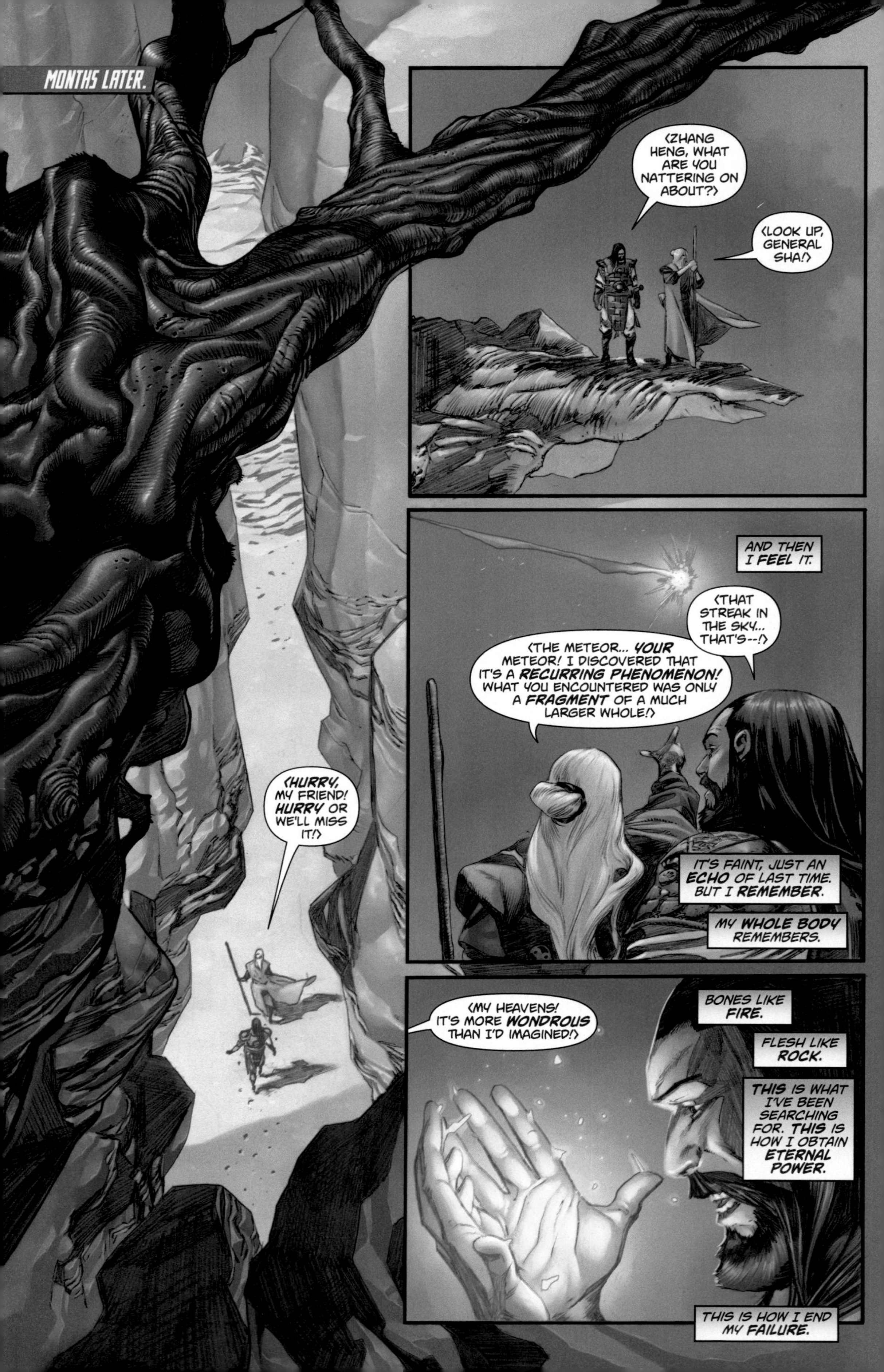
MONTHS LATER.
‹ZHANG HENG, WHAT ARE YOU NATTERING ON ABOUT?›
‹LOOK UP, GENERAL SHA!›
AND THEN I FEEL IT.
‹THAT STREAK IN THE SKY... THAT'S--!›
‹THE METEOR... YOUR METEOR! I DISCOVERED THAT IT'S A RECURRING PHENOMENON! WHAT YOU ENCOUNTERED WAS ONLY A FRAGMENT OF A MUCH LARGER WHOLE!›
‹HURRY, MY FRIEND! HURRY OR WE'LL MISS IT!›
IT'S FAINT, JUST AN ECHO OF LAST TIME. BUT I REMEMBER.
MY WHOLE BODY REMEMBERS.
‹MY HEAVENS! IT'S MORE WONDROUS THAN I'D IMAGINED!›
BONES LIKE FIRE.
FLESH LIKE ROCK.
THIS IS WHAT I'VE BEEN SEARCHING FOR. THIS IS HOW I OBTAIN ETERNAL POWER.
THIS IS HOW I END MY FAILURE.

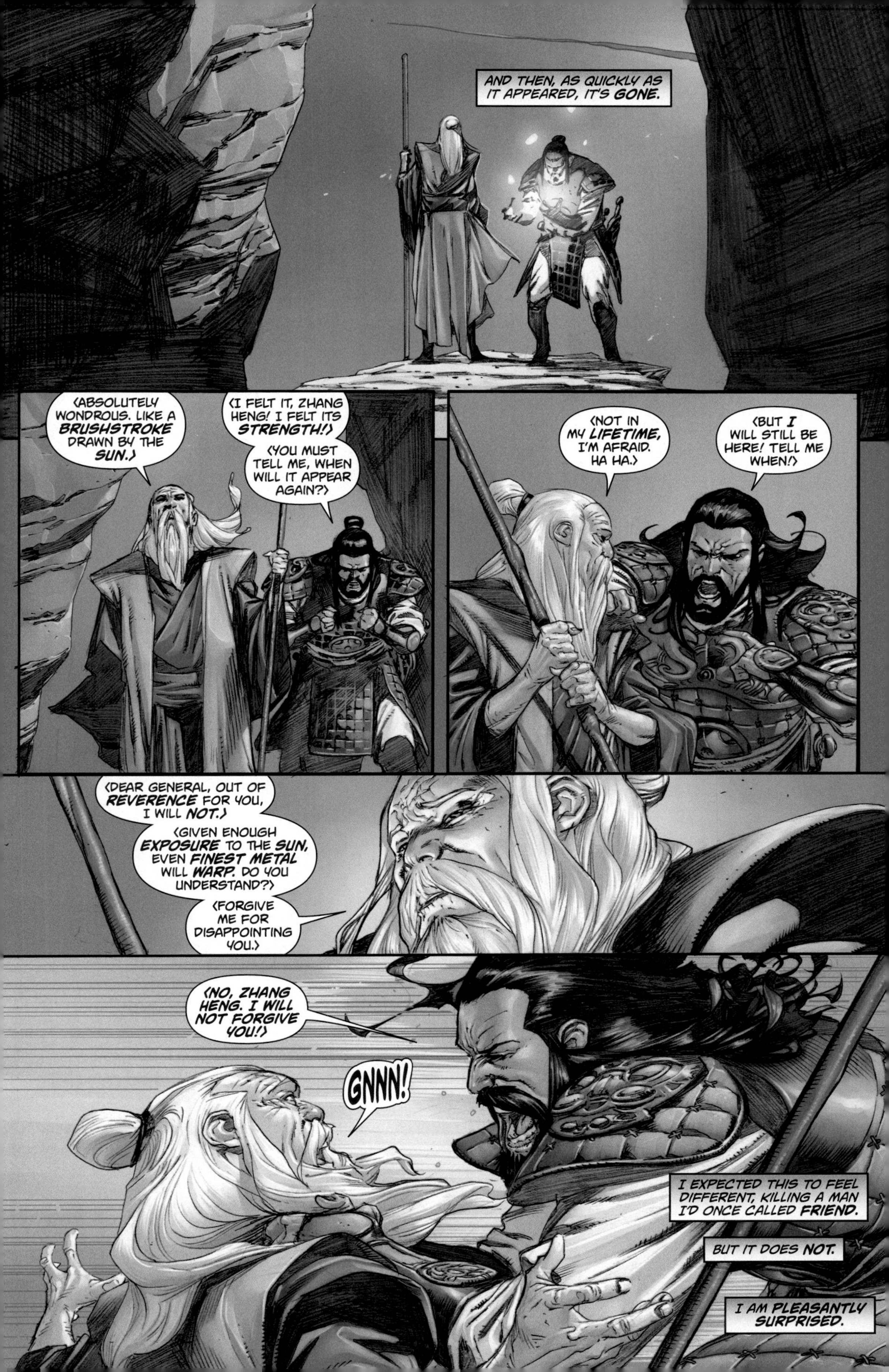
AND THEN, AS QUICKLY AS IT APPEARED, IT'S GONE.
‹ABSOLUTELY WONDROUS. LIKE A BRUSHSTROKE DRAWN BY THE SUN.›
‹I FELT IT, ZHANG HENG! I FELT ITS STRENGTH!›
‹YOU MUST TELL ME, WHEN WILL IT APPEAR AGAIN?›
‹NOT IN MY LIFETIME, I'M AFRAID. HA HA.›
‹BUT I WILL STILL BE HERE! TELL ME WHEN!›
‹DEAR GENERAL, OUT OF REVERENCE FOR YOU, I WILL NOT.›
‹GIVEN ENOUGH EXPOSURE TO THE SUN, EVEN FINEST METAL WILL WARP. DO YOU UNDERSTAND?›
‹FORGIVE ME FOR DISAPPOINTING YOU.›
‹NO, ZHANG HENG. I WILL NOT FORGIVE YOU!›
GNNN!
I EXPECTED THIS TO FEEL DIFFERENT, KILLING A MAN I'D ONCE CALLED FRIEND.
BUT IT DOES NOT.
I AM PLEASANTLY SURPRISED.

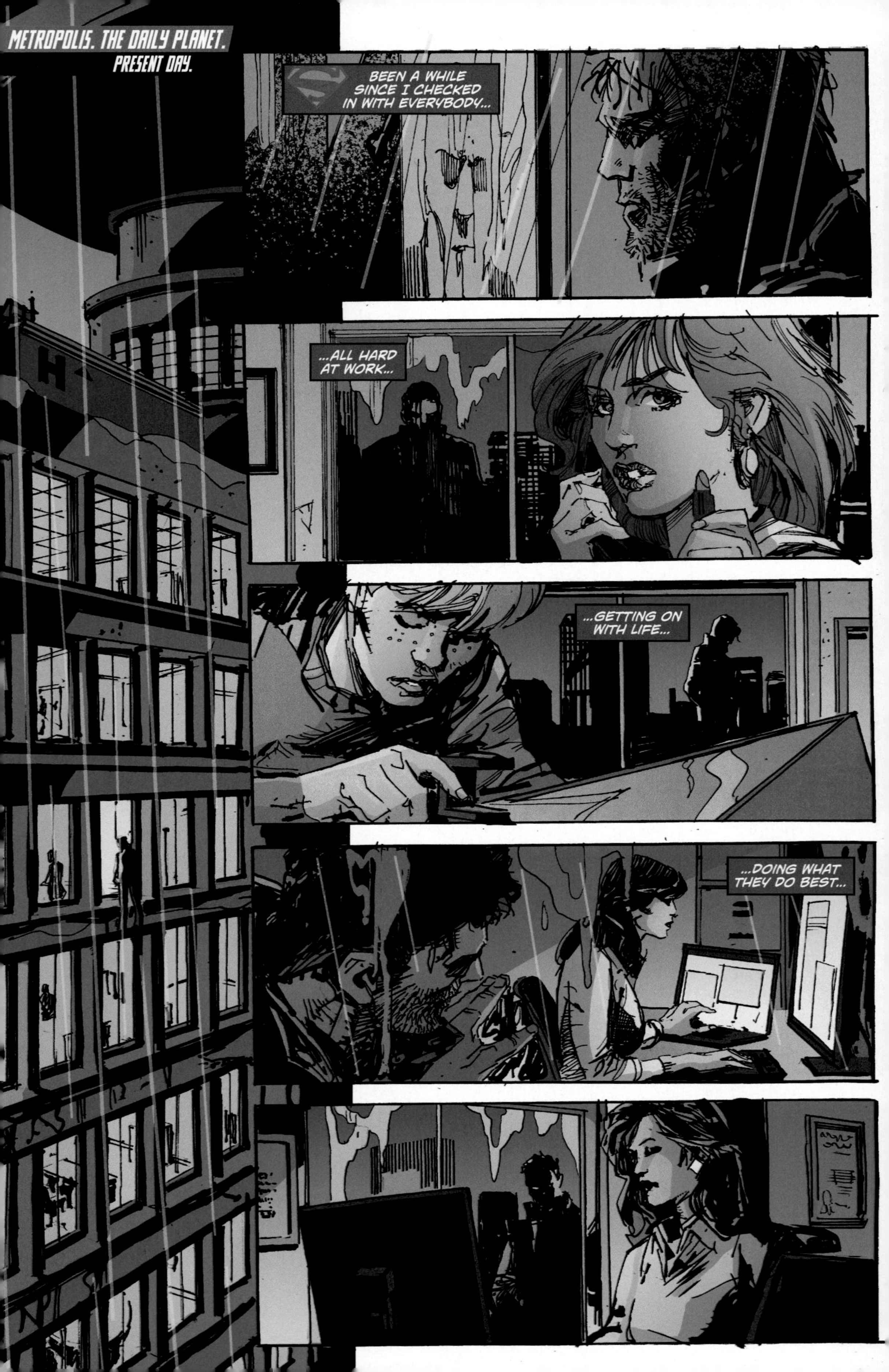
METROPOLIS. THE DAILY PLANET.
PRESENT DAY.
BEEN A WHILE SINCE I CHECKED IN WITH EVERYBODY...
...ALL HARD AT WORK...
...GETTING ON WITH LIFE...
...DOING WHAT THEY DO BEST...

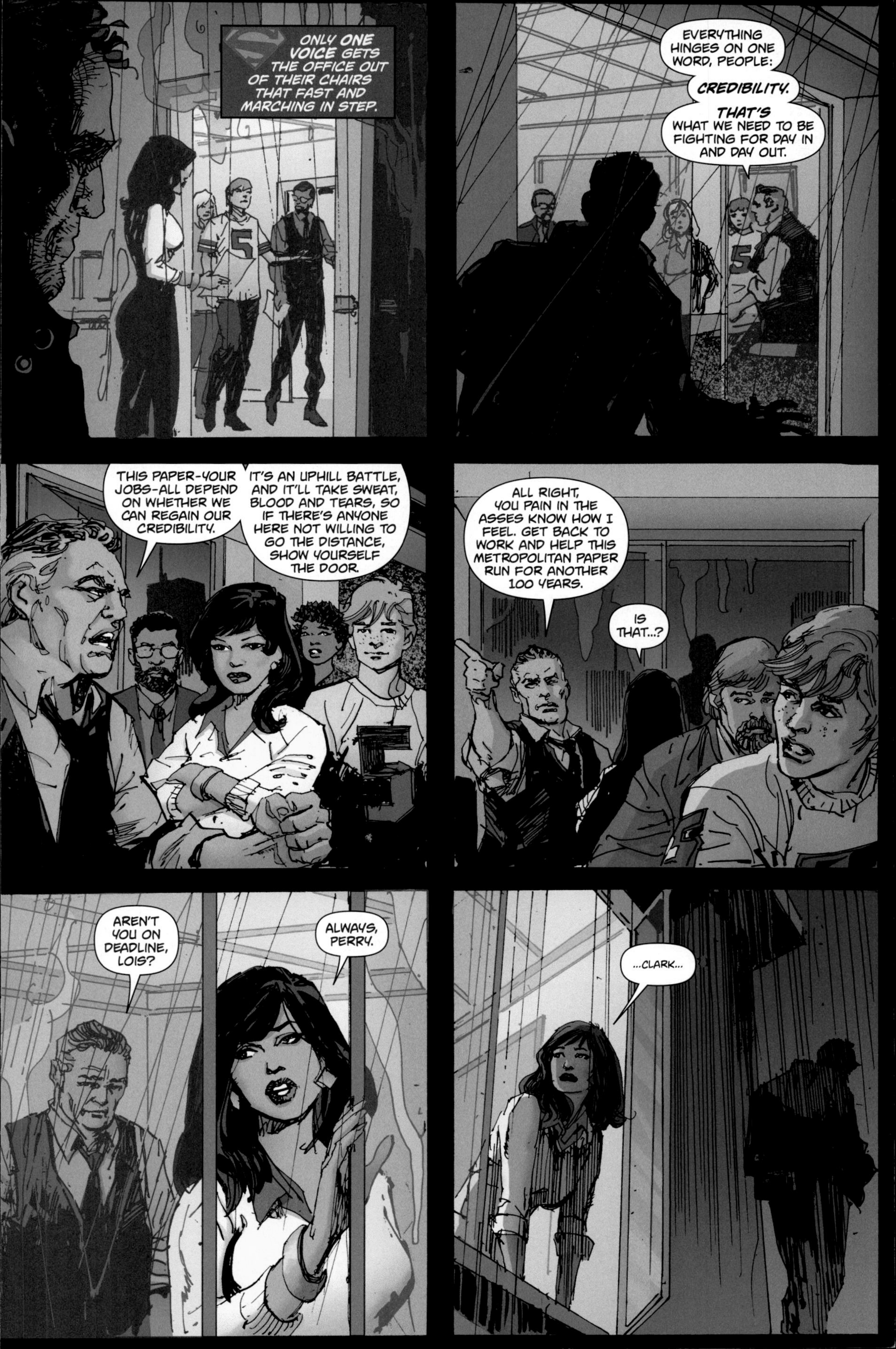
ONLY ONE VOICE GETS THE OFFICE OUT OF THEIR CHAIRS THAT FAST AND MARCHING IN STEP.
EVERYTHING HINGES ON ONE WORD, PEOPLE:
CREDIBILITY.
THAT'S WHAT WE NEED TO BE FIGHTING FOR DAY IN AND DAY OUT.
THIS PAPER--YOUR JOBS--ALL DEPEND ON WHETHER WE CAN REGAIN OUR CREDIBILITY.
IT'S AN UPHILL BATTLE, AND IT'LL TAKE SWEAT, BLOOD AND TEARS, SO IF THERE'S ANYONE HERE NOT WILLING TO GO THE DISTANCE, SHOW YOURSELF THE DOOR.
ALL RIGHT, YOU PAIN IN THE ASSES KNOW HOW I FEEL. GET BACK TO WORK AND HELP THIS METROPOLITAN PAPER RUN FOR ANOTHER 100 YEARS.
IS THAT...?
AREN'T YOU ON DEADLINE, LOIS?
ALWAYS, PERRY.
...CLARK...

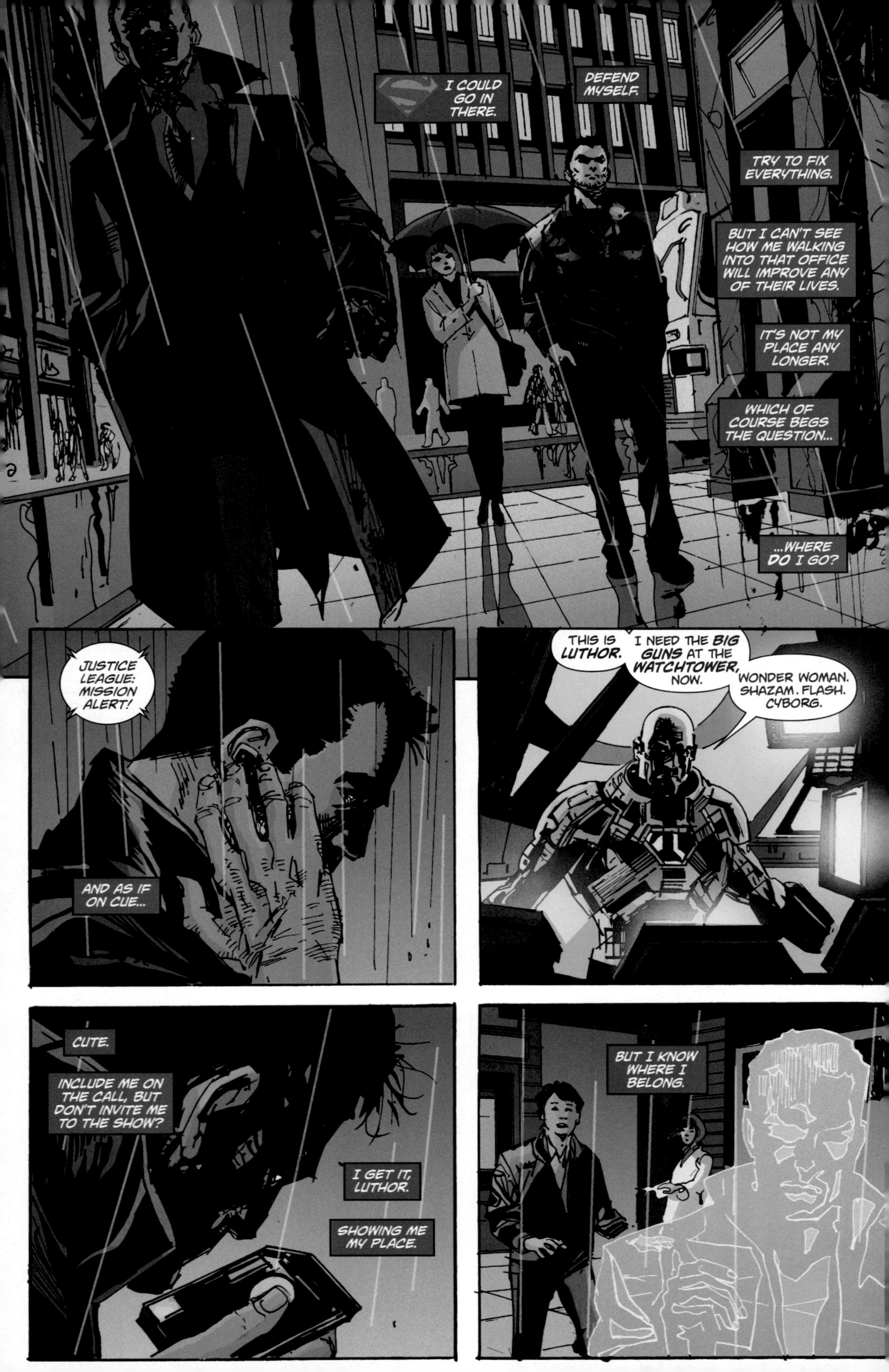
I COULD GO IN THERE.
DEFEND MYSELF.
TRY TO FIX EVERYTHING.
BUT I CAN'T SEE HOW ME WALKING INTO THAT OFFICE WILL IMPROVE ANY OF THEIR LIVES.
IT'S NOT MY PLACE ANY LONGER.
WHICH OF COURSE BEGS THE QUESTION...
...WHERE DO I GO?
JUSTICE LEAGUE: MISSION ALERT!
AND AS IF ON CUE...
THIS IS LUTHOR.
I NEED THE BIG GUNS AT THE WATCHTOWER, NOW.
WONDER WOMAN. SHAZAM. FLASH. CYBORG.
CUTE.
INCLUDE ME ON THE CALL, BUT DON'T INVITE ME TO THE SHOW?
I GET IT, LUTHOR.
SHOWING ME MY PLACE.
BUT I KNOW WHERE I BELONG.

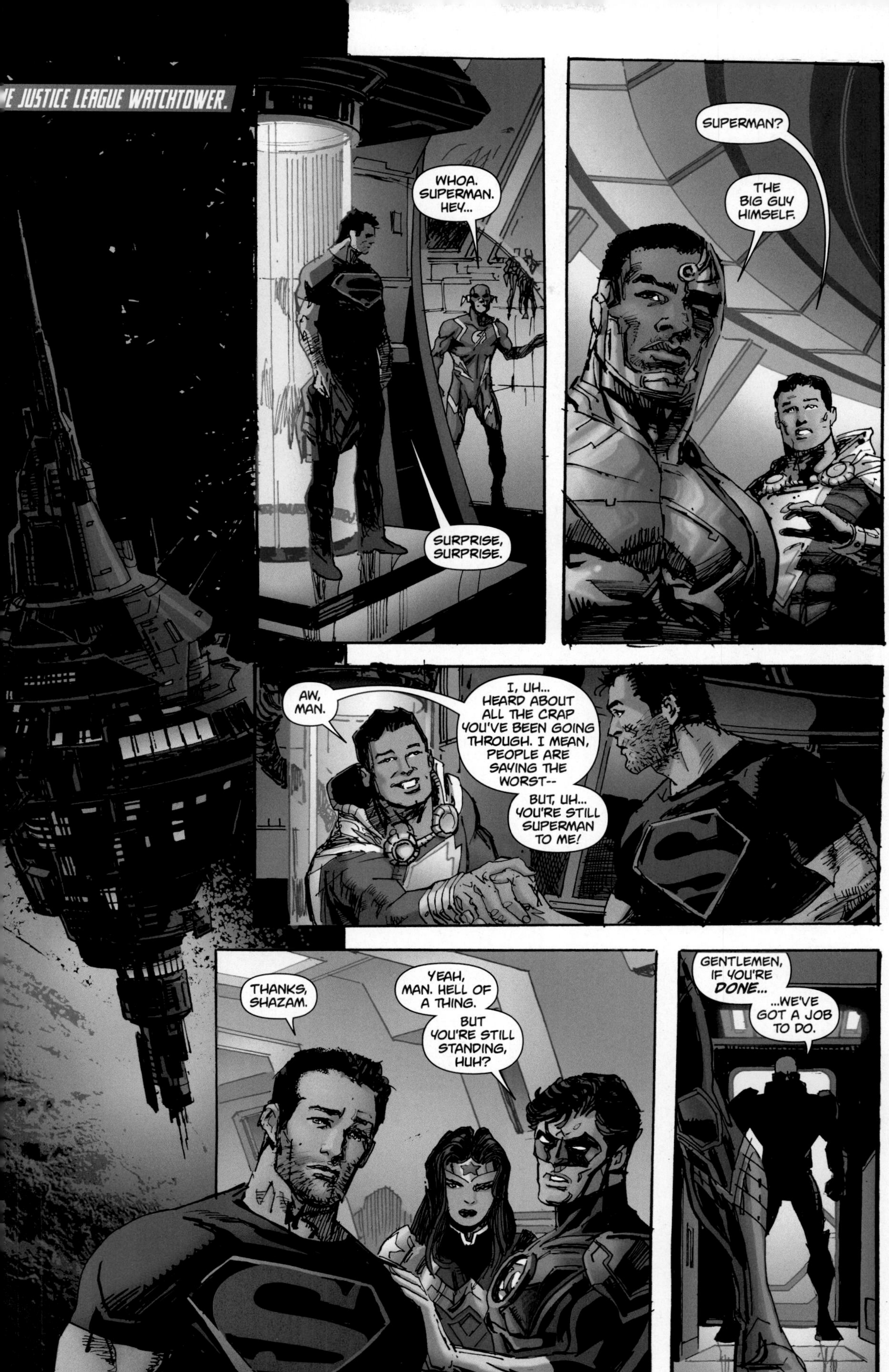

E JUSTICE LEAGUE WATCHTOWER.
WHOA. SUPERMAN. HEY...
SURPRISE, SURPRISE.
SUPERMAN?
THE BIG GUY HIMSELF.
AW, MAN.
I, UH... HEARD ABOUT ALL THE CRAP YOU'VE BEEN GOING THROUGH. I MEAN, PEOPLE ARE SAYING THE WORST--
BUT, UH... YOU'RE STILL SUPERMAN TO ME!
THANKS, SHAZAM.
YEAH, MAN. HELL OF A THING.
BUT YOU'RE STILL STANDING, HUH?
GENTLEMEN, IF YOU'RE *DONE*...
...WE'VE GOT A JOB TO DO.

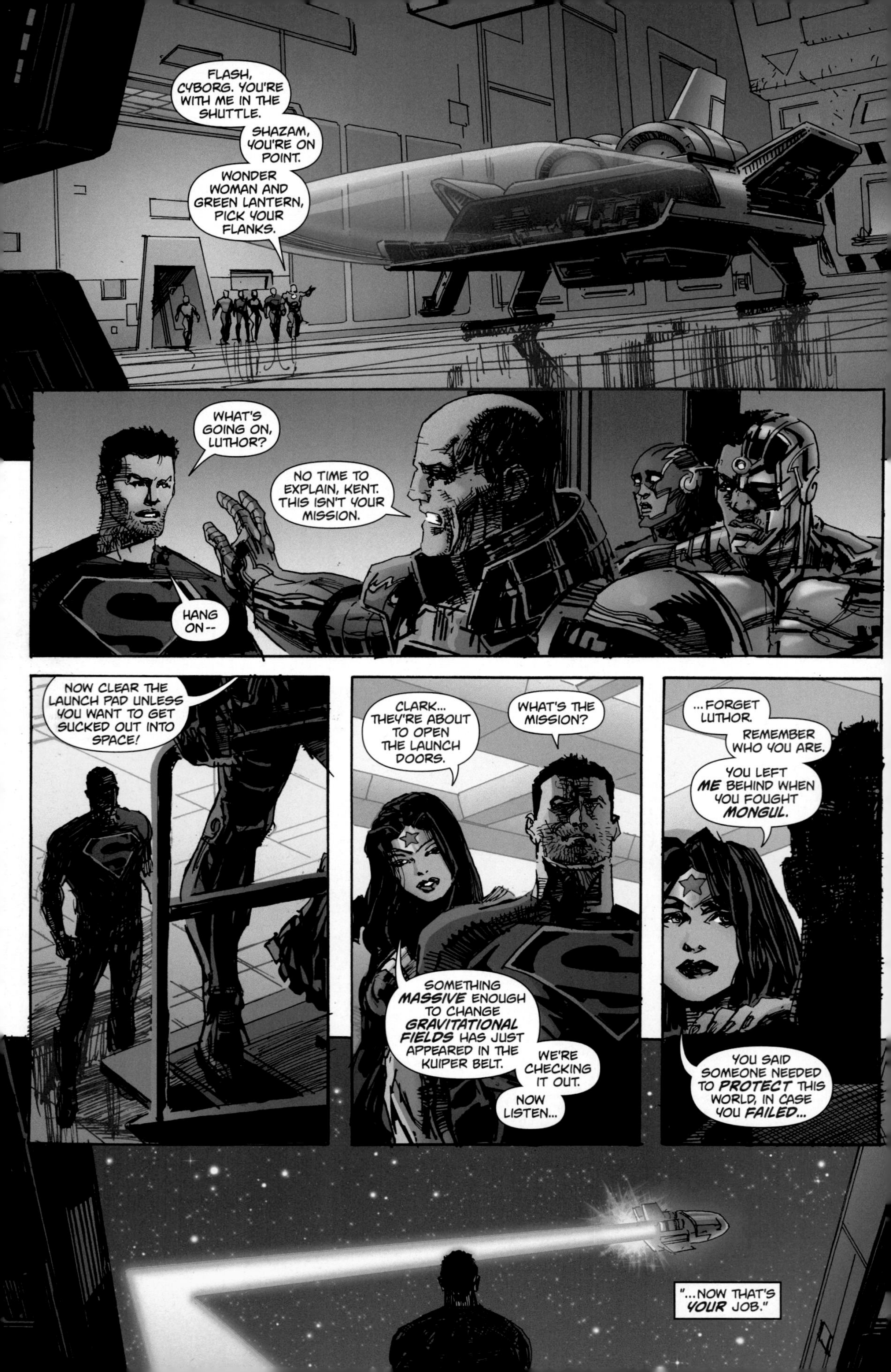
FLASH, CYBORG. YOU'RE WITH ME IN THE SHUTTLE.
SHAZAM, YOU'RE ON POINT.
WONDER WOMAN AND GREEN LANTERN, PICK YOUR FLANKS.
WHAT'S GOING ON, LUTHOR?
NO TIME TO EXPLAIN, KENT. THIS ISN'T YOUR MISSION.
HANG ON--
NOW CLEAR THE LAUNCH PAD UNLESS YOU WANT TO GET SUCKED OUT INTO SPACE!
CLARK... THEY'RE ABOUT TO OPEN THE LAUNCH DOORS.
WHAT'S THE MISSION?
SOMETHING MASSIVE ENOUGH TO CHANGE GRAVITATIONAL FIELDS HAS JUST APPEARED IN THE KUIPER BELT.
WE'RE CHECKING IT OUT.
NOW LISTEN...
...FORGET LUTHOR.
REMEMBER WHO YOU ARE.
YOU LEFT ME BEHIND WHEN YOU FOUGHT MONGUL.
YOU SAID SOMEONE NEEDED TO PROTECT THIS WORLD, IN CASE YOU FAILED...
"...NOW THAT'S YOUR JOB."

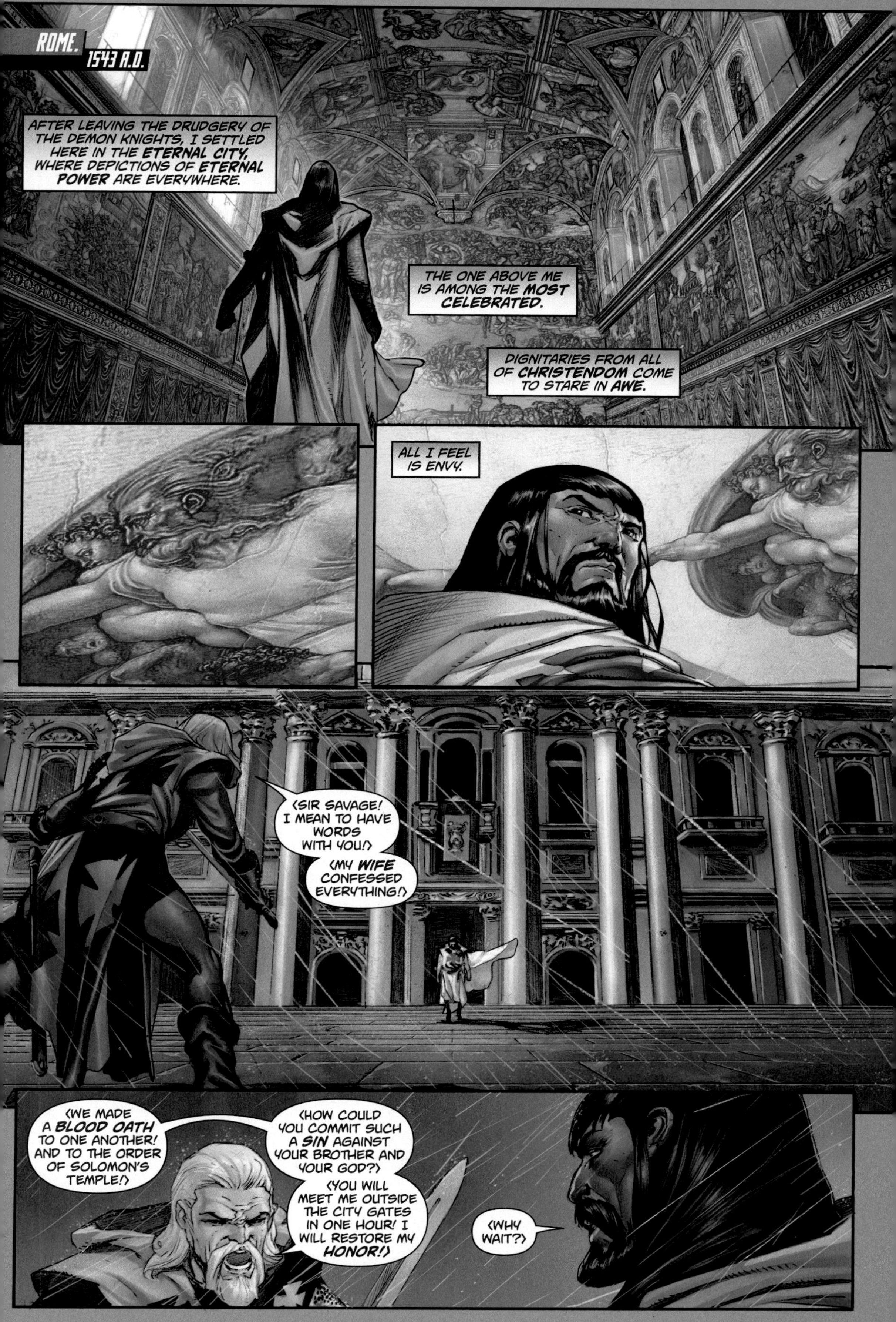
ROME.
1543 A.D.
AFTER LEAVING THE DRUDGERY OF THE DEMON KNIGHTS, I SETTLED HERE IN THE ETERNAL CITY, WHERE DEPICTIONS OF ETERNAL POWER ARE EVERYWHERE.
THE ONE ABOVE ME IS AMONG THE MOST CELEBRATED.
DIGNITARIES FROM ALL OF CHRISTENDOM COME TO STARE IN AWE.
ALL I FEEL IS ENVY.
<SIR SAVAGE! I MEAN TO HAVE WORDS WITH YOU!>
<MY WIFE CONFESSED EVERYTHING!>
<WE MADE A BLOOD OATH TO ONE ANOTHER! AND TO THE ORDER OF SOLOMON'S TEMPLE!>
<HOW COULD YOU COMMIT SUCH A SIN AGAINST YOUR BROTHER AND YOUR GOD?>
<YOU WILL MEET ME OUTSIDE THE CITY GATES IN ONE HOUR! I WILL RESTORE MY HONOR!>
<WHY WAIT?>

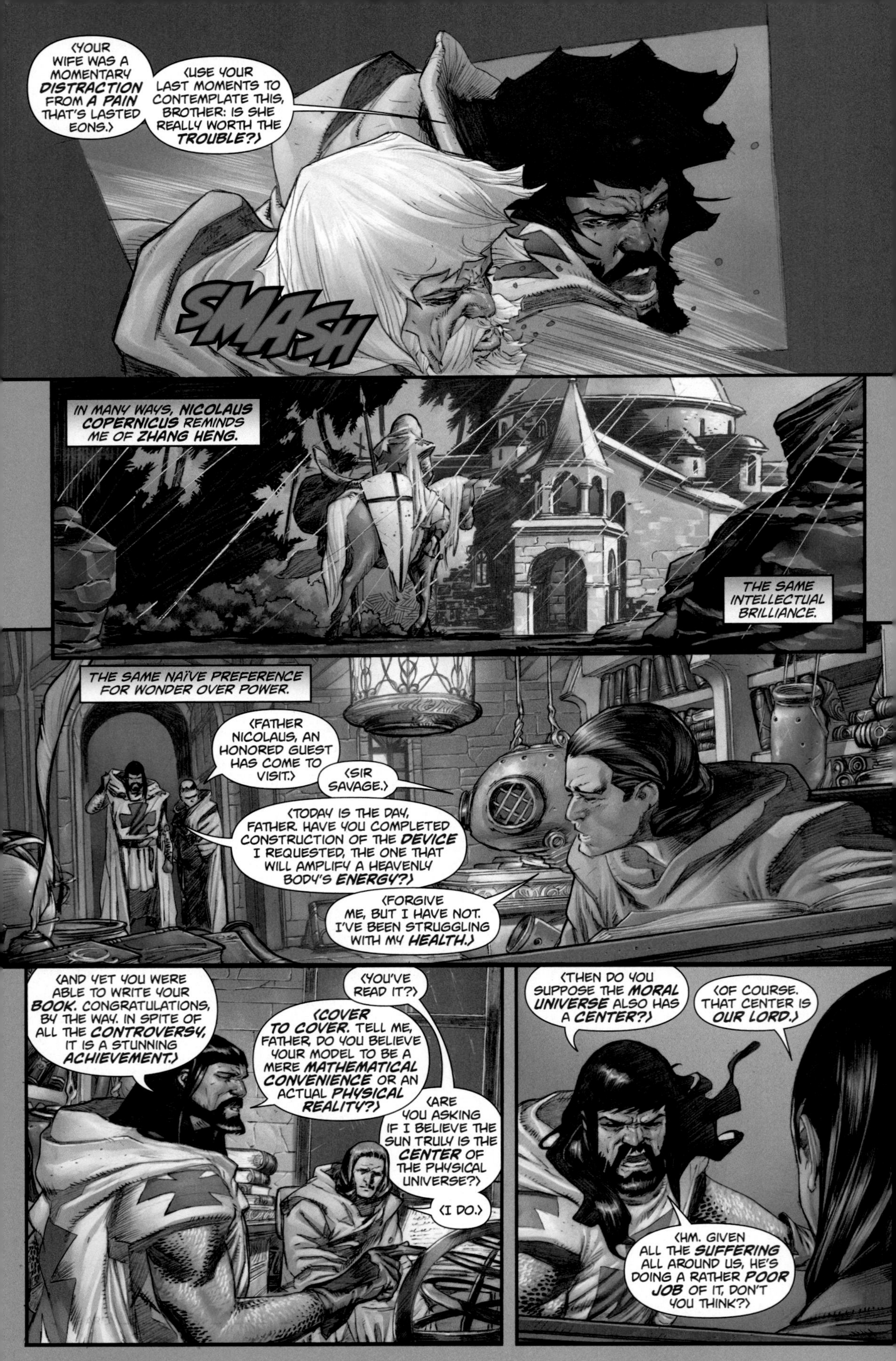
‹YOUR WIFE WAS A MOMENTARY DISTRACTION FROM A PAIN THAT'S LASTED EONS.›
‹USE YOUR LAST MOMENTS TO CONTEMPLATE THIS, BROTHER: IS SHE REALLY WORTH THE TROUBLE?›
SMASH
IN MANY WAYS, NICOLAUS COPERNICUS REMINDS ME OF ZHANG HENG.
THE SAME INTELLECTUAL BRILLIANCE.
THE SAME NAÏVE PREFERENCE FOR WONDER OVER POWER.
‹FATHER NICOLAUS, AN HONORED GUEST HAS COME TO VISIT.›
‹SIR SAVAGE.›
‹TODAY IS THE DAY, FATHER. HAVE YOU COMPLETED CONSTRUCTION OF THE DEVICE I REQUESTED, THE ONE THAT WILL AMPLIFY A HEAVENLY BODY'S ENERGY?›
‹FORGIVE ME, BUT I HAVE NOT. I'VE BEEN STRUGGLING WITH MY HEALTH.›
‹AND YET YOU WERE ABLE TO WRITE YOUR BOOK. CONGRATULATIONS, BY THE WAY. IN SPITE OF ALL THE CONTROVERSY, IT IS A STUNNING ACHIEVEMENT.›
‹YOU'VE READ IT?›
‹COVER TO COVER. TELL ME, FATHER, DO YOU BELIEVE YOUR MODEL TO BE A MERE MATHEMATICAL CONVENIENCE OR AN ACTUAL PHYSICAL REALITY?›
‹ARE YOU ASKING IF I BELIEVE THE SUN TRULY IS THE CENTER OF THE PHYSICAL UNIVERSE?›
‹I DO.›
‹THEN DO YOU SUPPOSE THE MORAL UNIVERSE ALSO HAS A CENTER?›
‹OF COURSE. THAT CENTER IS OUR LORD.›
‹HM. GIVEN ALL THE SUFFERING ALL AROUND US, HE'S DOING A RATHER POOR JOB OF IT, DON'T YOU THINK?›

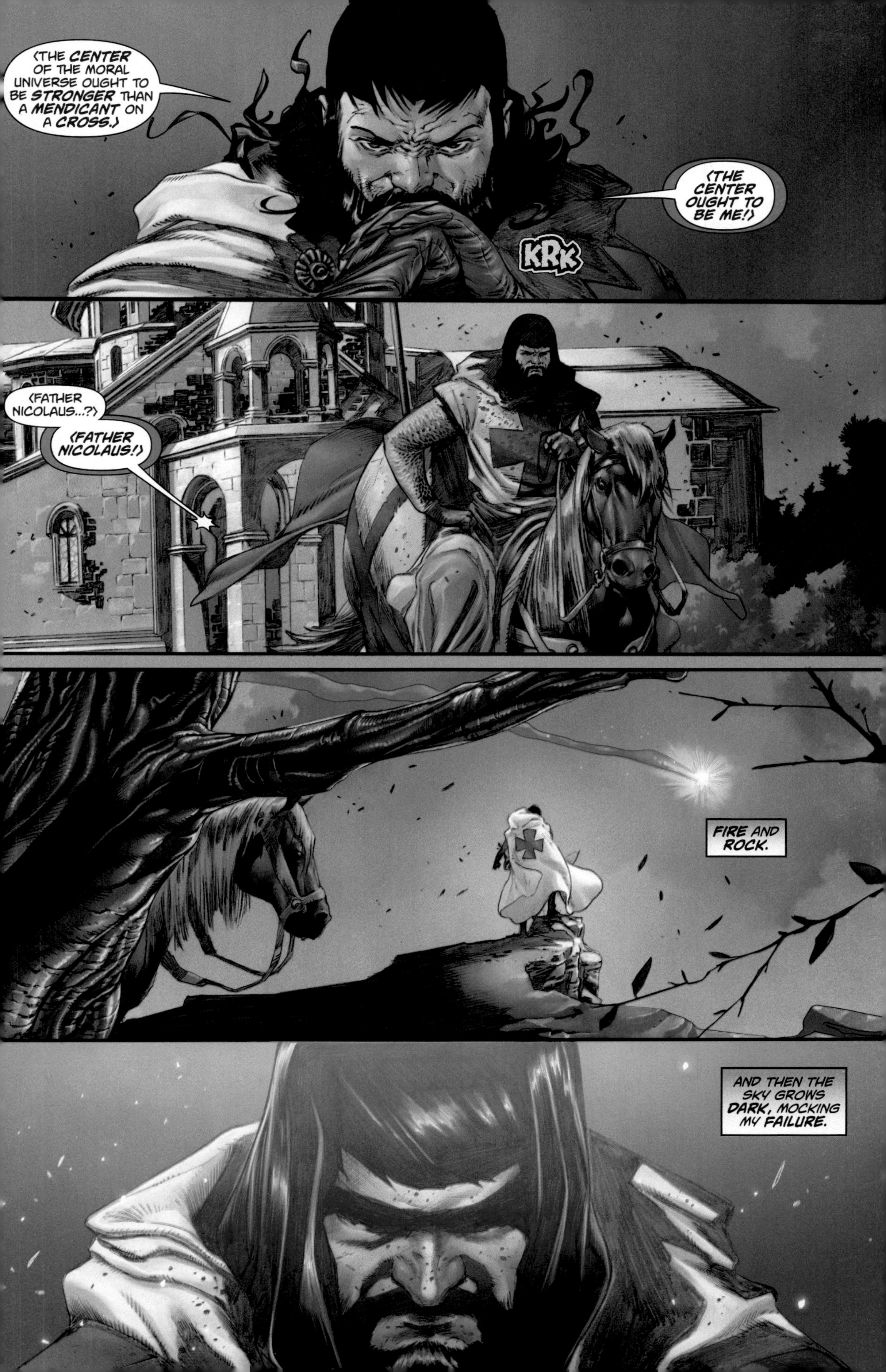

(THE CENTER OF THE MORAL UNIVERSE OUGHT TO BE STRONGER THAN A MENDICANT ON A CROSS.)
(THE CENTER OUGHT TO BE ME!)
KRK
(FATHER NICOLAUS...?)
(FATHER NICOLAUS!)
FIRE AND ROCK.
AND THEN THE SKY GROWS DARK, MOCKING MY FAILURE.

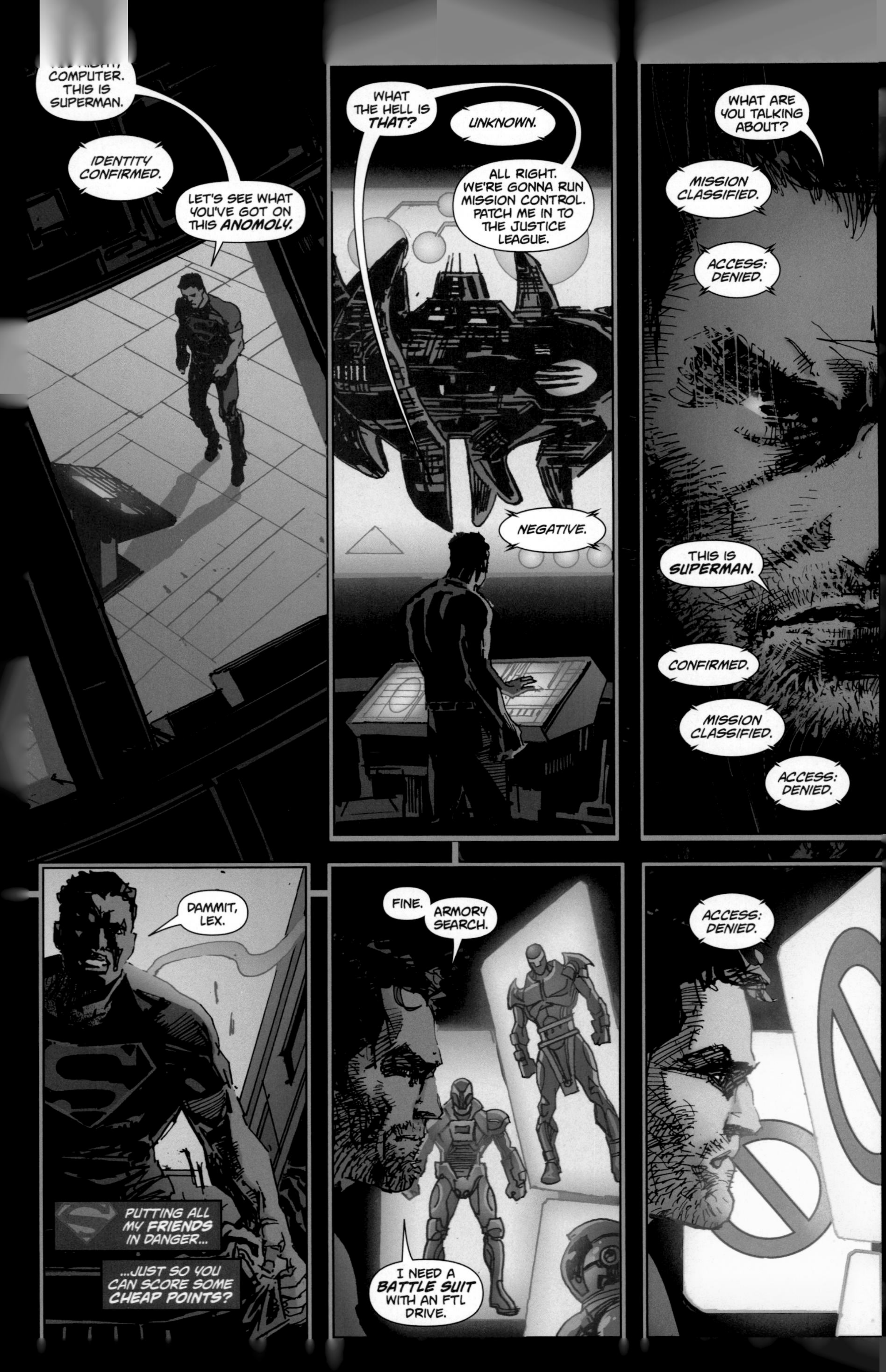

COMPUTER. THIS IS SUPERMAN.
IDENTITY CONFIRMED.
LET'S SEE WHAT YOU'VE GOT ON THIS ANOMOLY.
WHAT THE HELL IS THAT?
UNKNOWN.
ALL RIGHT. WE'RE GONNA RUN MISSION CONTROL. PATCH ME IN TO THE JUSTICE LEAGUE.
NEGATIVE.
WHAT ARE YOU TALKING ABOUT?
MISSION CLASSIFIED.
ACCESS: DENIED.
THIS IS SUPERMAN.
CONFIRMED.
MISSION CLASSIFIED.
ACCESS: DENIED.
DAMMIT, LEX.
PUTTING ALL MY FRIENDS IN DANGER...
...JUST SO YOU CAN SCORE SOME CHEAP POINTS?
FINE.
ARMORY SEARCH.
I NEED A BATTLE SUIT WITH AN FTL DRIVE.
ACCESS: DENIED.

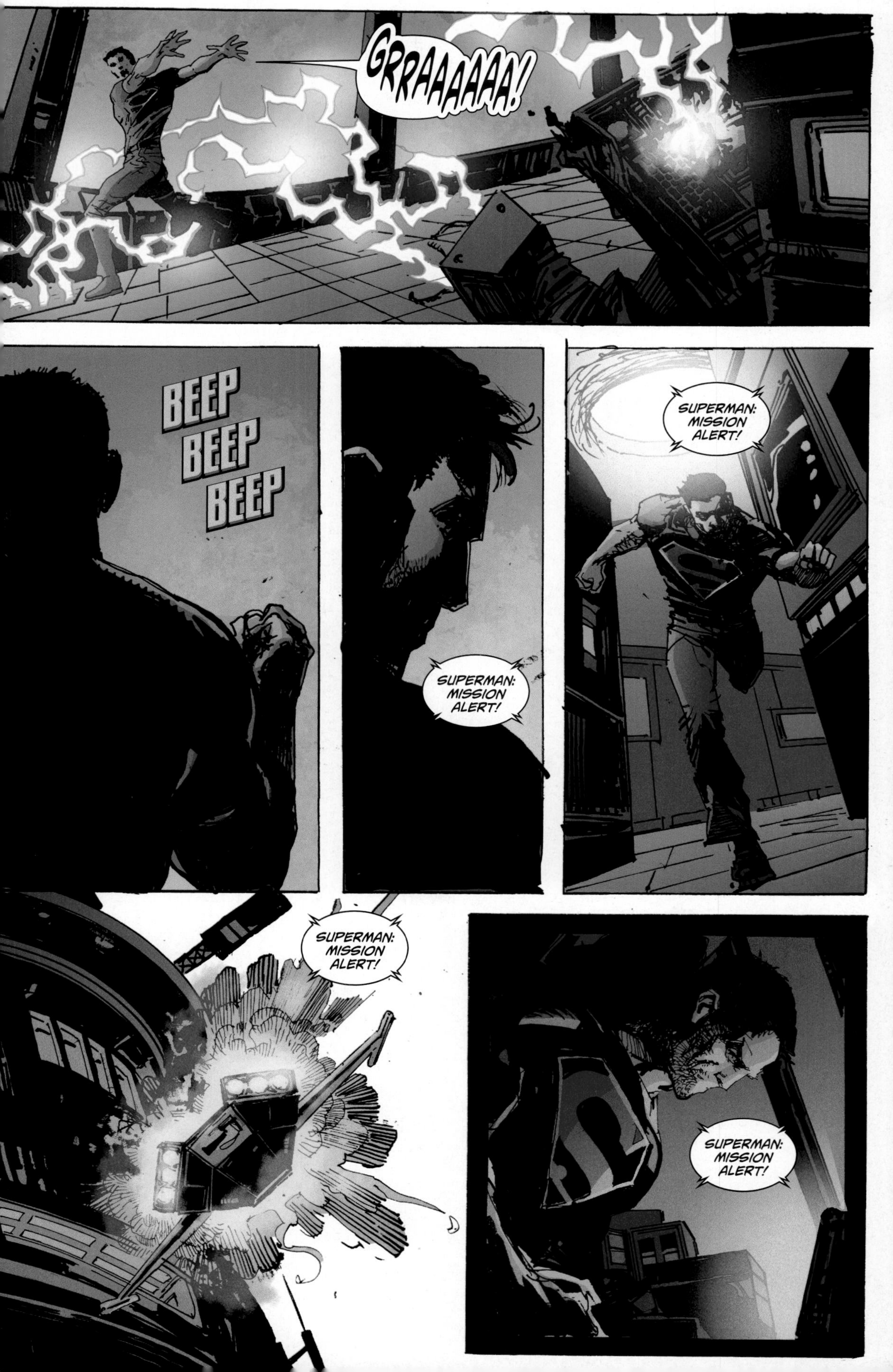
GRRAAAAAA!
BEEP
BEEP
BEEP
SUPERMAN: MISSION ALERT!
SUPERMAN: MISSION ALERT!
SUPERMAN: MISSION ALERT!
SUPERMAN: MISSION ALERT!

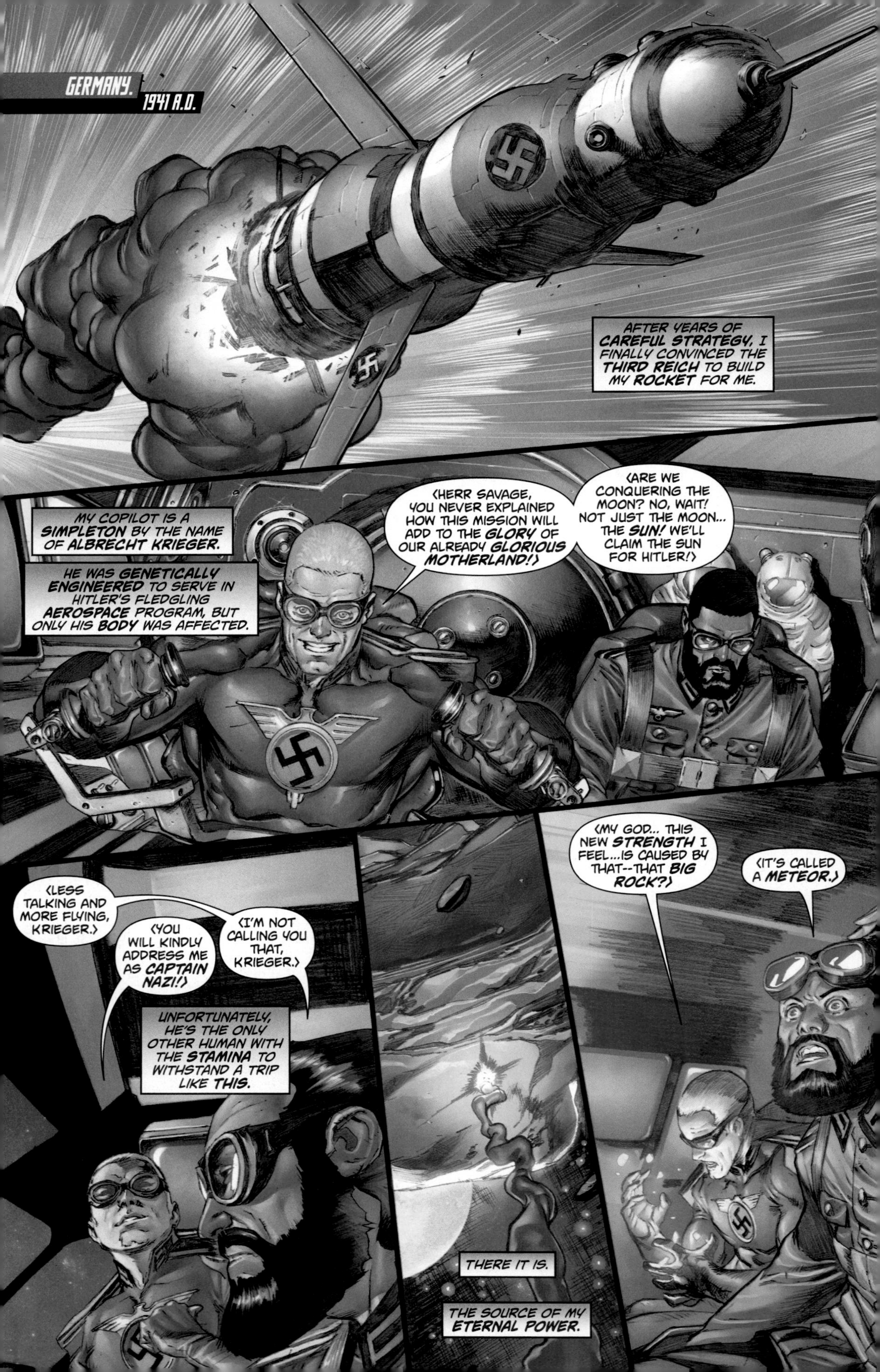
GERMANY.
1941 A.D.
AFTER YEARS OF CAREFUL STRATEGY, I FINALLY CONVINCED THE THIRD REICH TO BUILD MY ROCKET FOR ME.
MY COPILOT IS A SIMPLETON BY THE NAME OF ALBRECHT KRIEGER.
HE WAS GENETICALLY ENGINEERED TO SERVE IN HITLER'S FLEDGLING AEROSPACE PROGRAM, BUT ONLY HIS BODY WAS AFFECTED.
‹HERR SAVAGE, YOU NEVER EXPLAINED HOW THIS MISSION WILL ADD TO THE GLORY OF OUR ALREADY GLORIOUS MOTHERLAND!›
‹ARE WE CONQUERING THE MOON? NO, WAIT! NOT JUST THE MOON... THE SUN! WE'LL CLAIM THE SUN FOR HITLER!›
‹LESS TALKING AND MORE FLYING, KRIEGER.›
‹YOU WILL KINDLY ADDRESS ME AS CAPTAIN NAZI!›
‹I'M NOT CALLING YOU THAT, KRIEGER.›
UNFORTUNATELY, HE'S THE ONLY OTHER HUMAN WITH THE STAMINA TO WITHSTAND A TRIP LIKE THIS.
THERE IT IS.
THE SOURCE OF MY ETERNAL POWER.
‹MY GOD... THIS NEW STRENGTH I FEEL...IS CAUSED BY THAT--THAT BIG ROCK?›
‹IT'S CALLED A METEOR.›

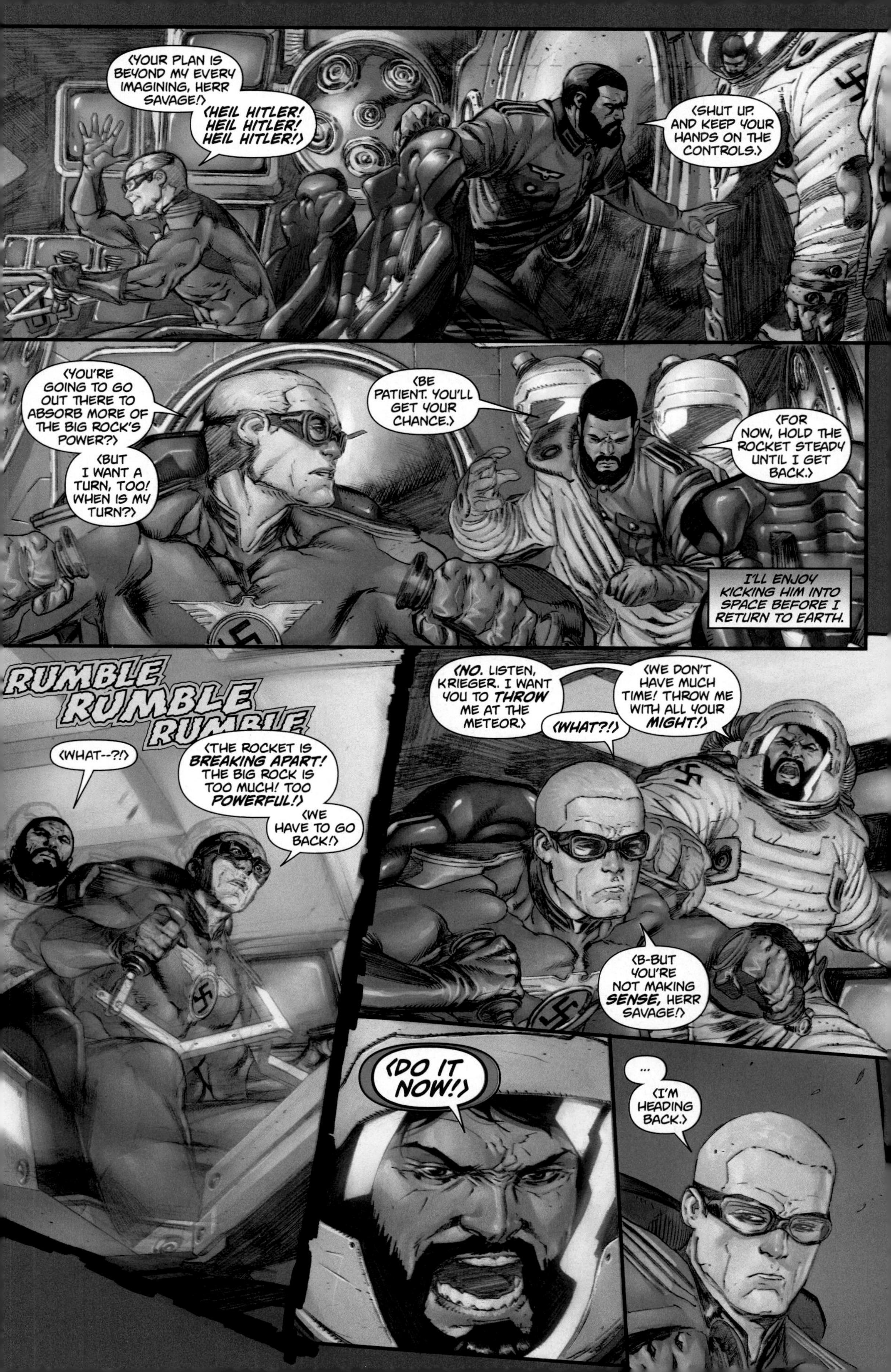
‹YOUR PLAN IS BEYOND MY EVERY IMAGINING, HERR SAVAGE!›
‹HEIL HITLER! HEIL HITLER! HEIL HITLER!›
‹SHUT UP. AND KEEP YOUR HANDS ON THE CONTROLS.›
‹YOU'RE GOING TO GO OUT THERE TO ABSORB MORE OF THE BIG ROCK'S POWER?›
‹BUT I WANT A TURN, TOO! WHEN IS MY TURN?›
‹BE PATIENT. YOU'LL GET YOUR CHANCE.›
‹FOR NOW, HOLD THE ROCKET STEADY UNTIL I GET BACK.›
I'LL ENJOY KICKING HIM INTO SPACE BEFORE I RETURN TO EARTH.
RUMBLE RUMBLE RUMBLE
‹WHAT--?!›
‹THE ROCKET IS BREAKING APART! THE BIG ROCK IS TOO MUCH! TOO POWERFUL!›
‹WE HAVE TO GO BACK!›
‹NO. LISTEN, KRIEGER. I WANT YOU TO THROW ME AT THE METEOR.›
‹WHAT?!›
‹WE DON'T HAVE MUCH TIME! THROW ME WITH ALL YOUR MIGHT!›
‹B-BUT YOU'RE NOT MAKING SENSE, HERR SAVAGE!›
‹DO IT NOW!›
...
‹I'M HEADING BACK.›

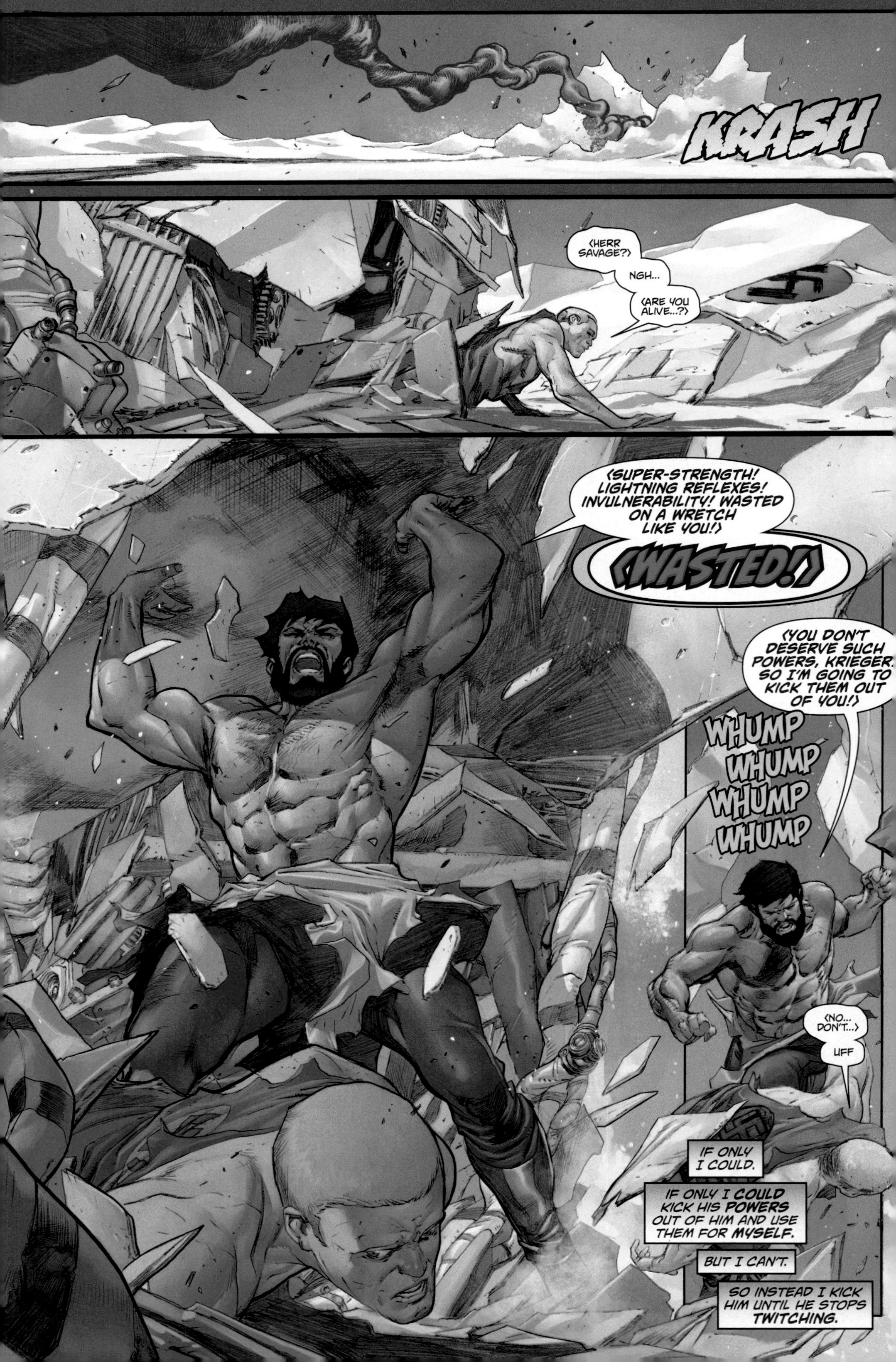
KRASH
‹HERR SAVAGE?›
NGH...
‹ARE YOU ALIVE...?›
‹SUPER-STRENGTH! LIGHTNING REFLEXES! INVULNERABILITY! WASTED ON A WRETCH LIKE YOU!›
‹WASTED!›
‹YOU DON'T DESERVE SUCH POWERS, KRIEGER. SO I'M GOING TO KICK THEM OUT OF YOU!›
WHUMP WHUMP WHUMP WHUMP
‹NO... DON'T...›
UFF
IF ONLY I COULD.
IF ONLY I COULD KICK HIS POWERS OUT OF HIM AND USE THEM FOR MYSELF.
BUT I CAN'T.
SO INSTEAD I KICK HIM UNTIL HE STOPS TWITCHING.

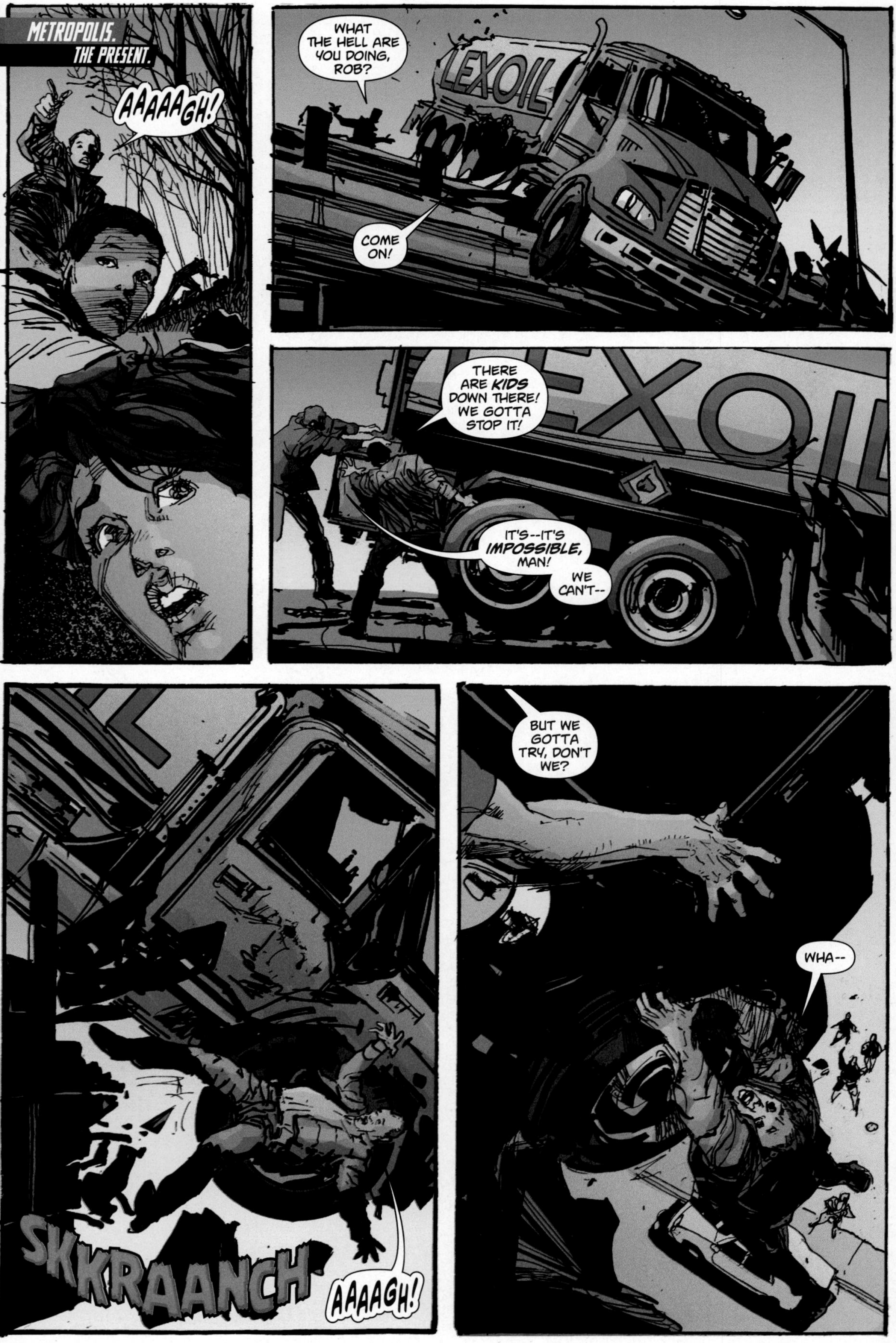
METROPOLIS.
THE PRESENT.
AAAAAGH!
WHAT THE HELL ARE YOU DOING, ROB?
COME ON!
THERE ARE KIDS DOWN THERE! WE GOTTA STOP IT!
IT'S--IT'S IMPOSSIBLE, MAN!
WE CAN'T--
SKKRAANCH
AAAAGH!
BUT WE GOTTA TRY, DON'T WE?
WHA--

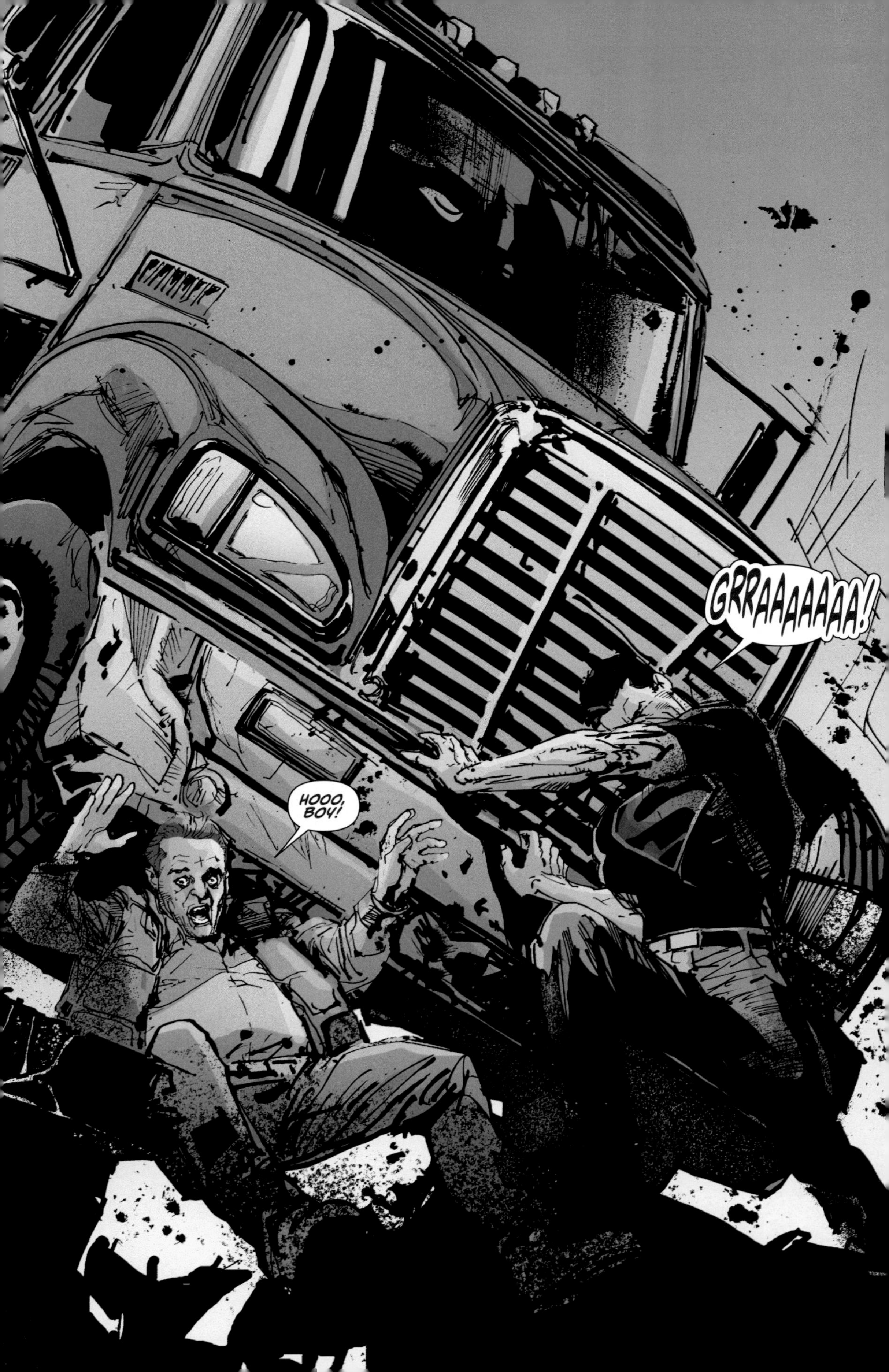
GRRAAAAAAA!
HOOO, BOY!

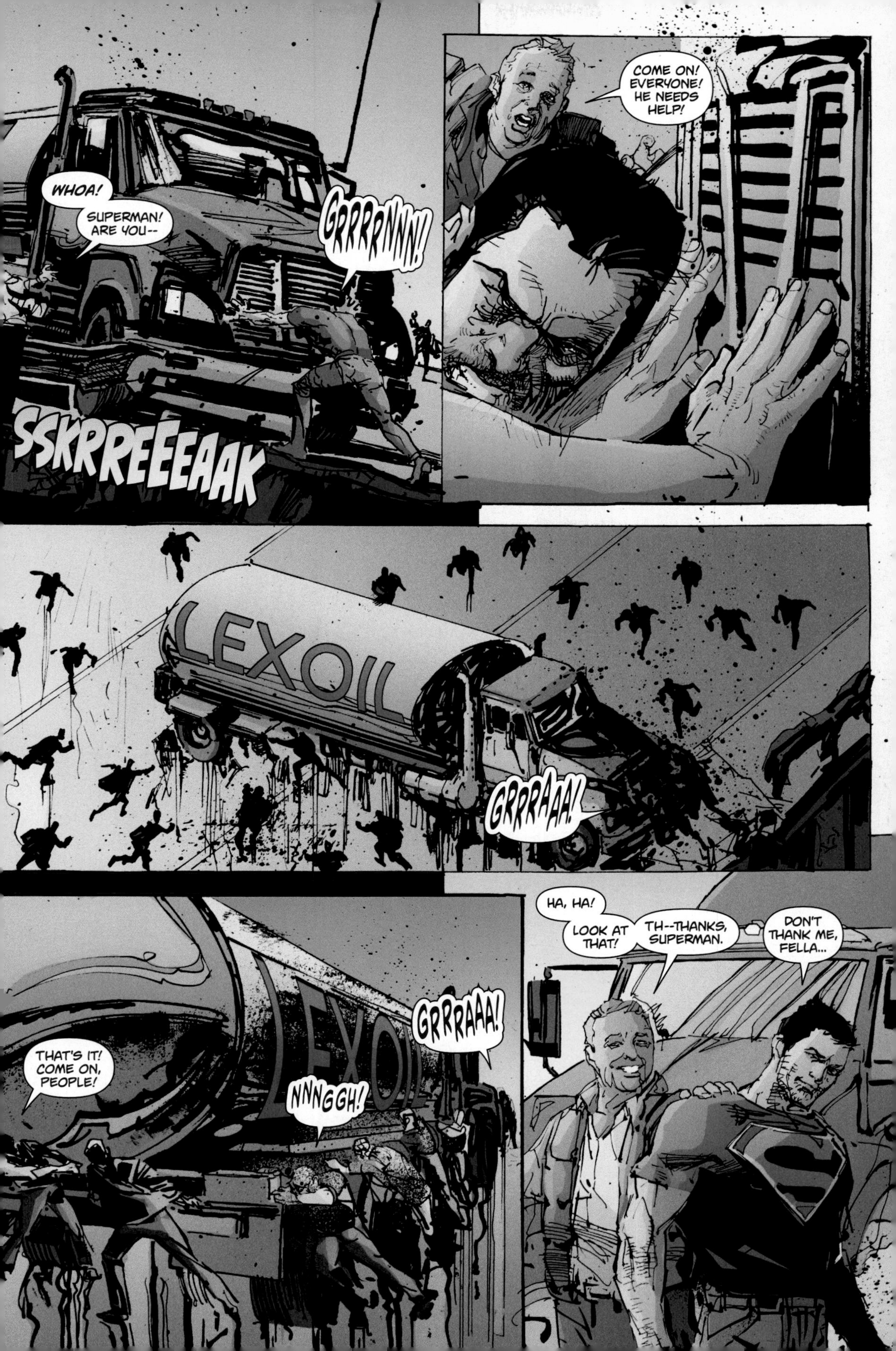
WHOA!
SUPERMAN! ARE YOU--
GRRRRNNN!
SSKRREEEAAK
COME ON! EVERYONE! HE NEEDS HELP!
LEXOIL
GRRRAAA!
LEXOIL
GRRRAAA!
THAT'S IT! COME ON, PEOPLE!
NNNGGH!
HA, HA!
LOOK AT THAT!
TH--THANKS, SUPERMAN.
DON'T THANK ME, FELLA...

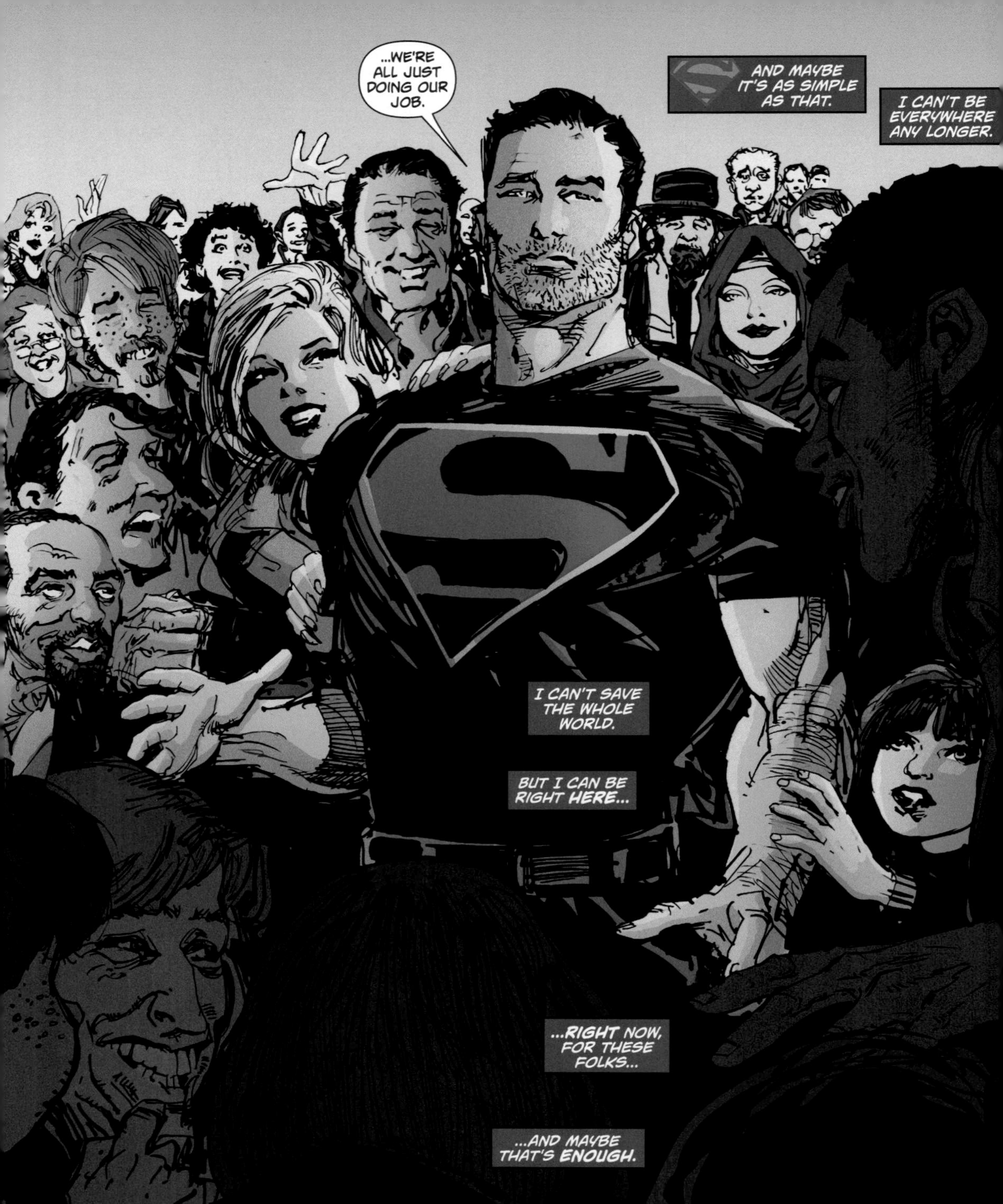
...WE'RE ALL JUST DOING OUR JOB.
AND MAYBE IT'S AS SIMPLE AS THAT.
I CAN'T BE EVERYWHERE ANY LONGER.
I CAN'T SAVE THE WHOLE WORLD.
BUT I CAN BE RIGHT HERE...
...RIGHT NOW, FOR THESE FOLKS...
...AND MAYBE THAT'S ENOUGH.

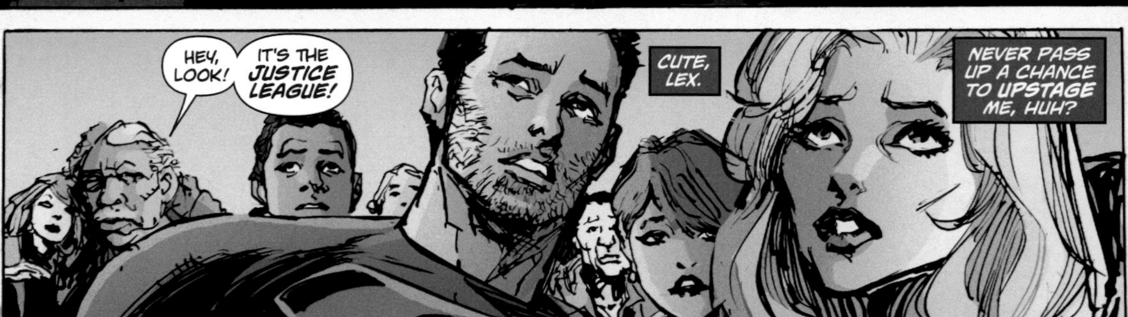
HEY, LOOK!
IT'S THE JUSTICE LEAGUE!
CUTE, LEX.
NEVER PASS UP A CHANCE TO UPSTAGE ME, HUH?

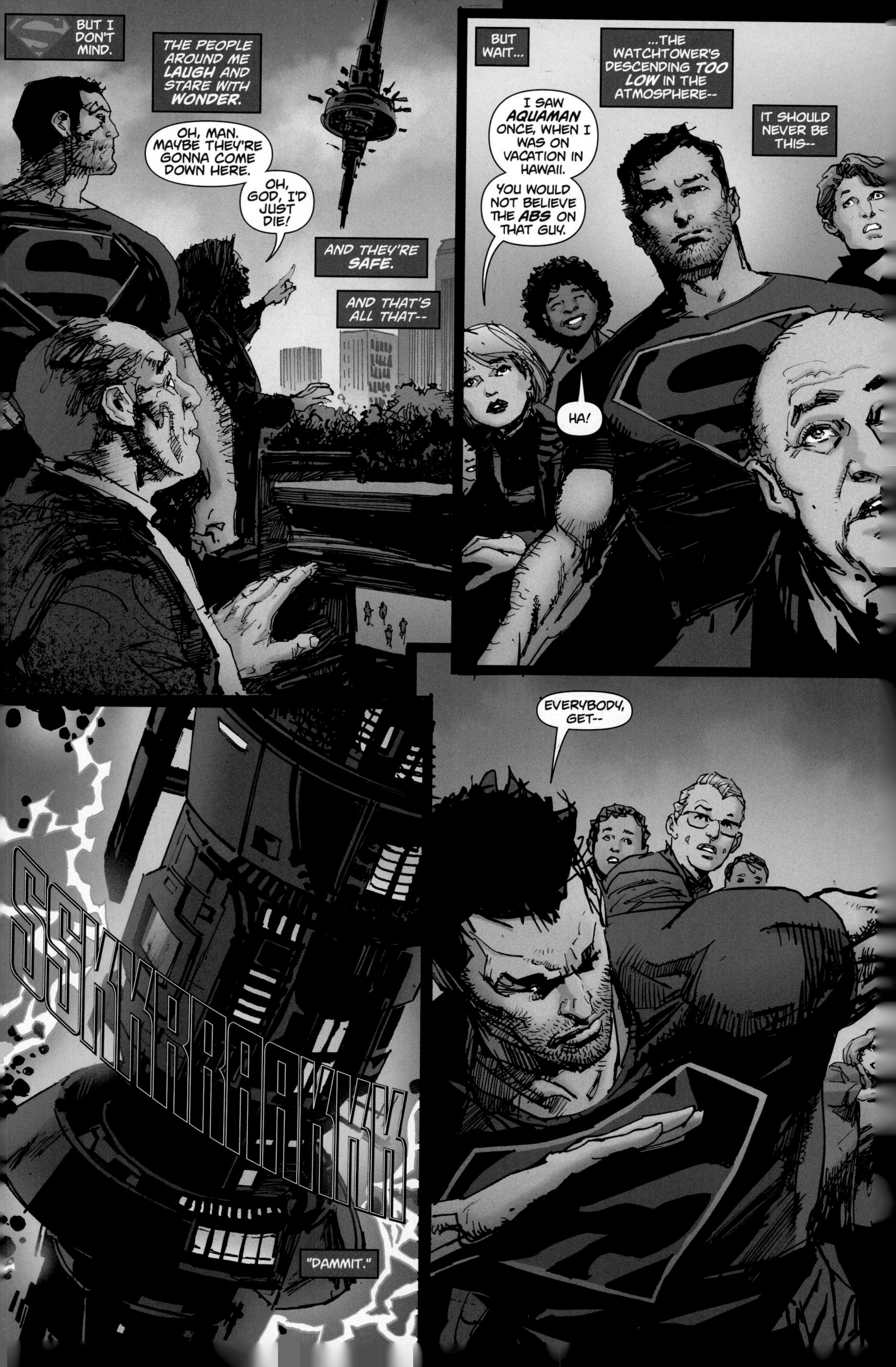
BUT I DON'T MIND.
THE PEOPLE AROUND ME LAUGH AND STARE WITH WONDER.
OH, MAN. MAYBE THEY'RE GONNA COME DOWN HERE.
OH, GOD, I'D JUST DIE!
AND THEY'RE SAFE.
AND THAT'S ALL THAT--
BUT WAIT...
...THE WATCHTOWER'S DESCENDING TOO LOW IN THE ATMOSPHERE--
I SAW AQUAMAN ONCE, WHEN I WAS ON VACATION IN HAWAII.
YOU WOULD NOT BELIEVE THE ABS ON THAT GUY.
IT SHOULD NEVER BE THIS--
HA!
SSKKRRAKKK
"DAMMIT."
EVERYBODY, GET--

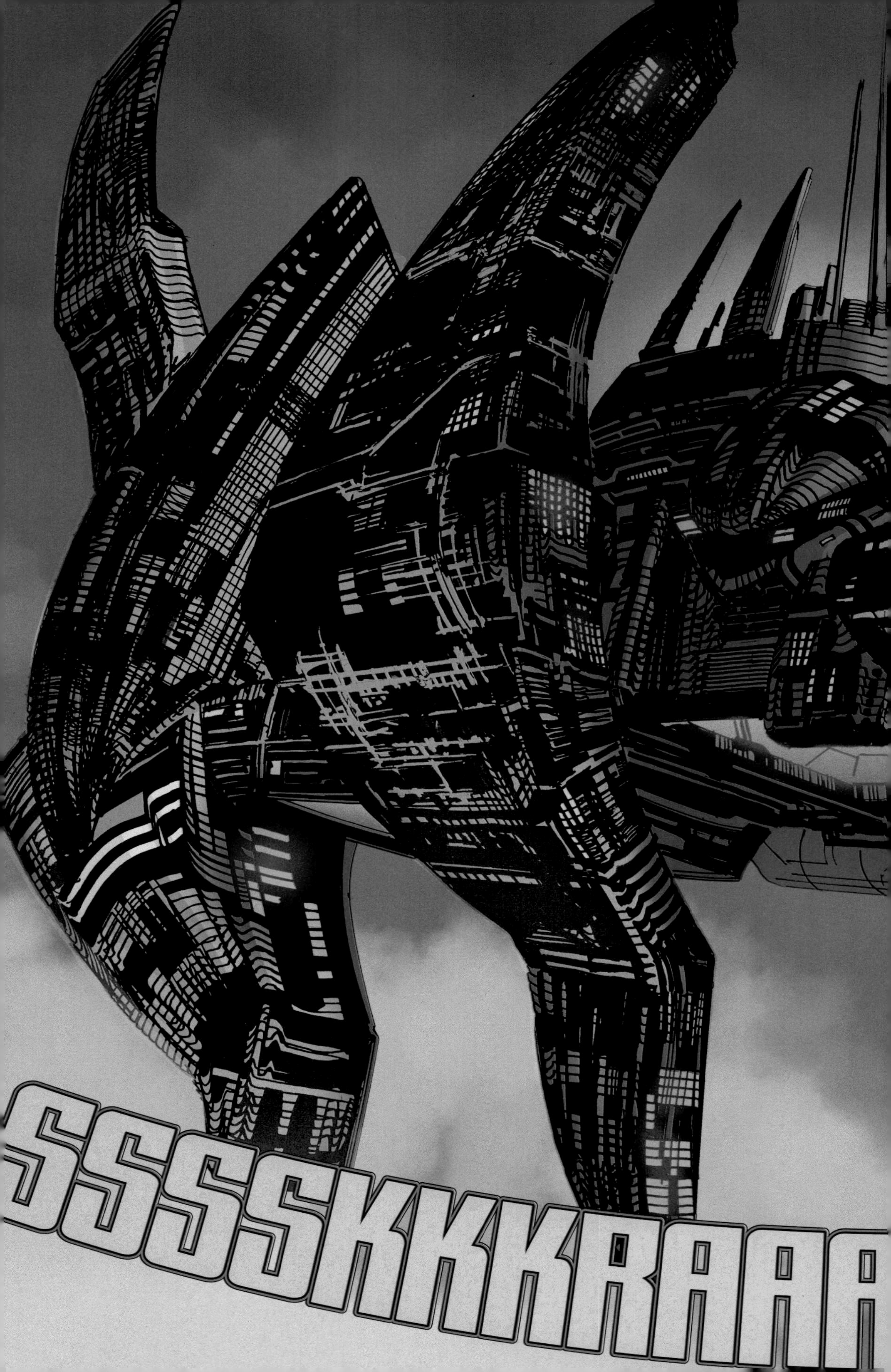
SSSSKKKRAAA

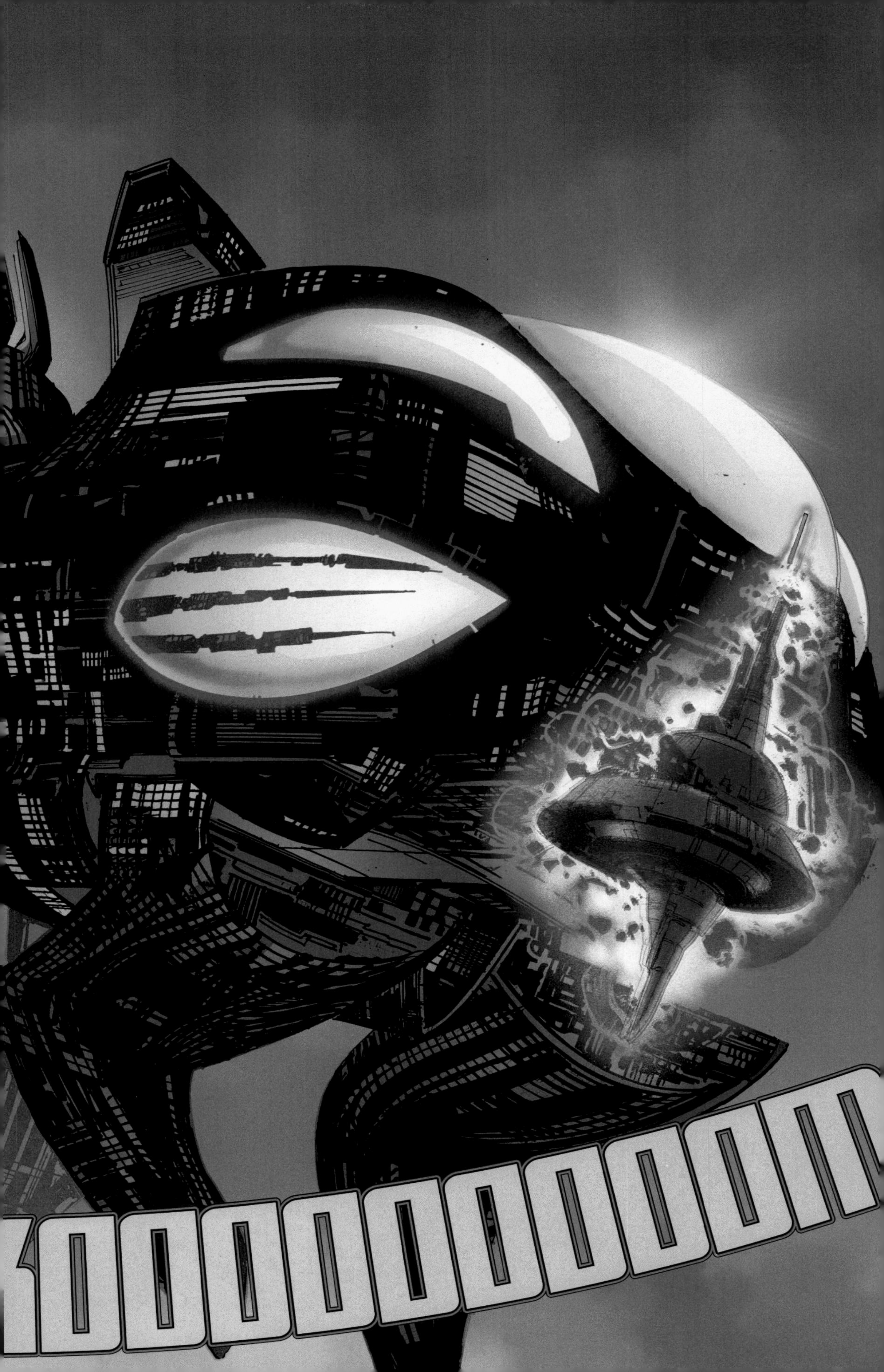
OOOOOOOOOM

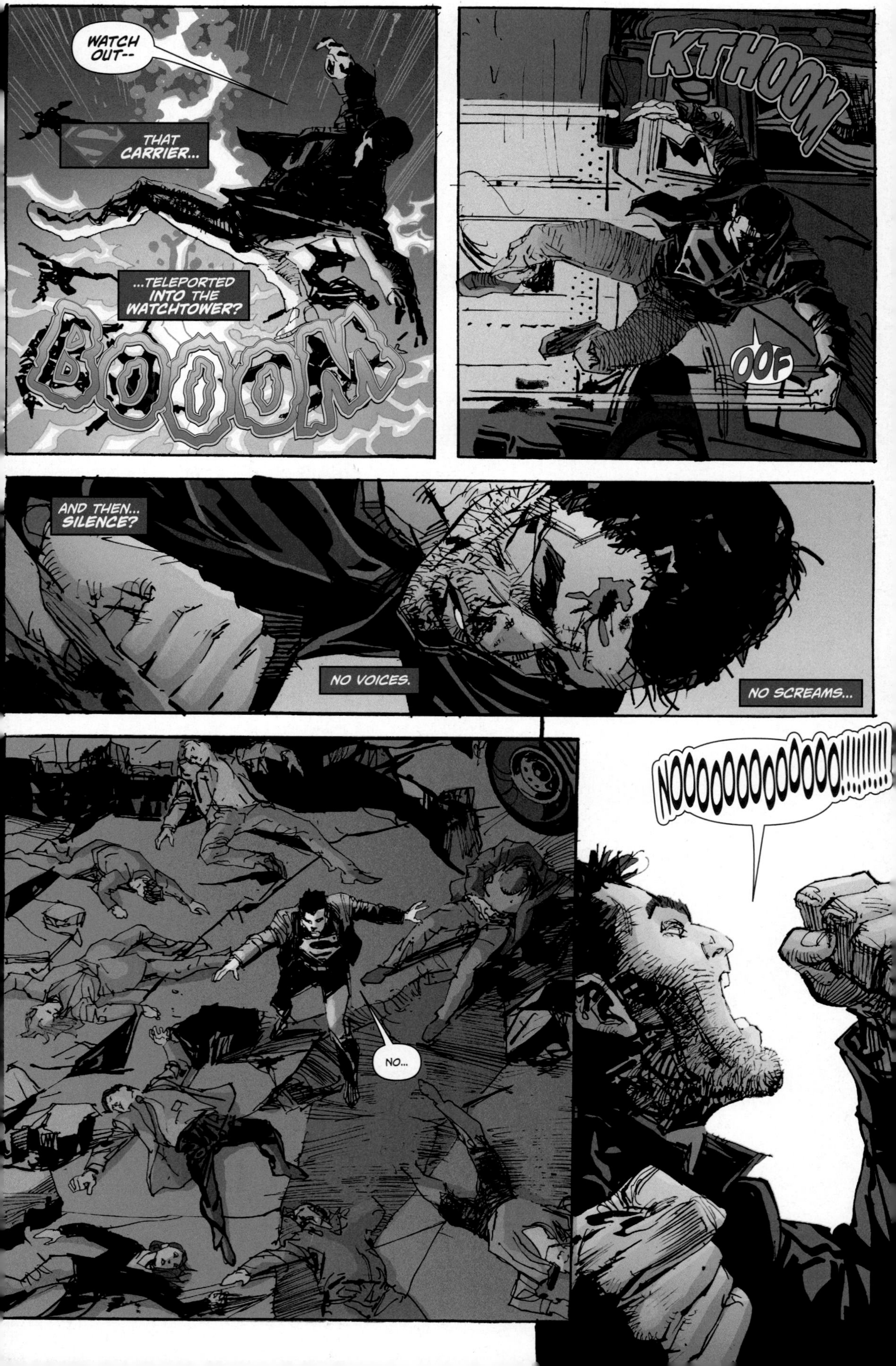
WATCH OUT--
THAT CARRIER...
...TELEPORTED INTO THE WATCHTOWER?
BOOOM
KTHOOM
OOF
AND THEN... SILENCE?
NO VOICES.
NO SCREAMS...
NO...
NOOOOOOOOOOOO!!!!!!!!

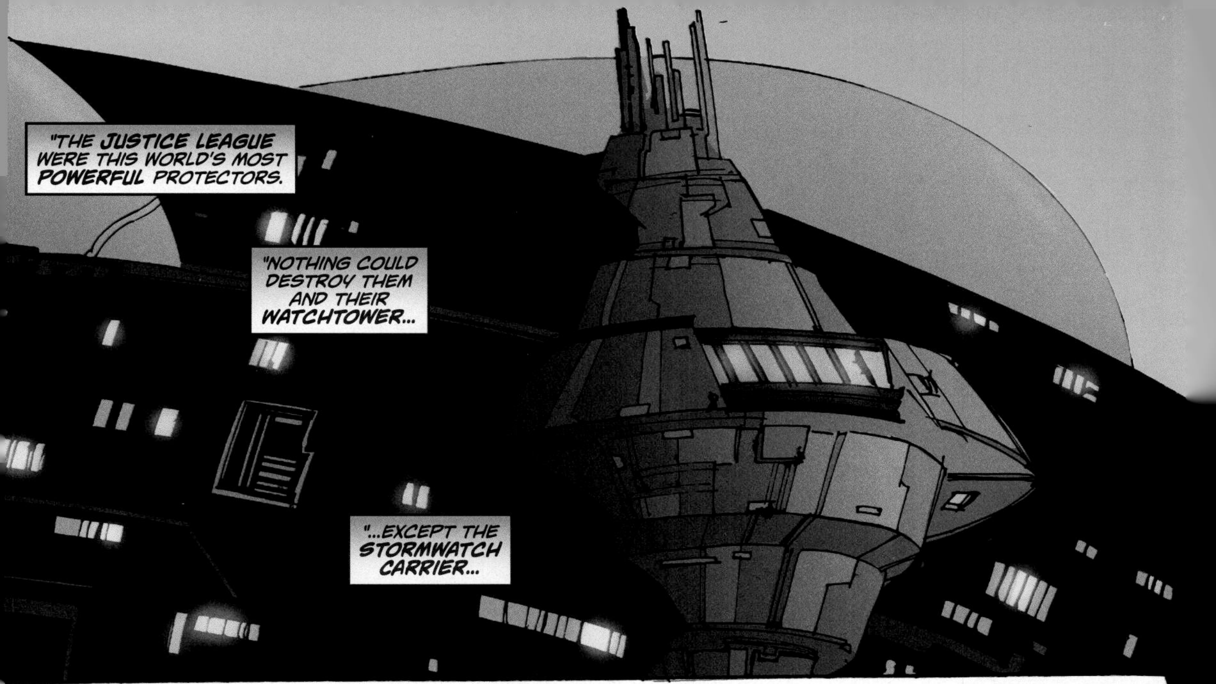
"THE JUSTICE LEAGUE WERE THIS WORLD'S MOST POWERFUL PROTECTORS.
"NOTHING COULD DESTROY THEM AND THEIR WATCHTOWER...
"...EXCEPT THE STORMWATCH CARRIER...

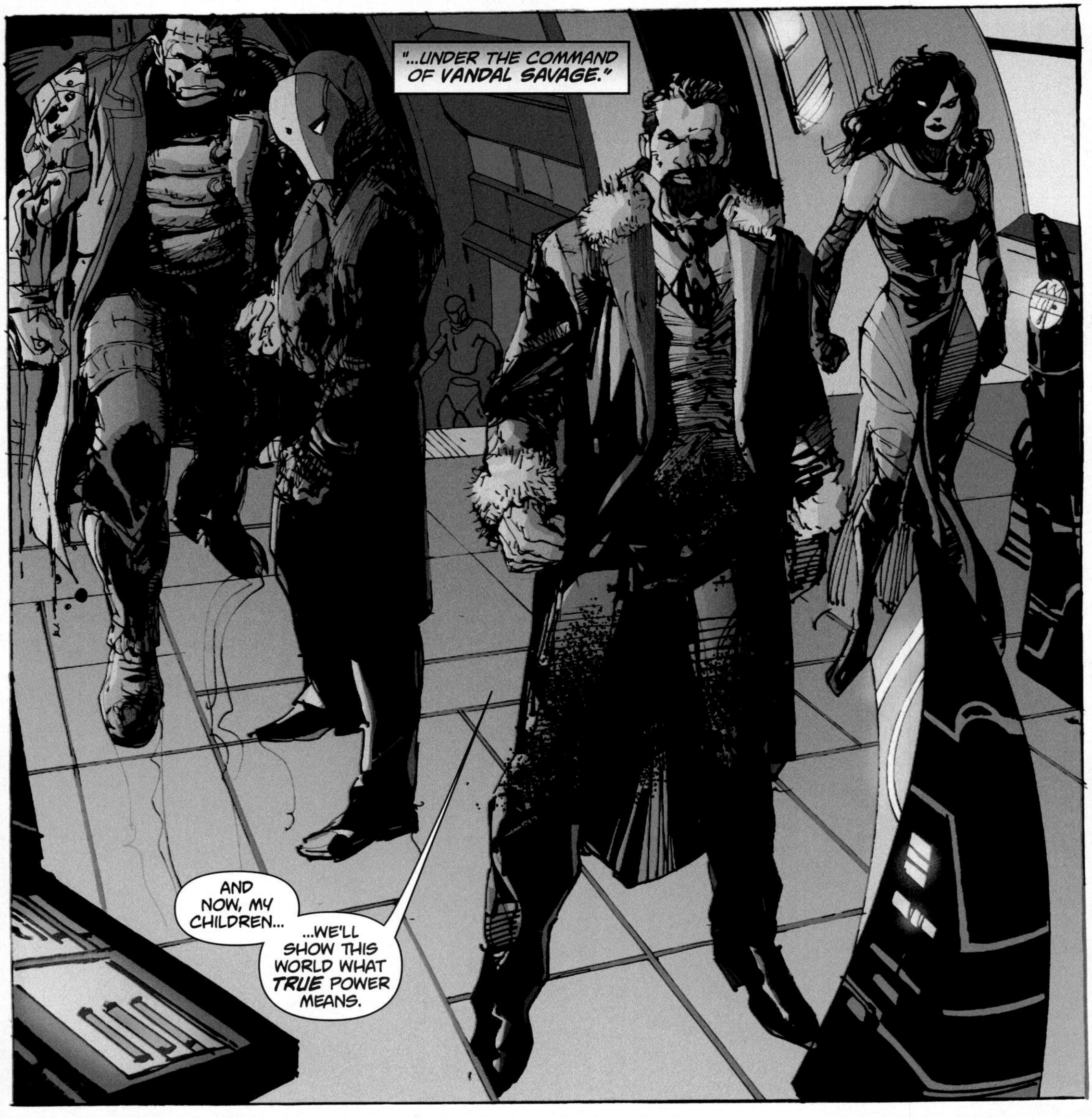
"...UNDER THE COMMAND OF VANDAL SAVAGE."
AND NOW, MY CHILDREN...
...WE'LL SHOW THIS WORLD WHAT TRUE POWER MEANS.

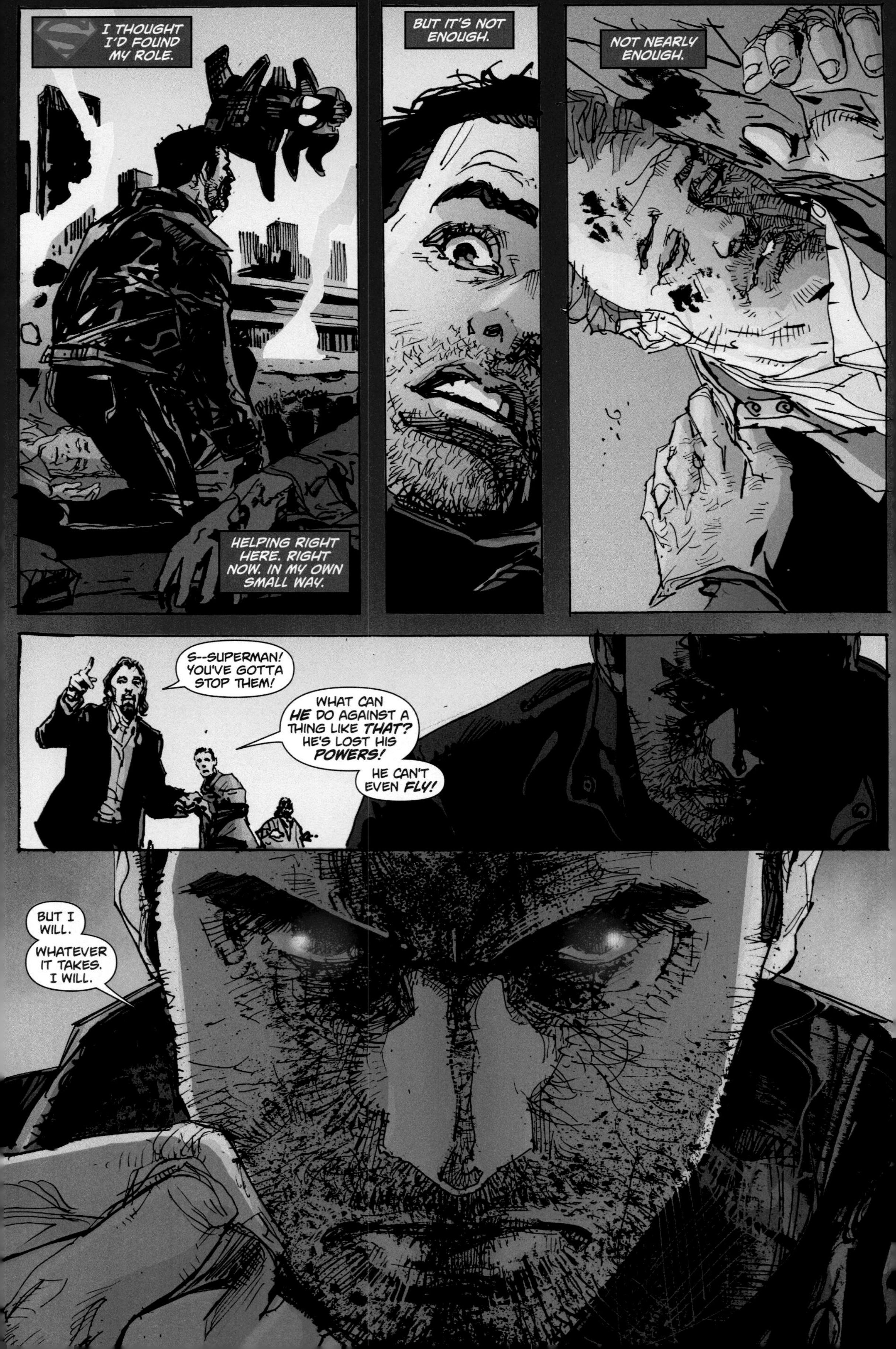
I THOUGHT I'D FOUND MY ROLE.
HELPING RIGHT HERE. RIGHT NOW. IN MY OWN SMALL WAY.
BUT IT'S NOT ENOUGH.
NOT NEARLY ENOUGH.
S--SUPERMAN! YOU'VE GOTTA STOP THEM!
WHAT CAN HE DO AGAINST A THING LIKE THAT? HE'S LOST HIS POWERS!
HE CAN'T EVEN FLY!
BUT I WILL.
WHATEVER IT TAKES. I WILL.

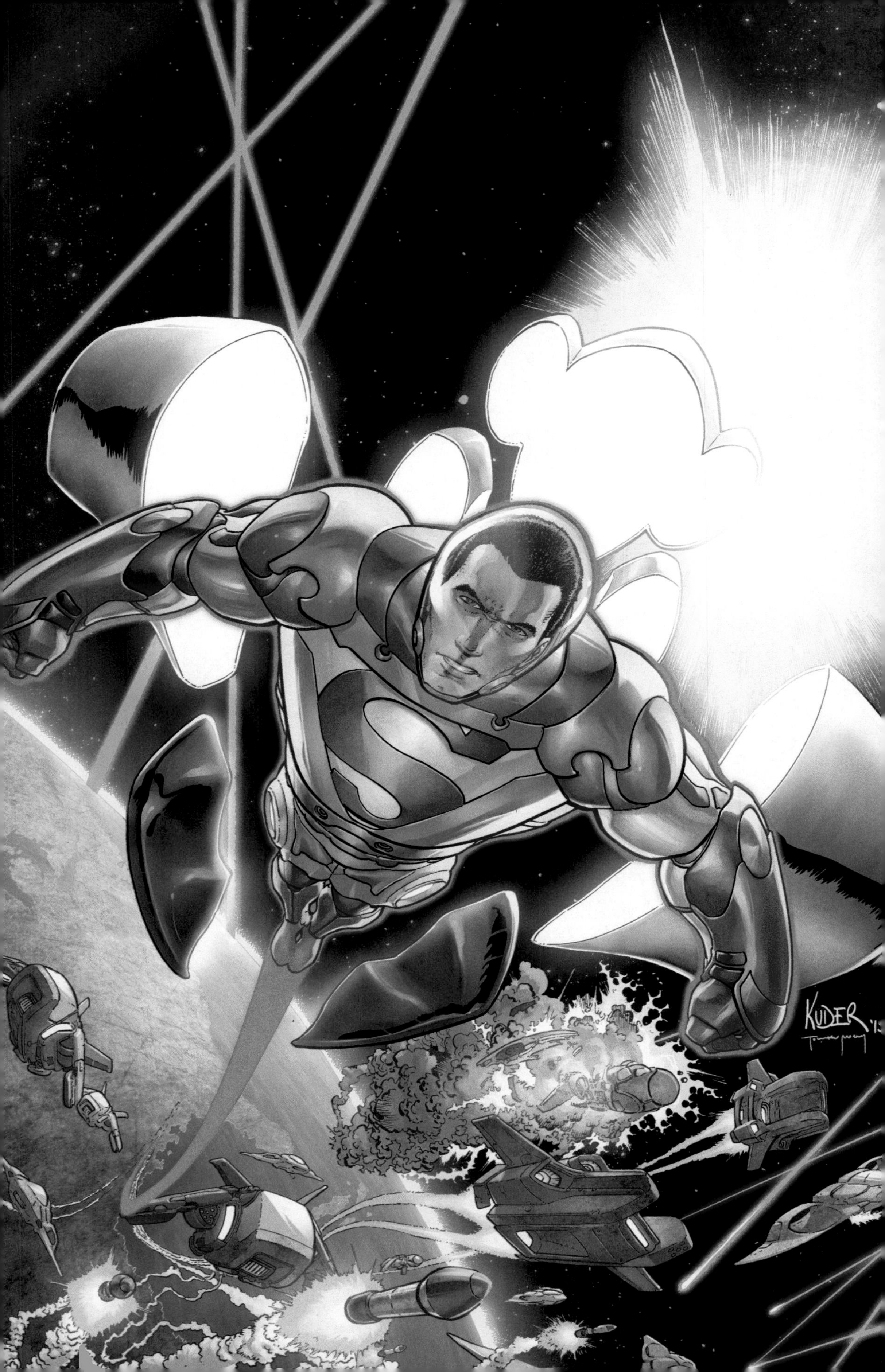
KUDER

SAVAGE DAWN: ASSAULT

GREK PAK AARON KUDER writers AARON KUDER RAFA SANDOVAL pencillers AARON KUDER JORDI TARRAGONA inkers TOMEU MOREY colorist STEVE WANDS letterer AARON KUDER TOMEU MOREY cover

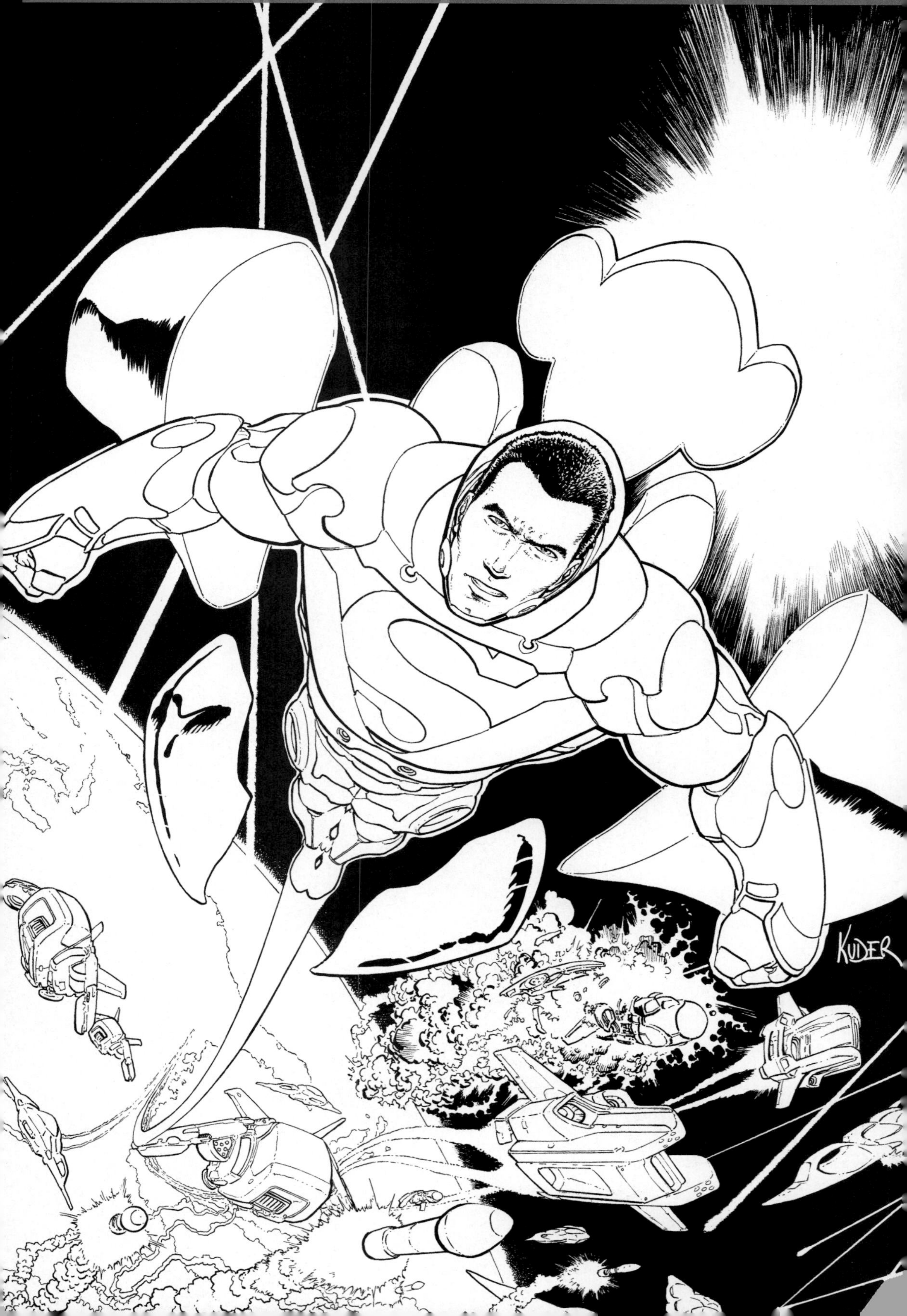
KUDER

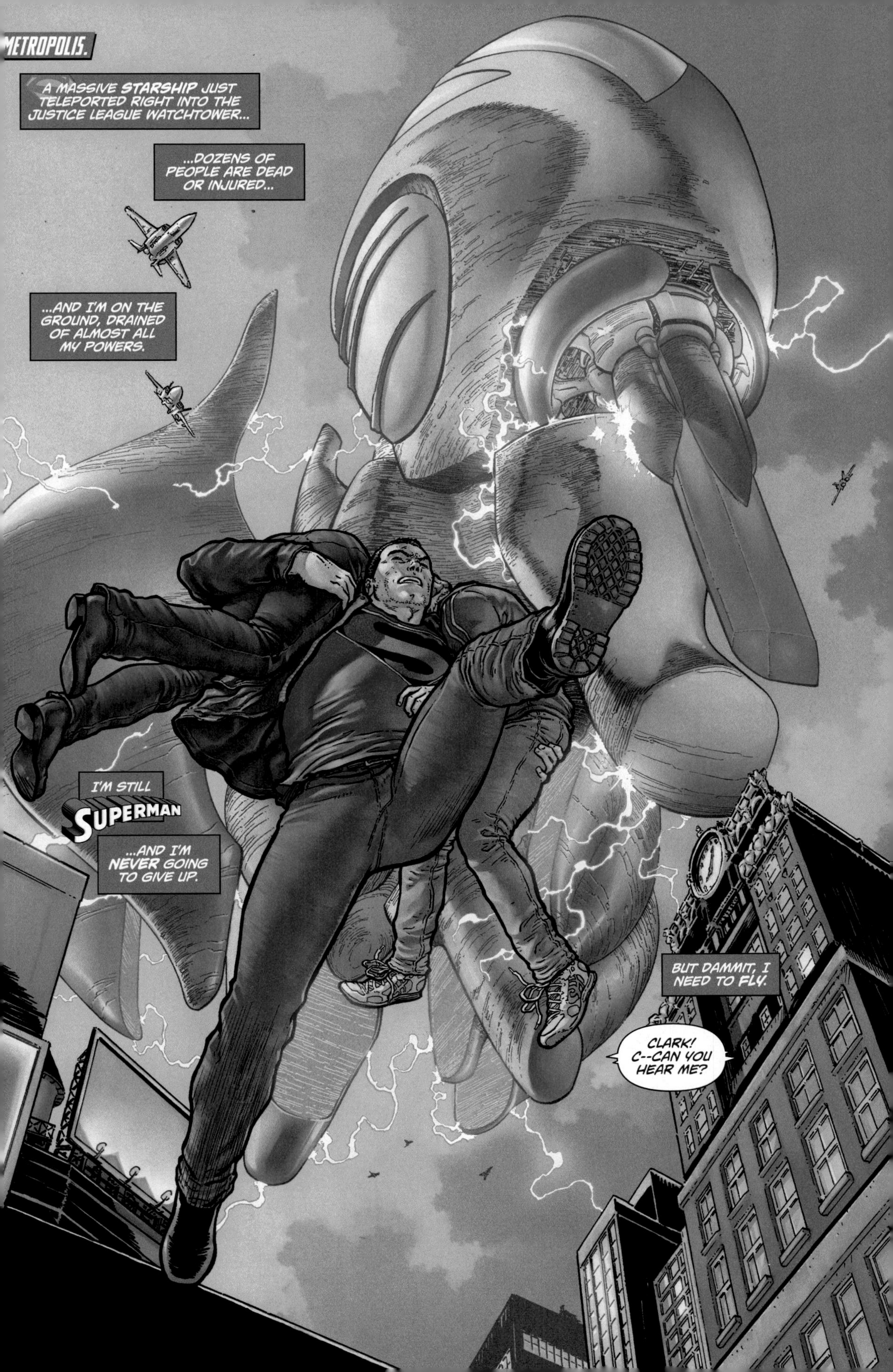
METROPOLIS.
A MASSIVE STARSHIP JUST TELEPORTED RIGHT INTO THE JUSTICE LEAGUE WATCHTOWER...
...DOZENS OF PEOPLE ARE DEAD OR INJURED...
...AND I'M ON THE GROUND, DRAINED OF ALMOST ALL MY POWERS.
I'M STILL
SUPERMAN
...AND I'M NEVER GOING TO GIVE UP.
BUT DAMMIT, I NEED TO FLY.
CLARK! C--CAN YOU HEAR ME?

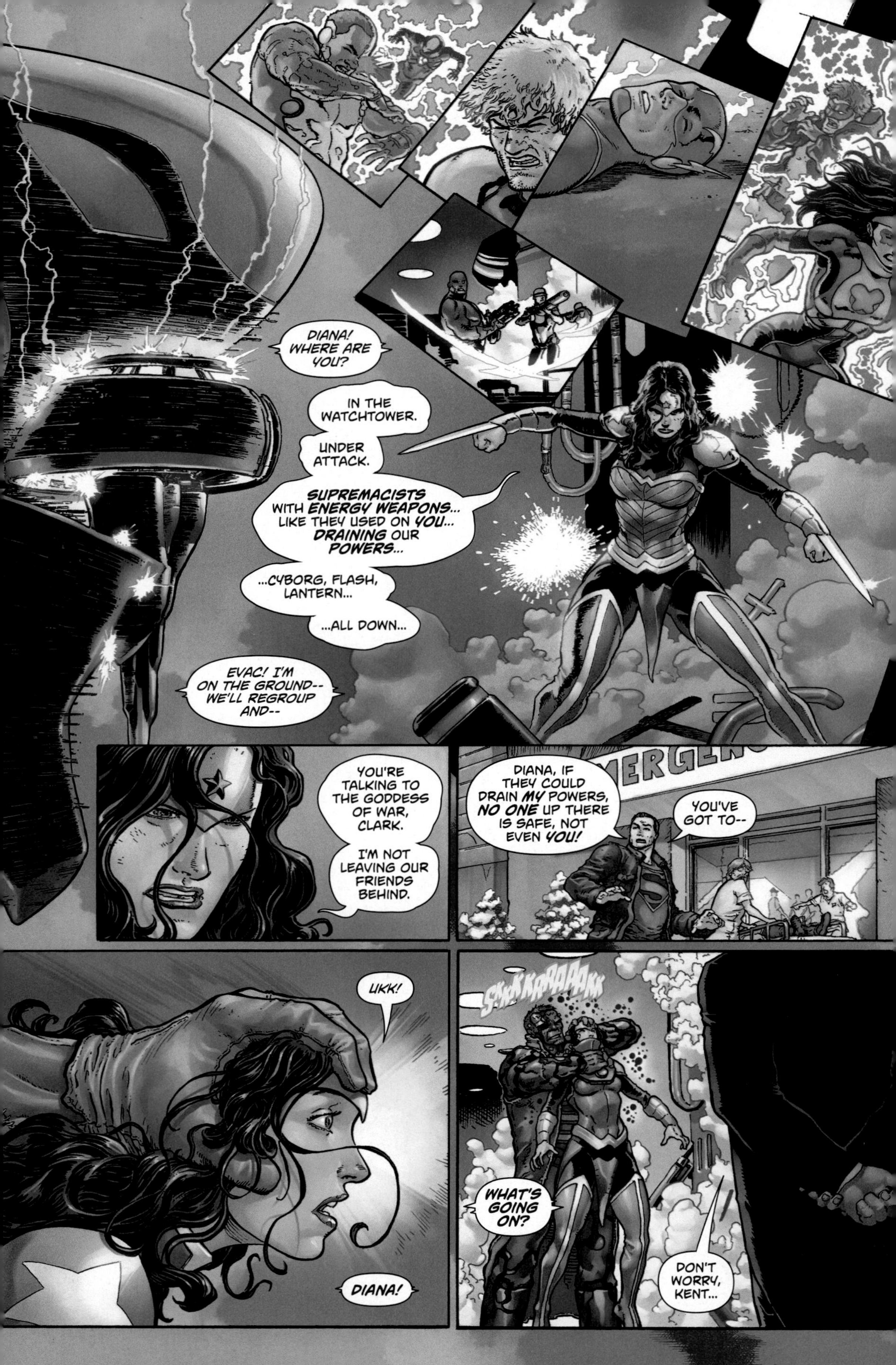
DIANA! WHERE ARE YOU?
IN THE WATCHTOWER.
UNDER ATTACK.
SUPREMACISTS WITH ENERGY WEAPONS... LIKE THEY USED ON YOU... DRAINING OUR POWERS...
...CYBORG, FLASH, LANTERN...
...ALL DOWN...
EVAC! I'M ON THE GROUND-- WE'LL REGROUP AND--
YOU'RE TALKING TO THE GODDESS OF WAR, CLARK.
I'M NOT LEAVING OUR FRIENDS BEHIND.
DIANA, IF THEY COULD DRAIN MY POWERS, NO ONE UP THERE IS SAFE, NOT EVEN YOU!
YOU'VE GOT TO--
UKK!
DIANA!
SKKKKRRAAAKK
WHAT'S GOING ON?
DON'T WORRY, KENT...

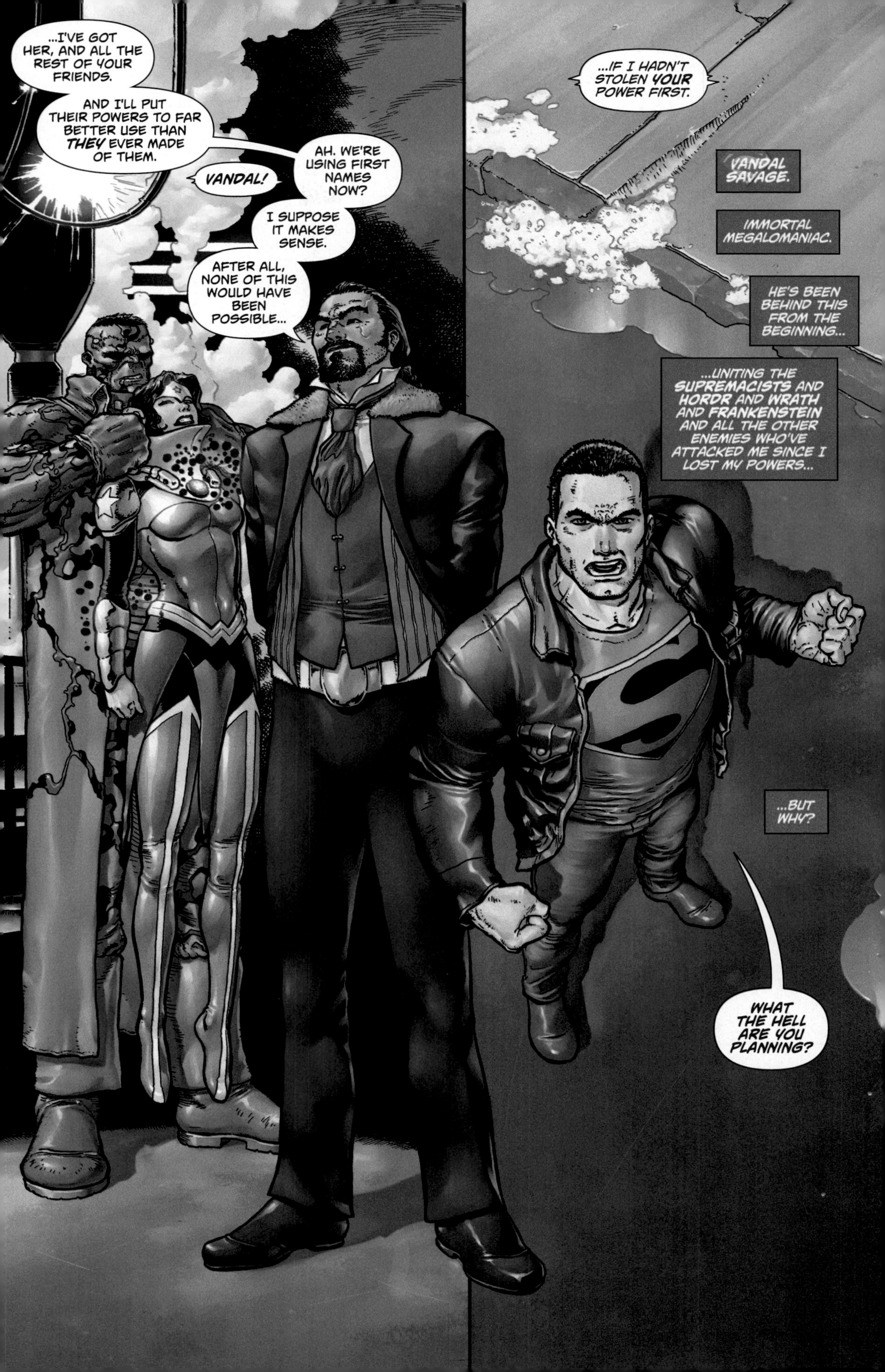
...I'VE GOT HER, AND ALL THE REST OF YOUR FRIENDS.
AND I'LL PUT THEIR POWERS TO FAR BETTER USE THAN THEY EVER MADE OF THEM.
VANDAL!
AH. WE'RE USING FIRST NAMES NOW?
I SUPPOSE IT MAKES SENSE.
AFTER ALL, NONE OF THIS WOULD HAVE BEEN POSSIBLE...
...IF I HADN'T STOLEN YOUR POWER FIRST.
VANDAL SAVAGE.
IMMORTAL MEGALOMANIAC.
HE'S BEEN BEHIND THIS FROM THE BEGINNING...
...UNITING THE SUPREMACISTS AND HORDR AND WRATH AND FRANKENSTEIN AND ALL THE OTHER ENEMIES WHO'VE ATTACKED ME SINCE I LOST MY POWERS...
...BUT WHY?
WHAT THE HELL ARE YOU PLANNING?

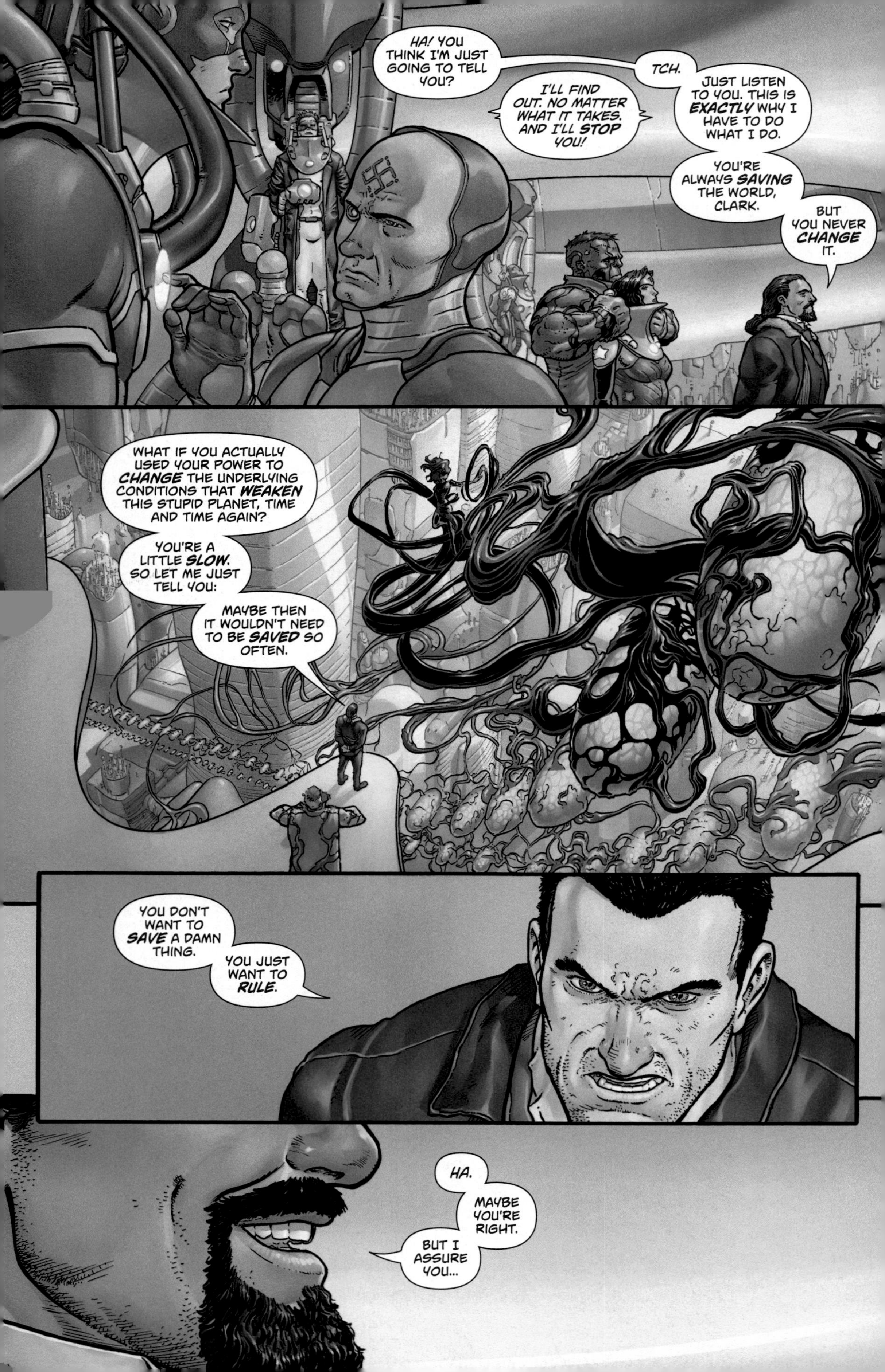
HA! YOU THINK I'M JUST GOING TO TELL YOU?
TCH.
I'LL FIND OUT. NO MATTER WHAT IT TAKES. AND I'LL STOP YOU!
JUST LISTEN TO YOU. THIS IS EXACTLY WHY I HAVE TO DO WHAT I DO.
YOU'RE ALWAYS SAVING THE WORLD, CLARK.
BUT YOU NEVER CHANGE IT.
WHAT IF YOU ACTUALLY USED YOUR POWER TO CHANGE THE UNDERLYING CONDITIONS THAT WEAKEN THIS STUPID PLANET, TIME AND TIME AGAIN?
YOU'RE A LITTLE SLOW. SO LET ME JUST TELL YOU:
MAYBE THEN IT WOULDN'T NEED TO BE SAVED SO OFTEN.
YOU DON'T WANT TO SAVE A DAMN THING.
YOU JUST WANT TO RULE.
HA.
MAYBE YOU'RE RIGHT.
BUT I ASSURE YOU...

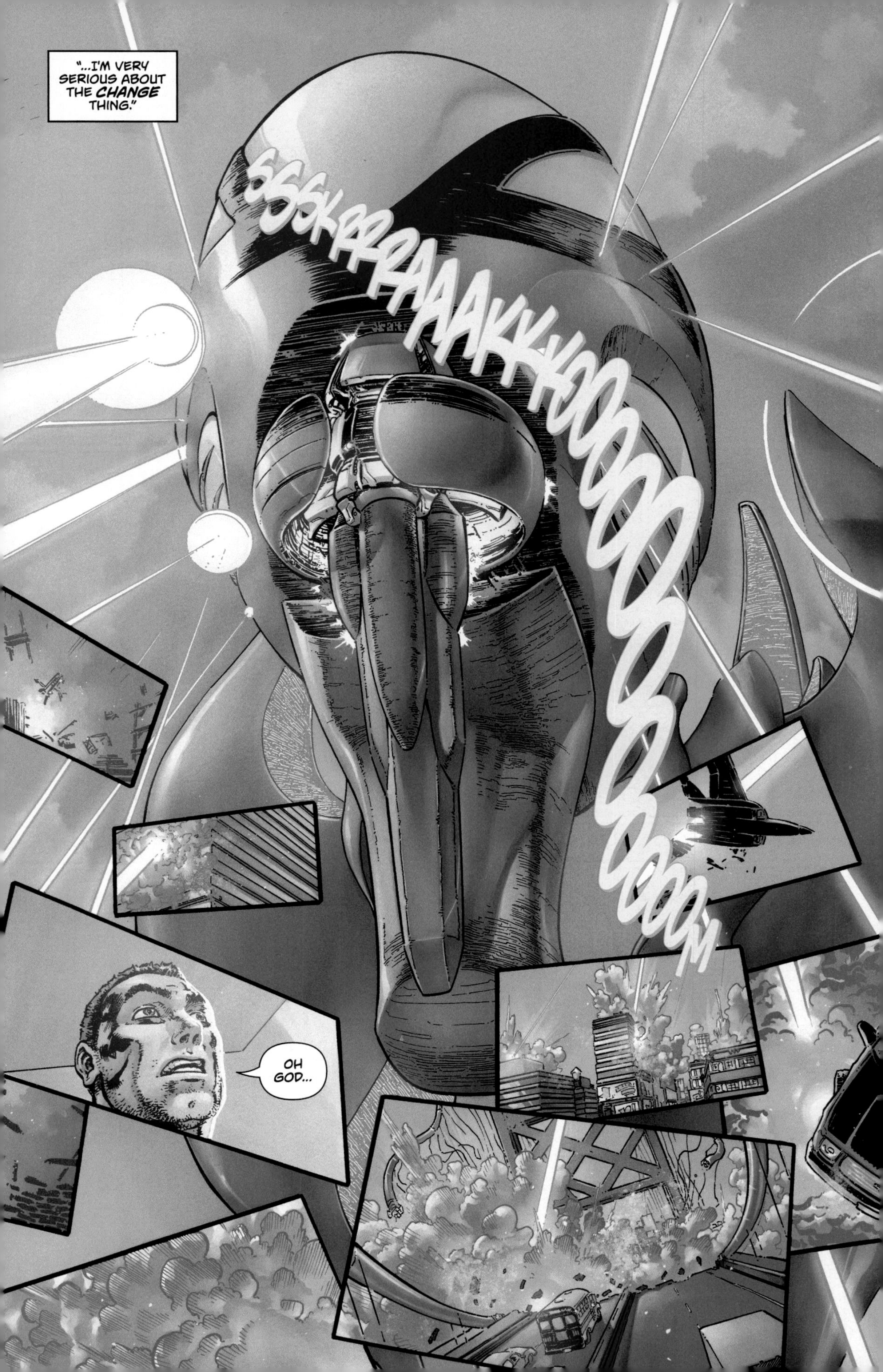
"...I'M VERY SERIOUS ABOUT THE *CHANGE* THING."
SSSKRRRAAAKKKOOOOOOOOOOOOOOM
OH GOD...

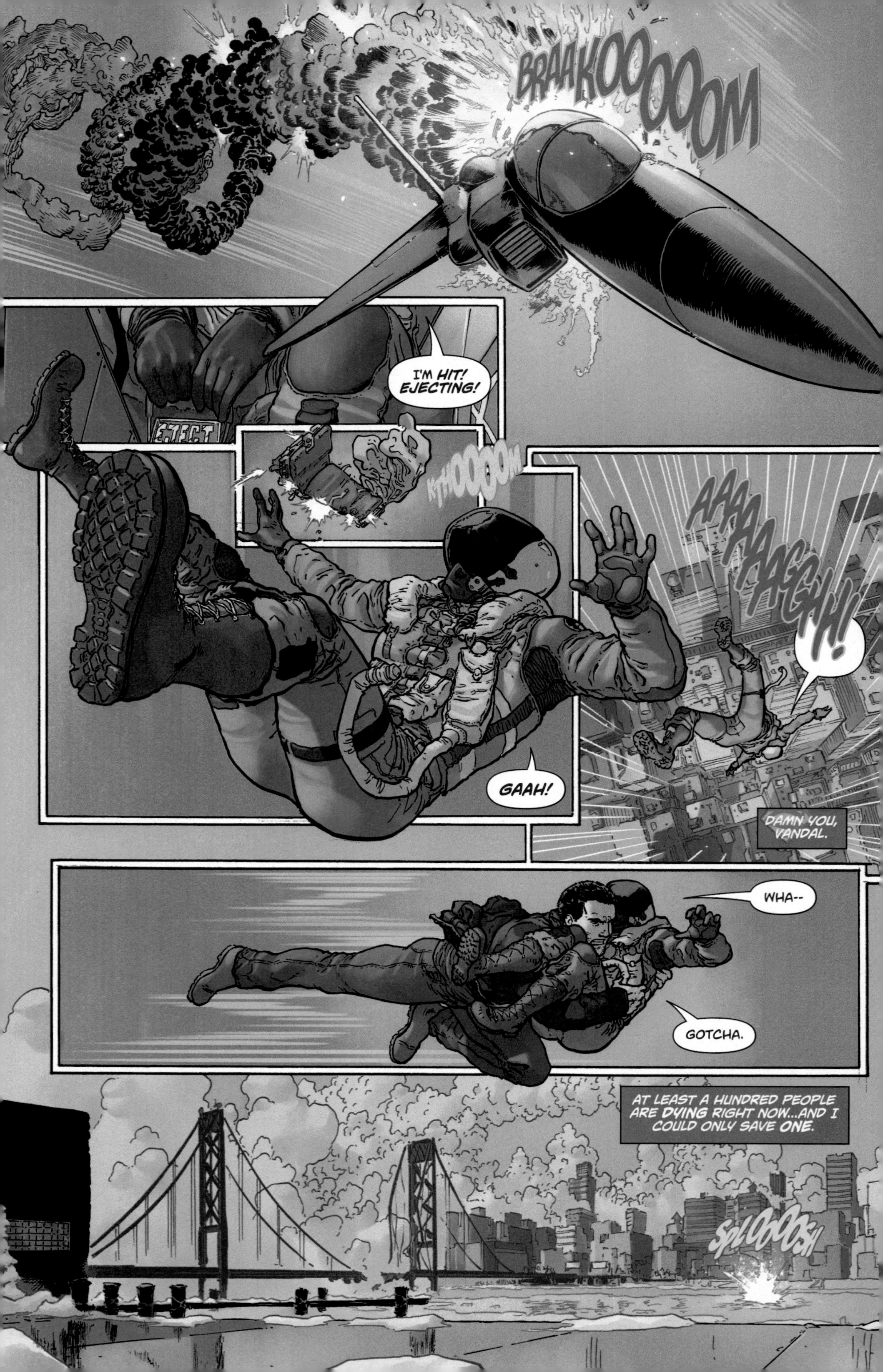
BRAAKOOOOOM
I'M HIT! EJECTING!
EJECT
KTHOOOOM
GAAH!
AAAAAAAGHH!
DAMN YOU, VANDAL.
WHA--
GOTCHA.
AT LEAST A HUNDRED PEOPLE ARE DYING RIGHT NOW...AND I COULD ONLY SAVE ONE.
SPLOOOOSH

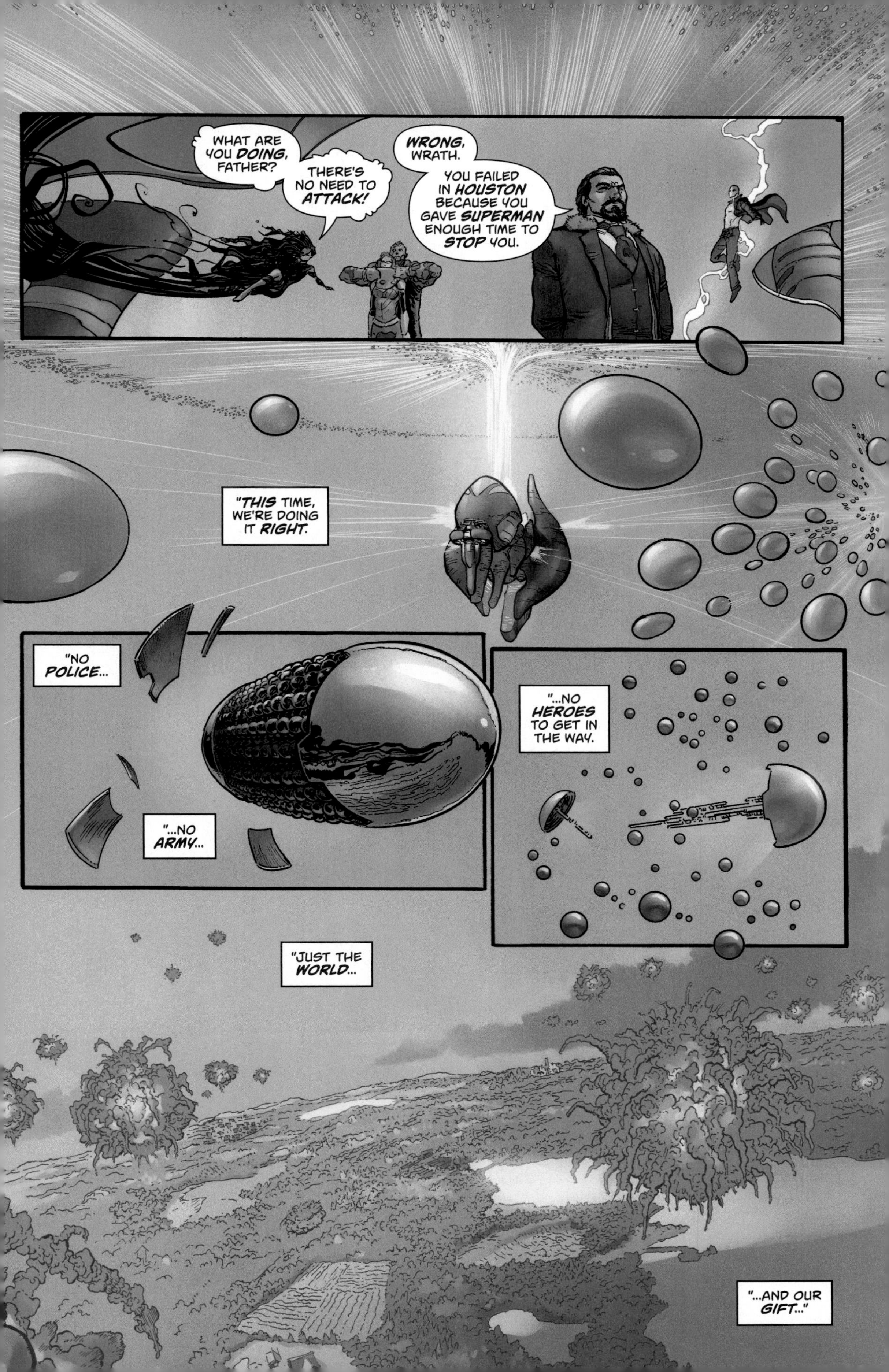
WHAT ARE YOU DOING, FATHER?
THERE'S NO NEED TO ATTACK!
WRONG, WRATH.
YOU FAILED IN HOUSTON BECAUSE YOU GAVE SUPERMAN ENOUGH TIME TO STOP YOU.
"THIS TIME, WE'RE DOING IT RIGHT.
"NO POLICE...
"...NO ARMY...
"...NO HEROES TO GET IN THE WAY.
"JUST THE WORLD...
"...AND OUR GIFT..."

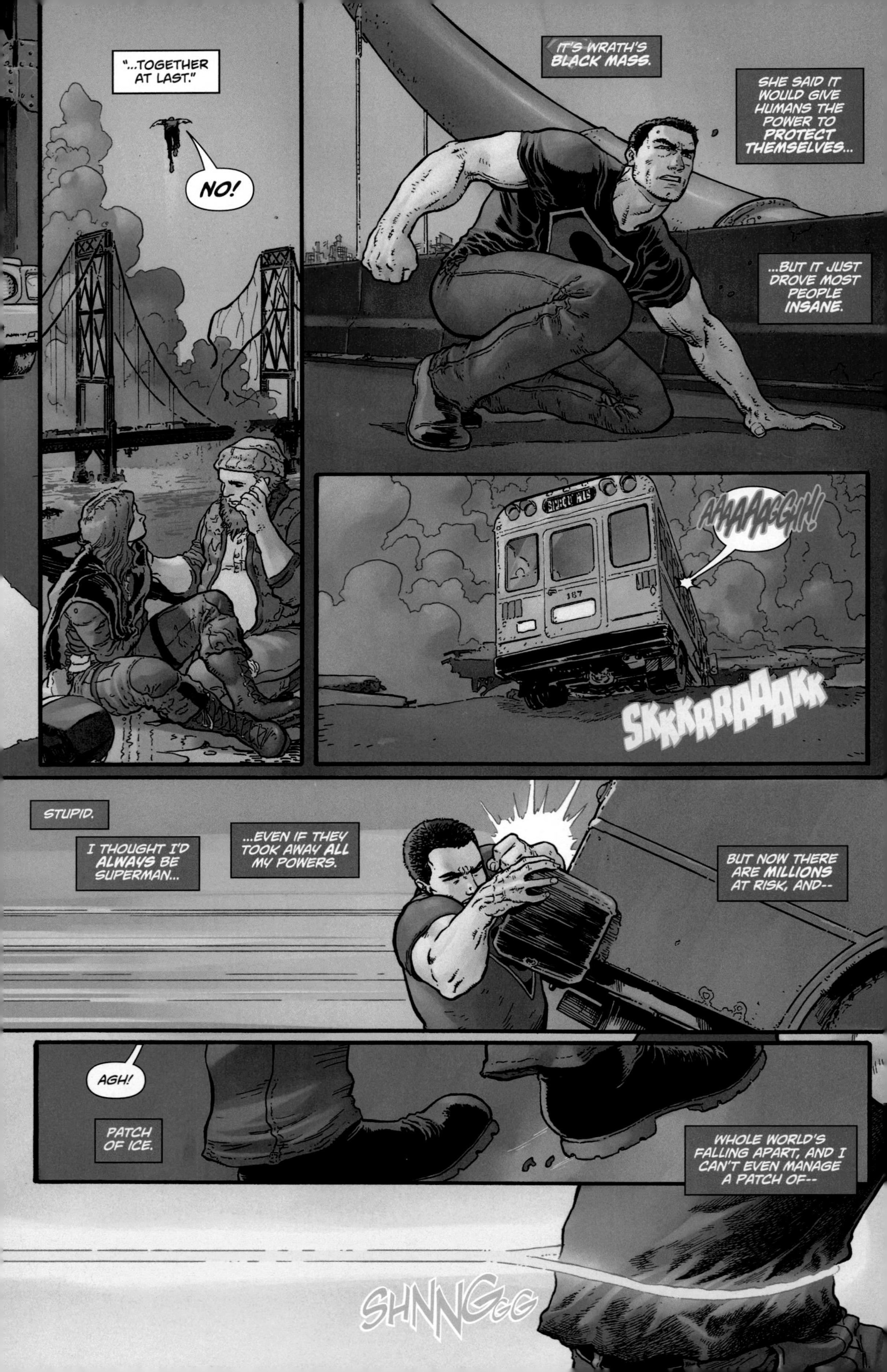
"...TOGETHER AT LAST."
NO!
IT'S WRATH'S BLACK MASS.
SHE SAID IT WOULD GIVE HUMANS THE POWER TO PROTECT THEMSELVES...
...BUT IT JUST DROVE MOST PEOPLE INSANE.
AAAAAAAGGHH!
SKKKRRAAAKK
STUPID.
I THOUGHT I'D ALWAYS BE SUPERMAN...
...EVEN IF THEY TOOK AWAY ALL MY POWERS.
BUT NOW THERE ARE MILLIONS AT RISK, AND--
AGH!
PATCH OF ICE.
WHOLE WORLD'S FALLING APART, AND I CAN'T EVEN MANAGE A PATCH OF--
SHNNGGG

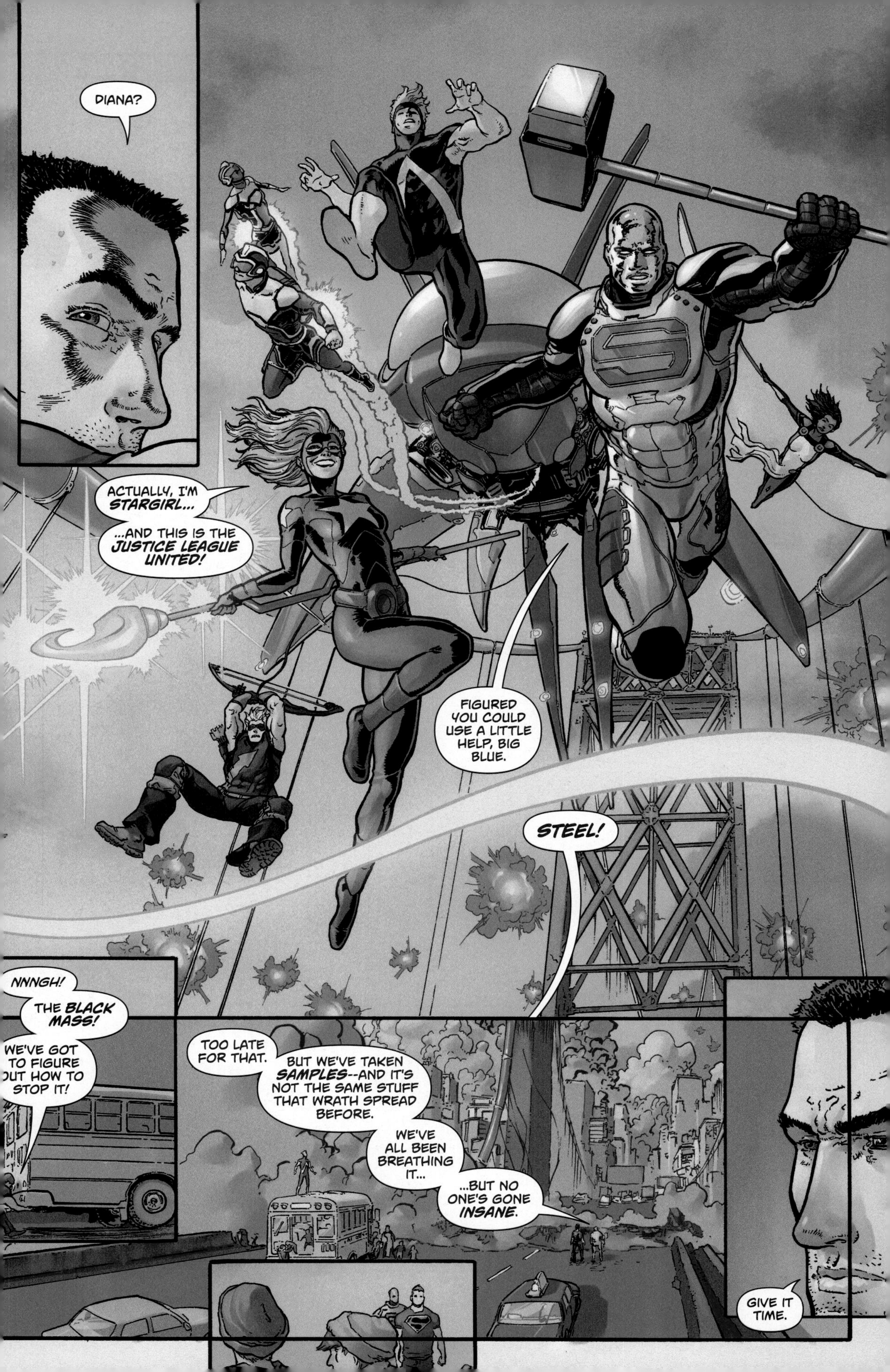
DIANA?
ACTUALLY, I'M STARGIRL...
...AND THIS IS THE JUSTICE LEAGUE UNITED!
FIGURED YOU COULD USE A LITTLE HELP, BIG BLUE.
STEEL!
NNNGH!
THE BLACK MASS!
WE'VE GOT TO FIGURE OUT HOW TO STOP IT!
TOO LATE FOR THAT.
BUT WE'VE TAKEN SAMPLES--AND IT'S NOT THE SAME STUFF THAT WRATH SPREAD BEFORE.
WE'VE ALL BEEN BREATHING IT...
...BUT NO ONE'S GONE INSANE.
GIVE IT TIME.

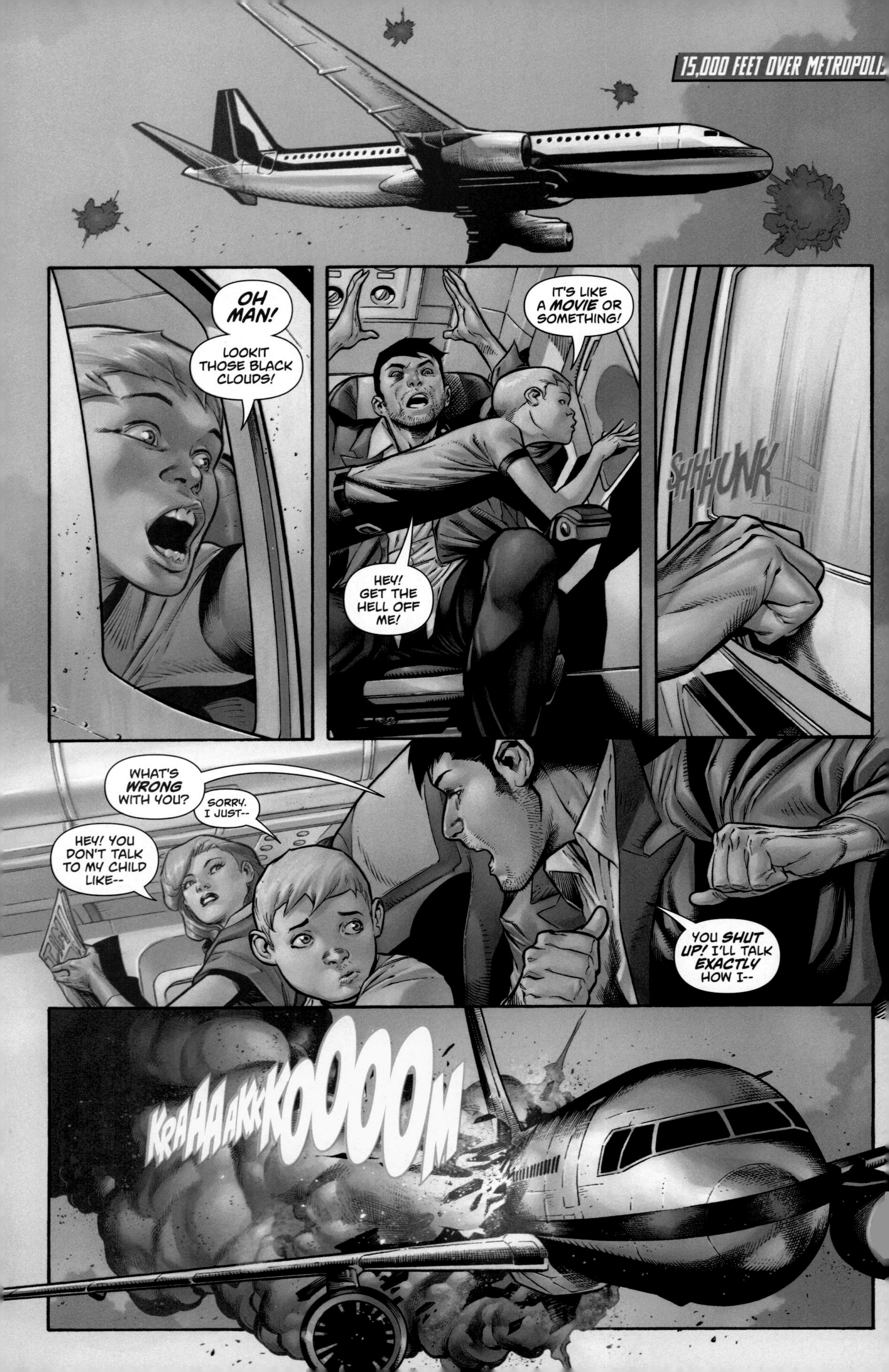
15,000 FEET OVER METROPOLIS
OH MAN!
LOOKIT THOSE BLACK CLOUDS!
IT'S LIKE A MOVIE OR SOMETHING!
HEY! GET THE HELL OFF ME!
SHHHUNK
WHAT'S WRONG WITH YOU?
SORRY. I JUST--
HEY! YOU DON'T TALK TO MY CHILD LIKE--
YOU SHUT UP! I'LL TALK EXACTLY HOW I--
KRAAAAKKKOOOOM

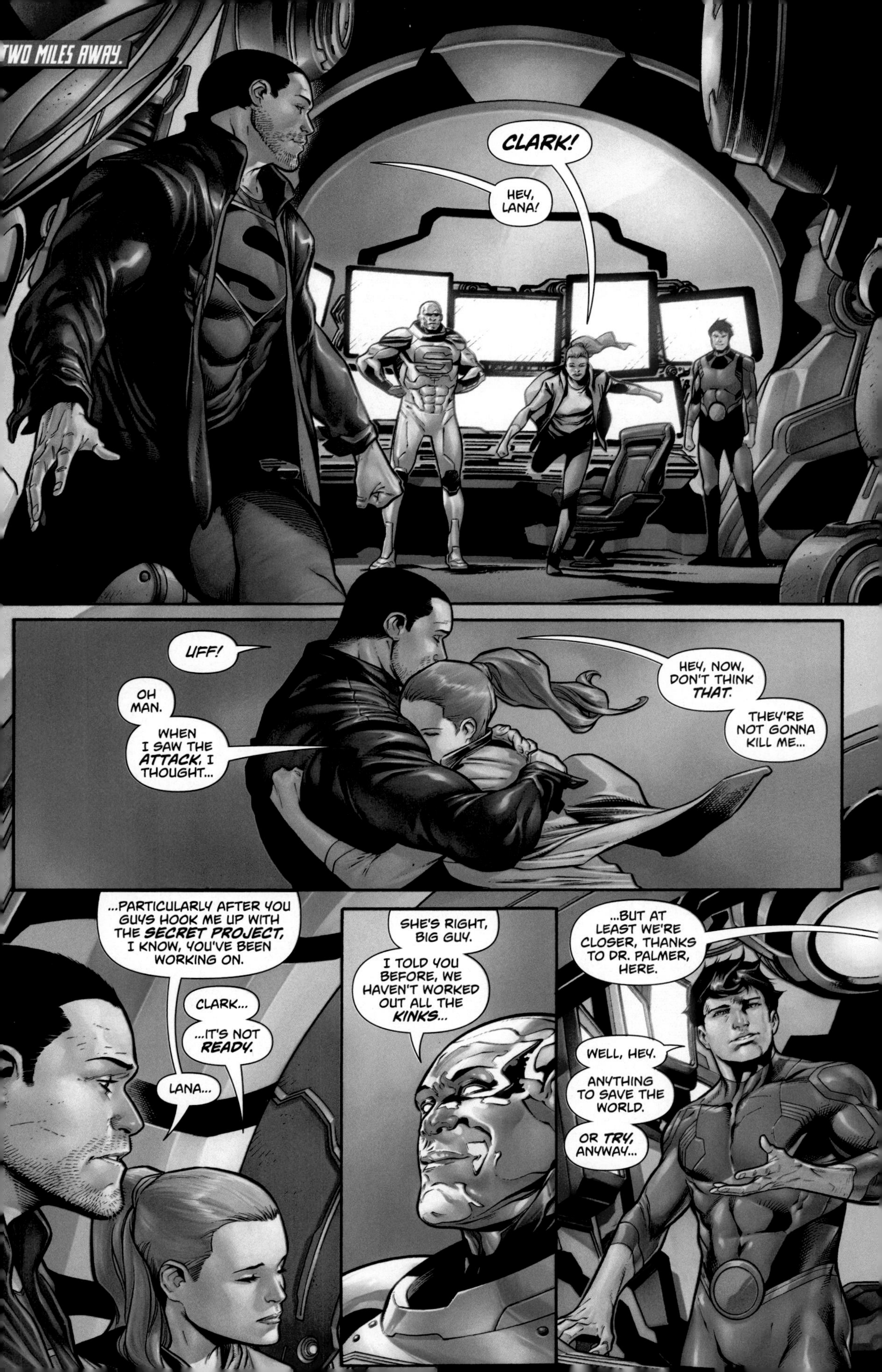
TWO MILES AWAY.
CLARK!
HEY, LANA!
UFF!
OH MAN.
WHEN I SAW THE ATTACK, I THOUGHT...
HEY, NOW, DON'T THINK THAT.
THEY'RE NOT GONNA KILL ME...
...PARTICULARLY AFTER YOU GUYS HOOK ME UP WITH THE SECRET PROJECT, I KNOW, YOU'VE BEEN WORKING ON.
CLARK...
...IT'S NOT READY.
LANA...
SHE'S RIGHT, BIG GUY.
I TOLD YOU BEFORE, WE HAVEN'T WORKED OUT ALL THE KINKS...
...BUT AT LEAST WE'RE CLOSER, THANKS TO DR. PALMER, HERE.
WELL, HEY.
ANYTHING TO SAVE THE WORLD.
OR TRY, ANYWAY...

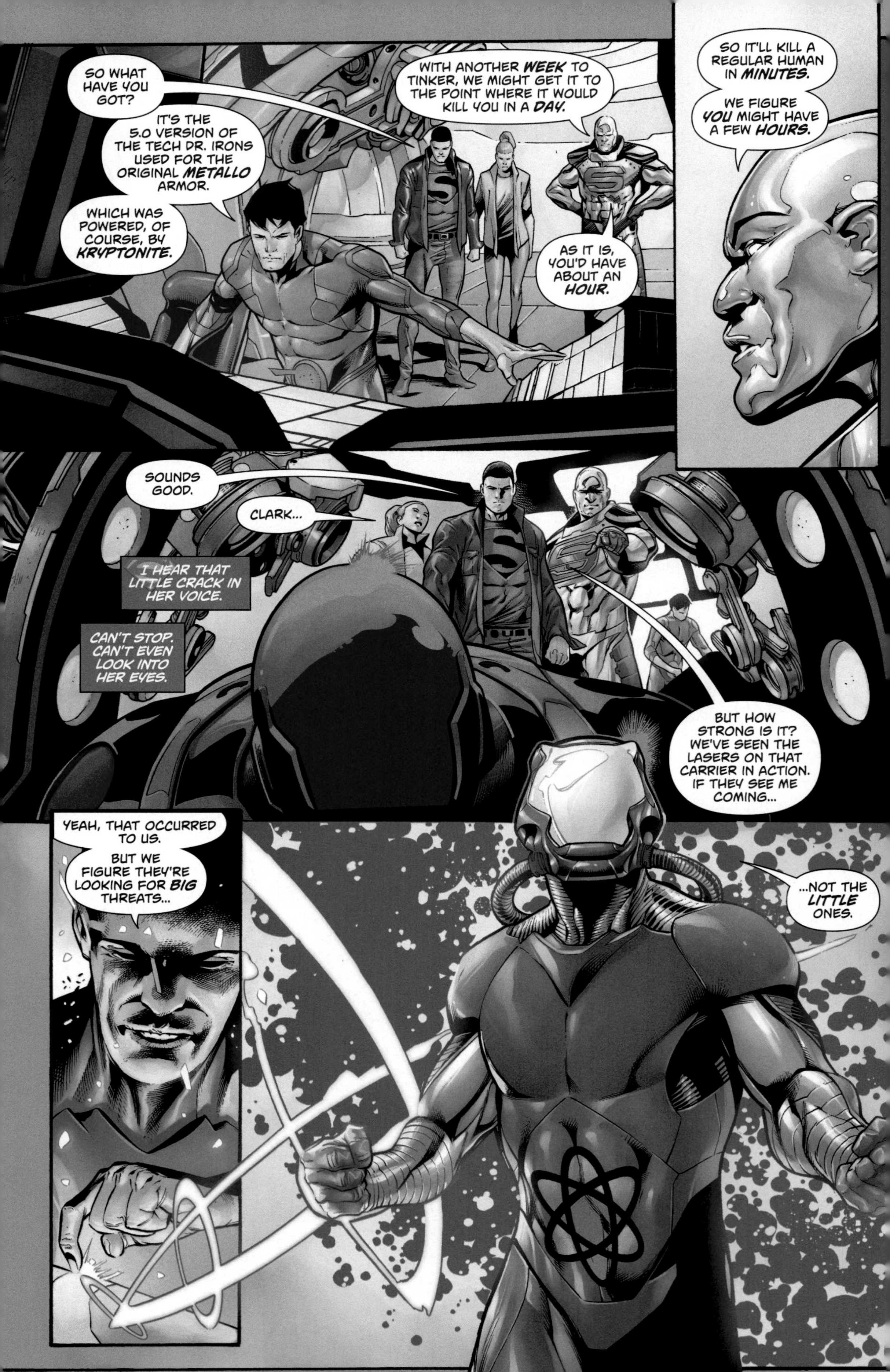
SO WHAT HAVE YOU GOT?
IT'S THE 5.0 VERSION OF THE TECH DR. IRONS USED FOR THE ORIGINAL METALLO ARMOR.
WHICH WAS POWERED, OF COURSE, BY KRYPTONITE.
WITH ANOTHER WEEK TO TINKER, WE MIGHT GET IT TO THE POINT WHERE IT WOULD KILL YOU IN A DAY.
AS IT IS, YOU'D HAVE ABOUT AN HOUR.
SO IT'LL KILL A REGULAR HUMAN IN MINUTES.
WE FIGURE YOU MIGHT HAVE A FEW HOURS.
SOUNDS GOOD.
CLARK...
I HEAR THAT LITTLE CRACK IN HER VOICE.
CAN'T STOP. CAN'T EVEN LOOK INTO HER EYES.
BUT HOW STRONG IS IT? WE'VE SEEN THE LASERS ON THAT CARRIER IN ACTION. IF THEY SEE ME COMING...
YEAH, THAT OCCURRED TO US.
BUT WE FIGURE THEY'RE LOOKING FOR BIG THREATS...
...NOT THE LITTLE ONES.

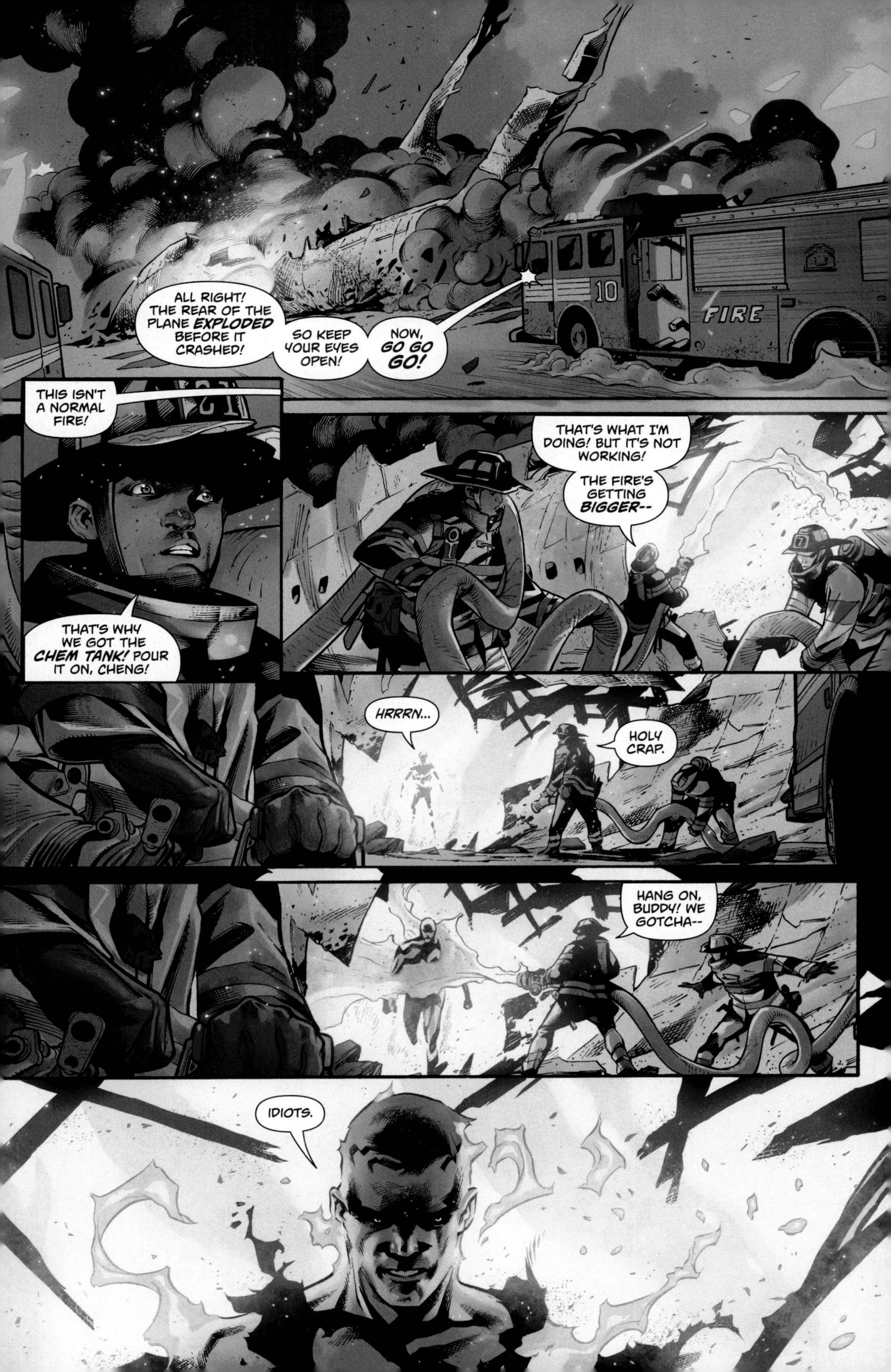
ALL RIGHT! THE REAR OF THE PLANE *EXPLODED* BEFORE IT CRASHED!
SO KEEP YOUR EYES OPEN!
NOW, *GO GO GO!*
THIS ISN'T A NORMAL FIRE!
THAT'S WHY WE GOT THE *CHEM TANK!* POUR IT ON, CHENG!
THAT'S WHAT I'M DOING! BUT IT'S NOT WORKING!
THE FIRE'S GETTING *BIGGER--*
HRRRN...
HOLY CRAP.
HANG ON, BUDDY! WE GOTCHA--
IDIOTS.

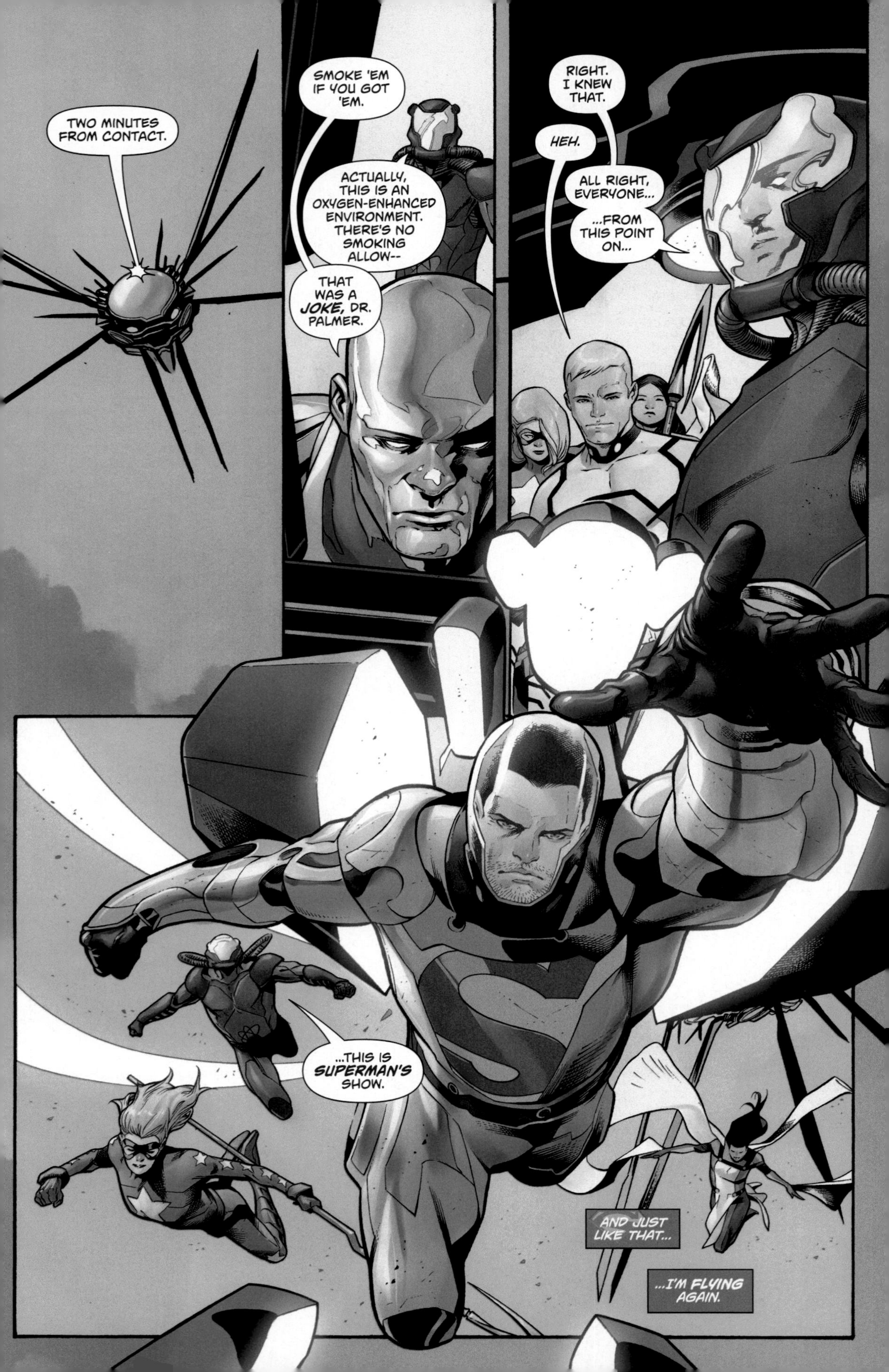
TWO MINUTES FROM CONTACT.
SMOKE 'EM IF YOU GOT 'EM.
ACTUALLY, THIS IS AN OXYGEN-ENHANCED ENVIRONMENT. THERE'S NO SMOKING ALLOW--
THAT WAS A JOKE, DR. PALMER.
RIGHT. I KNEW THAT.
HEH.
ALL RIGHT, EVERYONE...
...FROM THIS POINT ON...
...THIS IS SUPERMAN'S SHOW.
AND JUST LIKE THAT...
...I'M FLYING AGAIN.

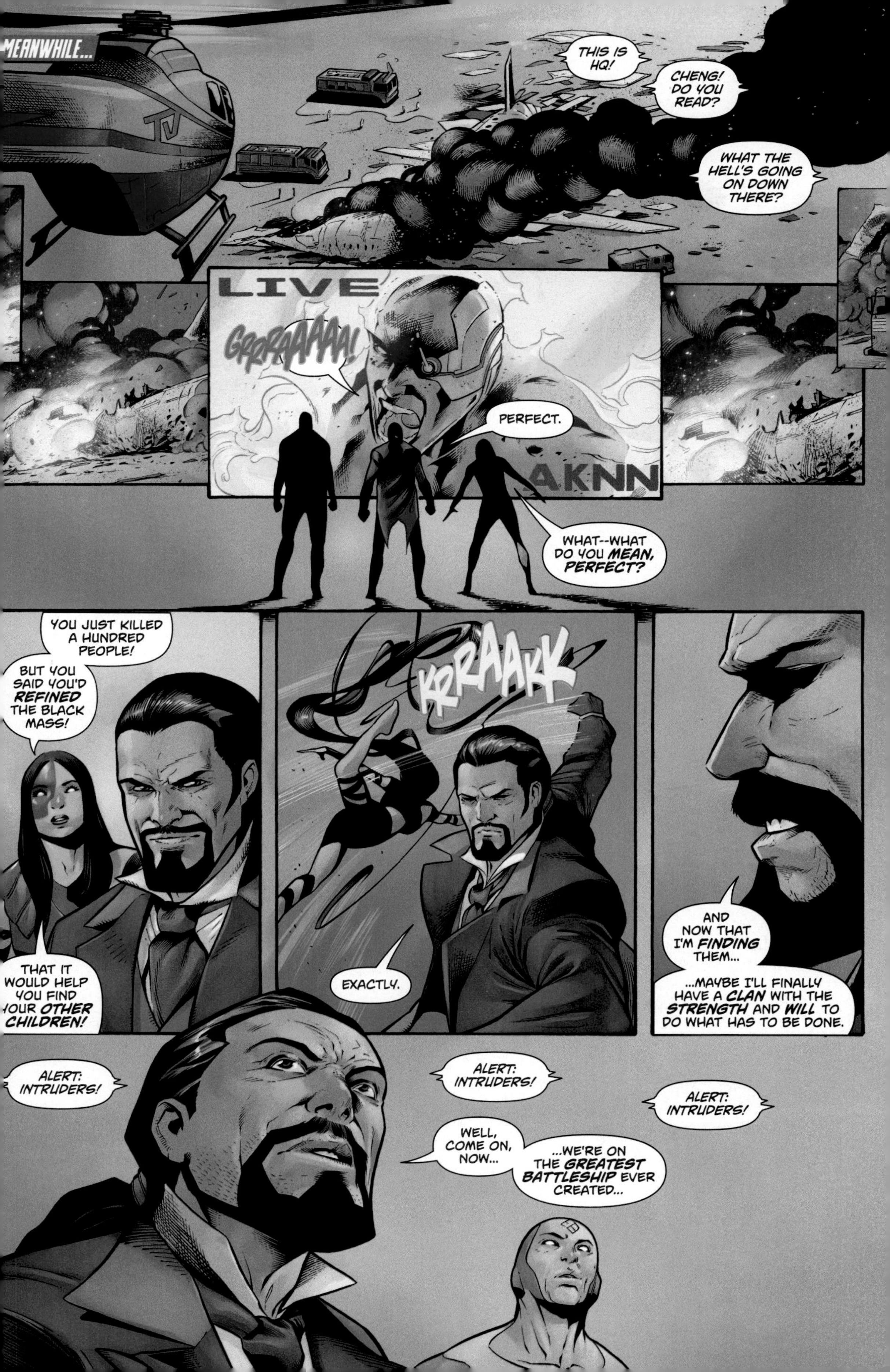
MEANWHILE...
THIS IS HQ!
CHENG! DO YOU READ?
WHAT THE HELL'S GOING ON DOWN THERE?
LIVE
GRRRAAAAA!
AKNN
PERFECT.
WHAT--WHAT DO YOU MEAN, PERFECT?
YOU JUST KILLED A HUNDRED PEOPLE!
BUT YOU SAID YOU'D REFINED THE BLACK MASS!
THAT IT WOULD HELP YOU FIND YOUR OTHER CHILDREN!
KRRAAKK
EXACTLY.
AND NOW THAT I'M FINDING THEM...
...MAYBE I'LL FINALLY HAVE A CLAN WITH THE STRENGTH AND WILL TO DO WHAT HAS TO BE DONE.
ALERT: INTRUDERS!
ALERT: INTRUDERS!
ALERT: INTRUDERS!
WELL, COME ON, NOW...
...WE'RE ON THE GREATEST BATTLESHIP EVER CREATED...

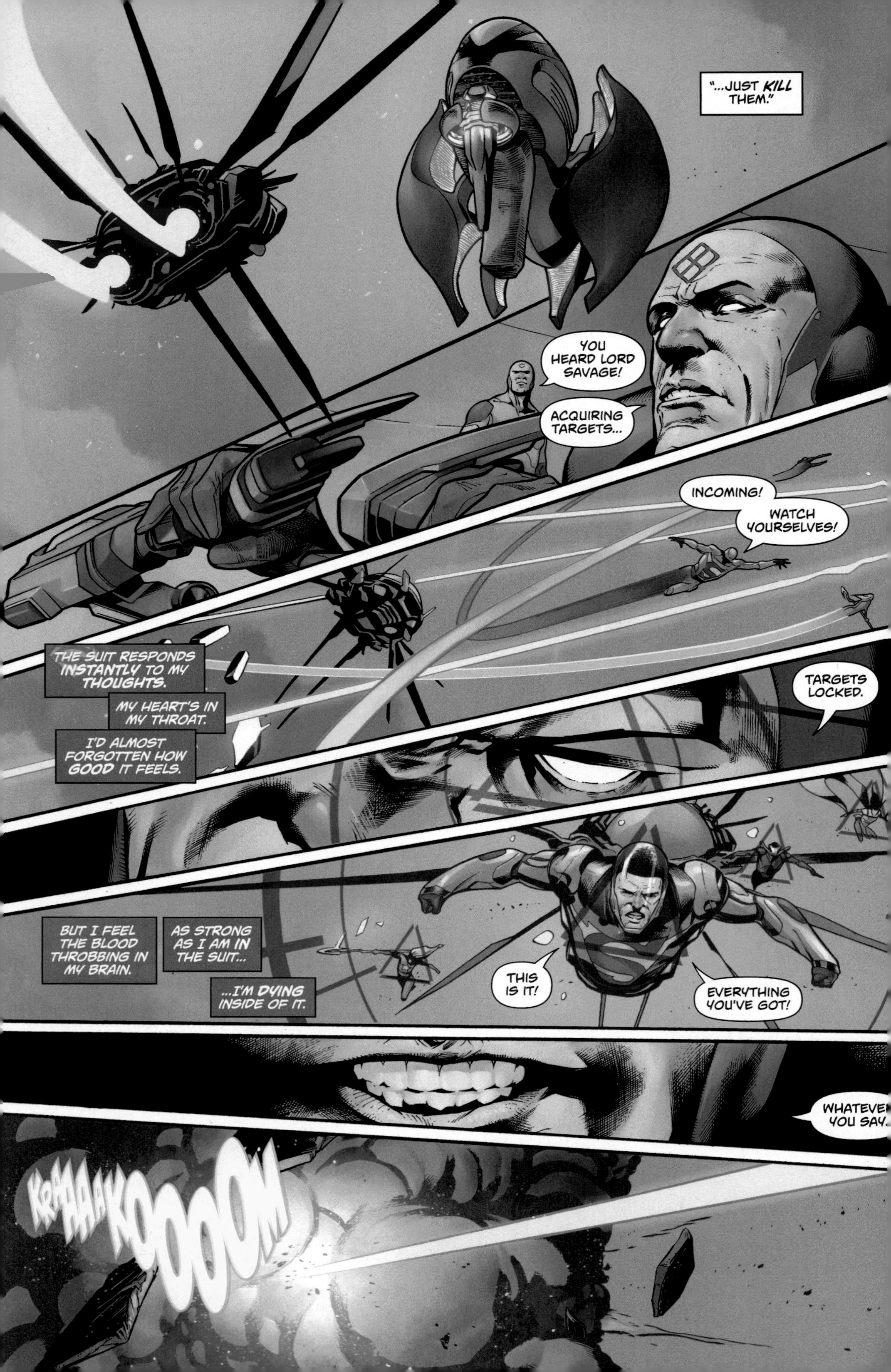
"...JUST KILL THEM."
YOU HEARD LORD SAVAGE!
ACQUIRING TARGETS...
INCOMING!
WATCH YOURSELVES!
THE SUIT RESPONDS INSTANTLY TO MY THOUGHTS.
MY HEART'S IN MY THROAT.
I'D ALMOST FORGOTTEN HOW GOOD IT FEELS.
TARGETS LOCKED.
BUT I FEEL THE BLOOD THROBBING IN MY BRAIN.
AS STRONG AS I AM IN THE SUIT...
...I'M DYING INSIDE OF IT.
THIS IS IT!
EVERYTHING YOU'VE GOT!
WHATEVER YOU SAY.
KRAAAAKOOOOM

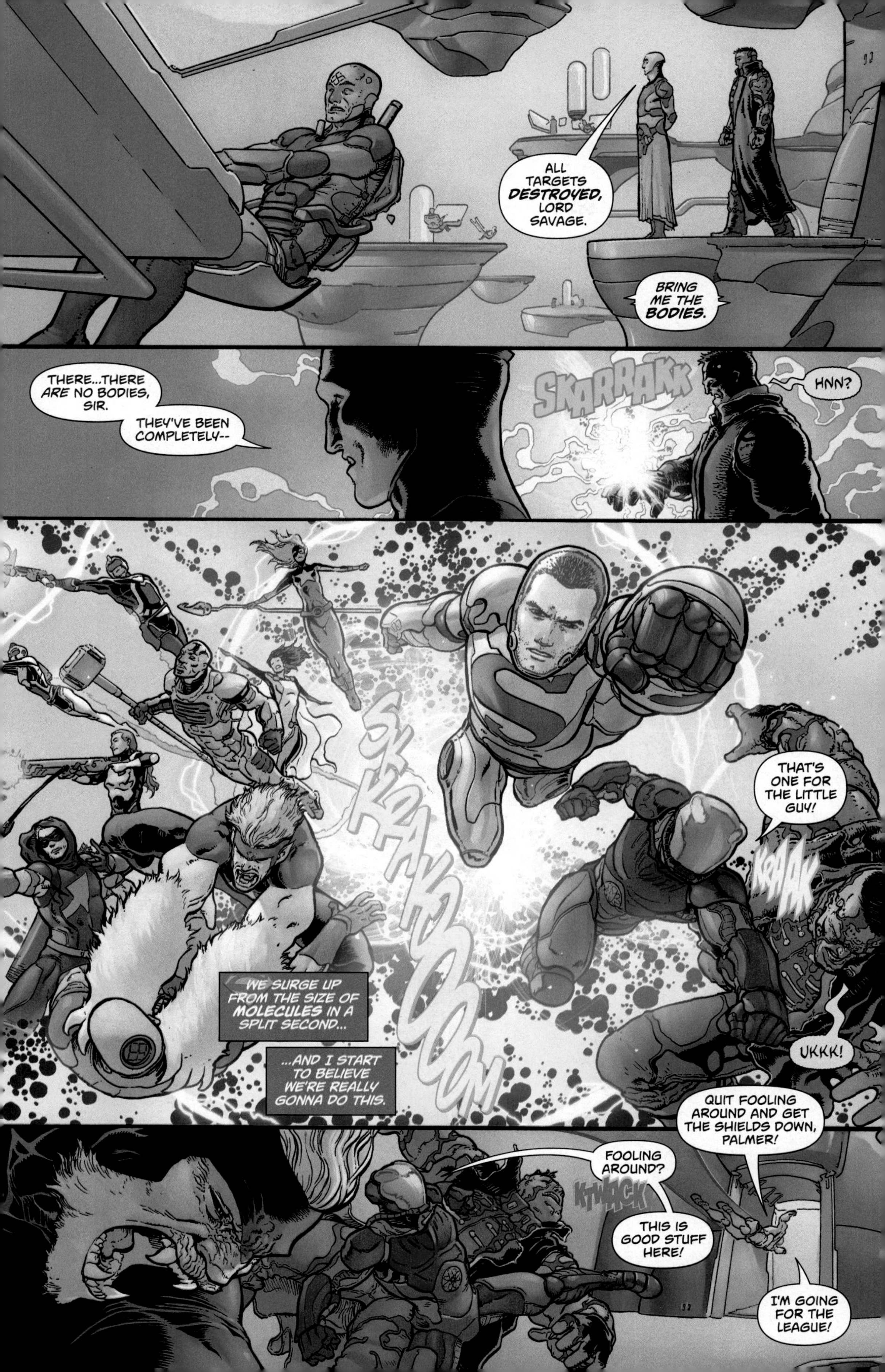
ALL TARGETS DESTROYED, LORD SAVAGE.
BRING ME THE BODIES.
THERE...THERE ARE NO BODIES, SIR.
THEY'VE BEEN COMPLETELY--
SKARRAKK
HNN?
WE SURGE UP FROM THE SIZE OF MOLECULES IN A SPLIT SECOND...
...AND I START TO BELIEVE WE'RE REALLY GONNA DO THIS.
THAT'S ONE FOR THE LITTLE GUY!
KRAAK
UKKK!
QUIT FOOLING AROUND AND GET THE SHIELDS DOWN, PALMER!
FOOLING AROUND?
KTWACK
THIS IS GOOD STUFF HERE!
I'M GOING FOR THE LEAGUE!

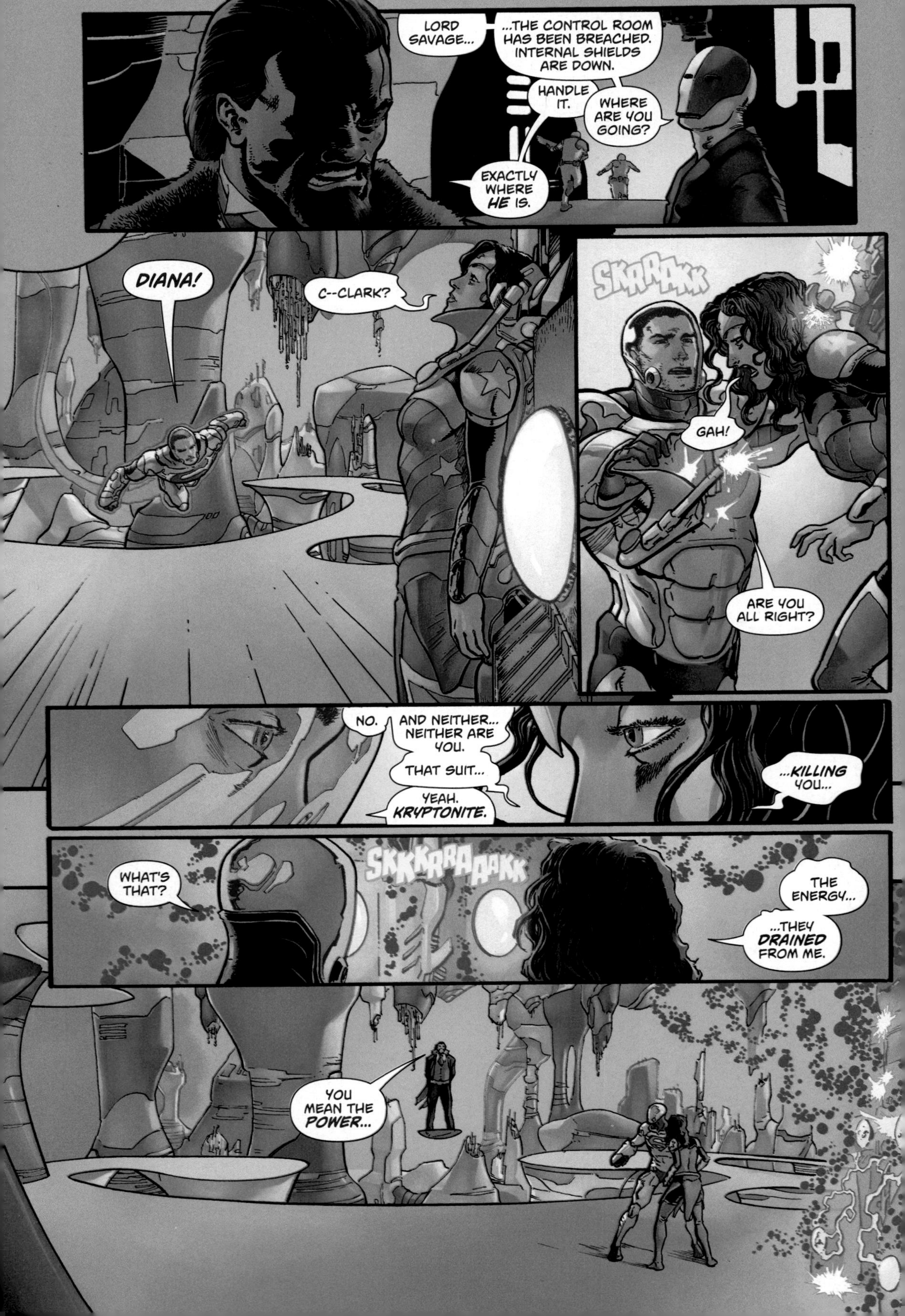
LORD SAVAGE...
...THE CONTROL ROOM HAS BEEN BREACHED. INTERNAL SHIELDS ARE DOWN.
HANDLE IT.
WHERE ARE YOU GOING?
EXACTLY WHERE HE IS.
DIANA!
C--CLARK?
SKRAAKK
GAH!
ARE YOU ALL RIGHT?
NO.
AND NEITHER... NEITHER ARE YOU.
THAT SUIT...
...KILLING YOU...
YEAH. KRYPTONITE.
SKKKRRAAAKK
WHAT'S THAT?
THE ENERGY...
...THEY DRAINED FROM ME.
YOU MEAN THE POWER...

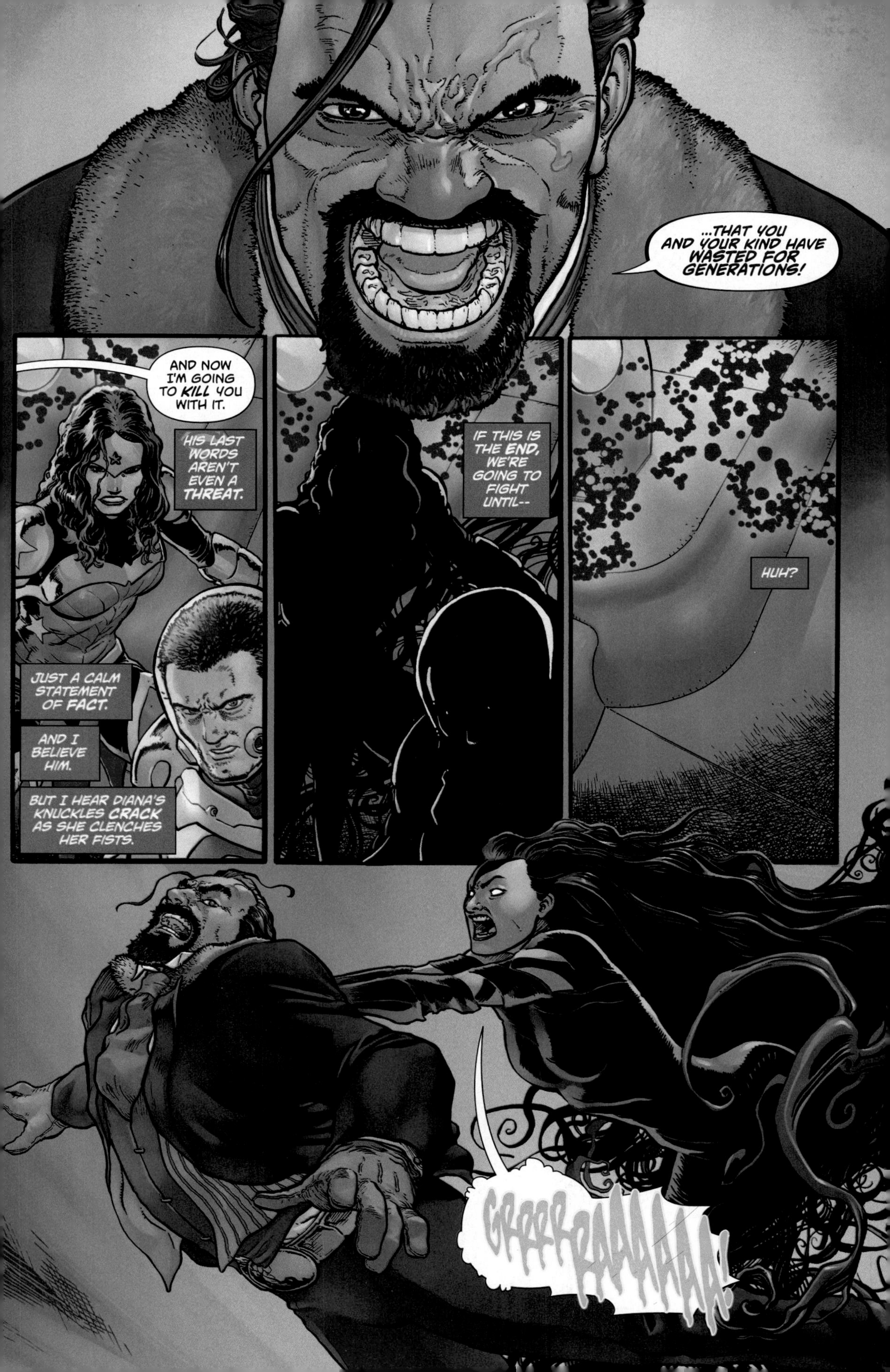
...THAT YOU AND YOUR KIND HAVE WASTED FOR GENERATIONS!
AND NOW I'M GOING TO KILL YOU WITH IT.
HIS LAST WORDS AREN'T EVEN A THREAT.
JUST A CALM STATEMENT OF FACT.
AND I BELIEVE HIM.
BUT I HEAR DIANA'S KNUCKLES CRACK AS SHE CLENCHES HER FISTS.
IF THIS IS THE END, WE'RE GOING TO FIGHT UNTIL--
HUH?
GRRRRAAAAAAA!

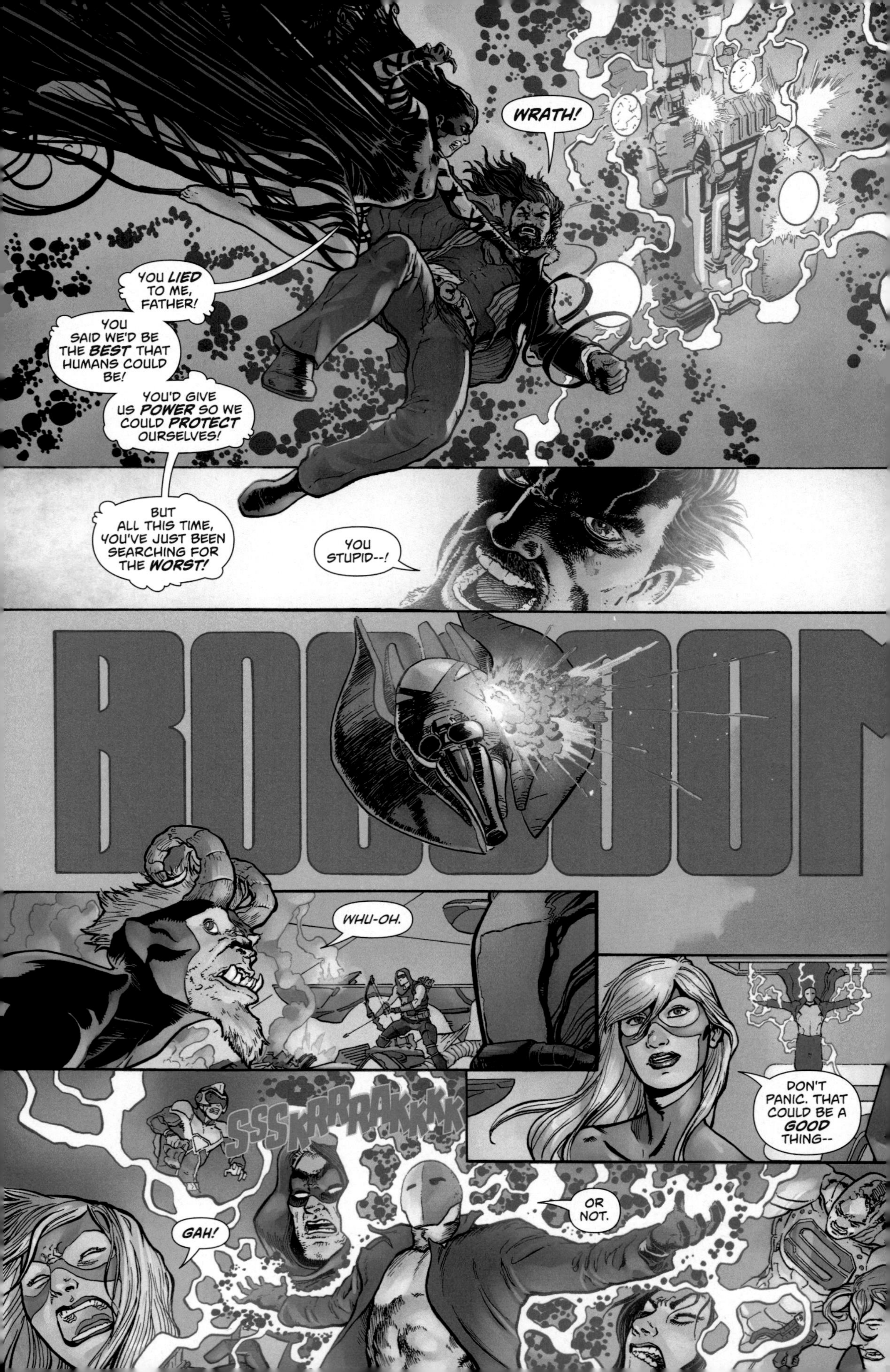

WRATH!
YOU LIED TO ME, FATHER!
YOU SAID WE'D BE THE BEST THAT HUMANS COULD BE!
YOU'D GIVE US POWER SO WE COULD PROTECT OURSELVES!
BUT ALL THIS TIME, YOU'VE JUST BEEN SEARCHING FOR THE WORST!
YOU STUPID--!
BOOOOOM
WHU-OH.
DON'T PANIC. THAT COULD BE A GOOD THING--
SSSKRRRAKKKK
OR NOT.
GAH!

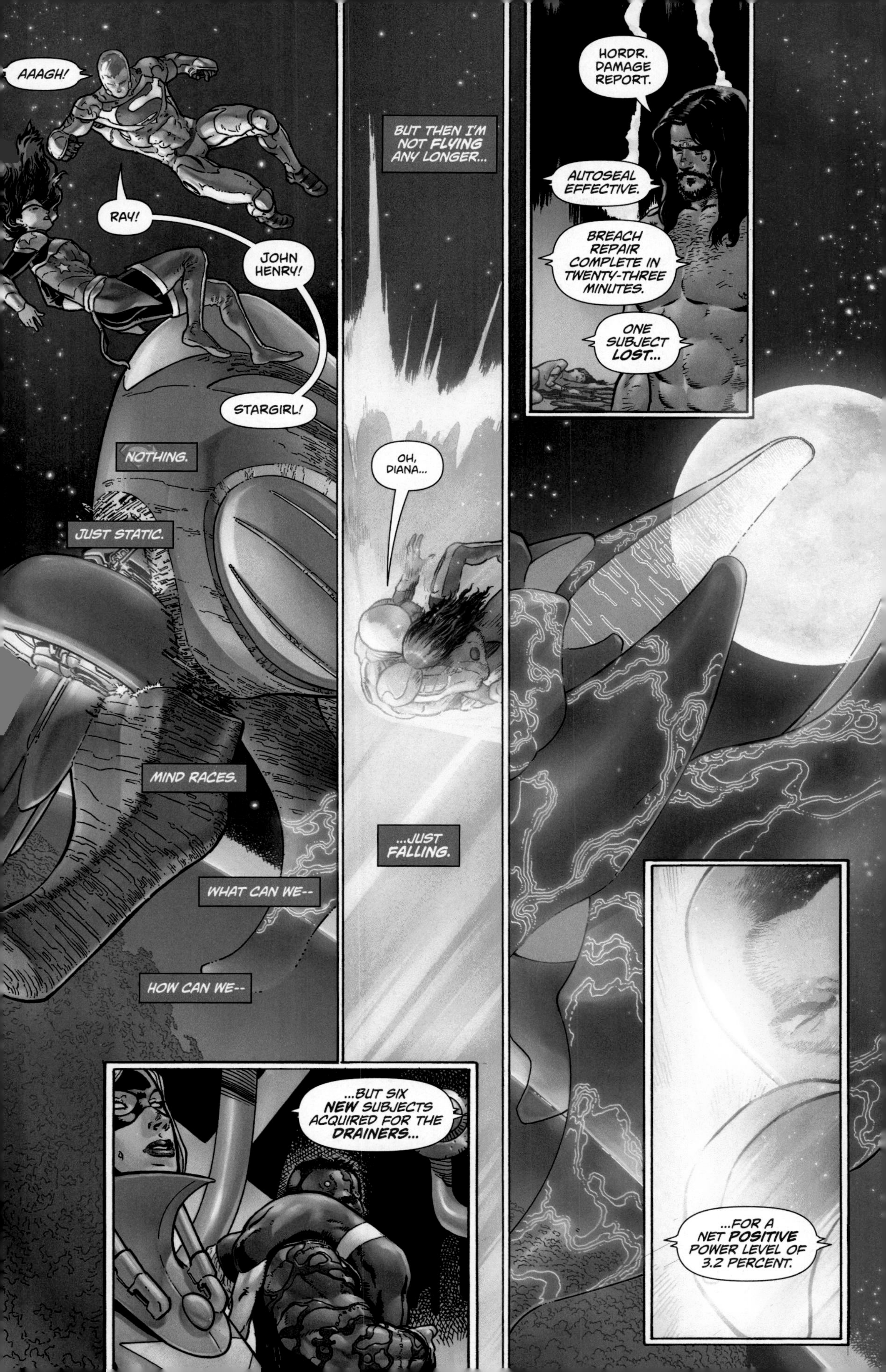
AAAGH!
RAY!
JOHN HENRY!
STARGIRL!
NOTHING.
JUST STATIC.
MIND RACES.
WHAT CAN WE--
HOW CAN WE--
BUT THEN I'M NOT FLYING ANY LONGER...
OH, DIANA...
...JUST FALLING.
HORDR. DAMAGE REPORT.
AUTOSEAL EFFECTIVE.
BREACH REPAIR COMPLETE IN TWENTY-THREE MINUTES.
ONE SUBJECT LOST...
...BUT SIX NEW SUBJECTS ACQUIRED FOR THE DRAINERS...
...FOR A NET POSITIVE POWER LEVEL OF 3.2 PERCENT.

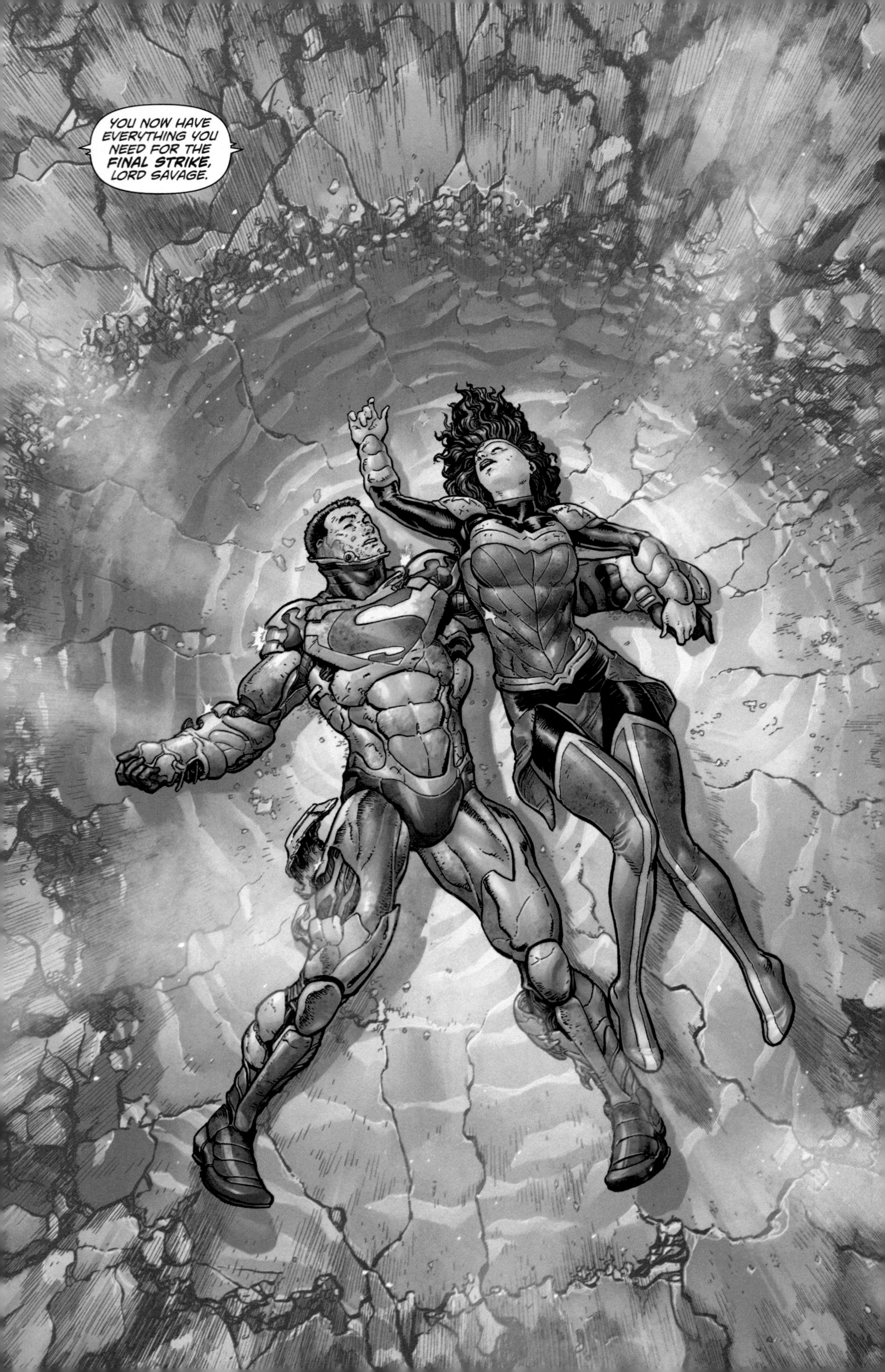
YOU NOW HAVE EVERYTHING YOU NEED FOR THE **FINAL STRIKE,** LORD SAVAGE.

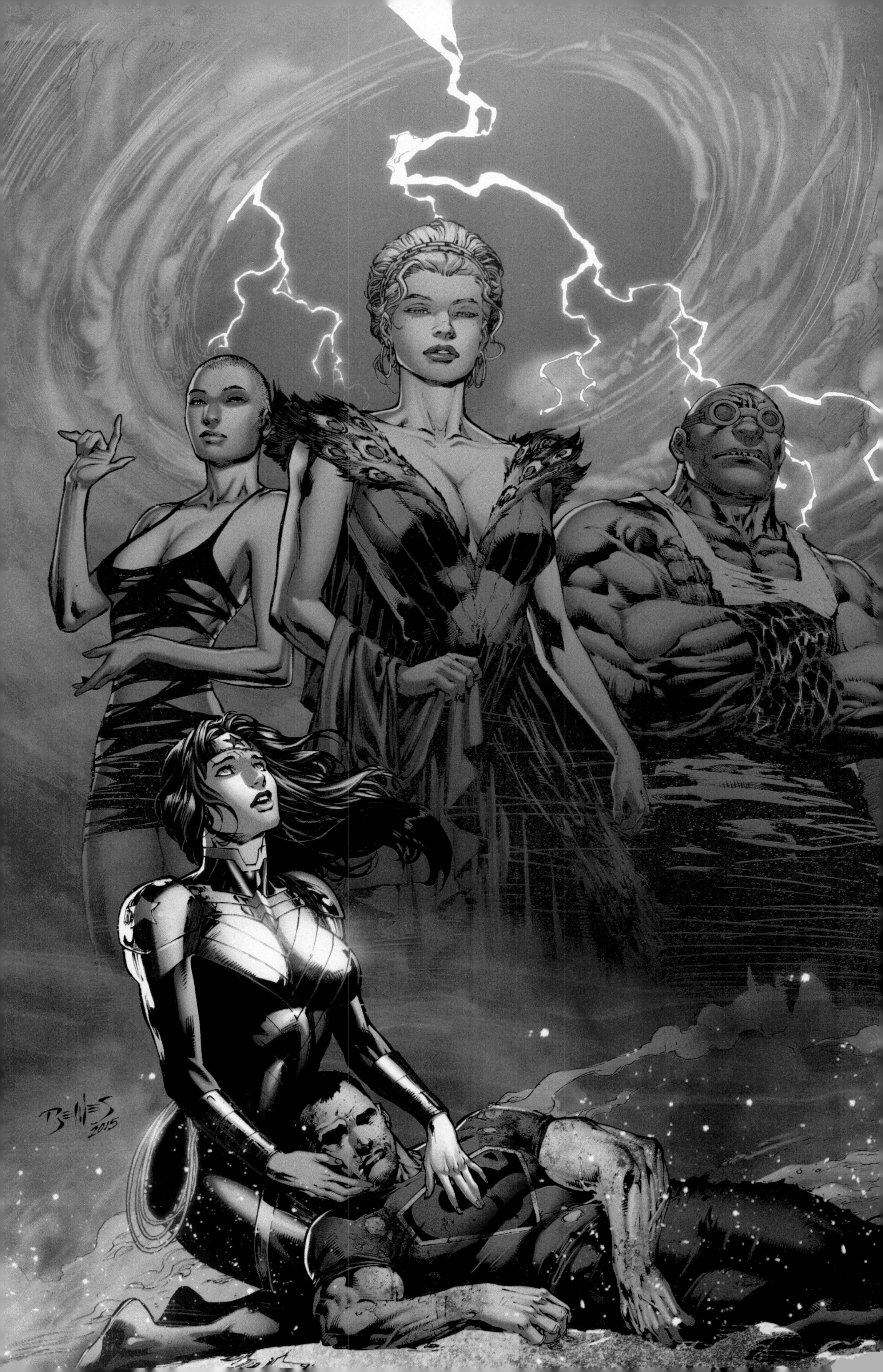
BENES 2015

A GOD SOMEWHERE

PETER J. TOMASI writer **DOUG MAHNKE** penciller **JAIME MENDOZA JONATHAN GLAPION SCOTT HANNA** inkers **WIL QUINTANA** colorist **ROB LEIGH** letterer
ED BENES WIL QUINTANA cover

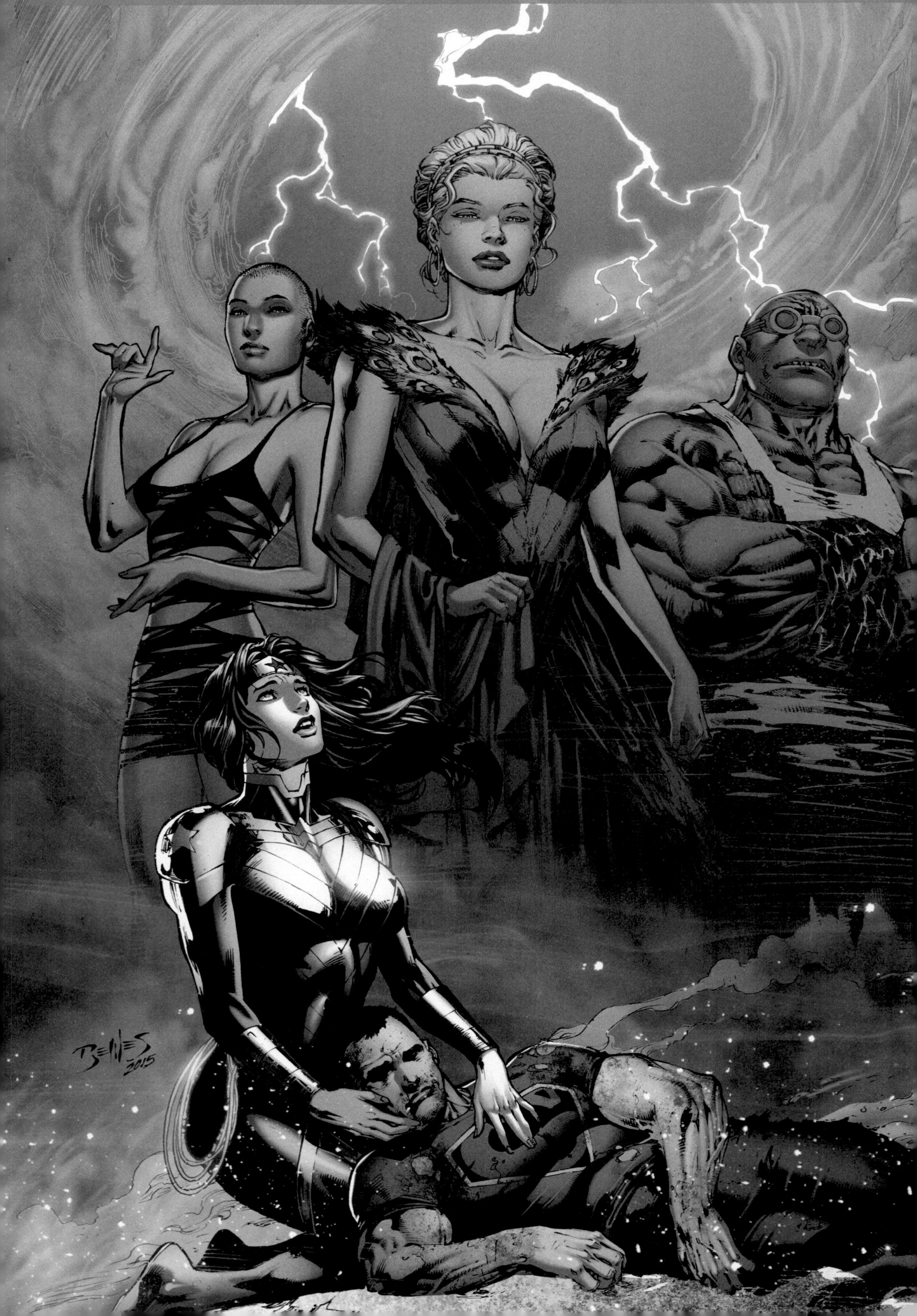
BENES 2015

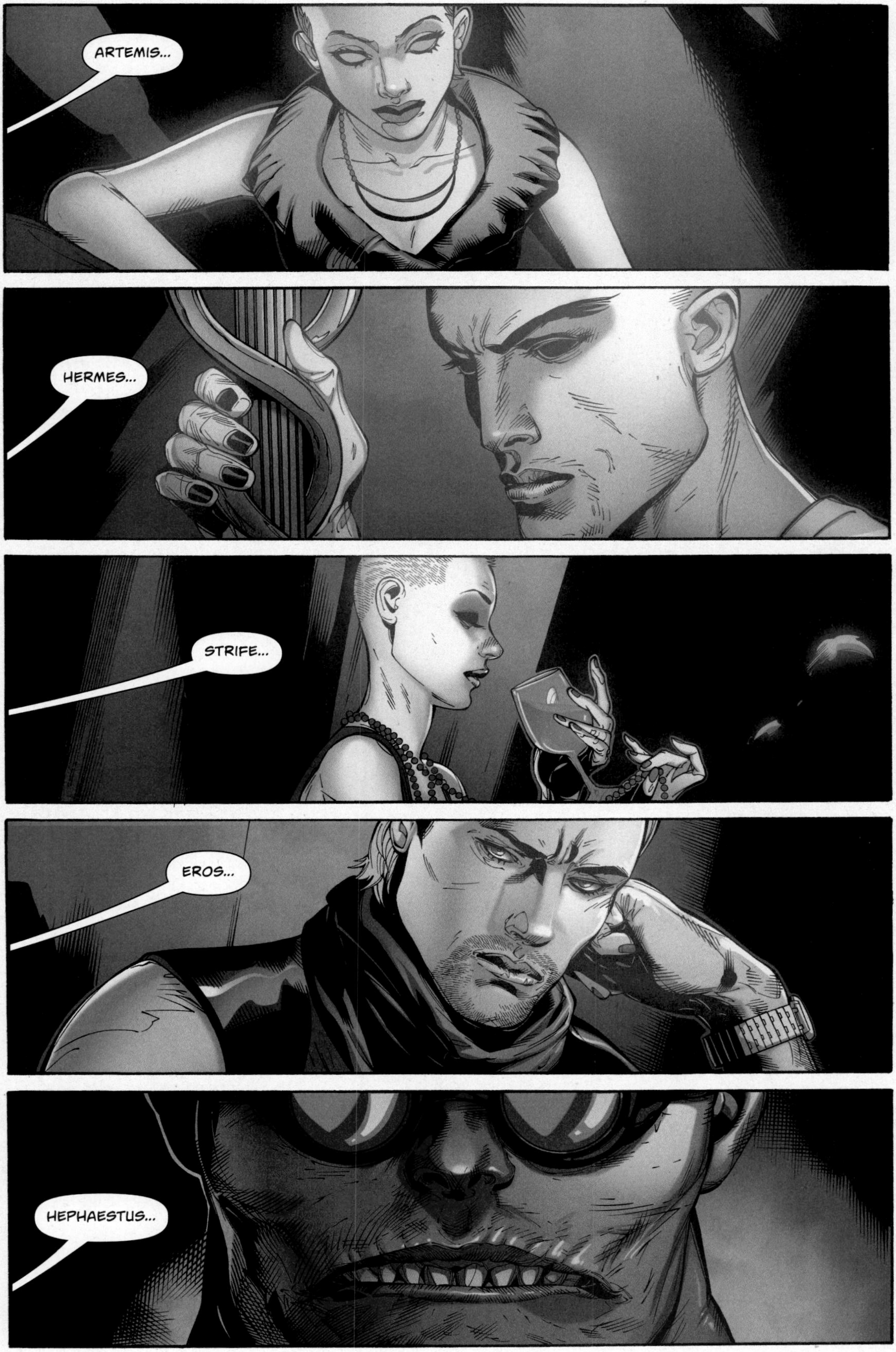
ARTEMIS...
HERMES...
STRIFE...
EROS...
HEPHAESTUS...

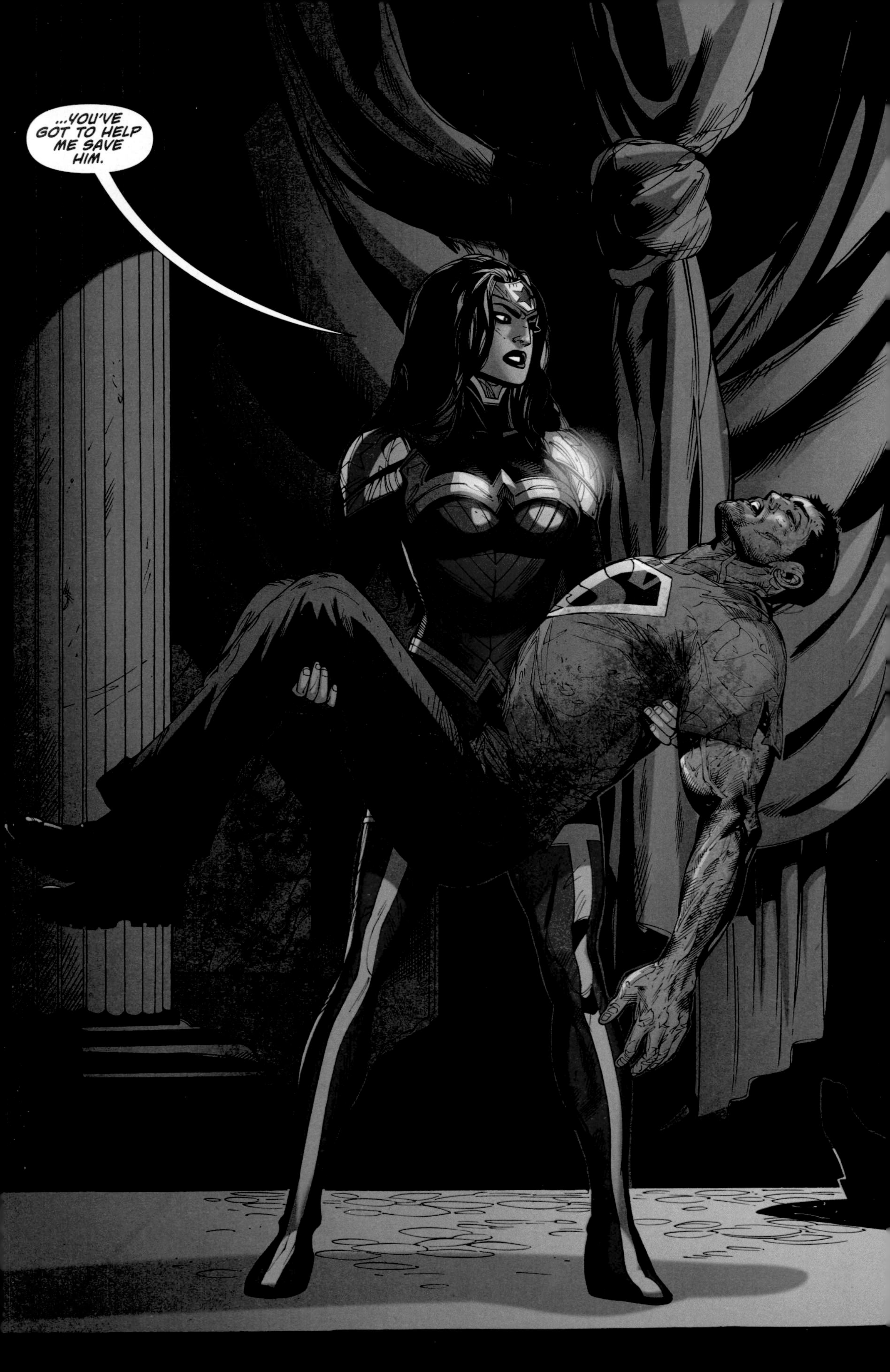
...YOU'VE GOT TO HELP ME SAVE HIM.

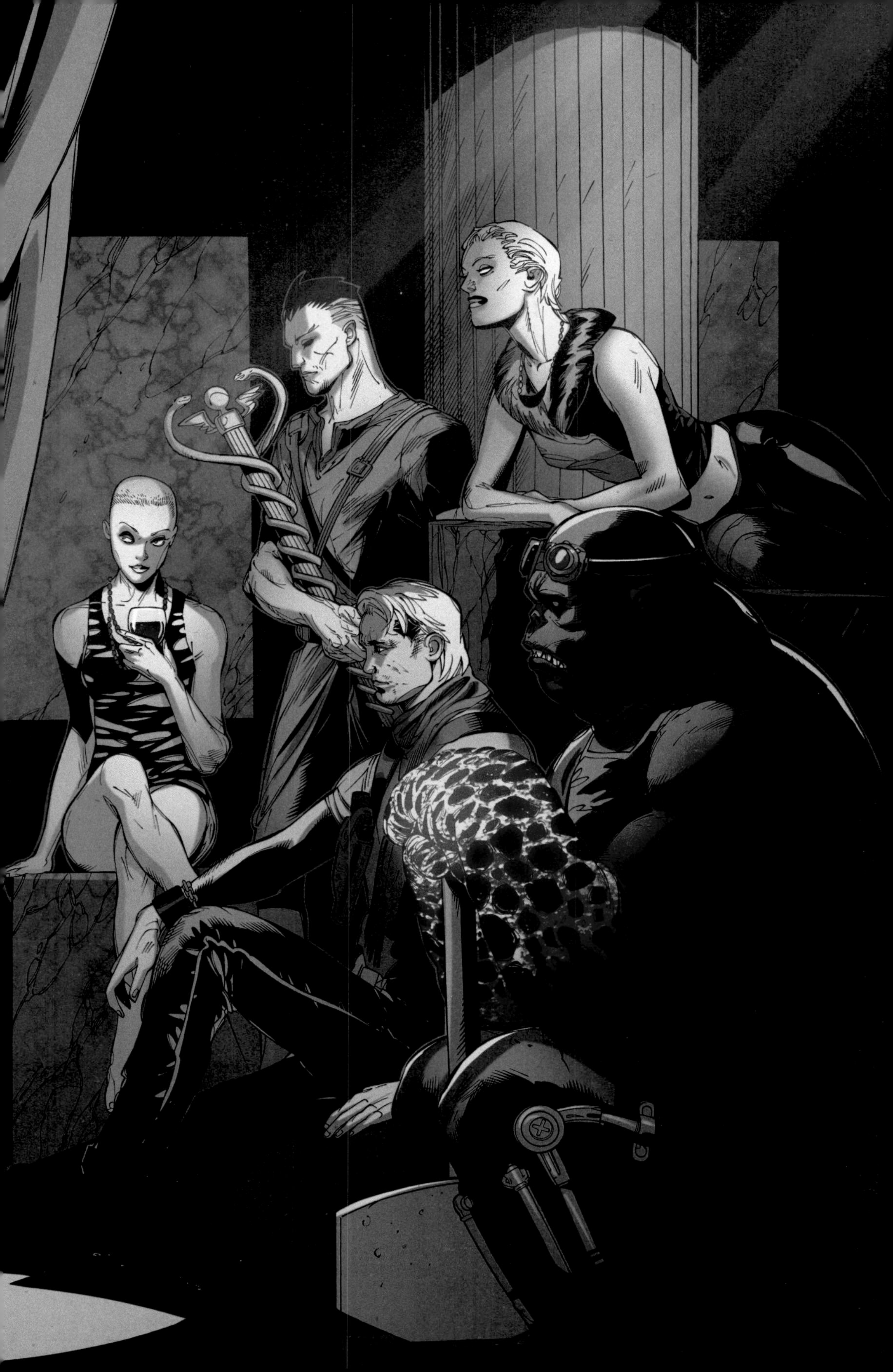

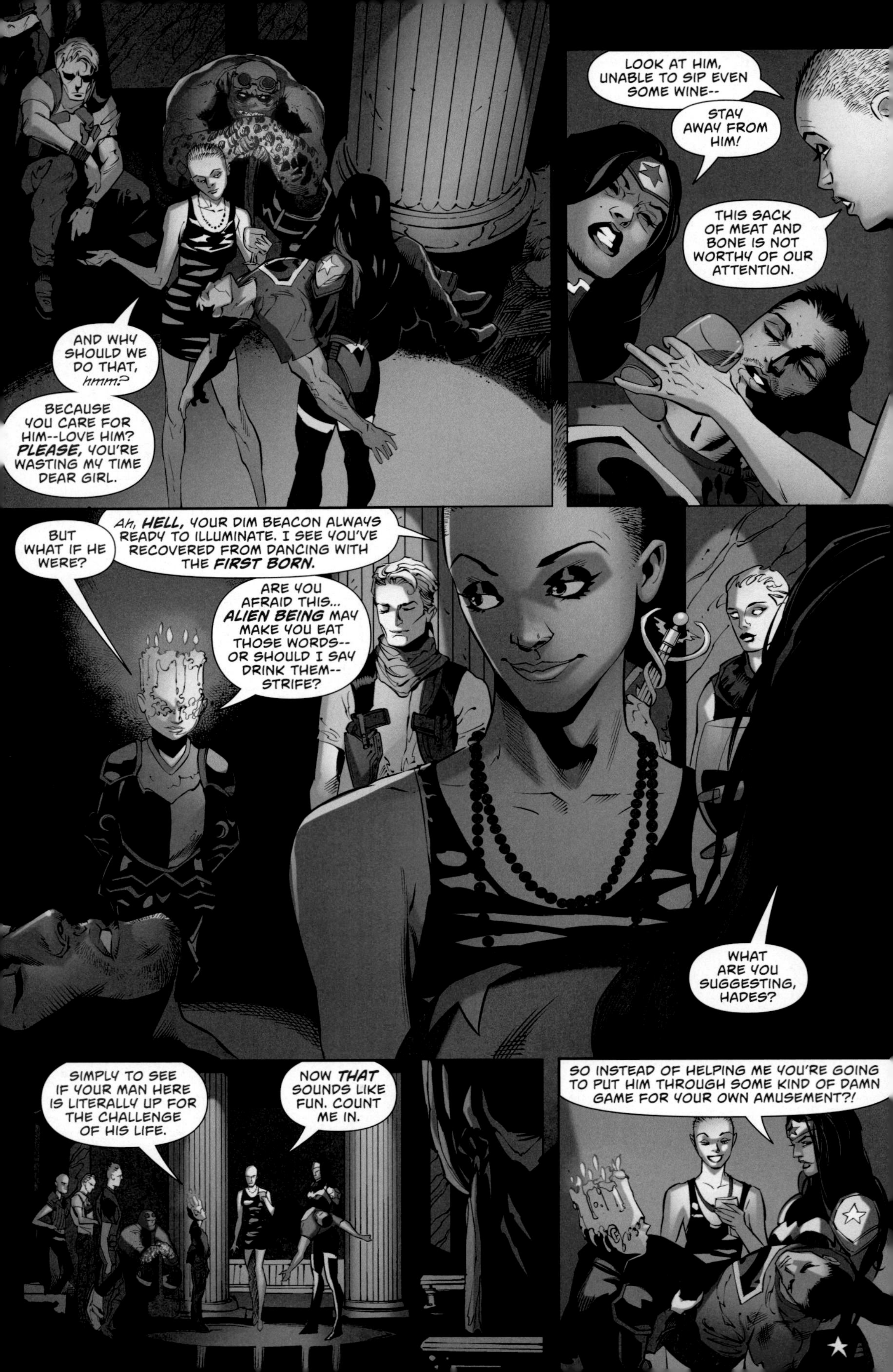
AND WHY SHOULD WE DO THAT, *hmm?*
BECAUSE YOU CARE FOR HIM--LOVE HIM? ***PLEASE,*** YOU'RE WASTING MY TIME DEAR GIRL.
LOOK AT HIM, UNABLE TO SIP EVEN SOME WINE--
STAY AWAY FROM HIM!
THIS SACK OF MEAT AND BONE IS NOT WORTHY OF OUR ATTENTION.
BUT WHAT IF HE WERE?
Ah, **HELL,** YOUR DIM BEACON ALWAYS READY TO ILLUMINATE. I SEE YOU'VE RECOVERED FROM DANCING WITH THE ***FIRST BORN.***
ARE YOU AFRAID THIS... ***ALIEN BEING*** MAY MAKE YOU EAT THOSE WORDS-- OR SHOULD I SAY DRINK THEM-- STRIFE?
WHAT ARE YOU SUGGESTING, HADES?
SIMPLY TO SEE IF YOUR MAN HERE IS LITERALLY UP FOR THE CHALLENGE OF HIS LIFE.
NOW ***THAT*** SOUNDS LIKE FUN. COUNT ME IN.
SO INSTEAD OF HELPING ME YOU'RE GOING TO PUT HIM THROUGH SOME KIND OF DAMN GAME FOR YOUR OWN AMUSEMENT?!

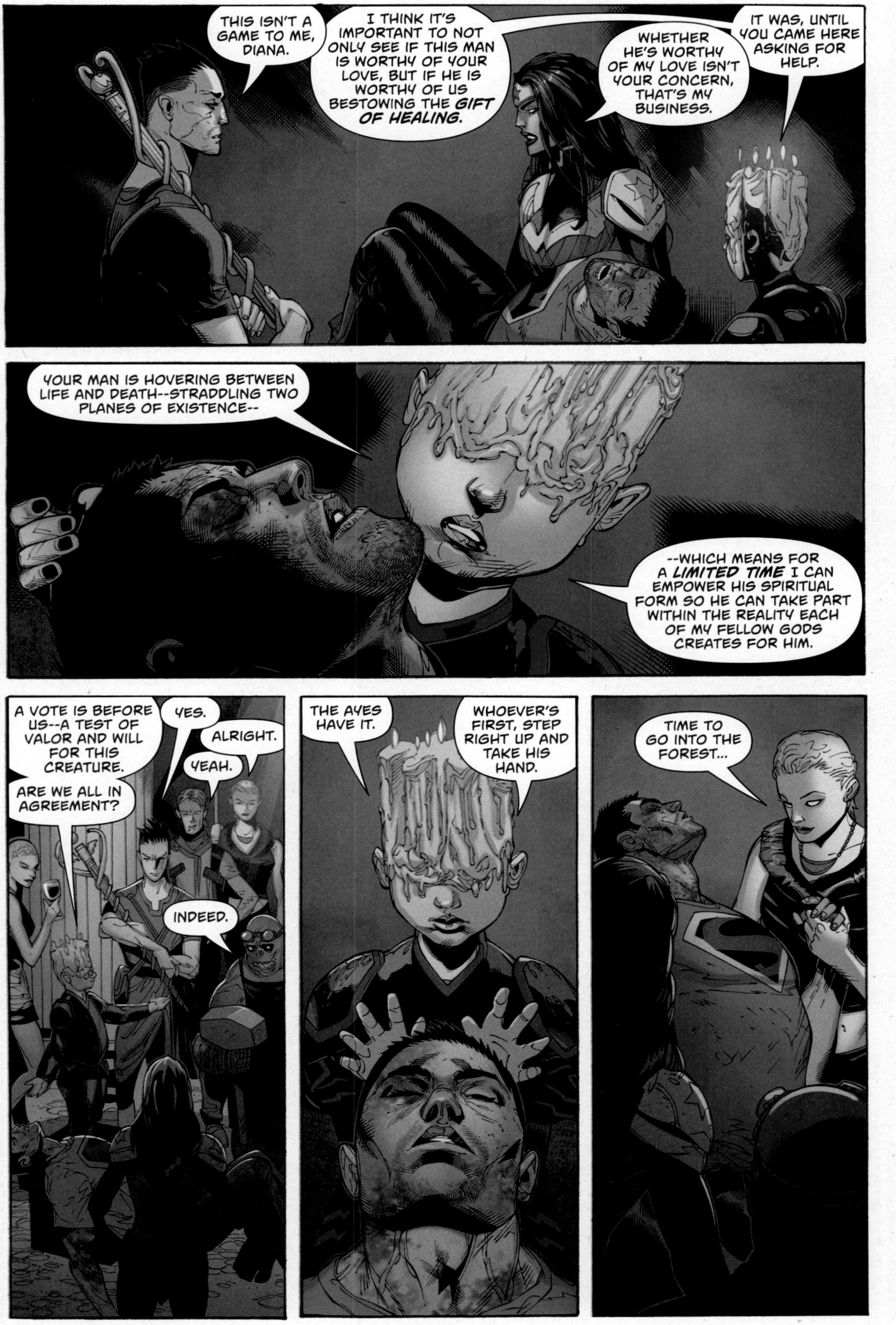
THIS ISN'T A GAME TO ME, DIANA.
I THINK IT'S IMPORTANT TO NOT ONLY SEE IF THIS MAN IS WORTHY OF YOUR LOVE, BUT IF HE IS WORTHY OF US BESTOWING THE GIFT OF HEALING.
WHETHER HE'S WORTHY OF MY LOVE ISN'T YOUR CONCERN, THAT'S MY BUSINESS.
IT WAS, UNTIL YOU CAME HERE ASKING FOR HELP.
YOUR MAN IS HOVERING BETWEEN LIFE AND DEATH--STRADDLING TWO PLANES OF EXISTENCE--
--WHICH MEANS FOR A LIMITED TIME I CAN EMPOWER HIS SPIRITUAL FORM SO HE CAN TAKE PART WITHIN THE REALITY EACH OF MY FELLOW GODS CREATES FOR HIM.
A VOTE IS BEFORE US--A TEST OF VALOR AND WILL FOR THIS CREATURE.
ARE WE ALL IN AGREEMENT?
YES.
ALRIGHT.
YEAH.
INDEED.
THE AYES HAVE IT.
WHOEVER'S FIRST, STEP RIGHT UP AND TAKE HIS HAND.
TIME TO GO INTO THE FOREST...

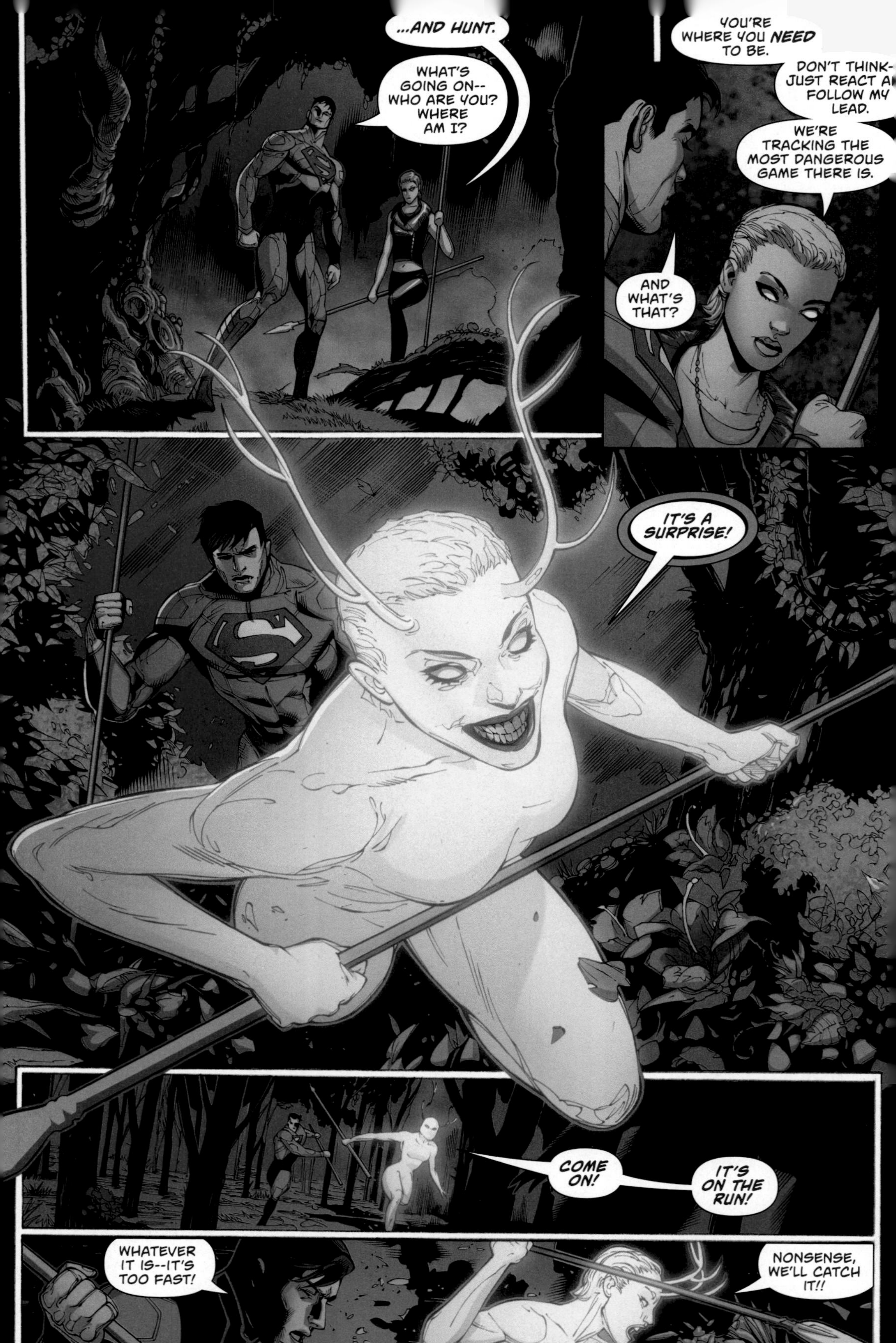
...AND HUNT.
WHAT'S GOING ON-- WHO ARE YOU? WHERE AM I?
YOU'RE WHERE YOU NEED TO BE.
DON'T THINK-- JUST REACT A FOLLOW MY LEAD.
WE'RE TRACKING THE MOST DANGEROUS GAME THERE IS.
AND WHAT'S THAT?
IT'S A SURPRISE!
COME ON!
IT'S ON THE RUN!
WHATEVER IT IS--IT'S TOO FAST!
NONSENSE, WE'LL CATCH IT!!

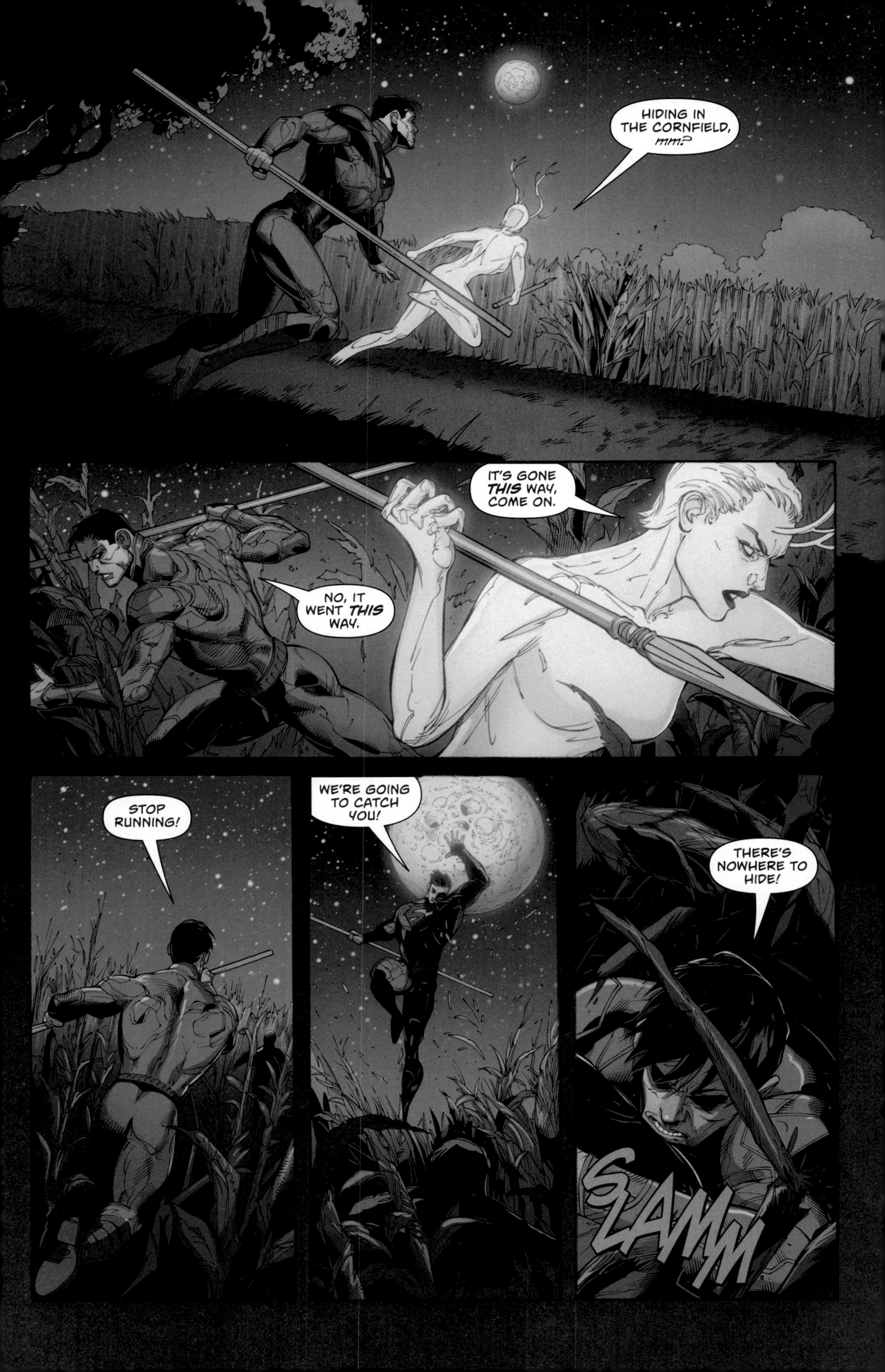
HIDING IN THE CORNFIELD, mmm?
IT'S GONE THIS WAY, COME ON.
NO, IT WENT THIS WAY.
STOP RUNNING!
WE'RE GOING TO CATCH YOU!
THERE'S NOWHERE TO HIDE!
SLAMM

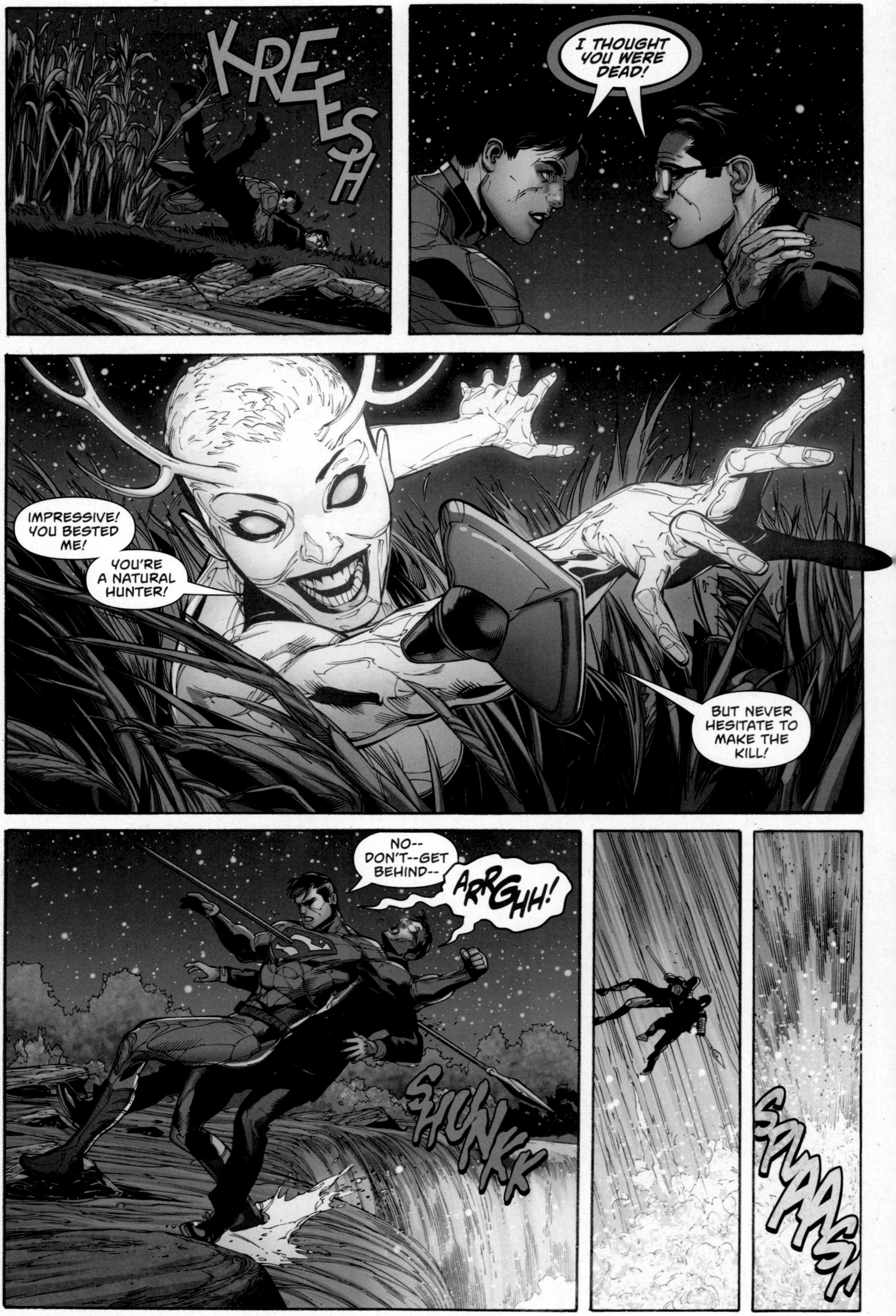
KREEESH
I THOUGHT YOU WERE DEAD!
IMPRESSIVE! YOU BESTED ME!
YOU'RE A NATURAL HUNTER!
BUT NEVER HESITATE TO MAKE THE KILL!
NO-- DON'T--GET BEHIND--
ARRGHH!
SHUNKK
SPLAASH

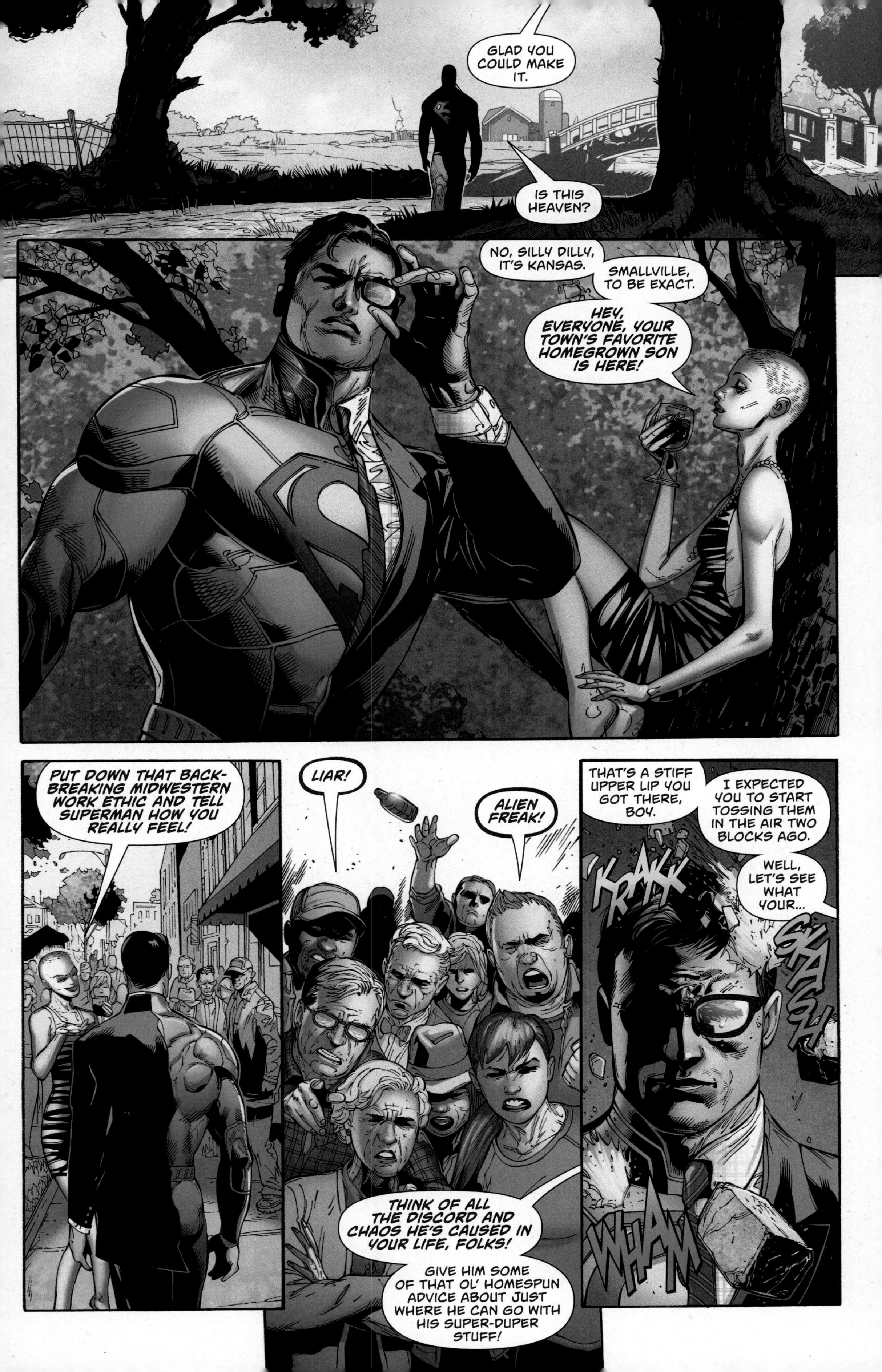
GLAD YOU COULD MAKE IT.
IS THIS HEAVEN?
NO, SILLY DILLY, IT'S KANSAS.
SMALLVILLE, TO BE EXACT.
HEY, EVERYONE, YOUR TOWN'S FAVORITE HOMEGROWN SON IS HERE!
PUT DOWN THAT BACK-BREAKING MIDWESTERN WORK ETHIC AND TELL SUPERMAN HOW YOU REALLY FEEL!
LIAR!
ALIEN FREAK!
THINK OF ALL THE DISCORD AND CHAOS HE'S CAUSED IN YOUR LIFE, FOLKS!
GIVE HIM SOME OF THAT OL' HOMESPUN ADVICE ABOUT JUST WHERE HE CAN GO WITH HIS SUPER-DUPER STUFF!
THAT'S A STIFF UPPER LIP YOU GOT THERE, BOY.
I EXPECTED YOU TO START TOSSING THEM IN THE AIR TWO BLOCKS AGO.
WELL, LET'S SEE WHAT YOUR...
KRAKK
SKASH
WHAM

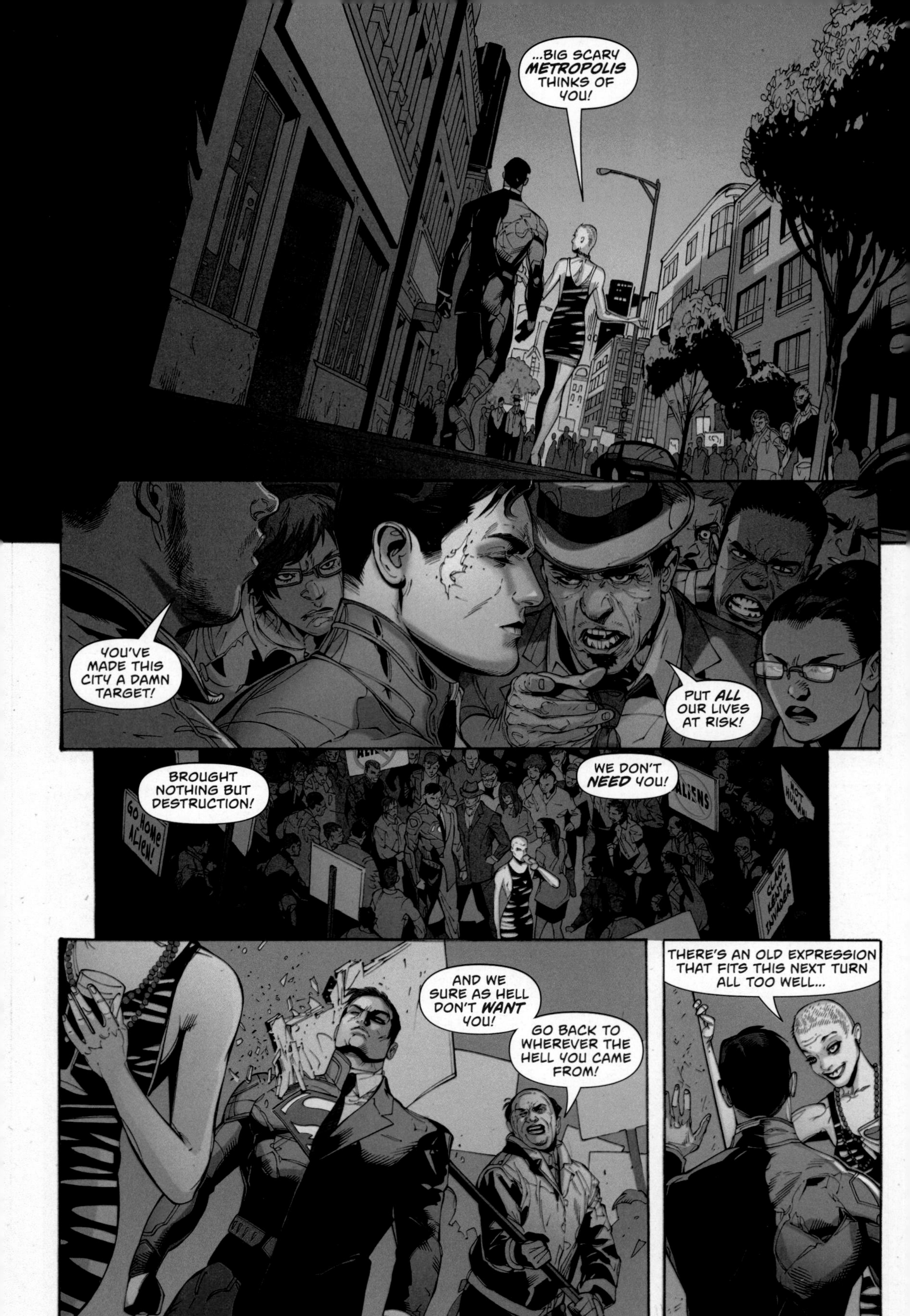

...BIG SCARY **METROPOLIS** THINKS OF YOU!
YOU'VE MADE THIS CITY A DAMN TARGET!
PUT **ALL** OUR LIVES AT RISK!
BROUGHT NOTHING BUT DESTRUCTION!
WE DON'T **NEED** YOU!
GO HOME ALIEN!
ALIENS
NOT HUMAN
AND WE SURE AS HELL DON'T **WANT** YOU!
GO BACK TO WHEREVER THE HELL YOU CAME FROM!
THERE'S AN OLD EXPRESSION THAT FITS THIS NEXT TURN ALL TOO WELL...

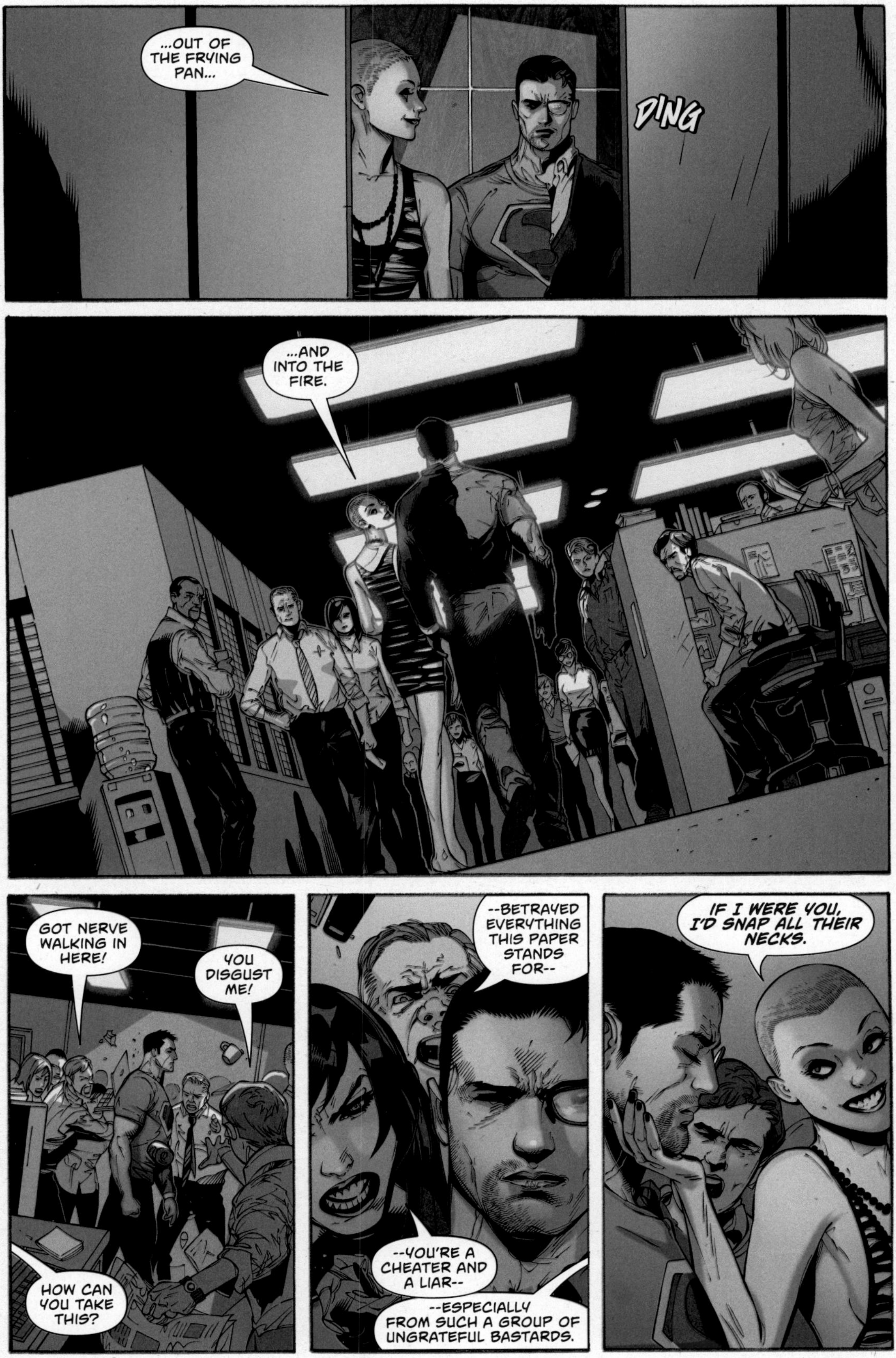
...OUT OF THE FRYING PAN...
DING
...AND INTO THE FIRE.
GOT NERVE WALKING IN HERE!
YOU DISGUST ME!
HOW CAN YOU TAKE THIS?
--BETRAYED EVERYTHING THIS PAPER STANDS FOR--
--YOU'RE A CHEATER AND A LIAR--
--ESPECIALLY FROM SUCH A GROUP OF UNGRATEFUL BASTARDS.
IF I WERE YOU, I'D SNAP ALL THEIR NECKS.

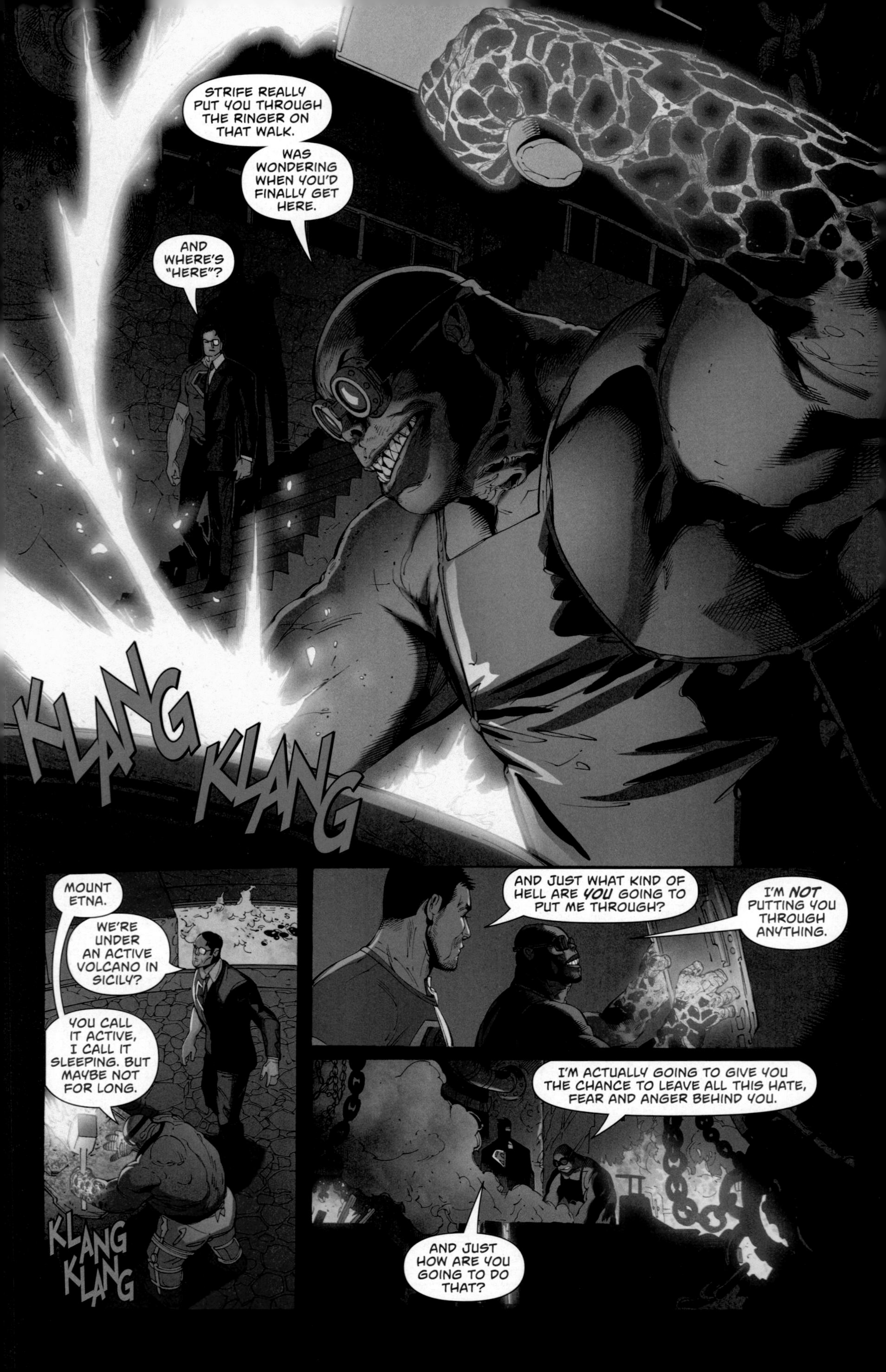
STRIFE REALLY PUT YOU THROUGH THE RINGER ON THAT WALK.
WAS WONDERING WHEN YOU'D FINALLY GET HERE.
AND WHERE'S "HERE"?
KLANG KLANG
MOUNT ETNA.
WE'RE UNDER AN ACTIVE VOLCANO IN SICILY?
YOU CALL IT ACTIVE, I CALL IT SLEEPING. BUT MAYBE NOT FOR LONG.
KLANG KLANG
AND JUST WHAT KIND OF HELL ARE *YOU* GOING TO PUT ME THROUGH?
I'M *NOT* PUTTING YOU THROUGH ANYTHING.
I'M ACTUALLY GOING TO GIVE YOU THE CHANCE TO LEAVE ALL THIS HATE, FEAR AND ANGER BEHIND YOU.
AND JUST HOW ARE YOU GOING TO DO THAT?

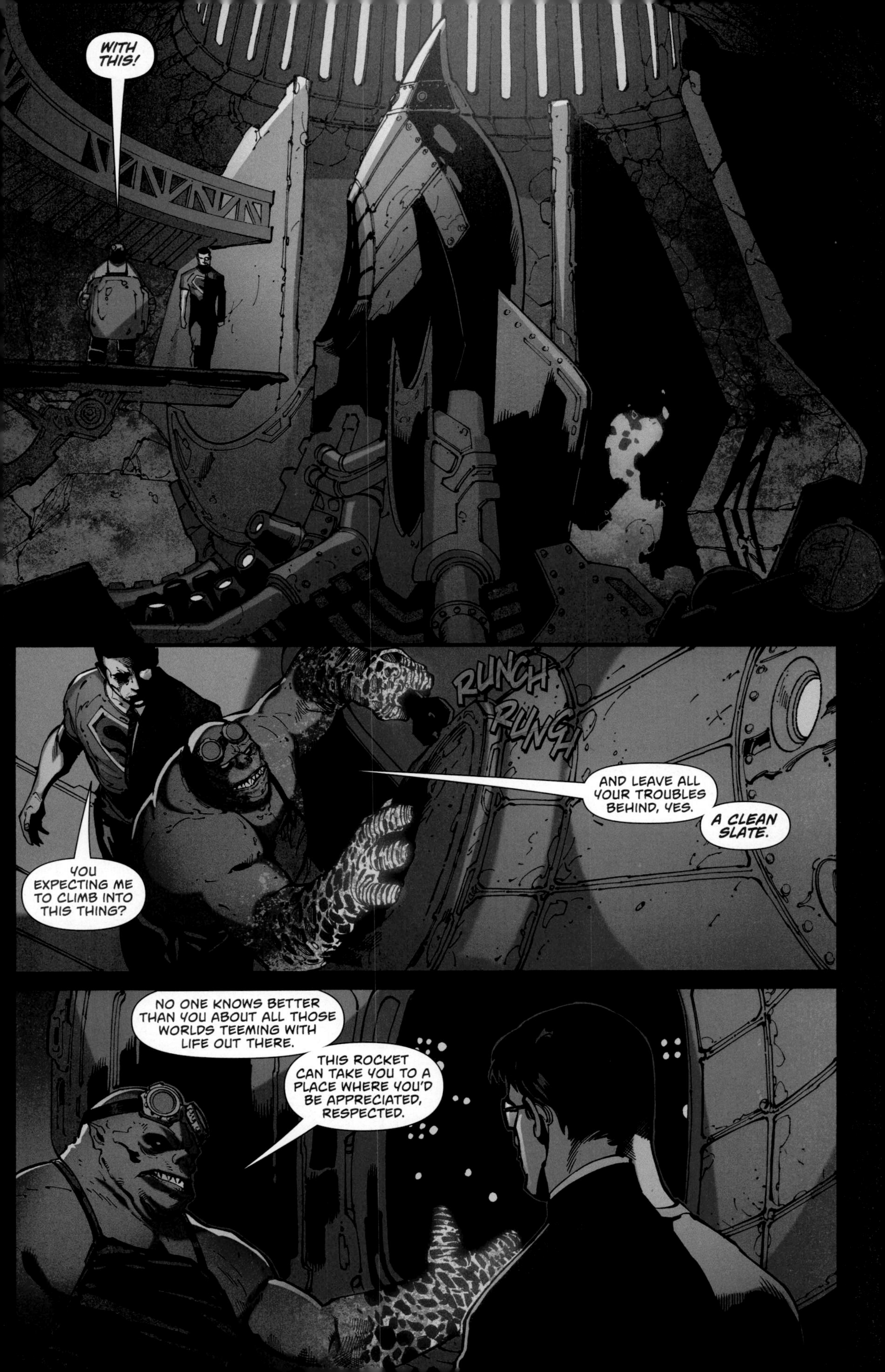
WITH THIS!
RUNCH RUNCH
AND LEAVE ALL YOUR TROUBLES BEHIND, YES.
A CLEAN SLATE.
YOU EXPECTING ME TO CLIMB INTO THIS THING?
NO ONE KNOWS BETTER THAN YOU ABOUT ALL THOSE WORLDS TEEMING WITH LIFE OUT THERE.
THIS ROCKET CAN TAKE YOU TO A PLACE WHERE YOU'D BE APPRECIATED, RESPECTED.

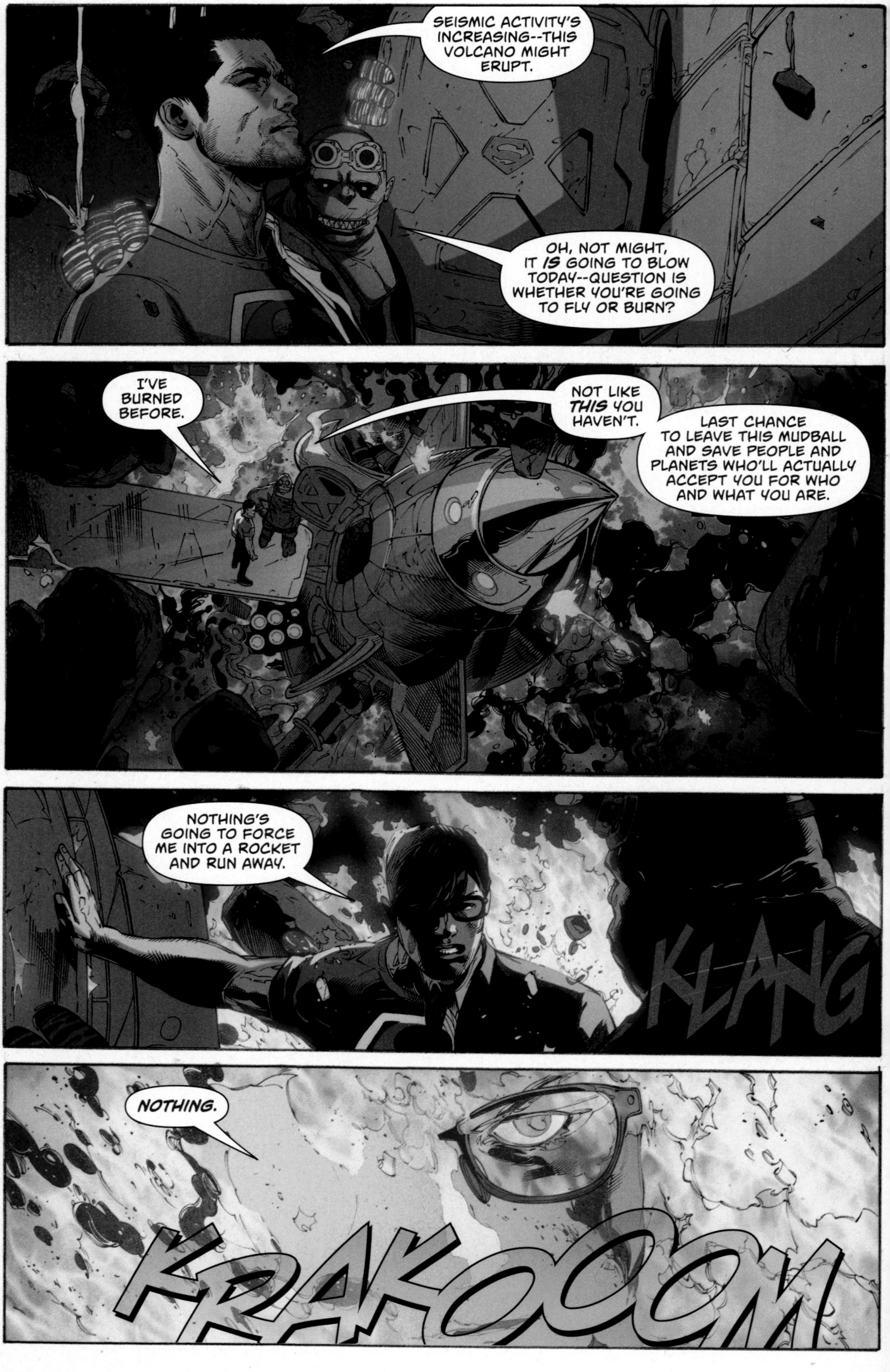
SEISMIC ACTIVITY'S INCREASING--THIS VOLCANO MIGHT ERUPT.
OH, NOT MIGHT, IT IS GOING TO BLOW TODAY--QUESTION IS WHETHER YOU'RE GOING TO FLY OR BURN?
I'VE BURNED BEFORE.
NOT LIKE THIS YOU HAVEN'T.
LAST CHANCE TO LEAVE THIS MUDBALL AND SAVE PEOPLE AND PLANETS WHO'LL ACTUALLY ACCEPT YOU FOR WHO AND WHAT YOU ARE.
NOTHING'S GOING TO FORCE ME INTO A ROCKET AND RUN AWAY.
KLANG
NOTHING.
KRAKOOOM

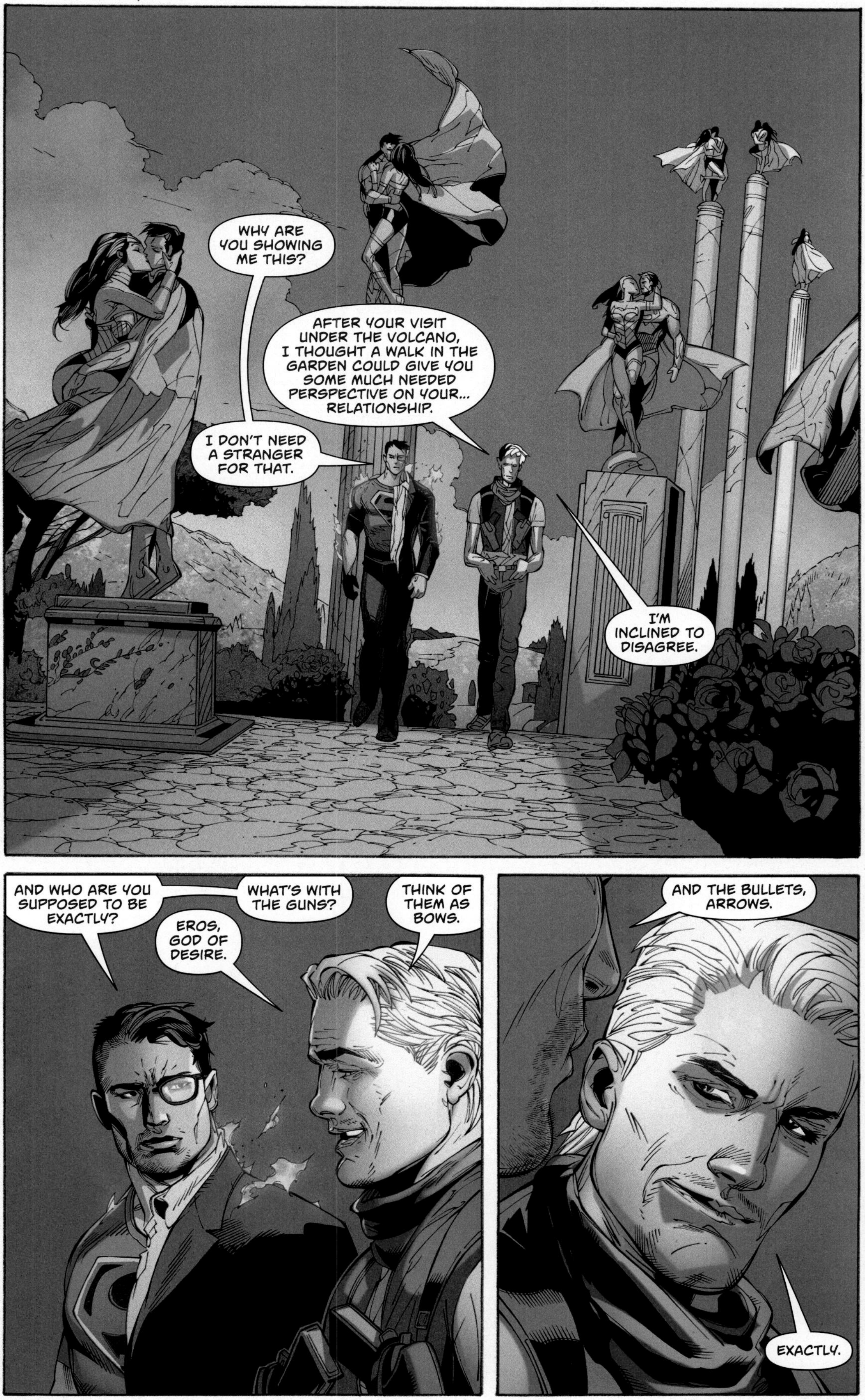
WHY ARE YOU SHOWING ME THIS?
AFTER YOUR VISIT UNDER THE VOLCANO, I THOUGHT A WALK IN THE GARDEN COULD GIVE YOU SOME MUCH NEEDED PERSPECTIVE ON YOUR... RELATIONSHIP.
I DON'T NEED A STRANGER FOR THAT.
I'M INCLINED TO DISAGREE.
AND WHO ARE YOU SUPPOSED TO BE EXACTLY?
EROS, GOD OF DESIRE.
WHAT'S WITH THE GUNS?
THINK OF THEM AS BOWS.
AND THE BULLETS, ARROWS.
EXACTLY.

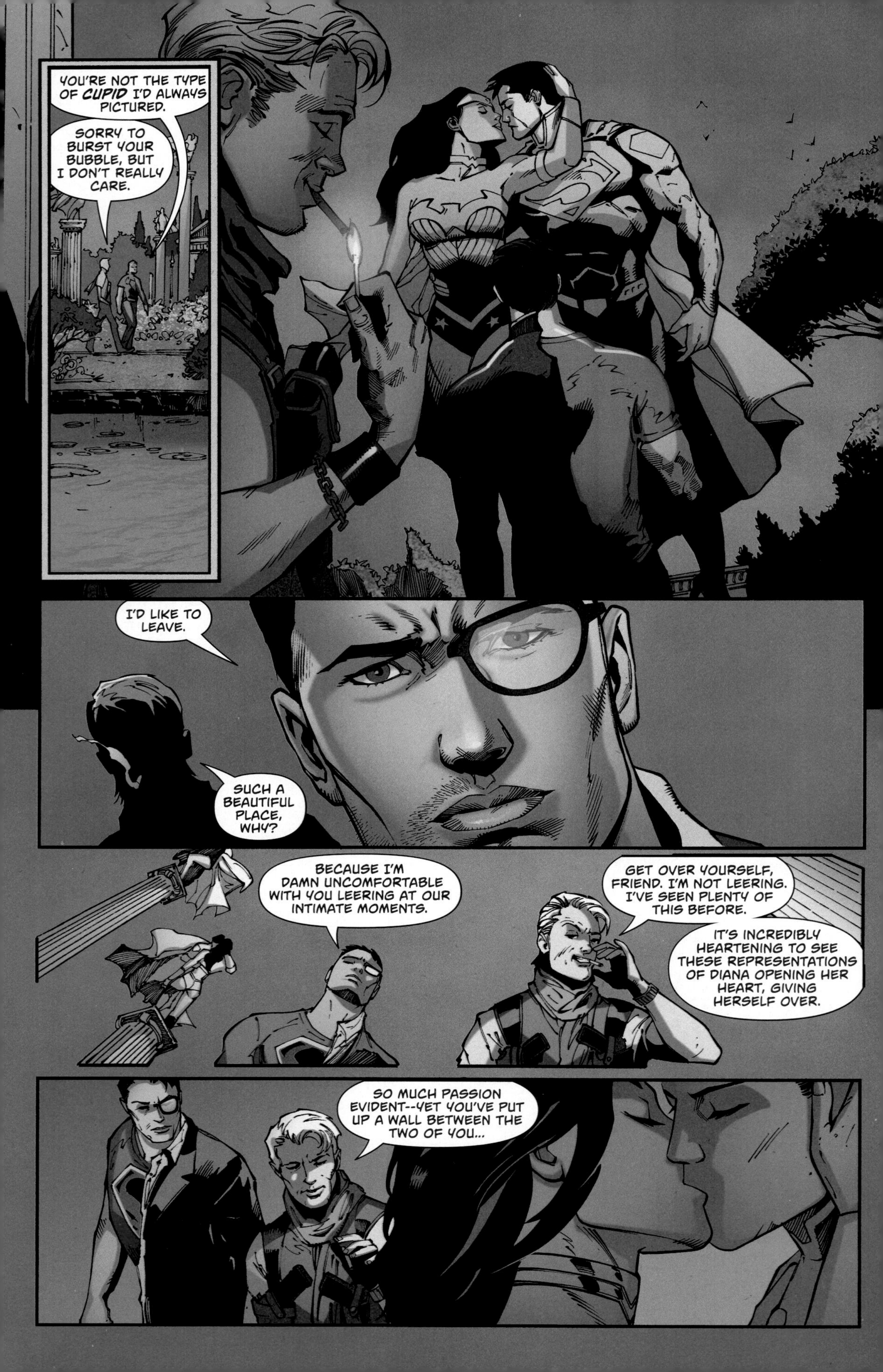
YOU'RE NOT THE TYPE OF CUPID I'D ALWAYS PICTURED.
SORRY TO BURST YOUR BUBBLE, BUT I DON'T REALLY CARE.
I'D LIKE TO LEAVE.
SUCH A BEAUTIFUL PLACE, WHY?
BECAUSE I'M DAMN UNCOMFORTABLE WITH YOU LEERING AT OUR INTIMATE MOMENTS.
GET OVER YOURSELF, FRIEND. I'M NOT LEERING. I'VE SEEN PLENTY OF THIS BEFORE.
IT'S INCREDIBLY HEARTENING TO SEE THESE REPRESENTATIONS OF DIANA OPENING HER HEART, GIVING HERSELF OVER.
SO MUCH PASSION EVIDENT--YET YOU'VE PUT UP A WALL BETWEEN THE TWO OF YOU...

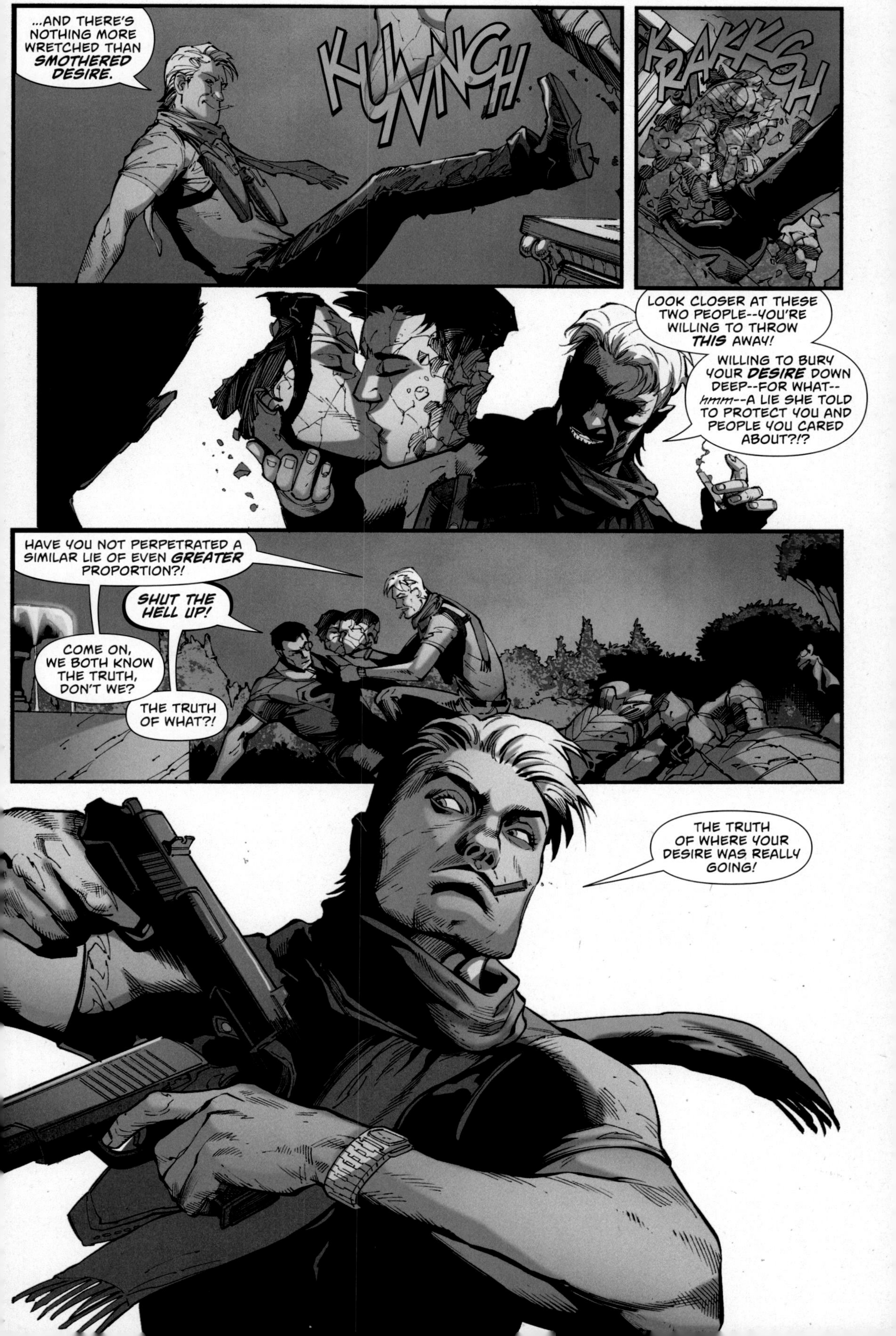

...AND THERE'S NOTHING MORE WRETCHED THAN SMOTHERED DESIRE.
KHWNCH
KRAKKSH
LOOK CLOSER AT THESE TWO PEOPLE--YOU'RE WILLING TO THROW THIS AWAY!
WILLING TO BURY YOUR DESIRE DOWN DEEP--FOR WHAT--hmm--A LIE SHE TOLD TO PROTECT YOU AND PEOPLE YOU CARED ABOUT?!?
HAVE YOU NOT PERPETRATED A SIMILAR LIE OF EVEN GREATER PROPORTION?!
SHUT THE HELL UP!
COME ON, WE BOTH KNOW THE TRUTH, DON'T WE?
THE TRUTH OF WHAT?!
THE TRUTH OF WHERE YOUR DESIRE WAS REALLY GOING!

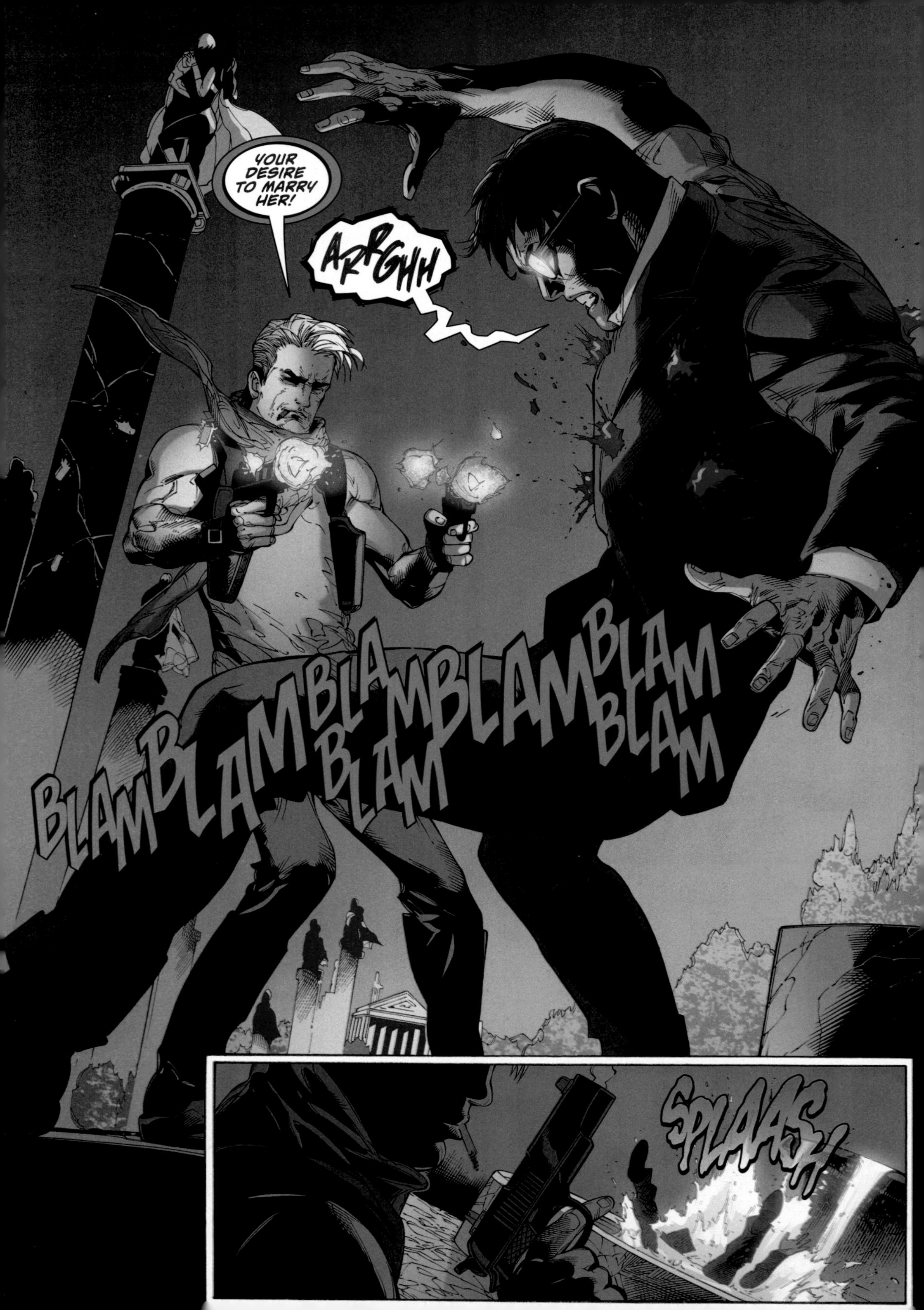
YOUR DESIRE TO MARRY HER!
ARRGHH
BLAMBLAMBLAMBLAMBLAMBLAM
BLAM
BLAM
SPLAASH

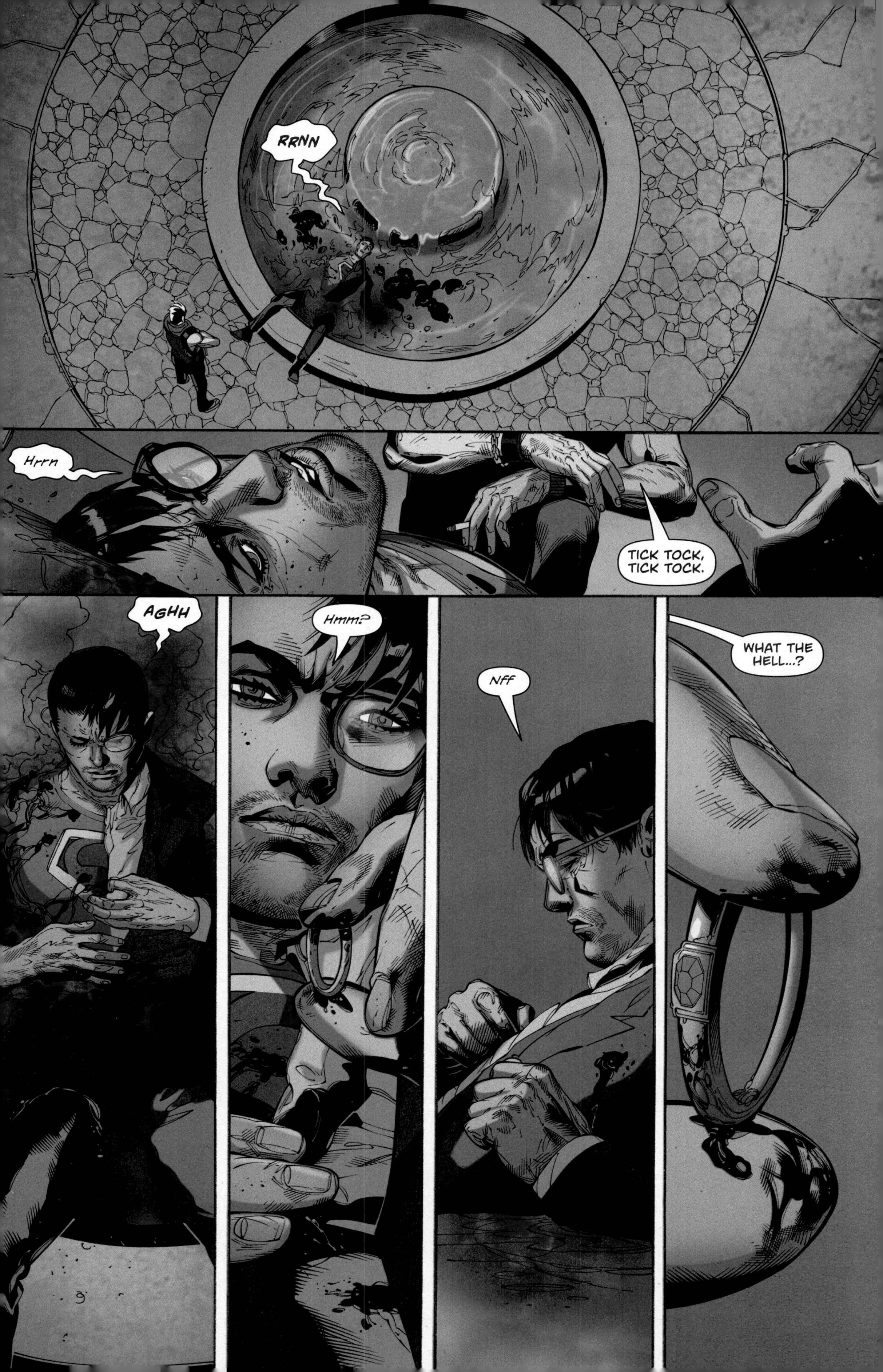

RRNN
Hrrn
TICK TOCK, TICK TOCK.
AGHH
Hmm?
Nff
WHAT THE HELL...?

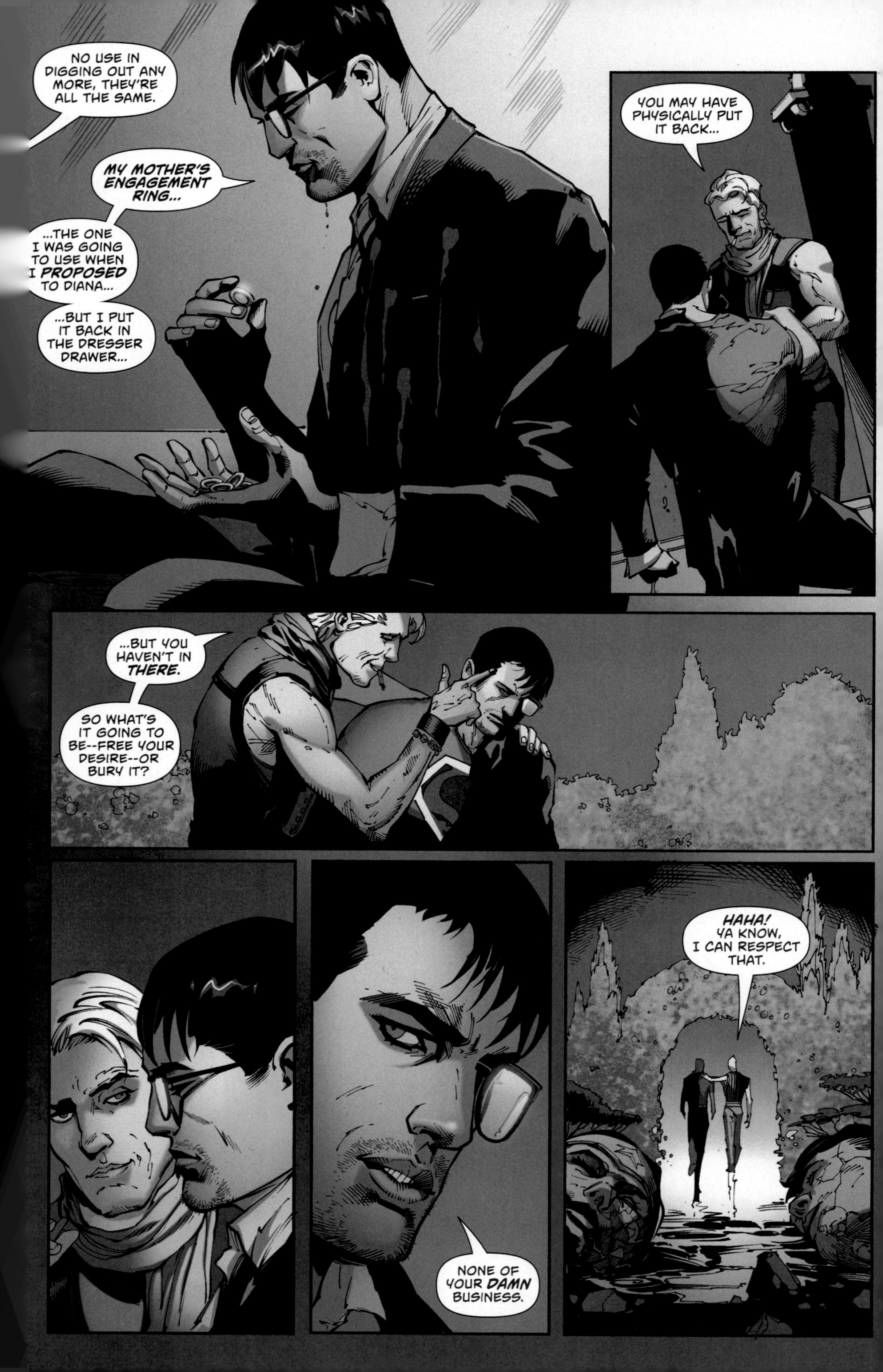
NO USE IN DIGGING OUT ANY MORE, THEY'RE ALL THE SAME.
MY MOTHER'S ENGAGEMENT RING...
...THE ONE I WAS GOING TO USE WHEN I PROPOSED TO DIANA...
...BUT I PUT IT BACK IN THE DRESSER DRAWER...
YOU MAY HAVE PHYSICALLY PUT IT BACK...
...BUT YOU HAVEN'T IN THERE.
SO WHAT'S IT GOING TO BE--FREE YOUR DESIRE--OR BURY IT?
NONE OF YOUR DAMN BUSINESS.
HAHA! YA KNOW, I CAN RESPECT THAT.

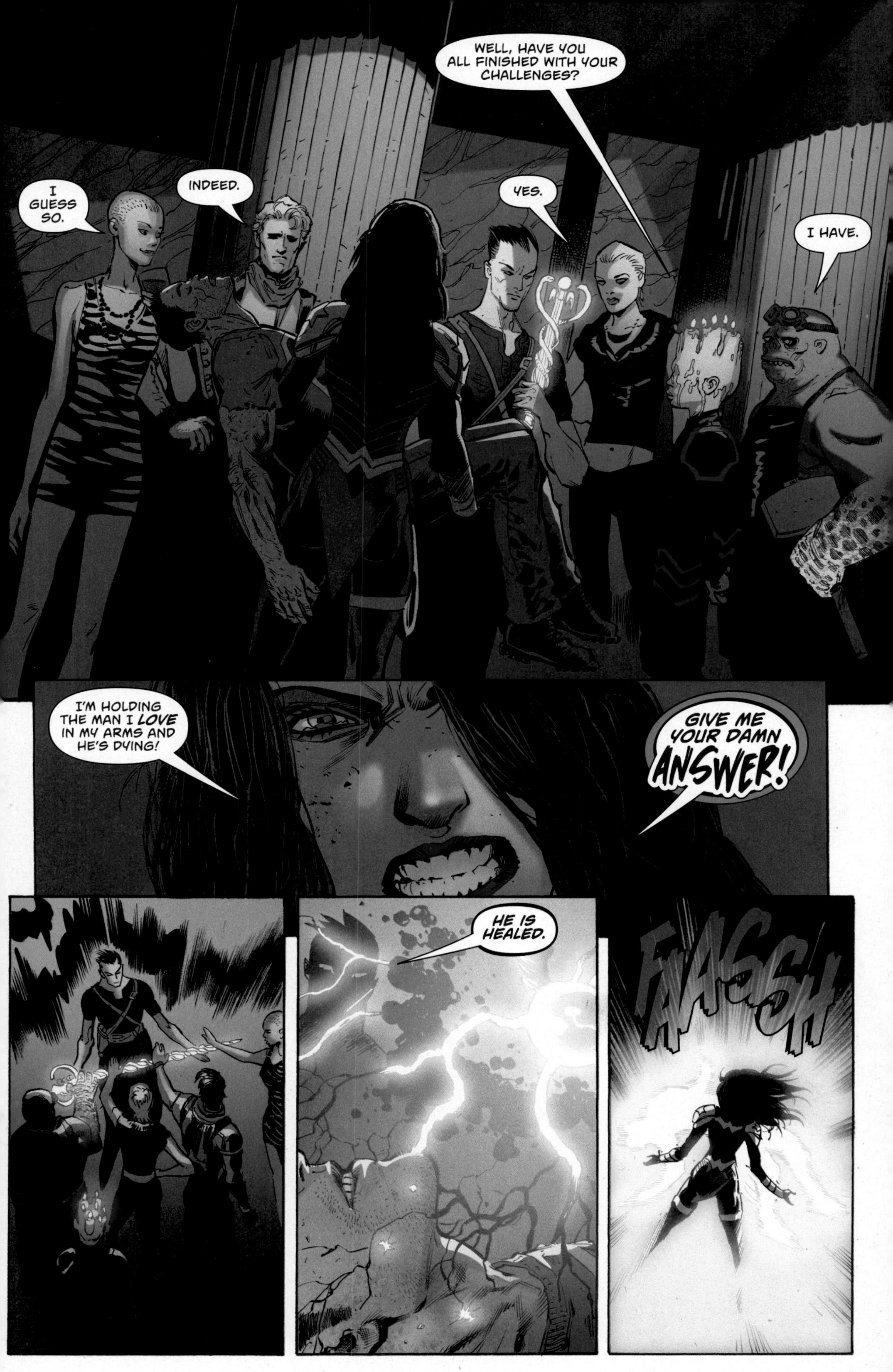

WELL, HAVE YOU ALL FINISHED WITH YOUR CHALLENGES?
I GUESS SO.
INDEED.
YES.
I HAVE.
I'M HOLDING THE MAN I LOVE IN MY ARMS AND HE'S DYING!
GIVE ME YOUR DAMN ANSWER!
HE IS HEALED.
FFASSH

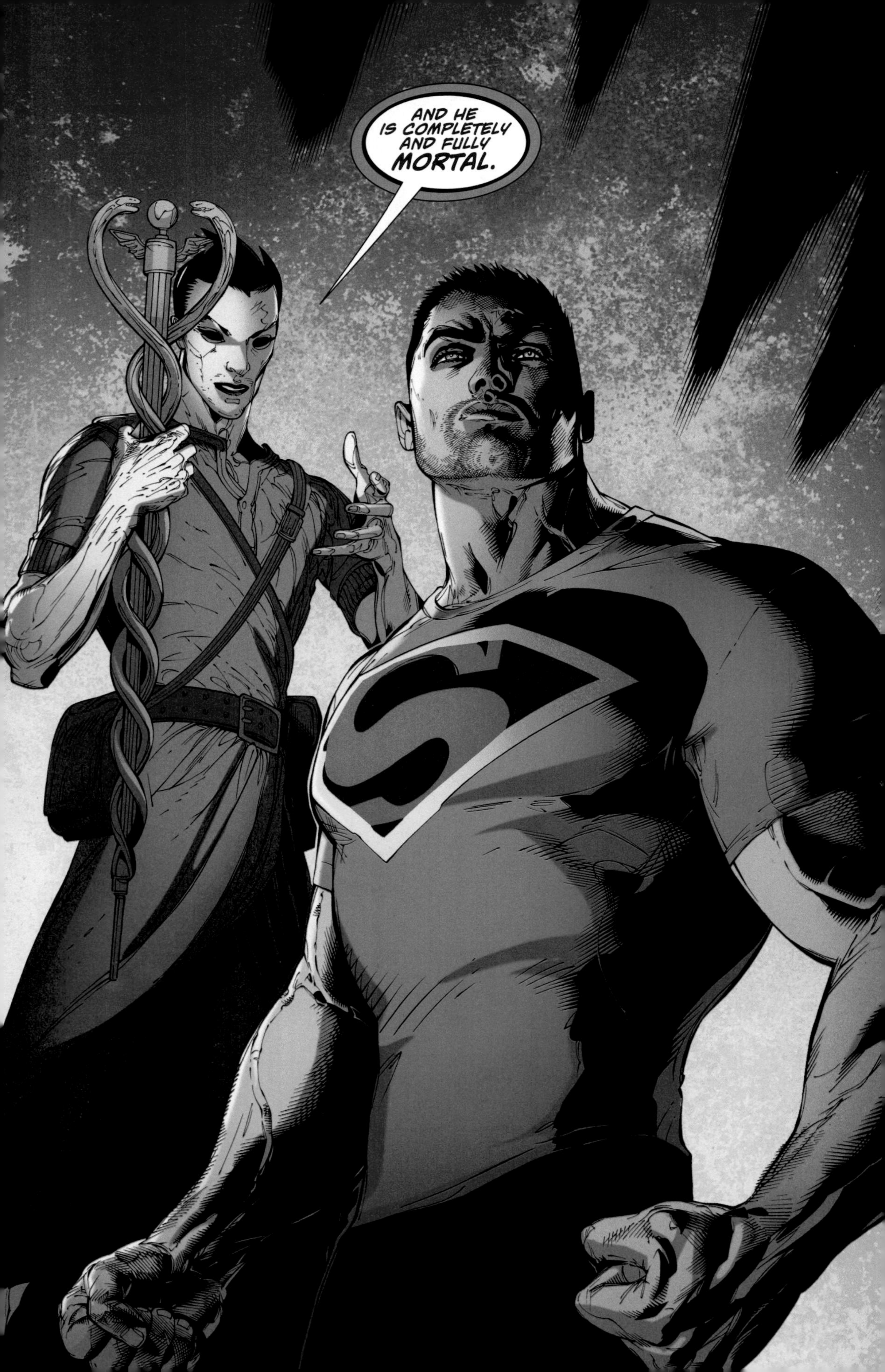
AND HE IS COMPLETELY AND FULLY MORTAL.

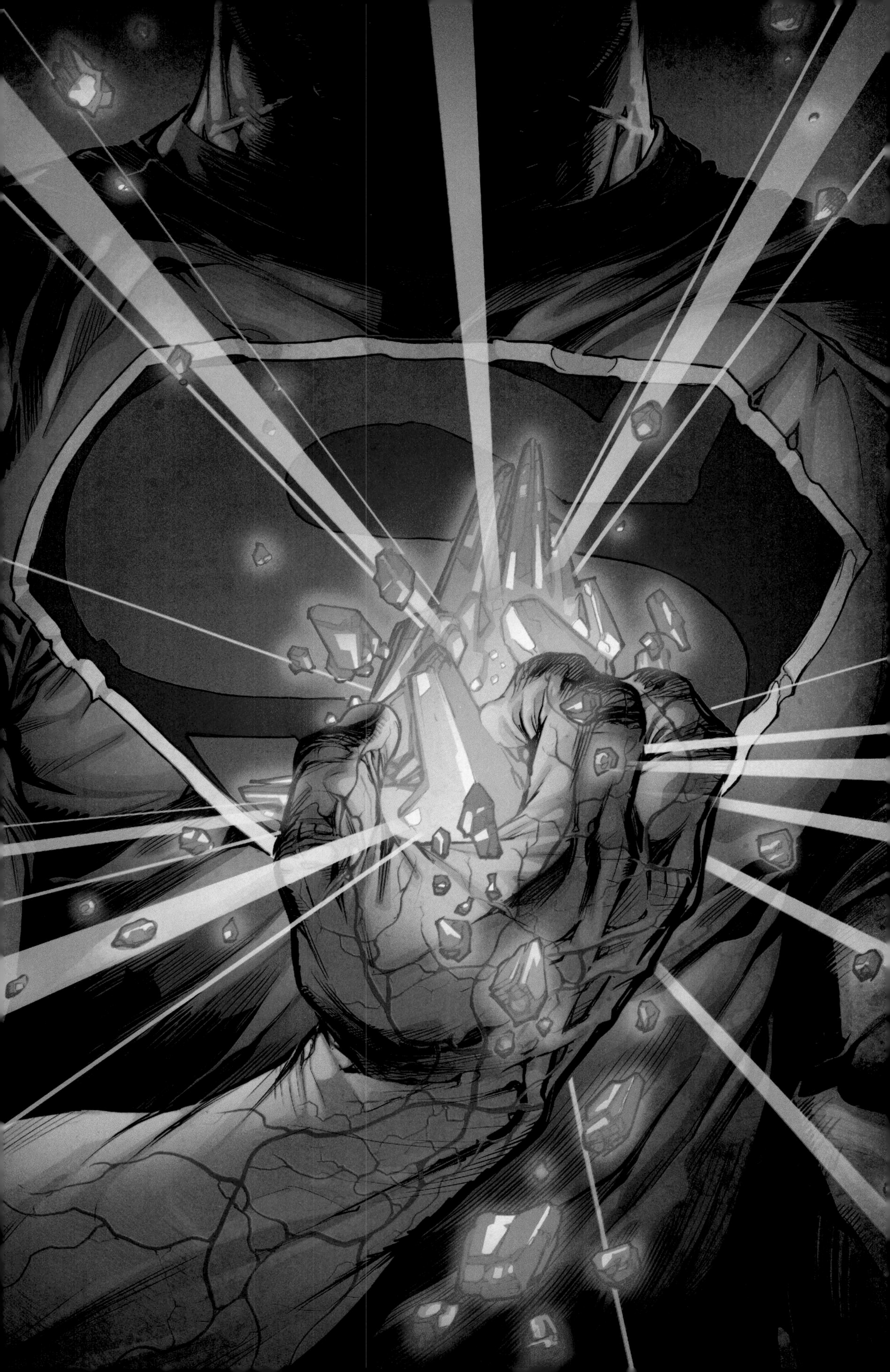

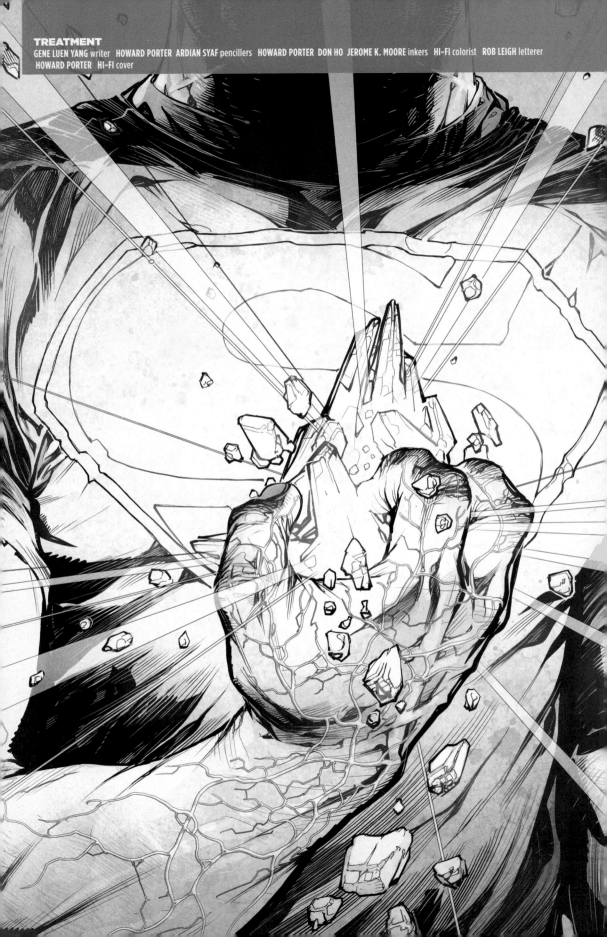

TREATMENT
GENE LUEN YANG writer HOWARD PORTER ARDIAN SYAF pencillers HOWARD PORTER DON HO JEROME K. MOORE inkers HI-FI colorist ROB LEIGH letterer
HOWARD PORTER HI-FI cover

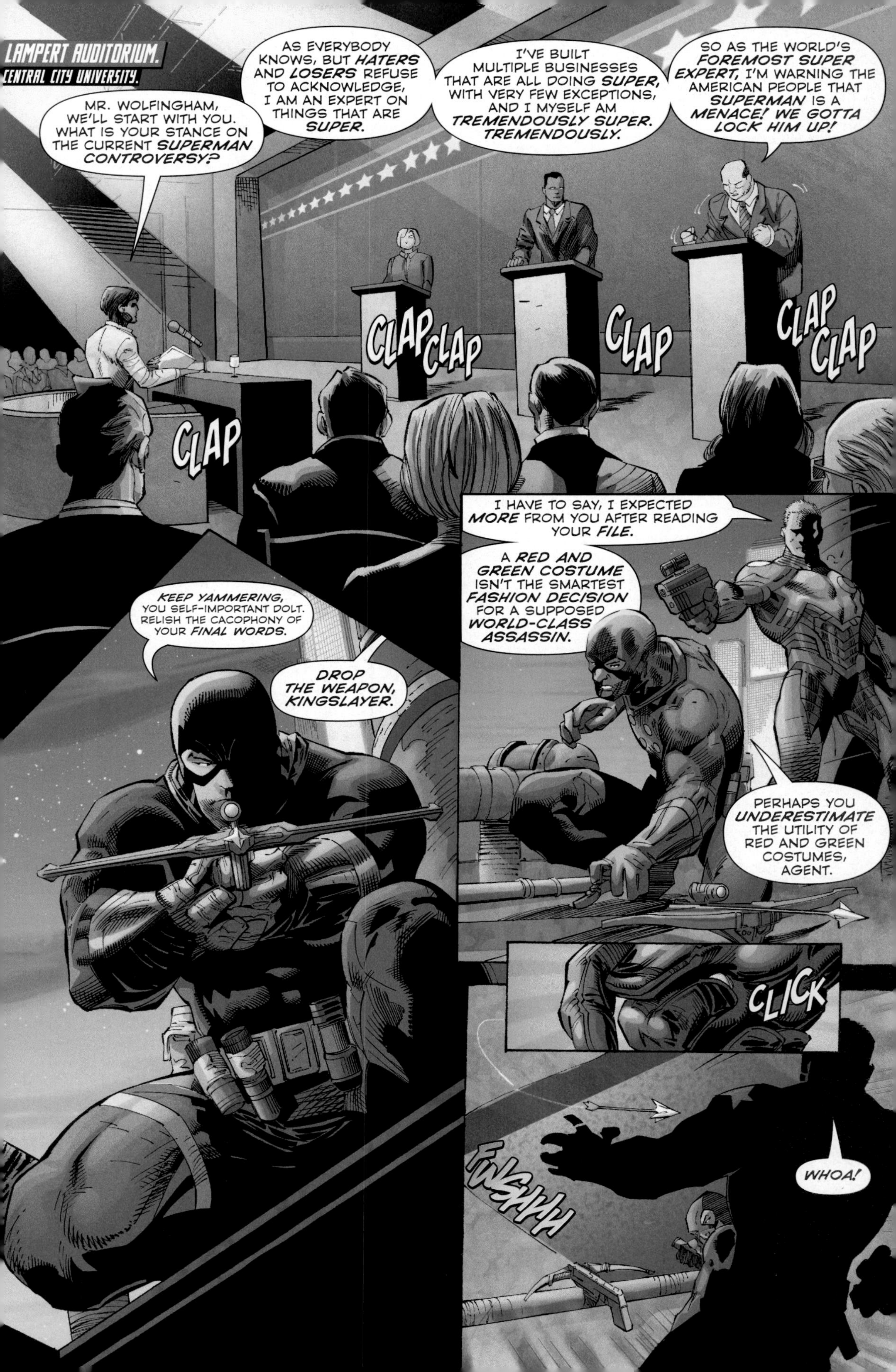
LAMPERT AUDITORIUM.
CENTRAL CITY UNIVERSITY.
MR. WOLFINGHAM, WE'LL START WITH YOU. WHAT IS YOUR STANCE ON THE CURRENT SUPERMAN CONTROVERSY?
AS EVERYBODY KNOWS, BUT HATERS AND LOSERS REFUSE TO ACKNOWLEDGE, I AM AN EXPERT ON THINGS THAT ARE SUPER.
I'VE BUILT MULTIPLE BUSINESSES THAT ARE ALL DOING SUPER, WITH VERY FEW EXCEPTIONS, AND I MYSELF AM TREMENDOUSLY SUPER. TREMENDOUSLY.
SO AS THE WORLD'S FOREMOST SUPER EXPERT, I'M WARNING THE AMERICAN PEOPLE THAT SUPERMAN IS A MENACE! WE GOTTA LOCK HIM UP!
CLAP
CLAP CLAP
CLAP
CLAP CLAP
KEEP YAMMERING, YOU SELF-IMPORTANT DOLT. RELISH THE CACOPHONY OF YOUR FINAL WORDS.
DROP THE WEAPON, KINGSLAYER.
I HAVE TO SAY, I EXPECTED MORE FROM YOU AFTER READING YOUR FILE.
A RED AND GREEN COSTUME ISN'T THE SMARTEST FASHION DECISION FOR A SUPPOSED WORLD-CLASS ASSASSIN.
PERHAPS YOU UNDERESTIMATE THE UTILITY OF RED AND GREEN COSTUMES, AGENT.
CLICK
FWSHHH
WHOA!

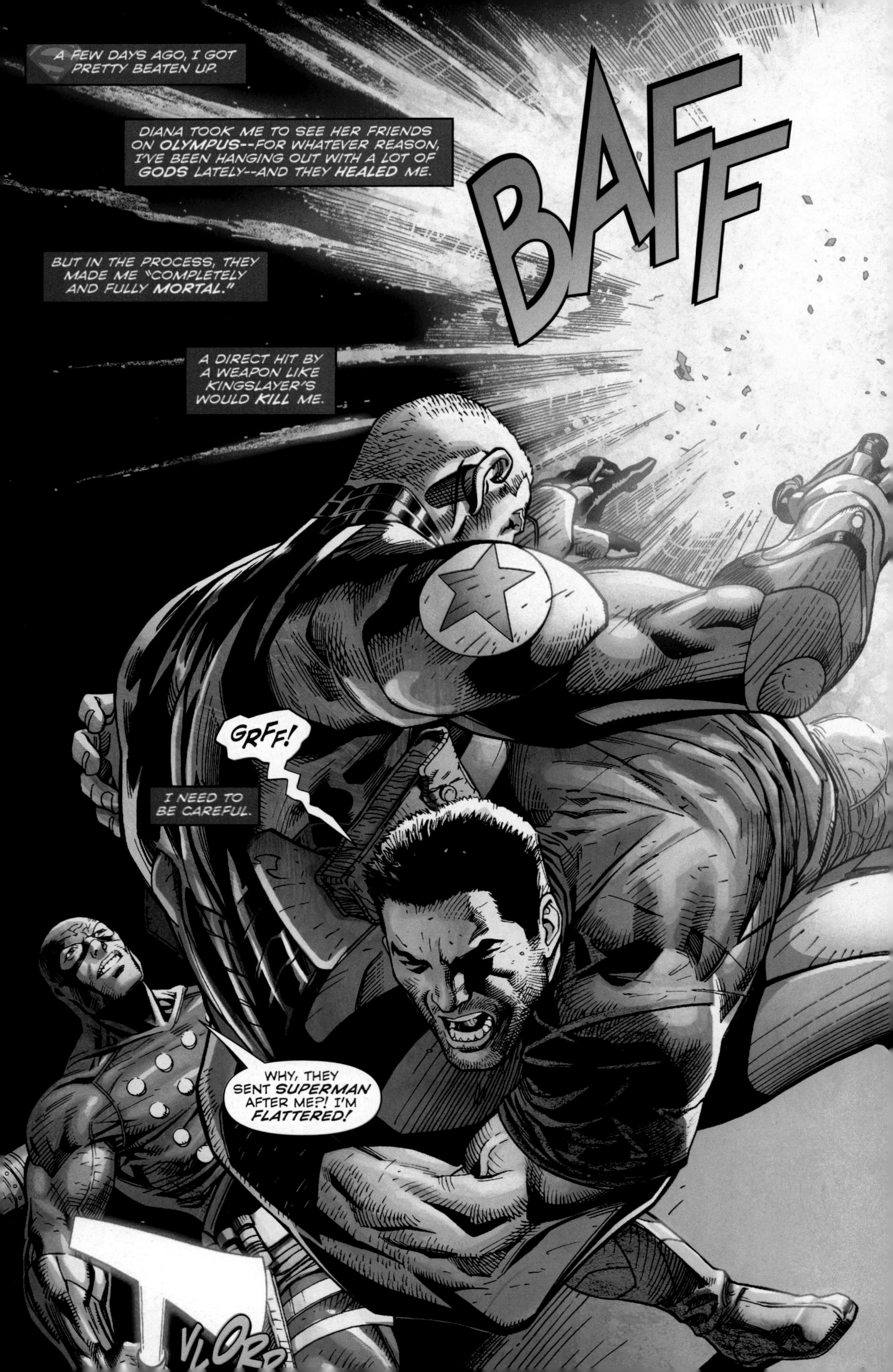
A FEW DAYS AGO, I GOT PRETTY BEATEN UP.
DIANA TOOK ME TO SEE HER FRIENDS ON OLYMPUS--FOR WHATEVER REASON, I'VE BEEN HANGING OUT WITH A LOT OF GODS LATELY--AND THEY HEALED ME.
BAFF
BUT IN THE PROCESS, THEY MADE ME "COMPLETELY AND FULLY MORTAL."
A DIRECT HIT BY A WEAPON LIKE KINGSLAYER'S WOULD KILL ME.
GRFF!
I NEED TO BE CAREFUL.
WHY, THEY SENT SUPERMAN AFTER ME?! I'M FLATTERED!

OOF!

WHUMP

SUPERMAN.

ACK!

BWAP

I JUST BAILED HIM OUT, BUT HE DOESN'T SEEM ALL THAT *THRILLED.*

UNDERSTANDABLE, I GUESS.

AGENT TREVOR.

IF I HAD TO PICK SOMEBODY TO BAIL ME OUT, MY *EX-GIRLFRIEND'S LATEST EX-BOYFRIEND* WOULDN'T BE AT THE TOP OF MY LIST, EITHER.

THAT RING AROUND HIM--?

A *PROTOTYPE* BUILT BY THE A.R.G.U.S. EGGHEADS, INSPIRED BY DIANA'S LASSO.

AFTER HER LAST VISIT TO OUR *EVALUATION LAB,* WE DECIDED THAT WE NEEDED A SIMILAR TOOL AT OUR DISPOSAL.

HOW'D YOU REPLICATE THE LASSO'S TRUTH-TELLING ABILITIES?

WE DIDN'T. WE USE *PAIN* INSTEAD.

WHAT YOU'RE FEELING RIGHT NOW IS JUST A *TENTH* OF WHAT THIS DEVICE IS CAPABLE OF. SO TELL ME: WHY ARE YOU GUNNING FOR *WILBUR WOLFINGHAM?*

RGh

WOLFINGHAM?

nGh

THAT *JESTER* WHO WOULD BE KING...? *HA.*

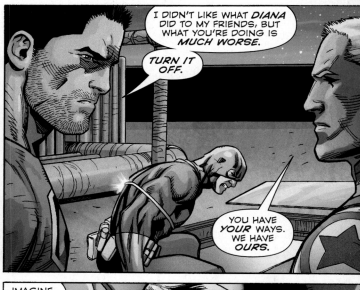

I DIDN'T LIKE WHAT *DIANA* DID TO MY FRIENDS, BUT WHAT YOU'RE DOING IS *MUCH WORSE.*

TURN IT OFF.

YOU HAVE *YOUR* WAYS. WE HAVE *OURS.*

IMAGINE A WORLD *FREE...*

ngh

NOT JUST OF *KINGS...*

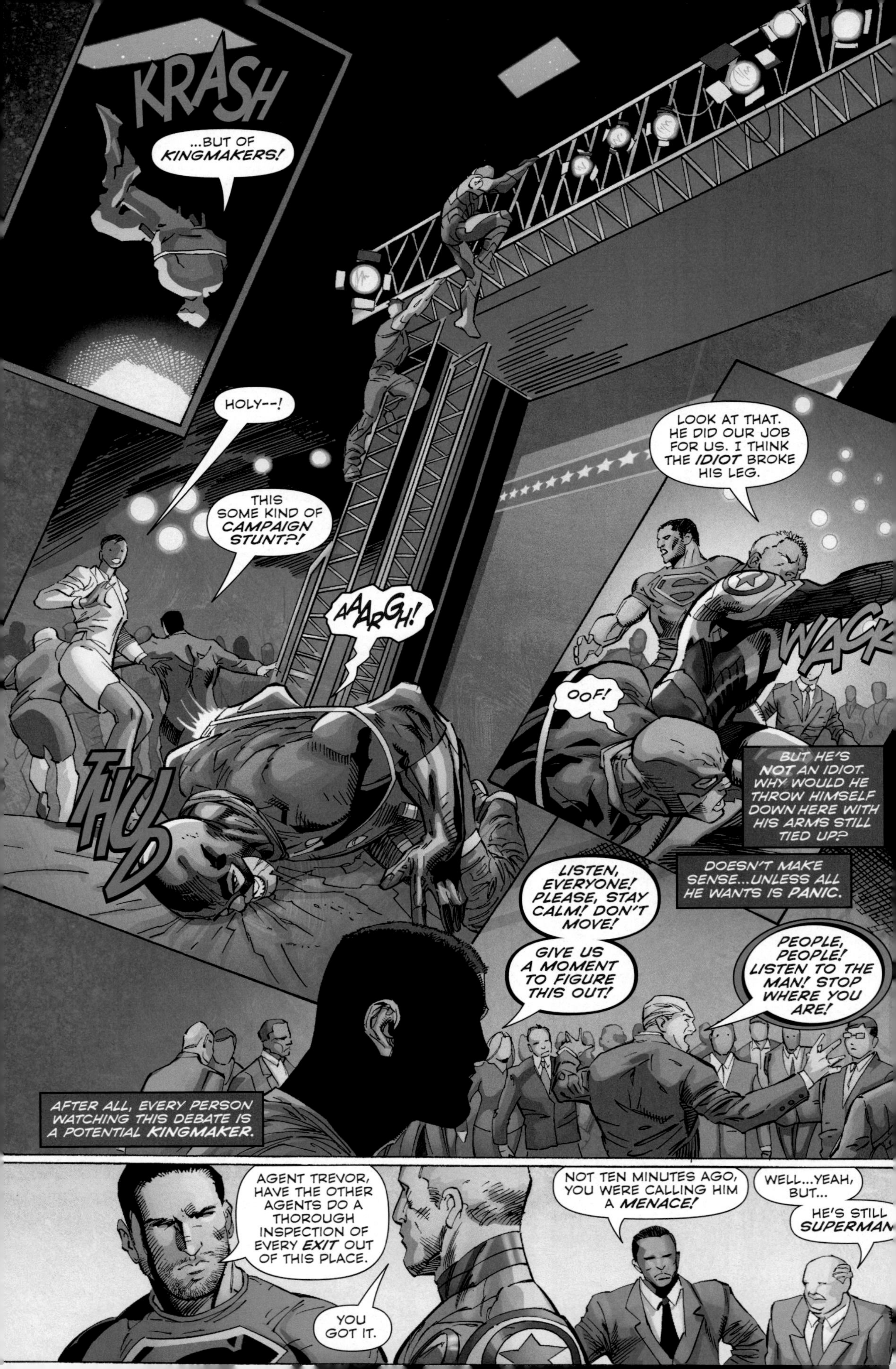
KRASH
...BUT OF KINGMAKERS!
HOLY--!
THIS SOME KIND OF CAMPAIGN STUNT?!
AAARGH!
THUD
LOOK AT THAT. HE DID OUR JOB FOR US. I THINK THE IDIOT BROKE HIS LEG.
WACK
OOF!
BUT HE'S NOT AN IDIOT. WHY WOULD HE THROW HIMSELF DOWN HERE WITH HIS ARMS STILL TIED UP?
DOESN'T MAKE SENSE...UNLESS ALL HE WANTS IS PANIC.
LISTEN, EVERYONE! PLEASE, STAY CALM! DON'T MOVE!
GIVE US A MOMENT TO FIGURE THIS OUT!
PEOPLE, PEOPLE! LISTEN TO THE MAN! STOP WHERE YOU ARE!
AFTER ALL, EVERY PERSON WATCHING THIS DEBATE IS A POTENTIAL KINGMAKER.
AGENT TREVOR, HAVE THE OTHER AGENTS DO A THOROUGH INSPECTION OF EVERY EXIT OUT OF THIS PLACE.
YOU GOT IT.
NOT TEN MINUTES AGO, YOU WERE CALLING HIM A MENACE!
WELL...YEAH, BUT...
HE'S STILL SUPERMAN

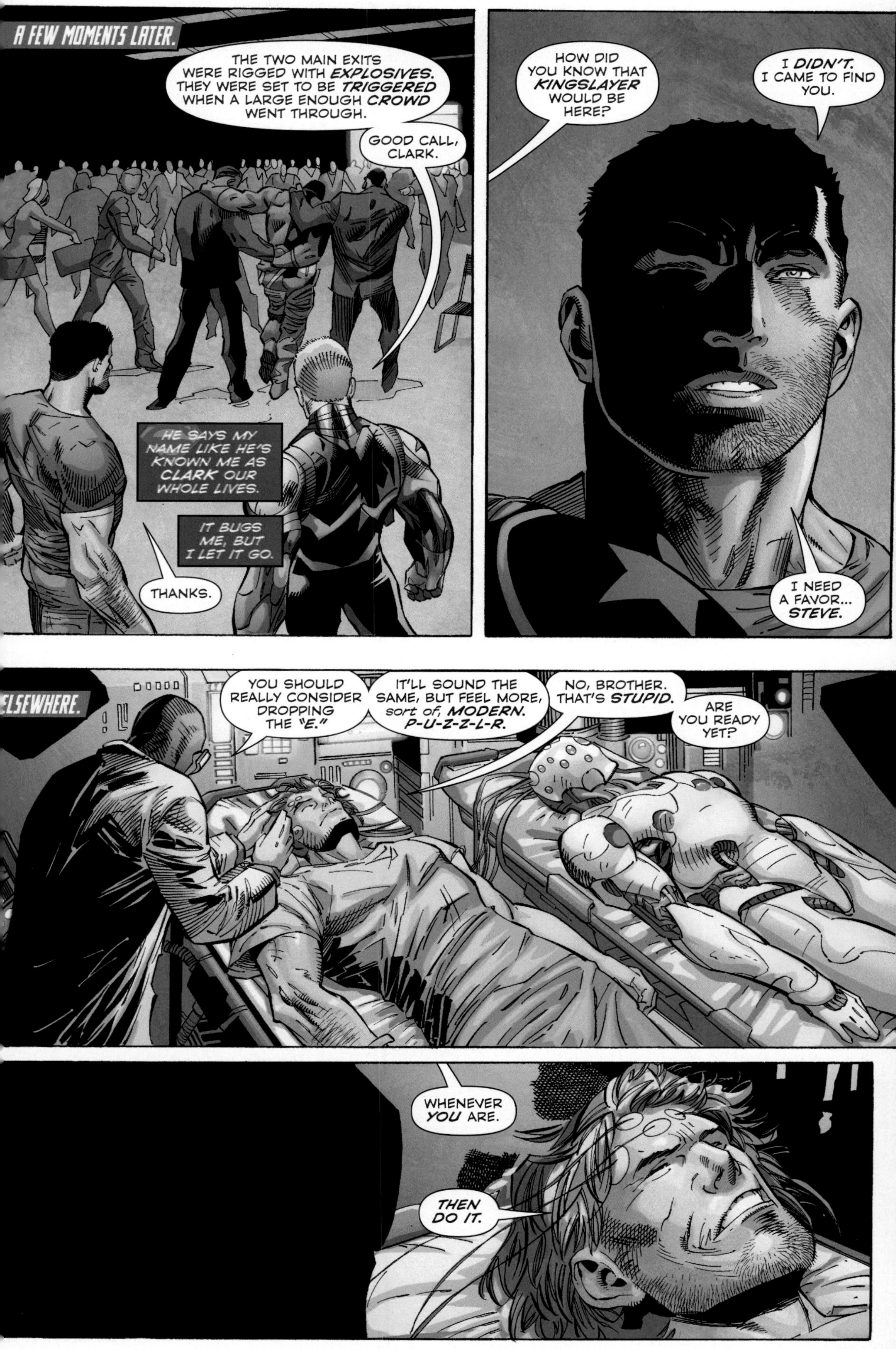
A FEW MOMENTS LATER.
THE TWO MAIN EXITS WERE RIGGED WITH EXPLOSIVES. THEY WERE SET TO BE TRIGGERED WHEN A LARGE ENOUGH CROWD WENT THROUGH.
GOOD CALL, CLARK.
HE SAYS MY NAME LIKE HE'S KNOWN ME AS CLARK OUR WHOLE LIVES.
IT BUGS ME, BUT I LET IT GO.
THANKS.
HOW DID YOU KNOW THAT KINGSLAYER WOULD BE HERE?
I DIDN'T. I CAME TO FIND YOU.
I NEED A FAVOR... STEVE.
ELSEWHERE.
YOU SHOULD REALLY CONSIDER DROPPING THE "E."
IT'LL SOUND THE SAME, BUT FEEL MORE, sort of, MODERN. P-U-Z-Z-L-R.
NO, BROTHER. THAT'S STUPID.
ARE YOU READY YET?
WHENEVER YOU ARE.
THEN DO IT.

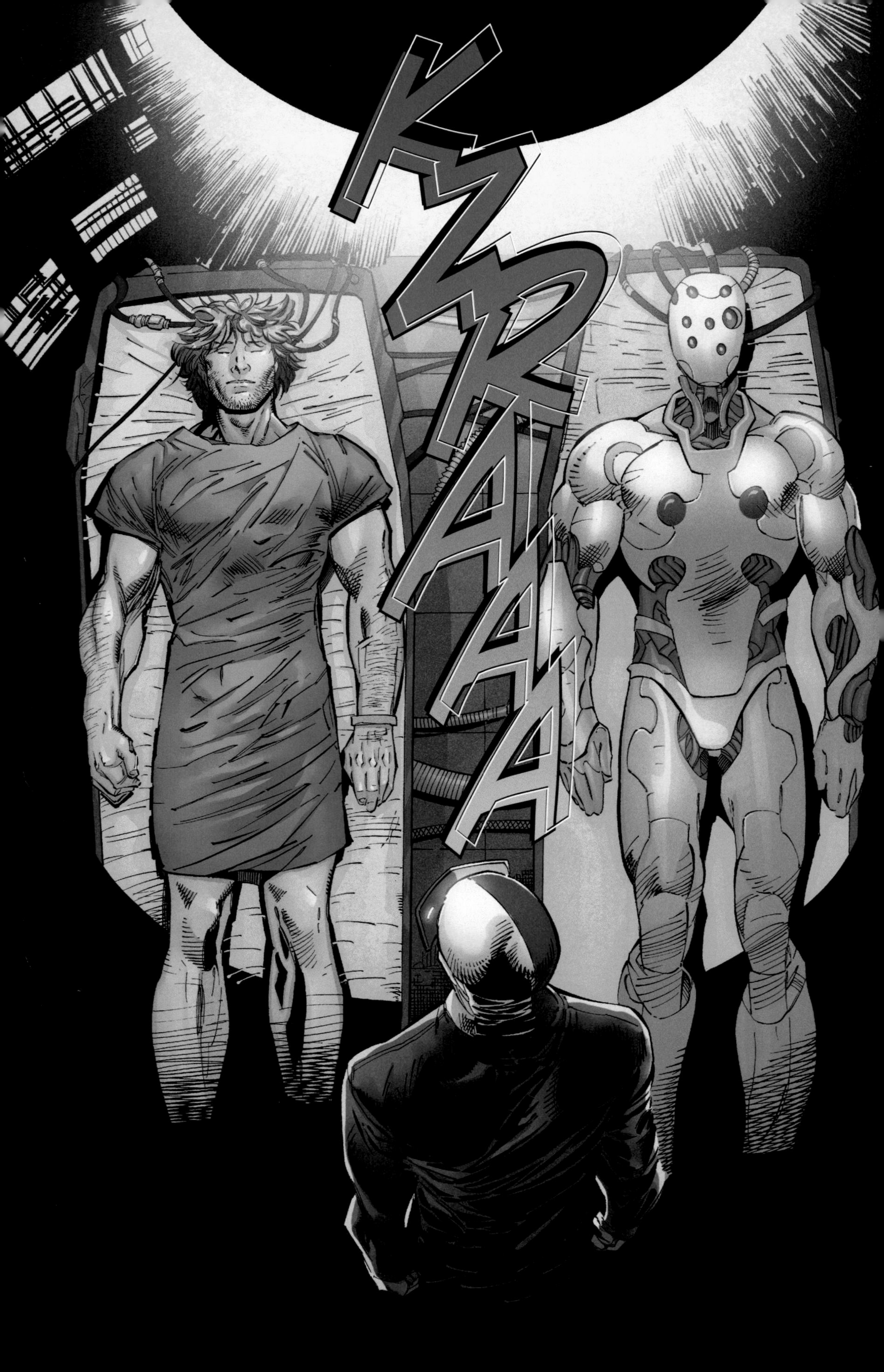
KZRAAAA

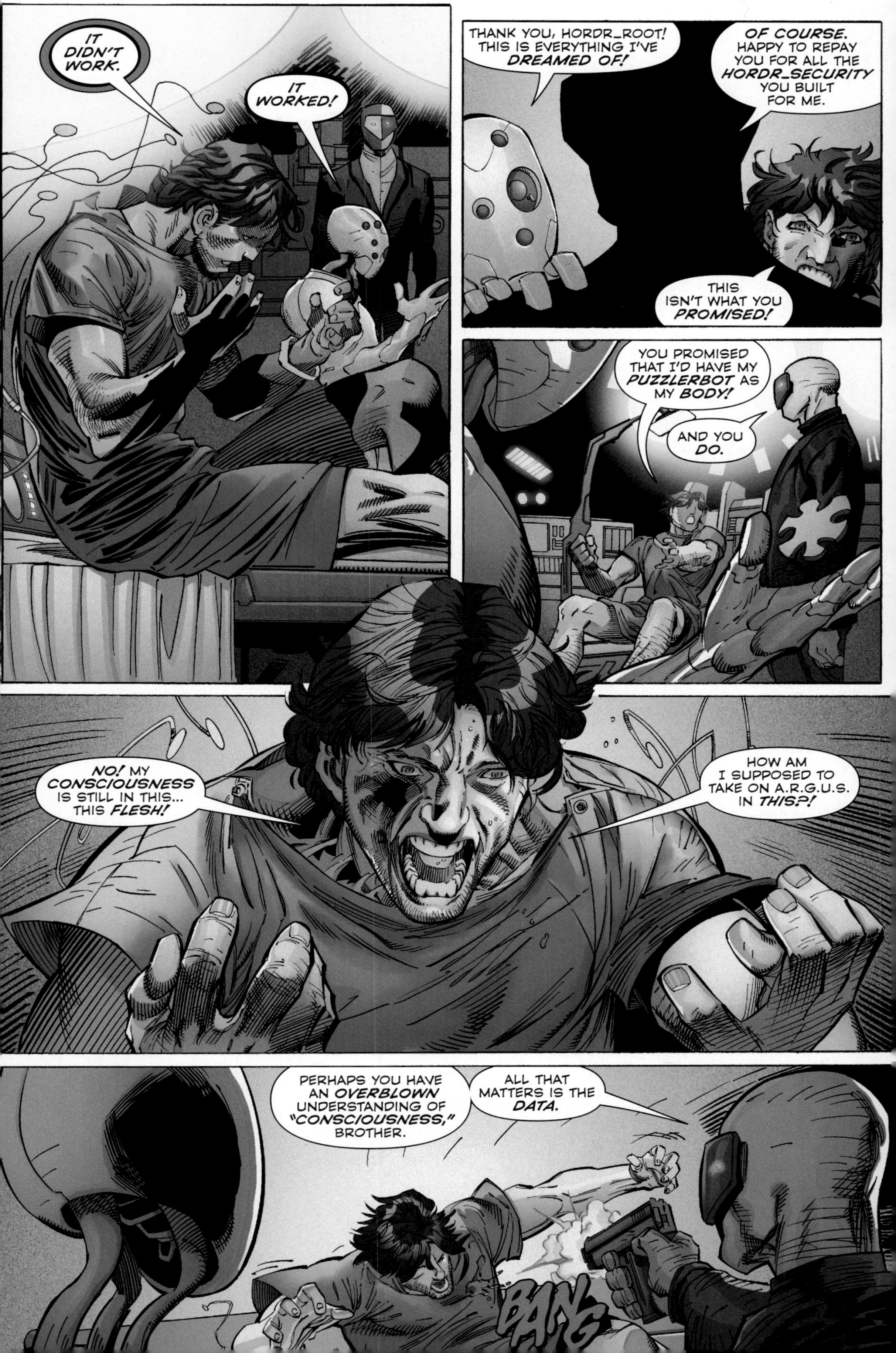
IT DIDN'T WORK.
IT WORKED!
THANK YOU, HORDR_ROOT! THIS IS EVERYTHING I'VE DREAMED OF!
OF COURSE. HAPPY TO REPAY YOU FOR ALL THE HORDR_SECURITY YOU BUILT FOR ME.
THIS ISN'T WHAT YOU PROMISED!
YOU PROMISED THAT I'D HAVE MY PUZZLERBOT AS MY BODY!
AND YOU DO.
NO! MY CONSCIOUSNESS IS STILL IN THIS... THIS FLESH!
HOW AM I SUPPOSED TO TAKE ON A.R.G.U.S. IN THIS?!
PERHAPS YOU HAVE AN OVERBLOWN UNDERSTANDING OF "CONSCIOUSNESS," BROTHER.
ALL THAT MATTERS IS THE DATA.
BANG

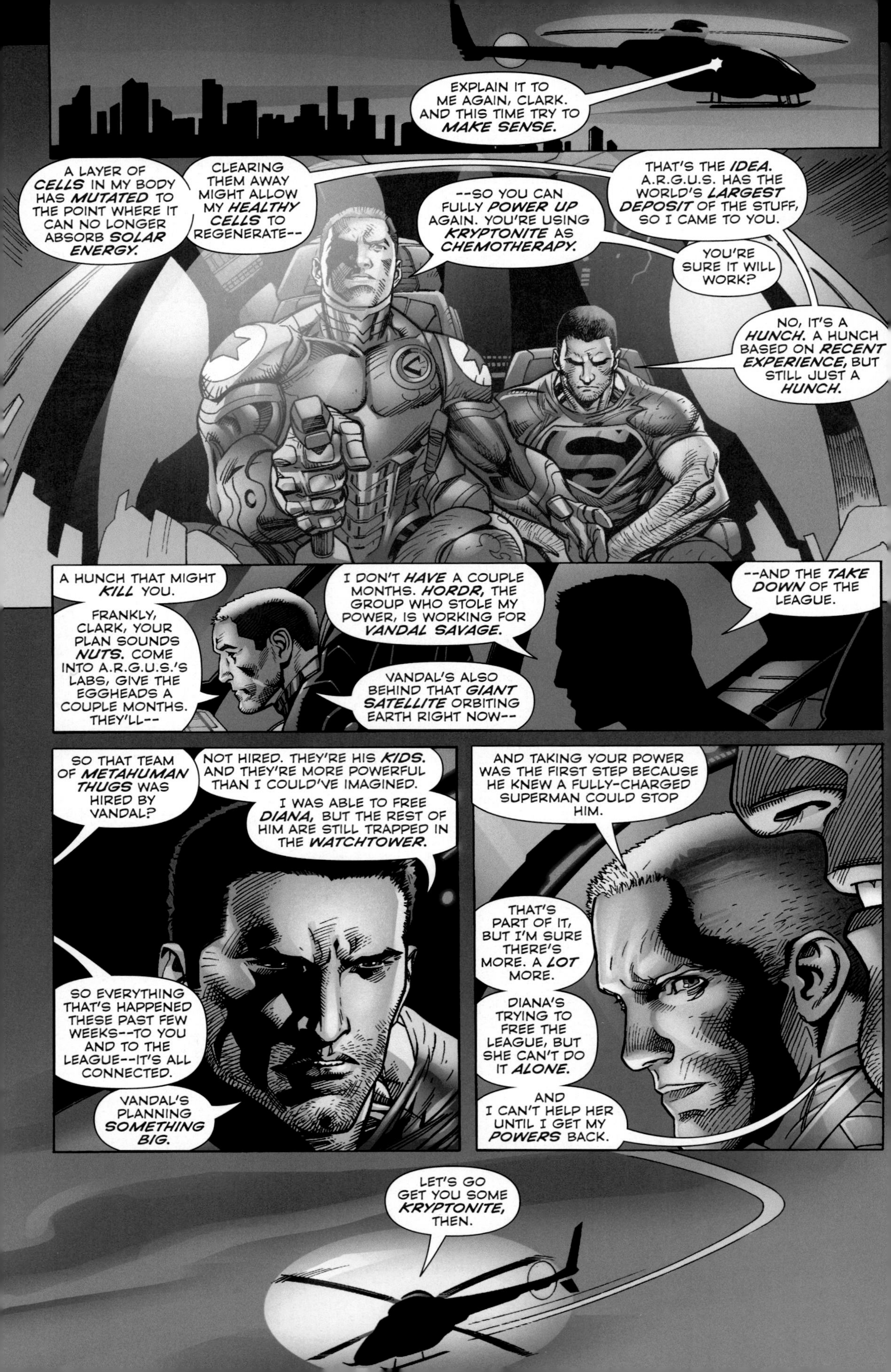
EXPLAIN IT TO ME AGAIN, CLARK. AND THIS TIME TRY TO *MAKE SENSE*.
A LAYER OF *CELLS* IN MY BODY HAS *MUTATED* TO THE POINT WHERE IT CAN NO LONGER ABSORB *SOLAR ENERGY*.
CLEARING THEM AWAY MIGHT ALLOW MY *HEALTHY CELLS* TO REGENERATE--
--SO YOU CAN FULLY *POWER UP* AGAIN. YOU'RE USING *KRYPTONITE* AS *CHEMOTHERAPY*.
THAT'S THE *IDEA*. A.R.G.U.S. HAS THE WORLD'S *LARGEST DEPOSIT* OF THE STUFF, SO I CAME TO YOU.
YOU'RE SURE IT WILL WORK?
NO, IT'S A *HUNCH*. A HUNCH BASED ON *RECENT EXPERIENCE*, BUT STILL JUST A *HUNCH*.
A HUNCH THAT MIGHT *KILL* YOU.
FRANKLY, CLARK, YOUR PLAN SOUNDS *NUTS*. COME INTO A.R.G.U.S.'S LABS, GIVE THE EGGHEADS A COUPLE MONTHS. THEY'LL--
I DON'T *HAVE* A COUPLE MONTHS. *HORDR*, THE GROUP WHO STOLE MY POWER, IS WORKING FOR *VANDAL SAVAGE*.
VANDAL'S ALSO BEHIND THAT *GIANT SATELLITE* ORBITING EARTH RIGHT NOW--
--AND THE *TAKE DOWN* OF THE LEAGUE.
SO THAT TEAM OF *METAHUMAN THUGS* WAS HIRED BY VANDAL?
NOT HIRED. THEY'RE HIS *KIDS*. AND THEY'RE MORE POWERFUL THAN I COULD'VE IMAGINED.
I WAS ABLE TO FREE *DIANA*, BUT THE REST OF HIM ARE STILL TRAPPED IN THE *WATCHTOWER*.
SO EVERYTHING THAT'S HAPPENED THE PAST FEW WEEKS--TO YOU AND TO THE LEAGUE--IT'S ALL CONNECTED.
VANDAL'S PLANNING *SOMETHING BIG*.
AND TAKING YOUR POWER WAS THE FIRST STEP BECAUSE HE KNEW A FULLY-CHARGED SUPERMAN COULD STOP HIM.
THAT'S PART OF IT, BUT I'M SURE THERE'S MORE. A *LOT* MORE.
DIANA'S TRYING TO FREE THE LEAGUE, BUT SHE CAN'T DO IT *ALONE*.
AND I CAN'T HELP HER UNTIL I GET MY *POWERS* BACK.
LET'S GO GET YOU SOME *KRYPTONITE*, THEN.

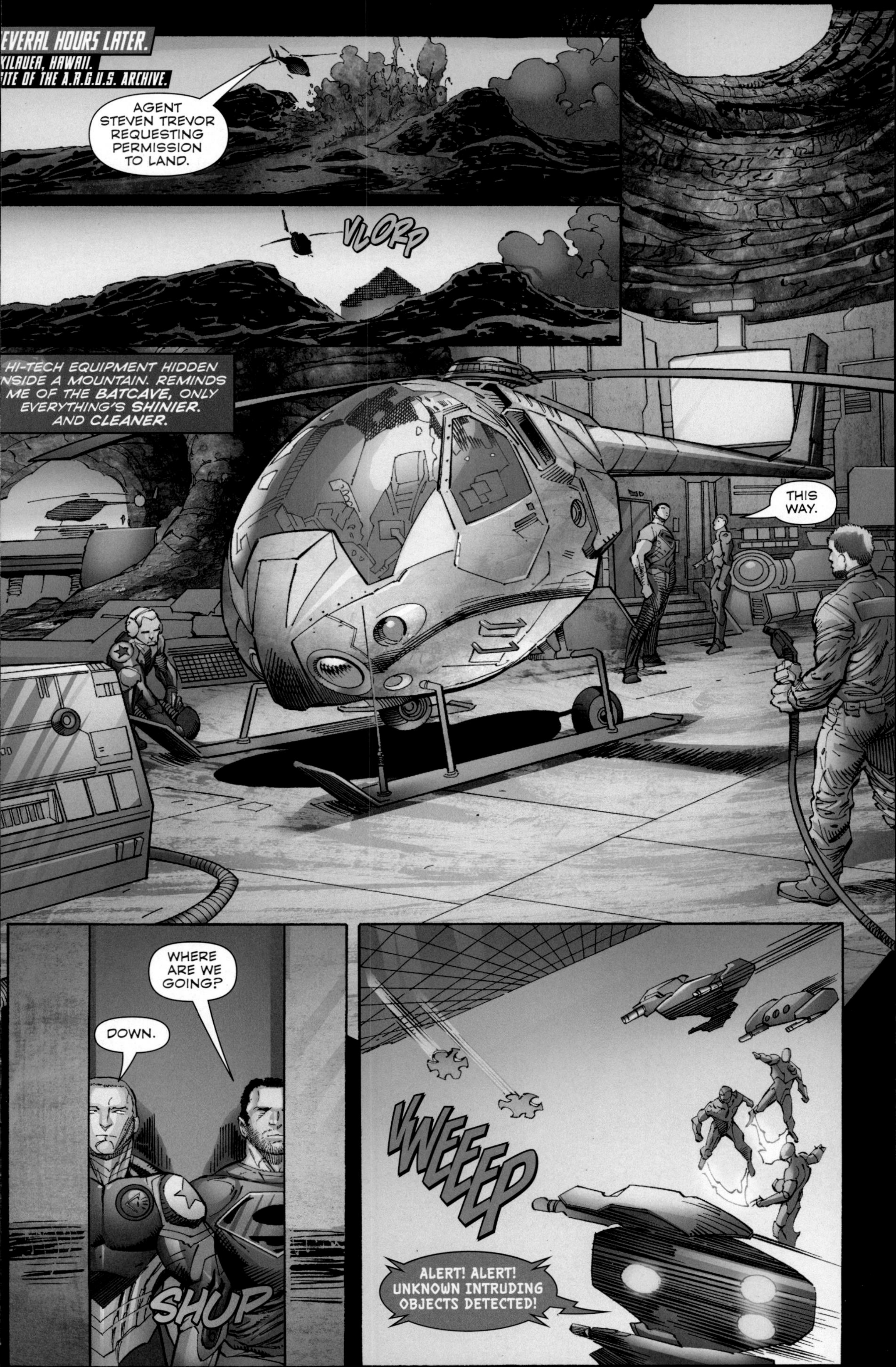

EVERAL HOURS LATER.
KILAUEA, HAWAII.
SITE OF THE A.R.G.U.S. ARCHIVE.
AGENT STEVEN TREVOR REQUESTING PERMISSION TO LAND.
VLORP
HI-TECH EQUIPMENT HIDDEN INSIDE A MOUNTAIN. REMINDS ME OF THE BATCAVE, ONLY EVERYTHING'S SHINIER. AND CLEANER.
THIS WAY.
WHERE ARE WE GOING?
DOWN.
SHUP
VWEEEP
ALERT! ALERT! UNKNOWN INTRUDING OBJECTS DETECTED!

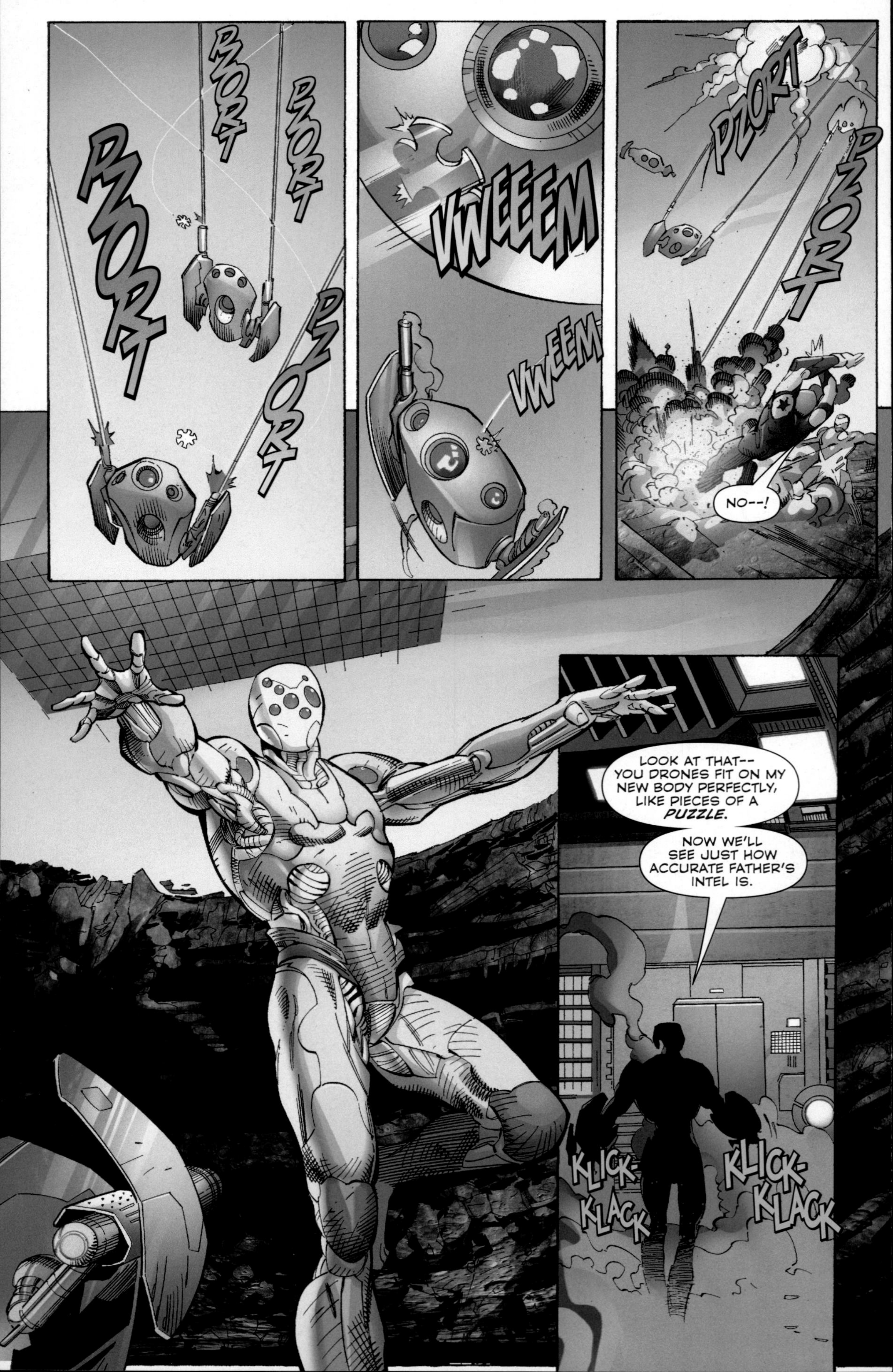
PZORT
PZORT
PZORT
PZORT
VWEEEM
VWEEM
PZORT
PZORT
NO--!
LOOK AT THAT-- YOU DRONES FIT ON MY NEW BODY PERFECTLY, LIKE PIECES OF A *PUZZLE*.
NOW WE'LL SEE JUST HOW ACCURATE FATHER'S INTEL IS.
KLICK-KLACK
KLICK-KLACK

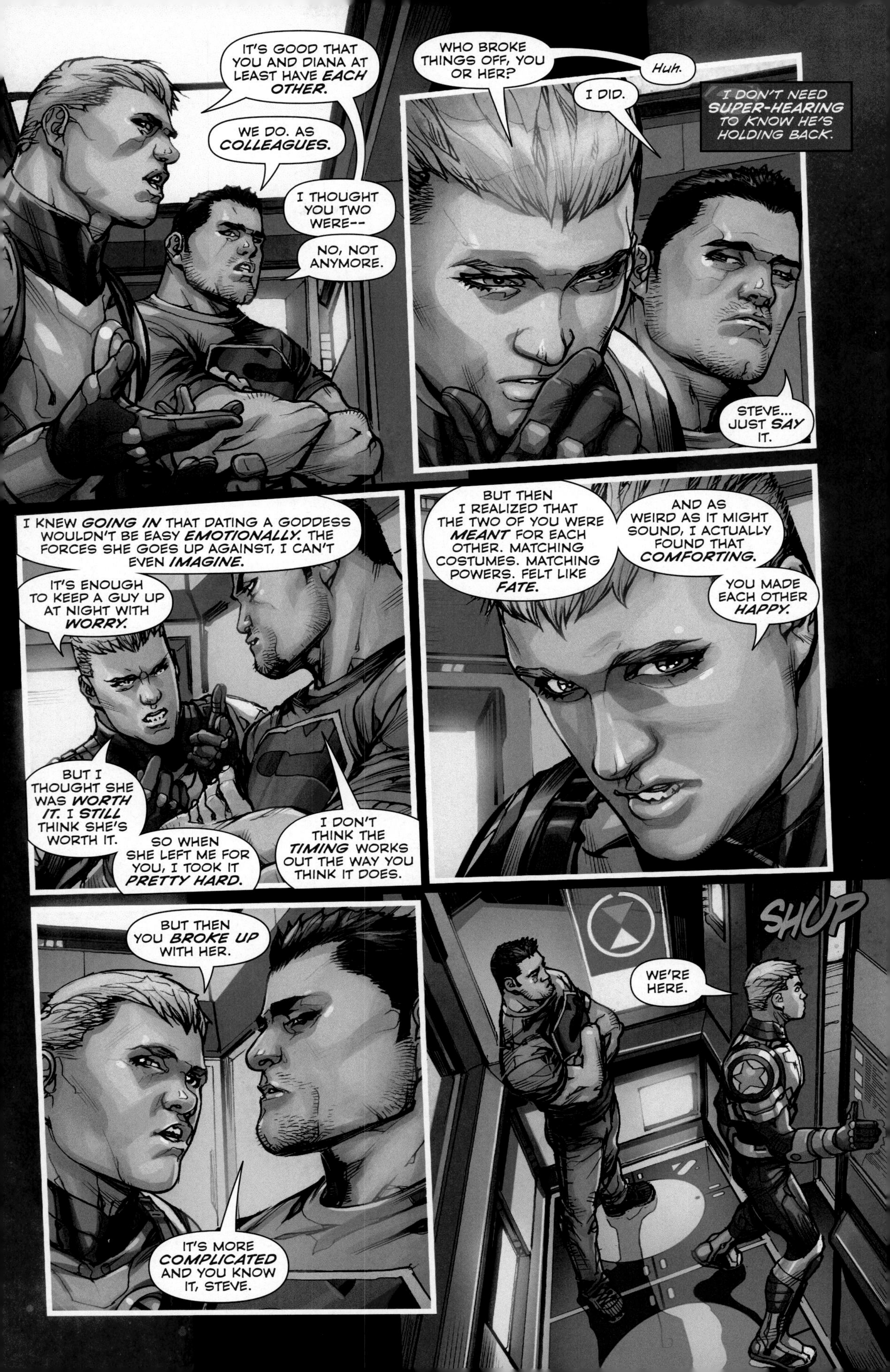
IT'S GOOD THAT YOU AND DIANA AT LEAST HAVE EACH OTHER.
WE DO. AS COLLEAGUES.
I THOUGHT YOU TWO WERE--
NO, NOT ANYMORE.
WHO BROKE THINGS OFF, YOU OR HER?
Huh.
I DID.
I DON'T NEED SUPER-HEARING TO KNOW HE'S HOLDING BACK.
STEVE... JUST SAY IT.
I KNEW GOING IN THAT DATING A GODDESS WOULDN'T BE EASY EMOTIONALLY. THE FORCES SHE GOES UP AGAINST, I CAN'T EVEN IMAGINE.
IT'S ENOUGH TO KEEP A GUY UP AT NIGHT WITH WORRY.
BUT I THOUGHT SHE WAS WORTH IT. I STILL THINK SHE'S WORTH IT.
SO WHEN SHE LEFT ME FOR YOU, I TOOK IT PRETTY HARD.
I DON'T THINK THE TIMING WORKS OUT THE WAY YOU THINK IT DOES.
BUT THEN I REALIZED THAT THE TWO OF YOU WERE MEANT FOR EACH OTHER. MATCHING COSTUMES. MATCHING POWERS. FELT LIKE FATE.
AND AS WEIRD AS IT MIGHT SOUND, I ACTUALLY FOUND THAT COMFORTING.
YOU MADE EACH OTHER HAPPY.
BUT THEN YOU BROKE UP WITH HER.
IT'S MORE COMPLICATED AND YOU KNOW IT, STEVE.
SHUP
WE'RE HERE.

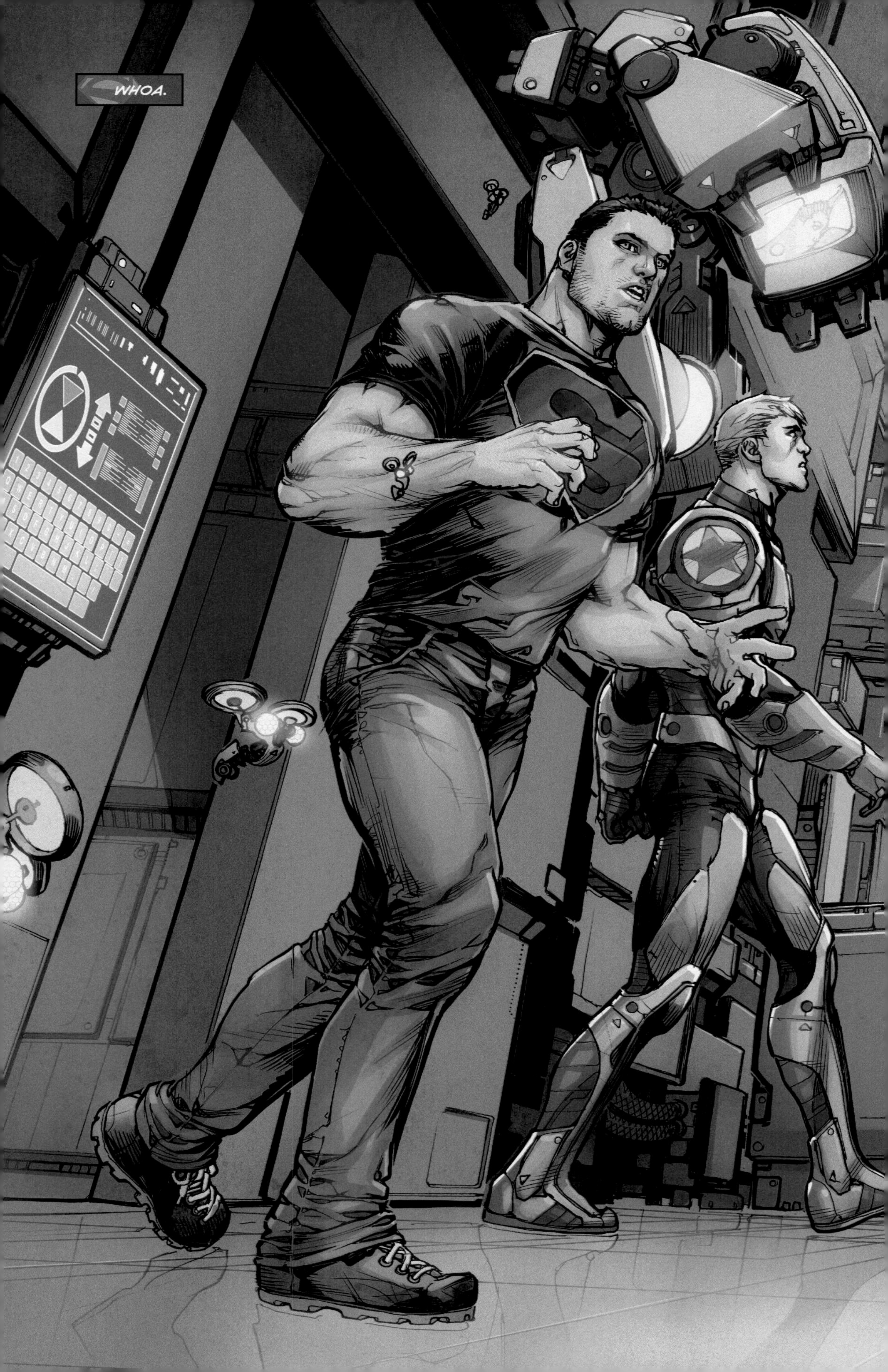
WHOA.

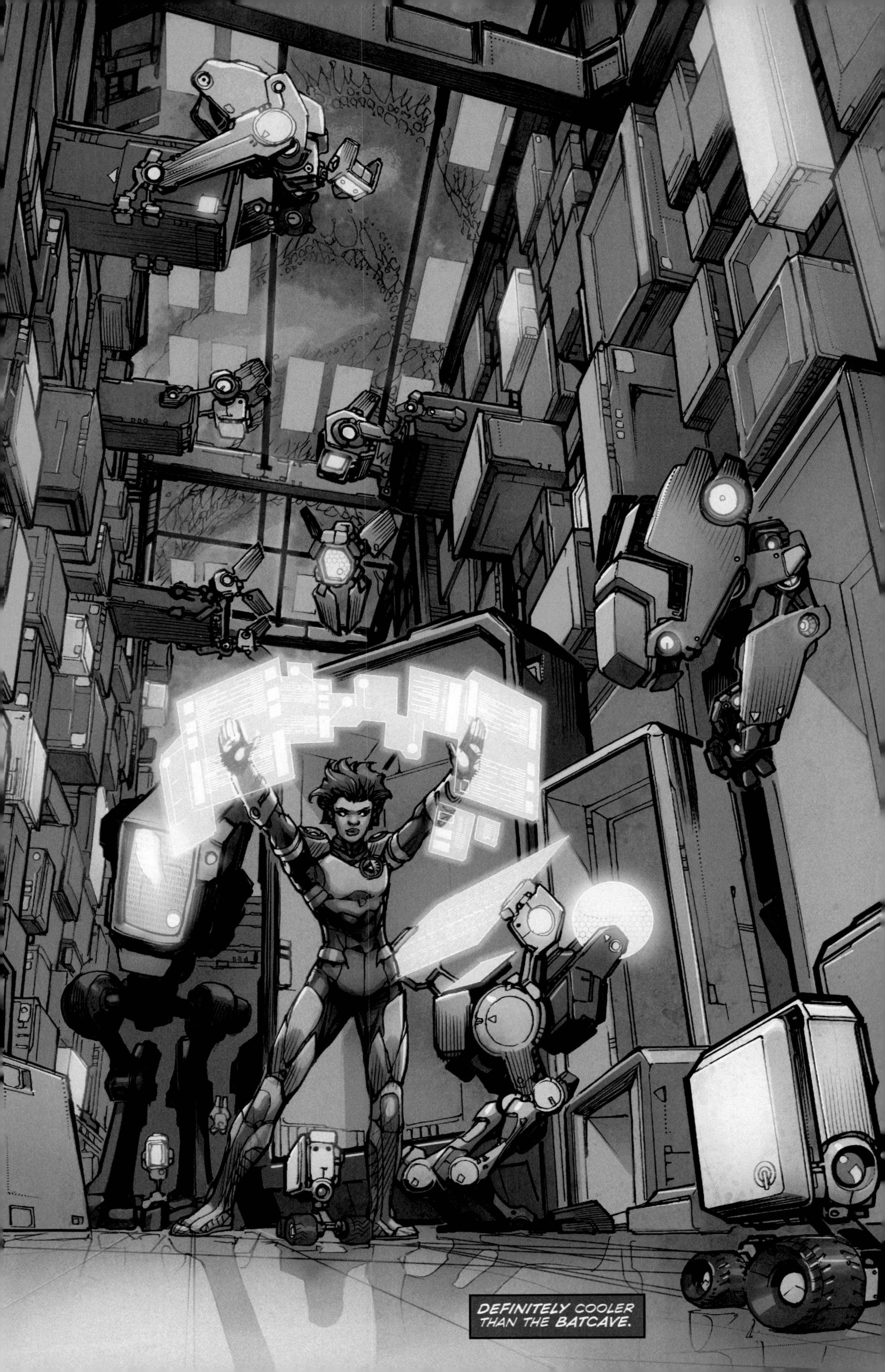
DEFINITELY COOLER THAN THE BATCAVE.

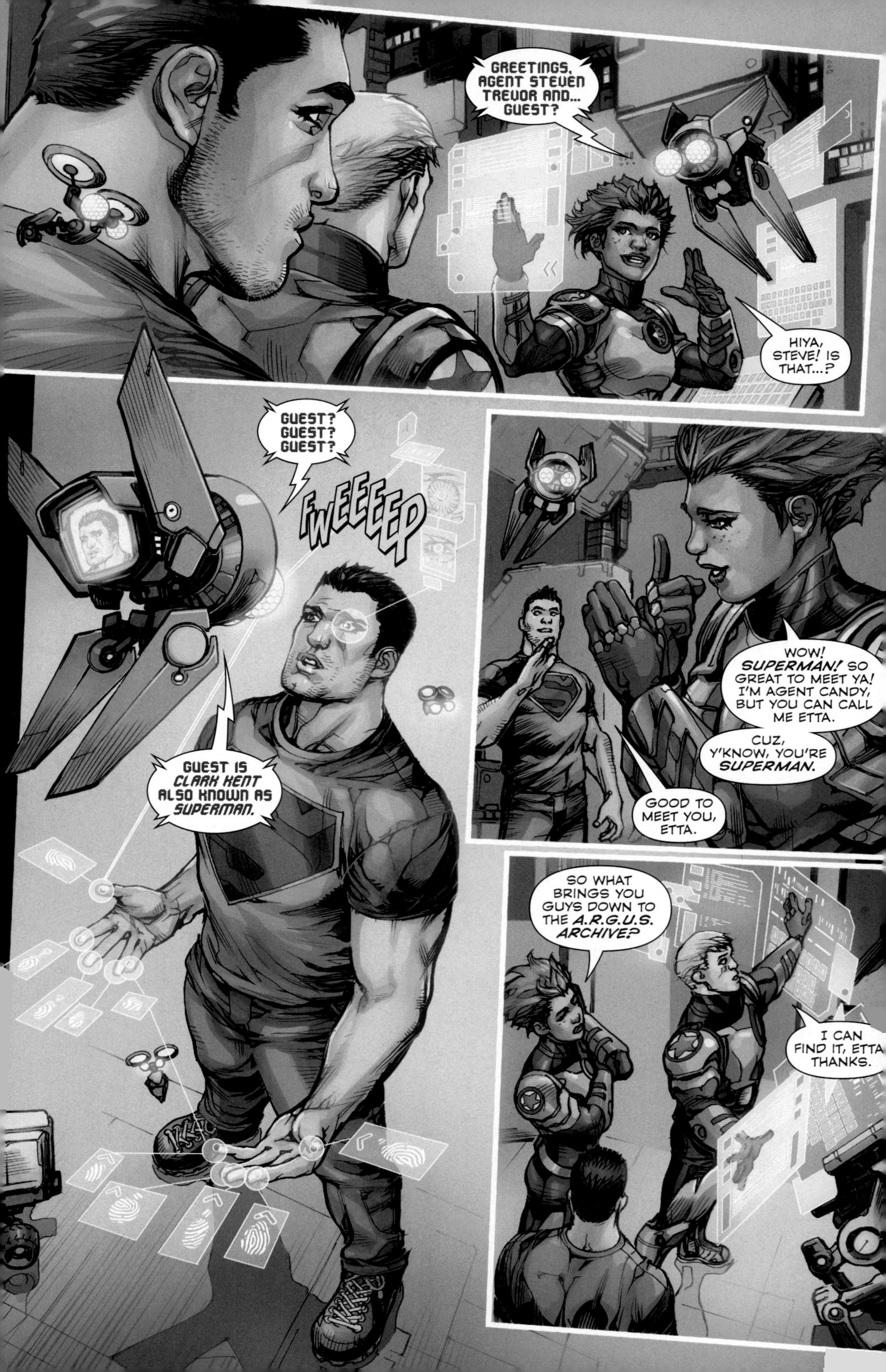
GREETINGS, AGENT STEVEN TREVOR AND... GUEST?
HIYA, STEVE! IS THAT...?
GUEST? GUEST? GUEST?
FWEEEEP
GUEST IS CLARK KENT ALSO KNOWN AS SUPERMAN.
WOW! SUPERMAN! SO GREAT TO MEET YA! I'M AGENT CANDY, BUT YOU CAN CALL ME ETTA.
CUZ, Y'KNOW, YOU'RE SUPERMAN.
GOOD TO MEET YOU, ETTA.
SO WHAT BRINGS YOU GUYS DOWN TO THE A.R.G.U.S. ARCHIVE?
I CAN FIND IT, ETTA THANKS.

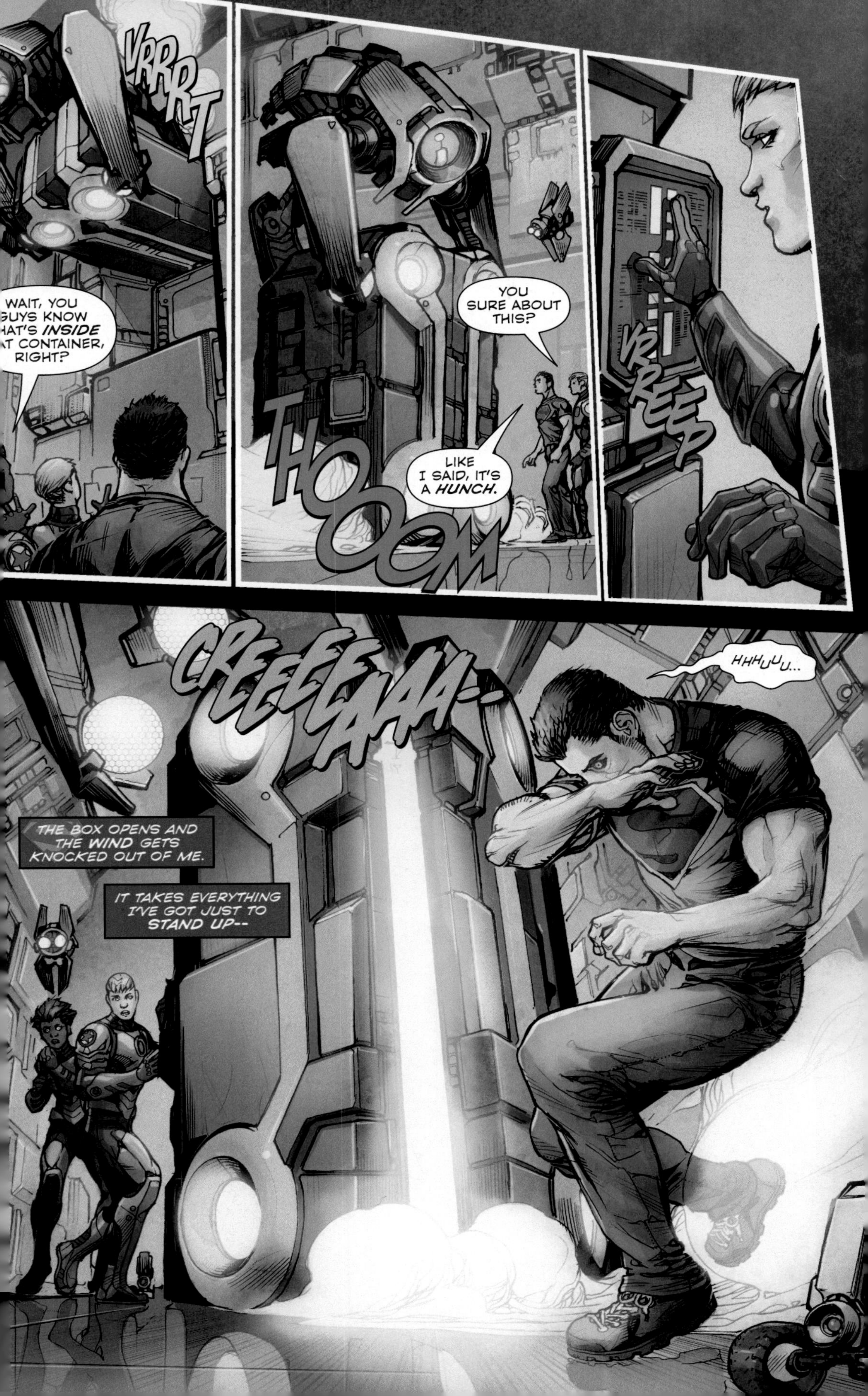

VRRRT
WAIT, YOU GUYS KNOW HAT'S *INSIDE* AT CONTAINER, RIGHT?
YOU SURE ABOUT THIS?
LIKE I SAID, IT'S A *HUNCH*.
THOOOOM
VRREEP
CREEEEAAAA--
HHHUUU...
THE BOX OPENS AND THE *WIND* GETS KNOCKED OUT OF ME.
IT TAKES EVERYTHING I'VE GOT JUST TO *STAND UP*--

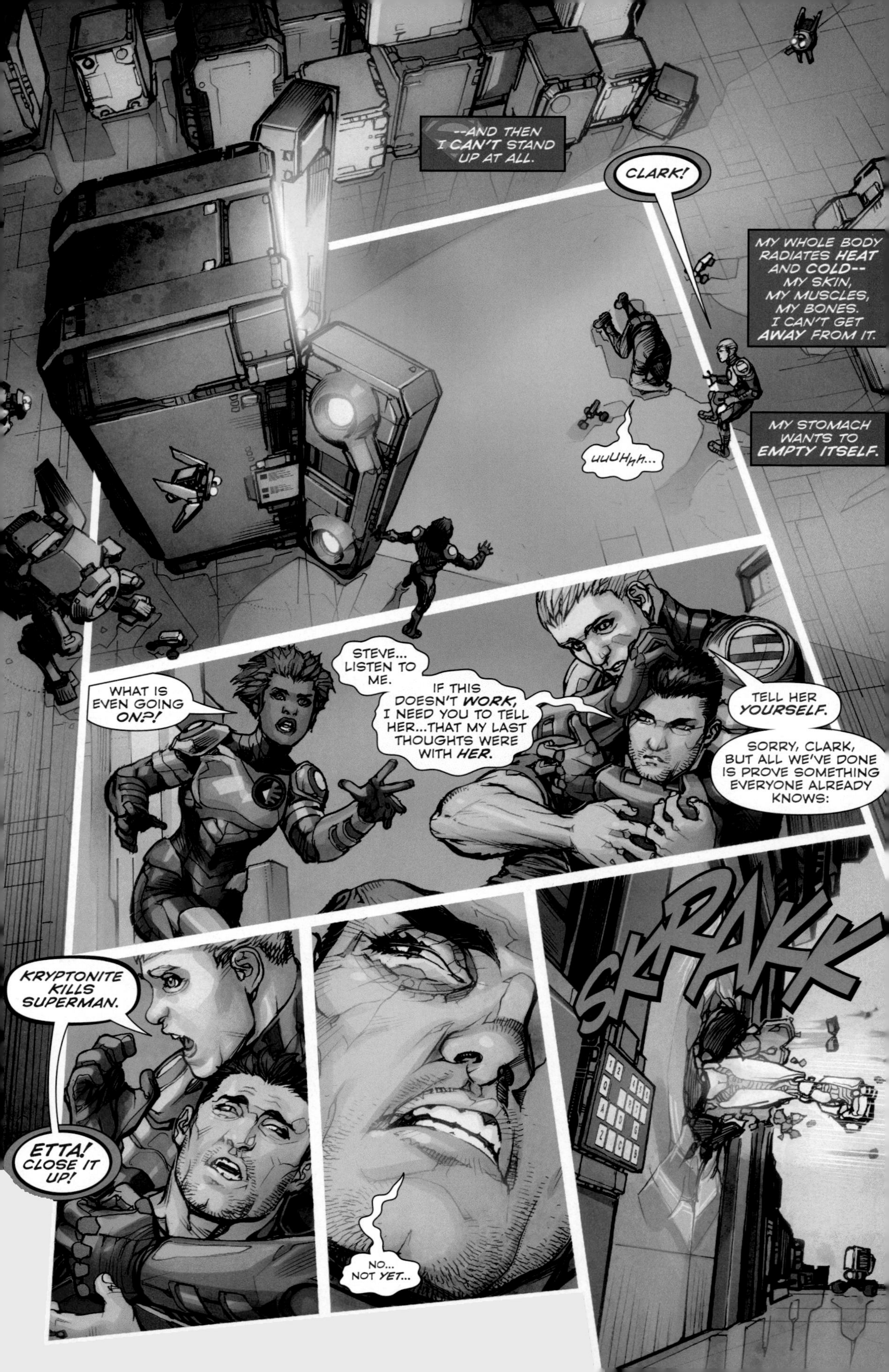
--AND THEN I CAN'T STAND UP AT ALL.
CLARK!
MY WHOLE BODY RADIATES HEAT AND COLD-- MY SKIN, MY MUSCLES, MY BONES. I CAN'T GET AWAY FROM IT.
MY STOMACH WANTS TO EMPTY ITSELF.
uuUHhh...
WHAT IS EVEN GOING ON?!
STEVE... LISTEN TO ME.
IF THIS DOESN'T WORK, I NEED YOU TO TELL HER...THAT MY LAST THOUGHTS WERE WITH HER.
TELL HER YOURSELF.
SORRY, CLARK, BUT ALL WE'VE DONE IS PROVE SOMETHING EVERYONE ALREADY KNOWS:
KRYPTONITE KILLS SUPERMAN.
ETTA! CLOSE IT UP!
NO... NOT YET...
SKRAKK

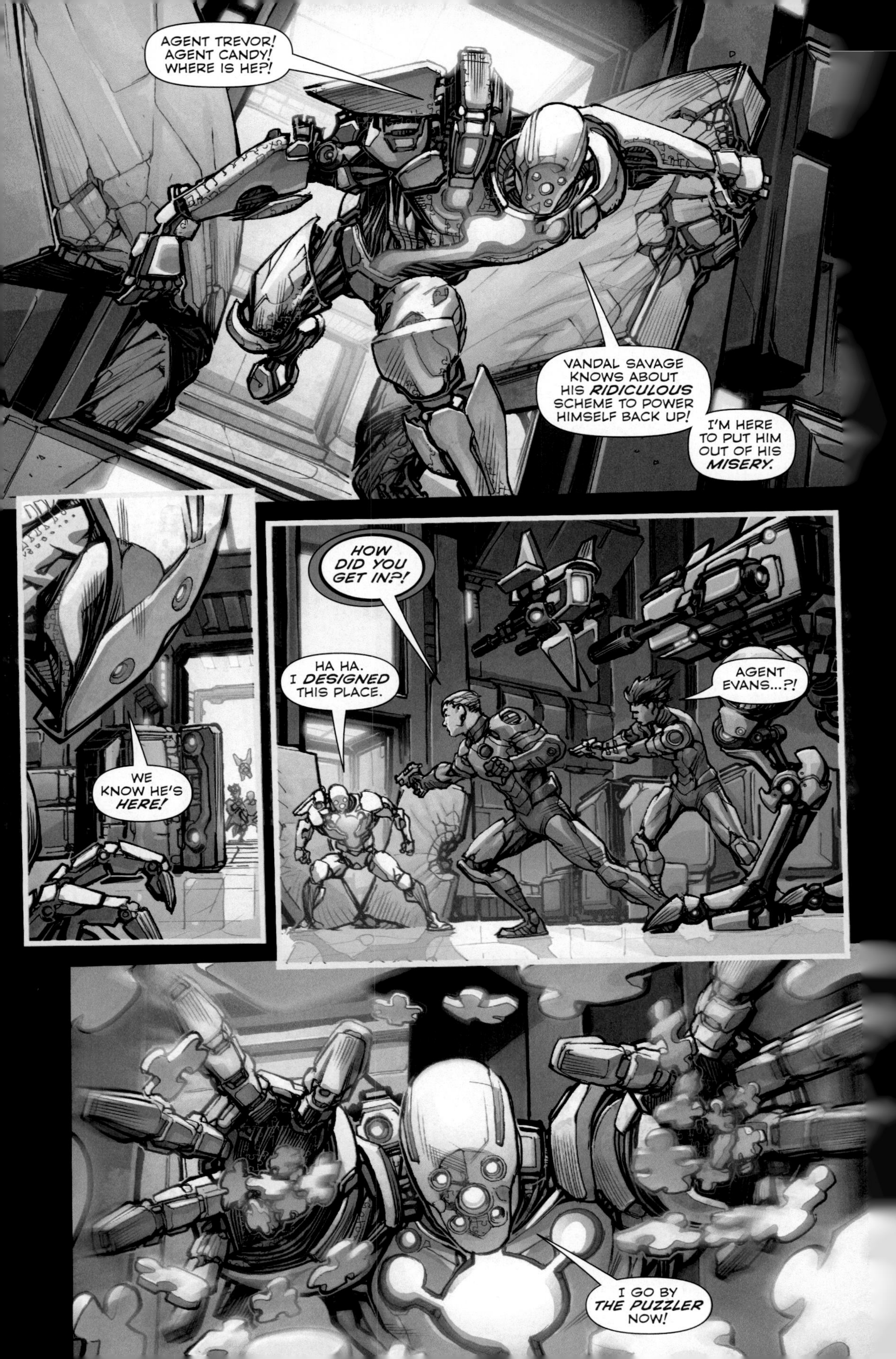
AGENT TREVOR! AGENT CANDY! WHERE IS HE?!
VANDAL SAVAGE KNOWS ABOUT HIS RIDICULOUS SCHEME TO POWER HIMSELF BACK UP!
I'M HERE TO PUT HIM OUT OF HIS MISERY.
WE KNOW HE'S HERE!
HOW DID YOU GET IN?!
HA HA. I DESIGNED THIS PLACE.
AGENT EVANS...?!
I GO BY THE PUZZLER NOW!

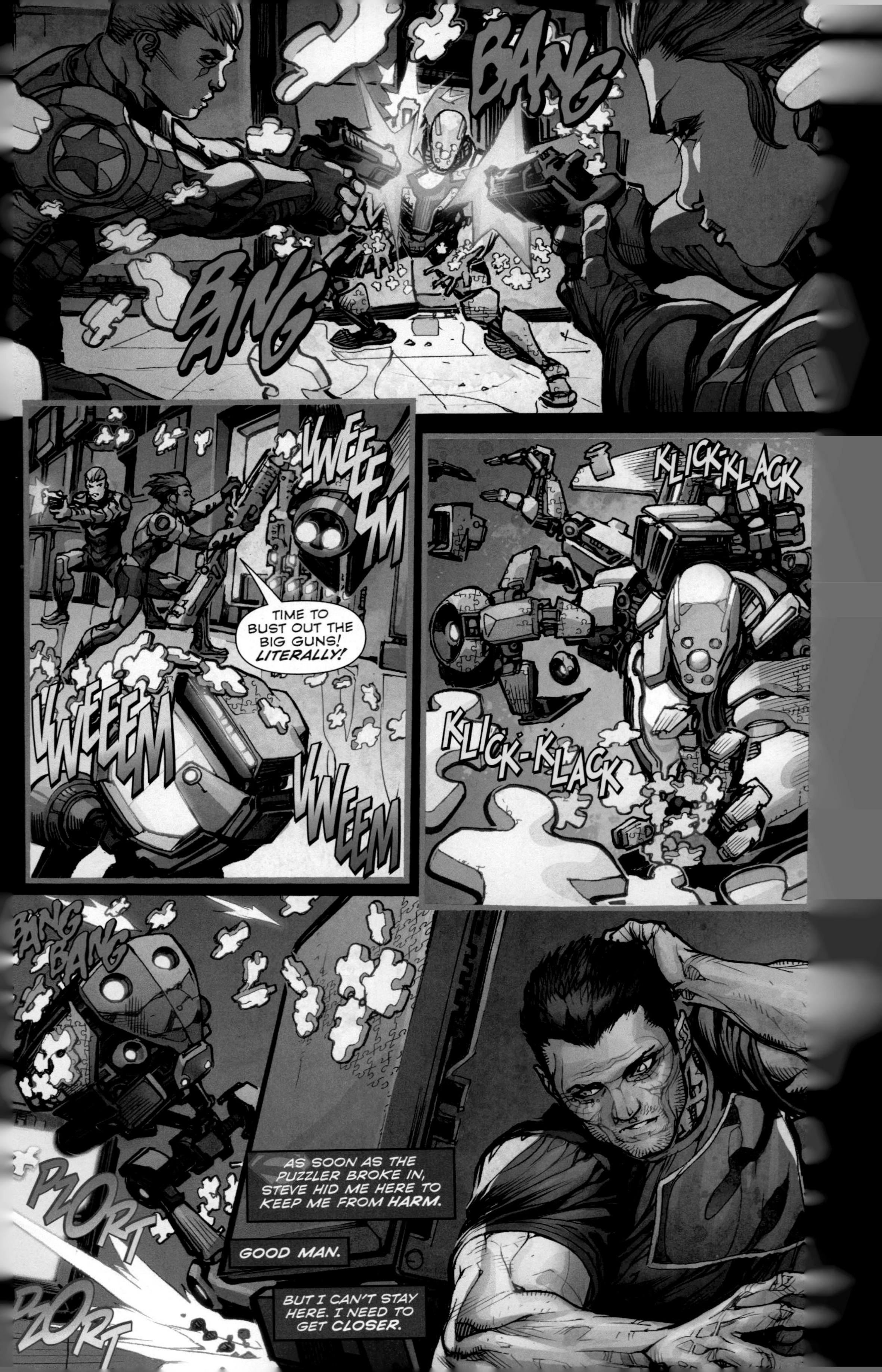
BANG
BANG
WEEEM
TIME TO BUST OUT THE BIG GUNS! LITERALLY!
WEEEM
WEEM
KLICK-KLACK
KLICK-KLACK
BANG
BANG
PLORT
AS SOON AS THE PUZZLER BROKE IN, STEVE HID ME HERE TO KEEP ME FROM HARM.
GOOD MAN.
BUT I CAN'T STAY HERE. I NEED TO GET CLOSER.
BLORT

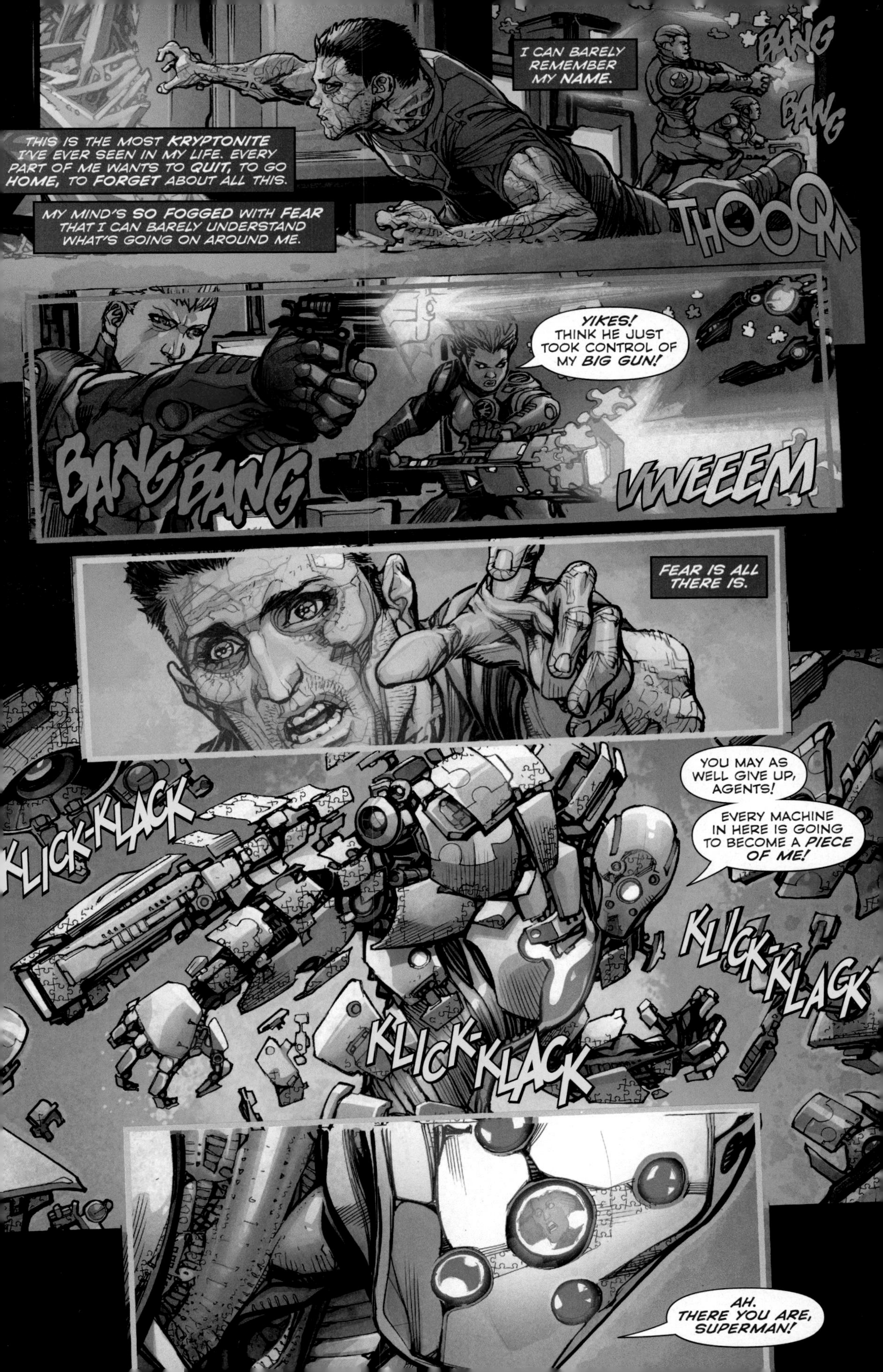

I CAN BARELY REMEMBER MY NAME.
BANG
BANG
THIS IS THE MOST KRYPTONITE I'VE EVER SEEN IN MY LIFE. EVERY PART OF ME WANTS TO QUIT, TO GO HOME, TO FORGET ABOUT ALL THIS.
MY MIND'S SO FOGGED WITH FEAR THAT I CAN BARELY UNDERSTAND WHAT'S GOING ON AROUND ME.
THOOOM
YIKES! THINK HE JUST TOOK CONTROL OF MY BIG GUN!
BANG BANG
VWEEEM
FEAR IS ALL THERE IS.
YOU MAY AS WELL GIVE UP, AGENTS!
EVERY MACHINE IN HERE IS GOING TO BECOME A PIECE OF ME!
KLICK-KLACK
KLICK-KLACK
KLICK-KLACK
AH. THERE YOU ARE, SUPERMAN!

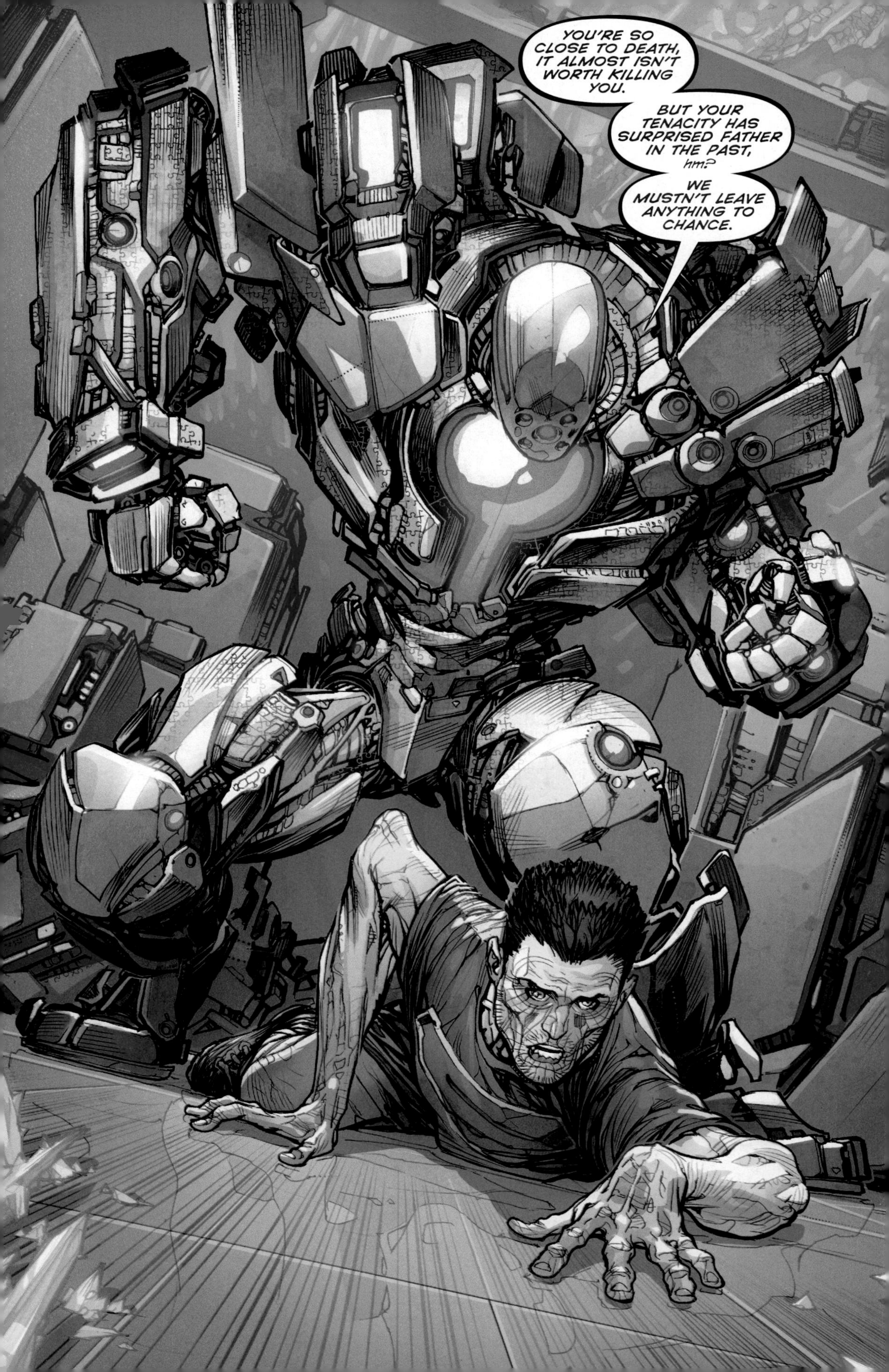
YOU'RE SO CLOSE TO DEATH, IT ALMOST ISN'T WORTH KILLING YOU.
BUT YOUR TENACITY HAS SURPRISED FATHER IN THE PAST, hm?
WE MUSTN'T LEAVE ANYTHING TO CHANCE.

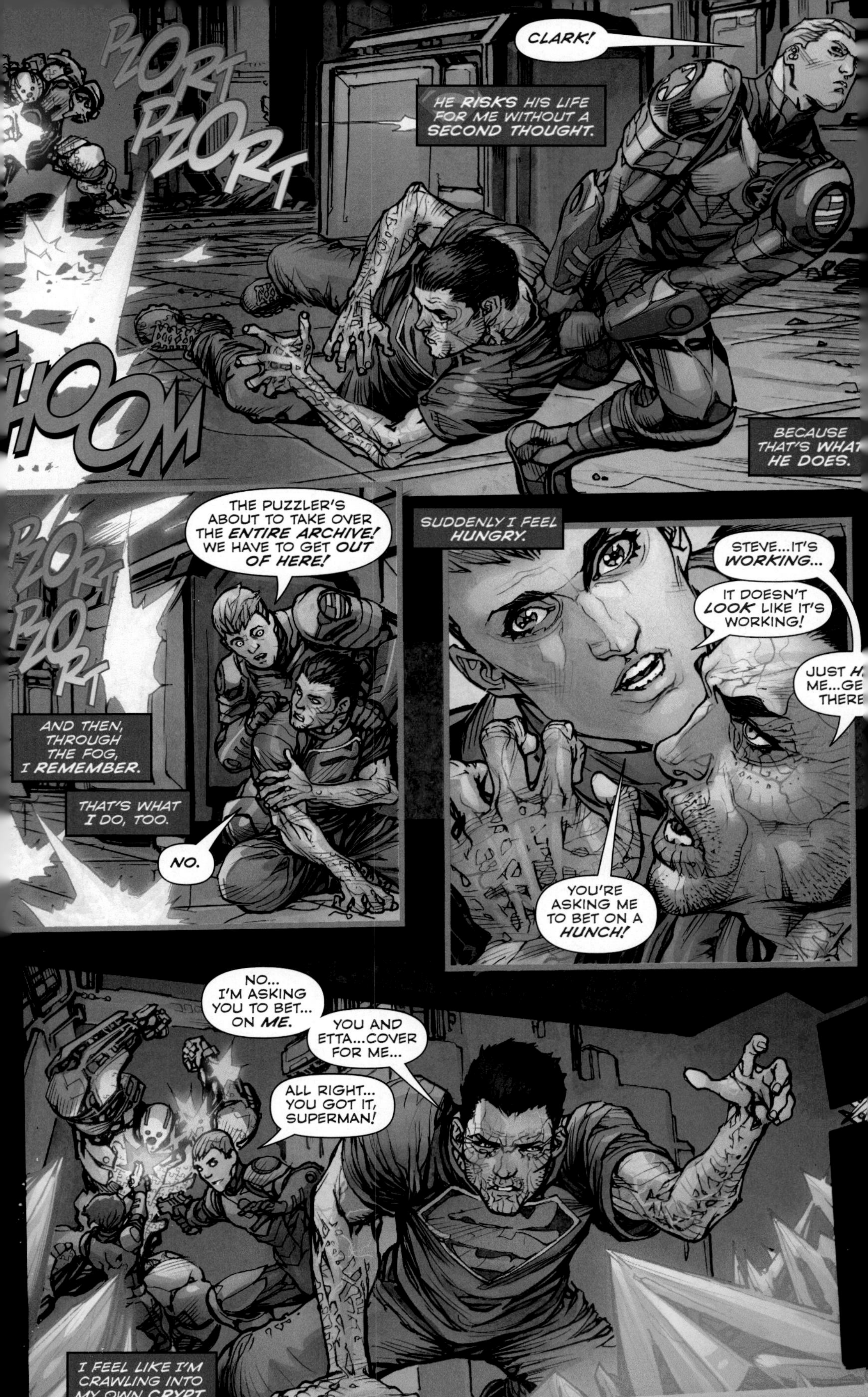

PZORT PZORT PZORT
CLARK!
HE RISKS HIS LIFE FOR ME WITHOUT A SECOND THOUGHT.
HOOM
BECAUSE THAT'S WHAT HE DOES.
PZORT PZORT
THE PUZZLER'S ABOUT TO TAKE OVER THE ENTIRE ARCHIVE! WE HAVE TO GET OUT OF HERE!
AND THEN, THROUGH THE FOG, I REMEMBER.
THAT'S WHAT I DO, TOO.
NO.
SUDDENLY I FEEL HUNGRY.
STEVE...IT'S WORKING...
IT DOESN'T LOOK LIKE IT'S WORKING!
YOU'RE ASKING ME TO BET ON A HUNCH!
NO... I'M ASKING YOU TO BET... ON ME.
YOU AND ETTA...COVER FOR ME...
ALL RIGHT... YOU GOT IT, SUPERMAN!
I FEEL LIKE I'M CRAWLING INTO MY OWN CRYPT.

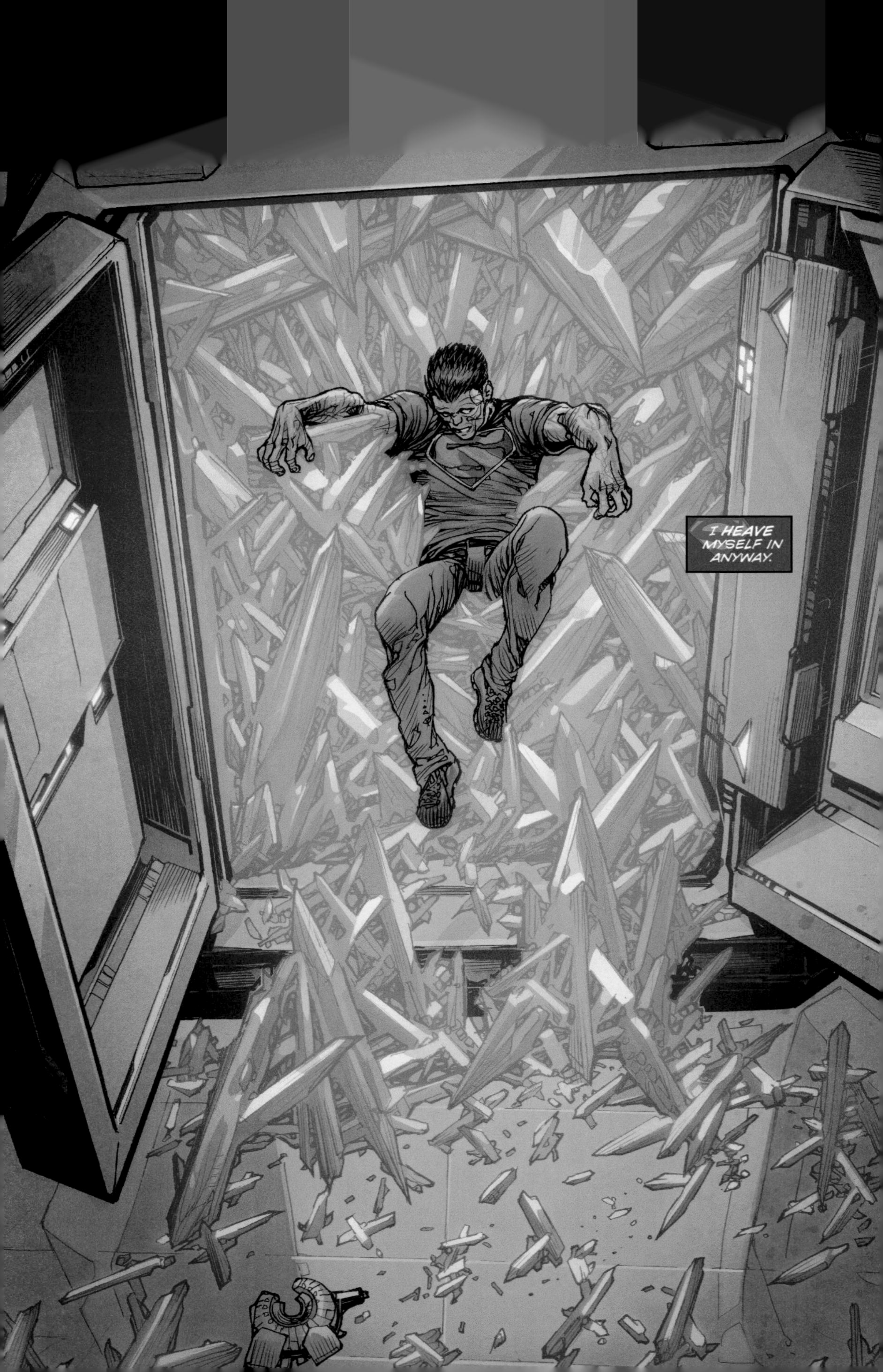
I HEAVE MYSELF IN ANYWAY.

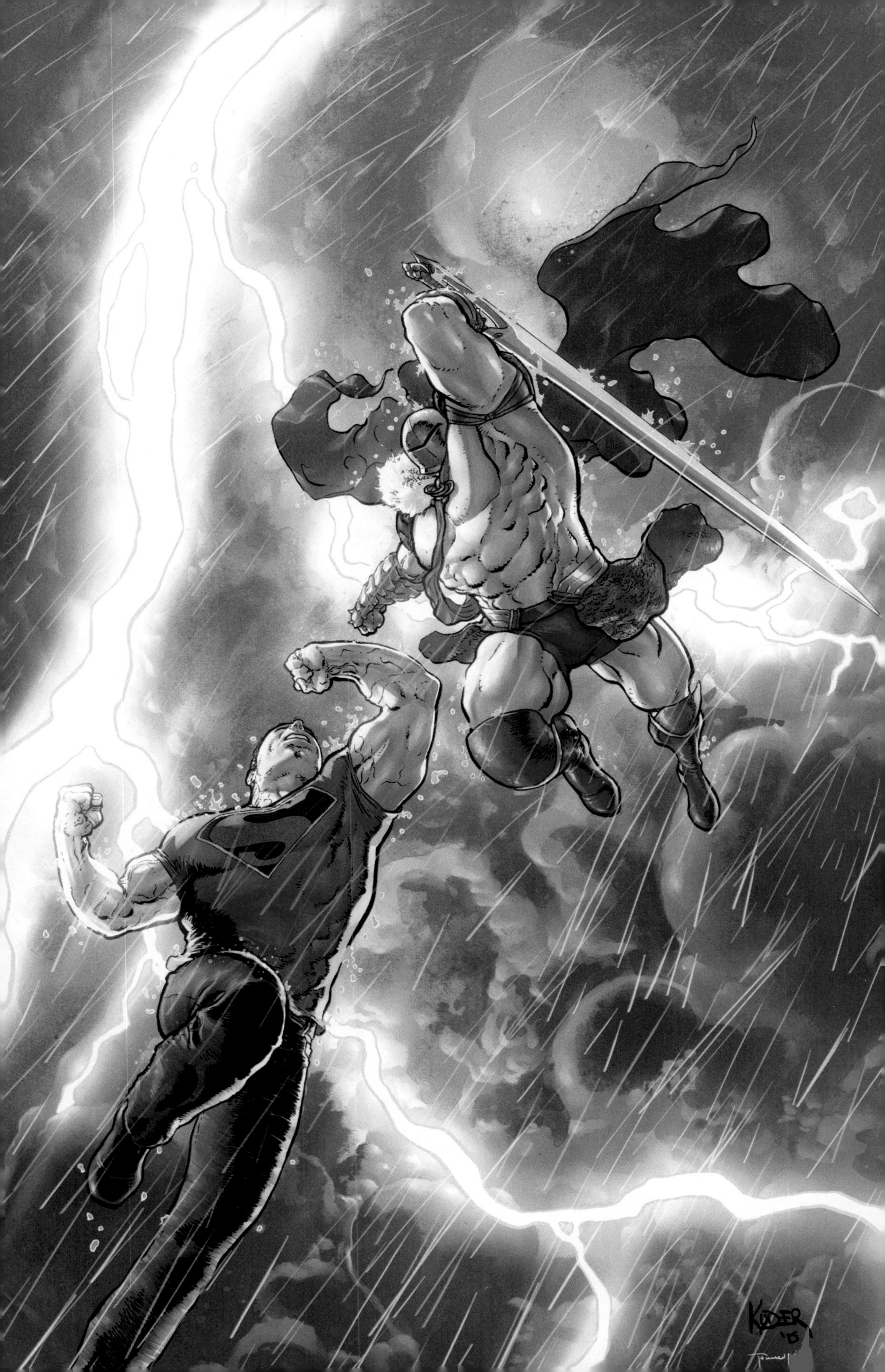
KUDER

SAVAGE DAWN: IMMORTAL COMBAT

GREK PAK AARON KUDER writers **AARON KUDER** layouts **ARDIAN SYAF** penciller **JONATHAN GLAPION SCOTT HANNA SANDRA HOPE** inkers **TOMEU MOREY WIL QUINTANA** colorists **STEVE WANDS** letterer **AARON KUDER TOMEU MOREY** cover

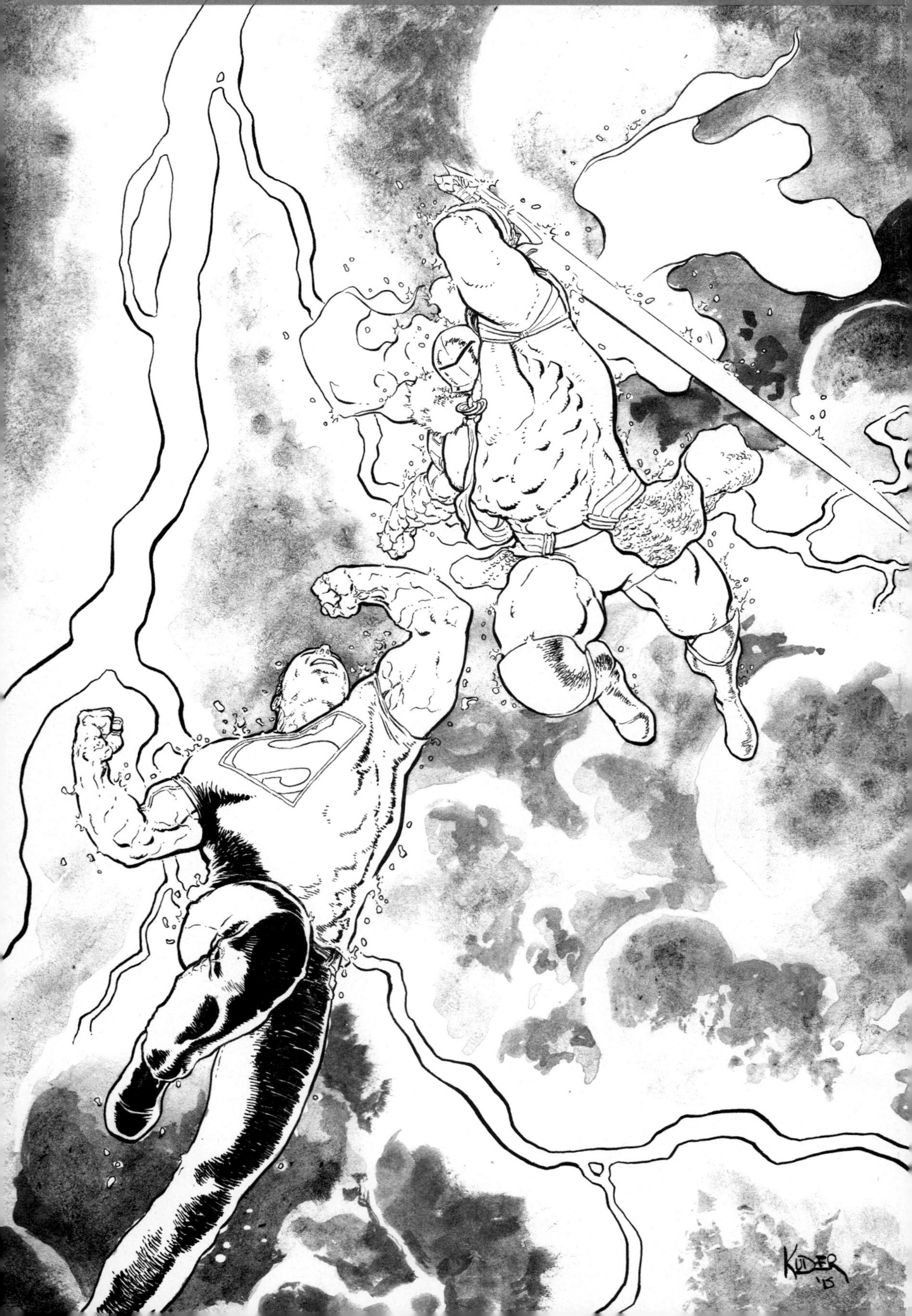
KUDER '15

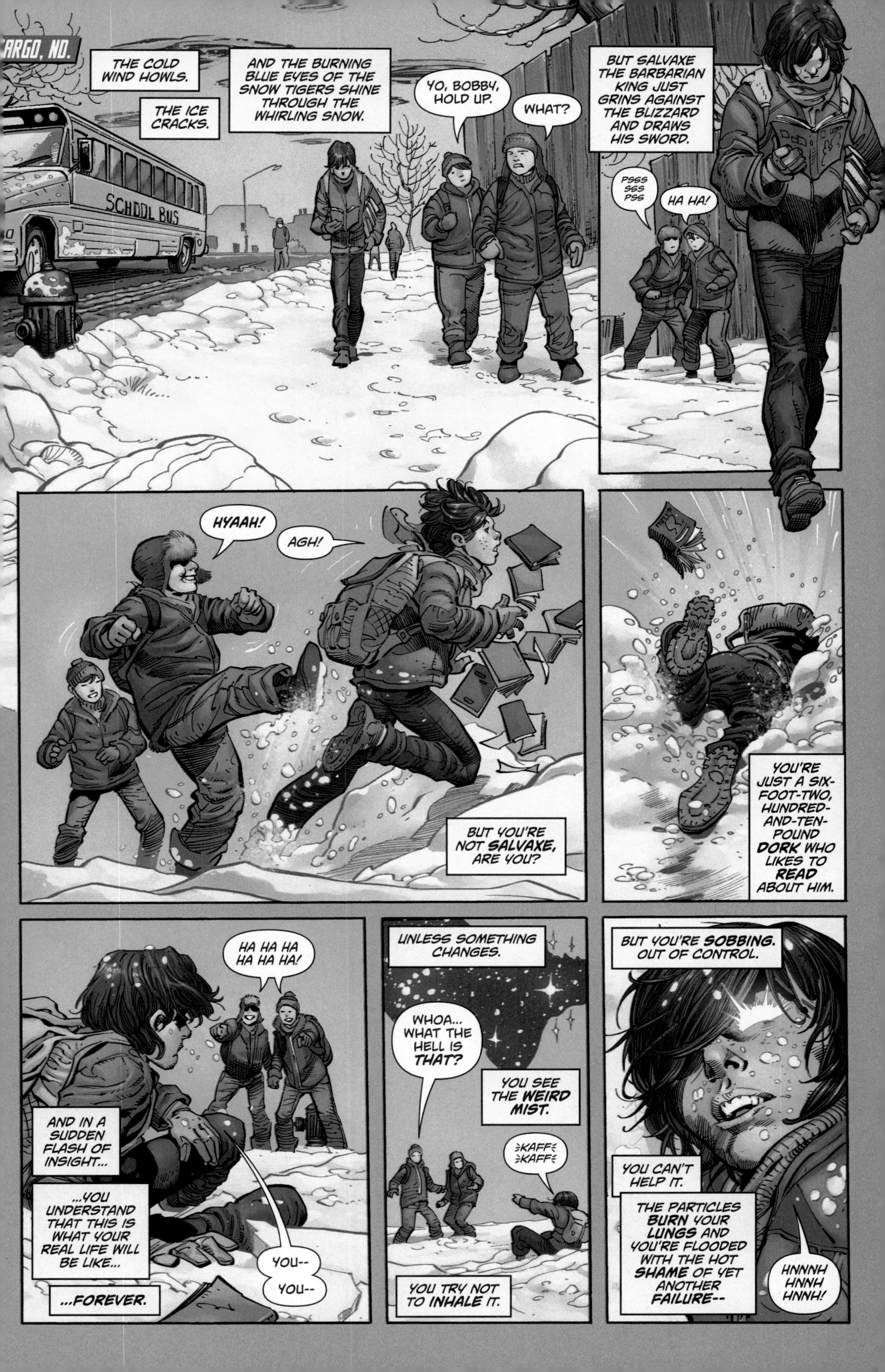
FARGO, ND.
THE COLD WIND HOWLS.
THE ICE CRACKS.
AND THE BURNING BLUE EYES OF THE SNOW TIGERS SHINE THROUGH THE WHIRLING SNOW.
SCHOOL BUS
YO, BOBBY, HOLD UP.
WHAT?
BUT SALVAXE THE BARBARIAN KING JUST GRINS AGAINST THE BLIZZARD AND DRAWS HIS SWORD.
PSSS SSS PSS
HA HA!
HYAAH!
AGH!
BUT YOU'RE NOT SALVAXE, ARE YOU?
YOU'RE JUST A SIX-FOOT-TWO, HUNDRED-AND-TEN-POUND DORK WHO LIKES TO READ ABOUT HIM.
HA HA HA HA HA HA!
AND IN A SUDDEN FLASH OF INSIGHT...
...YOU UNDERSTAND THAT THIS IS WHAT YOUR REAL LIFE WILL BE LIKE...
...FOREVER.
YOU--
YOU--
UNLESS SOMETHING CHANGES.
WHOA... WHAT THE HELL IS THAT?
YOU SEE THE WEIRD MIST.
KAFF KAFF
YOU TRY NOT TO INHALE IT.
BUT YOU'RE SOBBING. OUT OF CONTROL.
YOU CAN'T HELP IT.
THE PARTICLES BURN YOUR LUNGS AND YOU'RE FLOODED WITH THE HOT SHAME OF YET ANOTHER FAILURE--
HNNNH HNNH HNNH!

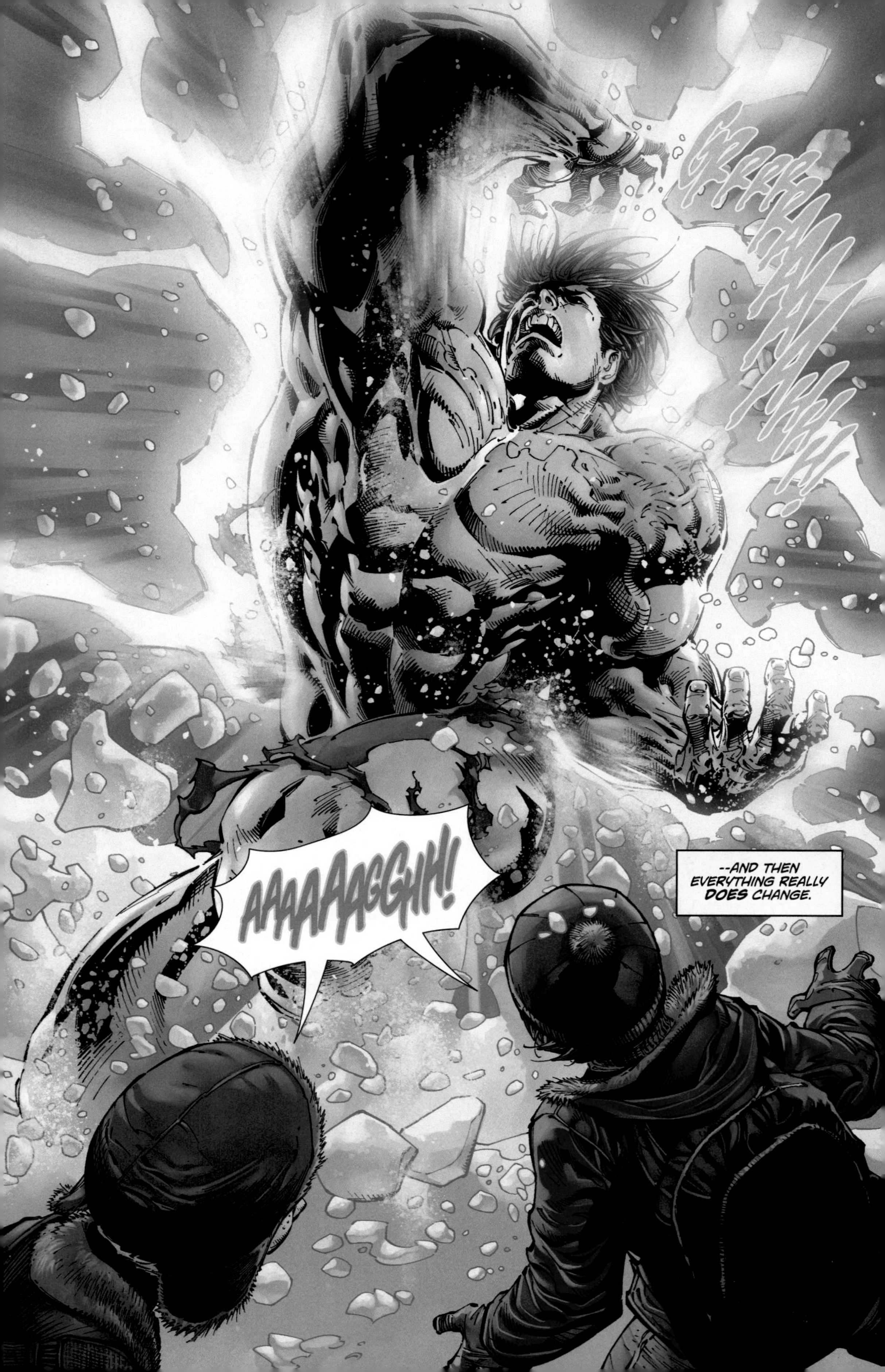
GRRRRAAAAAHHH!!
AAAAAAAGGHH!
--AND THEN EVERYTHING REALLY DOES CHANGE.

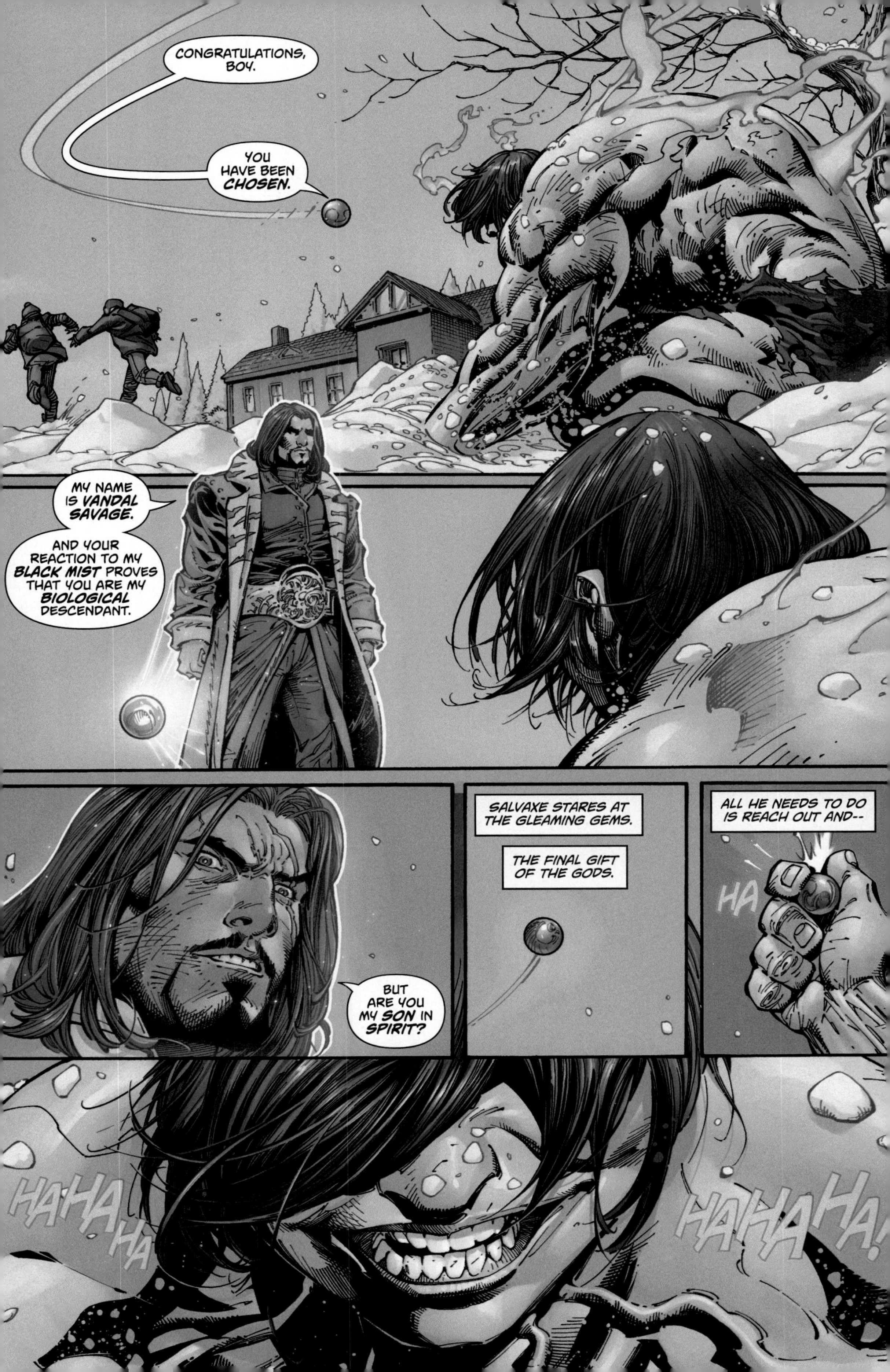
CONGRATULATIONS, BOY.
YOU HAVE BEEN CHOSEN.
MY NAME IS VANDAL SAVAGE.
AND YOUR REACTION TO MY BLACK MIST PROVES THAT YOU ARE MY BIOLOGICAL DESCENDANT.
BUT ARE YOU MY SON IN SPIRIT?
SALVAXE STARES AT THE GLEAMING GEMS.
THE FINAL GIFT OF THE GODS.
ALL HE NEEDS TO DO IS REACH OUT AND--
HA
HAHAHA
HAHAHA!

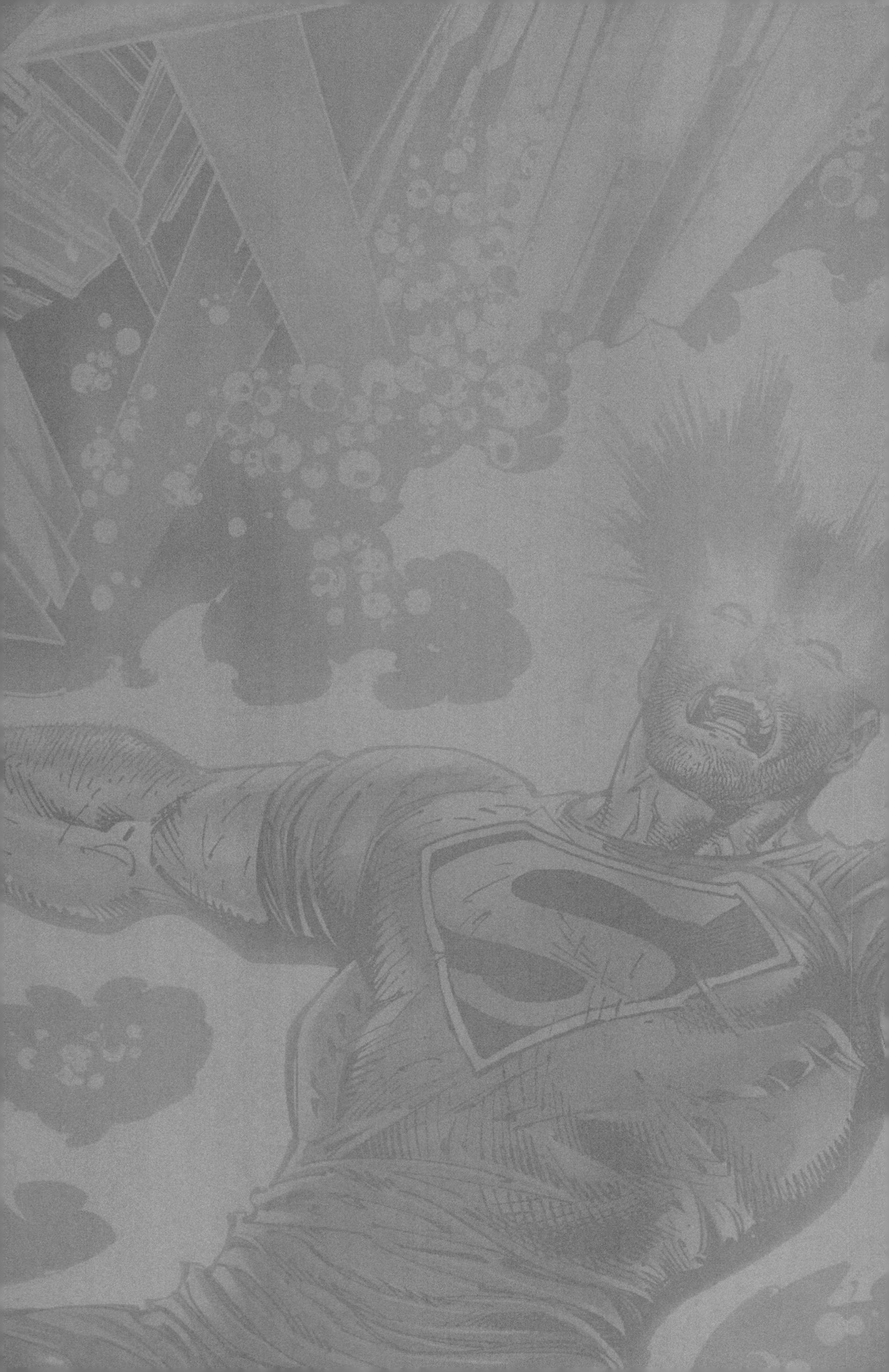

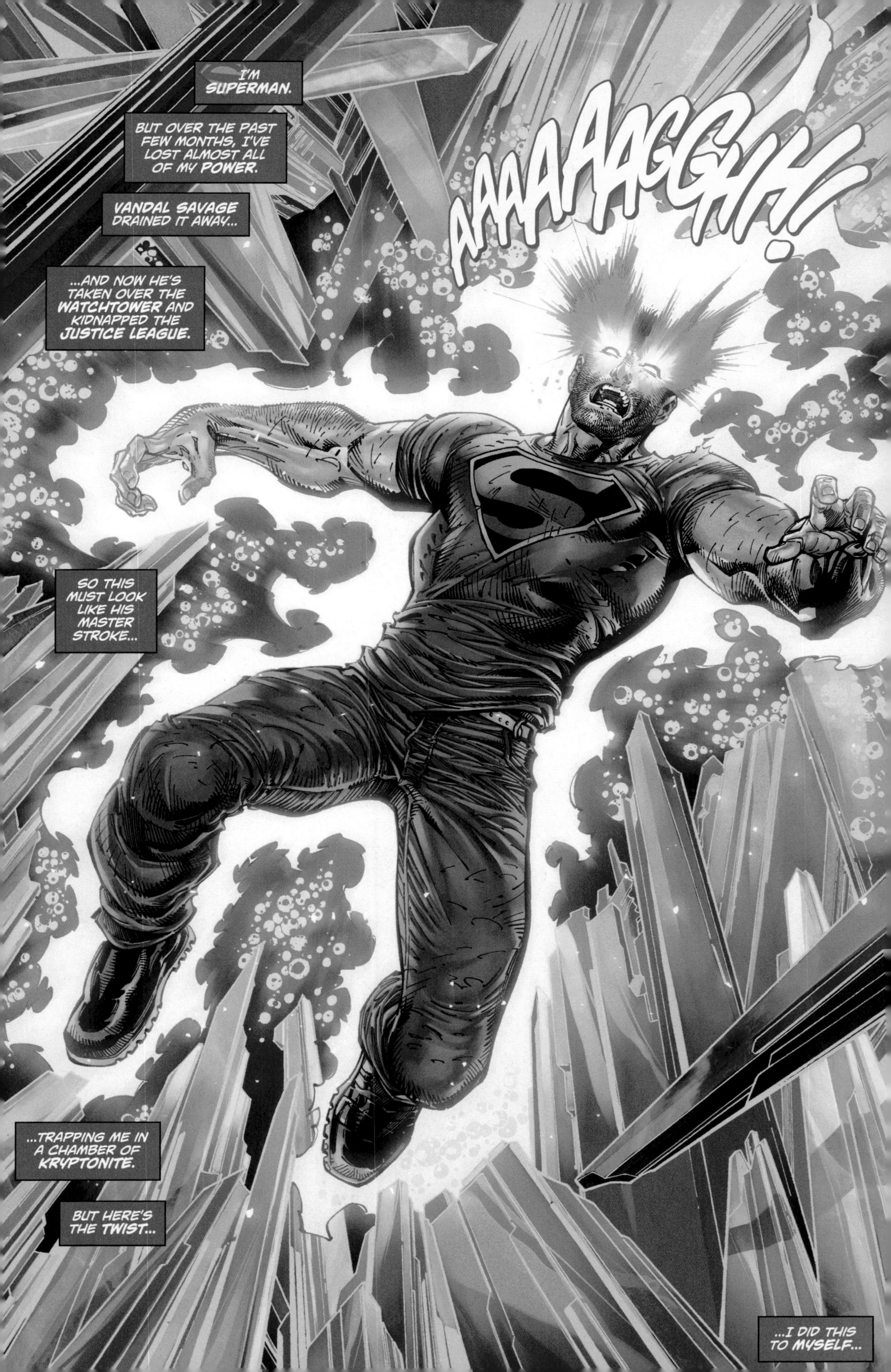
I'M SUPERMAN.
BUT OVER THE PAST FEW MONTHS, I'VE LOST ALMOST ALL OF MY POWER.
VANDAL SAVAGE DRAINED IT AWAY...
...AND NOW HE'S TAKEN OVER THE WATCHTOWER AND KIDNAPPED THE JUSTICE LEAGUE.
AAAAAAAGGHH!!
SO THIS MUST LOOK LIKE HIS MASTER STROKE...
...TRAPPING ME IN A CHAMBER OF KRYPTONITE.
BUT HERE'S THE TWIST...
...I DID THIS TO MYSELF...

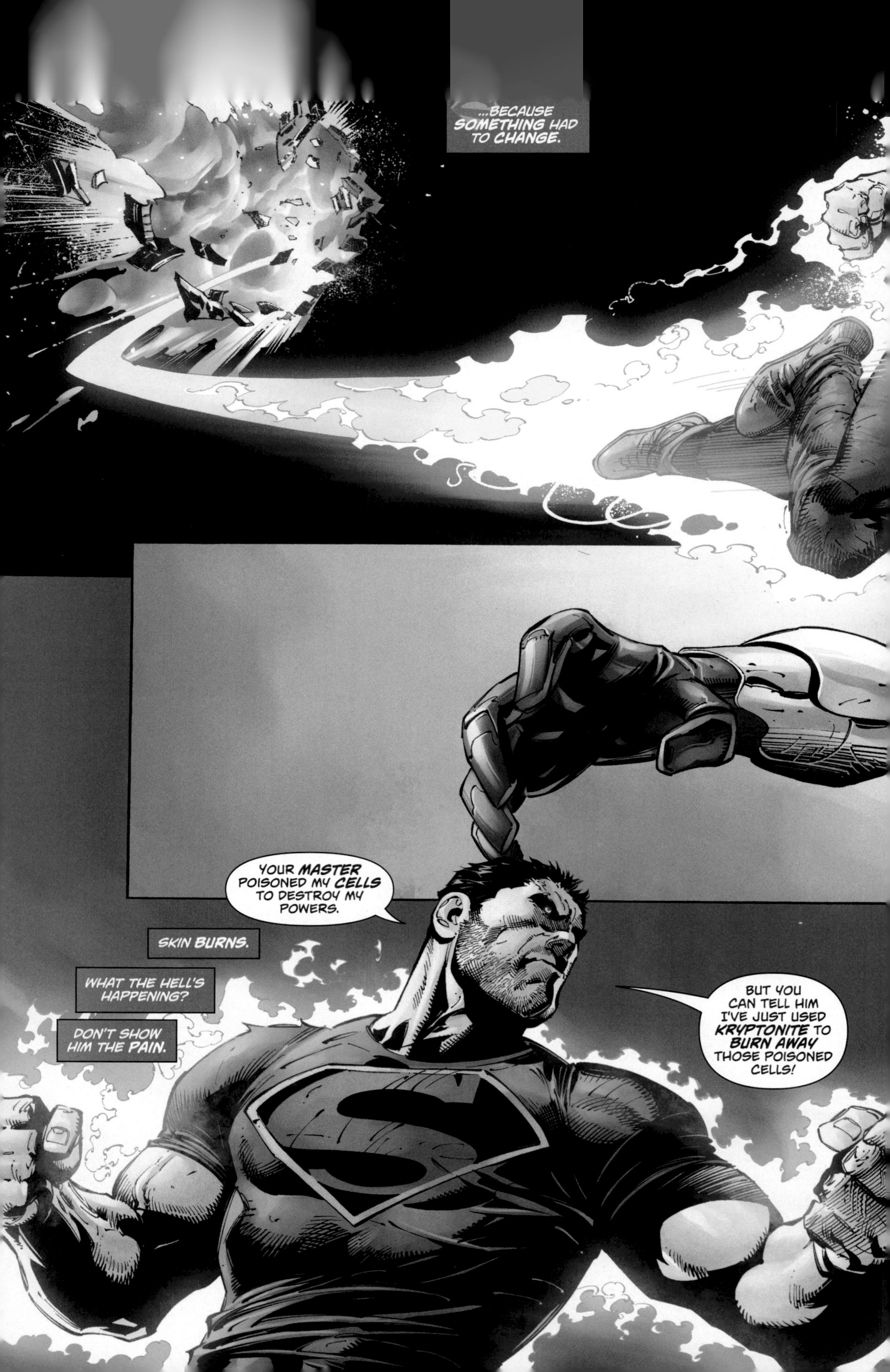
...BECAUSE SOMETHING HAD TO CHANGE.
YOUR MASTER POISONED MY CELLS TO DESTROY MY POWERS.
SKIN BURNS.
WHAT THE HELL'S HAPPENING?
DON'T SHOW HIM THE PAIN.
BUT YOU CAN TELL HIM I'VE JUST USED KRYPTONITE TO BURN AWAY THOSE POISONED CELLS!

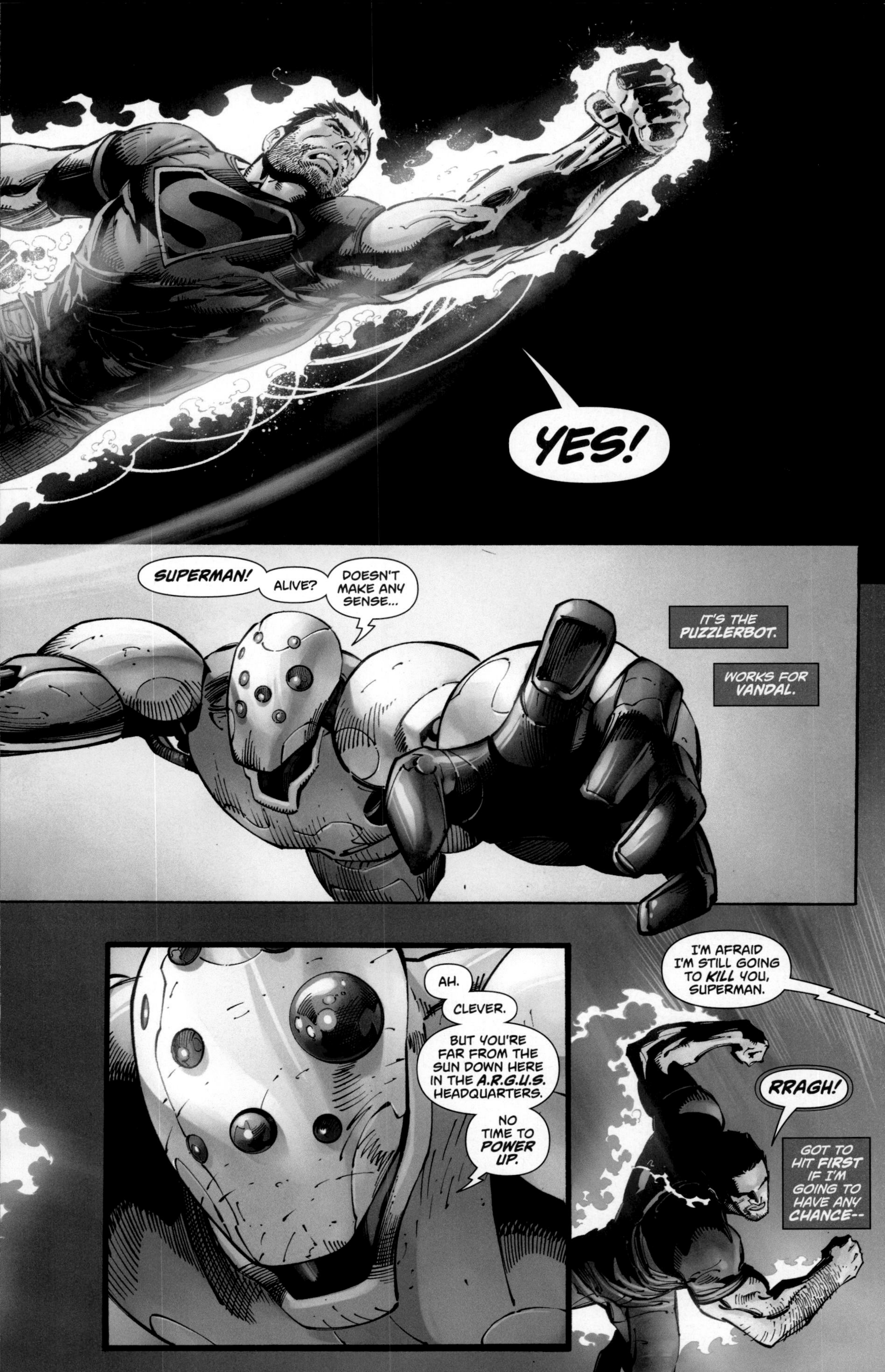
YES!
SUPERMAN!
ALIVE?
DOESN'T MAKE ANY SENSE...
IT'S THE PUZZLERBOT.
WORKS FOR VANDAL.
AH.
CLEVER.
BUT YOU'RE FAR FROM THE SUN DOWN HERE IN THE A.R.G.U.S. HEADQUARTERS.
NO TIME TO POWER UP.
I'M AFRAID I'M STILL GOING TO KILL YOU, SUPERMAN.
RRAGH!
GOT TO HIT FIRST IF I'M GOING TO HAVE ANY CHANCE--

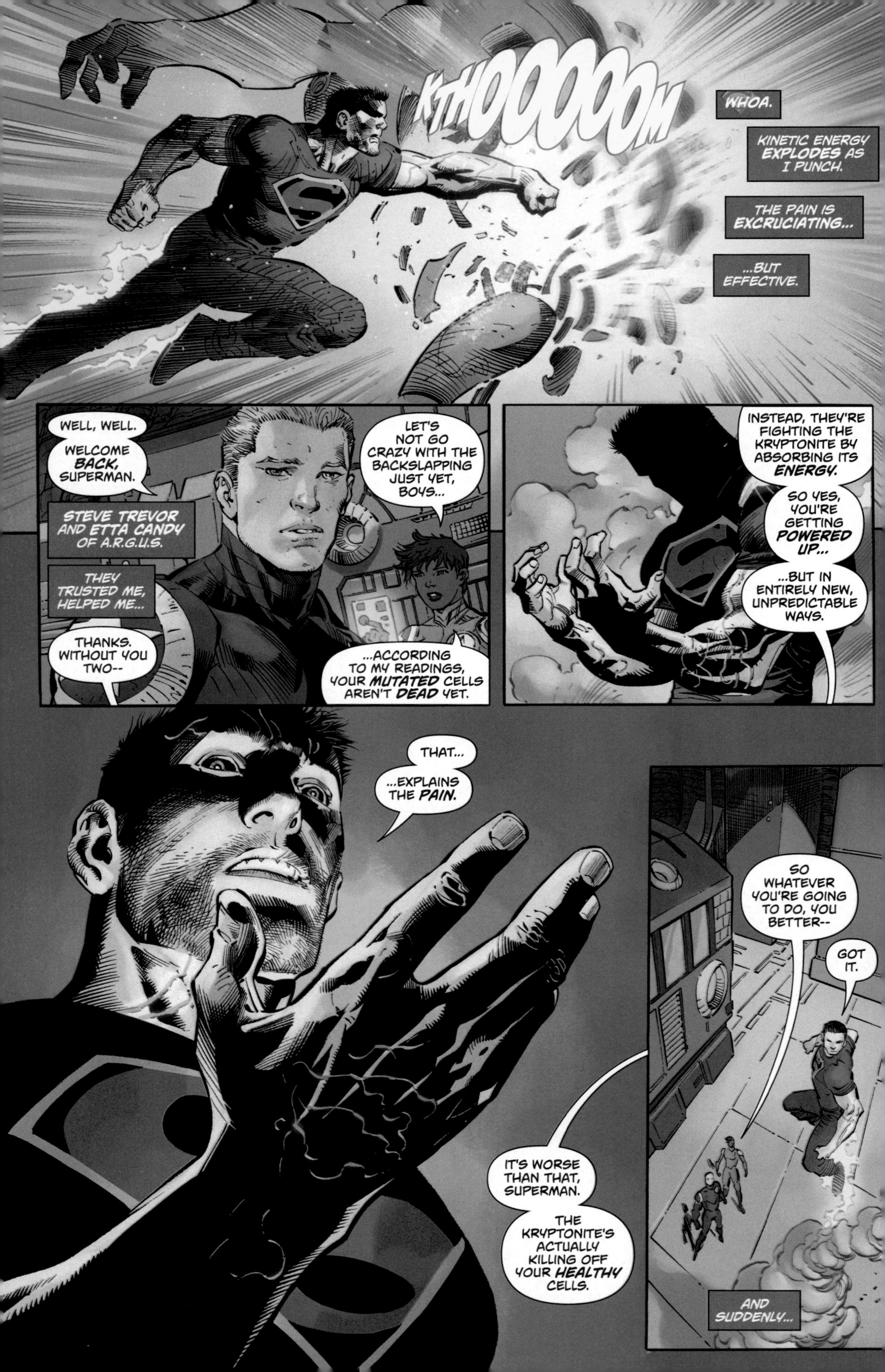
KTHOOOOOOM
WHOA.
KINETIC ENERGY EXPLODES AS I PUNCH.
THE PAIN IS EXCRUCIATING...
...BUT EFFECTIVE.
WELL, WELL.
WELCOME BACK, SUPERMAN.
LET'S NOT GO CRAZY WITH THE BACKSLAPPING JUST YET, BOYS...
STEVE TREVOR AND ETTA CANDY OF A.R.G.U.S.
THEY TRUSTED ME, HELPED ME...
THANKS. WITHOUT YOU TWO--
...ACCORDING TO MY READINGS, YOUR MUTATED CELLS AREN'T DEAD YET.
INSTEAD, THEY'RE FIGHTING THE KRYPTONITE BY ABSORBING ITS ENERGY.
SO YES, YOU'RE GETTING POWERED UP...
...BUT IN ENTIRELY NEW, UNPREDICTABLE WAYS.
THAT...
...EXPLAINS THE PAIN.
IT'S WORSE THAN THAT, SUPERMAN.
THE KRYPTONITE'S ACTUALLY KILLING OFF YOUR HEALTHY CELLS.
SO WHATEVER YOU'RE GOING TO DO, YOU BETTER--
GOT IT.
AND SUDDENLY...

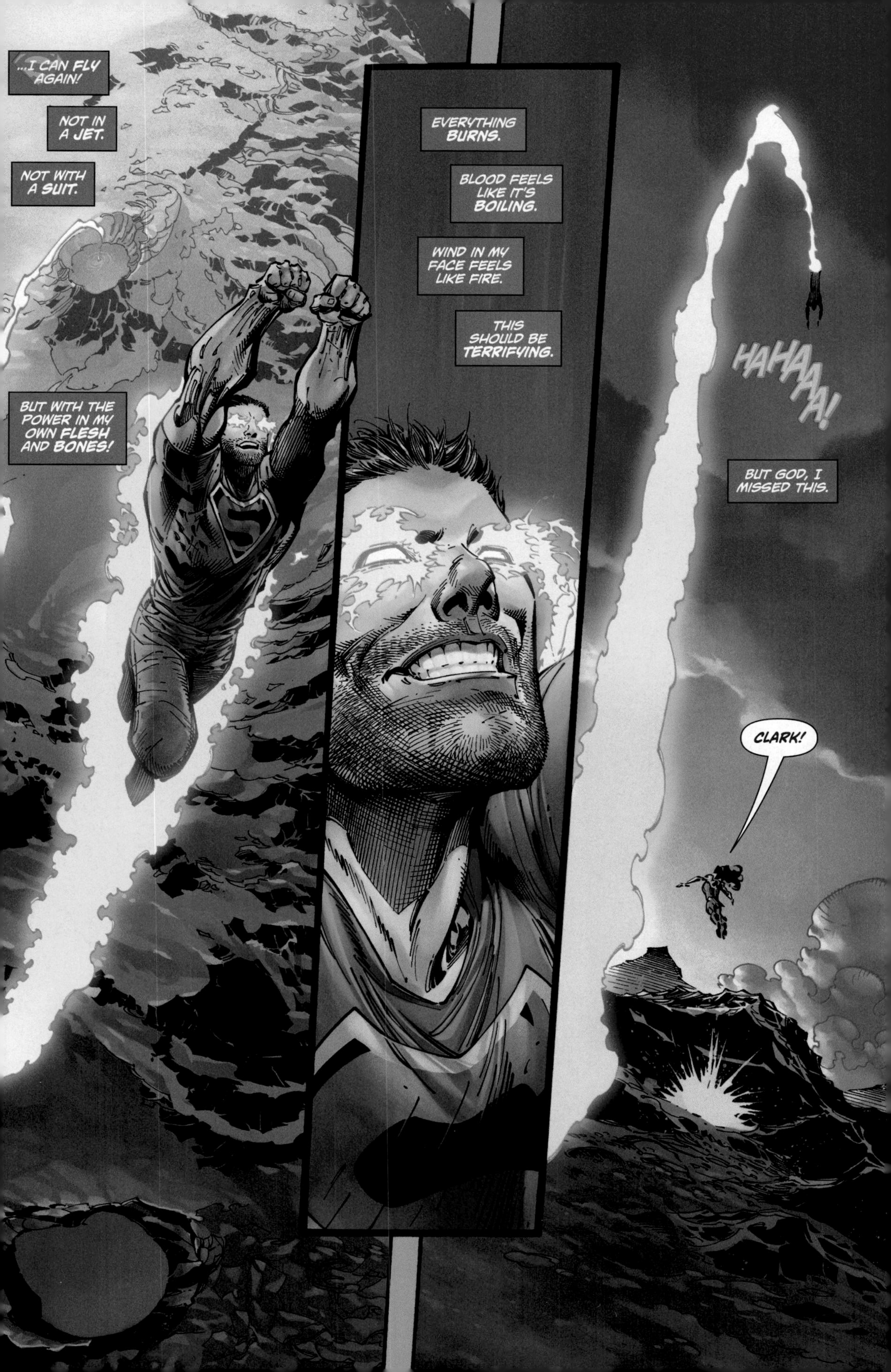
...I CAN FLY AGAIN!
NOT IN A JET.
NOT WITH A SUIT.
BUT WITH THE POWER IN MY OWN FLESH AND BONES!
EVERYTHING BURNS.
BLOOD FEELS LIKE IT'S BOILING.
WIND IN MY FACE FEELS LIKE FIRE.
THIS SHOULD BE TERRIFYING.
HAHAAA!
BUT GOD, I MISSED THIS.
CLARK!

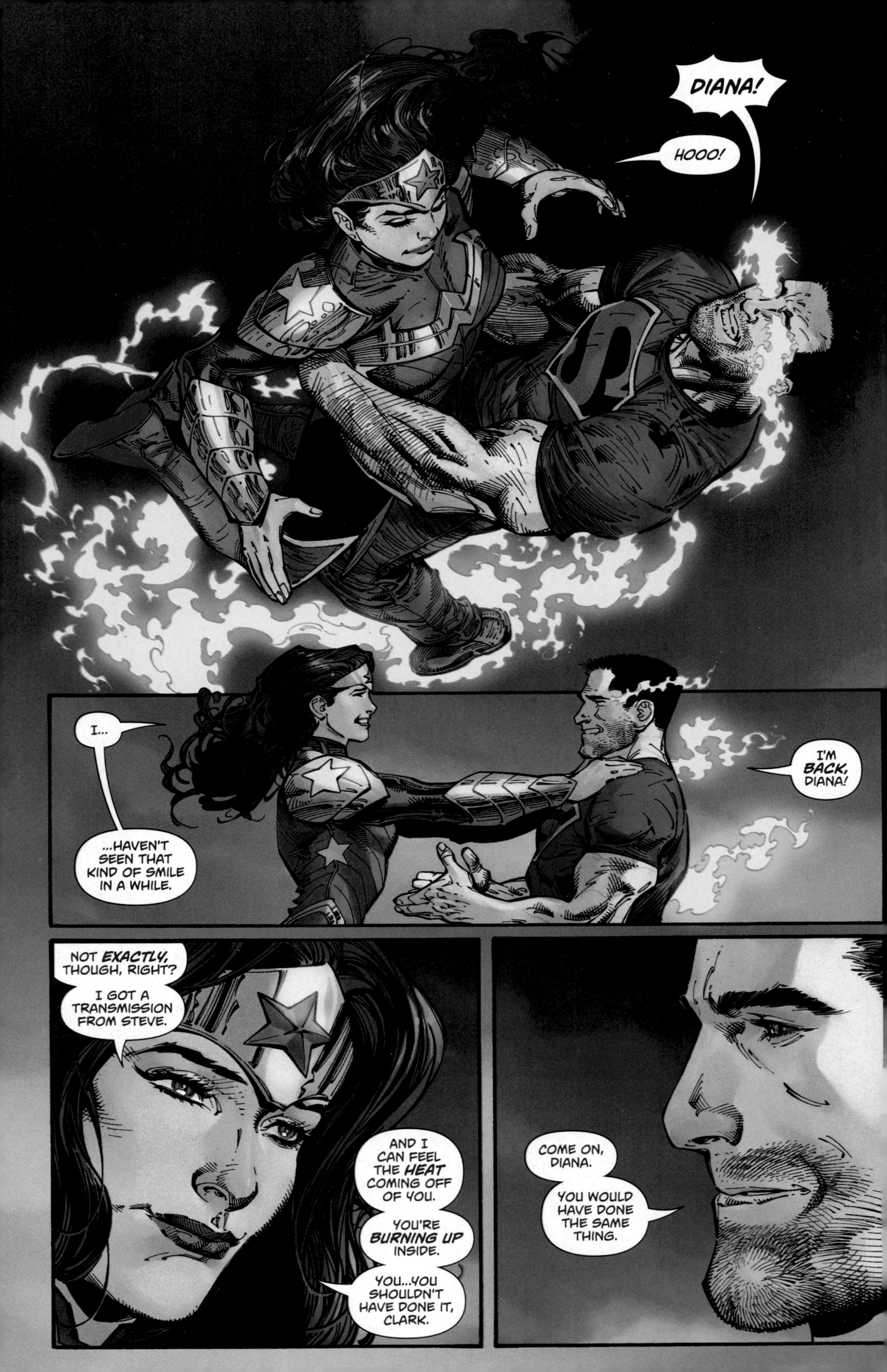
DIANA!
HOOO!
I...
...HAVEN'T SEEN THAT KIND OF SMILE IN A WHILE.
I'M *BACK,* DIANA!
NOT *EXACTLY,* THOUGH, RIGHT?
I GOT A TRANSMISSION FROM STEVE.
AND I CAN FEEL THE *HEAT* COMING OFF OF YOU.
YOU'RE *BURNING UP* INSIDE.
YOU...YOU SHOULDN'T HAVE DONE IT, CLARK.
COME ON, DIANA.
YOU WOULD HAVE DONE THE SAME THING.

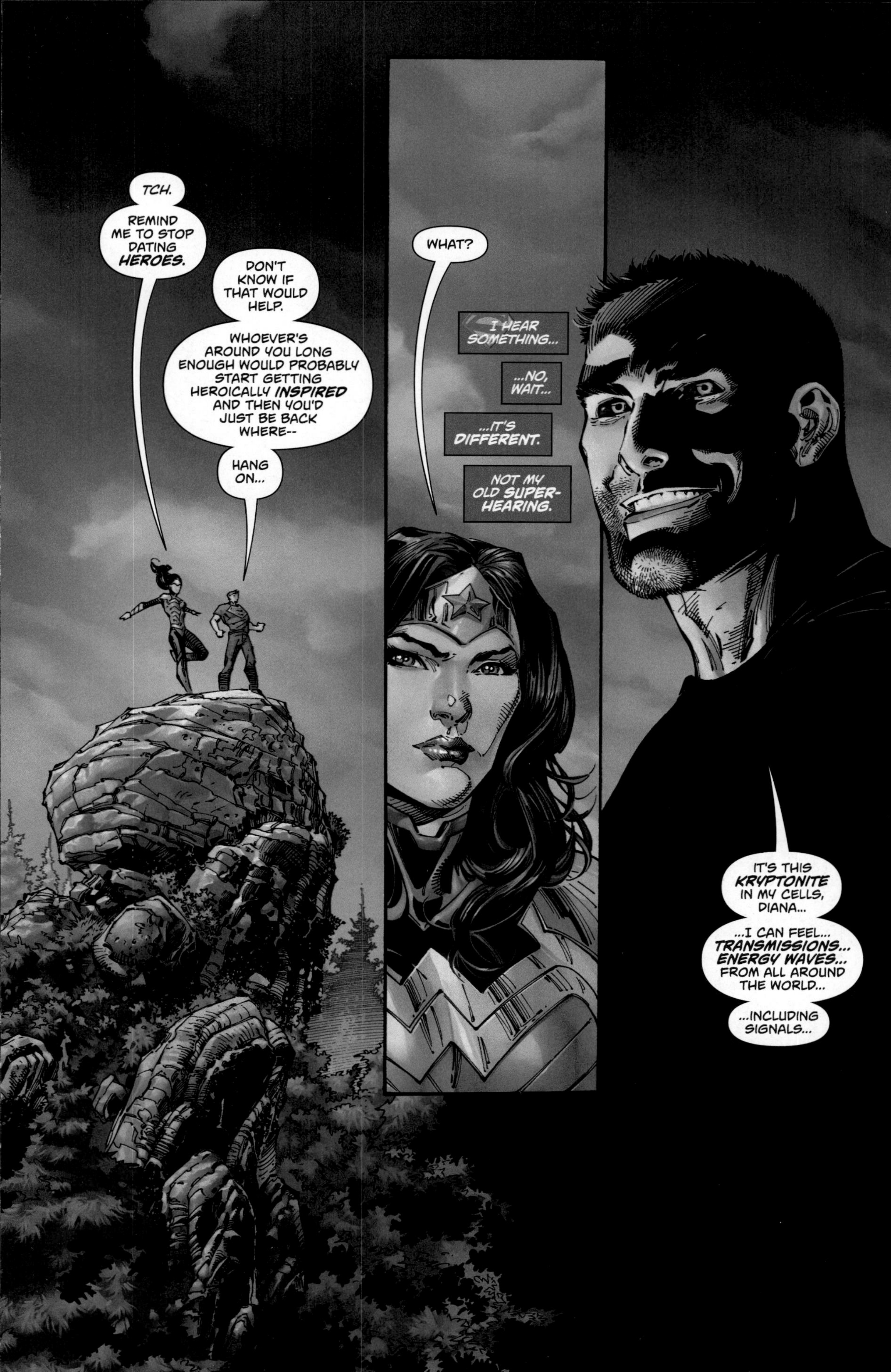
TCH.
REMIND ME TO STOP DATING HEROES.
DON'T KNOW IF THAT WOULD HELP.
WHOEVER'S AROUND YOU LONG ENOUGH WOULD PROBABLY START GETTING HEROICALLY INSPIRED AND THEN YOU'D JUST BE BACK WHERE--
HANG ON...
WHAT?
I HEAR SOMETHING...
...NO, WAIT...
...IT'S DIFFERENT.
NOT MY OLD SUPER-HEARING.
IT'S THIS KRYPTONITE IN MY CELLS, DIANA...
...I CAN FEEL... TRANSMISSIONS... ENERGY WAVES... FROM ALL AROUND THE WORLD...
...INCLUDING SIGNALS...

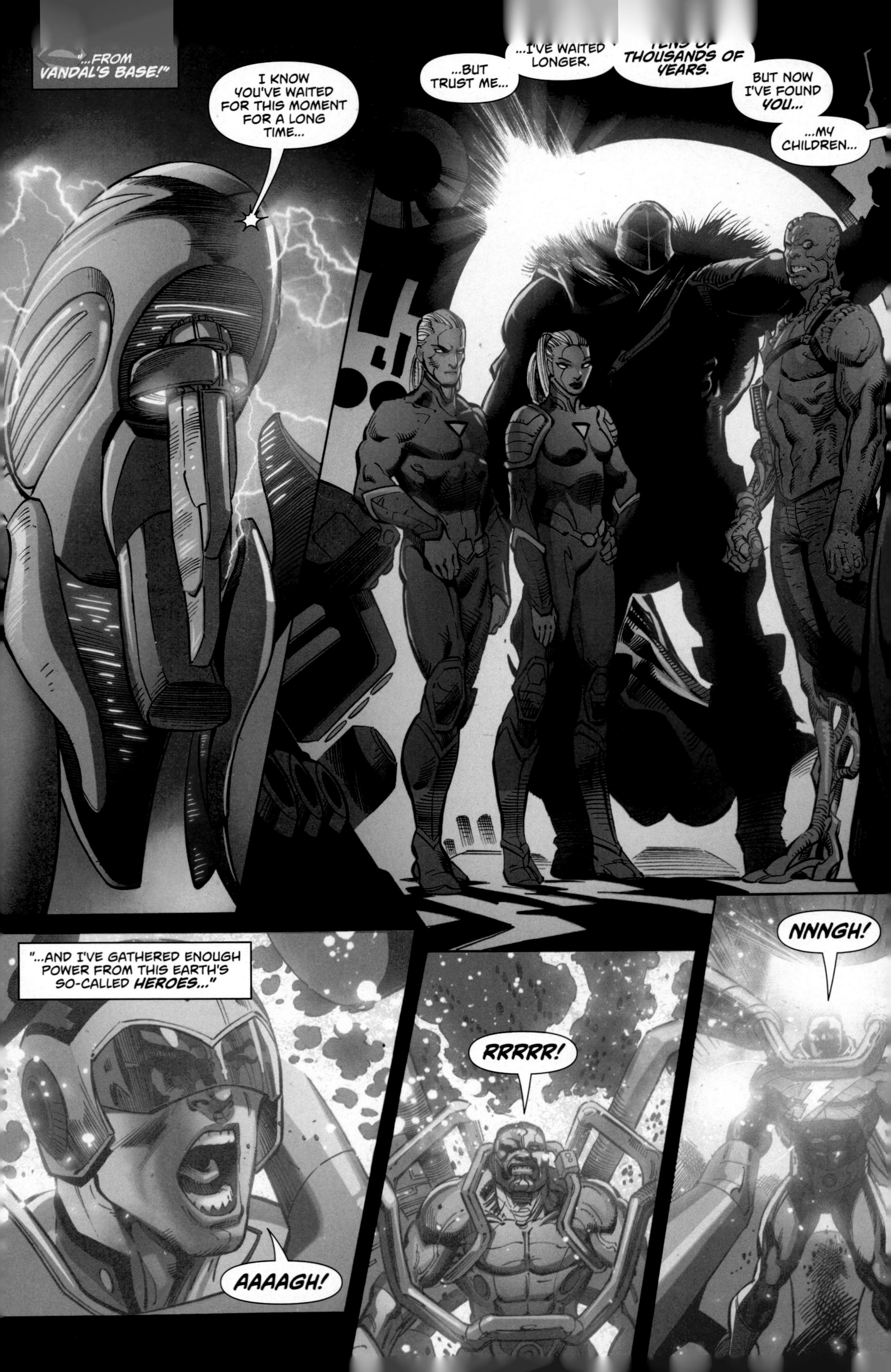
"...FROM VANDAL'S BASE!"
I KNOW YOU'VE WAITED FOR THIS MOMENT FOR A LONG TIME...
...BUT TRUST ME...
...I'VE WAITED LONGER.
THOUSANDS OF YEARS.
BUT NOW I'VE FOUND *YOU*...
...MY CHILDREN...
"...AND I'VE GATHERED ENOUGH POWER FROM THIS EARTH'S SO-CALLED *HEROES*..."
AAAAGH!
RRRRR!
NNNGH!

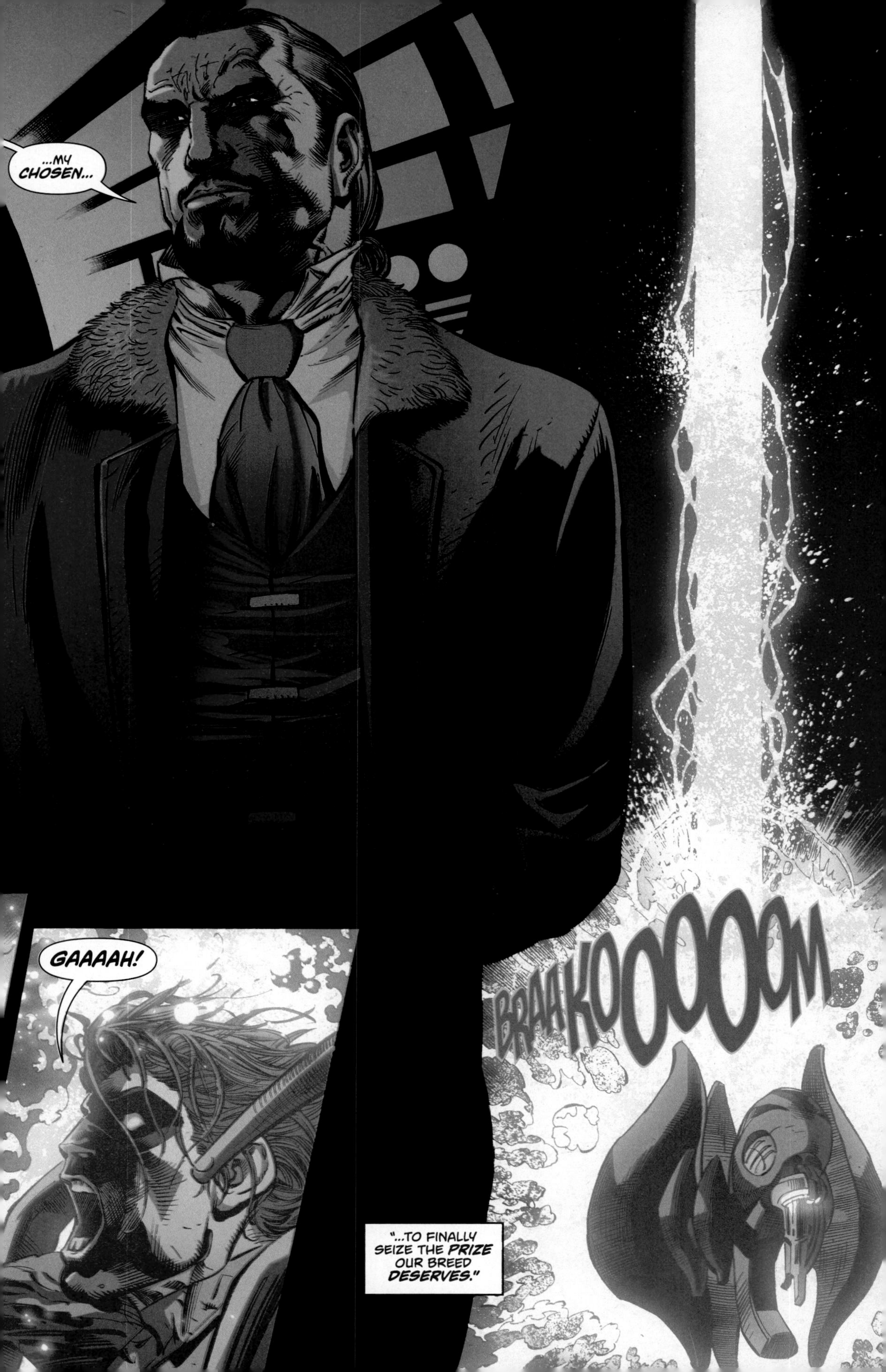
...MY CHOSEN...
GAAAAH!
BRAAKOOOOOM
"...TO FINALLY SEIZE THE *PRIZE* OUR BREED *DESERVES.*"

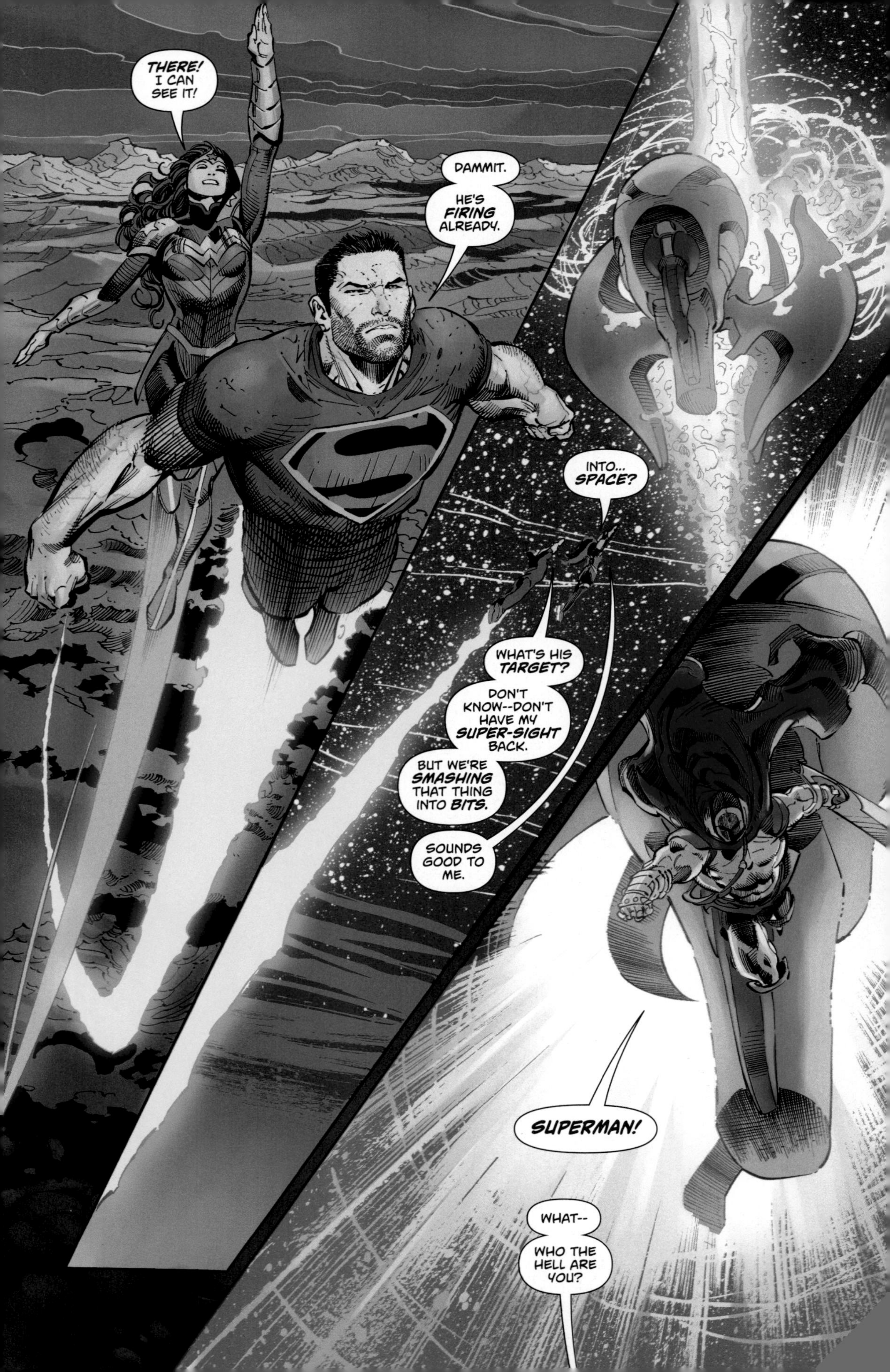
THERE! I CAN SEE IT!
DAMMIT.
HE'S FIRING ALREADY.
INTO... SPACE?
WHAT'S HIS TARGET?
DON'T KNOW--DON'T HAVE MY SUPER-SIGHT BACK.
BUT WE'RE SMASHING THAT THING INTO BITS.
SOUNDS GOOD TO ME.
SUPERMAN!
WHAT--
WHO THE HELL ARE YOU?

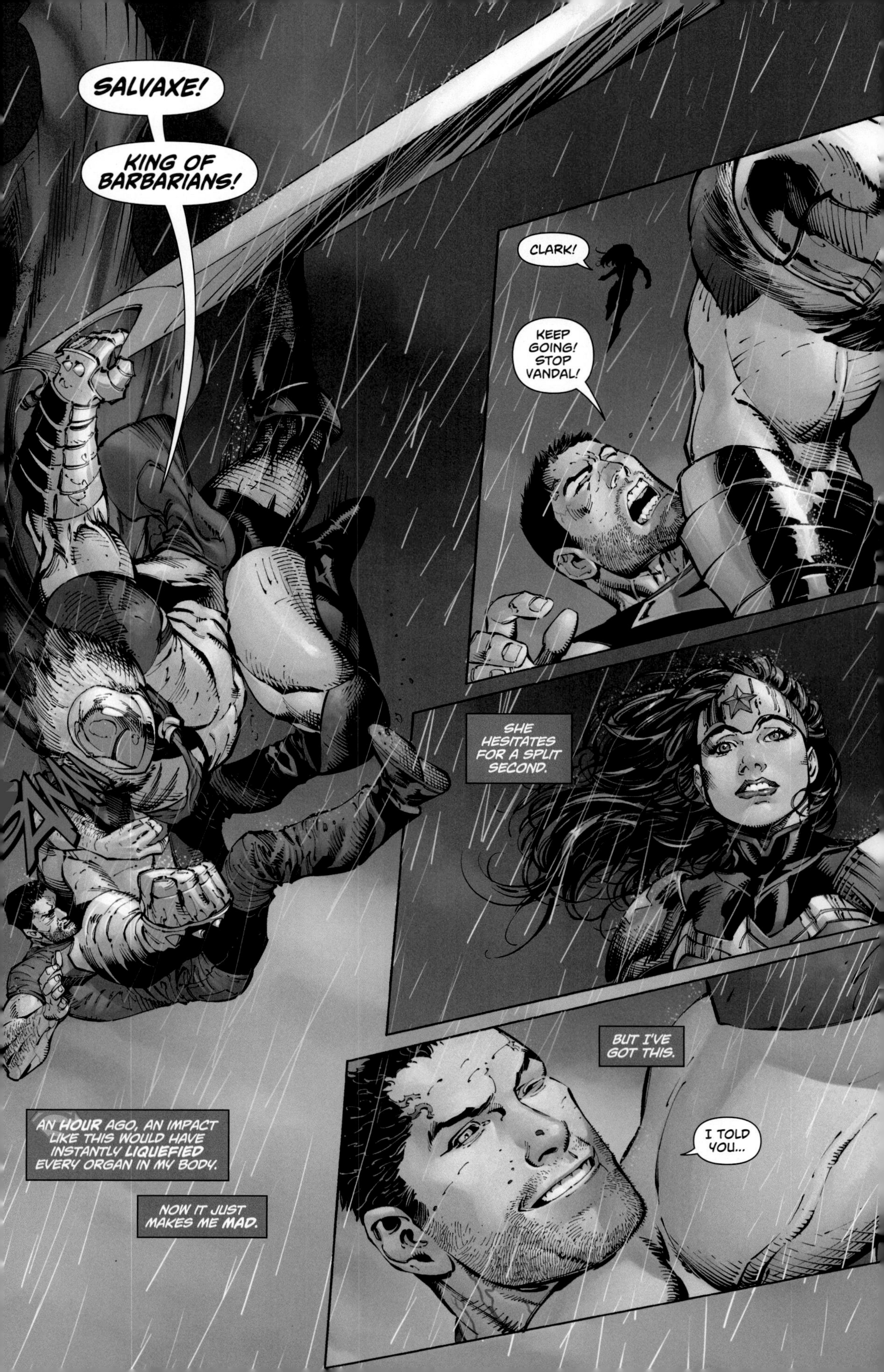
SALVAXE!
KING OF BARBARIANS!
CLARK!
KEEP GOING! STOP VANDAL!
SHE HESITATES FOR A SPLIT SECOND.
BUT I'VE GOT THIS.
AN HOUR AGO, AN IMPACT LIKE THIS WOULD HAVE INSTANTLY LIQUEFIED EVERY ORGAN IN MY BODY.
NOW IT JUST MAKES ME MAD.
I TOLD YOU...

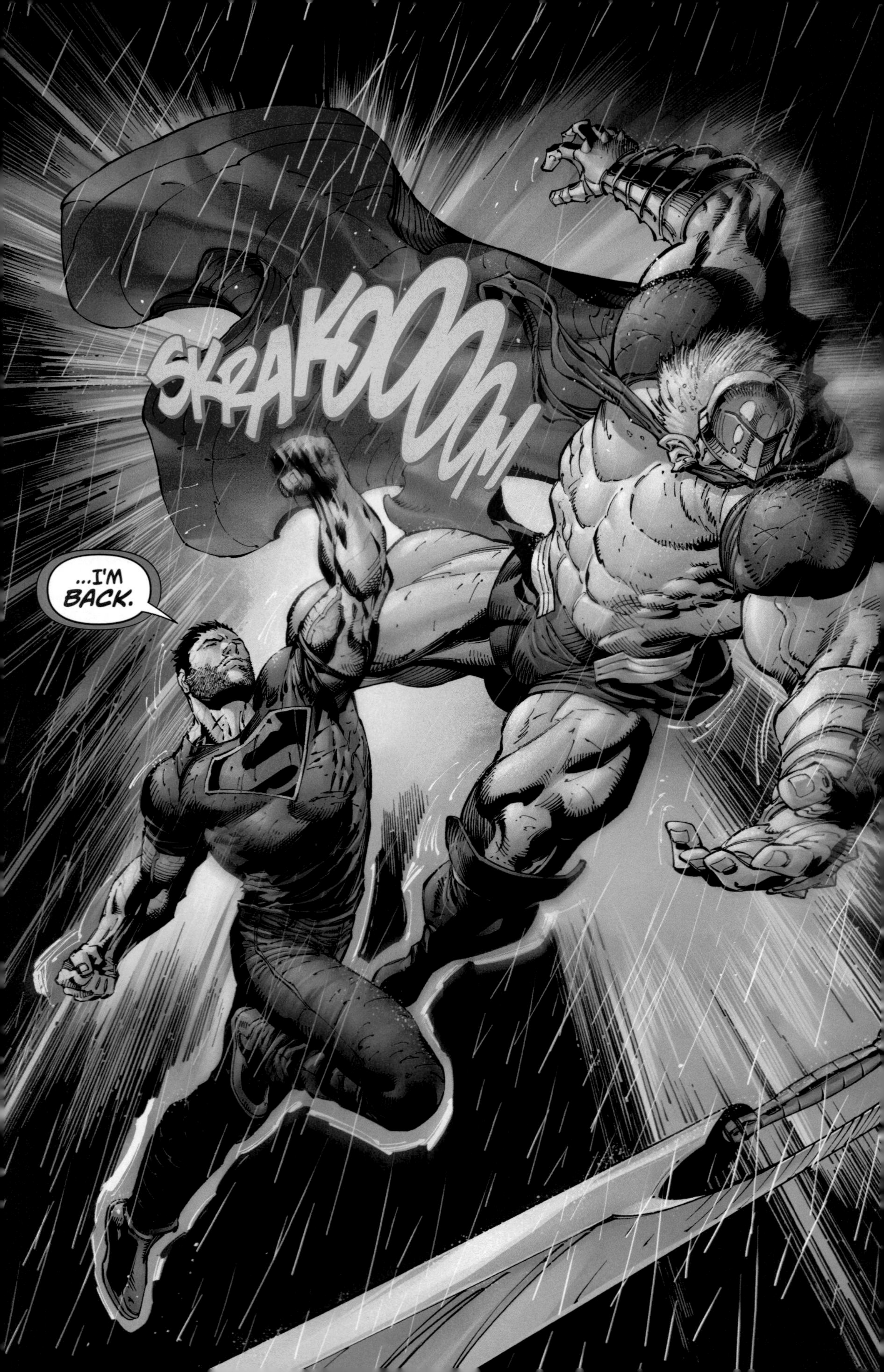
SKRAKOOOOOM
...I'M BACK.

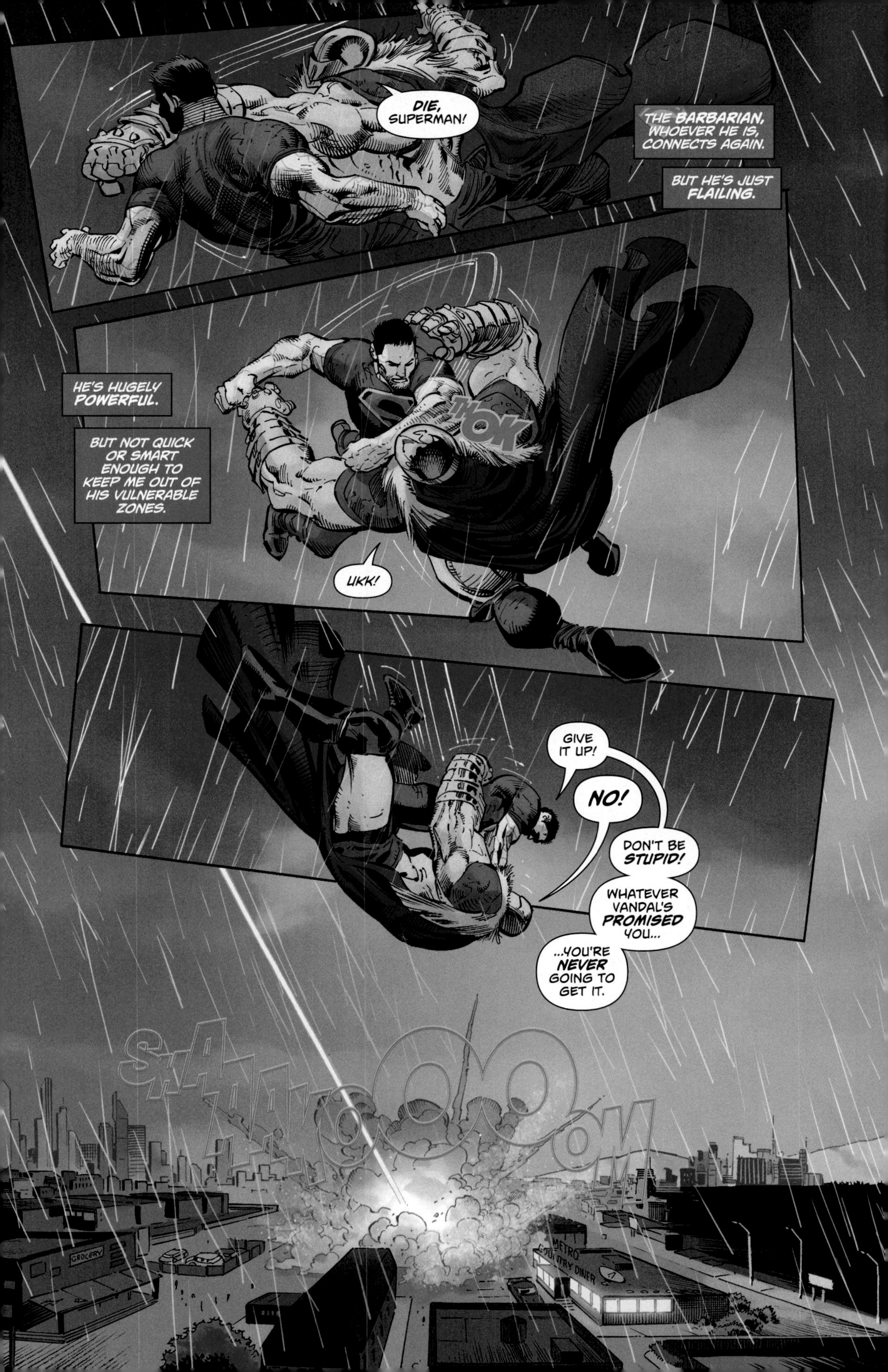

DIE, SUPERMAN!
THE BARBARIAN, WHOEVER HE IS, CONNECTS AGAIN.
BUT HE'S JUST FLAILING.
HE'S HUGELY POWERFUL.
BUT NOT QUICK OR SMART ENOUGH TO KEEP ME OUT OF HIS VULNERABLE ZONES.
THOK
UKK!
GIVE IT UP!
NO!
DON'T BE STUPID!
WHATEVER VANDAL'S PROMISED YOU...
...YOU'RE NEVER GOING TO GET IT.
SKABOOOOM
GROCERY
METRO COUNTRY DINER

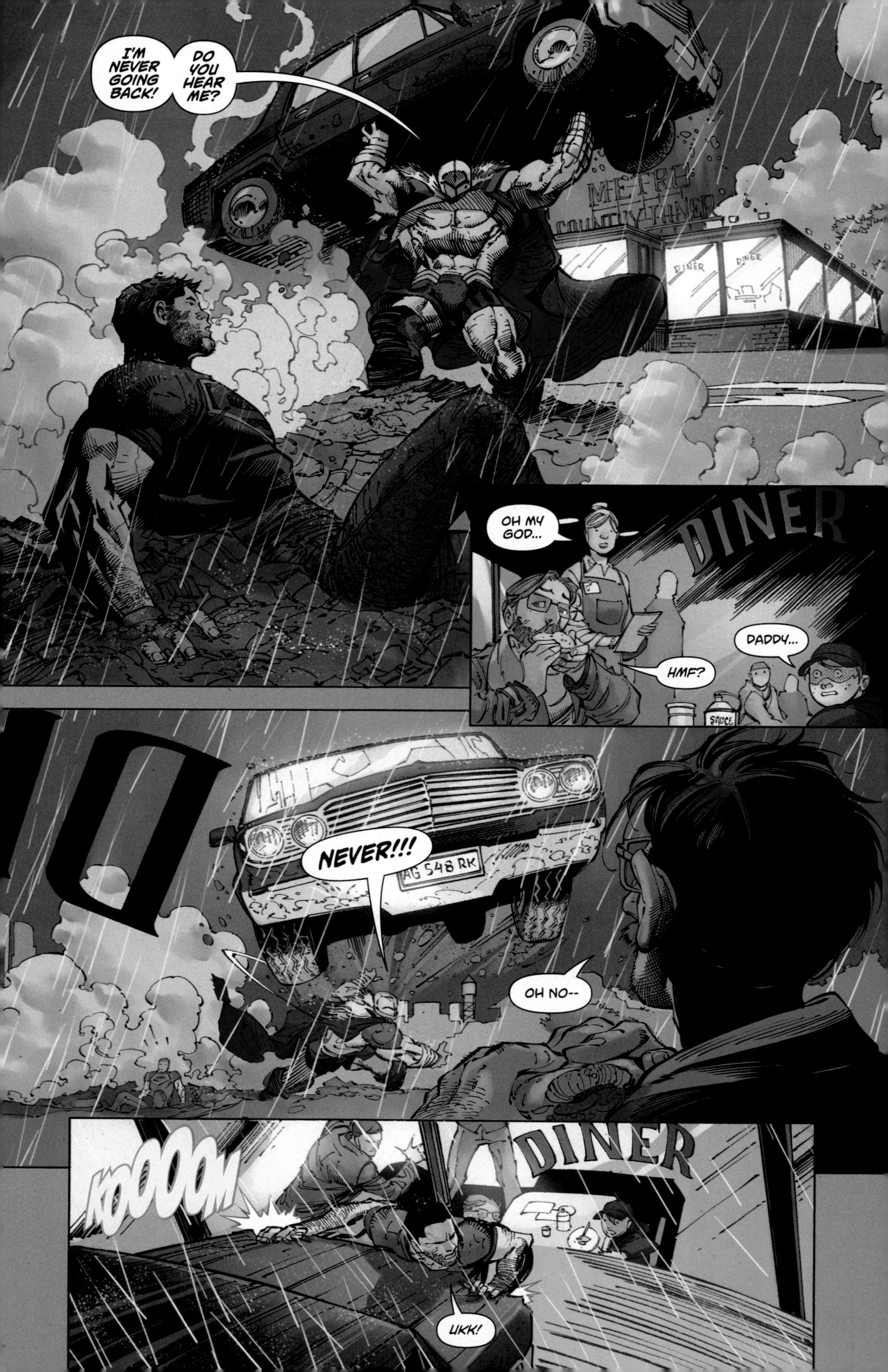
I'M NEVER GOING BACK!
DO YOU HEAR ME?
METRO
COUNTY DINER
DINER
DINER
DINER
OH MY GOD...
DADDY...
HMF?
SAUCE
NEVER!!!
AG 548 RK
OH NO--
KOOOOM
DINER
UKK!

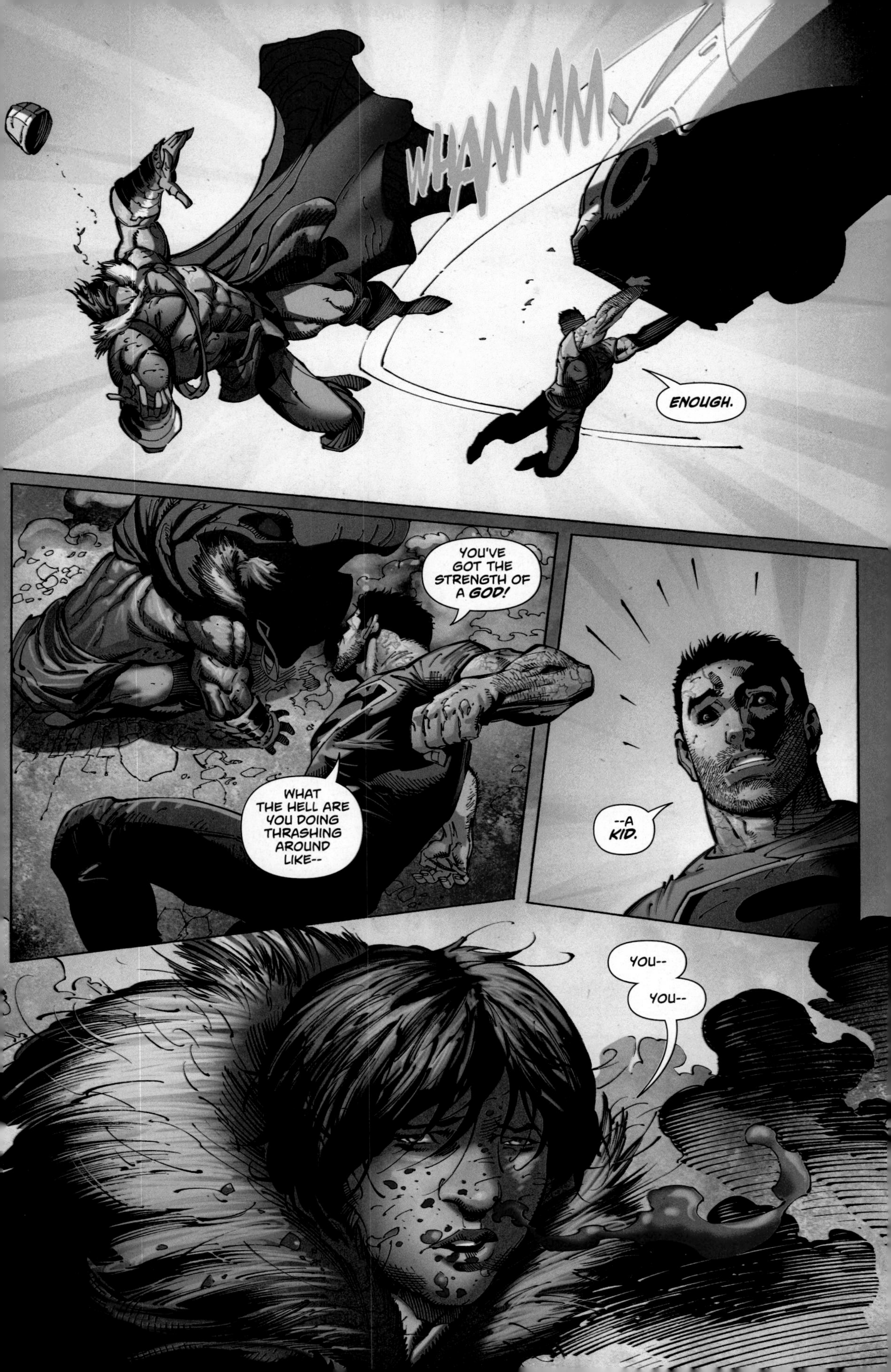
WHAMMM
ENOUGH.
YOU'VE GOT THE STRENGTH OF A GOD!
WHAT THE HELL ARE YOU DOING THRASHING AROUND LIKE--
--A KID.
YOU--
YOU--

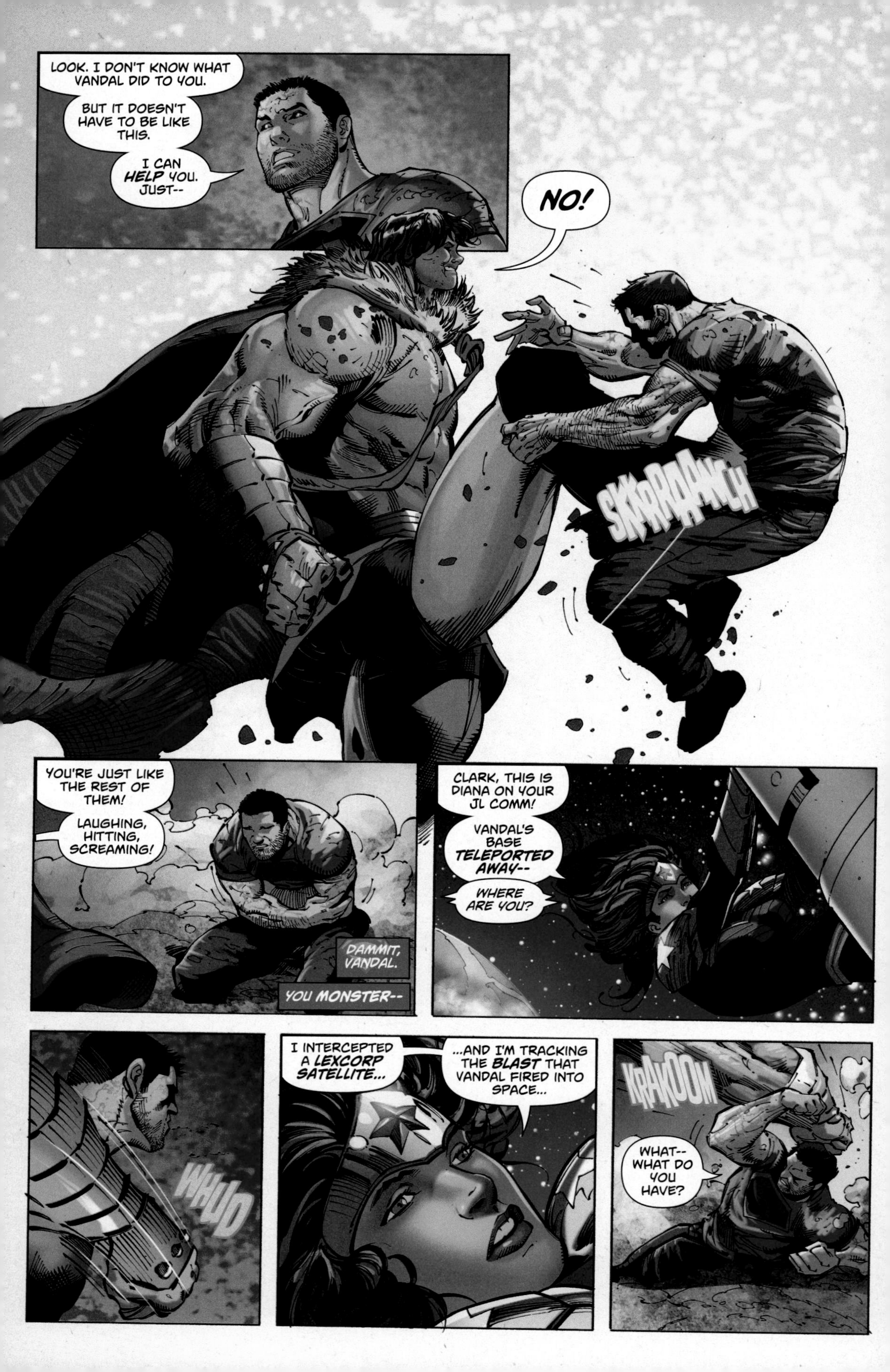
LOOK. I DON'T KNOW WHAT VANDAL DID TO YOU.
BUT IT DOESN'T HAVE TO BE LIKE THIS.
I CAN *HELP* YOU. JUST--
NO!
SKRRAANCH
YOU'RE JUST LIKE THE REST OF THEM!
LAUGHING, HITTING, SCREAMING!
DAMMIT, VANDAL.
YOU *MONSTER*--
CLARK, THIS IS DIANA ON YOUR JL COMM!
VANDAL'S BASE *TELEPORTED AWAY*--
WHERE ARE YOU?
WHUD
I INTERCEPTED A *LEXCORP SATELLITE*...
...AND I'M TRACKING THE *BLAST* THAT VANDAL FIRED INTO SPACE...
KRAKOOM
WHAT-- WHAT DO YOU HAVE?

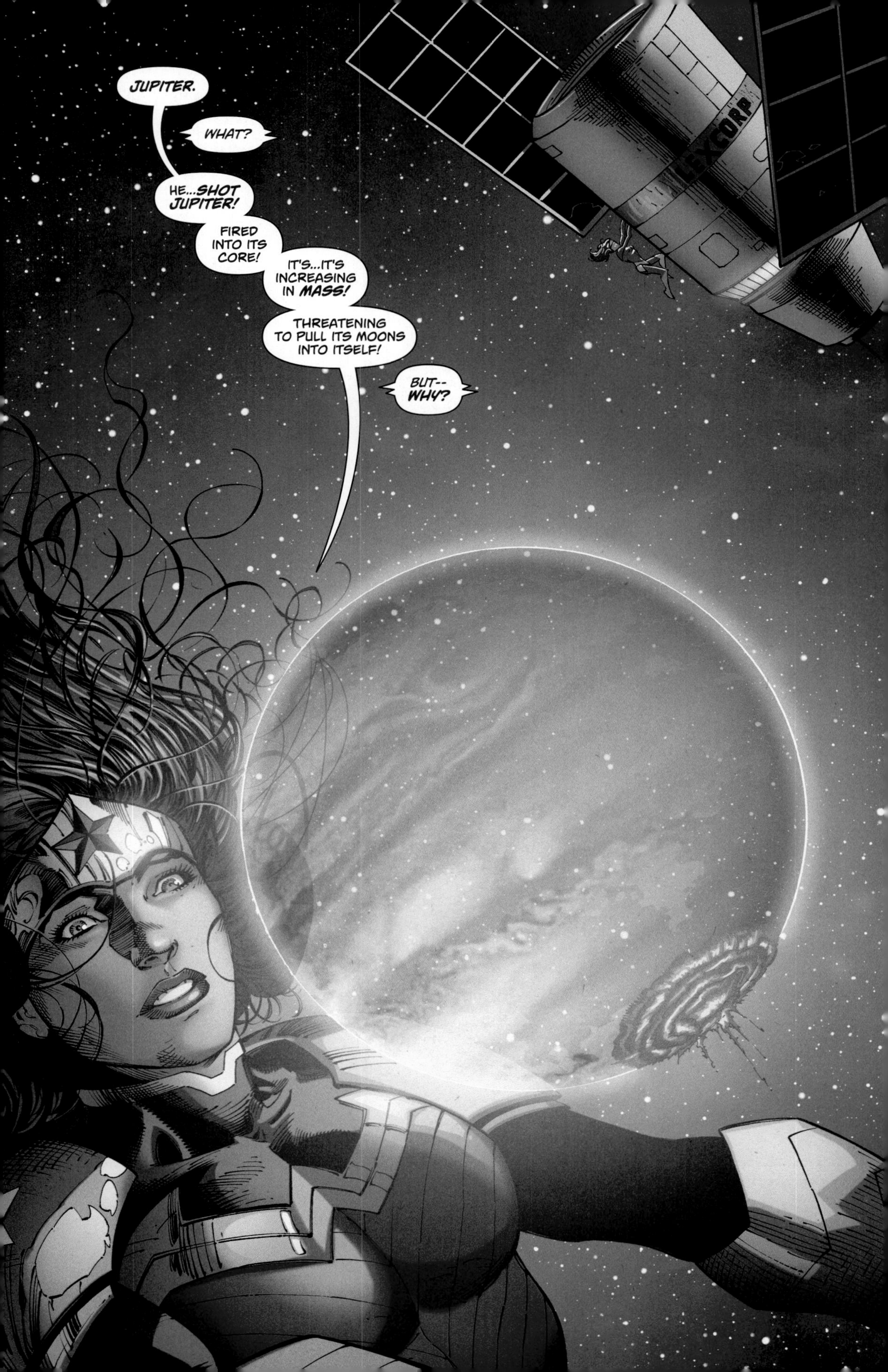
JUPITER.
WHAT?
HE...SHOT JUPITER!
FIRED INTO ITS CORE!
IT'S...IT'S INCREASING IN MASS!
THREATENING TO PULL ITS MOONS INTO ITSELF!
BUT-- WHY?
LEXCORP

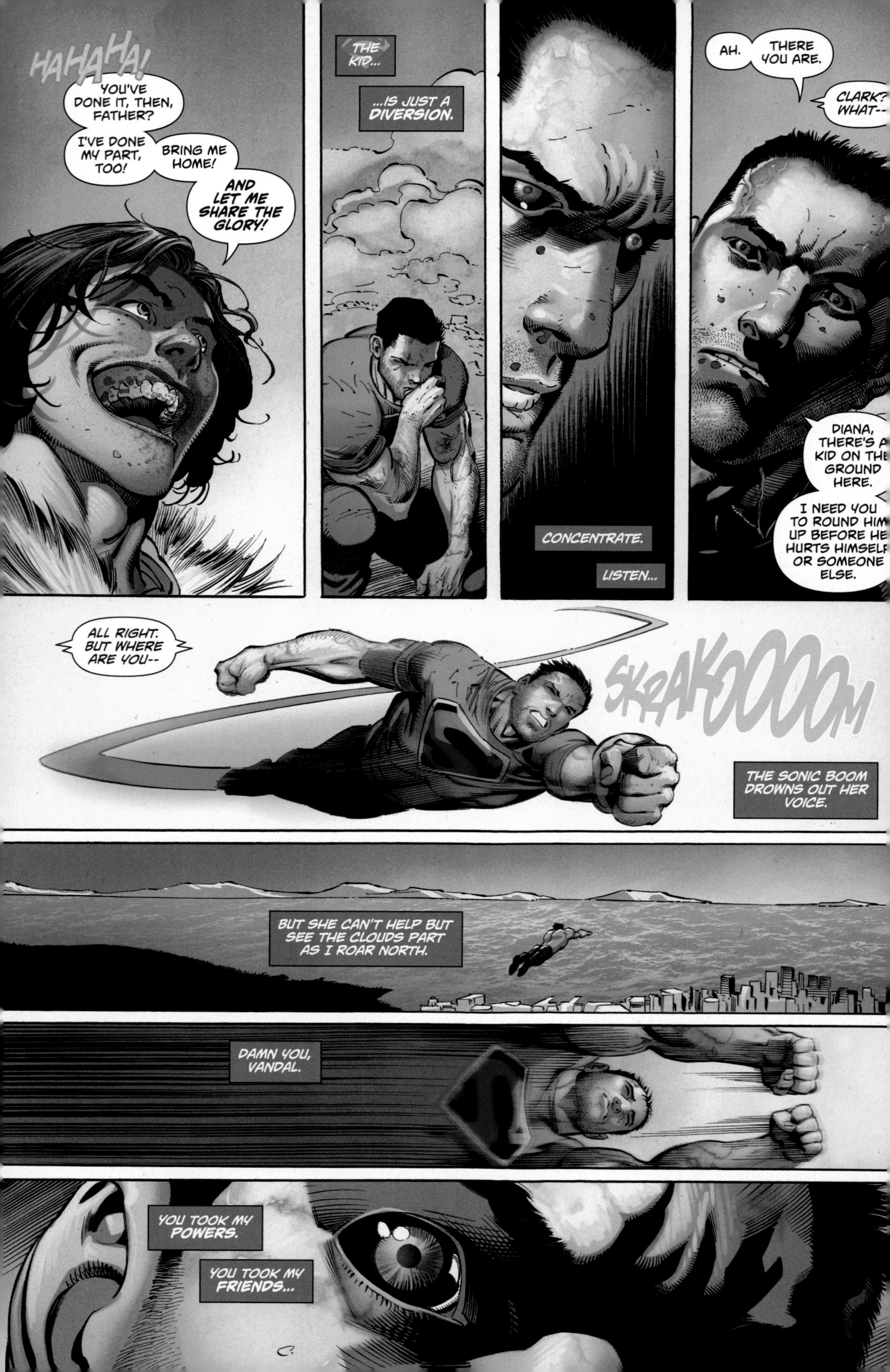
HAHAHA!
YOU'VE DONE IT, THEN, FATHER?
I'VE DONE MY PART, TOO!
BRING ME HOME!
AND LET ME SHARE THE GLORY!
THE KID...
...IS JUST A DIVERSION.
CONCENTRATE.
LISTEN...
AH.
THERE YOU ARE.
CLARK? WHAT--
DIANA, THERE'S A KID ON THE GROUND HERE.
I NEED YOU TO ROUND HIM UP BEFORE HE HURTS HIMSELF OR SOMEONE ELSE.
ALL RIGHT. BUT WHERE ARE YOU--
SKRAKOOOOM
THE SONIC BOOM DROWNS OUT HER VOICE.
BUT SHE CAN'T HELP BUT SEE THE CLOUDS PART AS I ROAR NORTH.
DAMN YOU, VANDAL.
YOU TOOK MY POWERS.
YOU TOOK MY FRIENDS...

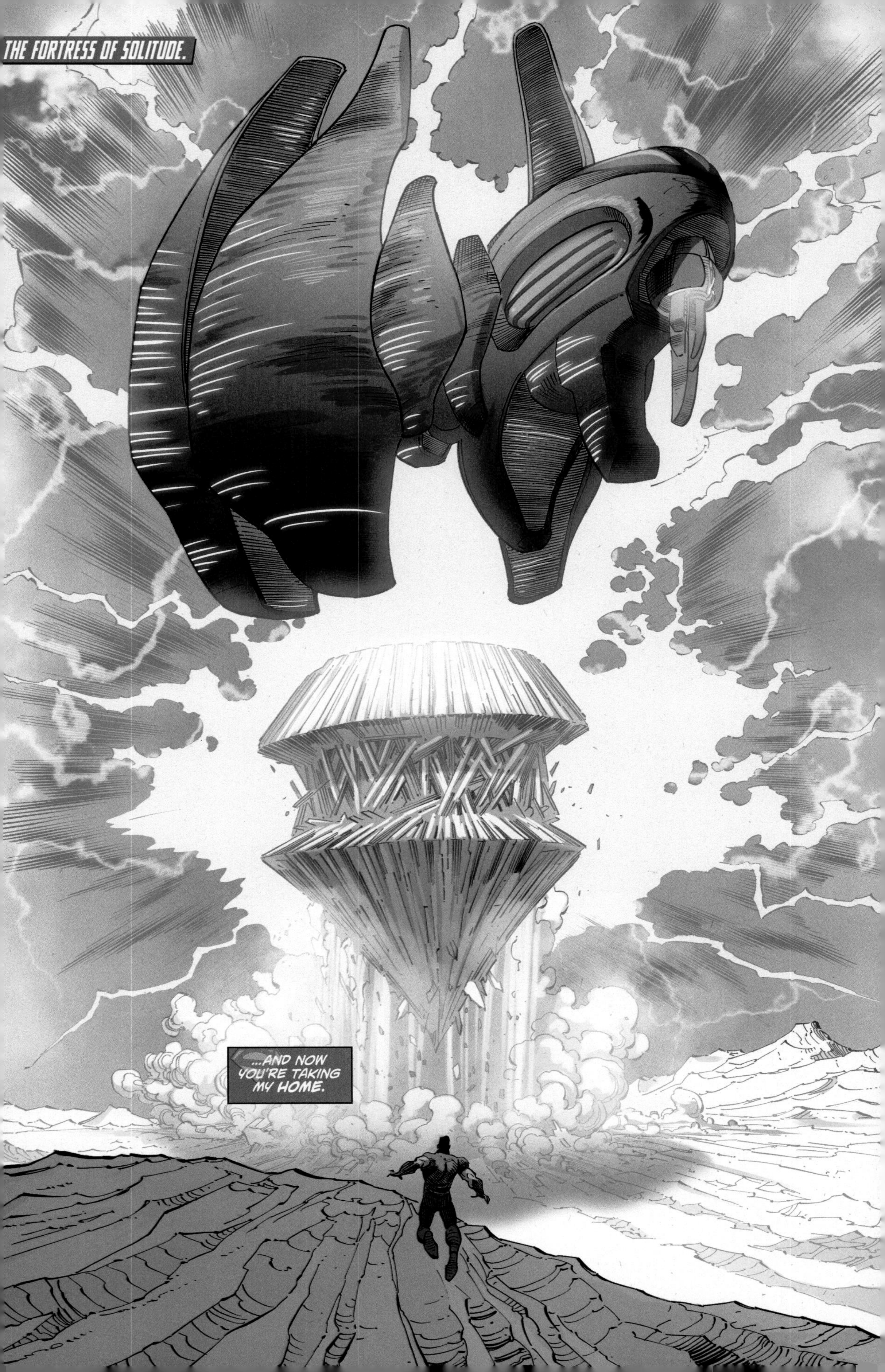
THE FORTRESS OF SOLITUDE.
...AND NOW YOU'RE TAKING MY HOME.

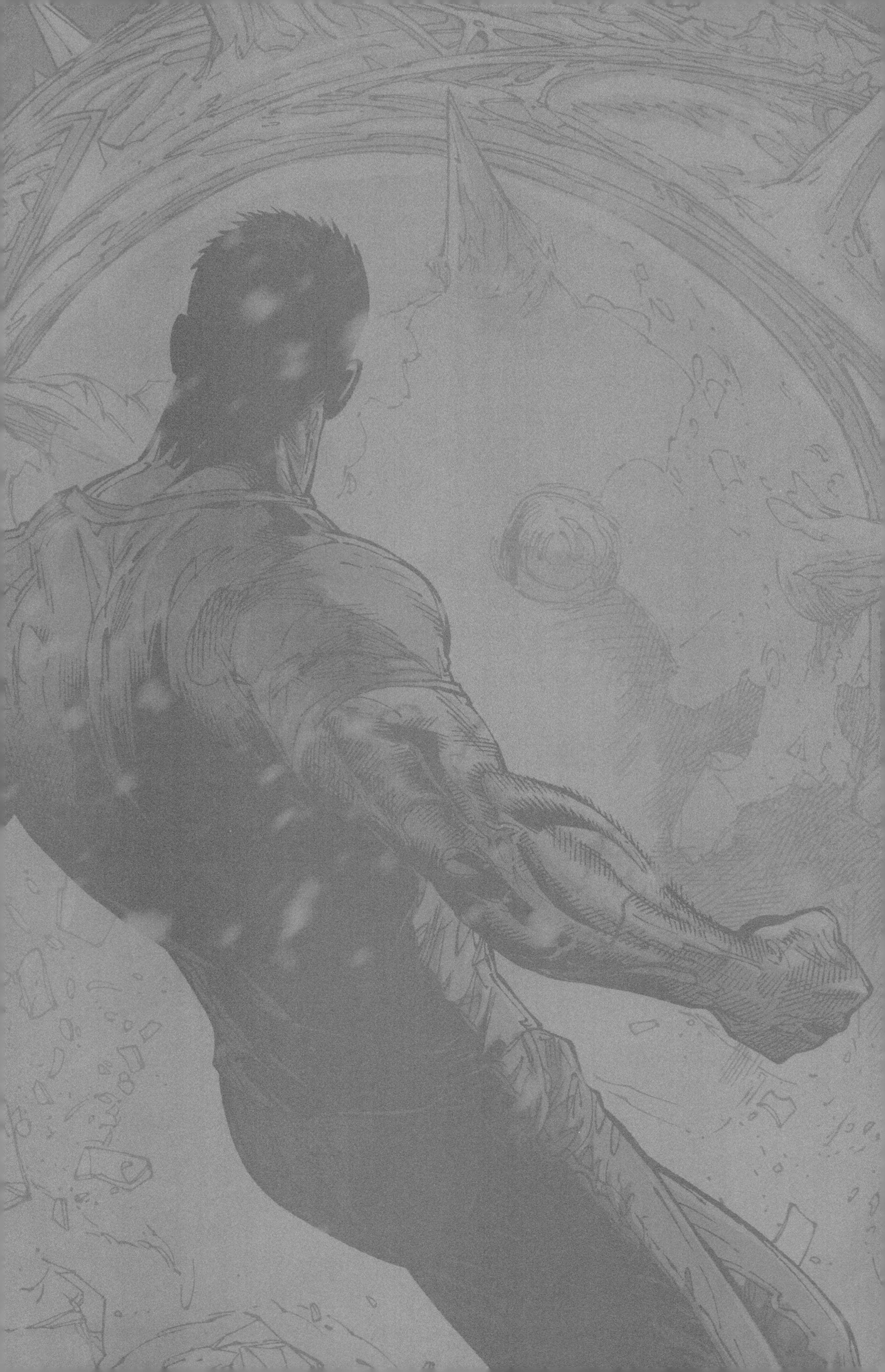

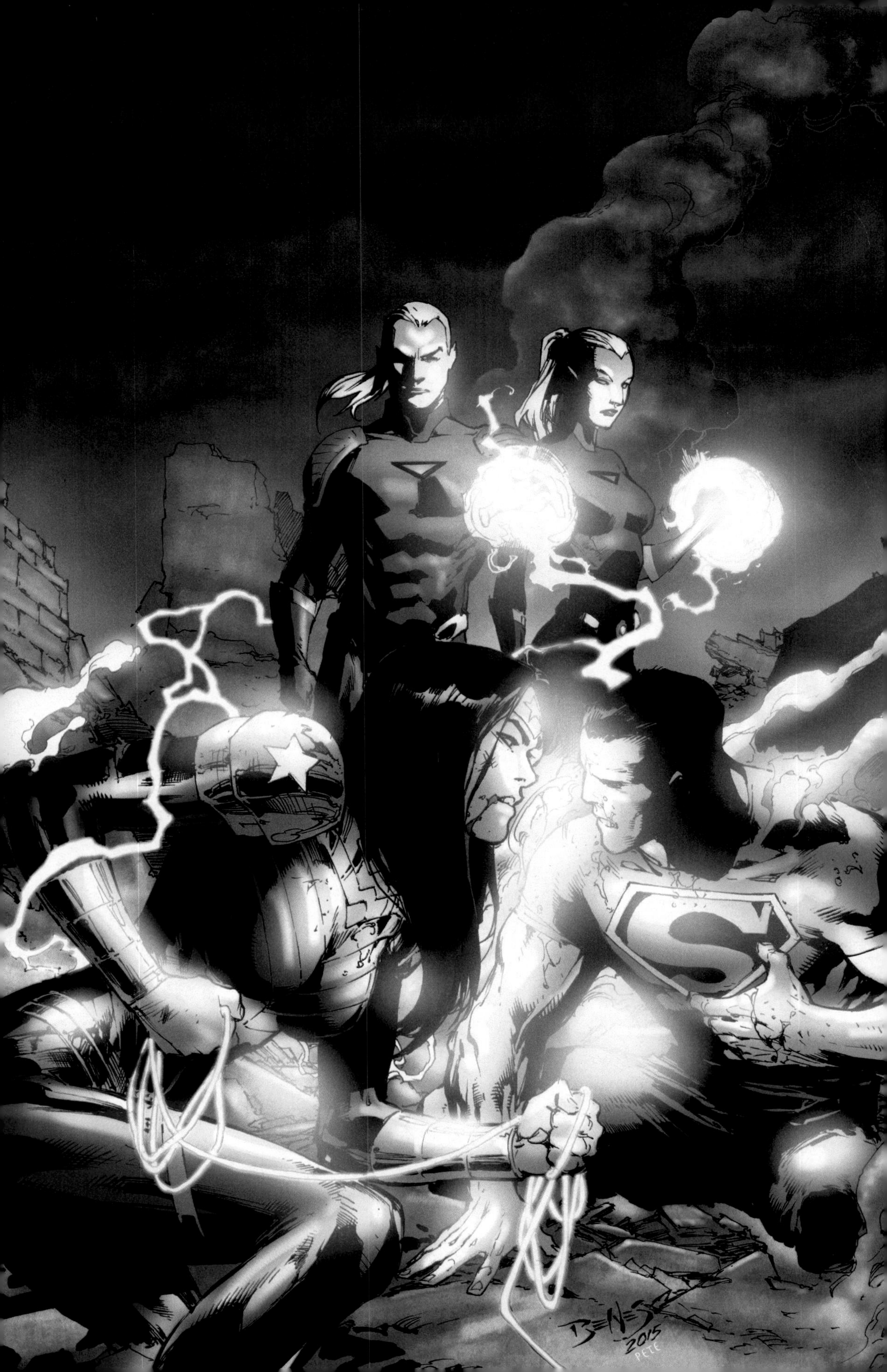
BENES
2015
PETE

SKYFALL

PETER J. TOMASI writer **DOUG MAHNKE** penciller **JAIME MENDOZA DOUG MAHNKE** inkers **WIL QUINTANA** colorist **ROB LEIGH** letterer **ED BENES PAT PANTAZIS** cover

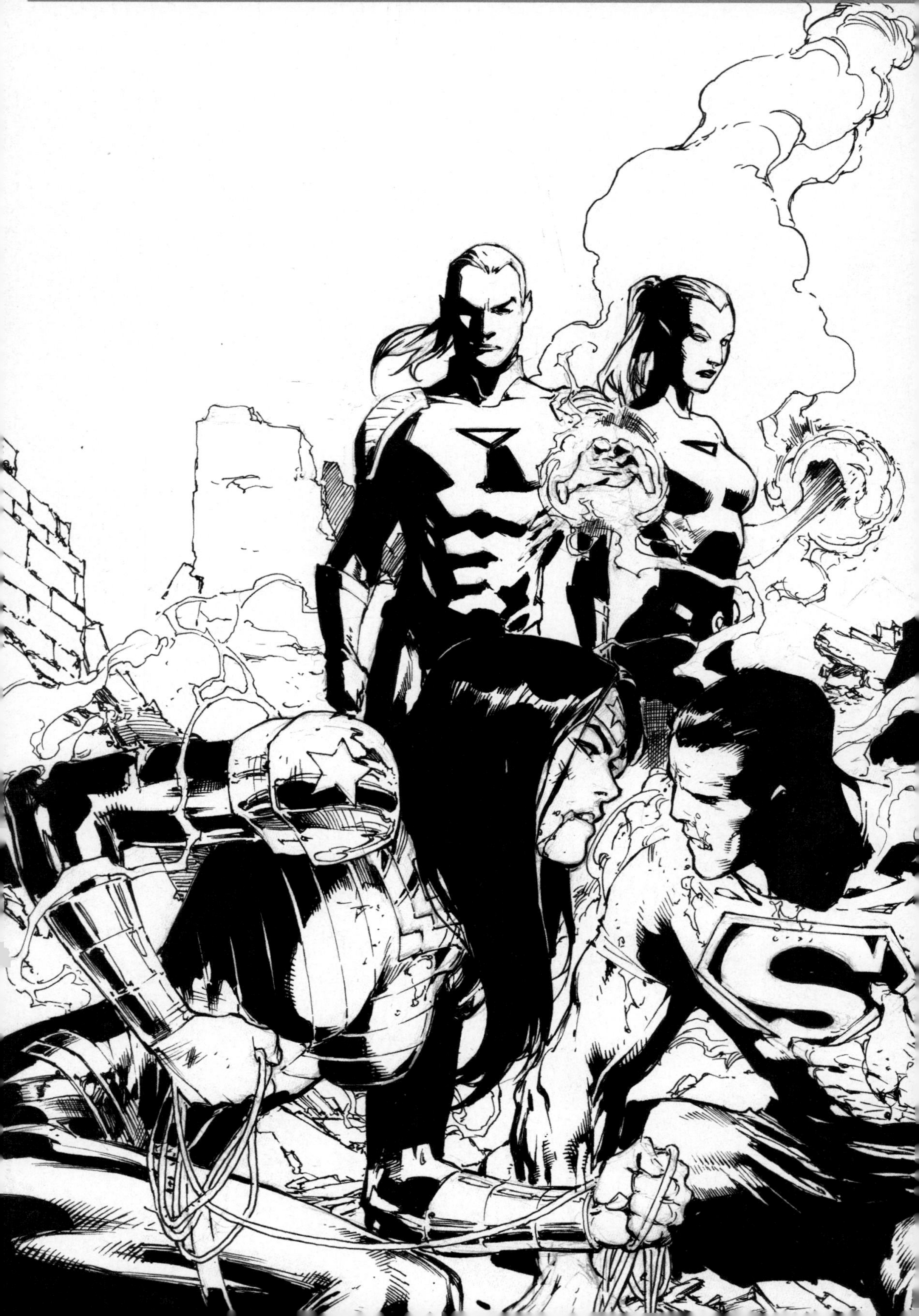

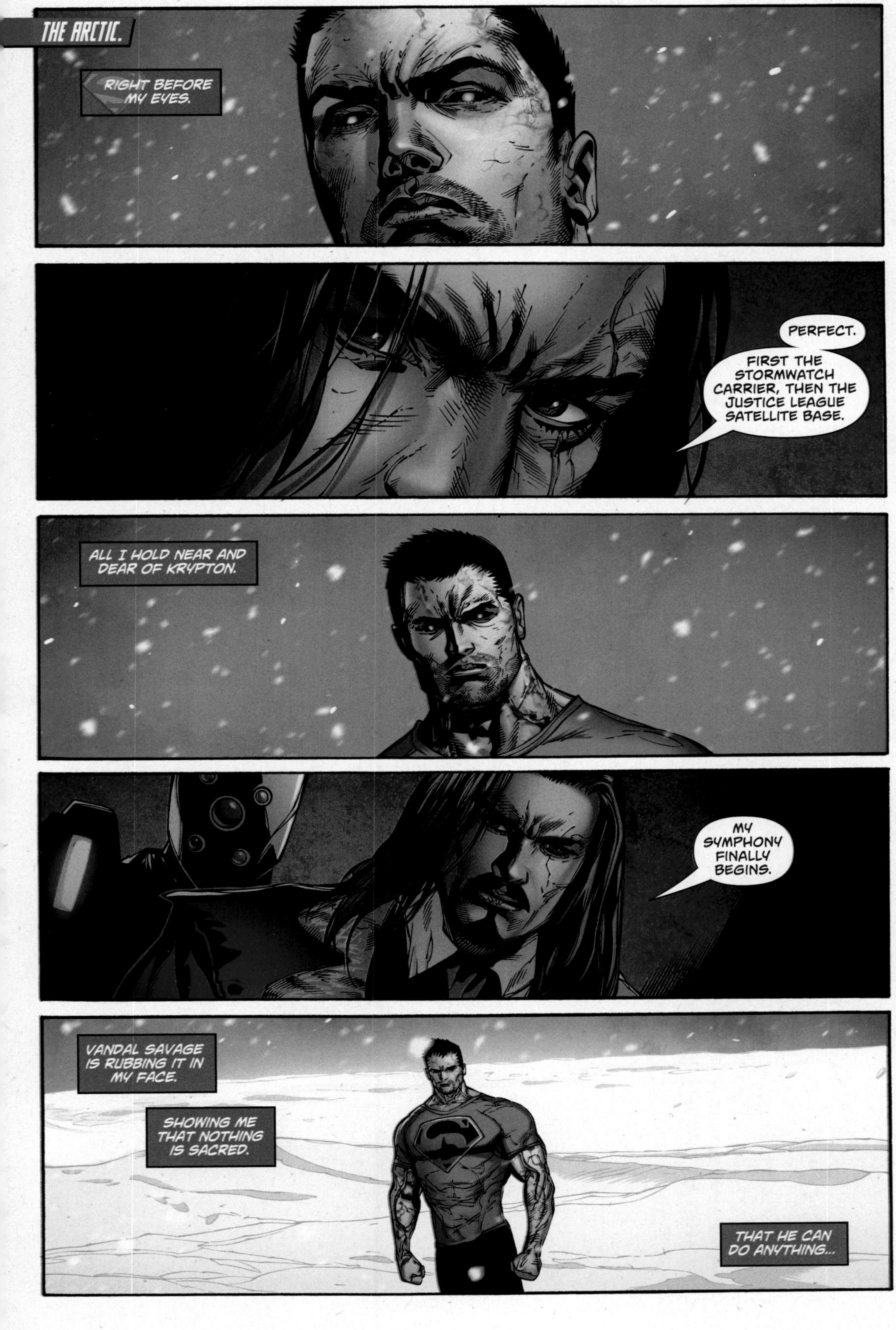
THE ARCTIC.
RIGHT BEFORE MY EYES.
PERFECT.
FIRST THE STORMWATCH CARRIER, THEN THE JUSTICE LEAGUE SATELLITE BASE.
ALL I HOLD NEAR AND DEAR OF KRYPTON.
MY SYMPHONY FINALLY BEGINS.
VANDAL SAVAGE IS RUBBING IT IN MY FACE.
SHOWING ME THAT NOTHING IS SACRED.
THAT HE CAN DO ANYTHING...

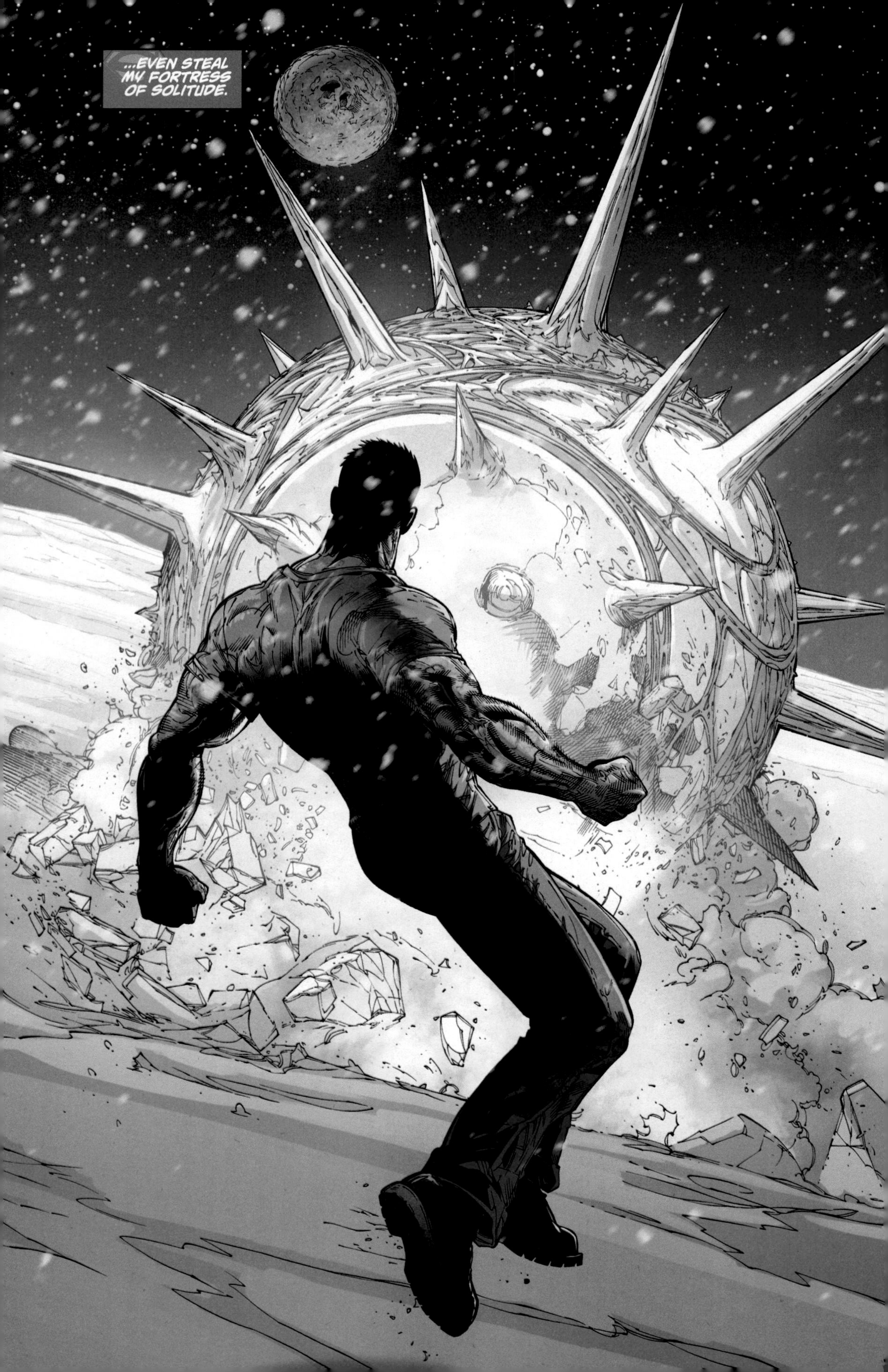
...EVEN STEAL MY FORTRESS OF SOLITUDE.

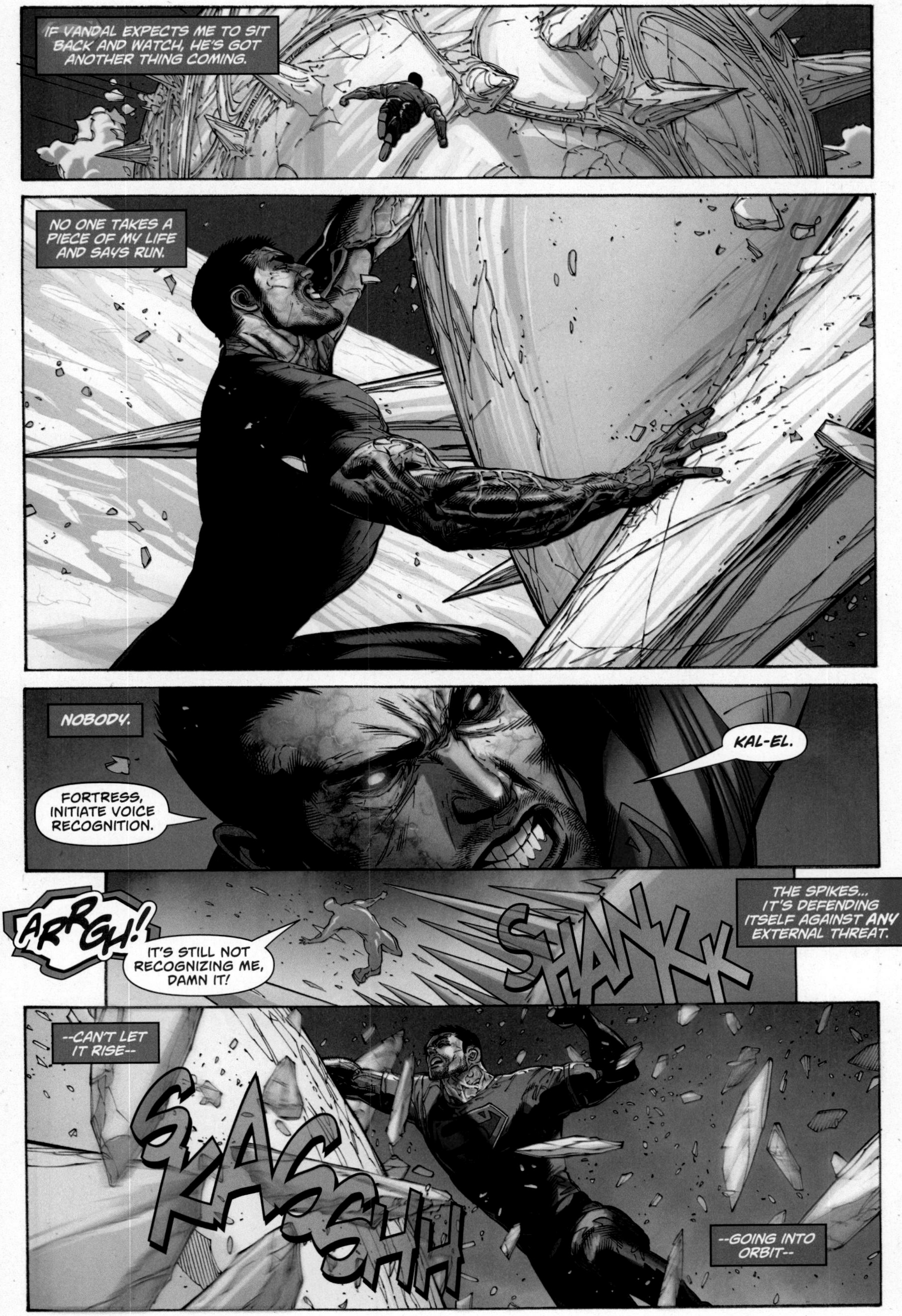
IF VANDAL EXPECTS ME TO SIT BACK AND WATCH, HE'S GOT ANOTHER THING COMING.
NO ONE TAKES A PIECE OF MY LIFE AND SAYS RUN.
NOBODY.
FORTRESS, INITIATE VOICE RECOGNITION.
KAL-EL.
ARRGH!
IT'S STILL NOT RECOGNIZING ME, DAMN IT!
SHANKK
THE SPIKES... IT'S DEFENDING ITSELF AGAINST ANY EXTERNAL THREAT.
--CAN'T LET IT RISE--
SKASCHH
--GOING INTO ORBIT--

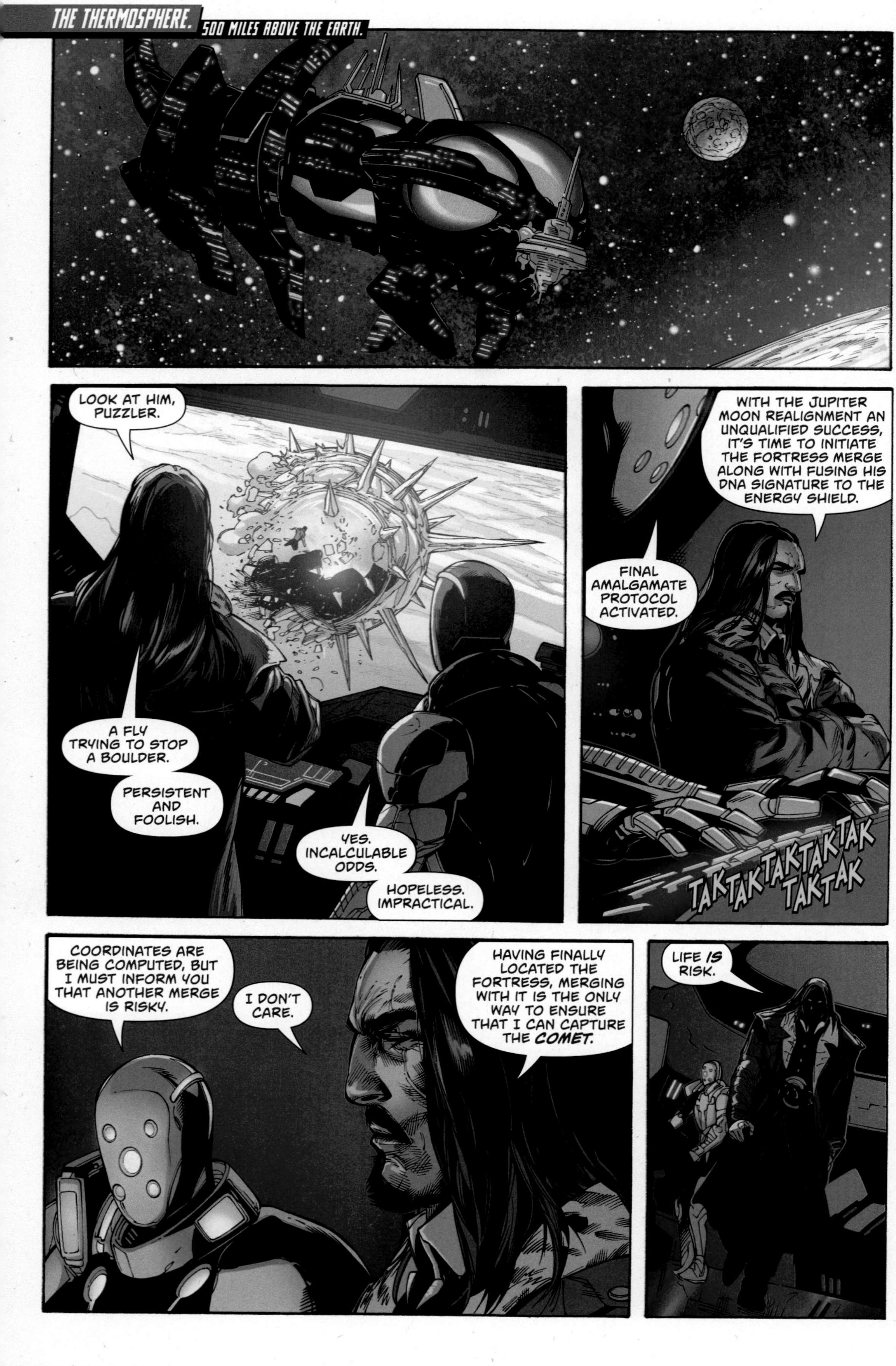
THE THERMOSPHERE.
500 MILES ABOVE THE EARTH.
LOOK AT HIM, PUZZLER.
A FLY TRYING TO STOP A BOULDER.
PERSISTENT AND FOOLISH.
YES. INCALCULABLE ODDS.
HOPELESS. IMPRACTICAL.
WITH THE JUPITER MOON REALIGNMENT AN UNQUALIFIED SUCCESS, IT'S TIME TO INITIATE THE FORTRESS MERGE ALONG WITH FUSING HIS DNA SIGNATURE TO THE ENERGY SHIELD.
FINAL AMALGAMATE PROTOCOL ACTIVATED.
TAKTAKTAKTAKTAK TAKTAK
COORDINATES ARE BEING COMPUTED, BUT I MUST INFORM YOU THAT ANOTHER MERGE IS RISKY.
I DON'T CARE.
HAVING FINALLY LOCATED THE FORTRESS, MERGING WITH IT IS THE ONLY WAY TO ENSURE THAT I CAN CAPTURE THE COMET.
LIFE IS RISK.

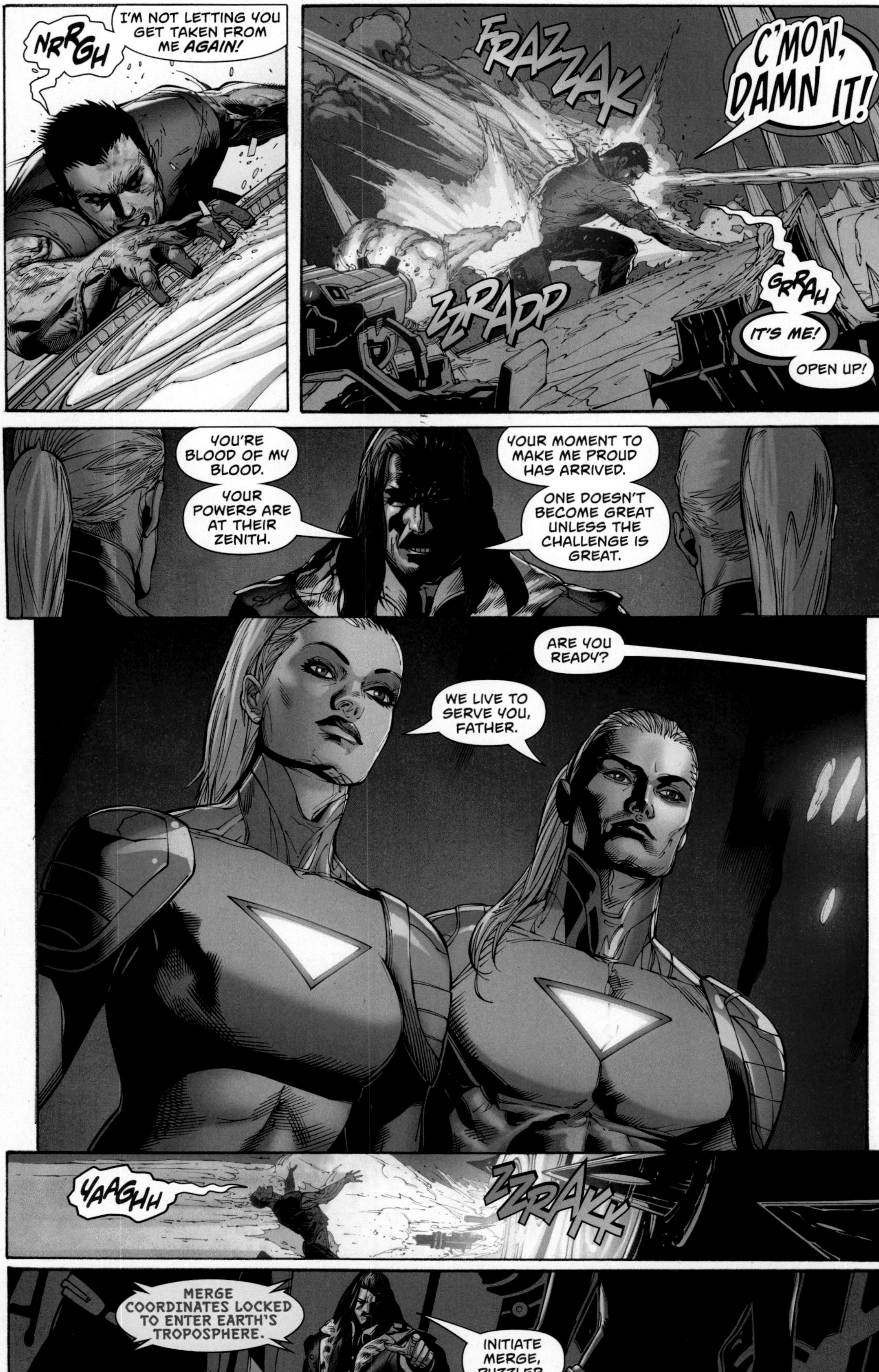
NRRGH
I'M NOT LETTING YOU GET TAKEN FROM ME AGAIN!
FRAZZAK
C'MON, DAMN IT!
ZZRADP
GRRAH
IT'S ME!
OPEN UP!
YOU'RE BLOOD OF MY BLOOD.
YOUR POWERS ARE AT THEIR ZENITH.
YOUR MOMENT TO MAKE ME PROUD HAS ARRIVED.
ONE DOESN'T BECOME GREAT UNLESS THE CHALLENGE IS GREAT.
ARE YOU READY?
WE LIVE TO SERVE YOU, FATHER.
YAAGHH
ZZRAKK
MERGE COORDINATES LOCKED TO ENTER EARTH'S TROPOSPHERE.
INITIATE MERGE, PUZZLER.

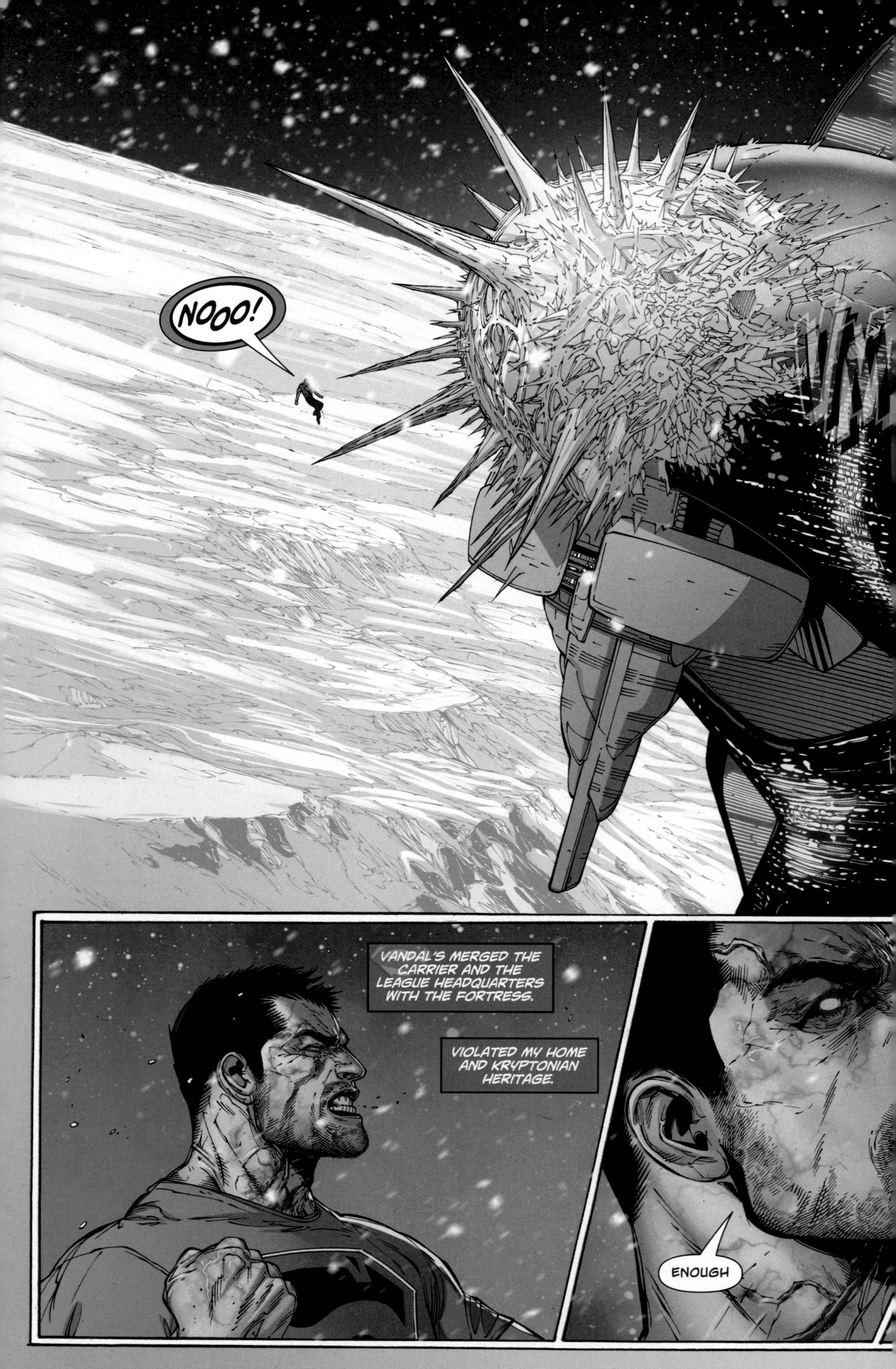
NOOO!
VANDAL'S MERGED THE CARRIER AND THE LEAGUE HEADQUARTERS WITH THE FORTRESS.
VIOLATED MY HOME AND KRYPTONIAN HERITAGE.
ENOUGH

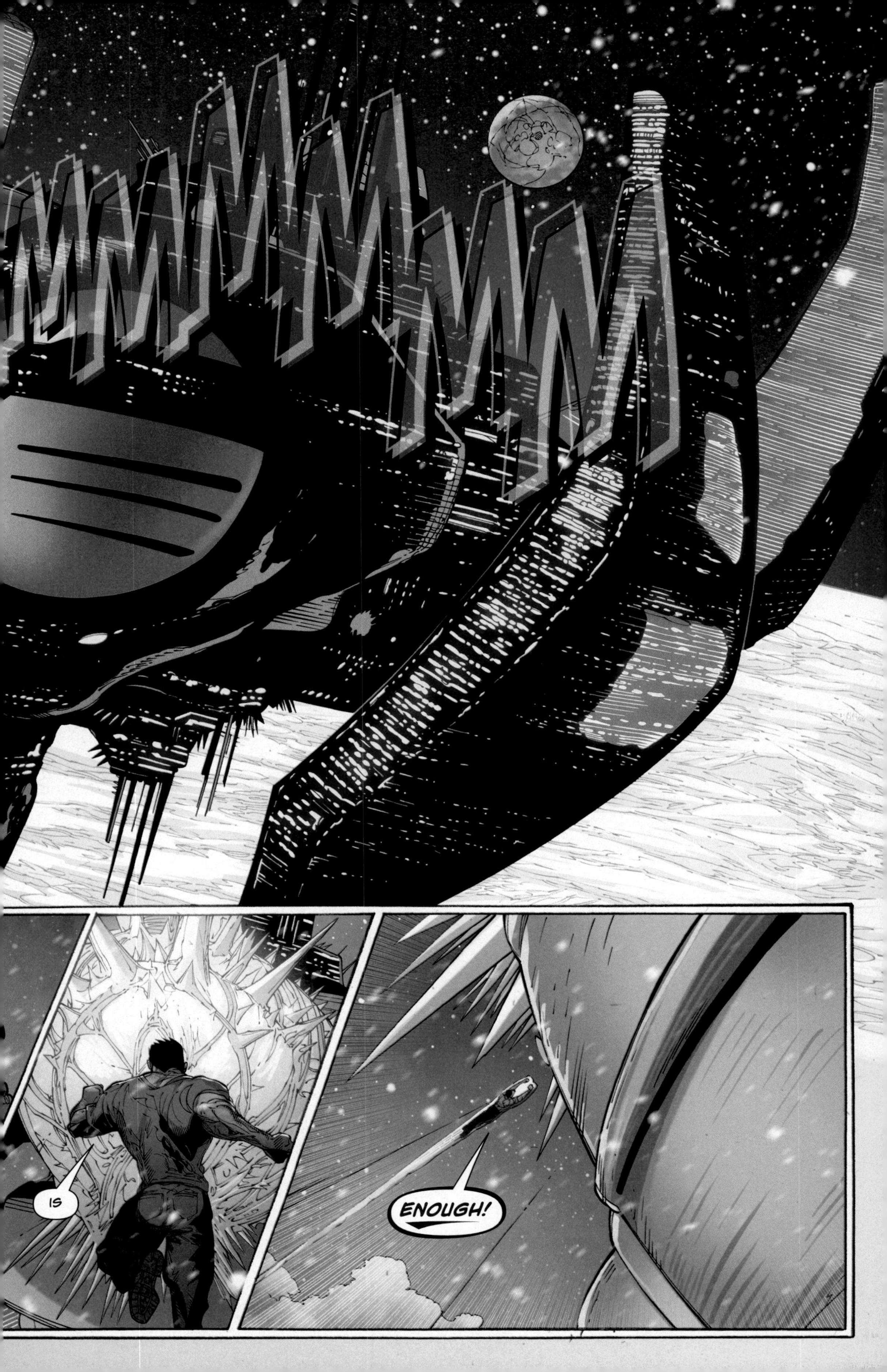

IS
ENOUGH!

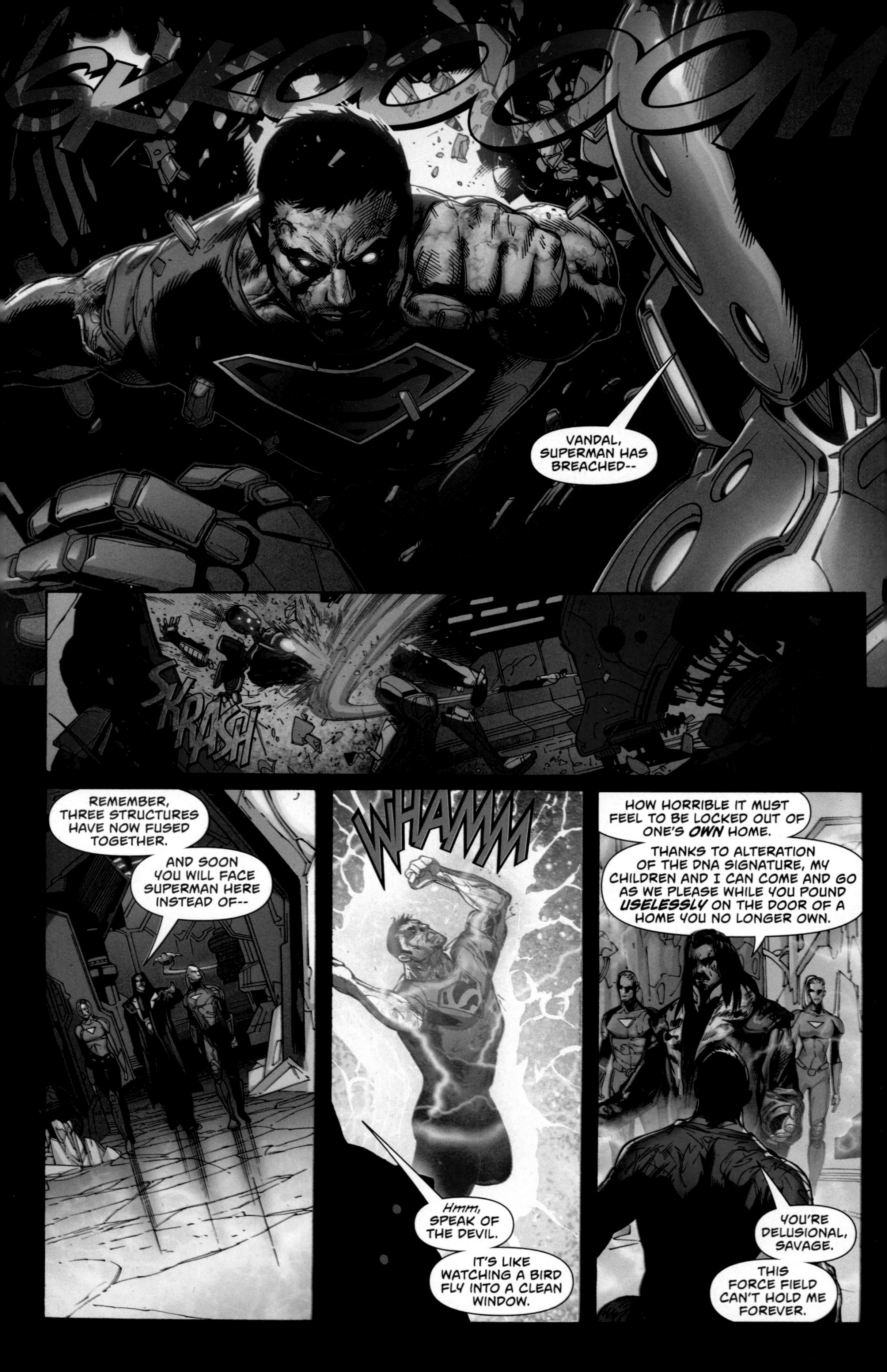

SKKOOOOOM
VANDAL, SUPERMAN HAS BREACHED--
SKRASH
REMEMBER, THREE STRUCTURES HAVE NOW FUSED TOGETHER.
AND SOON YOU WILL FACE SUPERMAN HERE INSTEAD OF--
WHAMM
Hmm, SPEAK OF THE DEVIL.
IT'S LIKE WATCHING A BIRD FLY INTO A CLEAN WINDOW.
HOW HORRIBLE IT MUST FEEL TO BE LOCKED OUT OF ONE'S ***OWN*** HOME.
THANKS TO ALTERATION OF THE DNA SIGNATURE, MY CHILDREN AND I CAN COME AND GO AS WE PLEASE WHILE YOU POUND ***USELESSLY*** ON THE DOOR OF A HOME YOU NO LONGER OWN.
YOU'RE DELUSIONAL, SAVAGE.
THIS FORCE FIELD CAN'T HOLD ME FOREVER.

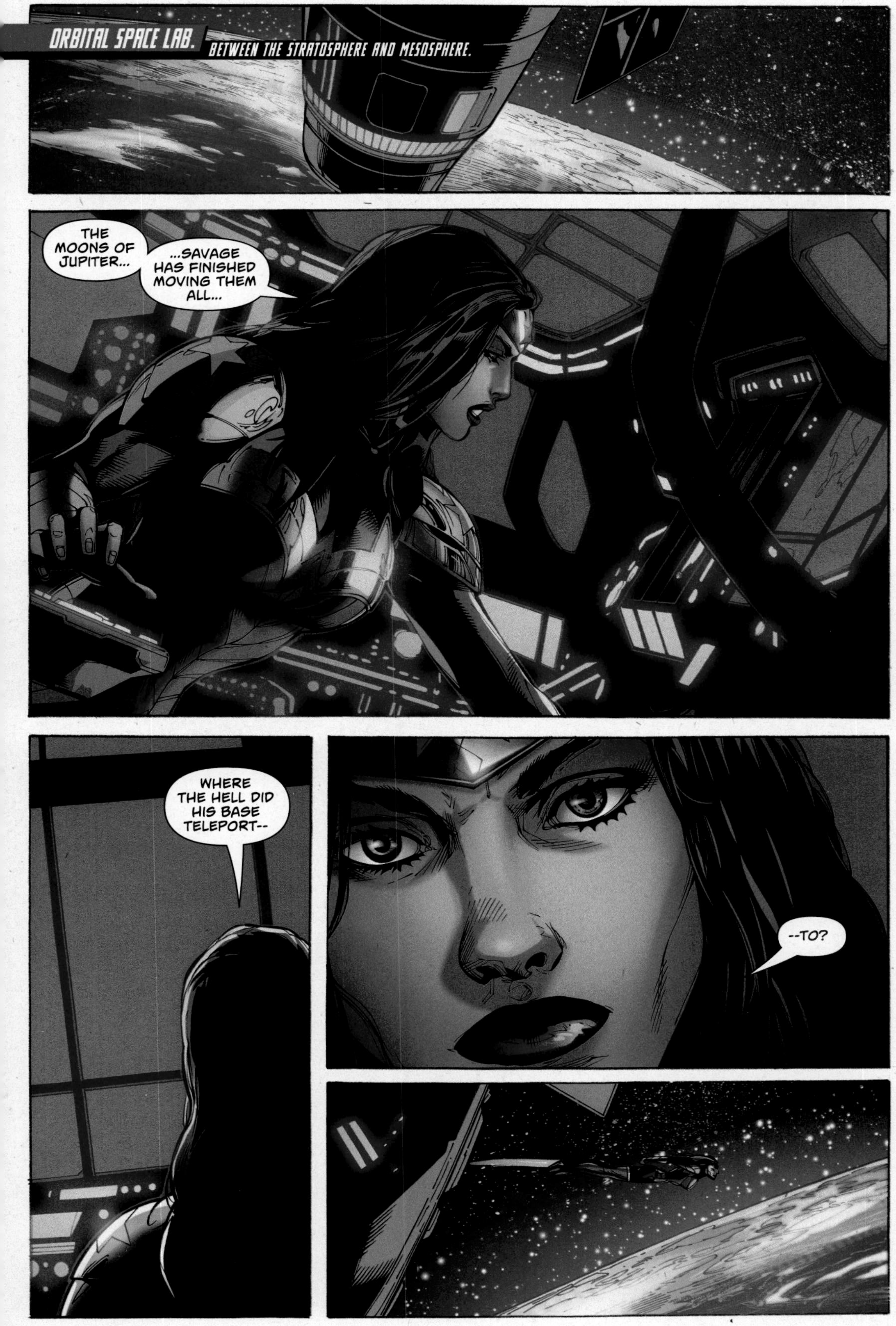
ORBITAL SPACE LAB. BETWEEN THE STRATOSPHERE AND MESOSPHERE.
THE MOONS OF JUPITER...
...SAVAGE HAS FINISHED MOVING THEM ALL...
WHERE THE HELL DID HIS BASE TELEPORT--
--TO?

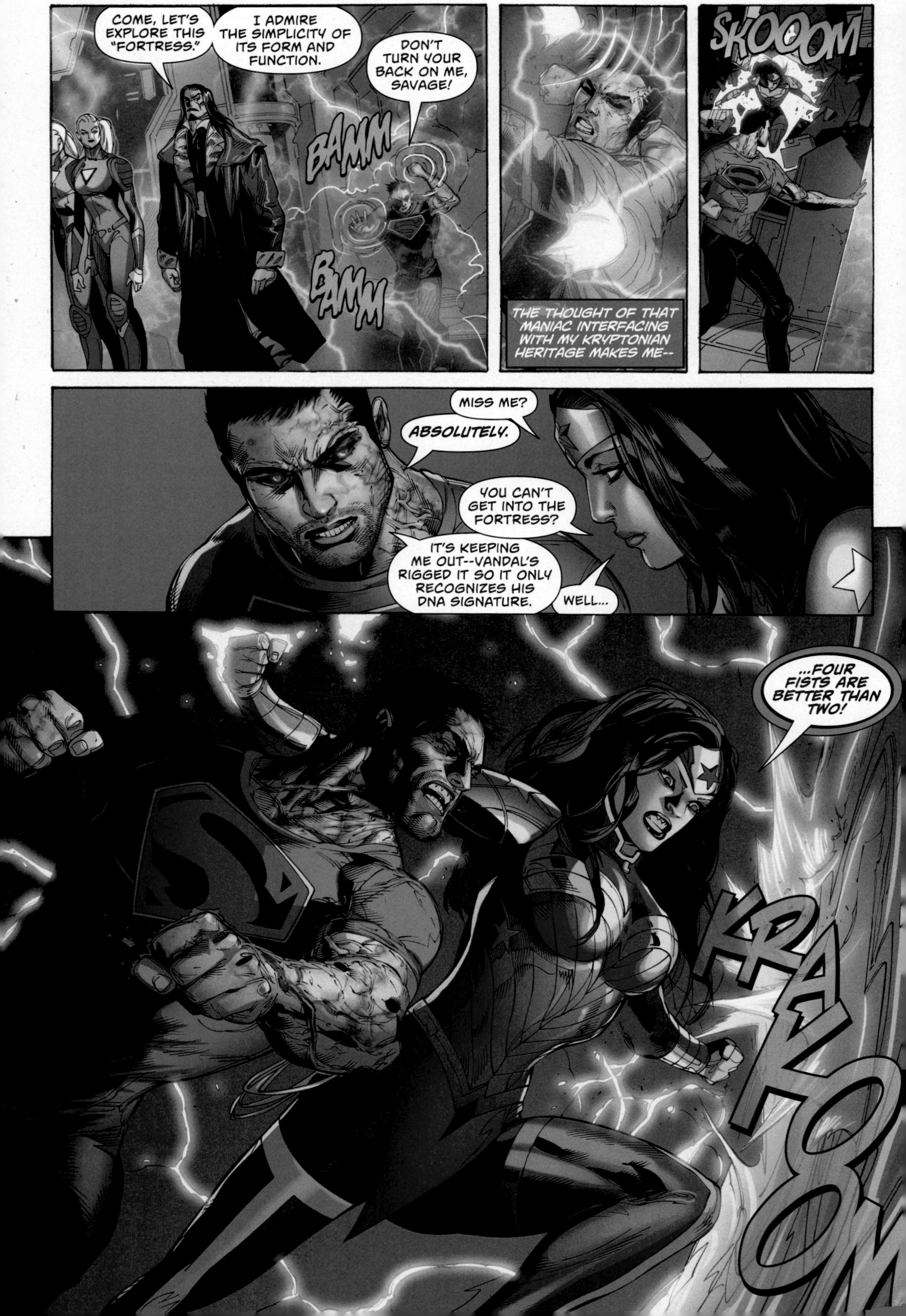

COME, LET'S EXPLORE THIS "FORTRESS."
I ADMIRE THE SIMPLICITY OF ITS FORM AND FUNCTION.
DON'T TURN YOUR BACK ON ME, SAVAGE!
BAMM
BAMM
THE THOUGHT OF THAT MANIAC INTERFACING WITH MY KRYPTONIAN HERITAGE MAKES ME--
SKOOOM
MISS ME?
ABSOLUTELY.
YOU CAN'T GET INTO THE FORTRESS?
IT'S KEEPING ME OUT--VANDAL'S RIGGED IT SO IT ONLY RECOGNIZES HIS DNA SIGNATURE.
WELL...
...FOUR FISTS ARE BETTER THAN TWO!
KRAKOOOM

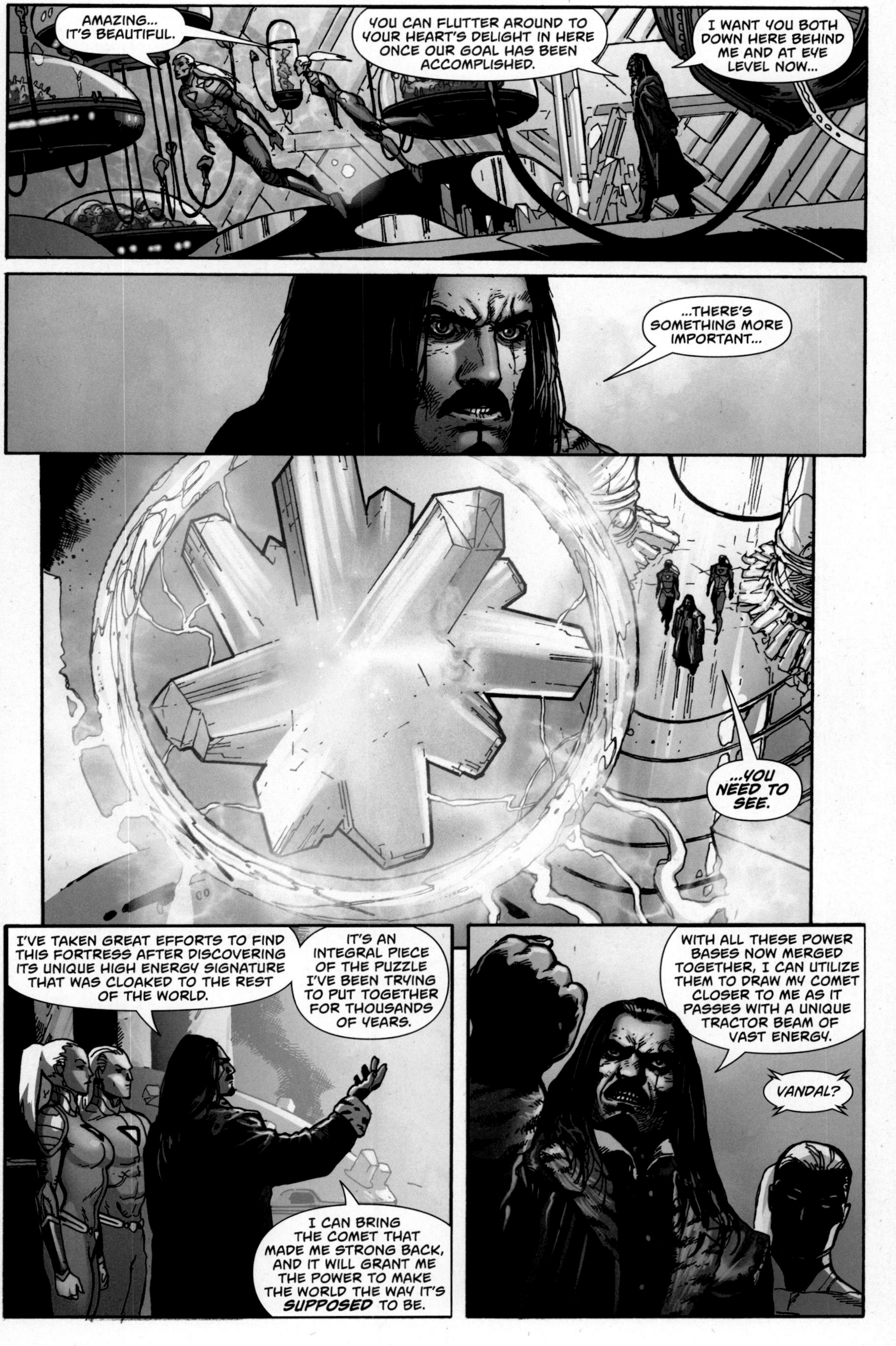
AMAZING... IT'S BEAUTIFUL.
YOU CAN FLUTTER AROUND TO YOUR HEART'S DELIGHT IN HERE ONCE OUR GOAL HAS BEEN ACCOMPLISHED.
I WANT YOU BOTH DOWN HERE BEHIND ME AND AT EYE LEVEL NOW...
...THERE'S SOMETHING MORE IMPORTANT...
...YOU NEED TO SEE.
I'VE TAKEN GREAT EFFORTS TO FIND THIS FORTRESS AFTER DISCOVERING ITS UNIQUE HIGH ENERGY SIGNATURE THAT WAS CLOAKED TO THE REST OF THE WORLD.
IT'S AN INTEGRAL PIECE OF THE PUZZLE I'VE BEEN TRYING TO PUT TOGETHER FOR THOUSANDS OF YEARS.
I CAN BRING THE COMET THAT MADE ME STRONG BACK, AND IT WILL GRANT ME THE POWER TO MAKE THE WORLD THE WAY IT'S SUPPOSED TO BE.
WITH ALL THESE POWER BASES NOW MERGED TOGETHER, I CAN UTILIZE THEM TO DRAW MY COMET CLOSER TO ME AS IT PASSES WITH A UNIQUE TRACTOR BEAM OF VAST ENERGY.
VANDAL?

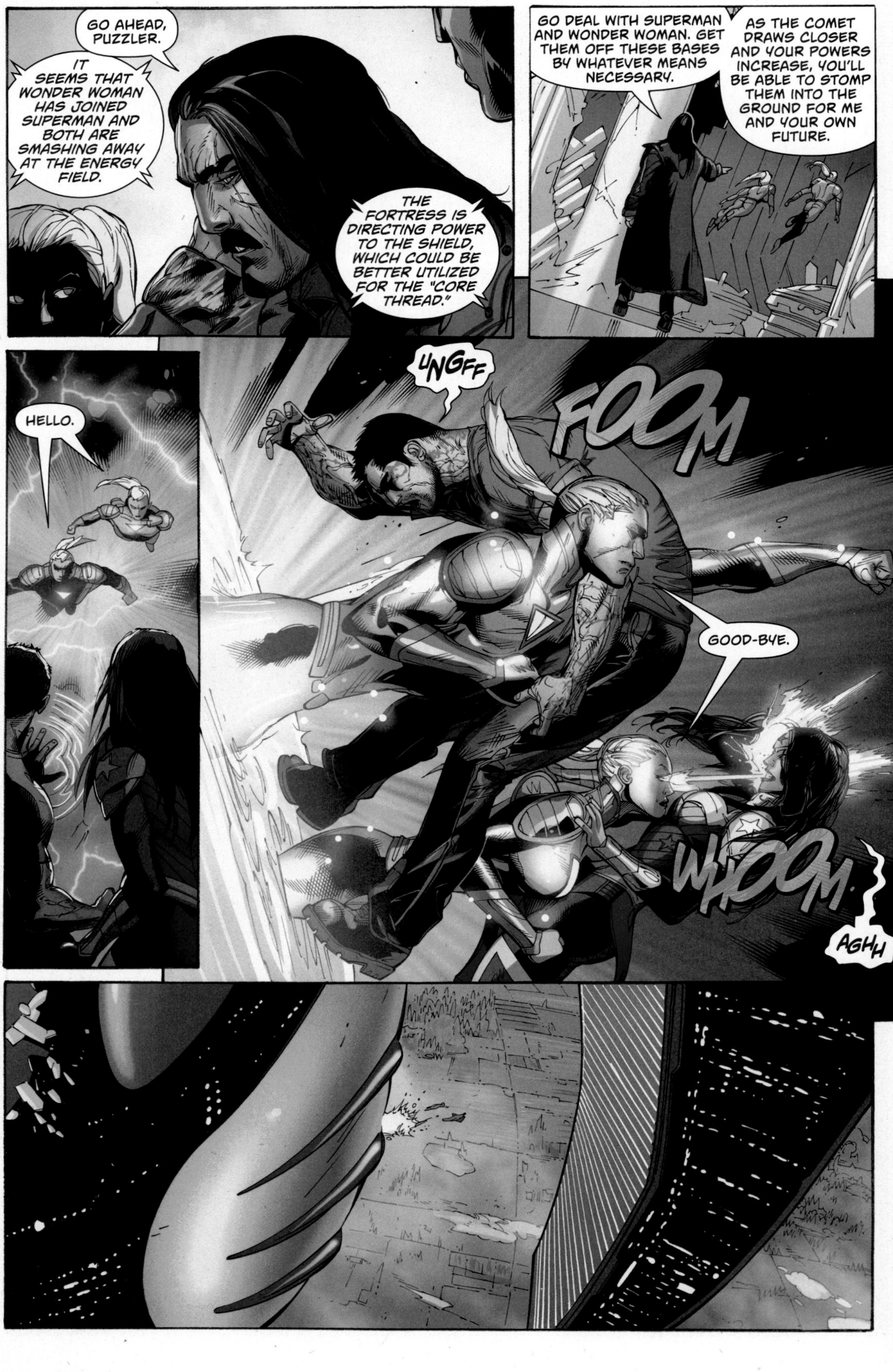
GO AHEAD, PUZZLER.
IT SEEMS THAT WONDER WOMAN HAS JOINED SUPERMAN AND BOTH ARE SMASHING AWAY AT THE ENERGY FIELD.
THE FORTRESS IS DIRECTING POWER TO THE SHIELD, WHICH COULD BE BETTER UTILIZED FOR THE "CORE THREAD."
GO DEAL WITH SUPERMAN AND WONDER WOMAN. GET THEM OFF THESE BASES BY WHATEVER MEANS NECESSARY.
AS THE COMET DRAWS CLOSER AND YOUR POWERS INCREASE, YOU'LL BE ABLE TO STOMP THEM INTO THE GROUND FOR ME AND YOUR OWN FUTURE.
HELLO.
UNGFF
FOOM
GOOD-BYE.
WHOOM
AGHH

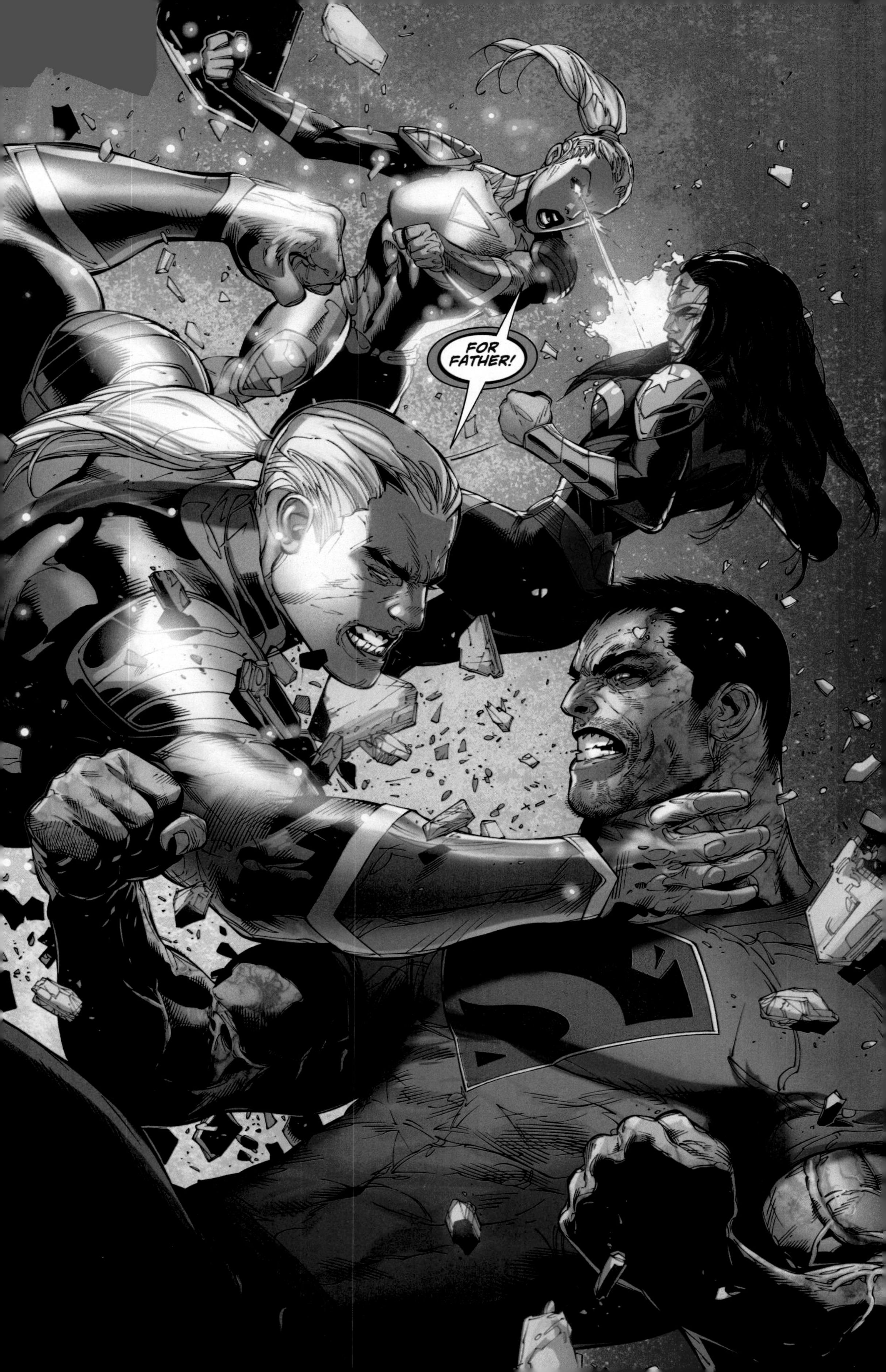
FOR FATHER!

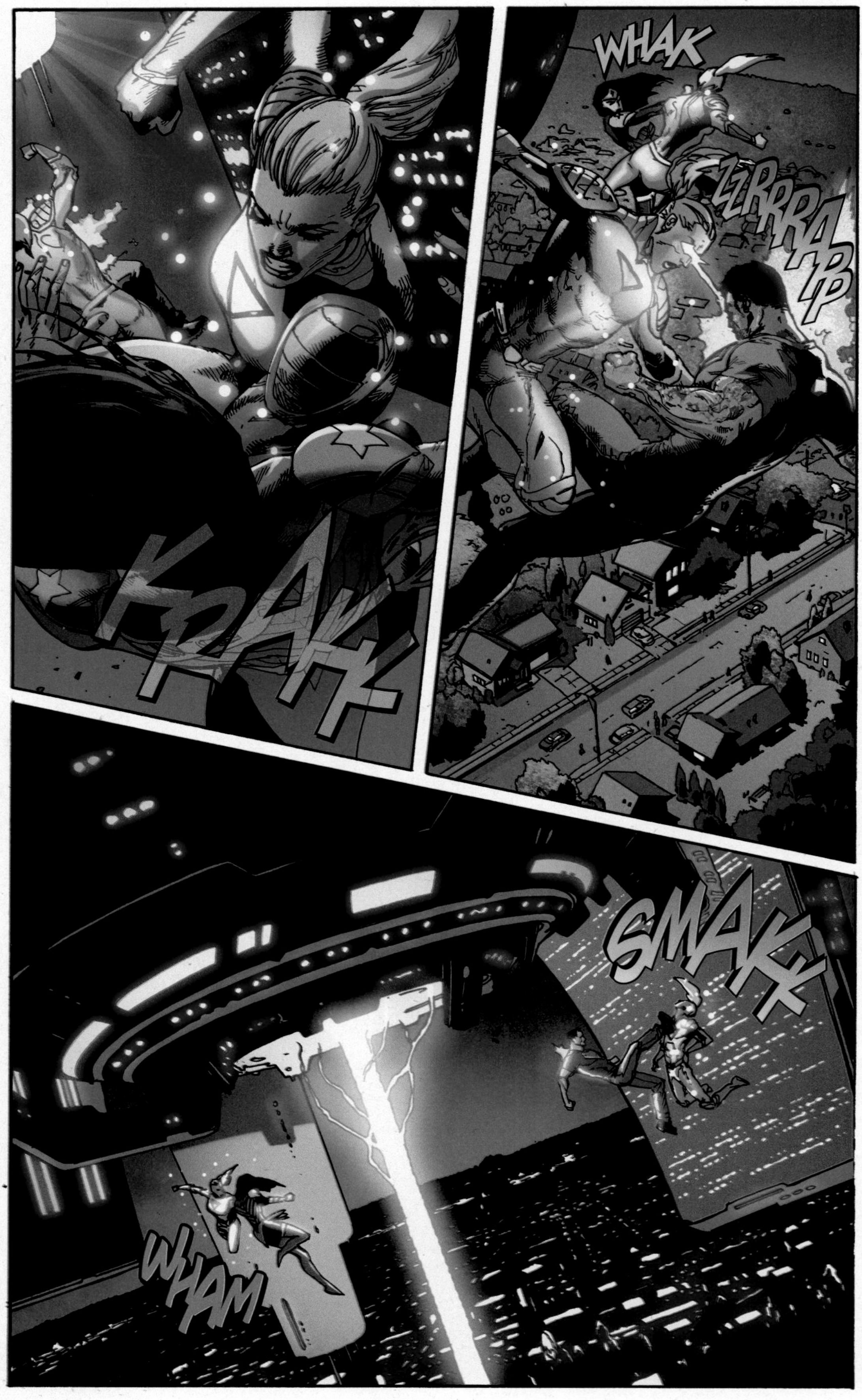
KRAKK
WHAK
ZZRRRAPP
SMAKK
WHAM

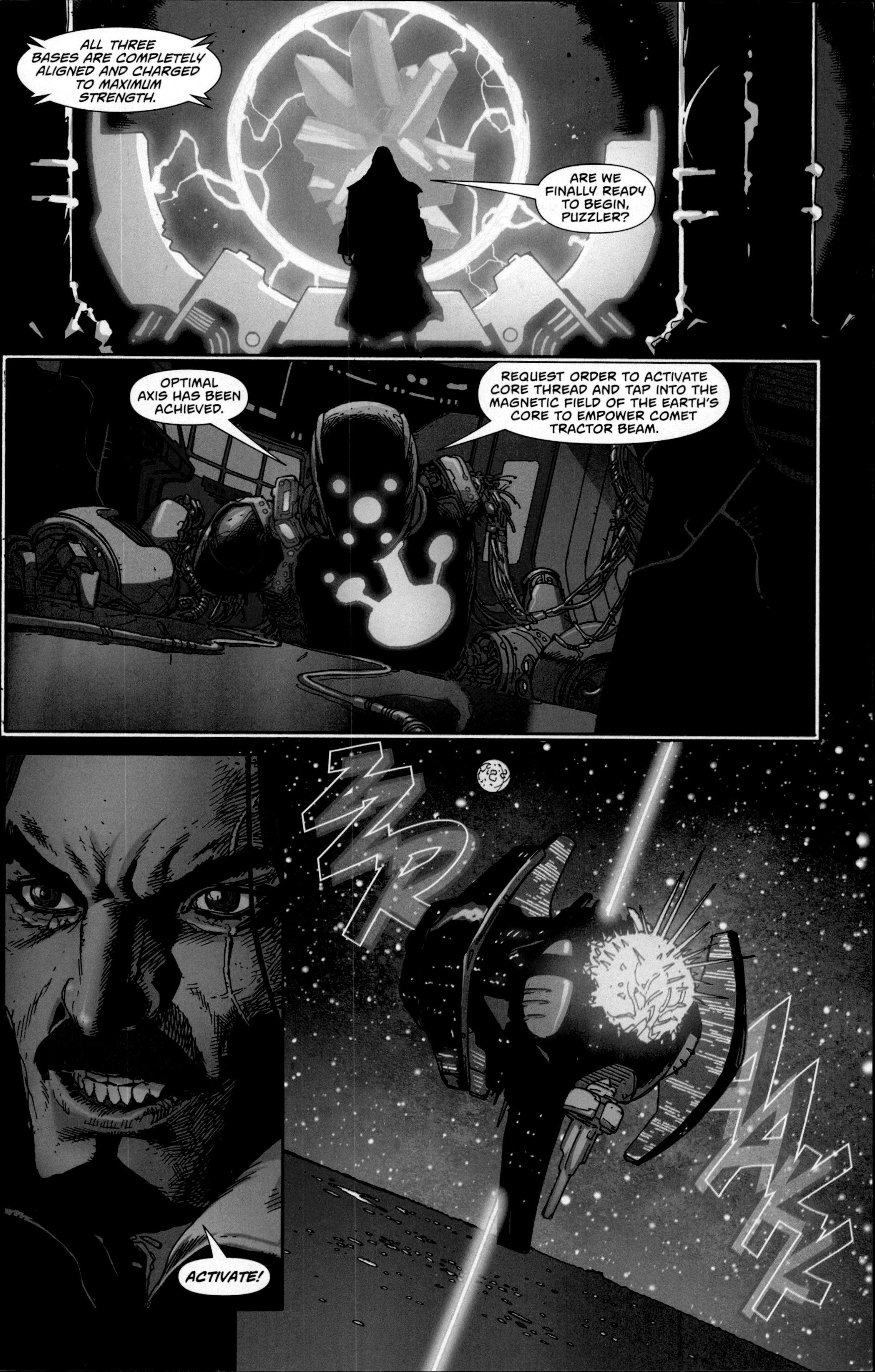
ALL THREE BASES ARE COMPLETELY ALIGNED AND CHARGED TO MAXIMUM STRENGTH.
ARE WE FINALLY READY TO BEGIN, PUZZLER?
OPTIMAL AXIS HAS BEEN ACHIEVED.
REQUEST ORDER TO ACTIVATE CORE THREAD AND TAP INTO THE MAGNETIC FIELD OF THE EARTH'S CORE TO EMPOWER COMET TRACTOR BEAM.
ACTIVATE!
ZZZRRAAAKK

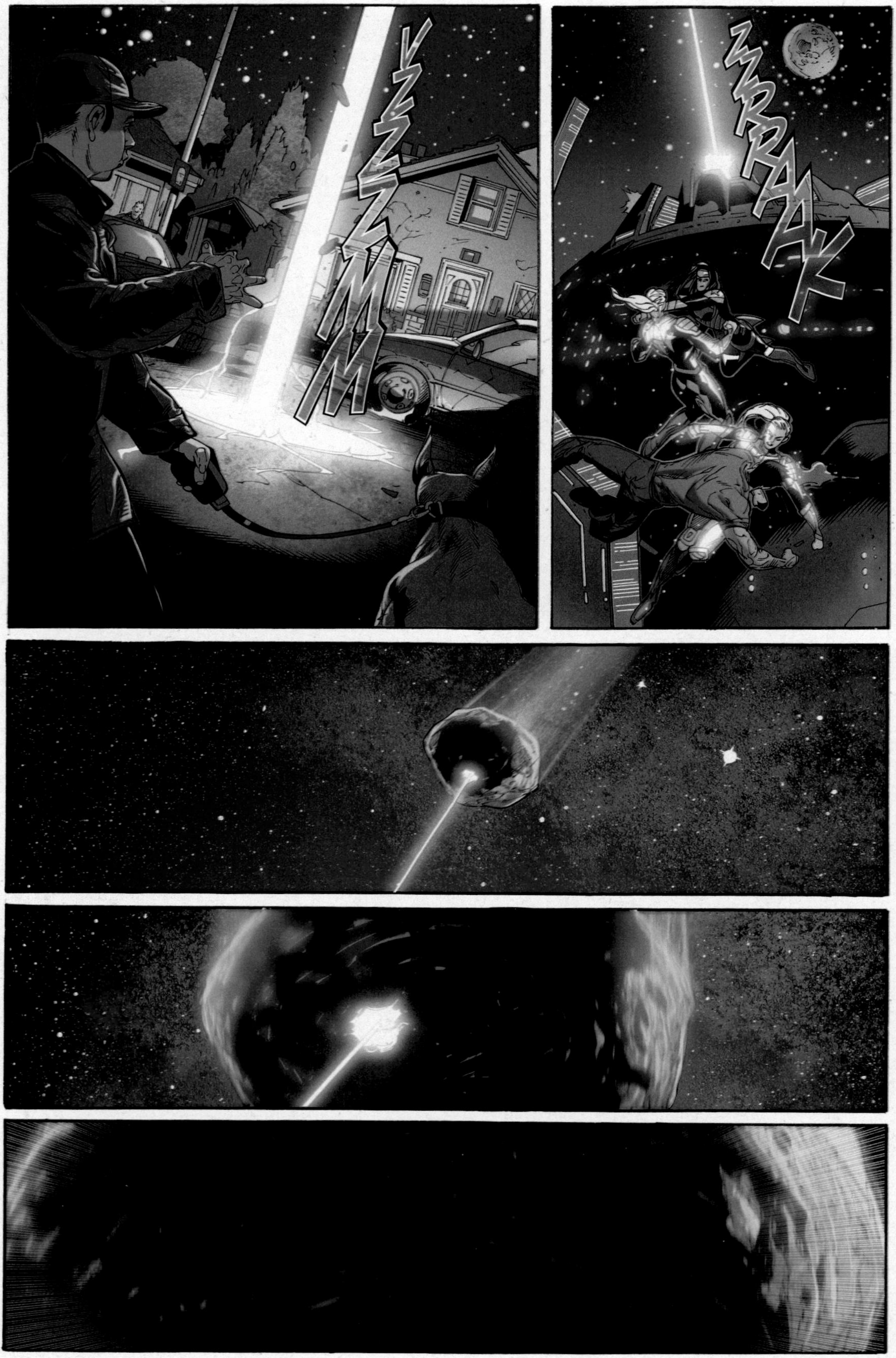
VZZZMMM
WRRAAK

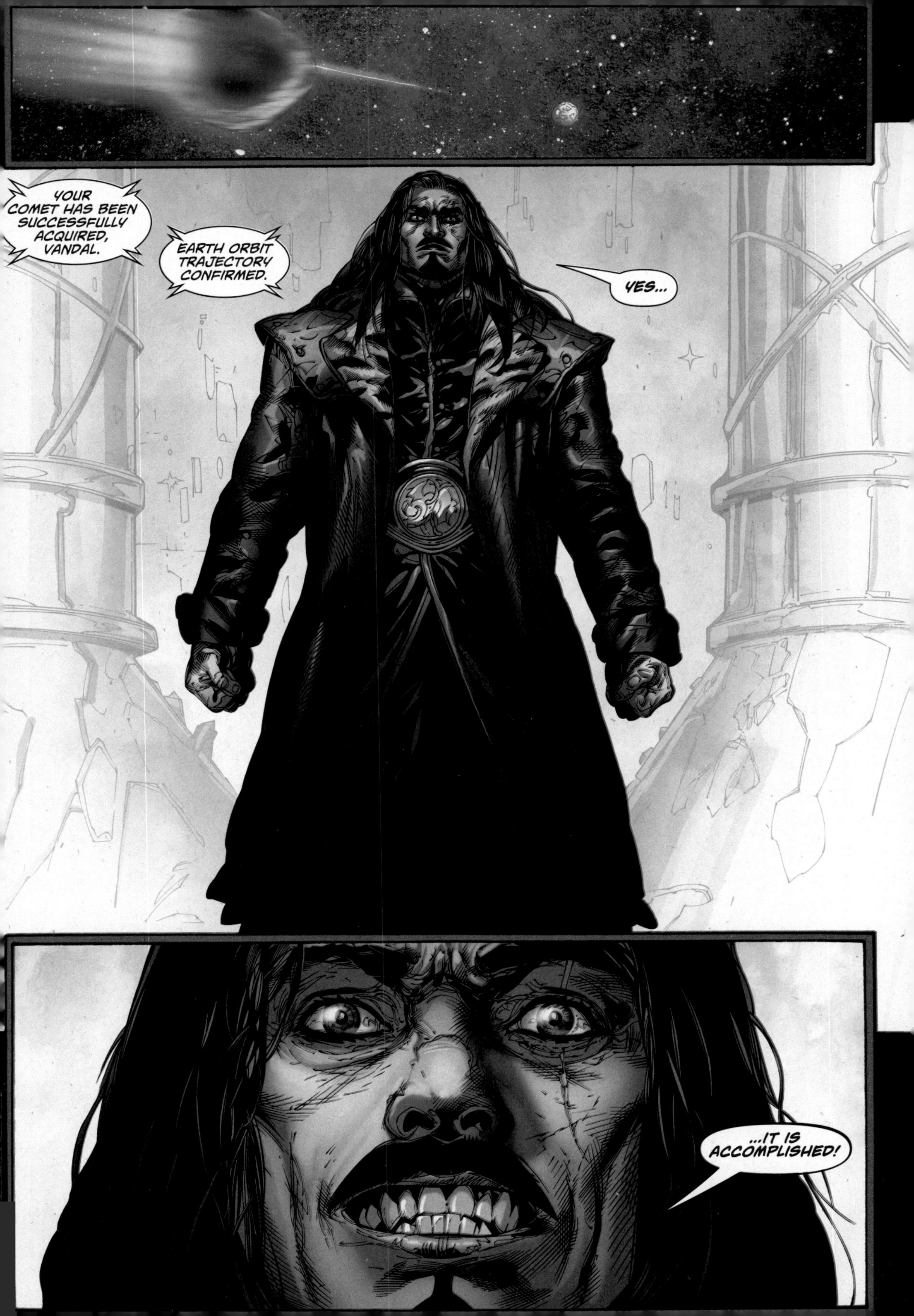
YOUR COMET HAS BEEN SUCCESSFULLY ACQUIRED, VANDAL.
EARTH ORBIT TRAJECTORY CONFIRMED.
YES...
...IT IS ACCOMPLISHED!

THE STRUCTURE'S DROPPING DOWN ON THAT ENERGY BEAM TOWARDS A POPULATED AREA BELOW!
WHAMM
AND THIS OTHER ENERGY BEAM CAN'T BE GOOD!
KRAKK
I'LL TAKE THE BASE--
AND I'LL TAKE THE TOP AND BLOCK THE BEAM!
KRAZAAK
RRGNN

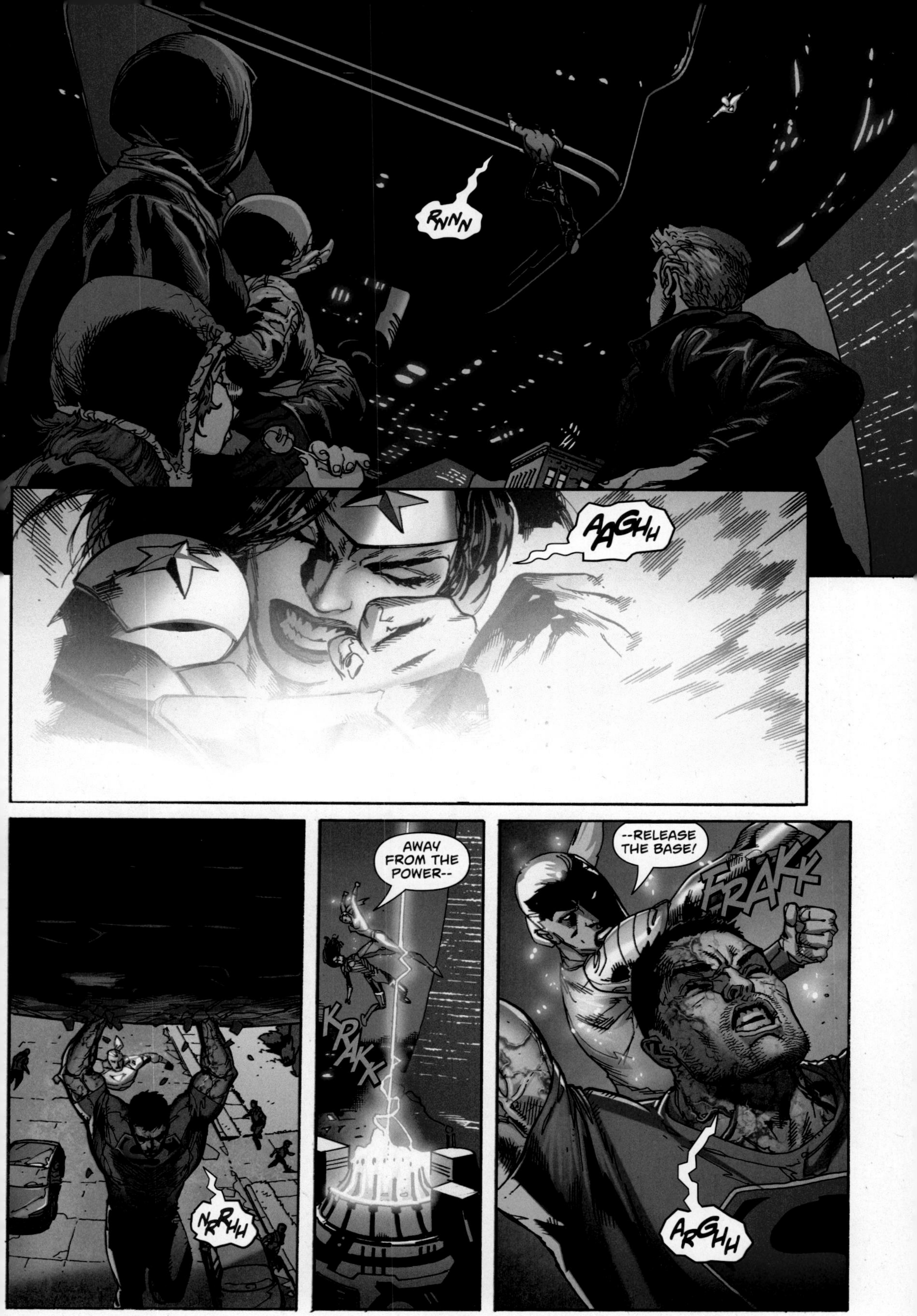
RNNN
AAGHH
NRRHH
AWAY FROM THE POWER--
KRAKK
--RELEASE THE BASE!
FRAKK
ARGHH

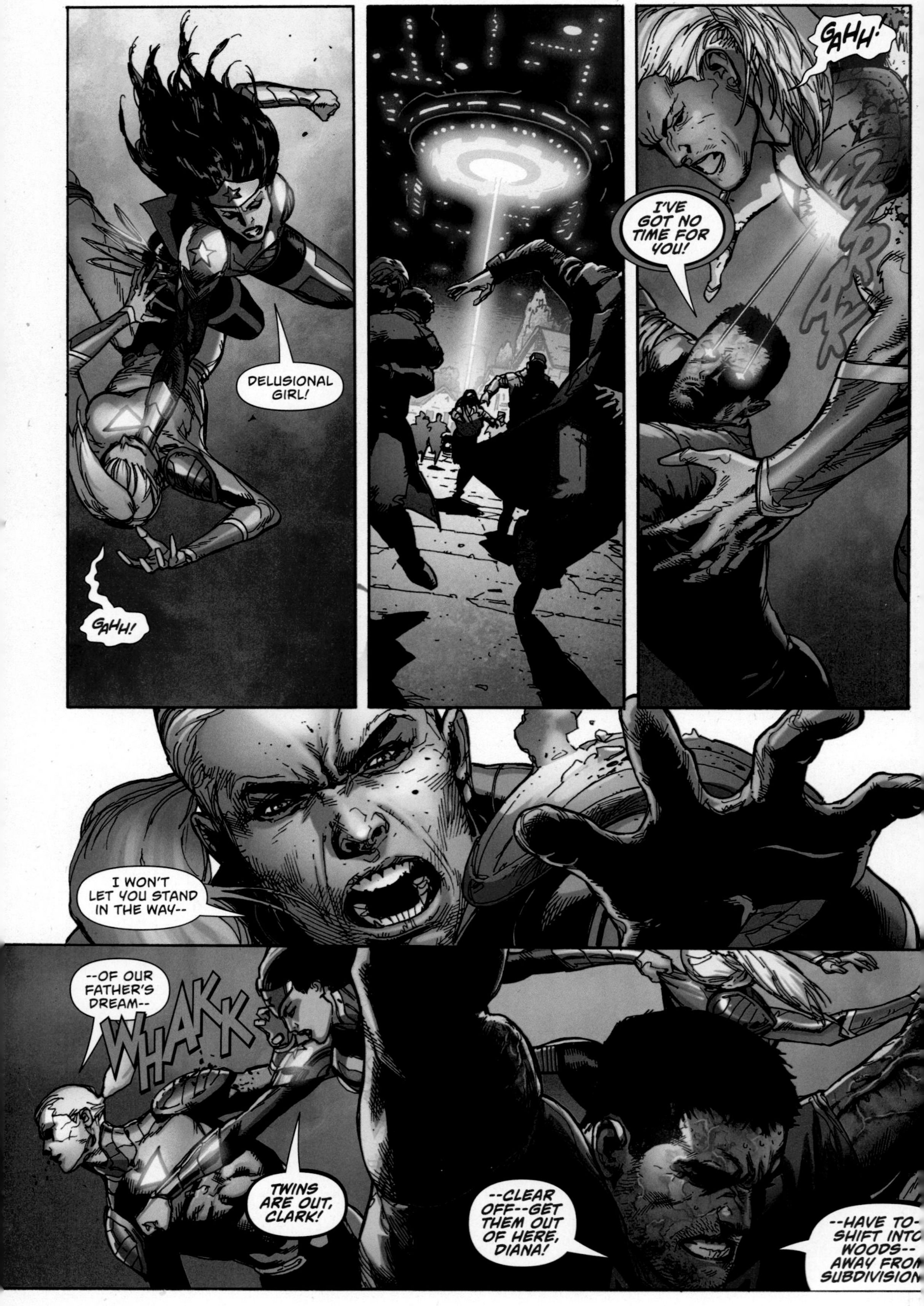
DELUSIONAL GIRL!
GAHH!
GAHH!
I'VE GOT NO TIME FOR YOU!
I WON'T LET YOU STAND IN THE WAY--
--OF OUR FATHER'S DREAM--
WHAKK
TWINS ARE OUT, CLARK!
--CLEAR OFF--GET THEM OUT OF HERE, DIANA!
--HAVE TO-SHIFT INTO WOODS--AWAY FROM SUBDIVISION

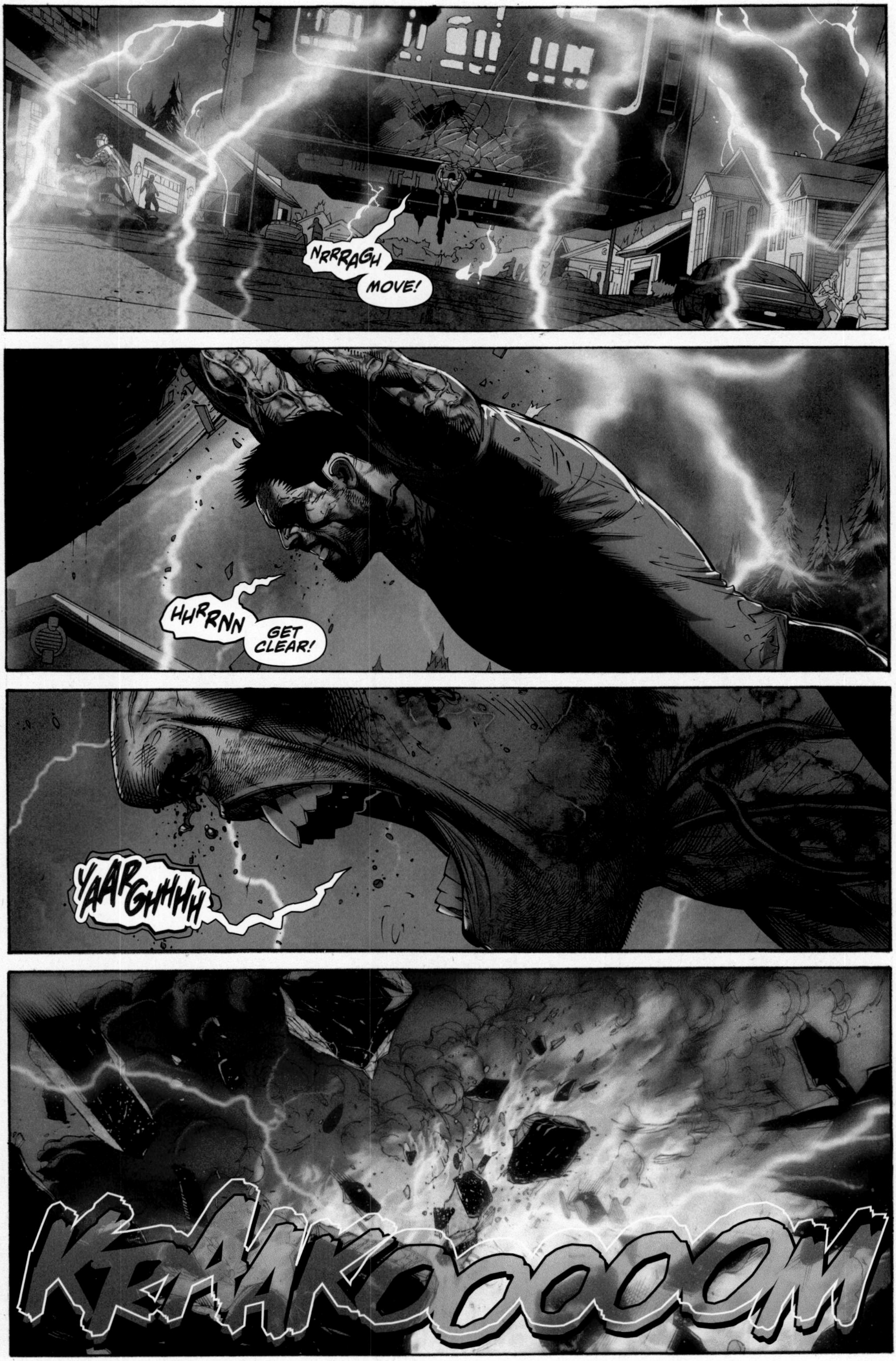
NRRRAGH
MOVE!
HHRRNN
GET CLEAR!
YAARGHHHH
KRAAKOOOOOM

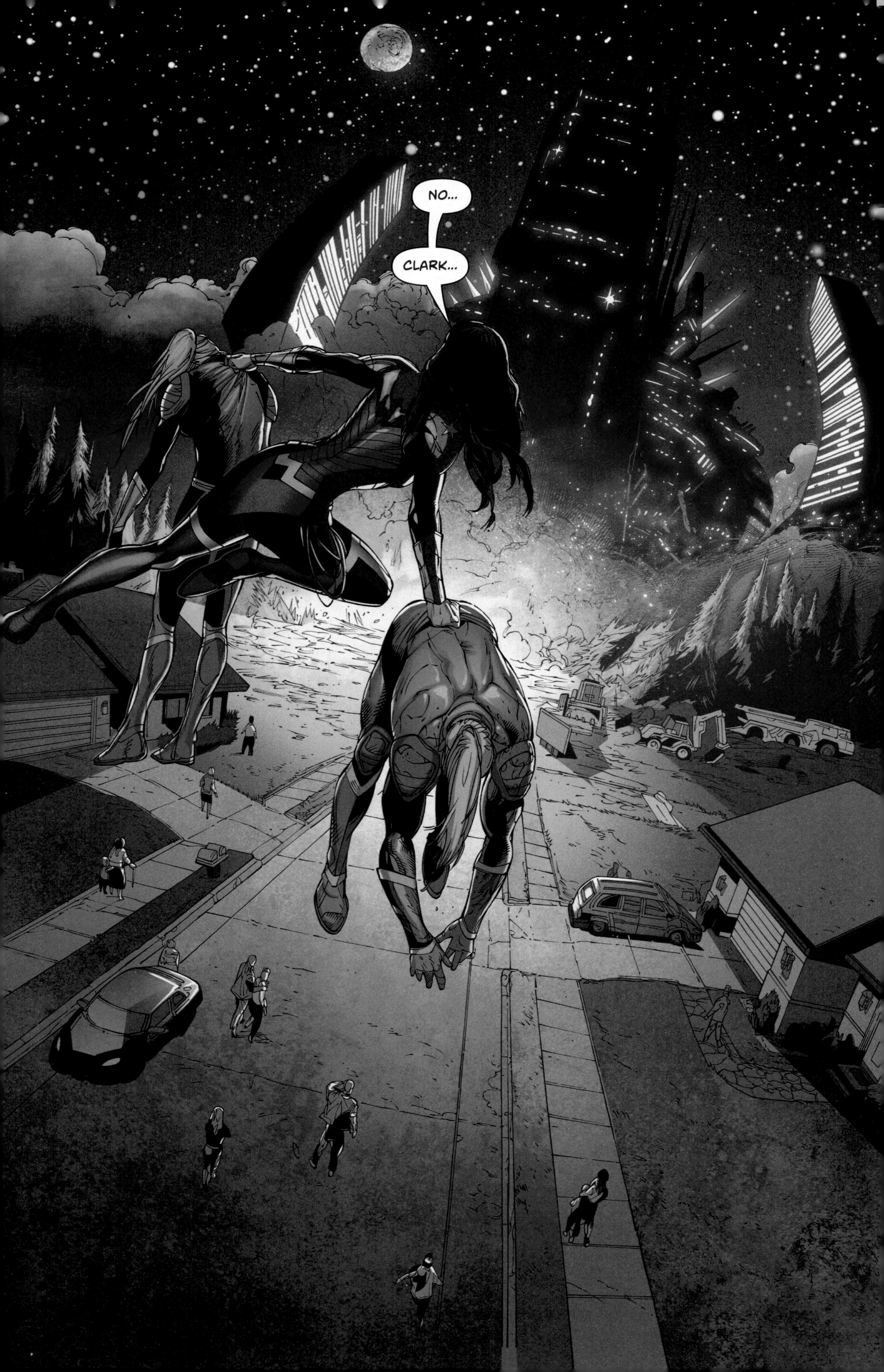
NO...
CLARK...

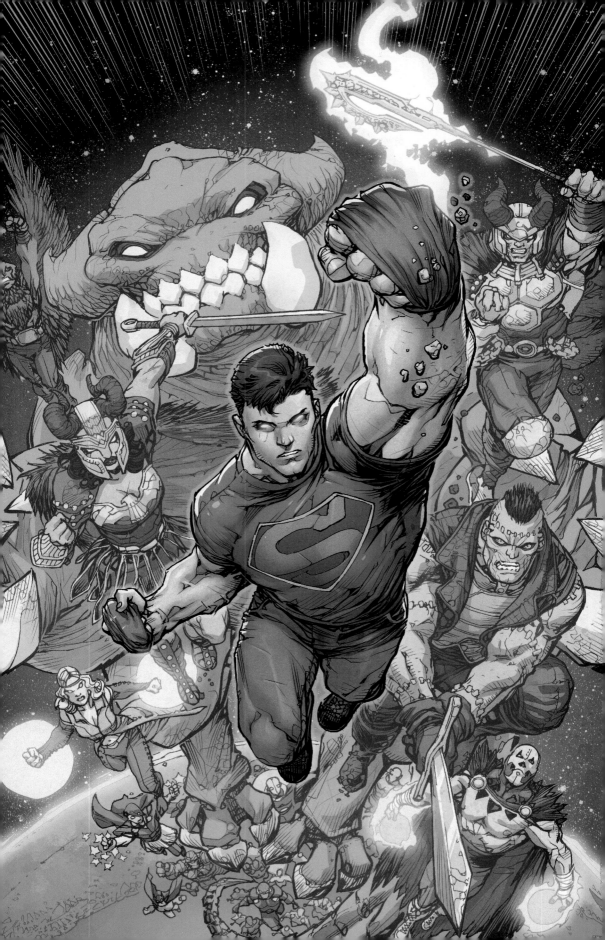

SACRIFICE

GENE LUEN YANG writer **JACK HERBERT** artist **HI-FI BLOND WIL QUINTANA** colorists **STEVE WANDS** letterer **HOWARD PORTER HI-FI** cover

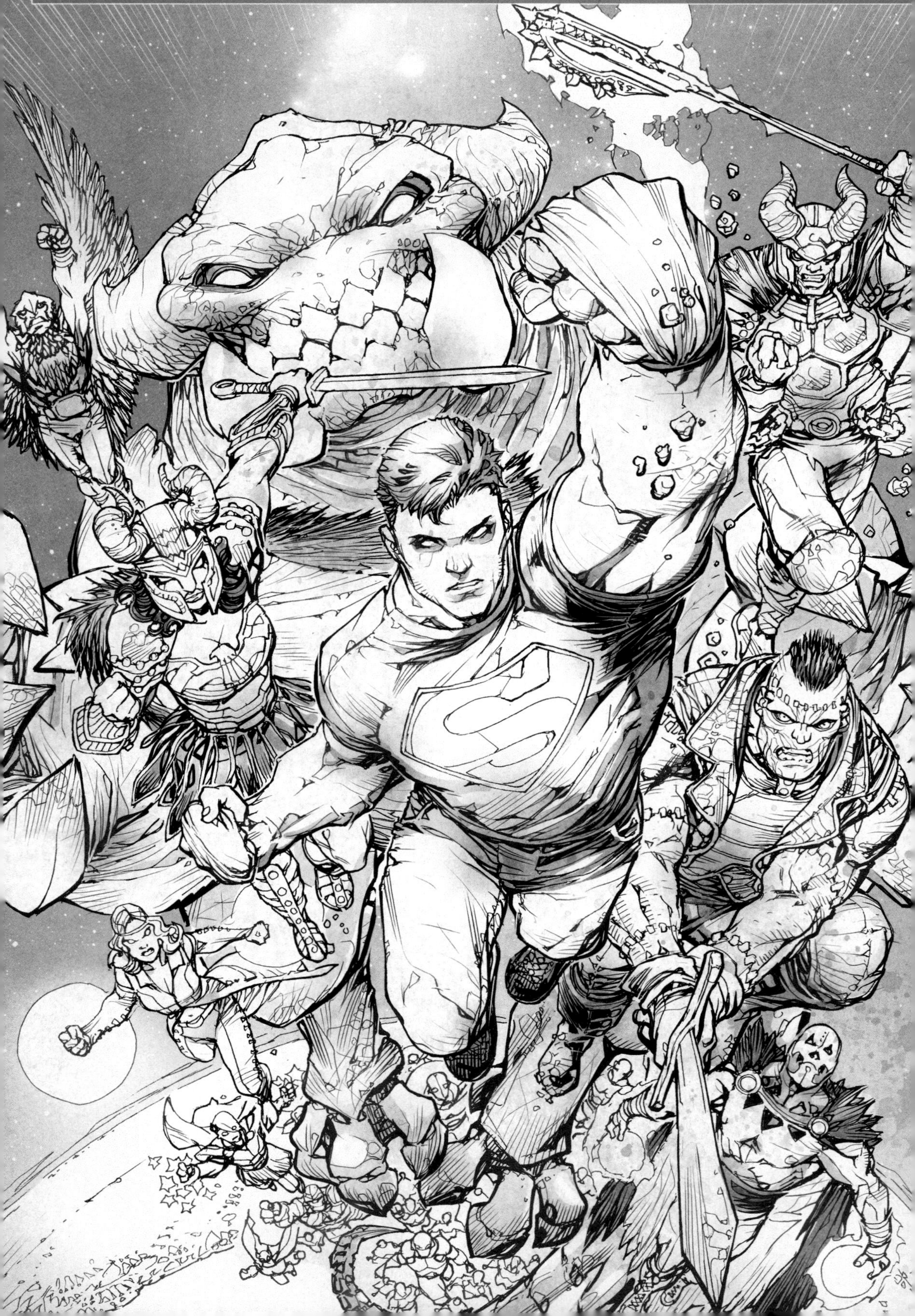

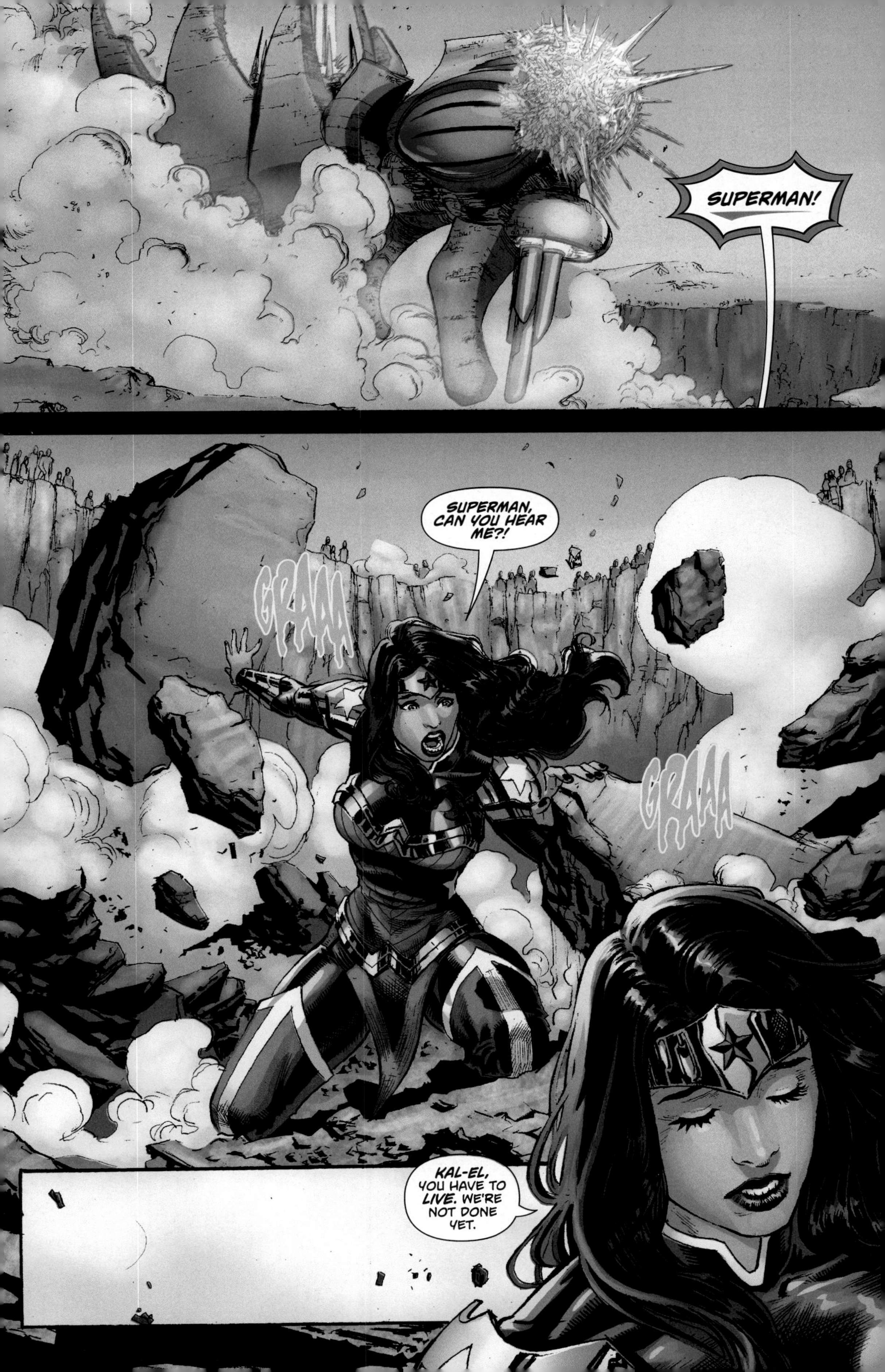
SUPERMAN!
SUPERMAN, CAN YOU HEAR ME?!
GRAAA
GRAAA
KAL-EL, YOU HAVE TO LIVE. WE'RE NOT DONE YET.

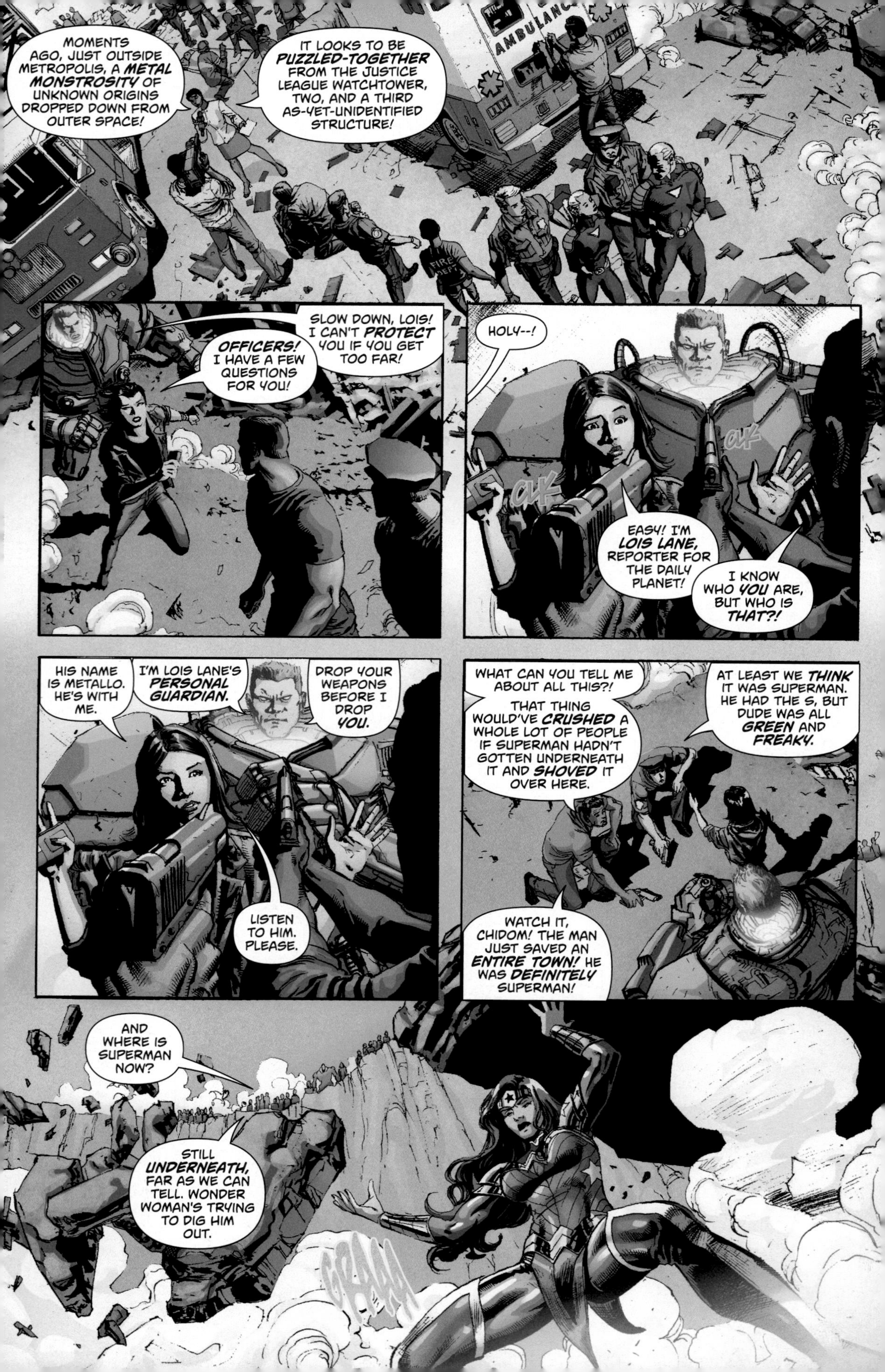
MOMENTS AGO, JUST OUTSIDE METROPOLIS, A METAL MONSTROSITY OF UNKNOWN ORIGINS DROPPED DOWN FROM OUTER SPACE!
IT LOOKS TO BE PUZZLED-TOGETHER FROM THE JUSTICE LEAGUE WATCHTOWER, TWO, AND A THIRD AS-YET-UNIDENTIFIED STRUCTURE!
AMBULANCE
FIRE DEPT
SLOW DOWN, LOIS! I CAN'T PROTECT YOU IF YOU GET TOO FAR!
OFFICERS! I HAVE A FEW QUESTIONS FOR YOU!
HOLY--!
CLK
CLK
EASY! I'M LOIS LANE, REPORTER FOR THE DAILY PLANET!
I KNOW WHO YOU ARE, BUT WHO IS THAT?!
HIS NAME IS METALLO. HE'S WITH ME.
I'M LOIS LANE'S PERSONAL GUARDIAN.
DROP YOUR WEAPONS BEFORE I DROP YOU.
LISTEN TO HIM. PLEASE.
WHAT CAN YOU TELL ME ABOUT ALL THIS?!
THAT THING WOULD'VE CRUSHED A WHOLE LOT OF PEOPLE IF SUPERMAN HADN'T GOTTEN UNDERNEATH IT AND SHOVED IT OVER HERE.
AT LEAST WE THINK IT WAS SUPERMAN. HE HAD THE S, BUT DUDE WAS ALL GREEN AND FREAKY.
WATCH IT, CHIDOM! THE MAN JUST SAVED AN ENTIRE TOWN! HE WAS DEFINITELY SUPERMAN!
AND WHERE IS SUPERMAN NOW?
STILL UNDERNEATH, FAR AS WE CAN TELL. WONDER WOMAN'S TRYING TO DIG HIM OUT.
GRAAA

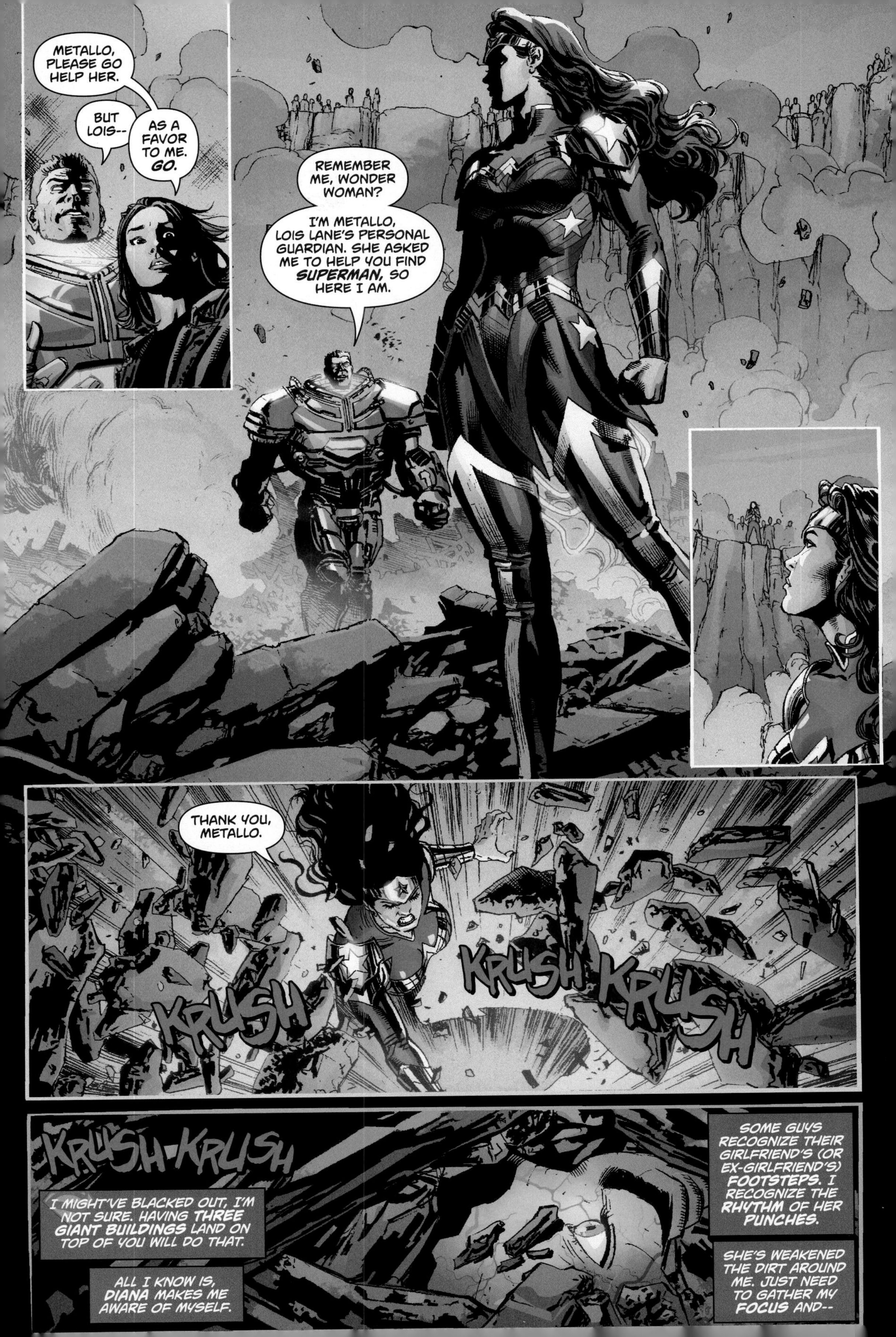

METALLO, PLEASE GO HELP HER.
BUT LOIS--
AS A FAVOR TO ME. GO.
REMEMBER ME, WONDER WOMAN?
I'M METALLO, LOIS LANE'S PERSONAL GUARDIAN. SHE ASKED ME TO HELP YOU FIND SUPERMAN, SO HERE I AM.
THANK YOU, METALLO.
KRUSH
KRUSH KRUSH
KRUSH-KRUSH
I MIGHT'VE BLACKED OUT, I'M NOT SURE. HAVING THREE GIANT BUILDINGS LAND ON TOP OF YOU WILL DO THAT.
ALL I KNOW IS, DIANA MAKES ME AWARE OF MYSELF.
SOME GUYS RECOGNIZE THEIR GIRLFRIEND'S (OR EX-GIRLFRIEND'S) FOOTSTEPS. I RECOGNIZE THE RHYTHM OF HER PUNCHES.
SHE'S WEAKENED THE DIRT AROUND ME. JUST NEED TO GATHER MY FOCUS AND--

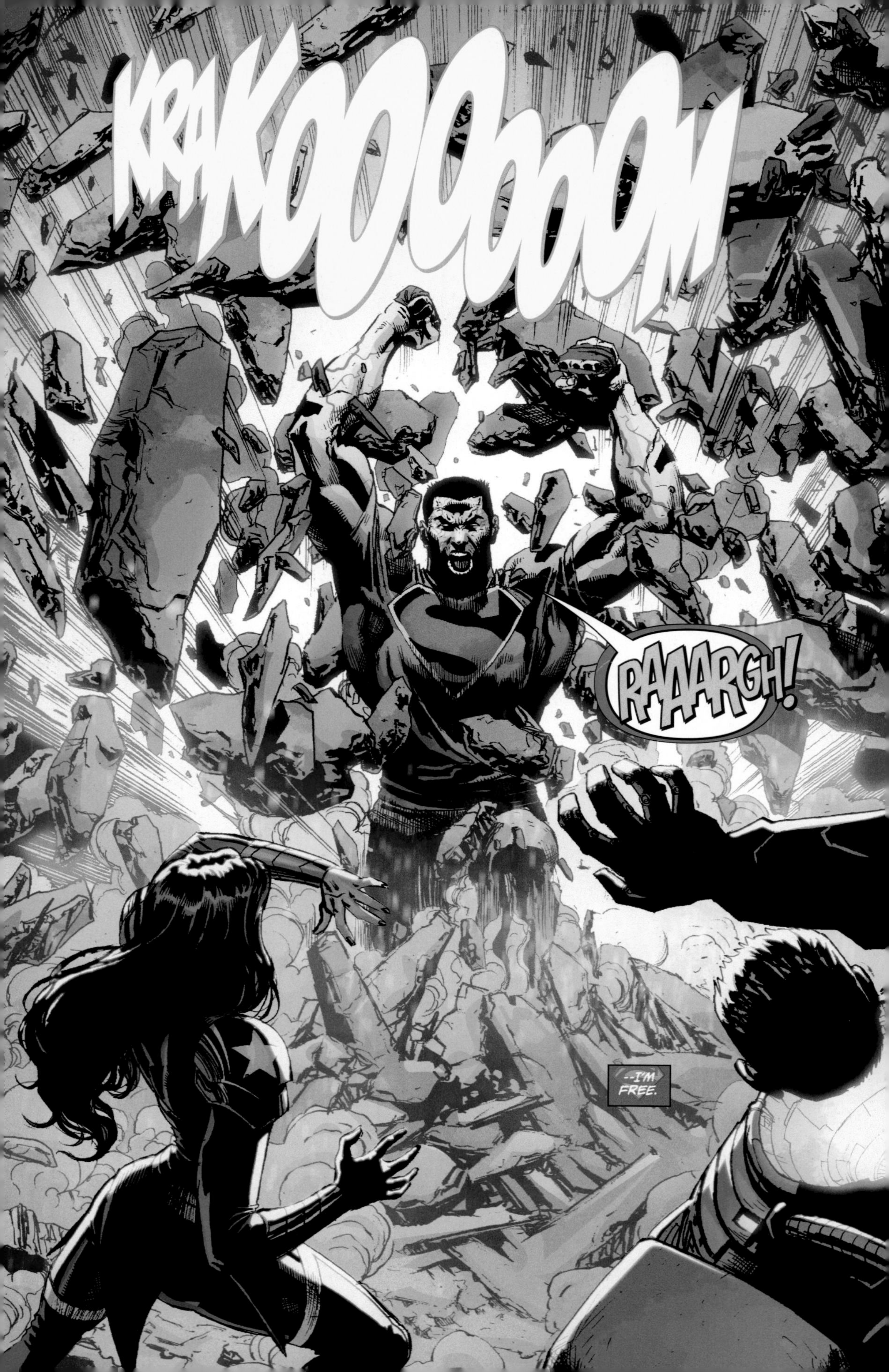
KRAKOOOOOOM
RAAARGH!
--I'M FREE.

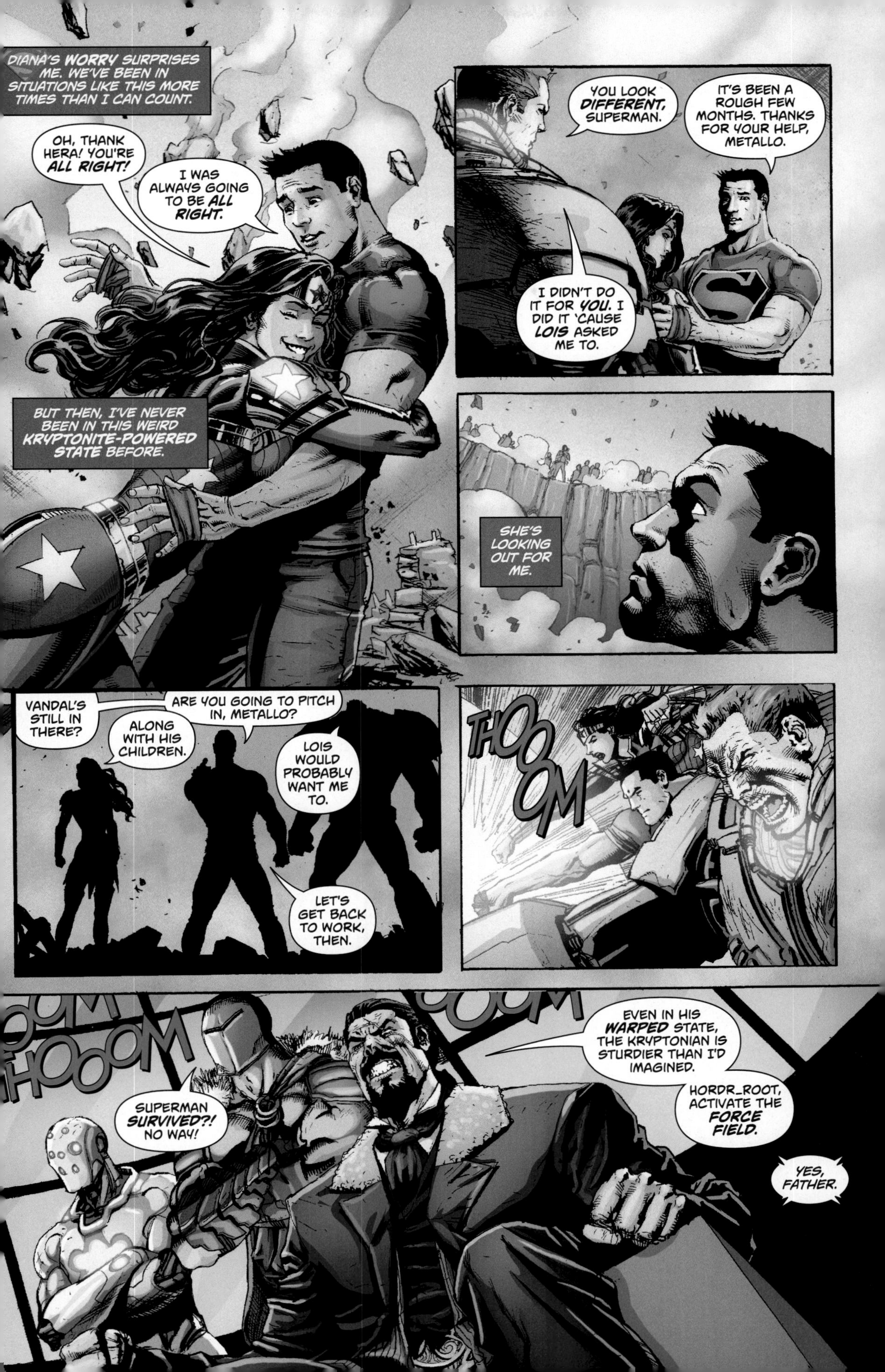
DIANA'S WORRY SURPRISES ME. WE'VE BEEN IN SITUATIONS LIKE THIS MORE TIMES THAN I CAN COUNT.
OH, THANK HERA! YOU'RE ALL RIGHT!
I WAS ALWAYS GOING TO BE ALL RIGHT.
BUT THEN, I'VE NEVER BEEN IN THIS WEIRD KRYPTONITE-POWERED STATE BEFORE.
YOU LOOK DIFFERENT, SUPERMAN.
IT'S BEEN A ROUGH FEW MONTHS. THANKS FOR YOUR HELP, METALLO.
I DIDN'T DO IT FOR YOU. I DID IT 'CAUSE LOIS ASKED ME TO.
SHE'S LOOKING OUT FOR ME.
VANDAL'S STILL IN THERE?
ALONG WITH HIS CHILDREN.
ARE YOU GOING TO PITCH IN, METALLO?
LOIS WOULD PROBABLY WANT ME TO.
LET'S GET BACK TO WORK, THEN.
THOOOM
OOOM
THOOOM
OOOM
EVEN IN HIS WARPED STATE, THE KRYPTONIAN IS STURDIER THAN I'D IMAGINED.
HORDR_ROOT, ACTIVATE THE FORCE FIELD.
SUPERMAN SURVIVED?! NO WAY!
YES, FATHER.

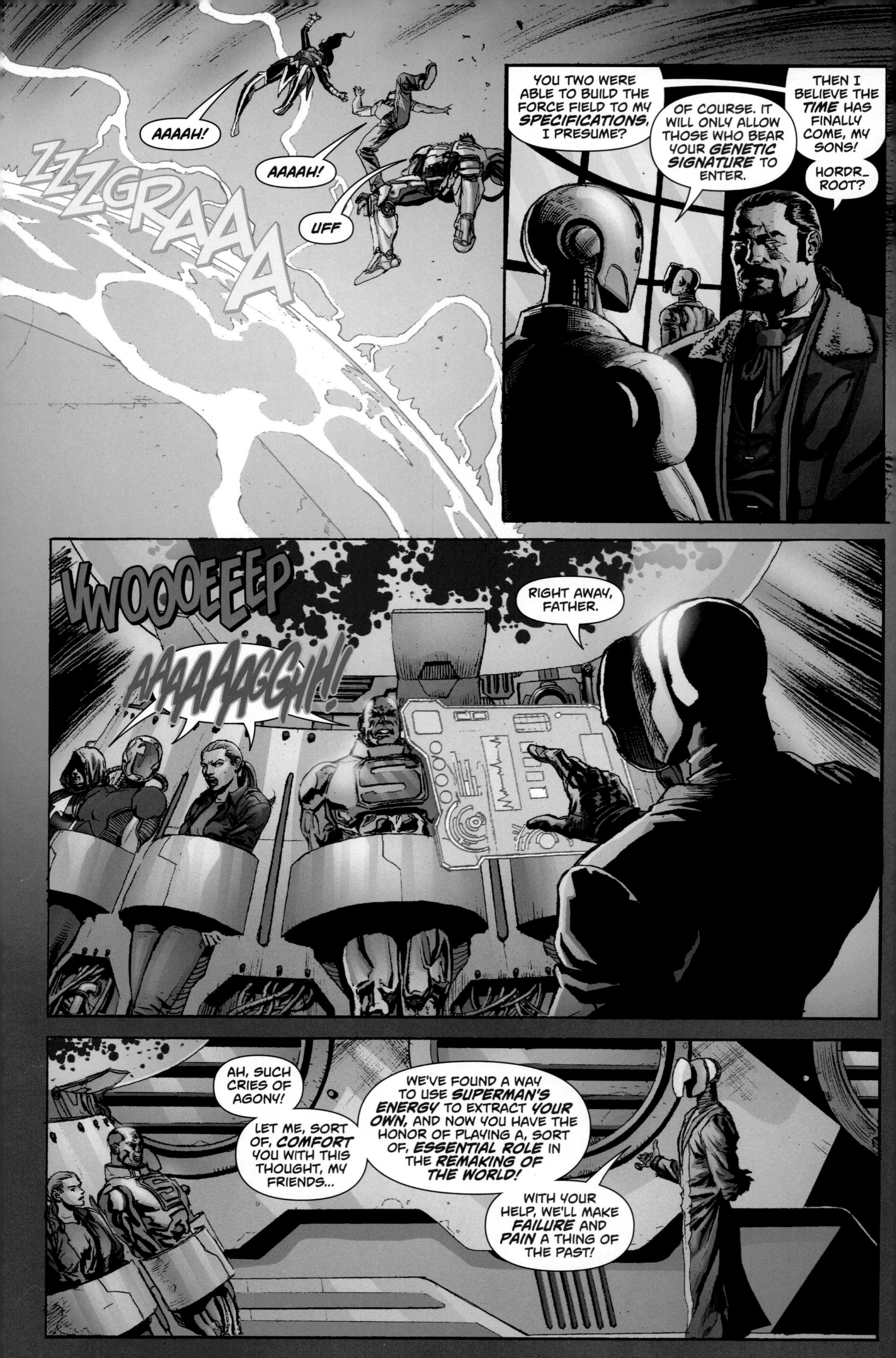
AAAAH!
AAAAH!
UFF
ZZZGRAAAA
YOU TWO WERE ABLE TO BUILD THE FORCE FIELD TO MY SPECIFICATIONS, I PRESUME?
OF COURSE. IT WILL ONLY ALLOW THOSE WHO BEAR YOUR GENETIC SIGNATURE TO ENTER.
THEN I BELIEVE THE TIME HAS FINALLY COME, MY SONS!
HORDR_ROOT?
VWOOOEEEP
AAAAAAGGHH!
RIGHT AWAY, FATHER.
AH, SUCH CRIES OF AGONY!
LET ME, SORT OF, COMFORT YOU WITH THIS THOUGHT, MY FRIENDS...
WE'VE FOUND A WAY TO USE SUPERMAN'S ENERGY TO EXTRACT YOUR OWN, AND NOW YOU HAVE THE HONOR OF PLAYING A, SORT OF, ESSENTIAL ROLE IN THE REMAKING OF THE WORLD!
WITH YOUR HELP, WE'LL MAKE FAILURE AND PAIN A THING OF THE PAST!

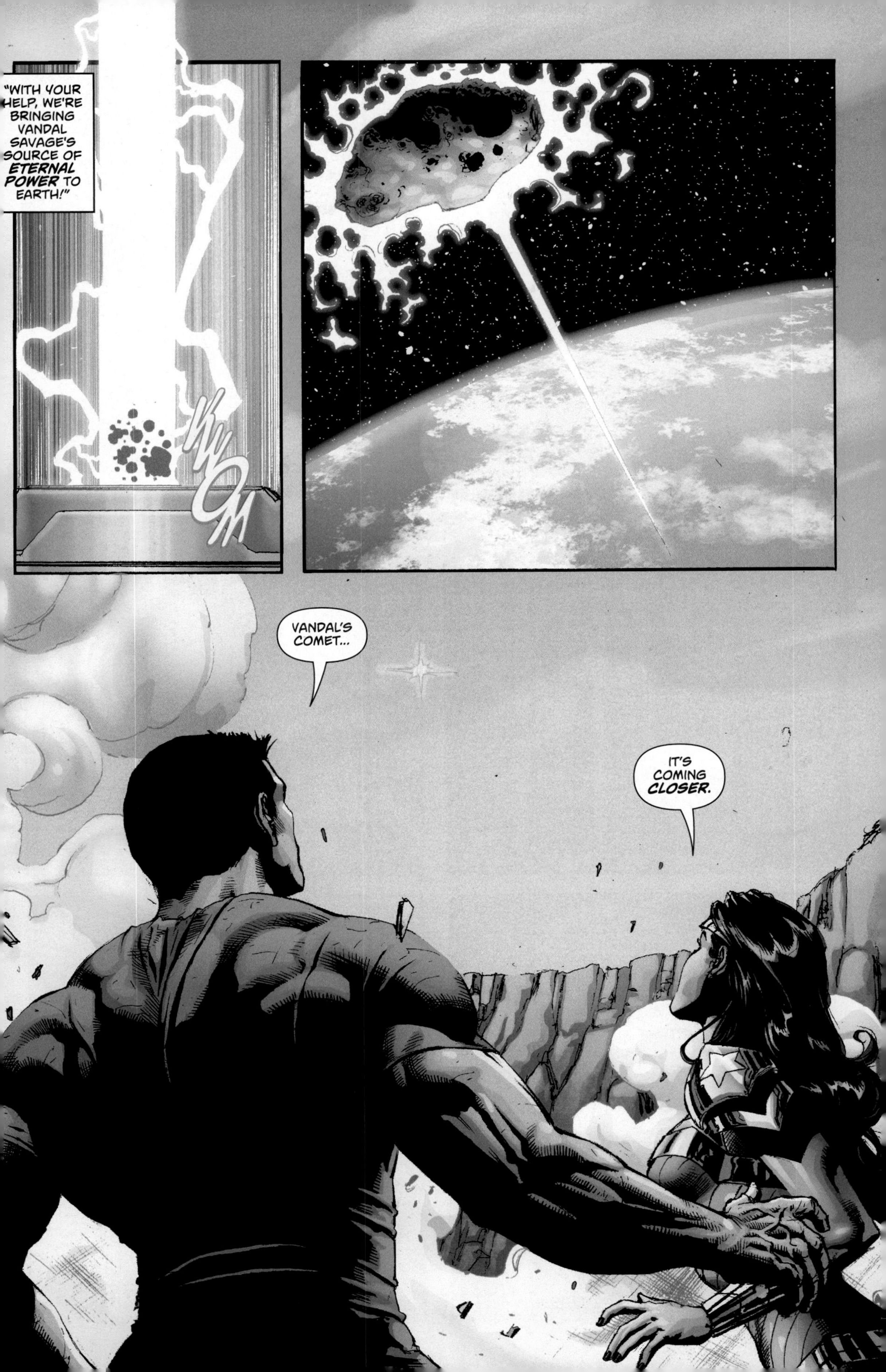
"WITH YOUR HELP, WE'RE BRINGING VANDAL SAVAGE'S SOURCE OF ETERNAL POWER TO EARTH!"
KWOM
VANDAL'S COMET...
IT'S COMING CLOSER.

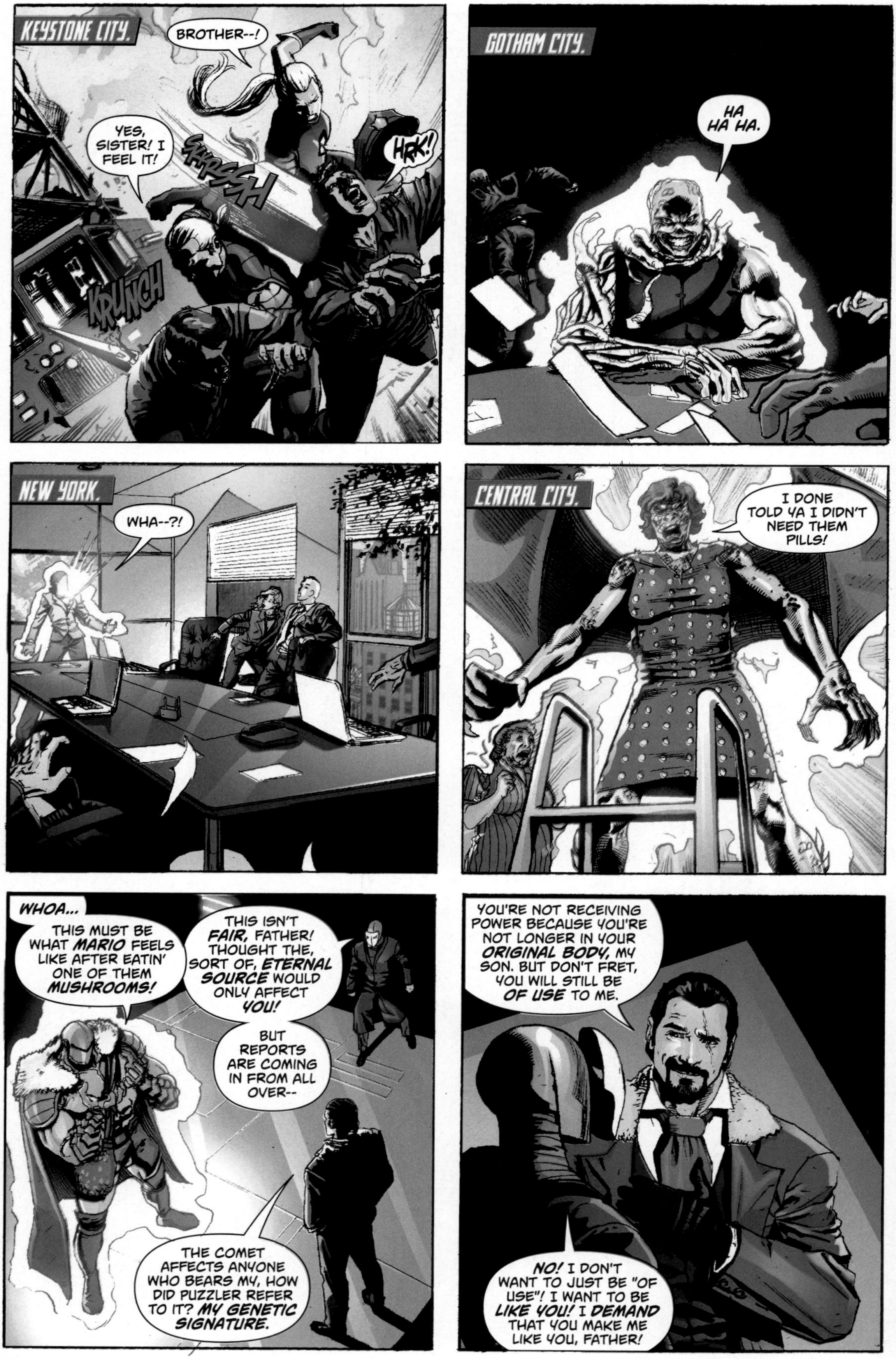
KEYSTONE CITY.
BROTHER--!
YES, SISTER! I FEEL IT!
SHRSSH
HRK!
KRUNCH
GOTHAM CITY.
HA HA HA.
NEW YORK.
WHA--?!
CENTRAL CITY.
I DONE TOLD YA I DIDN'T NEED THEM PILLS!
WHOA...
THIS MUST BE WHAT MARIO FEELS LIKE AFTER EATIN' ONE OF THEM MUSHROOMS!
THIS ISN'T FAIR, FATHER! THOUGHT THE, SORT OF, ETERNAL SOURCE WOULD ONLY AFFECT YOU!
BUT REPORTS ARE COMING IN FROM ALL OVER--
THE COMET AFFECTS ANYONE WHO BEARS MY, HOW DID PUZZLER REFER TO IT? MY GENETIC SIGNATURE.
YOU'RE NOT RECEIVING POWER BECAUSE YOU'RE NOT LONGER IN YOUR ORIGINAL BODY, MY SON. BUT DON'T FRET, YOU WILL STILL BE OF USE TO ME.
NO! I DON'T WANT TO JUST BE "OF USE"! I WANT TO BE LIKE YOU! I DEMAND THAT YOU MAKE ME LIKE YOU, FATHER!

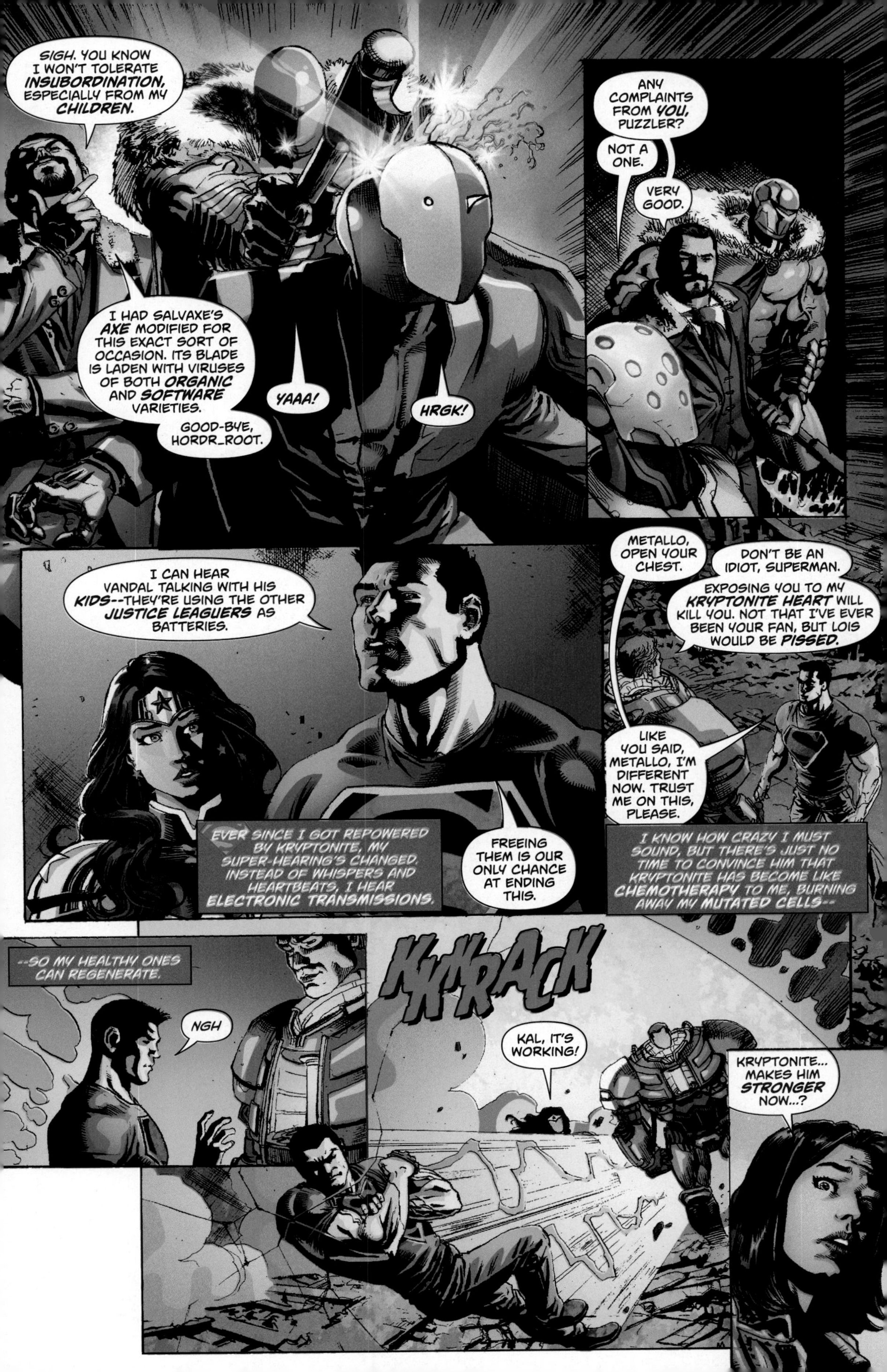
SIGH. YOU KNOW I WON'T TOLERATE INSUBORDINATION, ESPECIALLY FROM MY CHILDREN.
I HAD SALVAXE'S AXE MODIFIED FOR THIS EXACT SORT OF OCCASION. ITS BLADE IS LADEN WITH VIRUSES OF BOTH ORGANIC AND SOFTWARE VARIETIES.
GOOD-BYE, HORDR_ROOT.
YAAA!
HRGK!
ANY COMPLAINTS FROM YOU, PUZZLER?
NOT A ONE.
VERY GOOD.
I CAN HEAR VANDAL TALKING WITH HIS KIDS--THEY'RE USING THE OTHER JUSTICE LEAGUERS AS BATTERIES.
EVER SINCE I GOT REPOWERED BY KRYPTONITE, MY SUPER-HEARING'S CHANGED. INSTEAD OF WHISPERS AND HEARTBEATS, I HEAR ELECTRONIC TRANSMISSIONS.
FREEING THEM IS OUR ONLY CHANCE AT ENDING THIS.
METALLO, OPEN YOUR CHEST.
DON'T BE AN IDIOT, SUPERMAN.
EXPOSING YOU TO MY KRYPTONITE HEART WILL KILL YOU. NOT THAT I'VE EVER BEEN YOUR FAN, BUT LOIS WOULD BE PISSED.
LIKE YOU SAID, METALLO, I'M DIFFERENT NOW. TRUST ME ON THIS, PLEASE.
I KNOW HOW CRAZY I MUST SOUND, BUT THERE'S JUST NO TIME TO CONVINCE HIM THAT KRYPTONITE HAS BECOME LIKE CHEMOTHERAPY TO ME, BURNING AWAY MY MUTATED CELLS--
--SO MY HEALTHY ONES CAN REGENERATE.
NGH
KKHRACK
KAL, IT'S WORKING!
KRYPTONITE... MAKES HIM STRONGER NOW...?

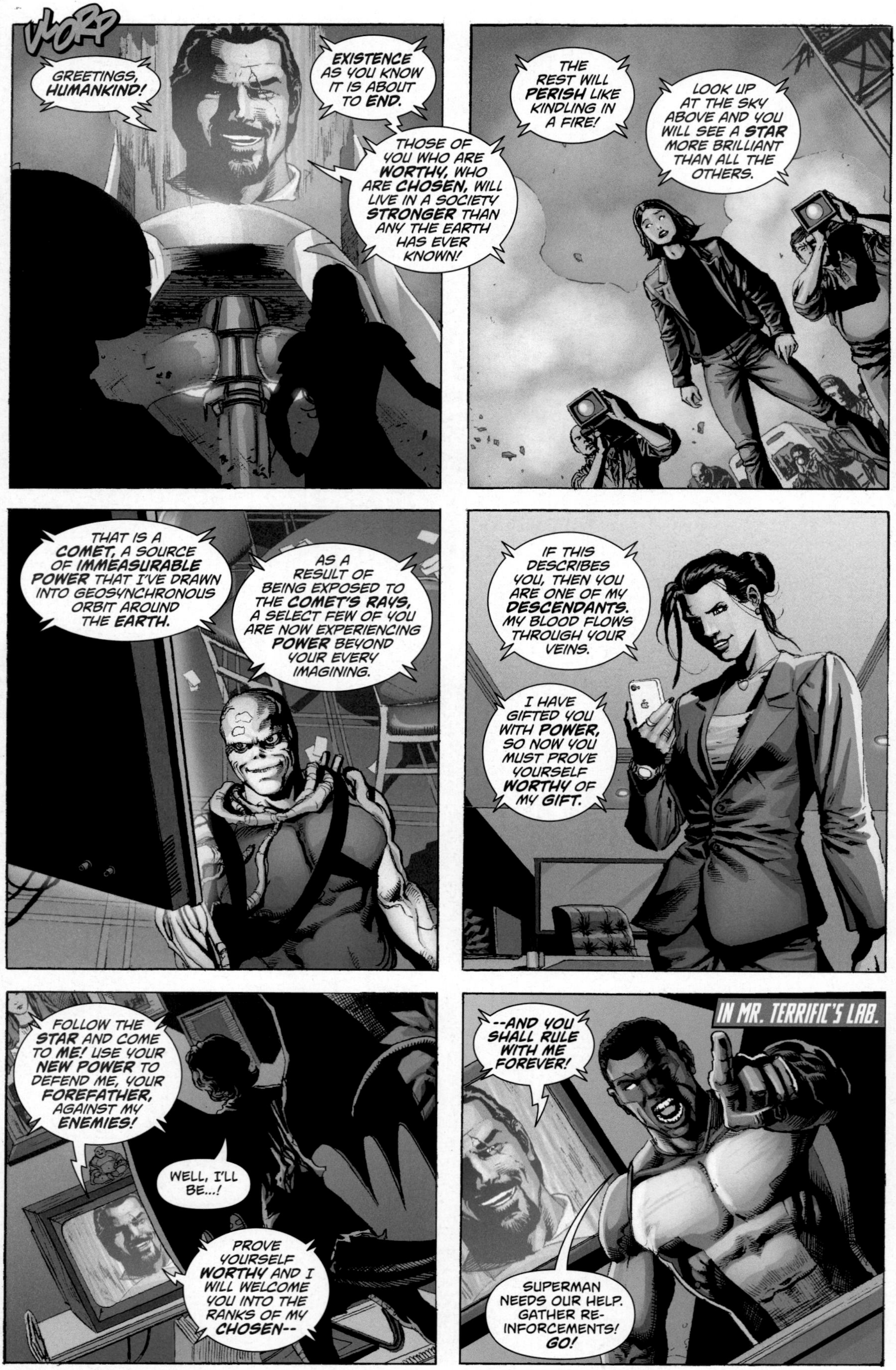
VWORP
GREETINGS, HUMANKIND!
EXISTENCE AS YOU KNOW IT IS ABOUT TO END.
THOSE OF YOU WHO ARE WORTHY, WHO ARE CHOSEN, WILL LIVE IN A SOCIETY STRONGER THAN ANY THE EARTH HAS EVER KNOWN!
THE REST WILL PERISH LIKE KINDLING IN A FIRE!
LOOK UP AT THE SKY ABOVE AND YOU WILL SEE A STAR MORE BRILLIANT THAN ALL THE OTHERS.
THAT IS A COMET, A SOURCE OF IMMEASURABLE POWER THAT I'VE DRAWN INTO GEOSYNCHRONOUS ORBIT AROUND THE EARTH.
AS A RESULT OF BEING EXPOSED TO THE COMET'S RAYS, A SELECT FEW OF YOU ARE NOW EXPERIENCING POWER BEYOND YOUR EVERY IMAGINING.
IF THIS DESCRIBES YOU, THEN YOU ARE ONE OF MY DESCENDANTS. MY BLOOD FLOWS THROUGH YOUR VEINS.
I HAVE GIFTED YOU WITH POWER, SO NOW YOU MUST PROVE YOURSELF WORTHY OF MY GIFT.
FOLLOW THE STAR AND COME TO ME! USE YOUR NEW POWER TO DEFEND ME, YOUR FOREFATHER, AGAINST MY ENEMIES!
WELL, I'LL BE...!
PROVE YOURSELF WORTHY AND I WILL WELCOME YOU INTO THE RANKS OF MY CHOSEN--
IN MR. TERRIFIC'S LAB.
--AND YOU SHALL RULE WITH ME FOREVER!
SUPERMAN NEEDS OUR HELP. GATHER RE-INFORCEMENTS! GO!

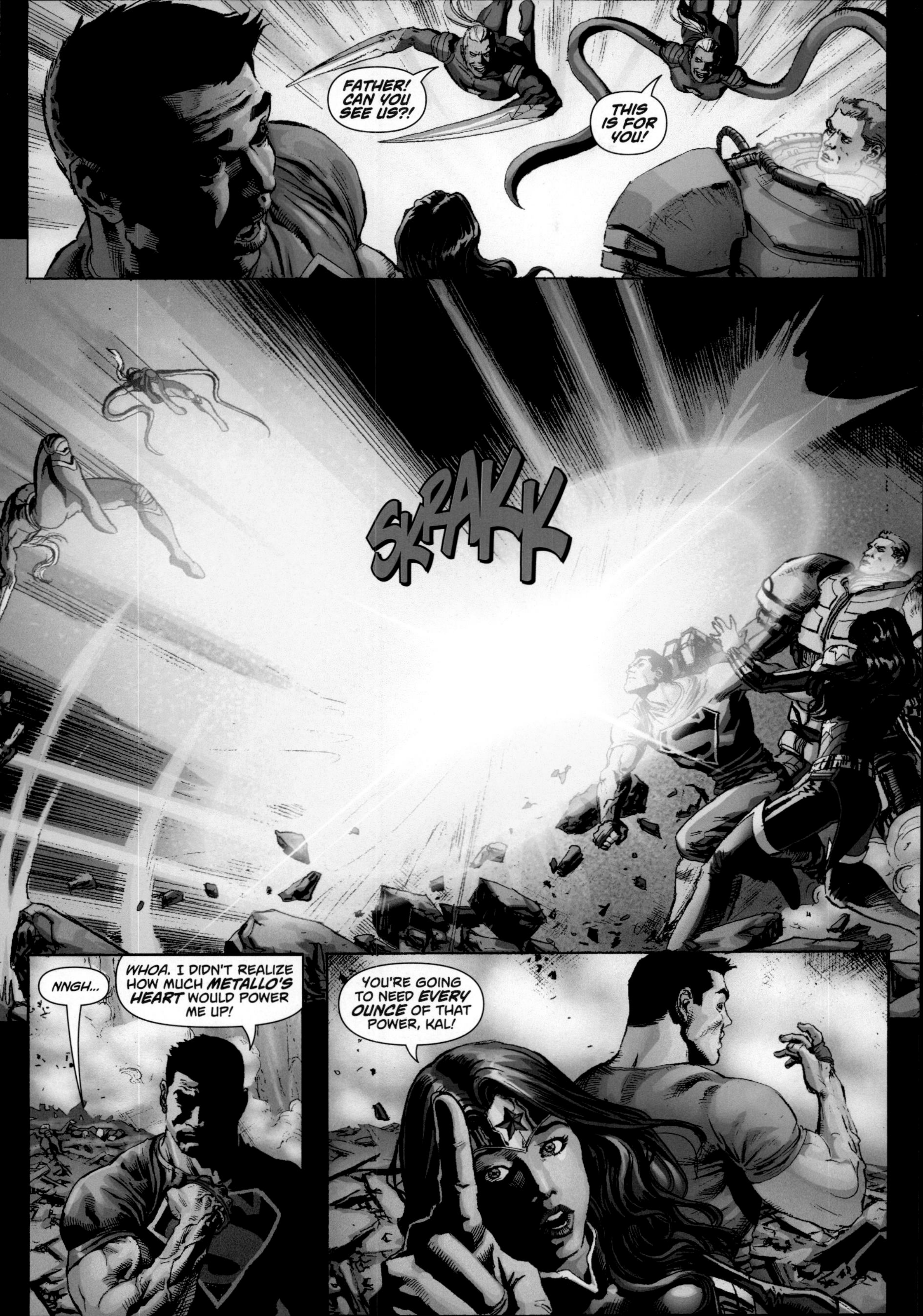
FATHER! CAN YOU SEE US?!
THIS IS FOR YOU!
SKRAKK
NNGH...
WHOA. I DIDN'T REALIZE HOW MUCH METALLO'S HEART WOULD POWER ME UP!
YOU'RE GOING TO NEED EVERY OUNCE OF THAT POWER, KAL!

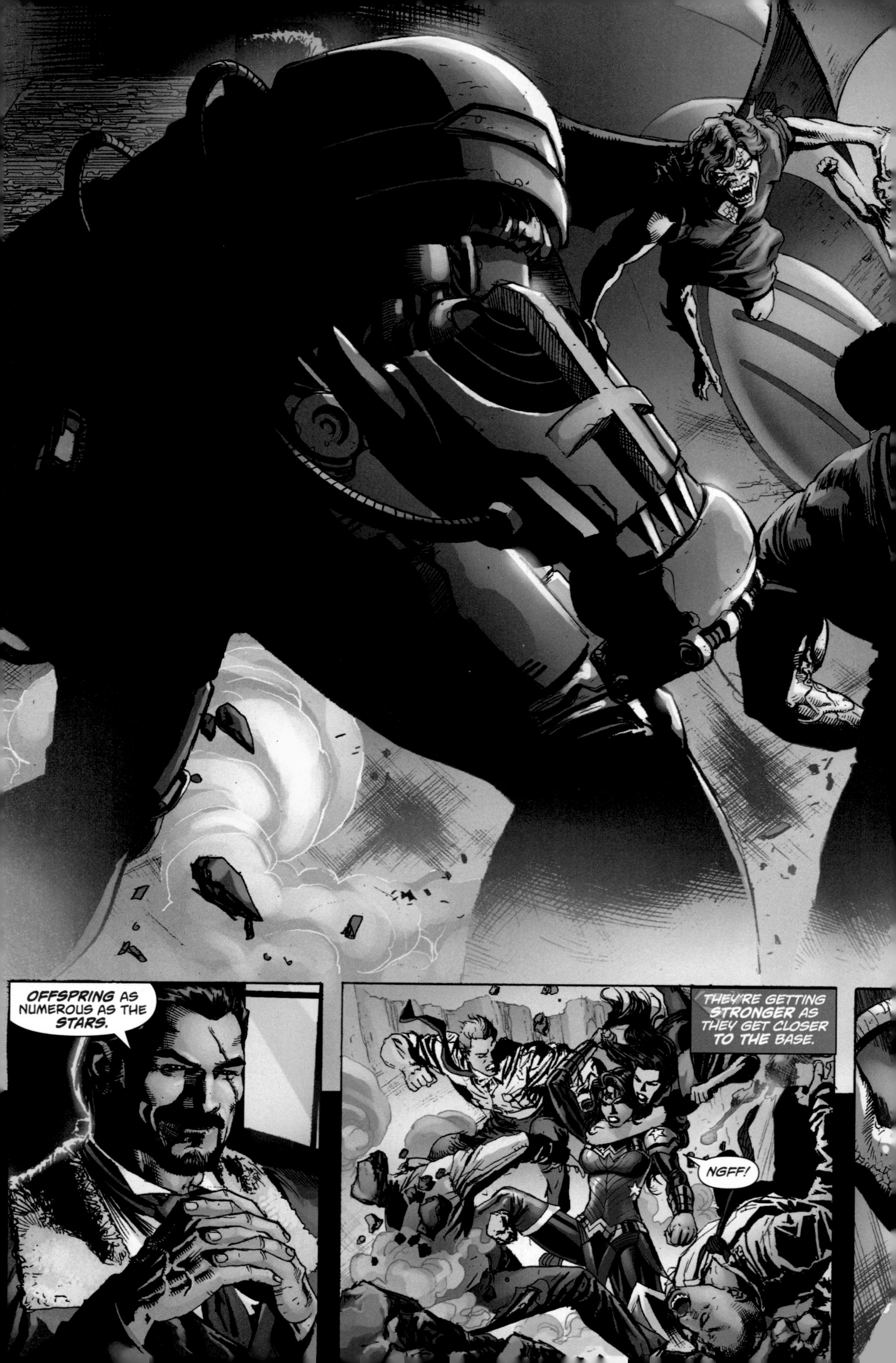
OFFSPRING AS NUMEROUS AS THE STARS.
THEY'RE GETTING STRONGER AS THEY GET CLOSER TO THE BASE.
NGFF!

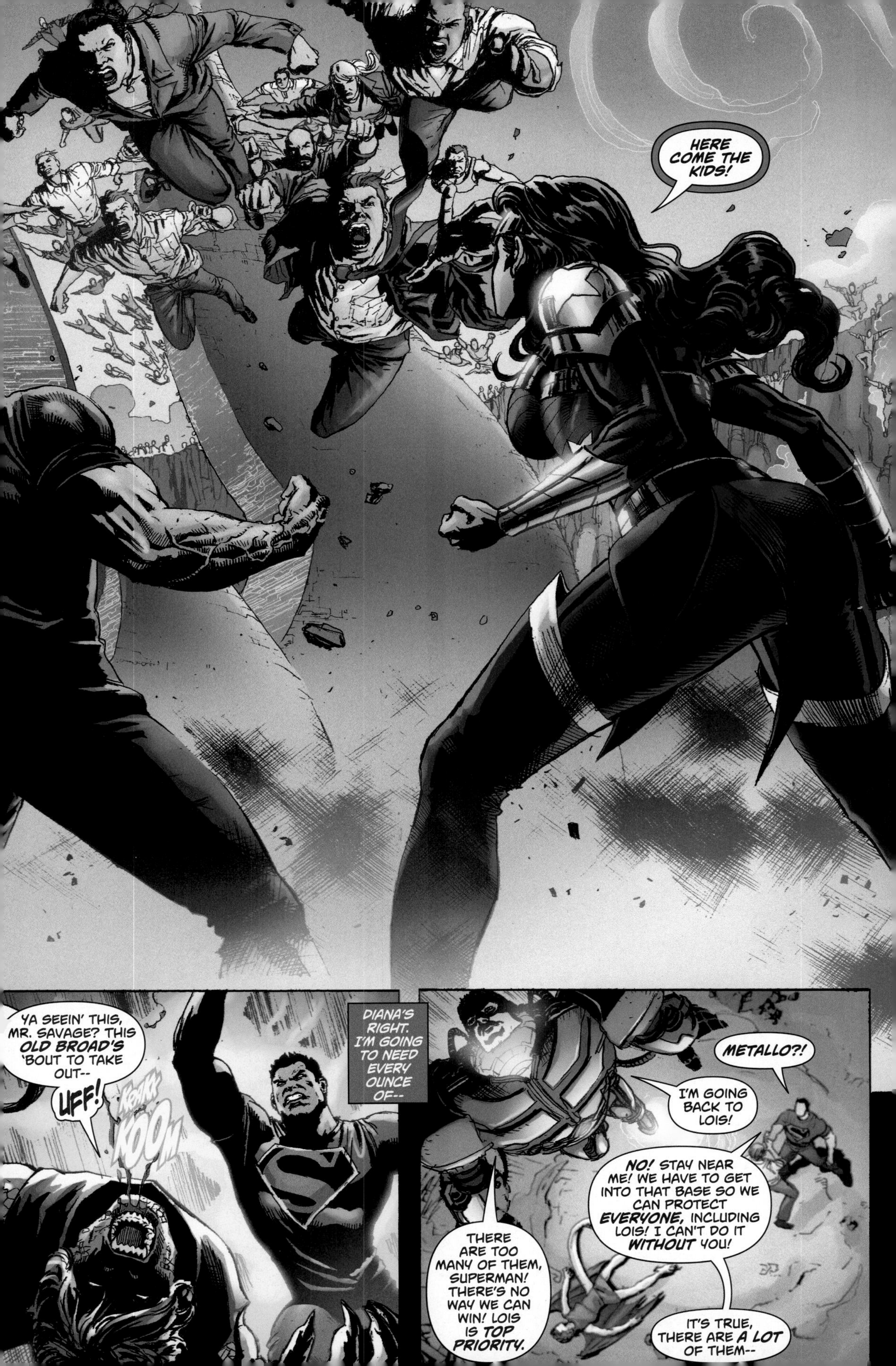
HERE COME THE KIDS!
YA SEEIN' THIS, MR. SAVAGE? THIS OLD BROAD'S 'BOUT TO TAKE OUT--
UFF!
KRAKK KOOM
DIANA'S RIGHT. I'M GOING TO NEED EVERY OUNCE OF--
METALLO?!
I'M GOING BACK TO LOIS!
THERE ARE TOO MANY OF THEM, SUPERMAN! THERE'S NO WAY WE CAN WIN! LOIS IS TOP PRIORITY.
NO! STAY NEAR ME! WE HAVE TO GET INTO THAT BASE SO WE CAN PROTECT EVERYONE, INCLUDING LOIS! I CAN'T DO IT WITHOUT YOU!
IT'S TRUE, THERE ARE A LOT OF THEM--

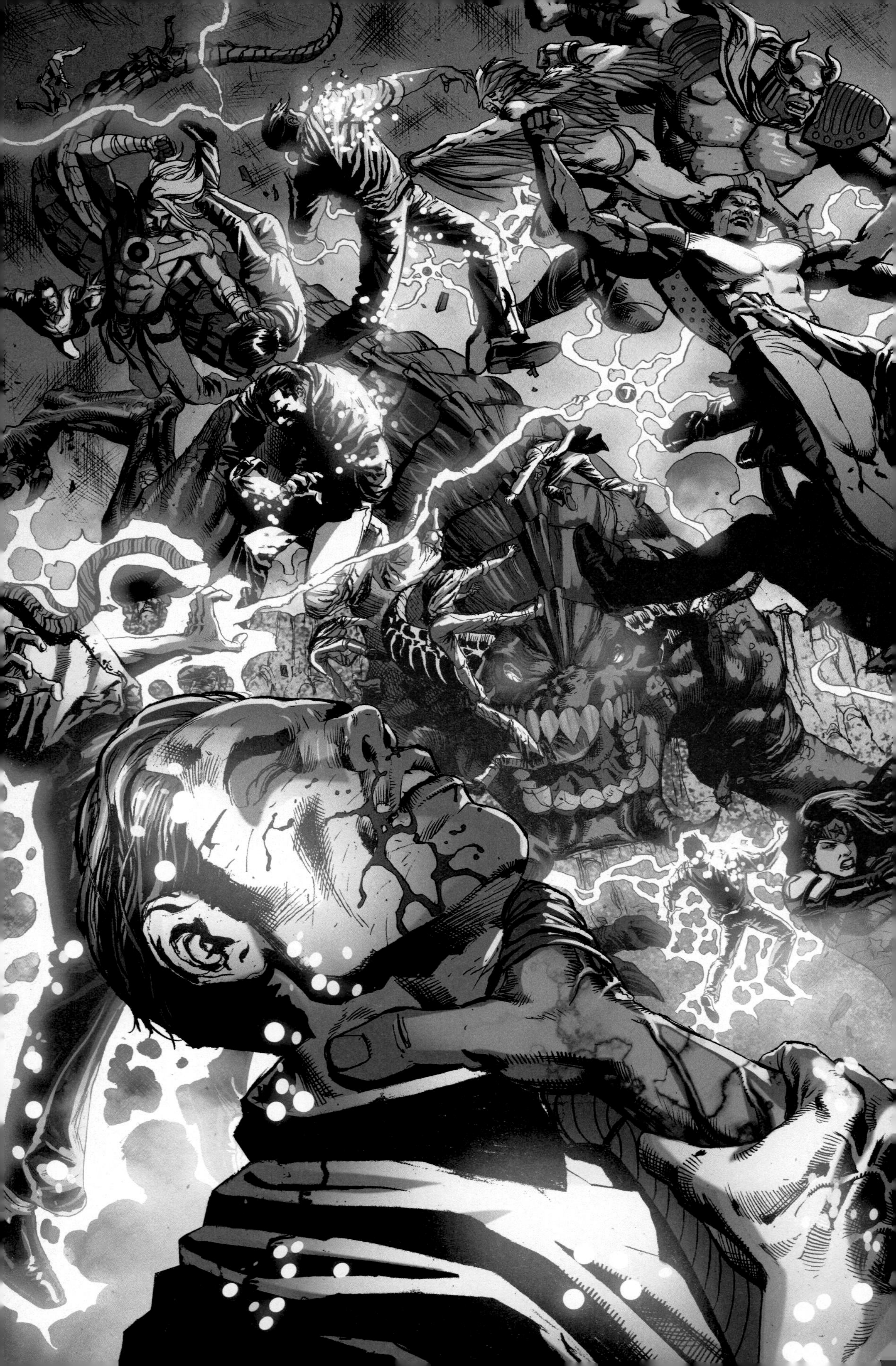

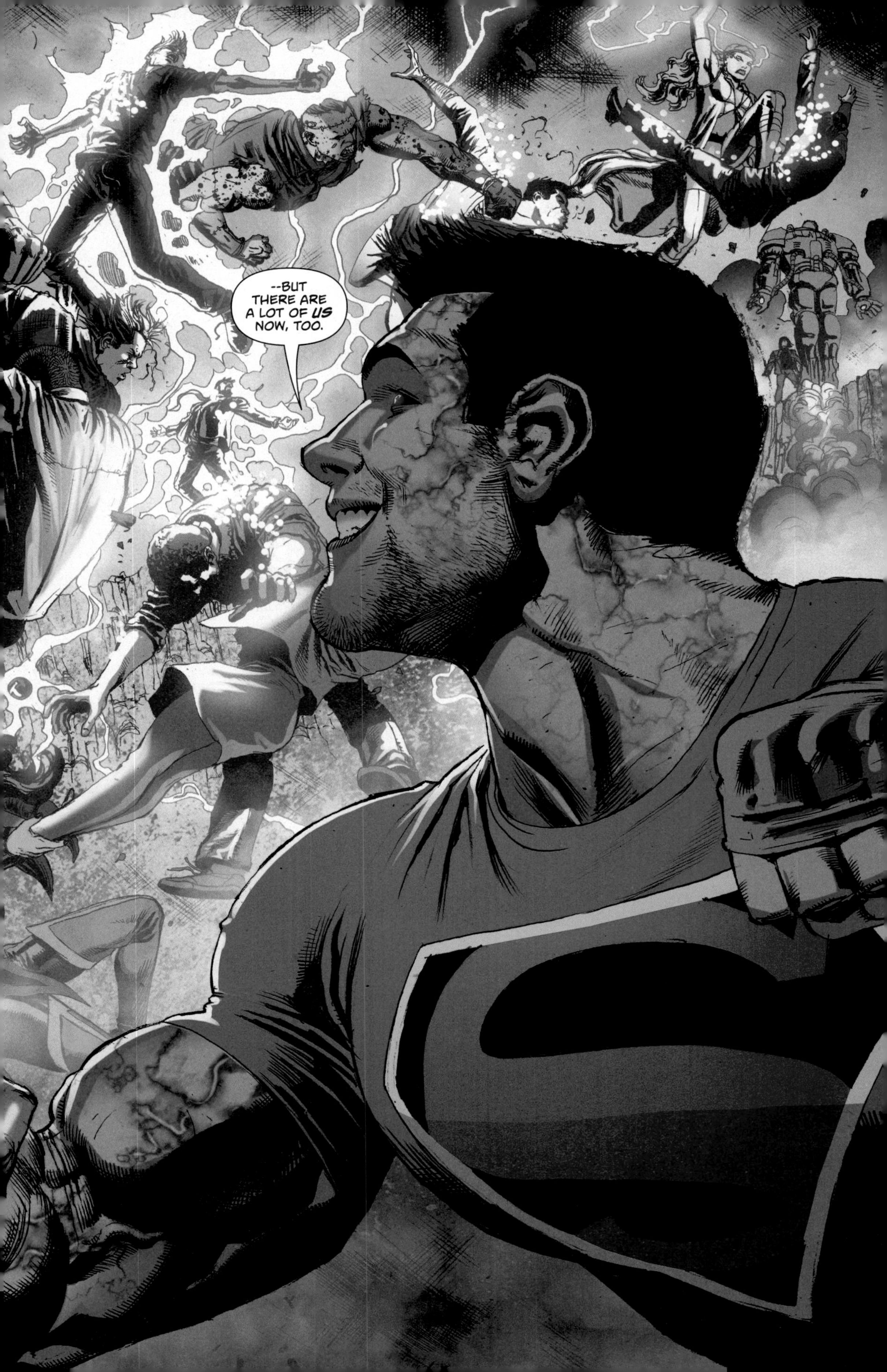
--BUT THERE ARE A LOT OF US NOW, TOO.

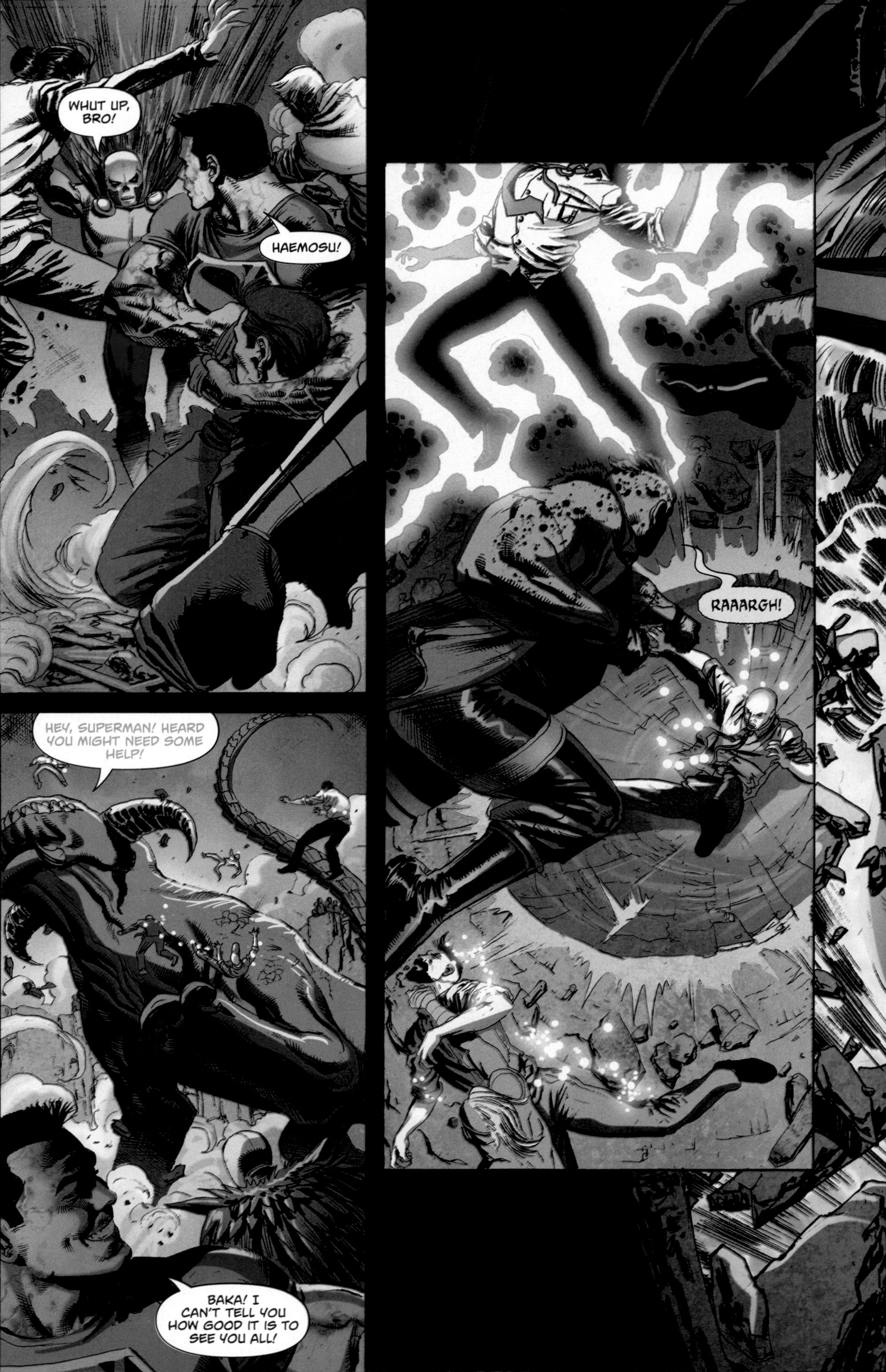
WHUT UP, BRO!
HAEMOSU!
HEY, SUPERMAN! HEARD YOU MIGHT NEED SOME HELP!
BAKA! I CAN'T TELL YOU HOW GOOD IT IS TO SEE YOU ALL!
RAAARGH!

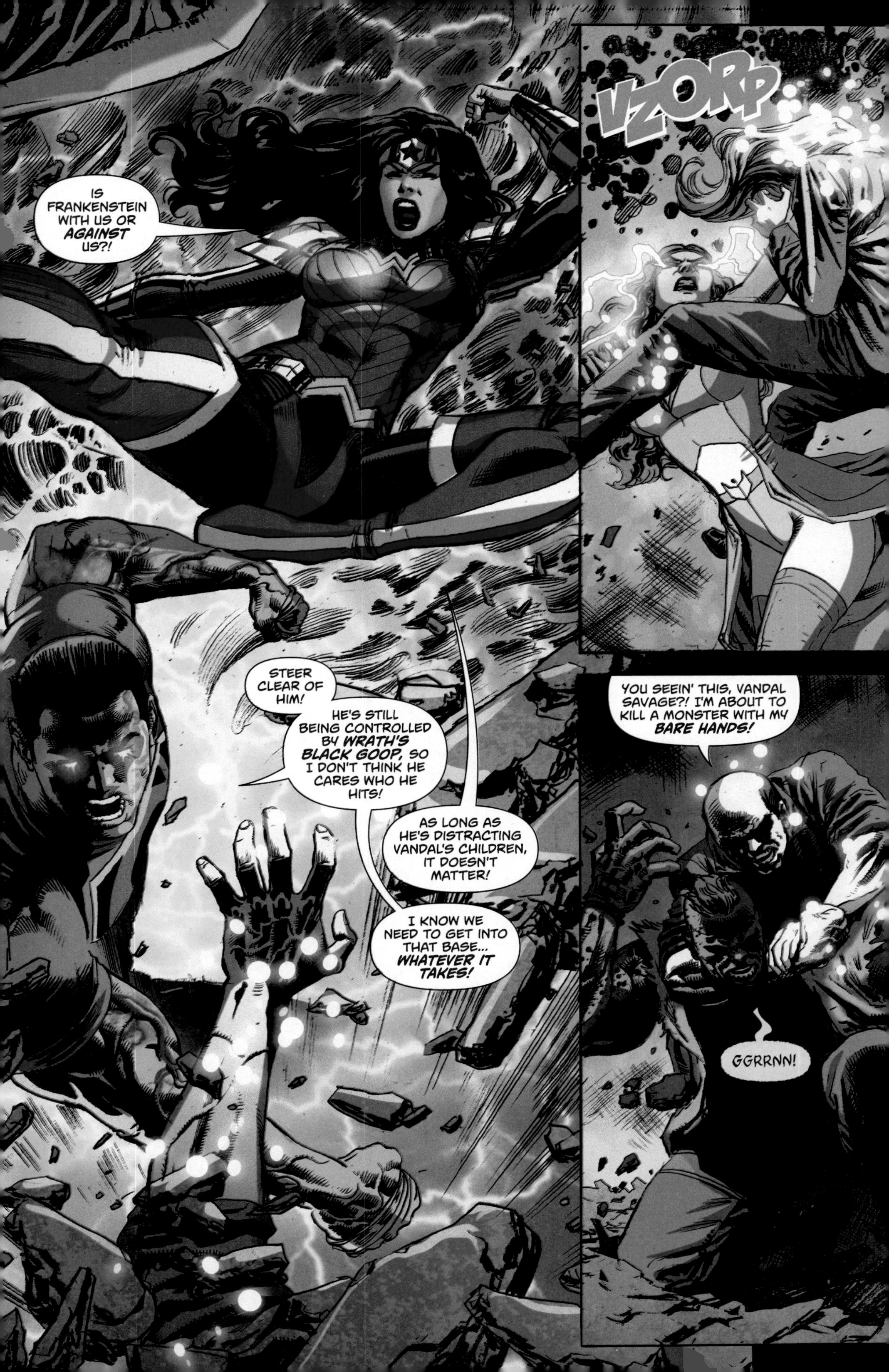
IS FRANKENSTEIN WITH US OR AGAINST US?!
VZORP
STEER CLEAR OF HIM!
HE'S STILL BEING CONTROLLED BY WRATH'S BLACK GOOP, SO I DON'T THINK HE CARES WHO HE HITS!
AS LONG AS HE'S DISTRACTING VANDAL'S CHILDREN, IT DOESN'T MATTER!
I KNOW WE NEED TO GET INTO THAT BASE... WHATEVER IT TAKES!
YOU SEEIN' THIS, VANDAL SAVAGE?! I'M ABOUT TO KILL A MONSTER WITH MY BARE HANDS!
GGRRNN!

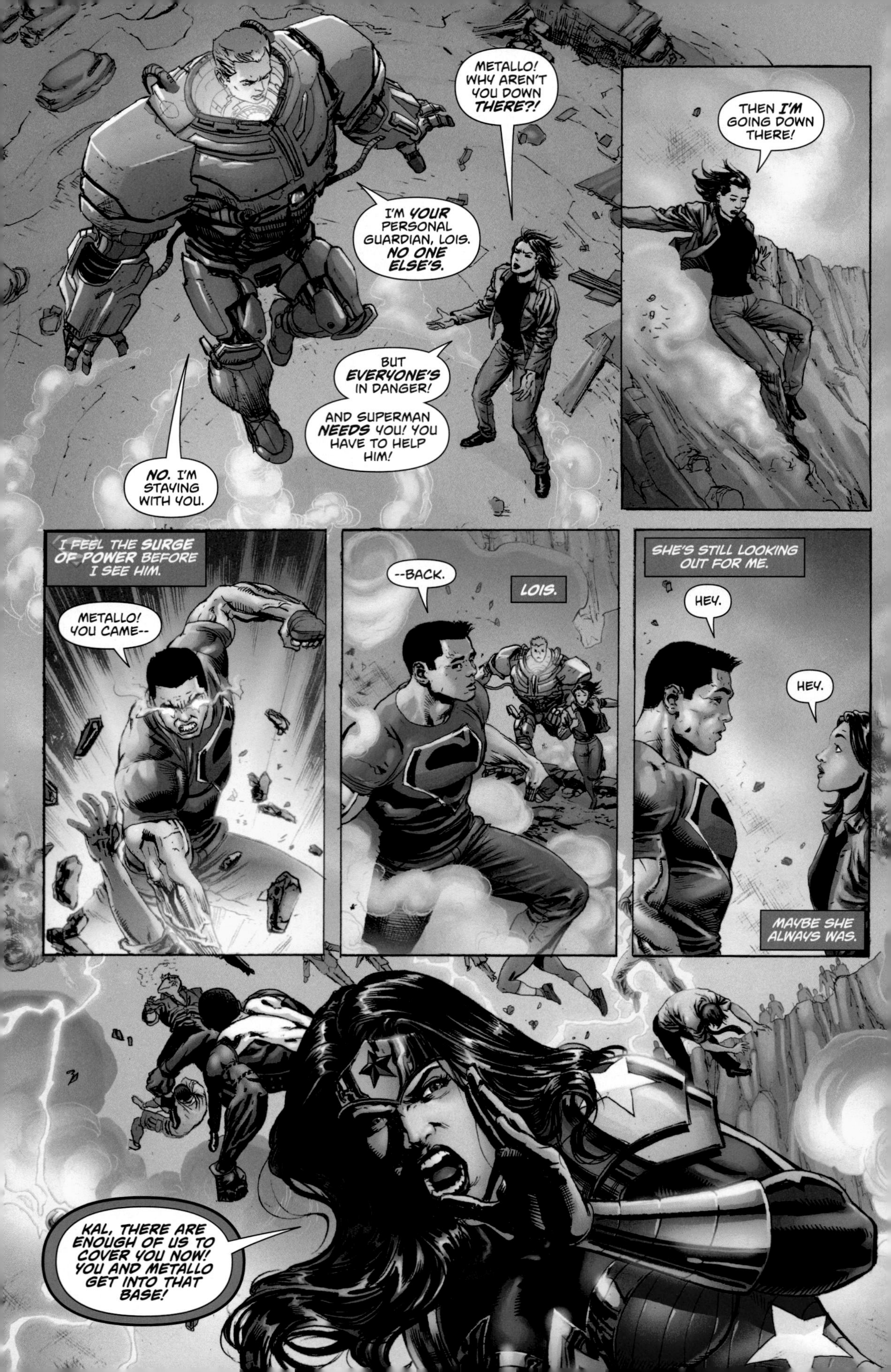
METALLO! WHY AREN'T YOU DOWN THERE?!
I'M YOUR PERSONAL GUARDIAN, LOIS. NO ONE ELSE'S.
BUT EVERYONE'S IN DANGER!
AND SUPERMAN NEEDS YOU! YOU HAVE TO HELP HIM!
NO. I'M STAYING WITH YOU.
THEN I'M GOING DOWN THERE!
I FEEL THE SURGE OF POWER BEFORE I SEE HIM.
METALLO! YOU CAME--
--BACK.
LOIS.
SHE'S STILL LOOKING OUT FOR ME.
HEY.
HEY.
MAYBE SHE ALWAYS WAS.
KAL, THERE ARE ENOUGH OF US TO COVER YOU NOW! YOU AND METALLO GET INTO THAT BASE!

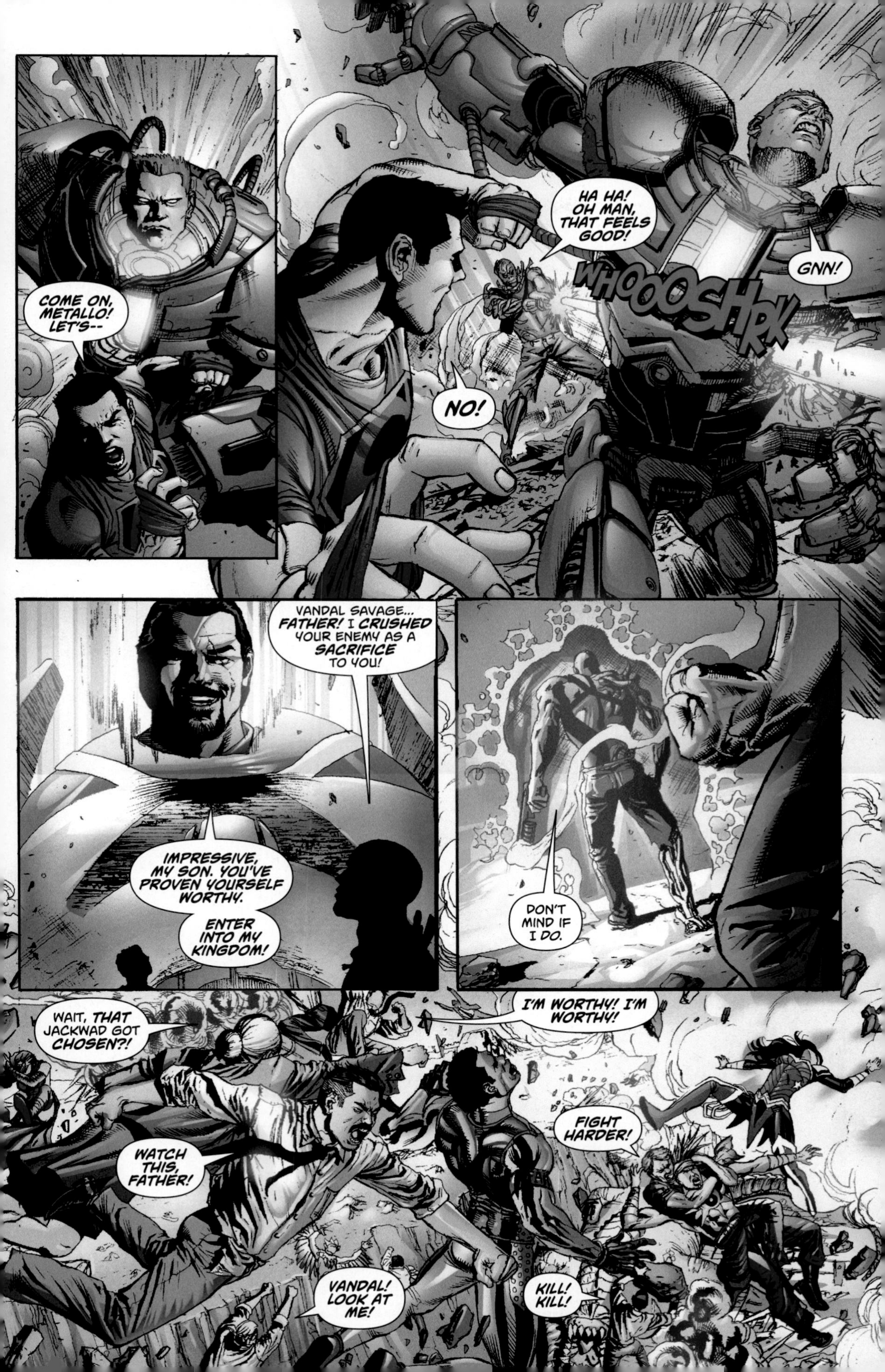
COME ON, METALLO! LET'S--
HA HA! OH MAN, THAT FEELS GOOD!
WHOOOSHRK
GNN!
NO!
VANDAL SAVAGE... FATHER! I CRUSHED YOUR ENEMY AS A SACRIFICE TO YOU!
IMPRESSIVE, MY SON. YOU'VE PROVEN YOURSELF WORTHY.
ENTER INTO MY KINGDOM!
DON'T MIND IF I DO.
WAIT, THAT JACKWAD GOT CHOSEN?!
I'M WORTHY! I'M WORTHY!
FIGHT HARDER!
WATCH THIS, FATHER!
VANDAL! LOOK AT ME!
KILL! KILL!

METALLO...*JOHN.* I'M HERE, OKAY? EVERYTHING'S GOING TO BE ALL RIGHT. WE'LL GET YOU OUT OF HERE.

I'VE DREAMED OF YOU HOLDING ME LIKE THIS, LOIS.

HANG IN THERE. MR. TERRIFIC'S T-SPHERES CAN GET YOU OFF THE *BATTLEFIELD* AND--

SUPERMAN, I'VE SCANNED YOUR VITALS. YOU'RE *DYING.*

THE *POWER* YOU'RE GETTING FROM KRYPTONITE EXPOSURE IS *TEMPORARY,* AND THE SIDE EFFECT IS *DEATH.*

IS THAT TRUE?

...I HAVE TO STOP VANDAL. WHATEVER IT TAKES.

SO YOU'RE WILLING TO PROTECT OTHERS-- INCLUDING PEOPLE YOU'VE NEVER MET-- EVEN IF IT MEANS YOU'RE GOING TO *DIE?*

...YES.

SUPERMAN, *TAKE MY HEART.*

WHAT?!

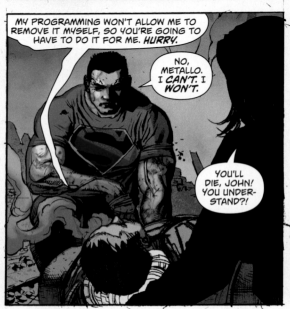

MY PROGRAMMING WON'T ALLOW ME TO REMOVE IT MYSELF, SO YOU'RE GOING TO HAVE TO DO IT FOR ME. *HURRY.*

NO, METALLO. I *CAN'T.* I *WON'T.*

YOU'LL DIE, JOHN! YOU UNDER-STAND?!

MY HEART HAS ALWAYS BEEN FOR *LOIS* ALONE. BUT SUPERMAN--

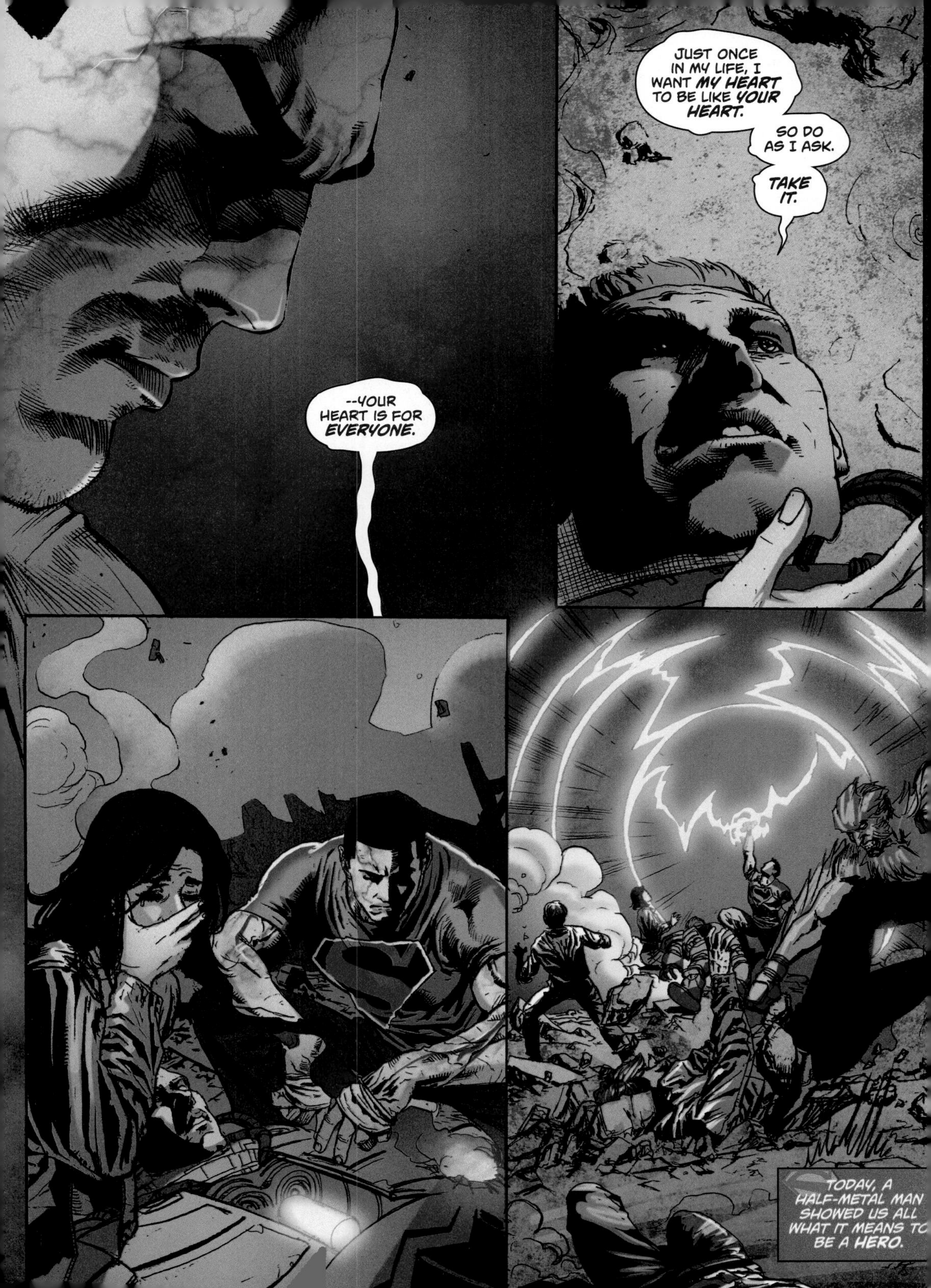
--YOUR HEART IS FOR EVERYONE.
JUST ONCE IN MY LIFE, I WANT MY HEART TO BE LIKE YOUR HEART.
SO DO AS I ASK.
TAKE IT.
TODAY, A HALF-METAL MAN SHOWED US ALL WHAT IT MEANS TO BE A HERO.

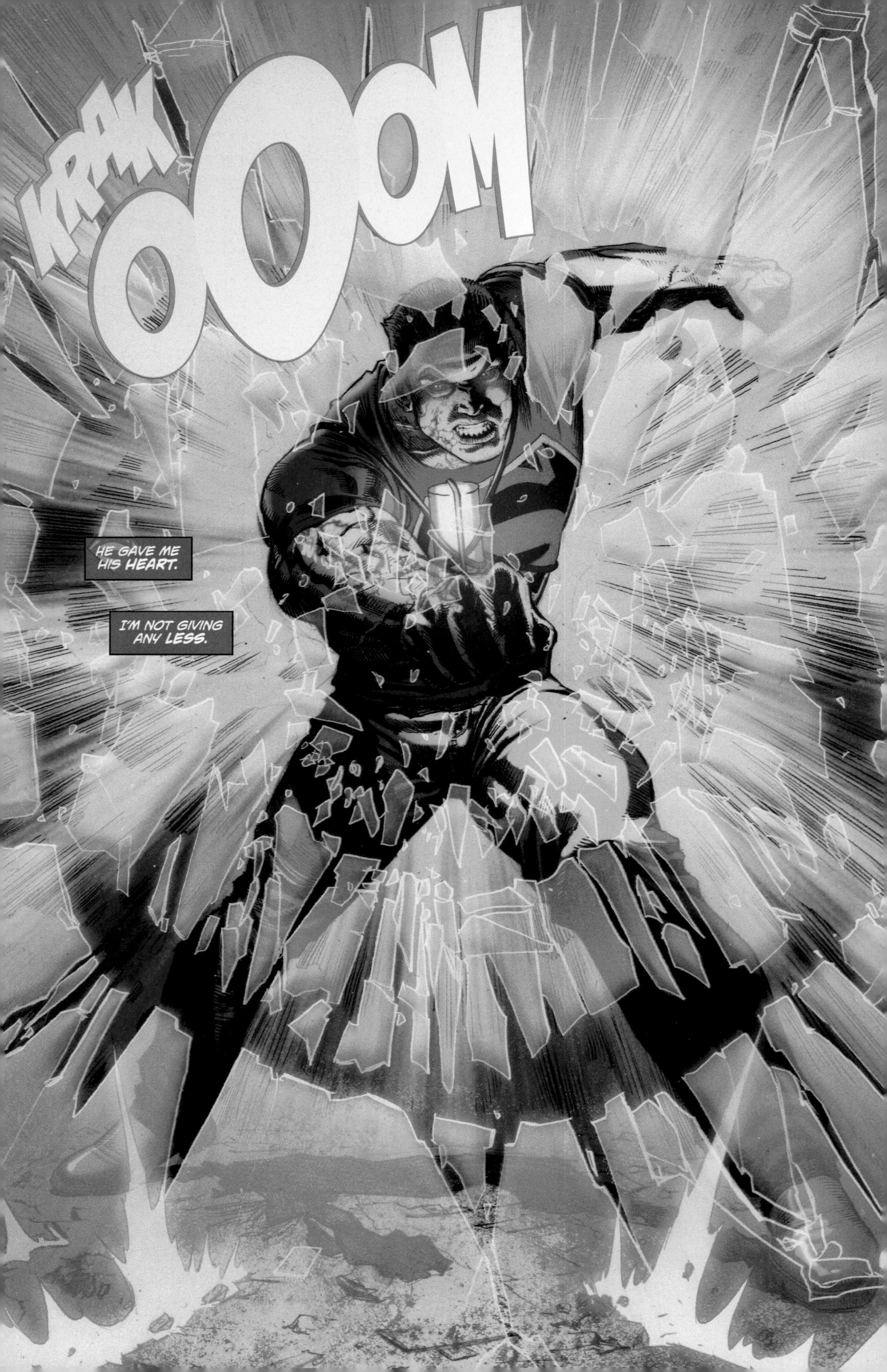
KRAKOOOM
HE GAVE ME HIS HEART.
I'M NOT GIVING ANY LESS.

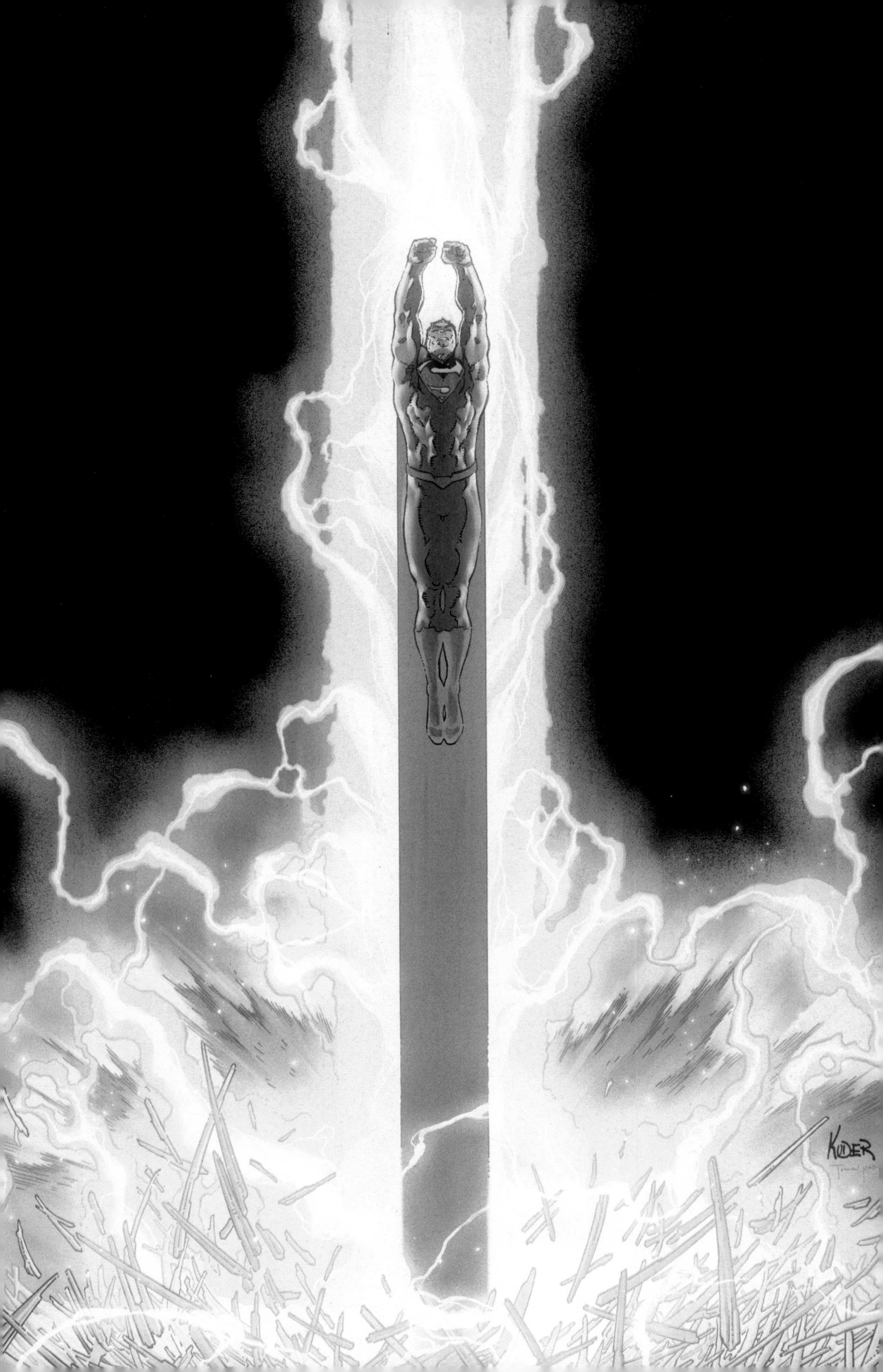

RESURRECTION

GREK PAK AARON KUDER writers AARON KUDER layouts AARON KUDER DAVID MESSINA JAVI FERNANDEZ BRUNO REDONDO VICENTE CIFUENTES pencillers AARON KUDER GAETANO CARLUCCI JUAN ALBARRAN JAVI FERNANDEZ VICENTE CIFUENTES inkers TOMEU MOREY ARIF PRIANTO WIL QUINTANA colorists STEVE WANDS letterer AARON KUDER TOMEU MOREY cover

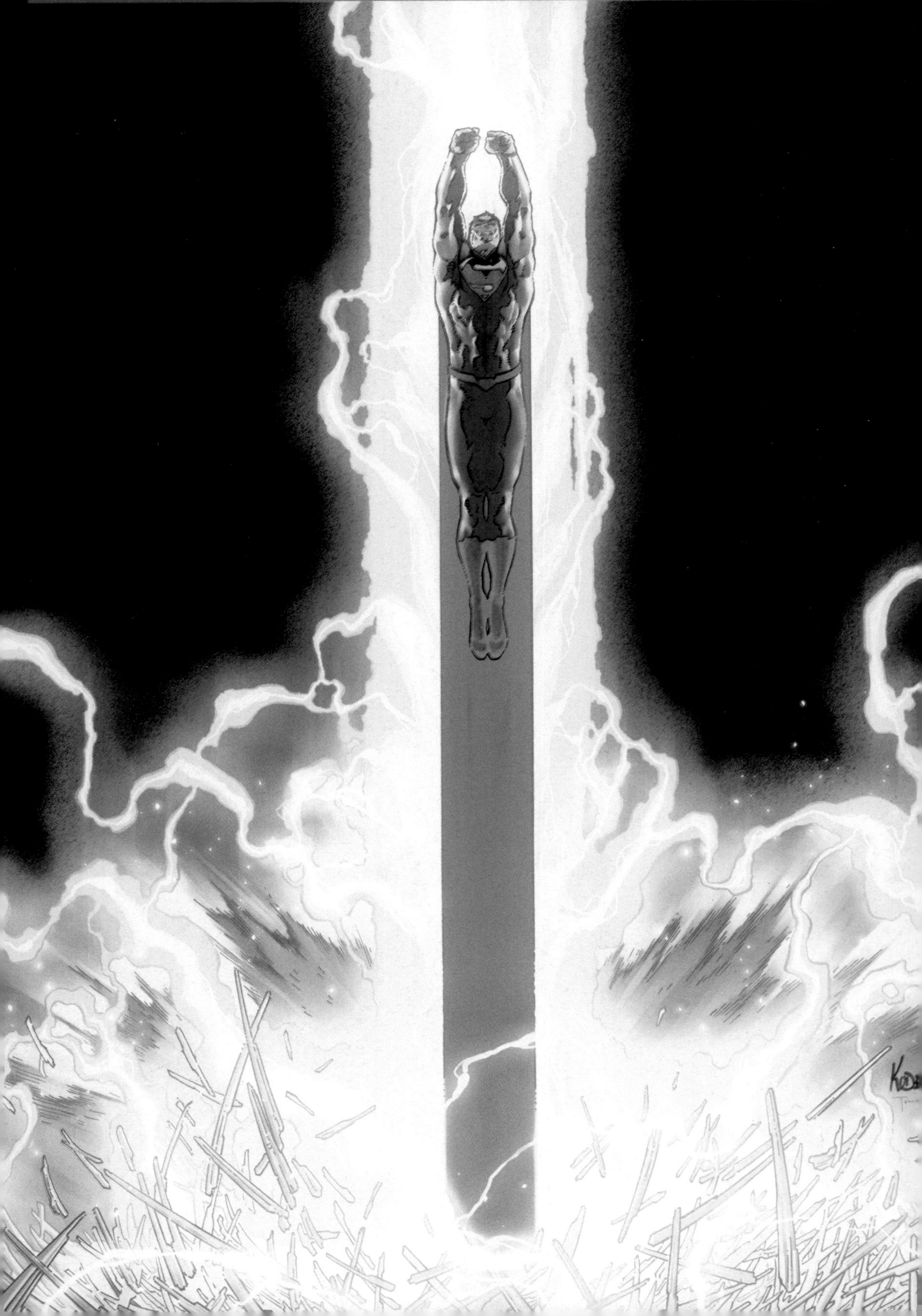

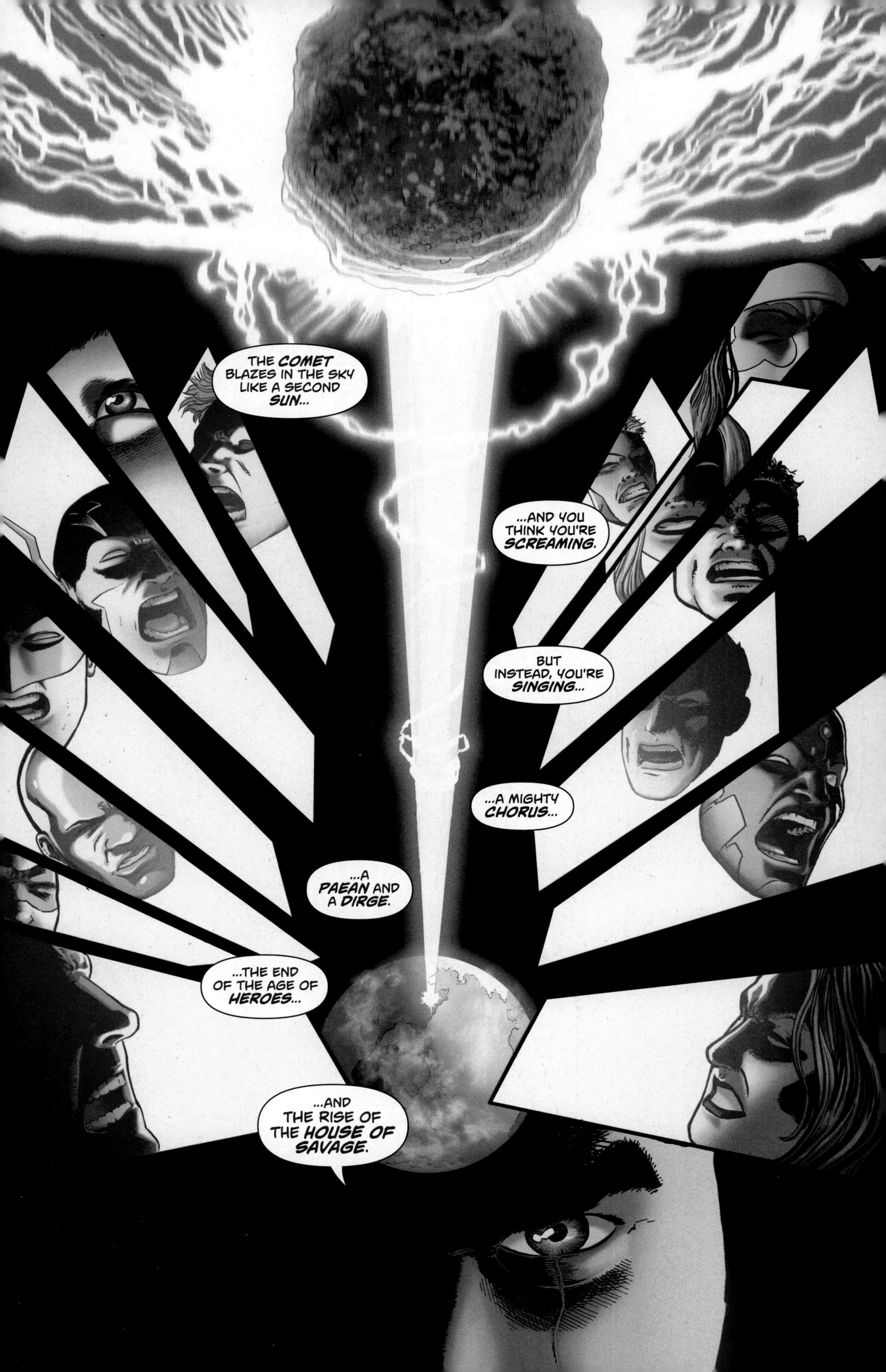
THE COMET BLAZES IN THE SKY LIKE A SECOND SUN...
...AND YOU THINK YOU'RE SCREAMING.
BUT INSTEAD, YOU'RE SINGING...
...A MIGHTY CHORUS...
...A PAEAN AND A DIRGE.
...THE END OF THE AGE OF HEROES...
...AND THE RISE OF THE HOUSE OF SAVAGE.

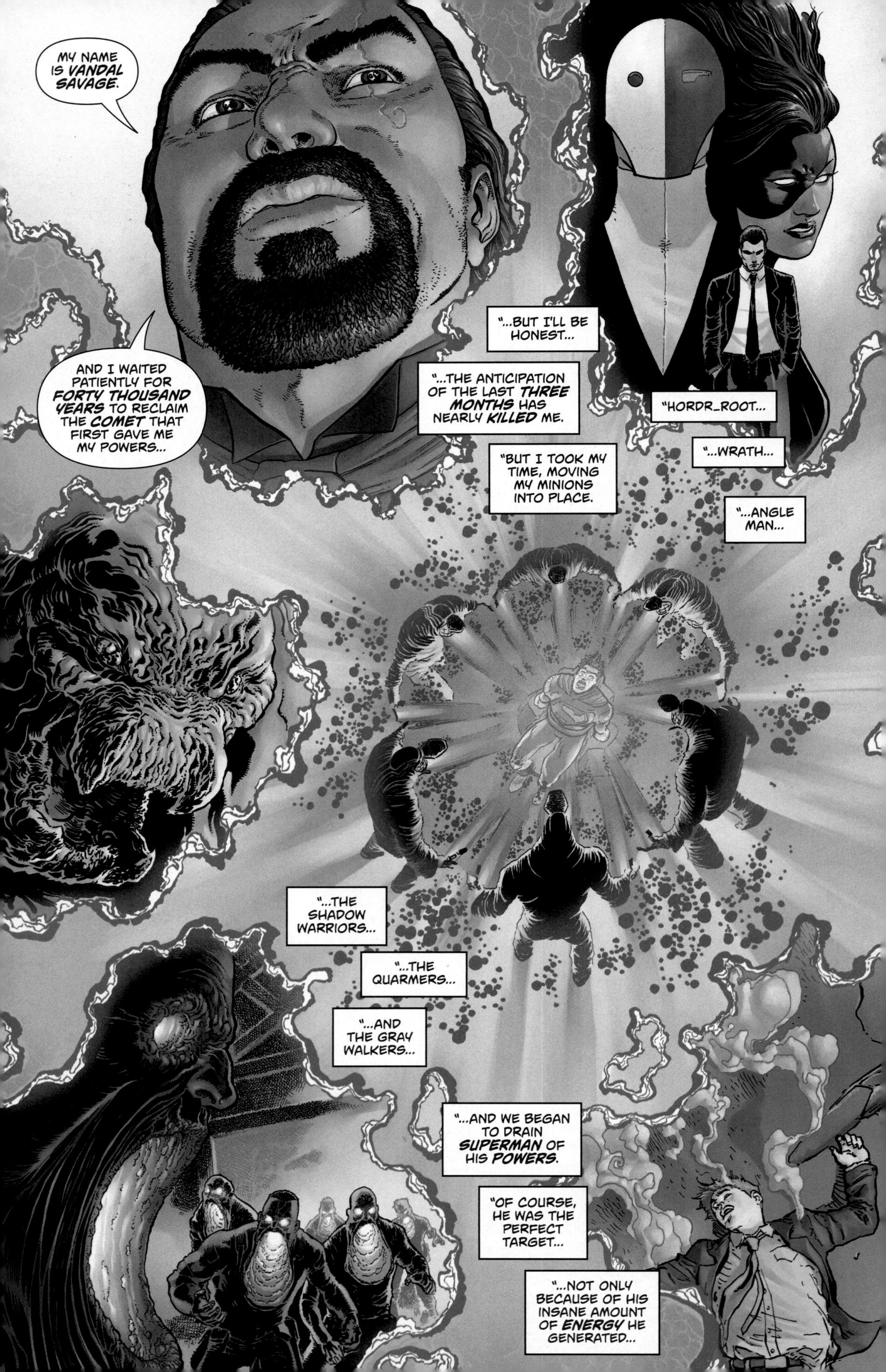
MY NAME IS VANDAL SAVAGE.
AND I WAITED PATIENTLY FOR FORTY THOUSAND YEARS TO RECLAIM THE COMET THAT FIRST GAVE ME MY POWERS...
"...BUT I'LL BE HONEST...
"...THE ANTICIPATION OF THE LAST THREE MONTHS HAS NEARLY KILLED ME.
"BUT I TOOK MY TIME, MOVING MY MINIONS INTO PLACE.
"HORDR_ROOT...
"...WRATH...
"...ANGLE MAN...
"...THE SHADOW WARRIORS...
"...THE QUARMERS...
"...AND THE GRAY WALKERS...
"...AND WE BEGAN TO DRAIN SUPERMAN OF HIS POWERS.
"OF COURSE, HE WAS THE PERFECT TARGET...
"...NOT ONLY BECAUSE OF HIS INSANE AMOUNT OF ENERGY HE GENERATED...

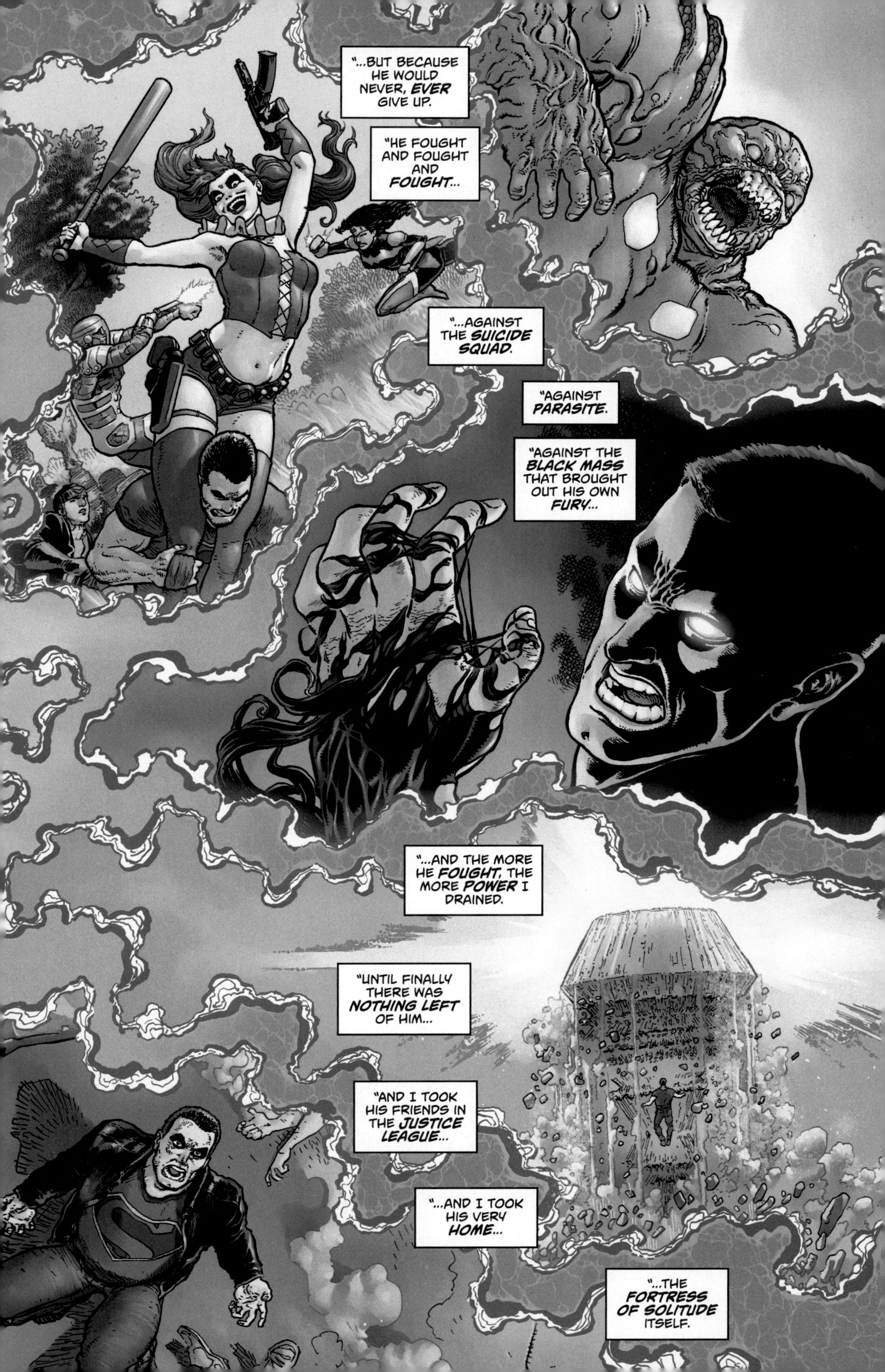
"...BUT BECAUSE HE WOULD NEVER, EVER GIVE UP.
"HE FOUGHT AND FOUGHT AND FOUGHT...
"...AGAINST THE SUICIDE SQUAD.
"AGAINST PARASITE.
"AGAINST THE BLACK MASS THAT BROUGHT OUT HIS OWN FURY...
"...AND THE MORE HE FOUGHT, THE MORE POWER I DRAINED.
"UNTIL FINALLY THERE WAS NOTHING LEFT OF HIM...
"AND I TOOK HIS FRIENDS IN THE JUSTICE LEAGUE...
"...AND I TOOK HIS VERY HOME...
"...THE FORTRESS OF SOLITUDE ITSELF.

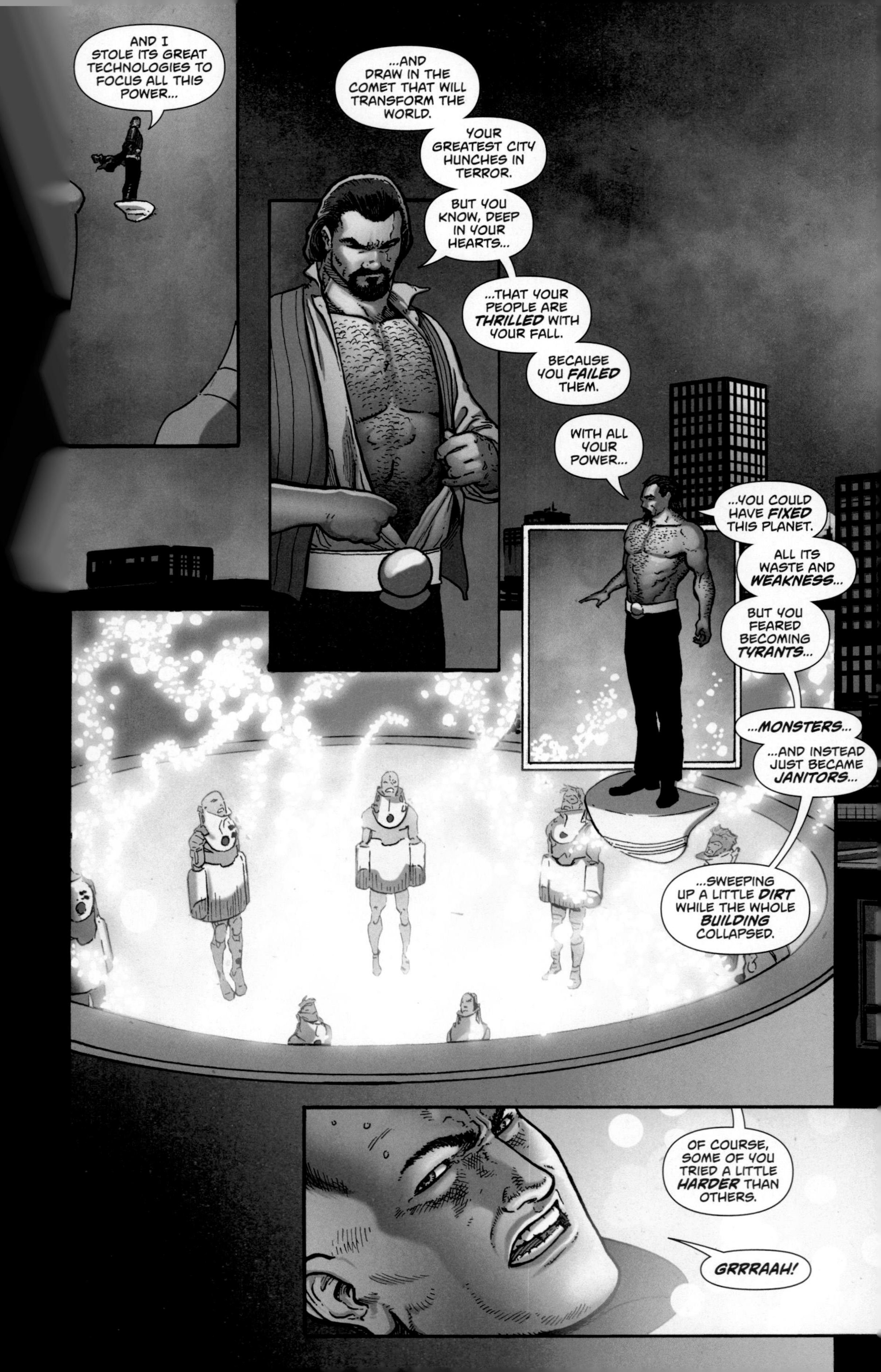
AND I STOLE ITS GREAT TECHNOLOGIES TO FOCUS ALL THIS POWER...
...AND DRAW IN THE COMET THAT WILL TRANSFORM THE WORLD.
YOUR GREATEST CITY HUNCHES IN TERROR.
BUT YOU KNOW, DEEP IN YOUR HEARTS...
...THAT YOUR PEOPLE ARE THRILLED WITH YOUR FALL.
BECAUSE YOU FAILED THEM.
WITH ALL YOUR POWER...
...YOU COULD HAVE FIXED THIS PLANET.
ALL ITS WASTE AND WEAKNESS...
BUT YOU FEARED BECOMING TYRANTS...
...MONSTERS...
...AND INSTEAD JUST BECAME JANITORS...
...SWEEPING UP A LITTLE DIRT WHILE THE WHOLE BUILDING COLLAPSED.
OF COURSE, SOME OF YOU TRIED A LITTLE HARDER THAN OTHERS.
GRRRAAH!

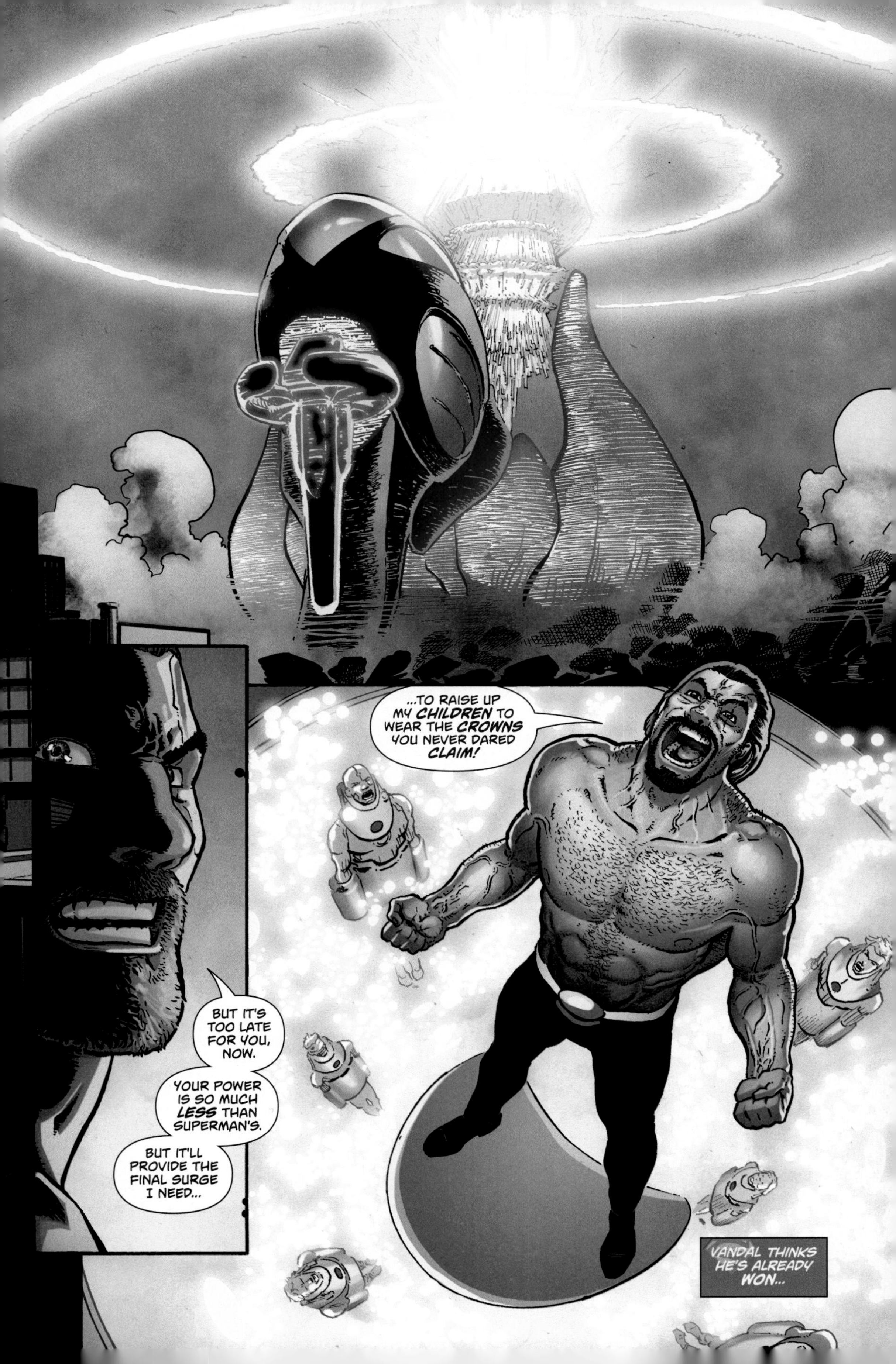
...TO RAISE UP MY CHILDREN TO WEAR THE CROWNS YOU NEVER DARED CLAIM!
BUT IT'S TOO LATE FOR YOU, NOW.
YOUR POWER IS SO MUCH LESS THAN SUPERMAN'S.
BUT IT'LL PROVIDE THE FINAL SURGE I NEED...
VANDAL THINKS HE'S ALREADY WON...

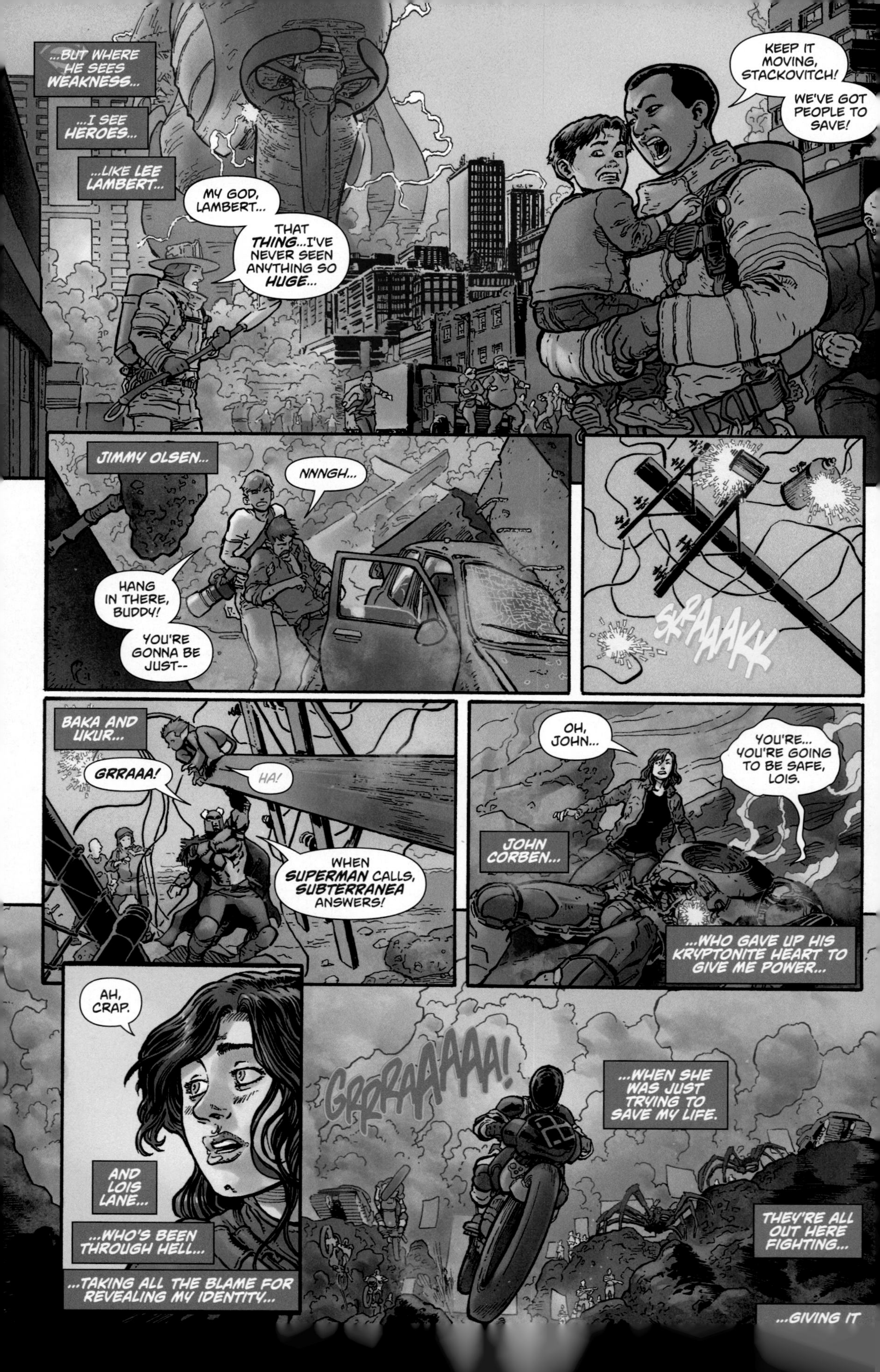
...BUT WHERE HE SEES WEAKNESS...
...I SEE HEROES...
...LIKE LEE LAMBERT...
MY GOD, LAMBERT...
THAT THING...I'VE NEVER SEEN ANYTHING SO HUGE...
KEEP IT MOVING, STACKOVITCH!
WE'VE GOT PEOPLE TO SAVE!
JIMMY OLSEN...
NNNGH...
HANG IN THERE, BUDDY!
YOU'RE GONNA BE JUST--
SKRAAAKK
BAKA AND UKUR...
GRRAAA!
HA!
WHEN SUPERMAN CALLS, SUBTERRANEA ANSWERS!
OH, JOHN...
YOU'RE... YOU'RE GOING TO BE SAFE, LOIS.
JOHN CORBEN...
...WHO GAVE UP HIS KRYPTONITE HEART TO GIVE ME POWER...
AH, CRAP.
GRRRAAAAAA!
...WHEN SHE WAS JUST TRYING TO SAVE MY LIFE.
AND LOIS LANE...
...WHO'S BEEN THROUGH HELL...
...TAKING ALL THE BLAME FOR REVEALING MY IDENTITY...
THEY'RE ALL OUT HERE FIGHTING...
...GIVING IT

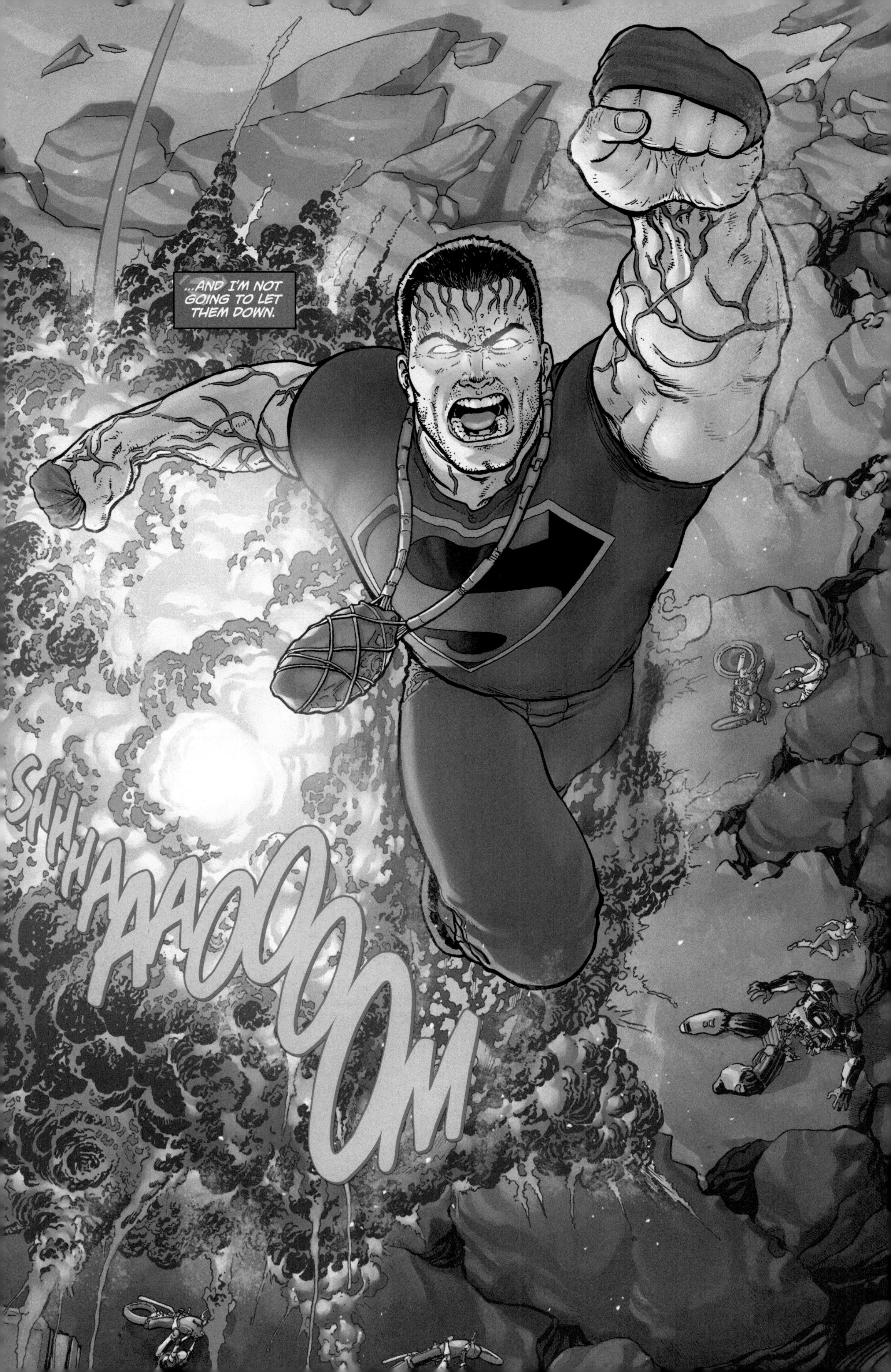
...AND I'M NOT GOING TO LET THEM DOWN.
SHHHAAAOOOOOM

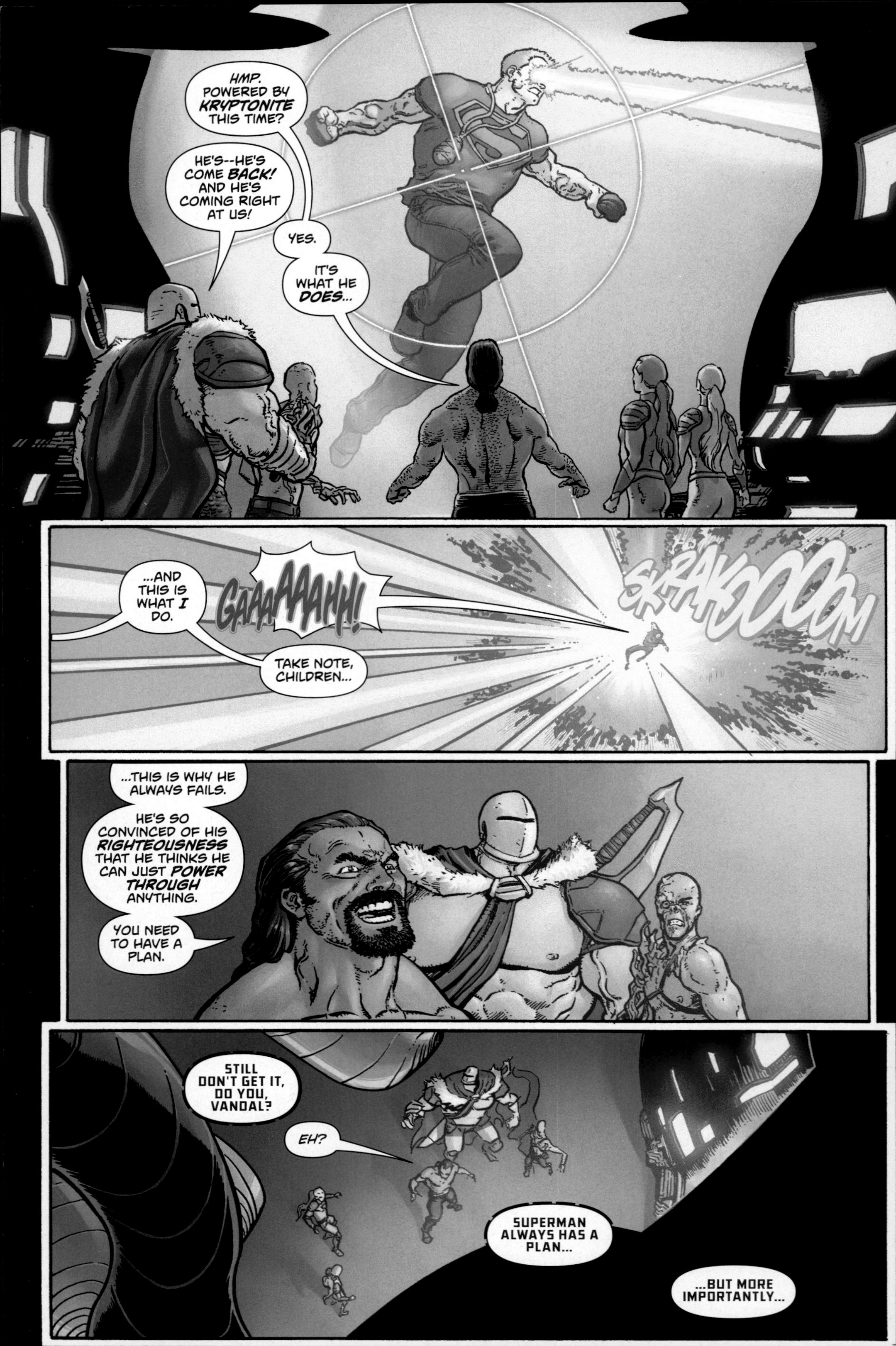
HMP. POWERED BY KRYPTONITE THIS TIME?
HE'S--HE'S COME BACK! AND HE'S COMING RIGHT AT US!
YES.
IT'S WHAT HE DOES...
...AND THIS IS WHAT I DO.
GAAAAAAHH!
SKRAKOOOOM
TAKE NOTE, CHILDREN...
...THIS IS WHY HE ALWAYS FAILS.
HE'S SO CONVINCED OF HIS RIGHTEOUSNESS THAT HE THINKS HE CAN JUST POWER THROUGH ANYTHING.
YOU NEED TO HAVE A PLAN.
STILL DON'T GET IT, DO YOU, VANDAL?
EH?
SUPERMAN ALWAYS HAS A PLAN...
...BUT MORE IMPORTANTLY...

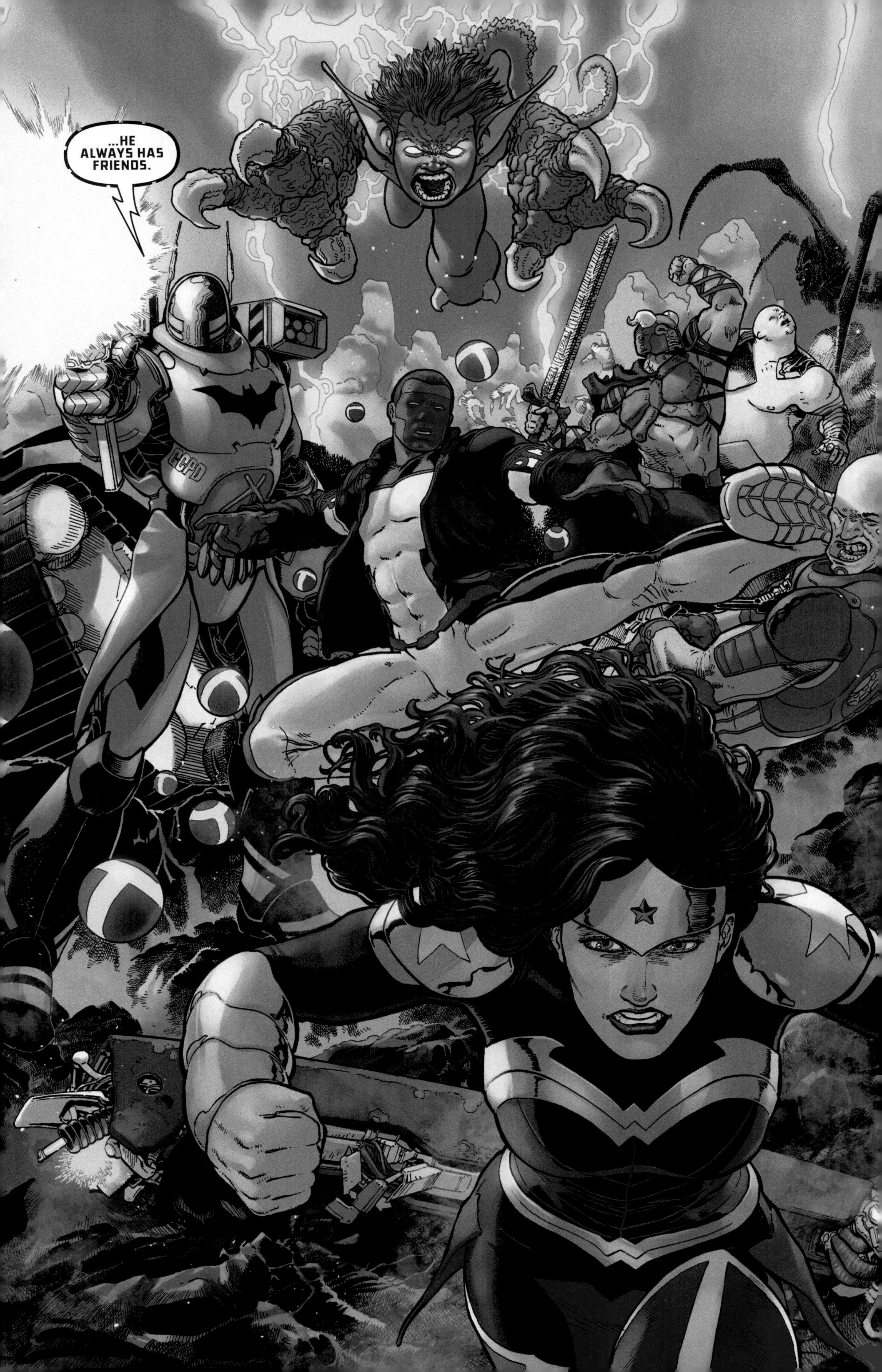
...HE ALWAYS HAS FRIENDS.

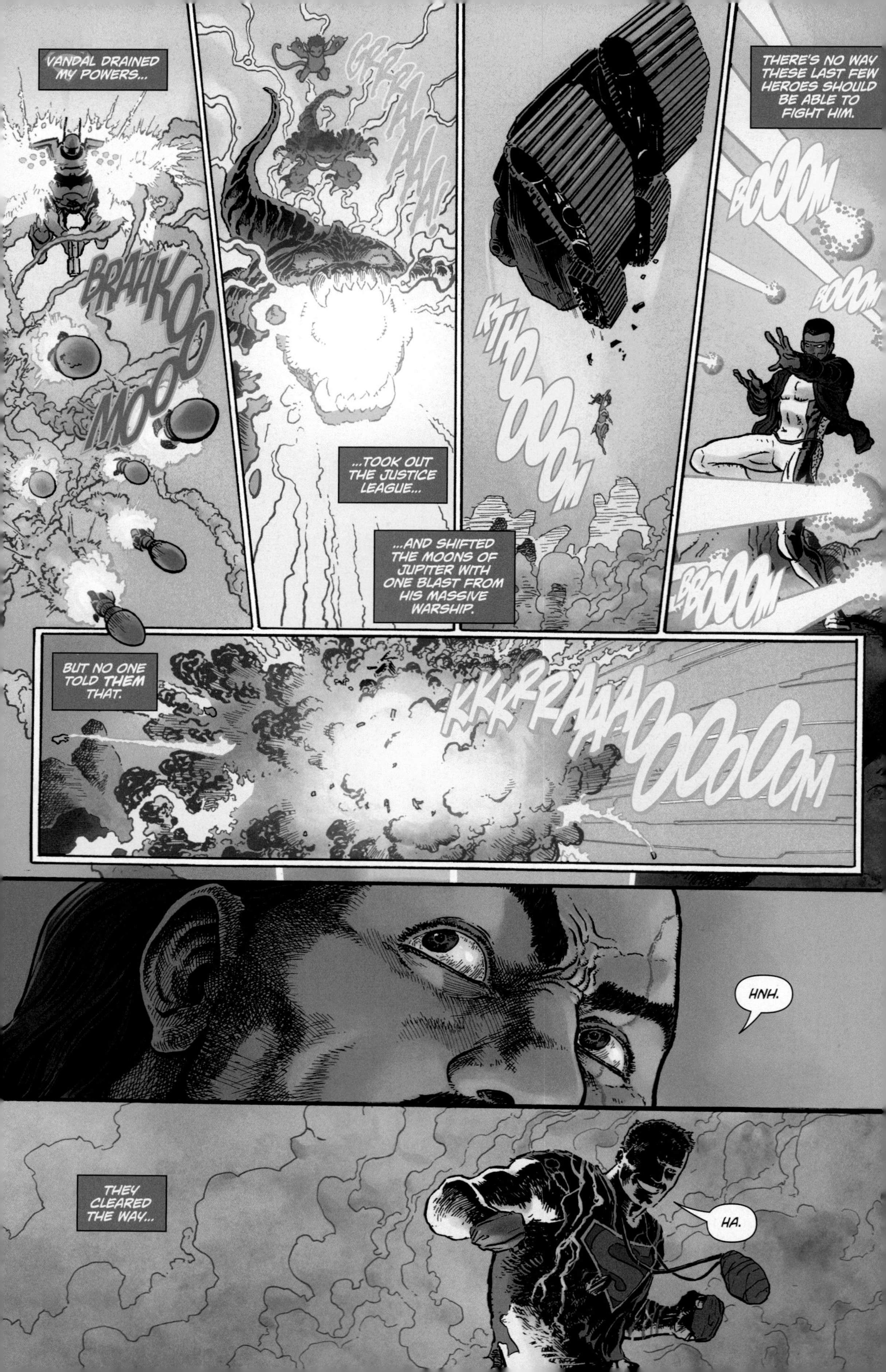
VANDAL DRAINED MY POWERS...
BRAAKOOOM
GRRRAAAAA!
...TOOK OUT THE JUSTICE LEAGUE...
KTHOOOOOOM
...AND SHIFTED THE MOONS OF JUPITER WITH ONE BLAST FROM HIS MASSIVE WARSHIP.
THERE'S NO WAY THESE LAST FEW HEROES SHOULD BE ABLE TO FIGHT HIM.
BOOOM
BOOOM
BBOOOM
BUT NO ONE TOLD THEM THAT.
KKKRRAAAOOOOOOM
HNH.
THEY CLEARED THE WAY...
HA.

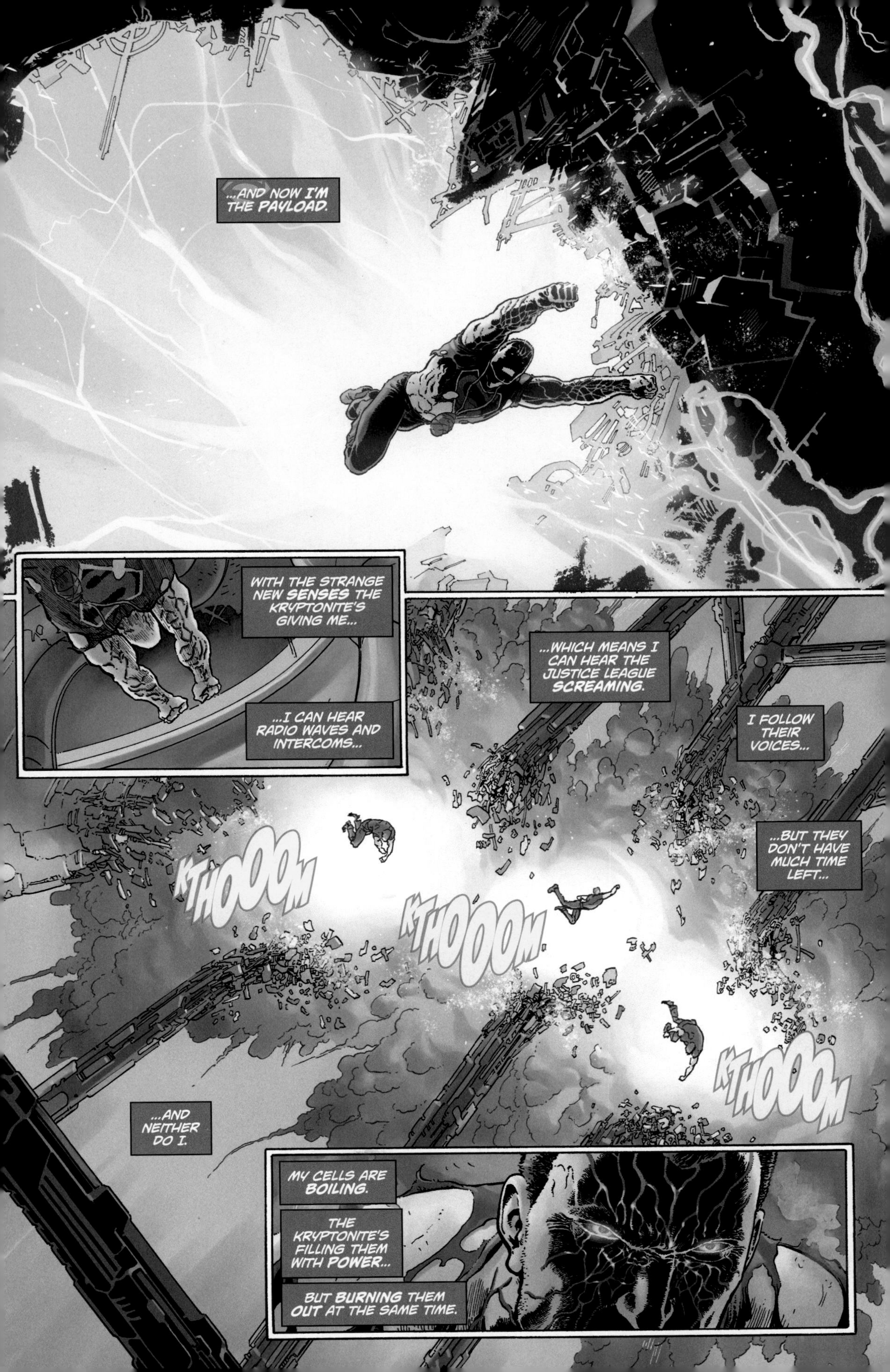
...AND NOW I'M THE PAYLOAD.
WITH THE STRANGE NEW SENSES THE KRYPTONITE'S GIVING ME...
...I CAN HEAR RADIO WAVES AND INTERCOMS...
...WHICH MEANS I CAN HEAR THE JUSTICE LEAGUE SCREAMING.
I FOLLOW THEIR VOICES...
...BUT THEY DON'T HAVE MUCH TIME LEFT...
KTHOOOM
KTHOOOM
KTHOOOM
...AND NEITHER DO I.
MY CELLS ARE BOILING.
THE KRYPTONITE'S FILLING THEM WITH POWER...
BUT BURNING THEM OUT AT THE SAME TIME.

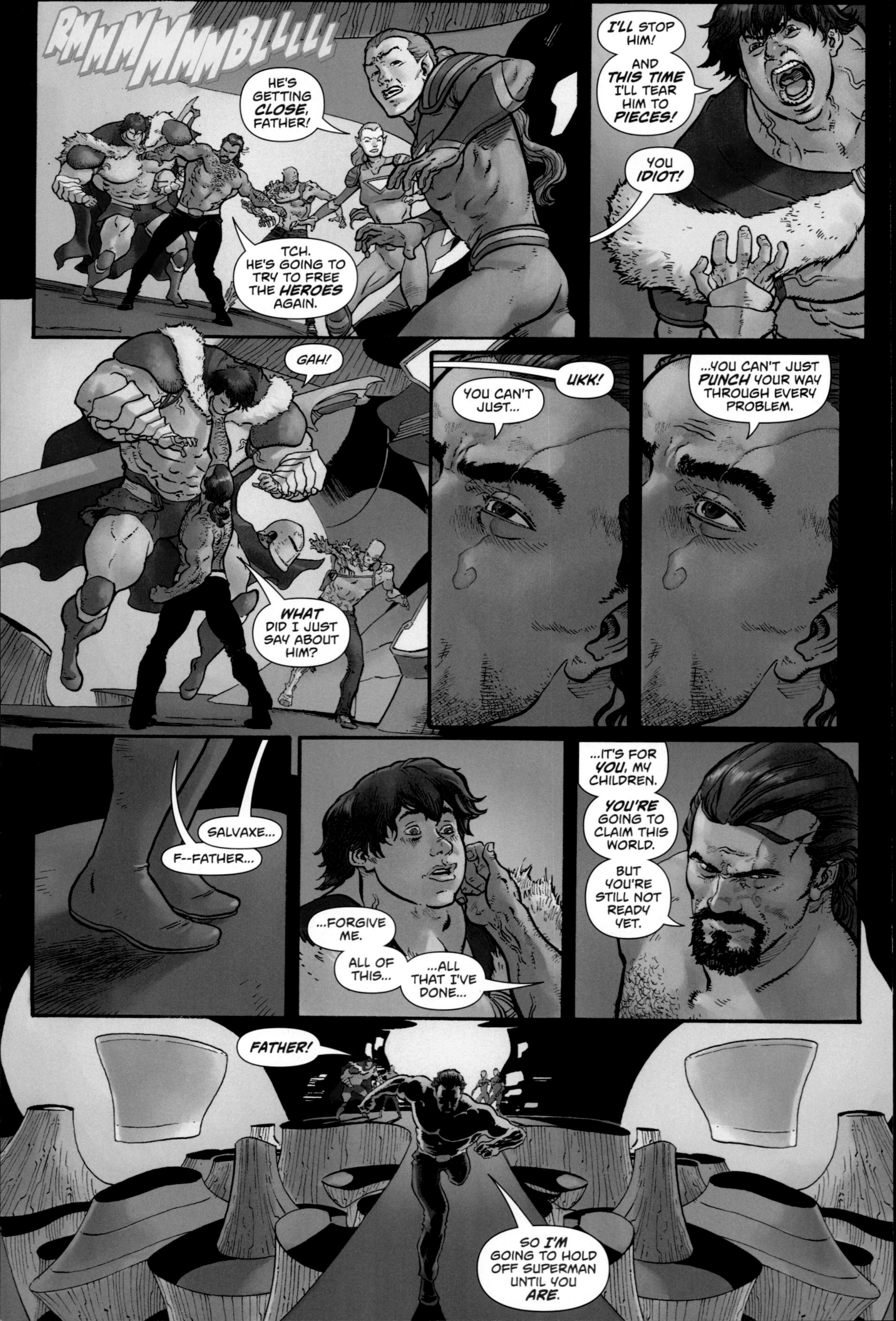
RMMMMMMBLLLLL
HE'S GETTING CLOSE, FATHER!
TCH. HE'S GOING TO TRY TO FREE THE HEROES AGAIN.
I'LL STOP HIM!
AND THIS TIME I'LL TEAR HIM TO PIECES!
YOU IDIOT!
GAH!
WHAT DID I JUST SAY ABOUT HIM?
UKK!
YOU CAN'T JUST...
...YOU CAN'T JUST PUNCH YOUR WAY THROUGH EVERY PROBLEM.
SALVAXE...
F--FATHER...
...FORGIVE ME.
ALL OF THIS...
...ALL THAT I'VE DONE...
...IT'S FOR YOU, MY CHILDREN.
YOU'RE GOING TO CLAIM THIS WORLD.
BUT YOU'RE STILL NOT READY YET.
FATHER!
SO I'M GOING TO HOLD OFF SUPERMAN UNTIL YOU ARE.

ALL RIGHT, SUPES! I'VE ACCESSED THE CARRIER'S COMPUTER SYSTEM! TRANSMITTING THE LOCATION OF THE JUSTICE LEAGUE...

...GOT IT. CROSS-CHECKS WITH WHAT I'M PICKING UP. I'M COMING IN FROM THE NORTH...

...AND WE'RE COMING UP FROM THE EAST!

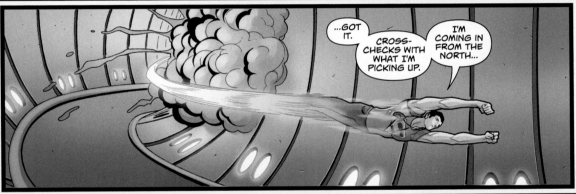

SHOULD BE A CLEAR PATHWAY. I'M DISARMING THE AUTOMATED CANNONS.

DAMMIT. THIS IS BAD.

WHAT? WHY?

VANDAL'S TOO SMART TO MAKE IT THIS EASY. WHERE THE HELL IS HE?

MR. TERRIFIC?

MY NANO-PROBES HAVE JUST PICKED UP TRACES OF HIS DNA... ...OH NO...

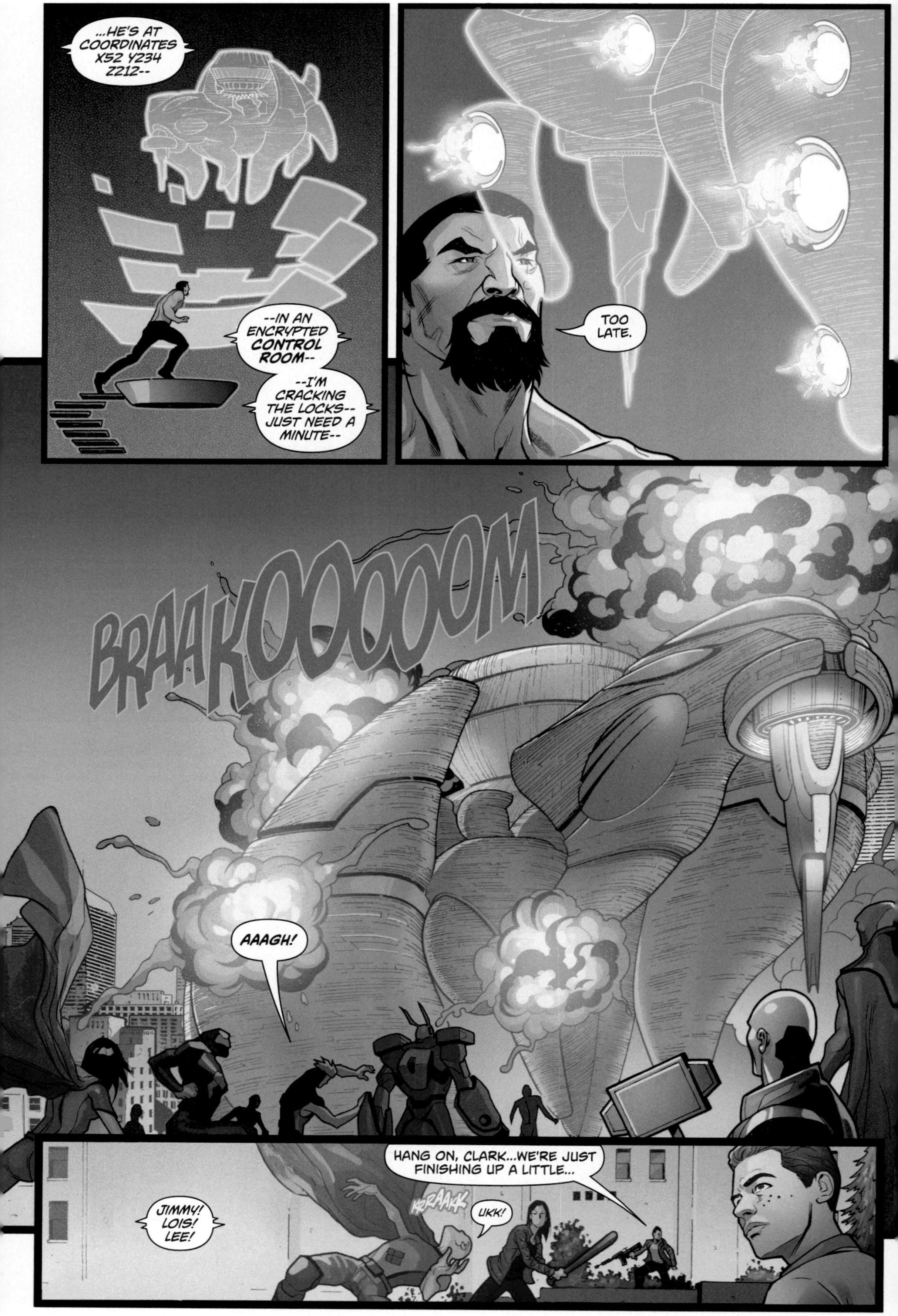
...HE'S AT COORDINATES X52 Y234 Z212--
--IN AN ENCRYPTED CONTROL ROOM--
--I'M CRACKING THE LOCKS-- JUST NEED A MINUTE--
TOO LATE.
BRAAKOOOOOM
AAAGH!
JIMMY! LOIS! LEE!
KRAAKK
UKK!
HANG ON, CLARK...WE'RE JUST FINISHING UP A LITTLE...

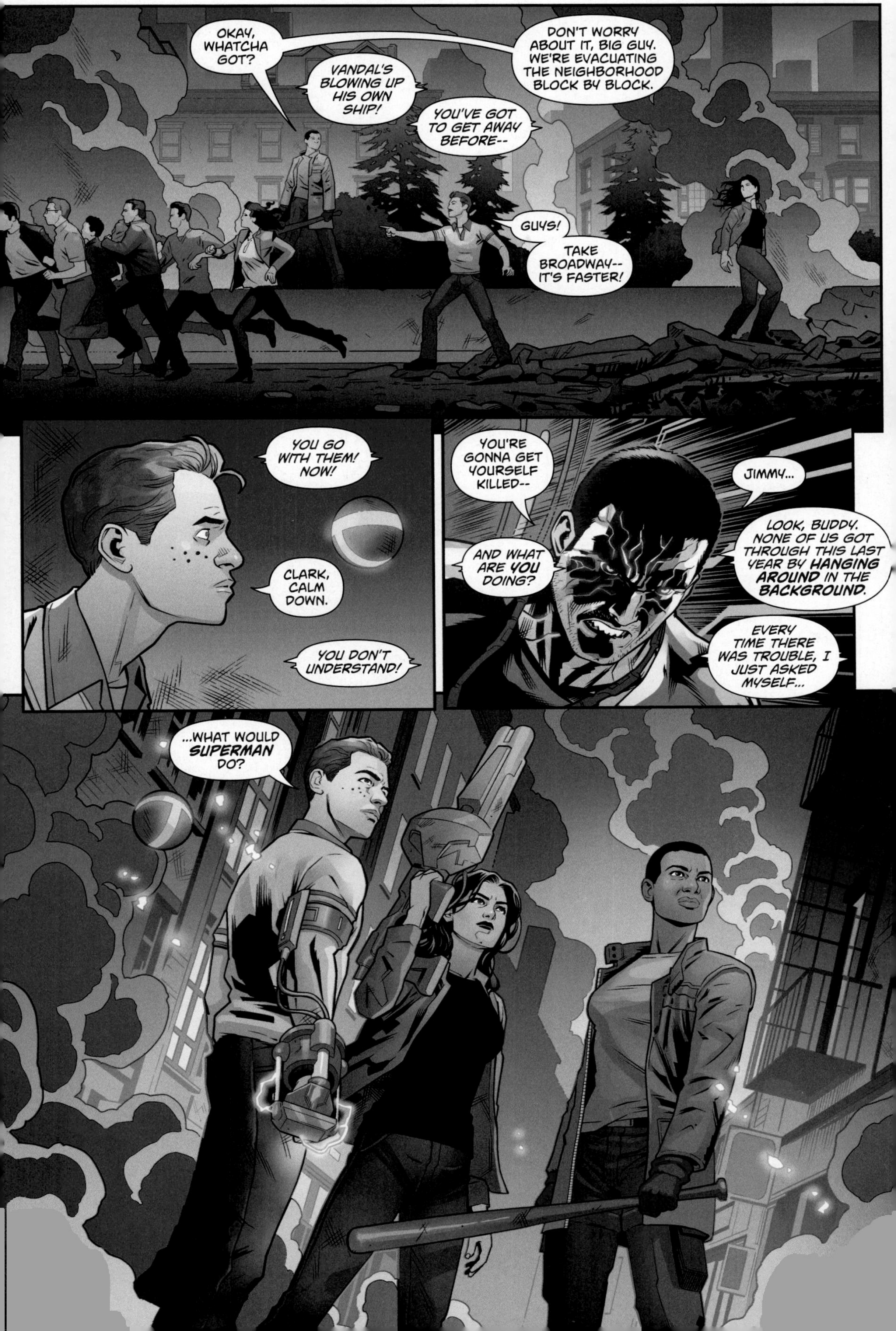
OKAY, WHATCHA GOT?
DON'T WORRY ABOUT IT, BIG GUY. WE'RE EVACUATING THE NEIGHBORHOOD BLOCK BY BLOCK.
VANDAL'S BLOWING UP HIS OWN SHIP!
YOU'VE GOT TO GET AWAY BEFORE--
GUYS!
TAKE BROADWAY-- IT'S FASTER!
YOU GO WITH THEM! NOW!
CLARK, CALM DOWN.
YOU DON'T UNDERSTAND!
YOU'RE GONNA GET YOURSELF KILLED--
JIMMY...
AND WHAT ARE YOU DOING?
LOOK, BUDDY. NONE OF US GOT THROUGH THIS LAST YEAR BY HANGING AROUND IN THE BACKGROUND.
EVERY TIME THERE WAS TROUBLE, I JUST ASKED MYSELF...
...WHAT WOULD SUPERMAN DO?

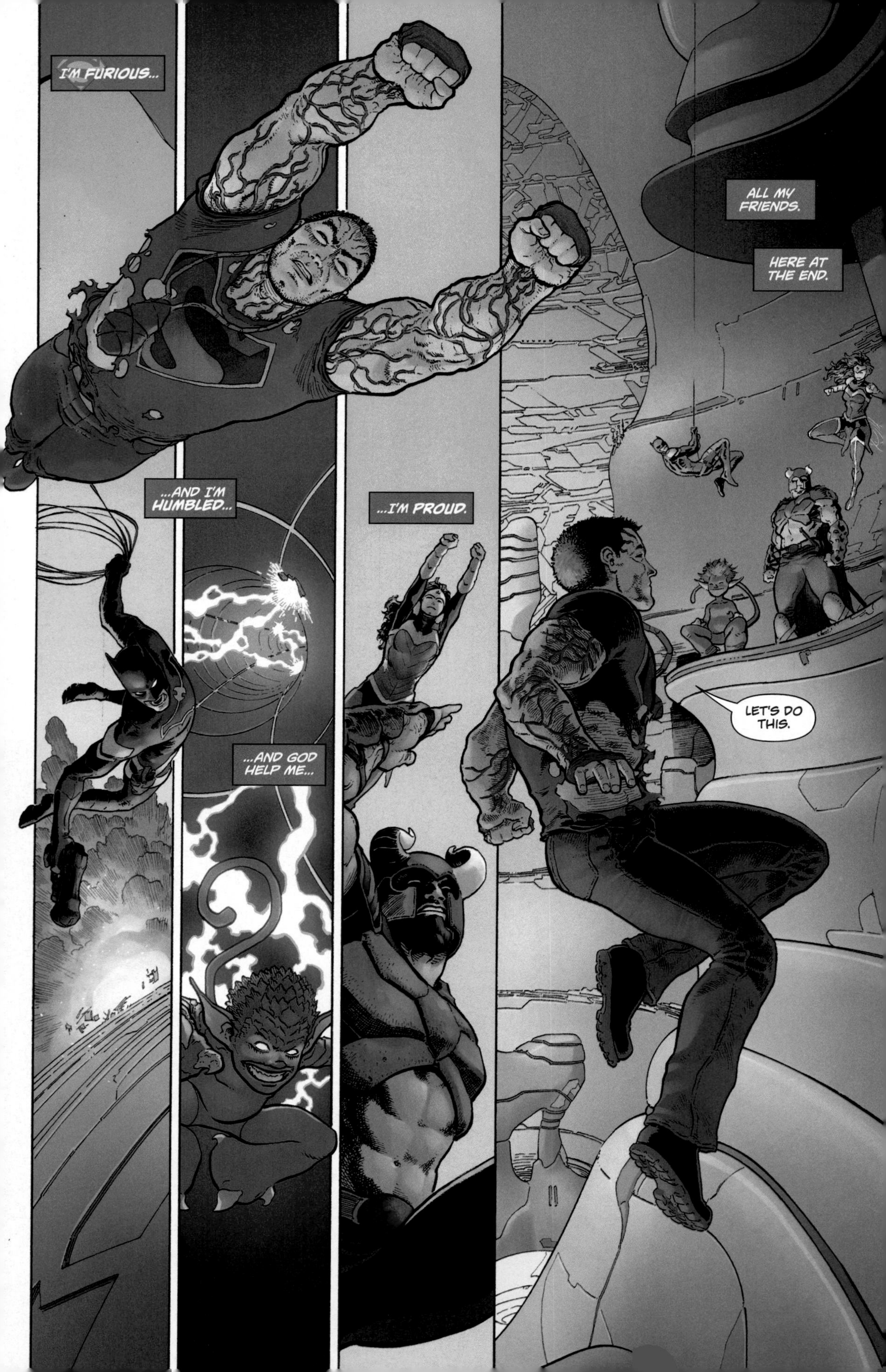
I'M FURIOUS...
...AND I'M HUMBLED...
...AND GOD HELP ME...
...I'M PROUD.
ALL MY FRIENDS.
HERE AT THE END.
LET'S DO THIS.

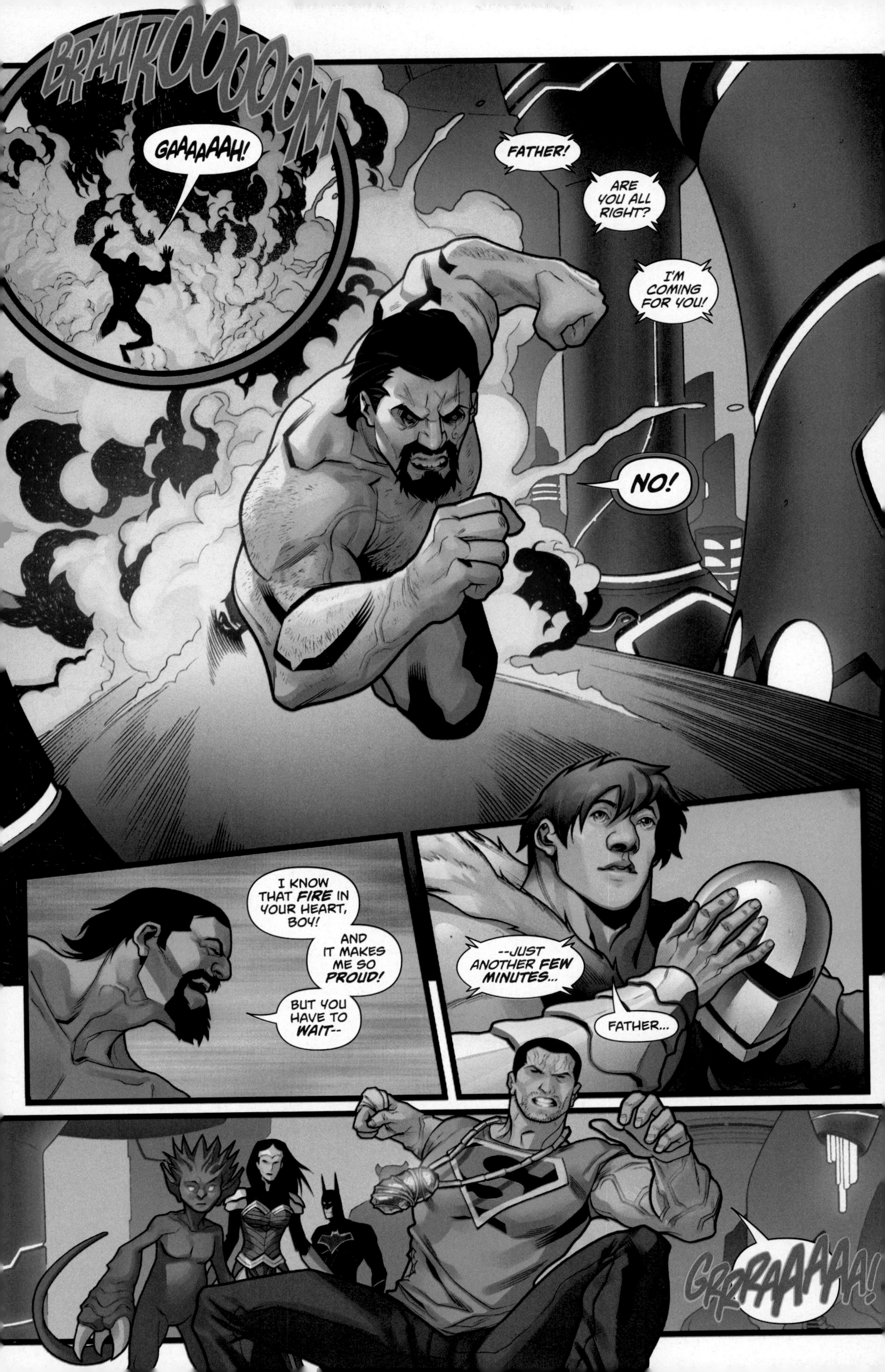
BRAAKOOOOOM
GAAAAAAH!
FATHER!
ARE YOU ALL RIGHT?
I'M COMING FOR YOU!
NO!
I KNOW THAT FIRE IN YOUR HEART, BOY!
AND IT MAKES ME SO PROUD!
BUT YOU HAVE TO WAIT--
--JUST ANOTHER FEW MINUTES...
FATHER...
GRRRAAAAAA!

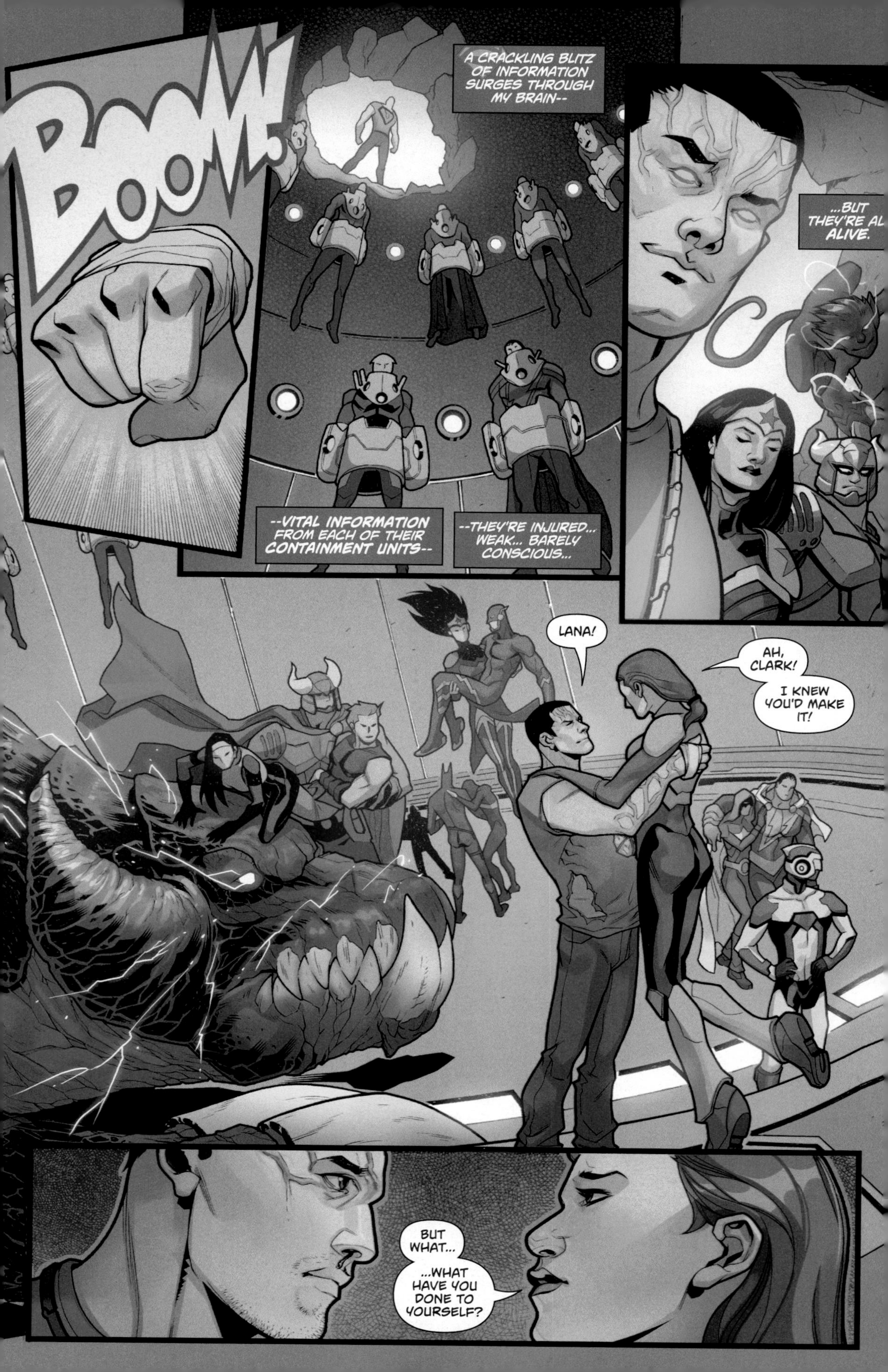
BOOM!
A CRACKLING BLITZ OF INFORMATION SURGES THROUGH MY BRAIN--
--VITAL INFORMATION FROM EACH OF THEIR CONTAINMENT UNITS--
--THEY'RE INJURED... WEAK... BARELY CONSCIOUS...
...BUT THEY'RE AL ALIVE.
LANA!
AH, CLARK!
I KNEW YOU'D MAKE IT!
BUT WHAT...
...WHAT HAVE YOU DONE TO YOURSELF?

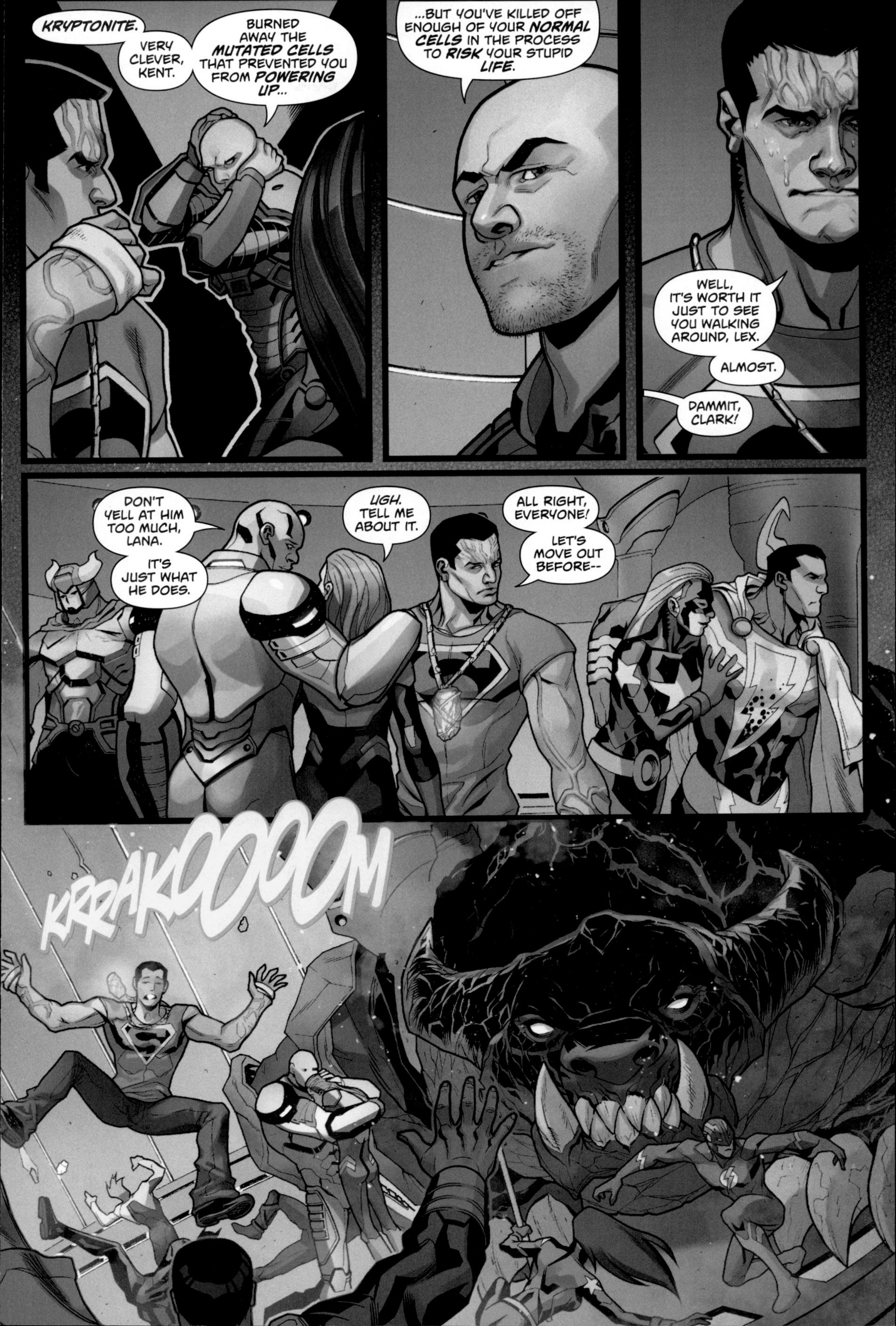
KRYPTONITE.
VERY CLEVER, KENT.
BURNED AWAY THE MUTATED CELLS THAT PREVENTED YOU FROM POWERING UP...
...BUT YOU'VE KILLED OFF ENOUGH OF YOUR NORMAL CELLS IN THE PROCESS TO RISK YOUR STUPID LIFE.
WELL, IT'S WORTH IT JUST TO SEE YOU WALKING AROUND, LEX.
ALMOST.
DAMMIT, CLARK!
DON'T YELL AT HIM TOO MUCH, LANA.
IT'S JUST WHAT HE DOES.
UGH. TELL ME ABOUT IT.
ALL RIGHT, EVERYONE!
LET'S MOVE OUT BEFORE--
KRRAKOOOOM

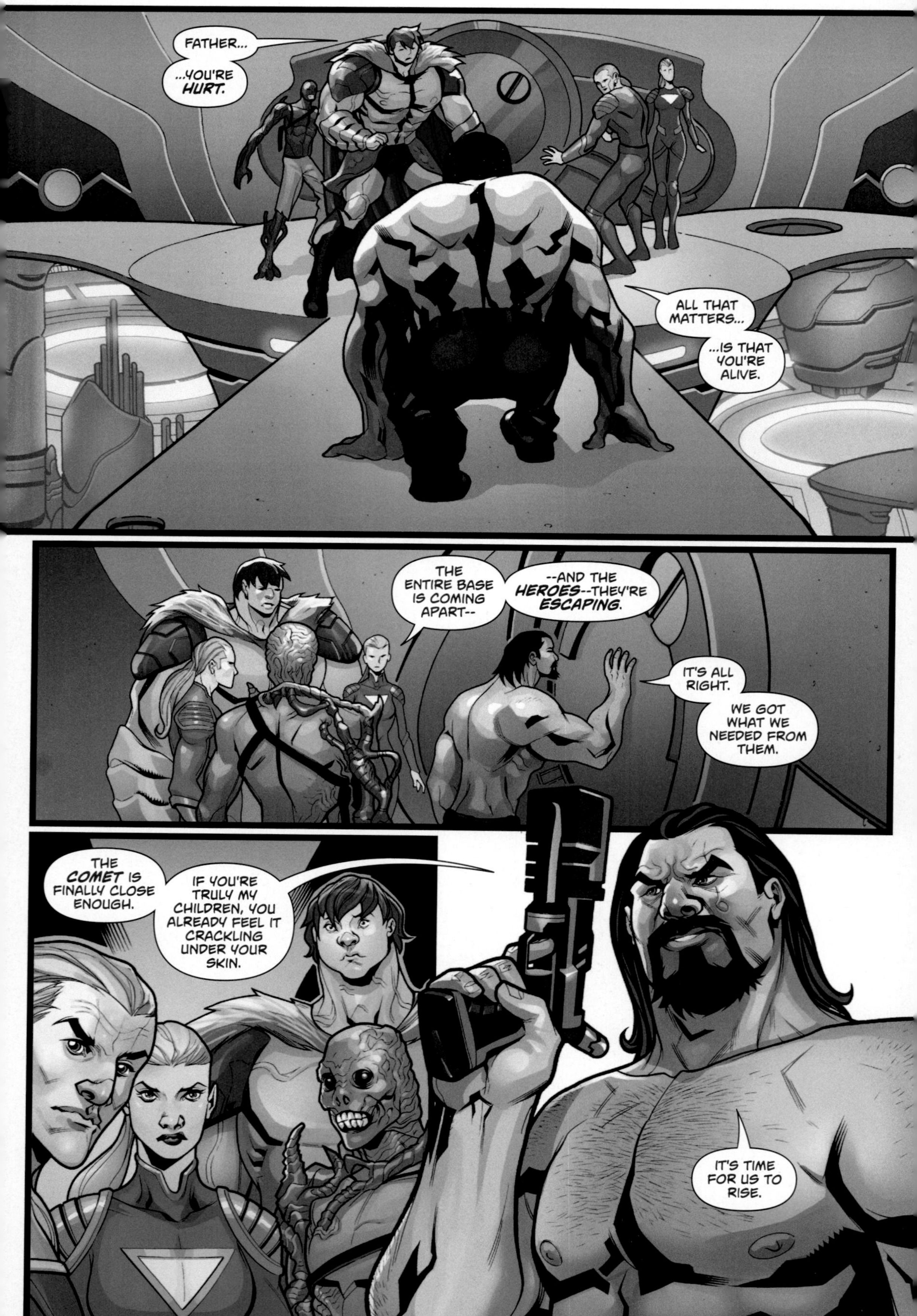
FATHER...
...YOU'RE *HURT.*
ALL THAT MATTERS...
...IS THAT YOU'RE ALIVE.
THE ENTIRE BASE IS COMING APART--
--AND THE *HEROES*--THEY'RE *ESCAPING*.
IT'S ALL RIGHT.
WE GOT WHAT WE NEEDED FROM THEM.
THE *COMET* IS FINALLY CLOSE ENOUGH.
IF YOU'RE TRULY MY CHILDREN, YOU ALREADY FEEL IT CRACKLING UNDER YOUR SKIN.
IT'S TIME FOR US TO RISE.

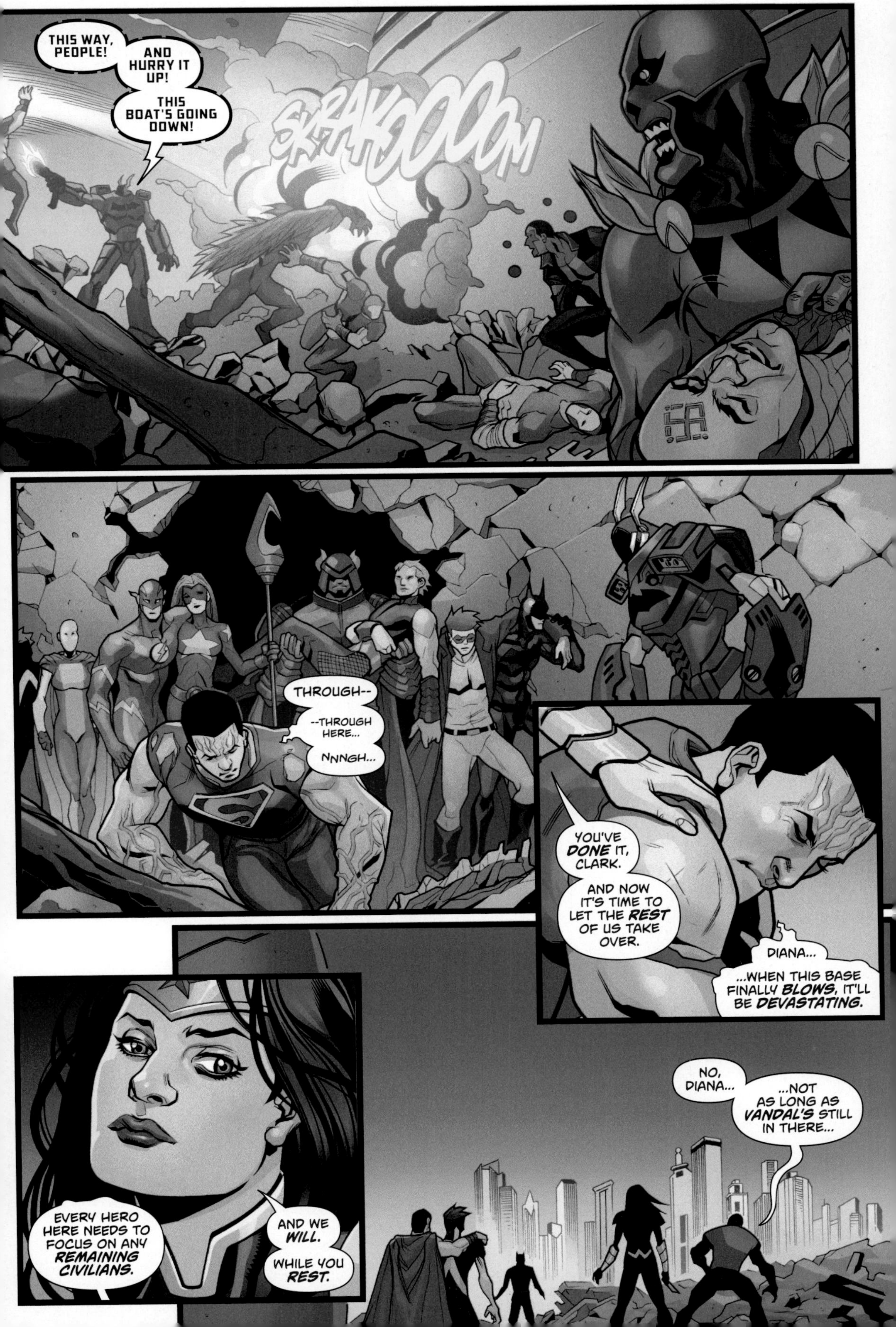
THIS WAY, PEOPLE!
AND HURRY IT UP!
THIS BOAT'S GOING DOWN!
SKRAKOOOOOM
THROUGH--
--THROUGH HERE...
NNNGH...
YOU'VE *DONE* IT, CLARK.
AND NOW IT'S TIME TO LET THE *REST* OF US TAKE OVER.
DIANA...
...WHEN THIS BASE FINALLY *BLOWS*, IT'LL BE *DEVASTATING*.
EVERY HERO HERE NEEDS TO FOCUS ON ANY *REMAINING CIVILIANS*.
AND WE *WILL*.
WHILE YOU *REST*.
NO, DIANA...
...NOT AS LONG AS *VANDAL'S* STILL IN THERE...

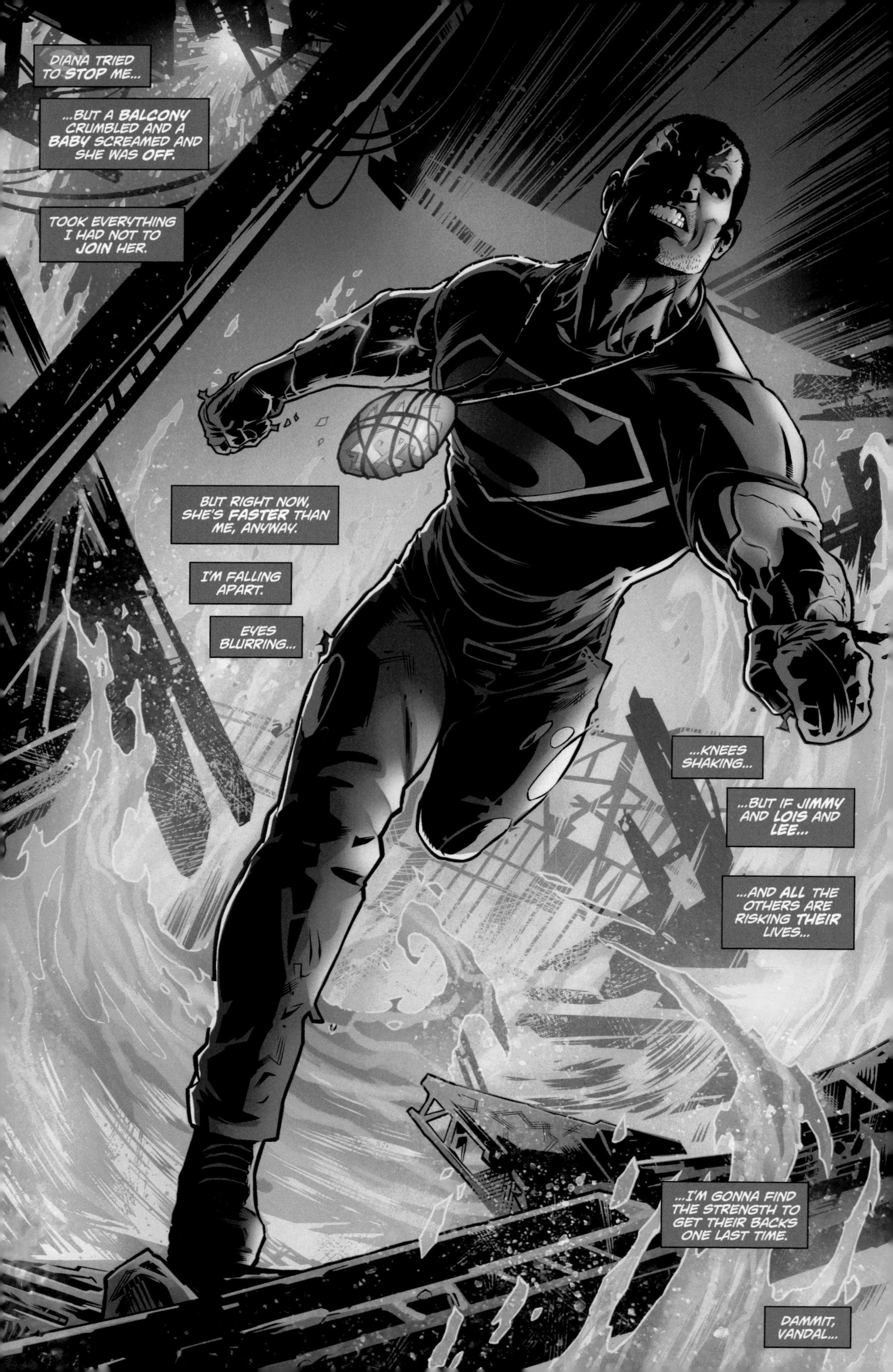
DIANA TRIED TO STOP ME...
...BUT A BALCONY CRUMBLED AND A BABY SCREAMED AND SHE WAS OFF.
TOOK EVERYTHING I HAD NOT TO JOIN HER.
BUT RIGHT NOW, SHE'S FASTER THAN ME, ANYWAY.
I'M FALLING APART.
EYES BLURRING...
...KNEES SHAKING...
...BUT IF JIMMY AND LOIS AND LEE...
...AND ALL THE OTHERS ARE RISKING THEIR LIVES...
...I'M GONNA FIND THE STRENGTH TO GET THEIR BACKS ONE LAST TIME.
DAMMIT, VANDAL...

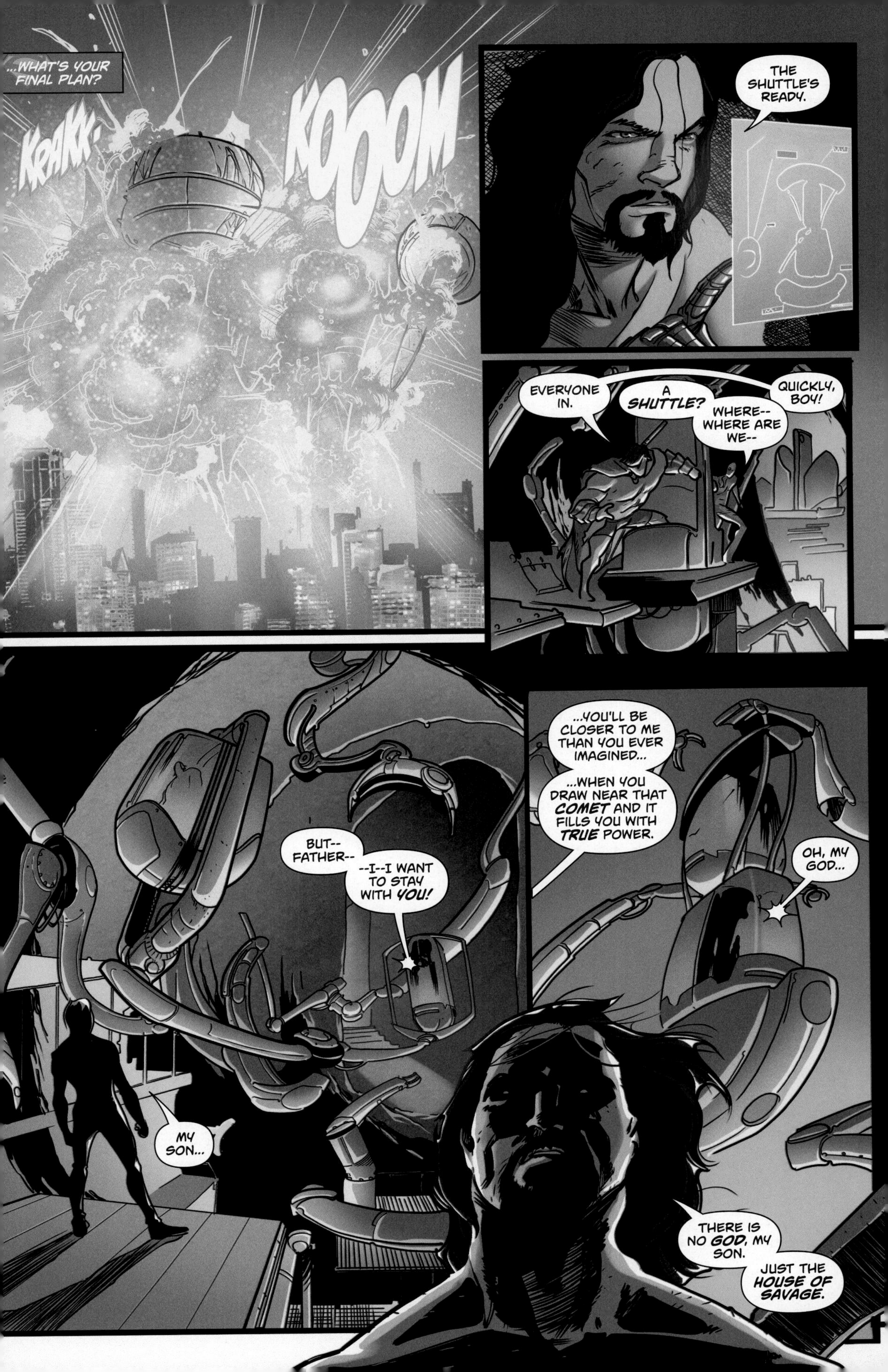
...WHAT'S YOUR FINAL PLAN?
KRAKK
KOOOM
THE SHUTTLE'S READY.
EVERYONE IN.
A SHUTTLE?
QUICKLY, BOY!
WHERE-- WHERE ARE WE--
MY SON...
BUT-- FATHER--
--I--I WANT TO STAY WITH YOU!
...YOU'LL BE CLOSER TO ME THAN YOU EVER IMAGINED...
...WHEN YOU DRAW NEAR THAT COMET AND IT FILLS YOU WITH TRUE POWER.
OH, MY GOD...
THERE IS NO GOD, MY SON.
JUST THE HOUSE OF SAVAGE.

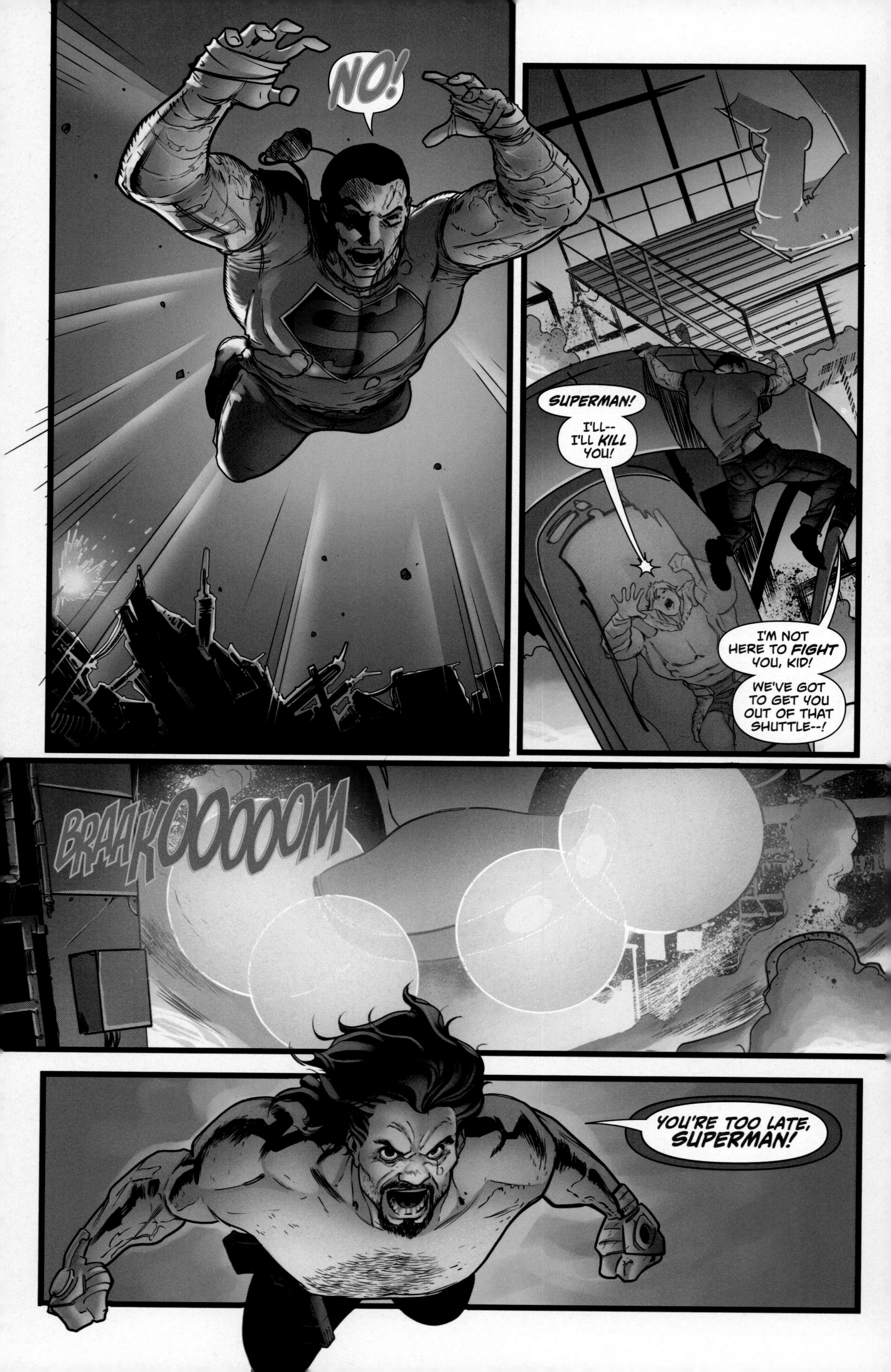
NO!
SUPERMAN!
I'LL-- I'LL KILL YOU!
I'M NOT HERE TO FIGHT YOU, KID!
WE'VE GOT TO GET YOU OUT OF THAT SHUTTLE--!
BRAAKOOOOOM
YOU'RE TOO LATE, SUPERMAN!

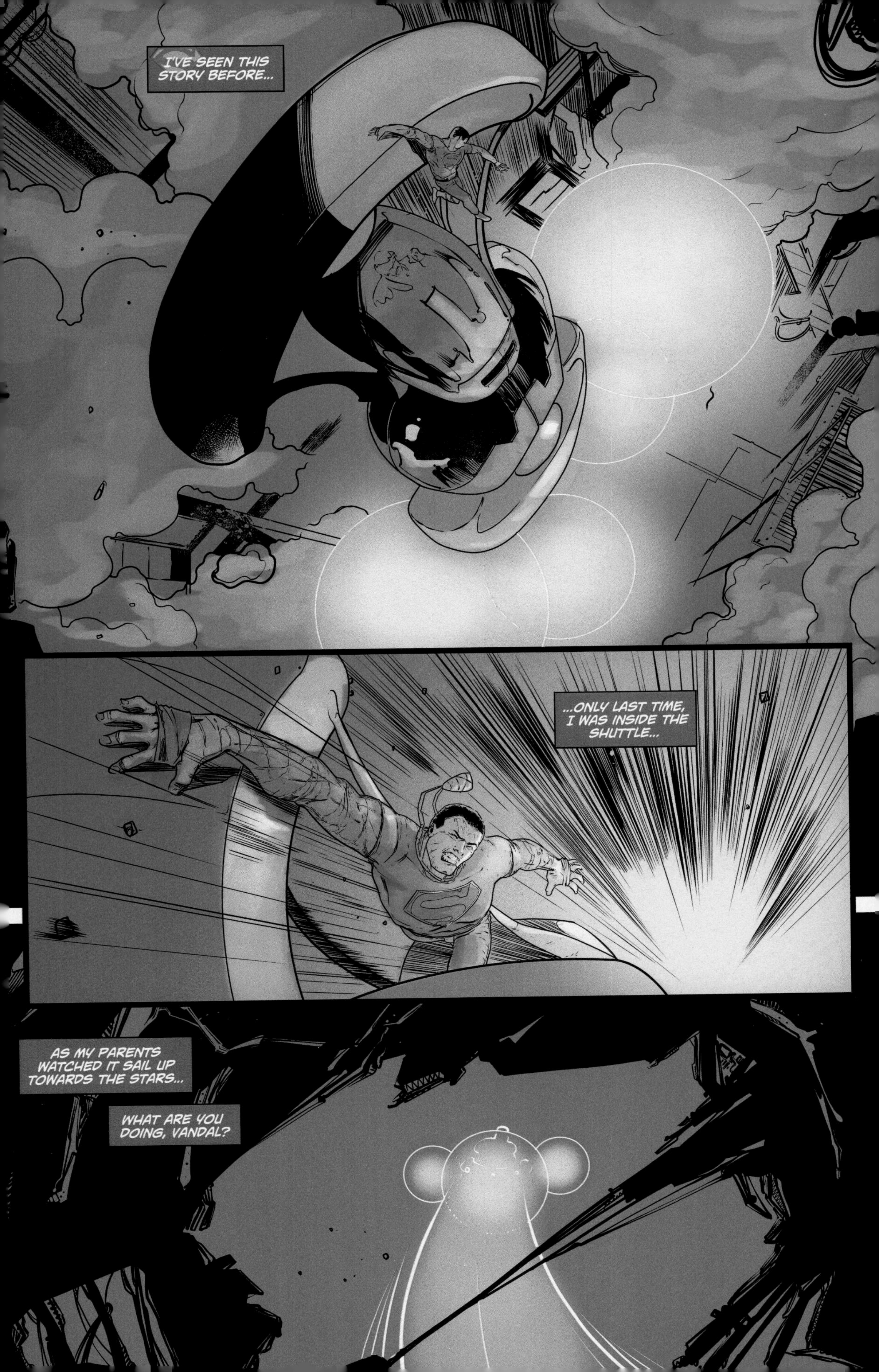
I'VE SEEN THIS STORY BEFORE...
...ONLY LAST TIME, I WAS INSIDE THE SHUTTLE...
AS MY PARENTS WATCHED IT SAIL UP TOWARDS THE STARS...
WHAT ARE YOU DOING, VANDAL?

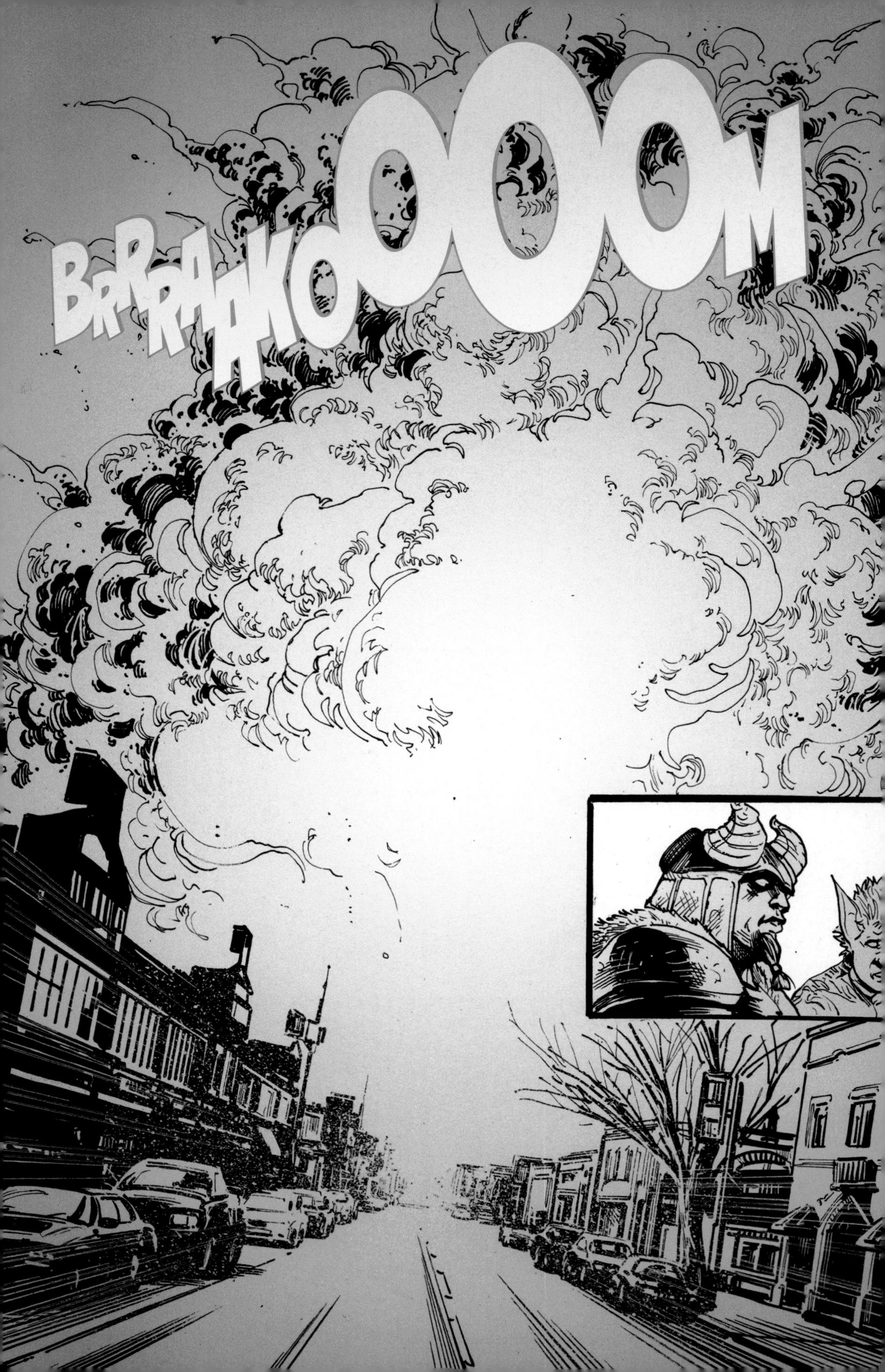
BRRRAAKOOOOM

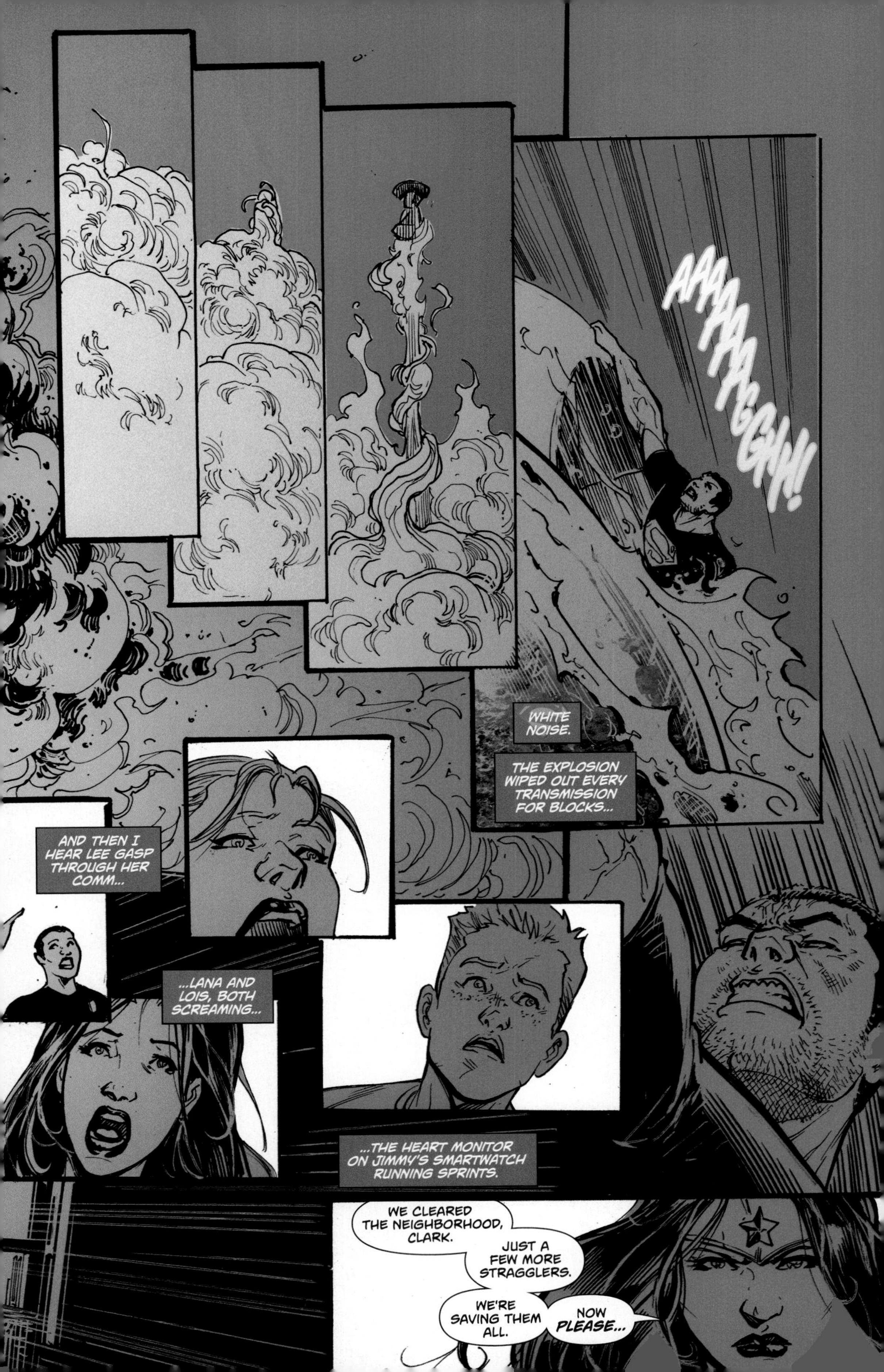
AAAAAAAAAGGHH!
WHITE NOISE.
THE EXPLOSION WIPED OUT EVERY TRANSMISSION FOR BLOCKS...
AND THEN I HEAR LEE GASP THROUGH HER COMM...
...LANA AND LOIS, BOTH SCREAMING...
...THE HEART MONITOR ON JIMMY'S SMARTWATCH RUNNING SPRINTS.
WE CLEARED THE NEIGHBORHOOD, CLARK.
JUST A FEW MORE STRAGGLERS.
WE'RE SAVING THEM ALL.
NOW PLEASE...

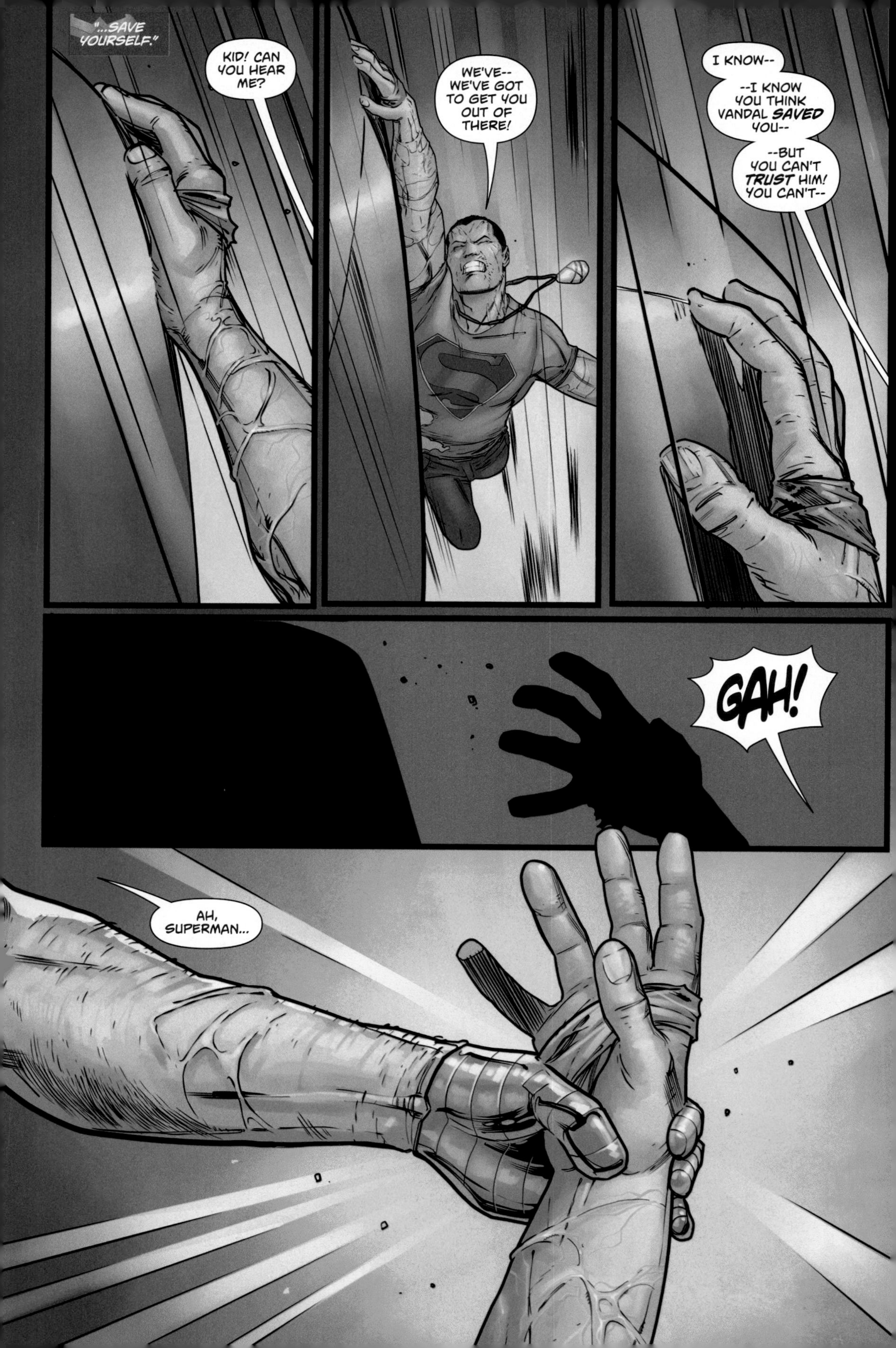
"...SAVE YOURSELF."
KID! CAN YOU HEAR ME?
WE'VE-- WE'VE GOT TO GET YOU OUT OF THERE!
I KNOW--
--I KNOW YOU THINK VANDAL SAVED YOU--
--BUT YOU CAN'T TRUST HIM! YOU CAN'T--
GAH!
AH, SUPERMAN...

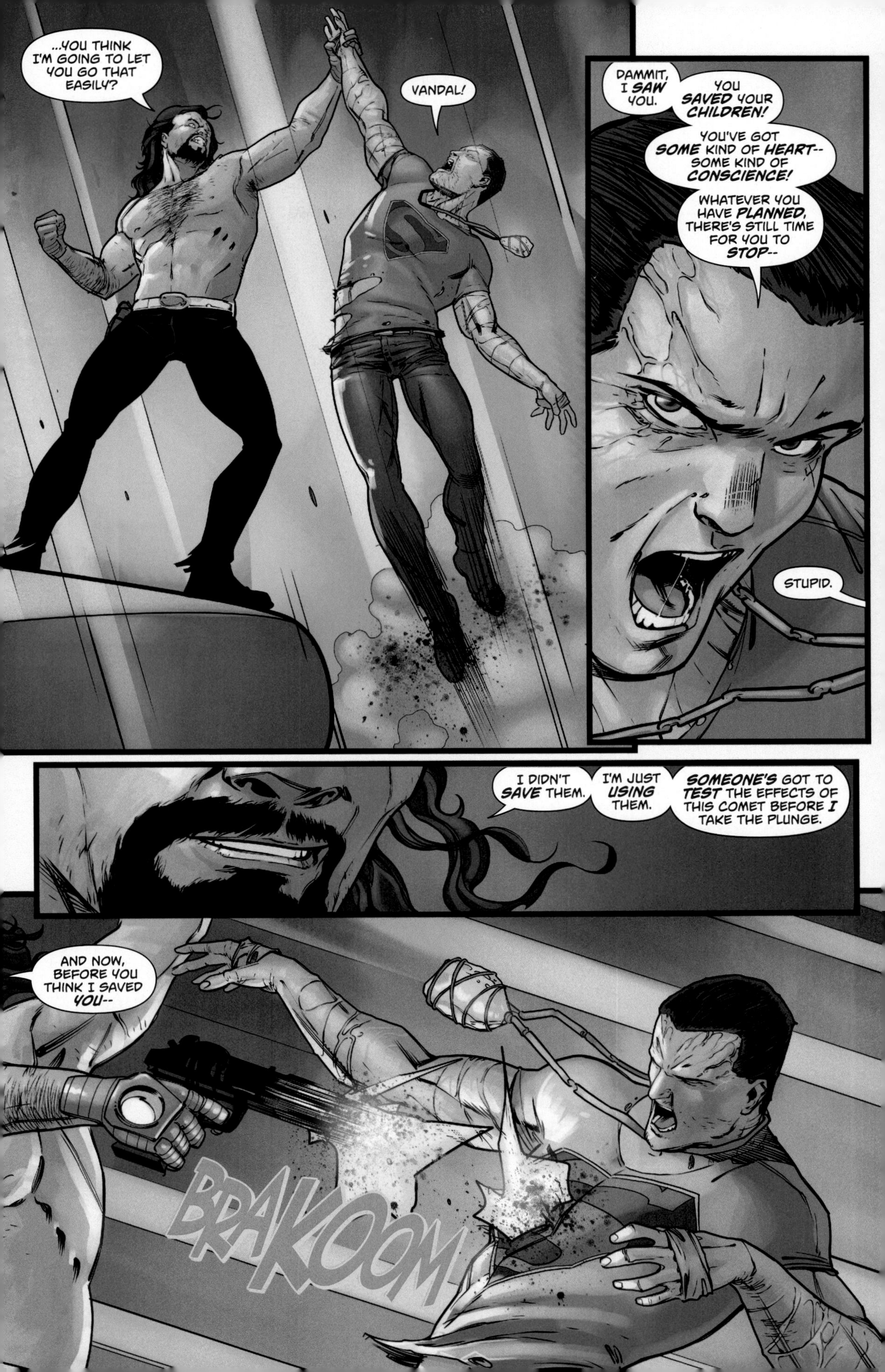
...YOU THINK I'M GOING TO LET YOU GO THAT EASILY?
VANDAL!
DAMMIT, I SAW YOU.
YOU SAVED YOUR CHILDREN!
YOU'VE GOT SOME KIND OF HEART-- SOME KIND OF CONSCIENCE!
WHATEVER YOU HAVE PLANNED, THERE'S STILL TIME FOR YOU TO STOP--
STUPID.
I DIDN'T SAVE THEM.
I'M JUST USING THEM.
SOMEONE'S GOT TO TEST THE EFFECTS OF THIS COMET BEFORE I TAKE THE PLUNGE.
AND NOW, BEFORE YOU THINK I SAVED YOU--
BRAKOOM

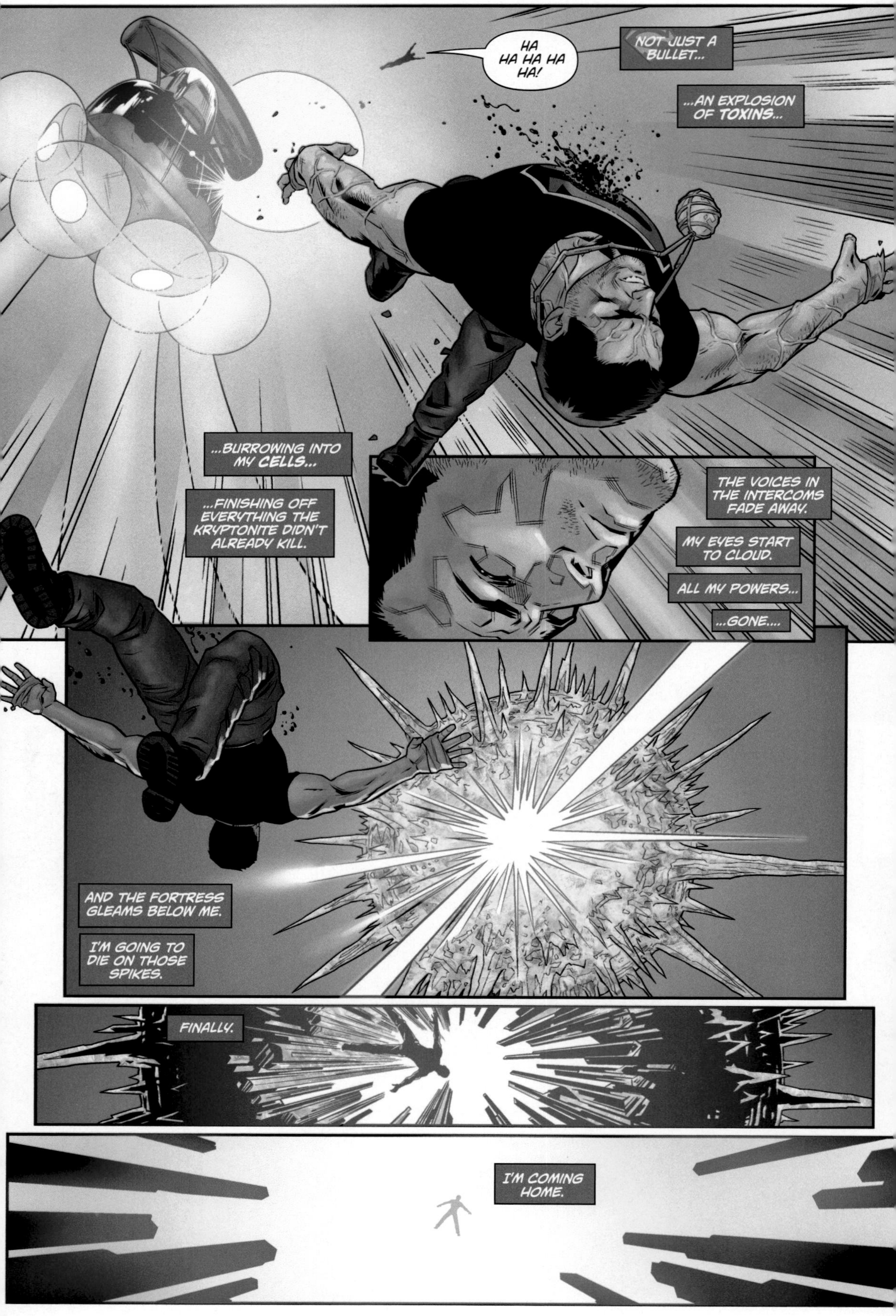
HA HA HA HA HA!
NOT JUST A BULLET...
...AN EXPLOSION OF TOXINS...
...BURROWING INTO MY CELLS...
...FINISHING OFF EVERYTHING THE KRYPTONITE DIDN'T ALREADY KILL.
THE VOICES IN THE INTERCOMS FADE AWAY.
MY EYES START TO CLOUD.
ALL MY POWERS...
...GONE....
AND THE FORTRESS GLEAMS BELOW ME.
I'M GOING TO DIE ON THOSE SPIKES.
FINALLY.
I'M COMING HOME.

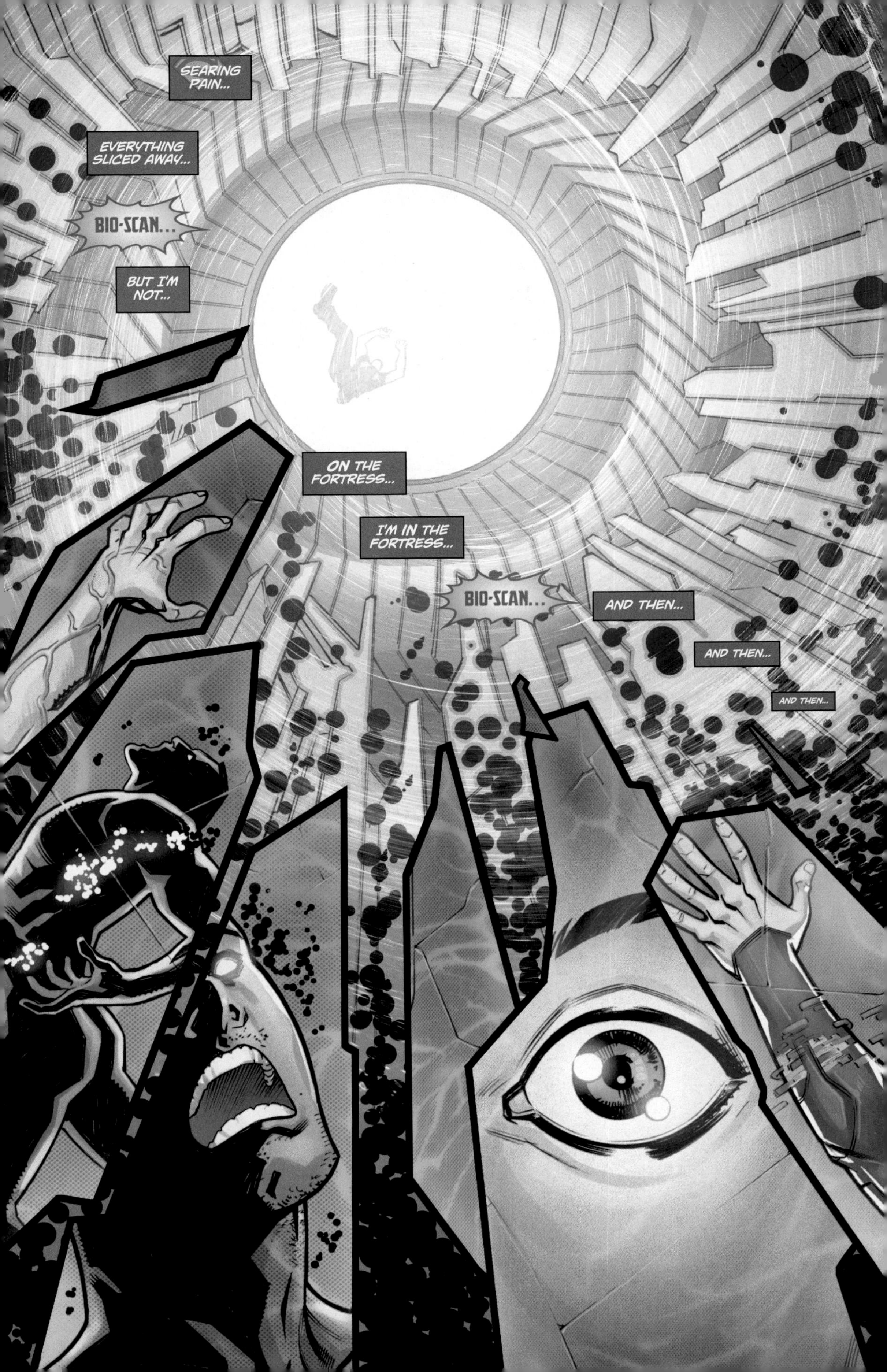
SEARING PAIN...
EVERYTHING SLICED AWAY...
BIO-SCAN...
BUT I'M NOT...
ON THE FORTRESS...
I'M IN THE FORTRESS...
BIO-SCAN...
AND THEN...
AND THEN...
AND THEN...

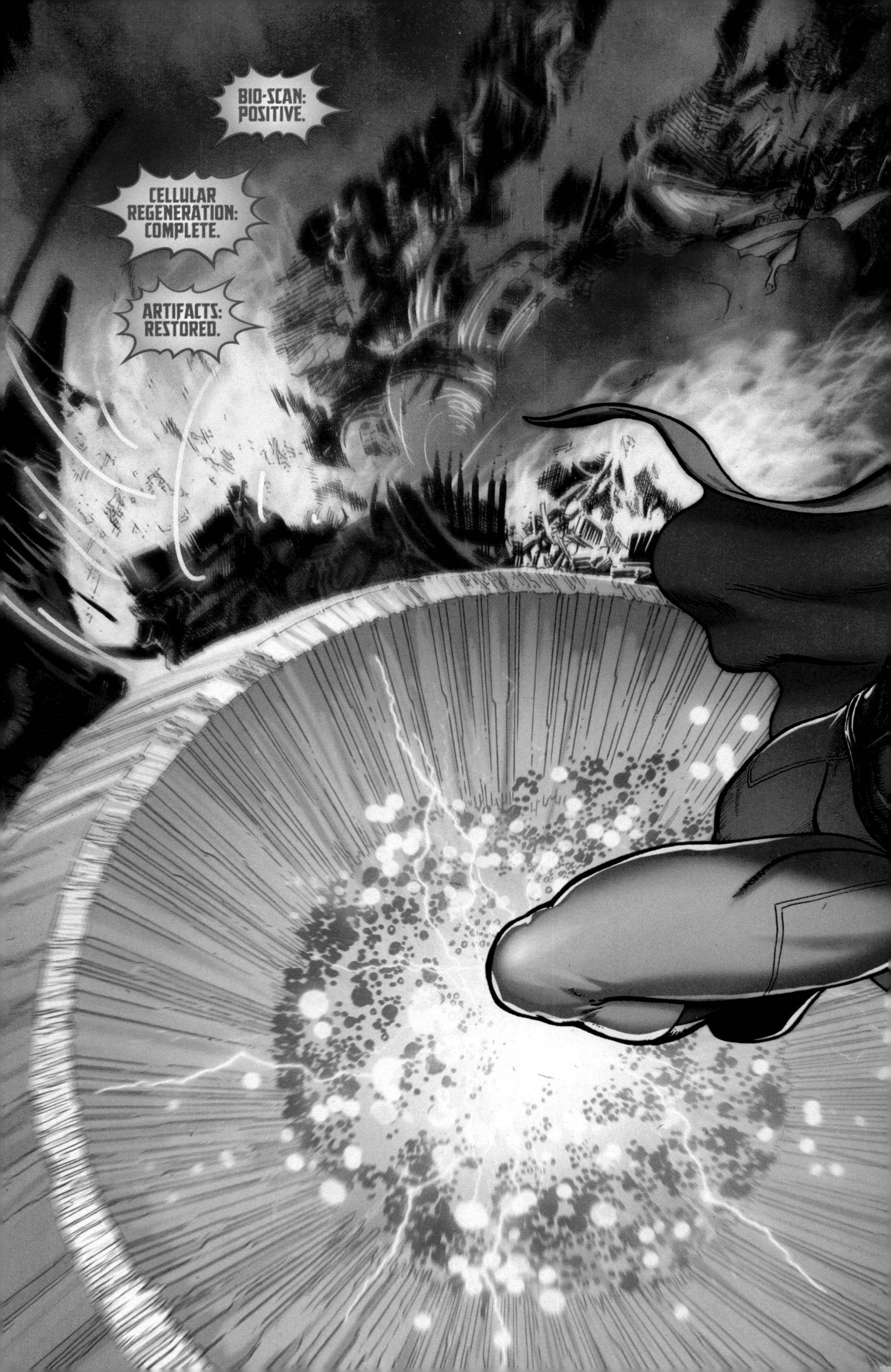
BIO-SCAN: POSITIVE.
CELLULAR REGENERATION: COMPLETE.
ARTIFACTS: RESTORED.

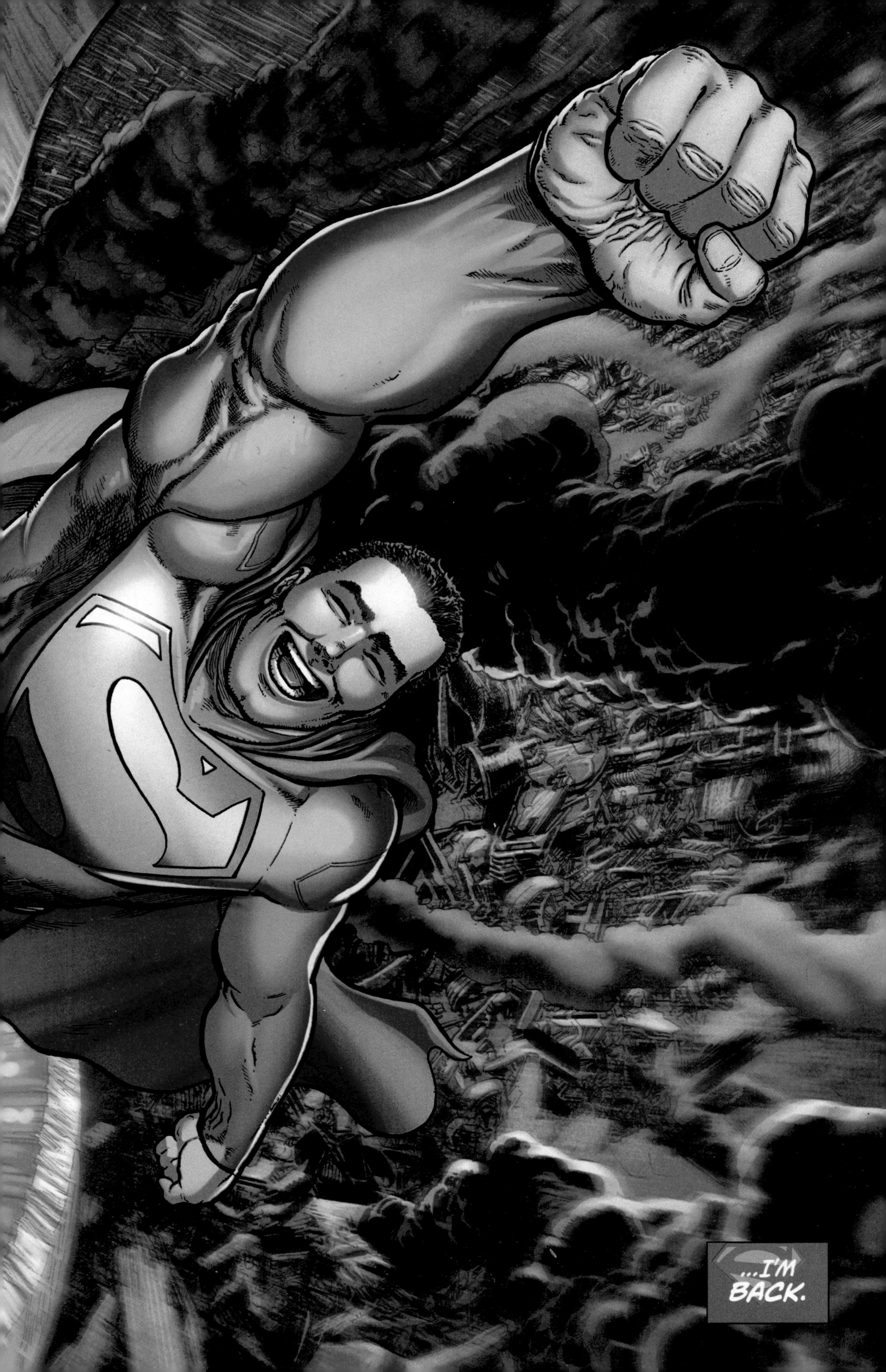
...I'M BACK.

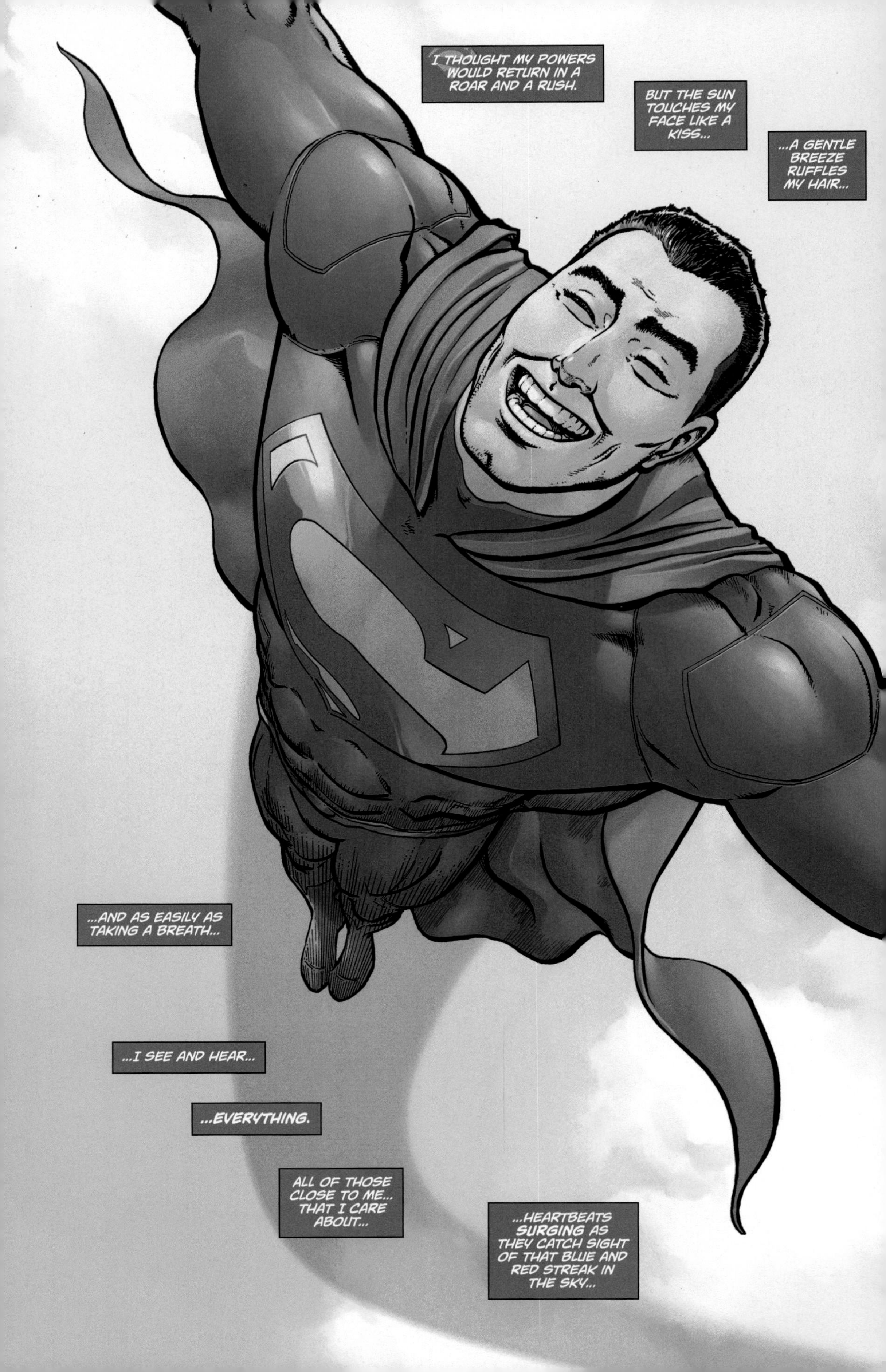
I THOUGHT MY POWERS WOULD RETURN IN A ROAR AND A RUSH.
BUT THE SUN TOUCHES MY FACE LIKE A KISS...
...A GENTLE BREEZE RUFFLES MY HAIR...
...AND AS EASILY AS TAKING A BREATH...
...I SEE AND HEAR...
...EVERYTHING.
ALL OF THOSE CLOSE TO ME... THAT I CARE ABOUT...
...HEARTBEATS SURGING AS THEY CATCH SIGHT OF THAT BLUE AND RED STREAK IN THE SKY...

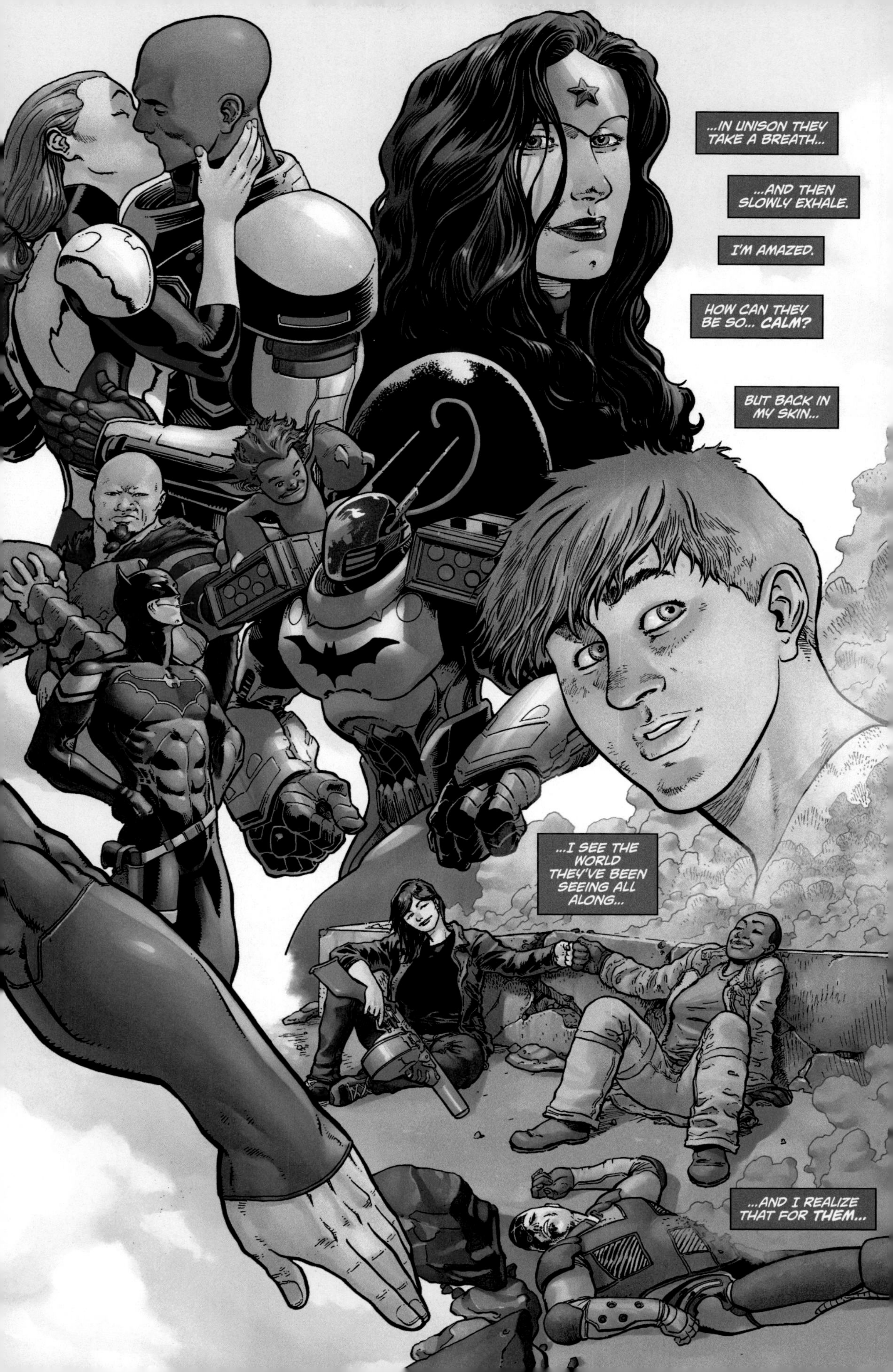
...IN UNISON THEY TAKE A BREATH...
...AND THEN SLOWLY EXHALE.
I'M AMAZED.
HOW CAN THEY BE SO... CALM?
BUT BACK IN MY SKIN...
...I SEE THE WORLD THEY'VE BEEN SEEING ALL ALONG...
...AND I REALIZE THAT FOR THEM...

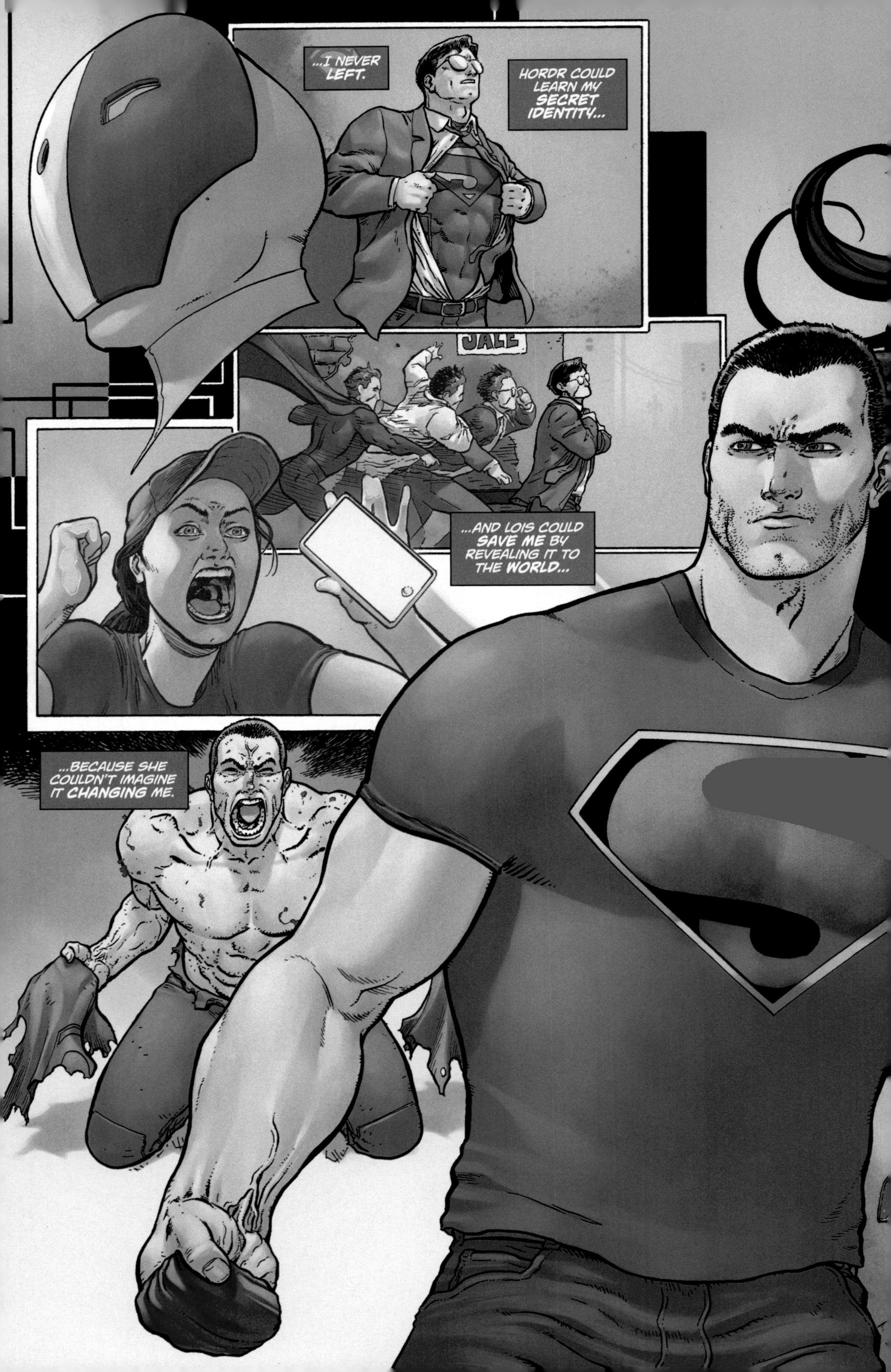
...I NEVER LEFT.
HORDR COULD LEARN MY SECRET IDENTITY...
...AND LOIS COULD SAVE ME BY REVEALING IT TO THE WORLD...
...BECAUSE SHE COULDN'T IMAGINE IT CHANGING ME.

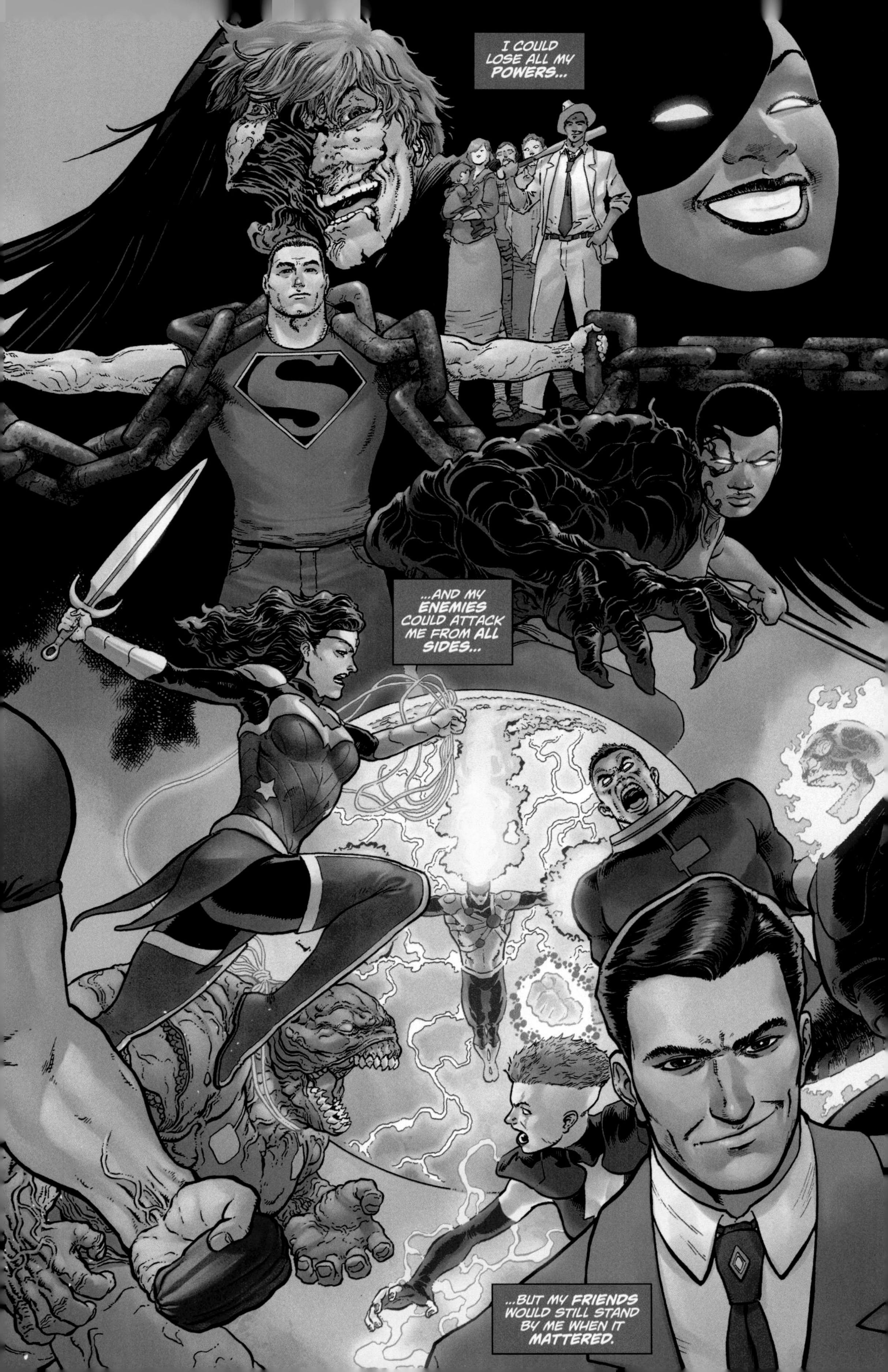
I COULD LOSE ALL MY POWERS...
...AND MY ENEMIES COULD ATTACK ME FROM ALL SIDES...
...BUT MY FRIENDS WOULD STILL STAND BY ME WHEN IT MATTERED.

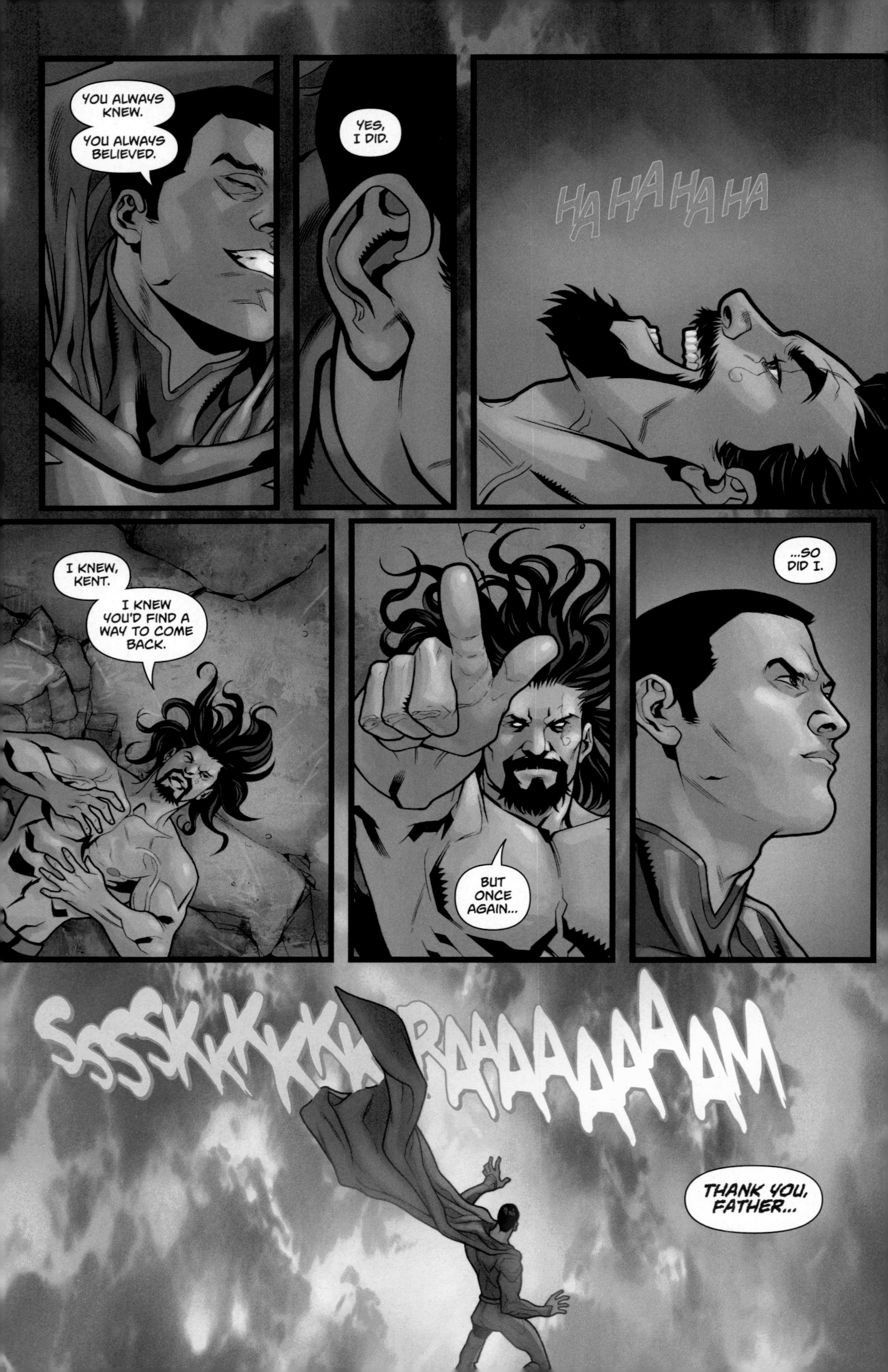
YOU ALWAYS KNEW.
YOU ALWAYS BELIEVED.
YES, I DID.
HA HA HA HA HA
I KNEW, KENT.
I KNEW YOU'D FIND A WAY TO COME BACK.
BUT ONCE AGAIN...
...SO DID I.
SSSSKKKKKRAAAAAAAAAM
THANK YOU, FATHER...

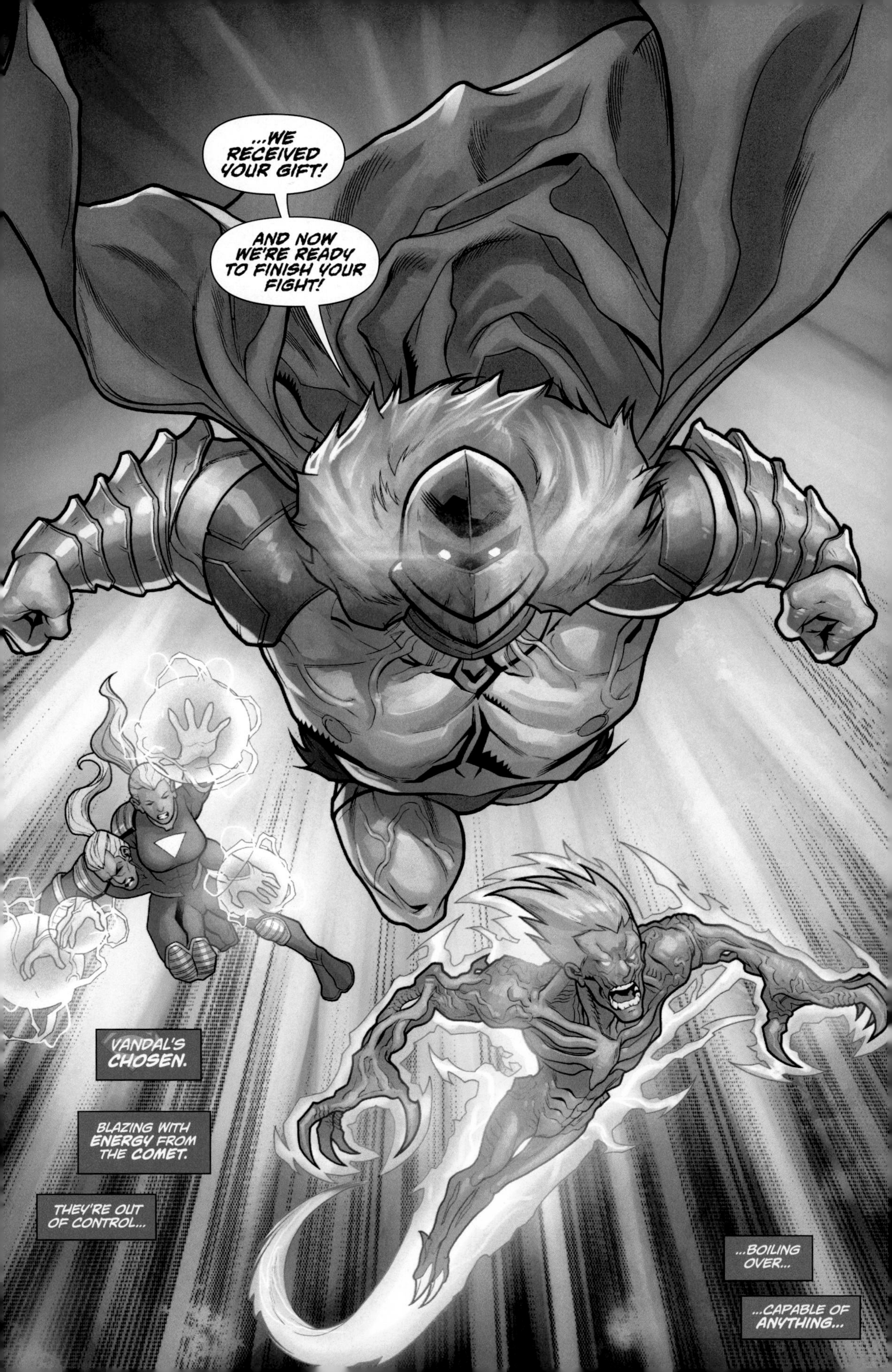
...WE RECEIVED YOUR GIFT!
AND NOW WE'RE READY TO FINISH YOUR FIGHT!
VANDAL'S CHOSEN.
BLAZING WITH ENERGY FROM THE COMET.
THEY'RE OUT OF CONTROL...
...BOILING OVER...
...CAPABLE OF ANYTHING...

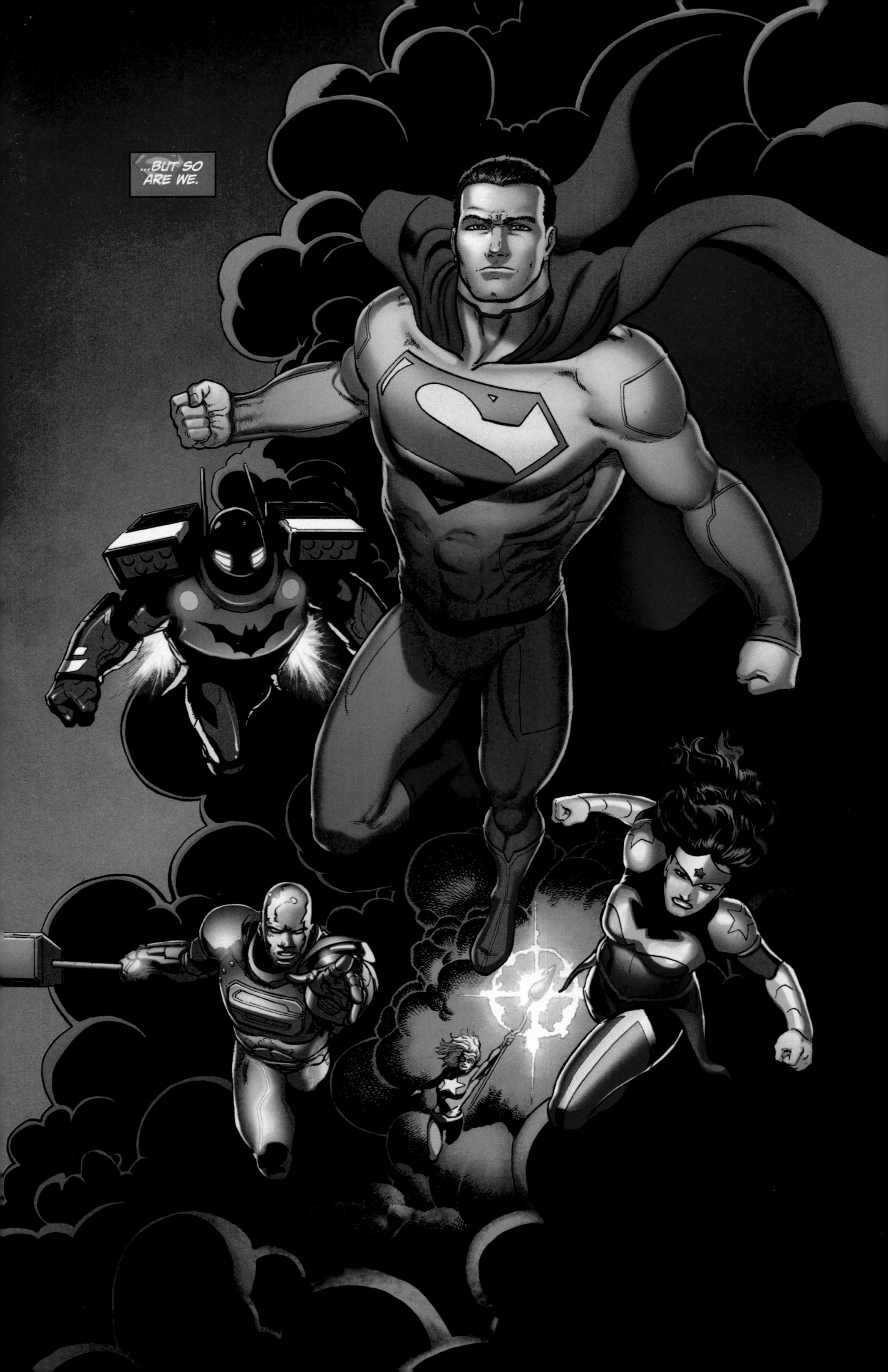
...BUT SO ARE WE.

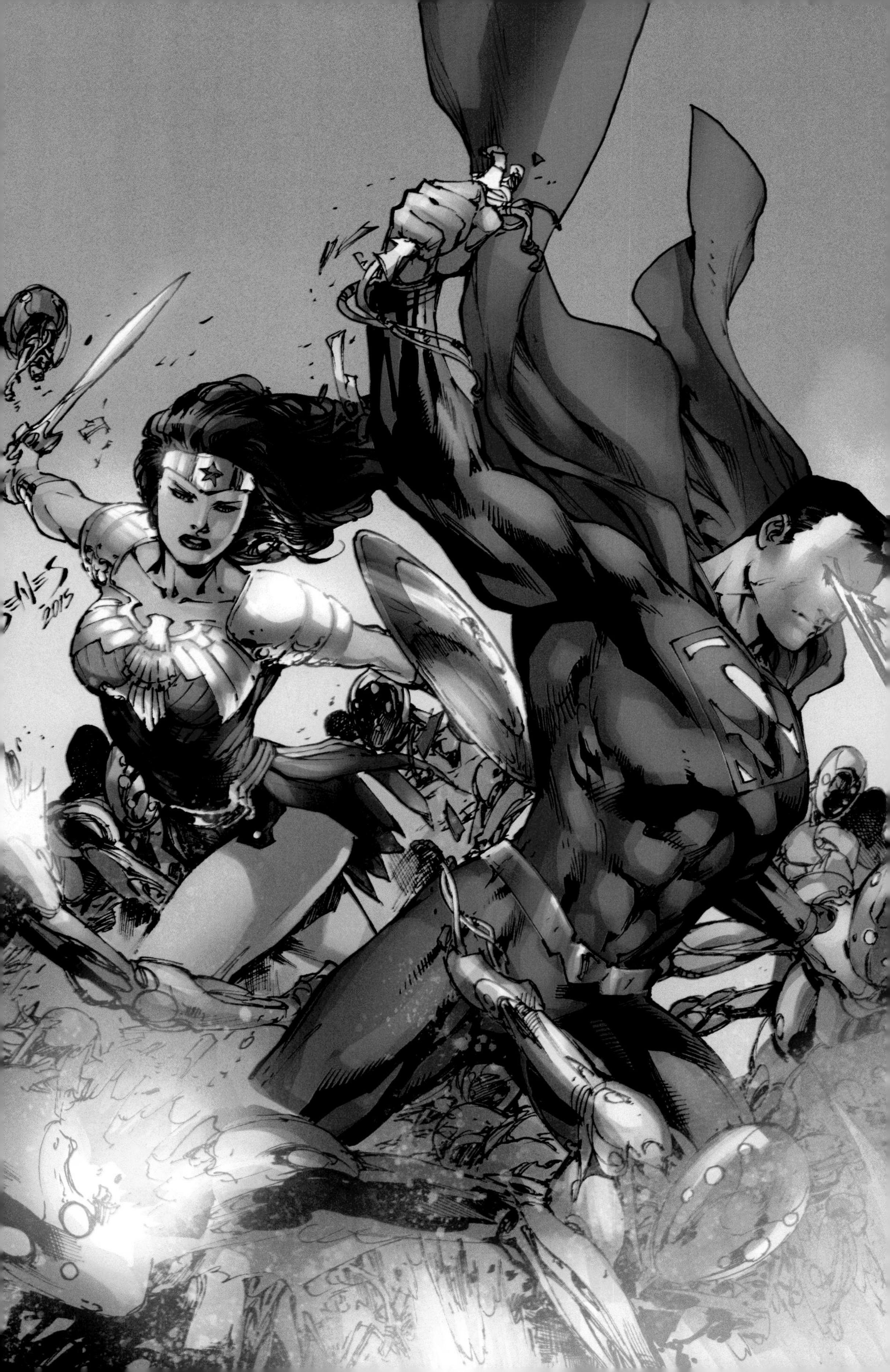

SLAM BANG

PETER J. TOMASI writer **CLIFF RICHARDS** artist **WIL QUINTANA** colorist **ROB LEIGH** letterer **ED BENES ALEX SINCLAIR** cover

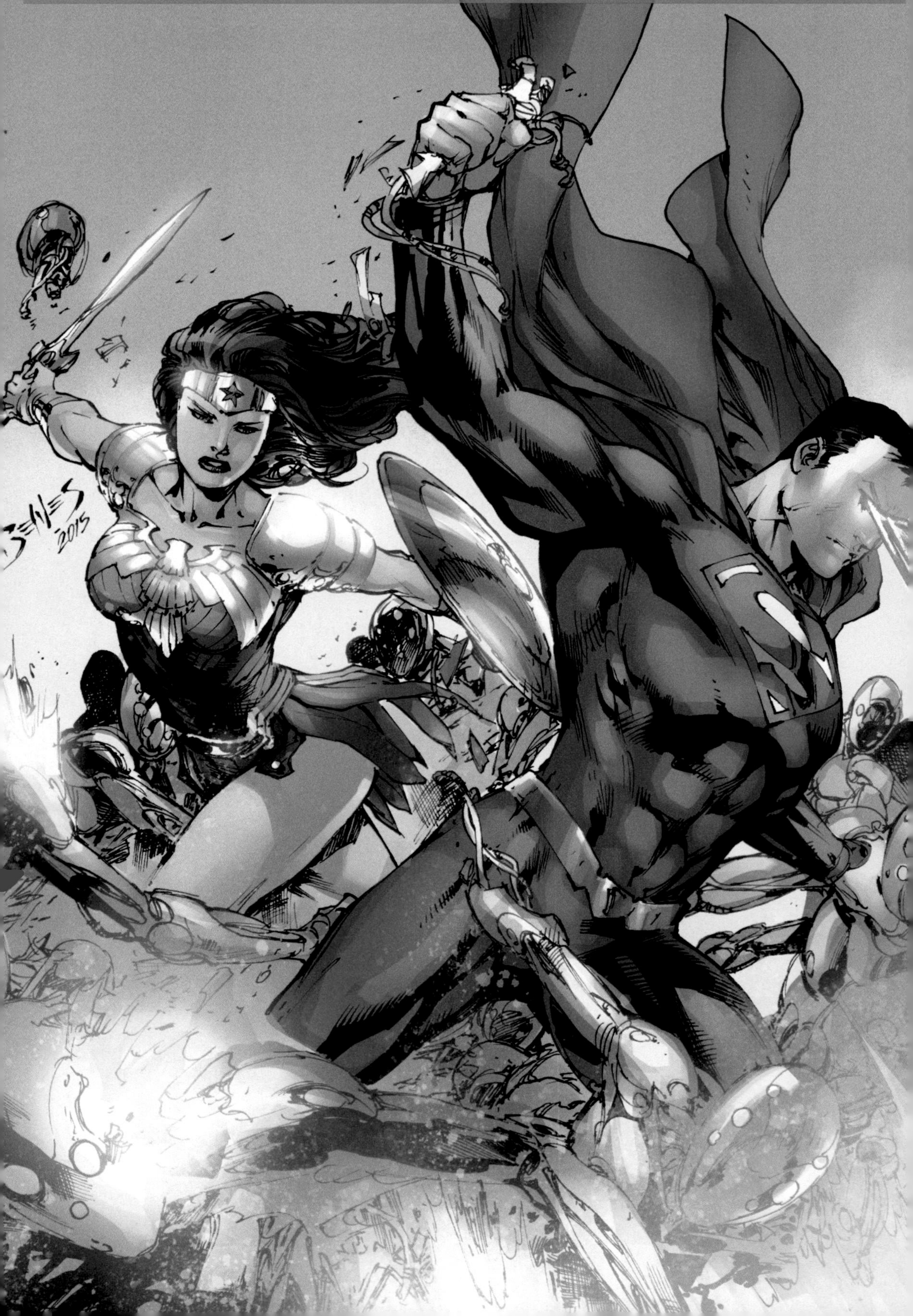
BENES
2015

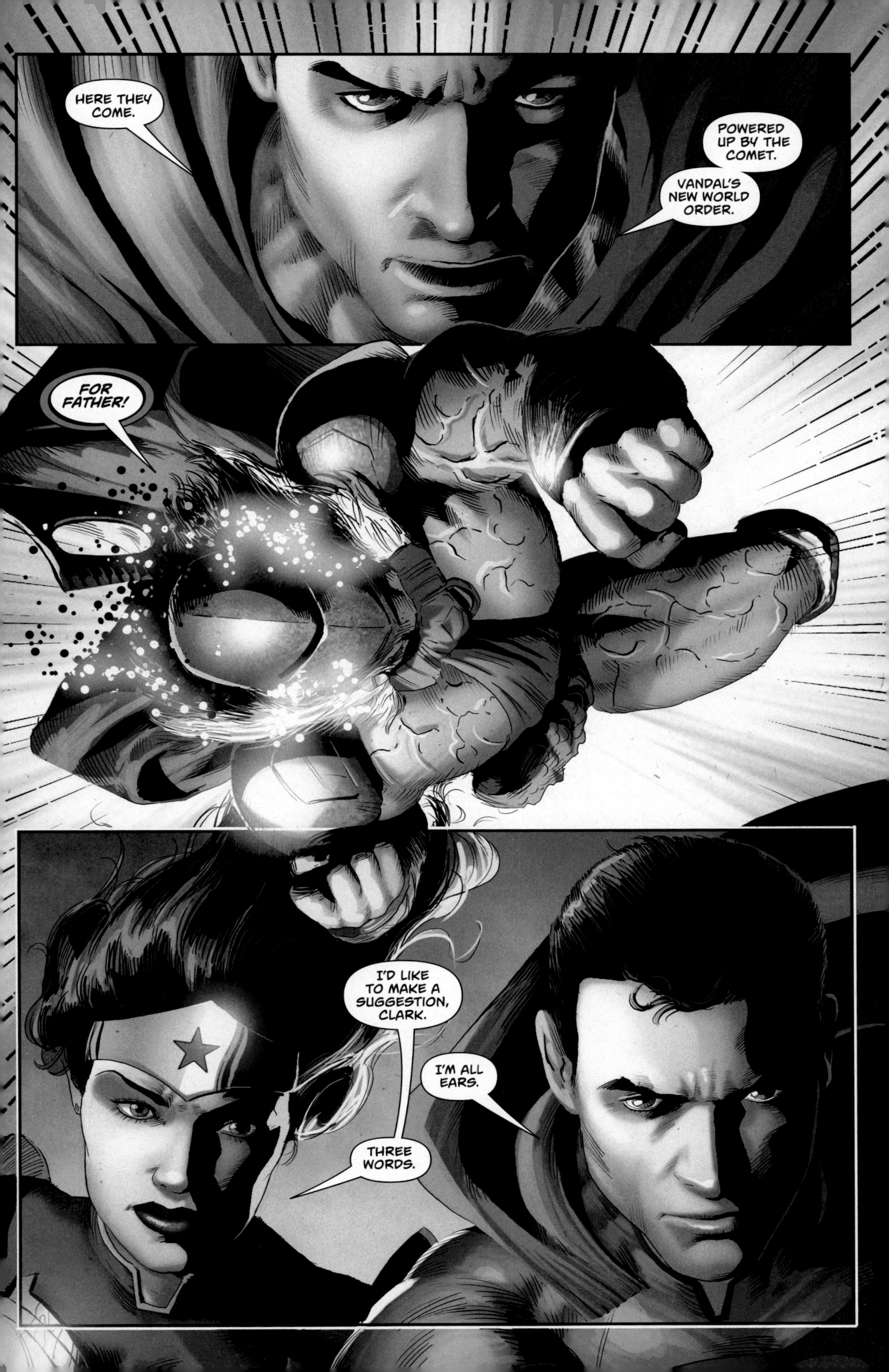
HERE THEY COME.
POWERED UP BY THE COMET.
VANDAL'S NEW WORLD ORDER.
FOR FATHER!
I'D LIKE TO MAKE A SUGGESTION, CLARK.
I'M ALL EARS.
THREE WORDS.

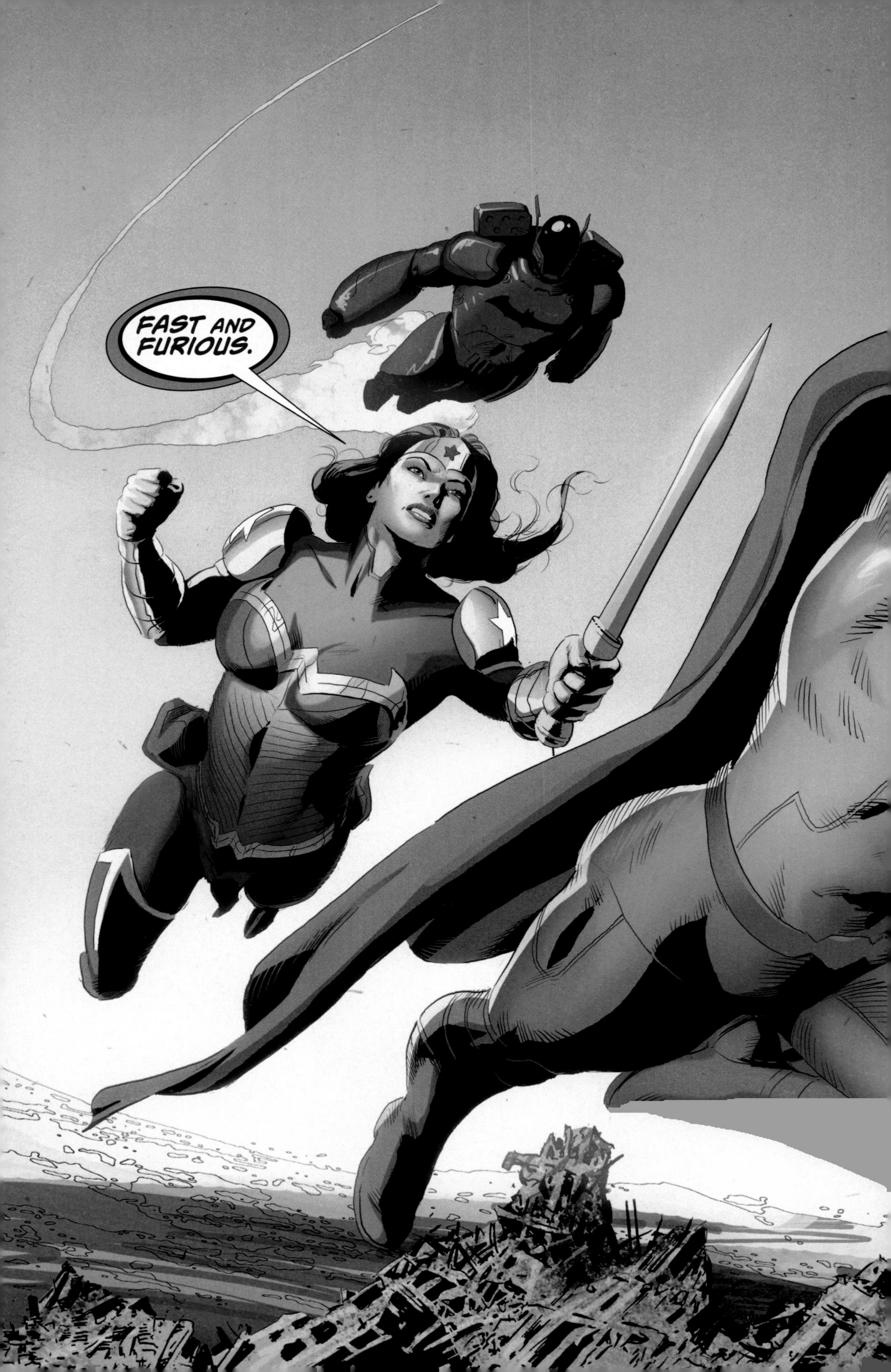
FAST AND FURIOUS.

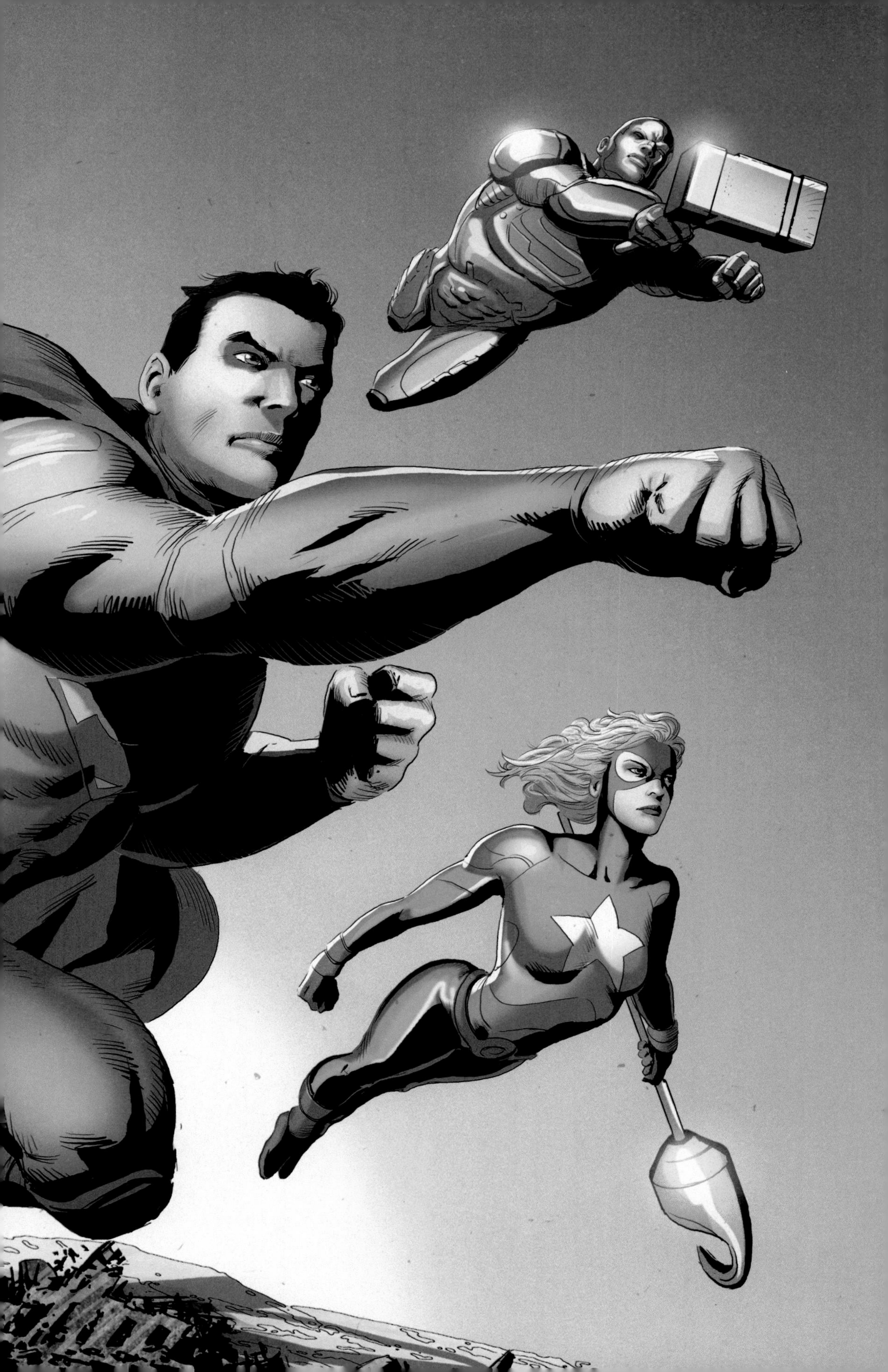

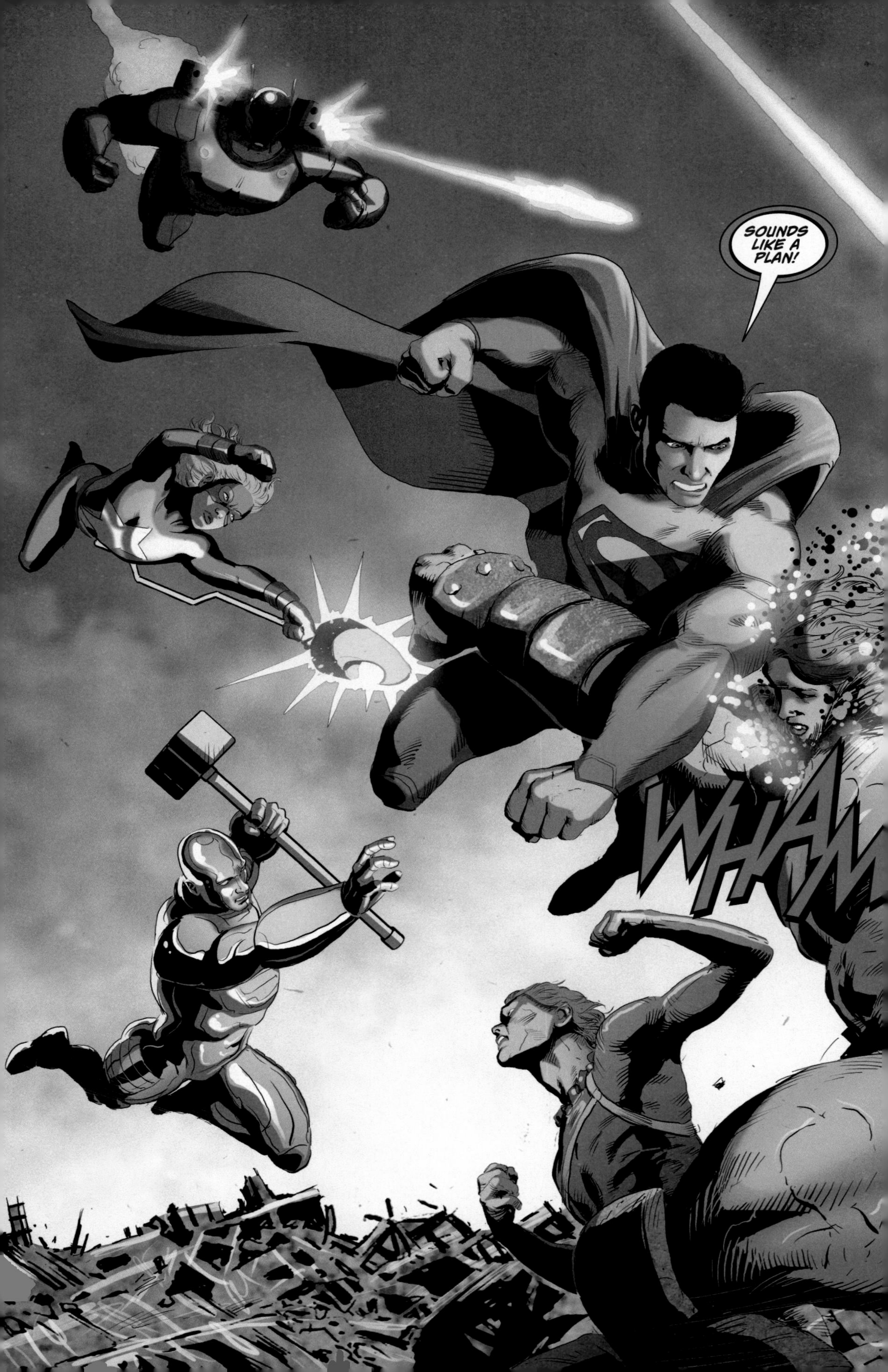
SOUNDS LIKE A PLAN!
WHAM

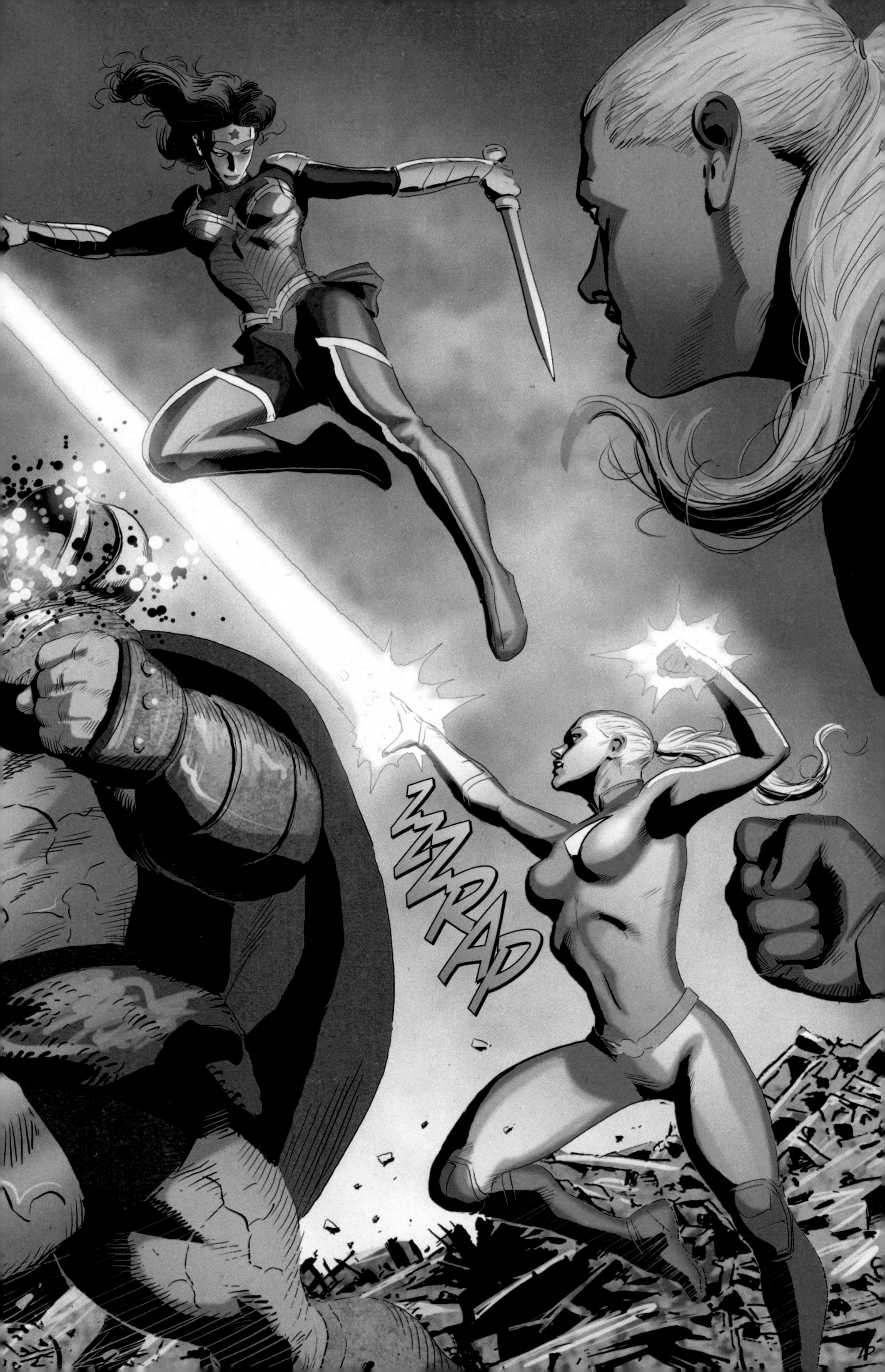
ZZZRAP

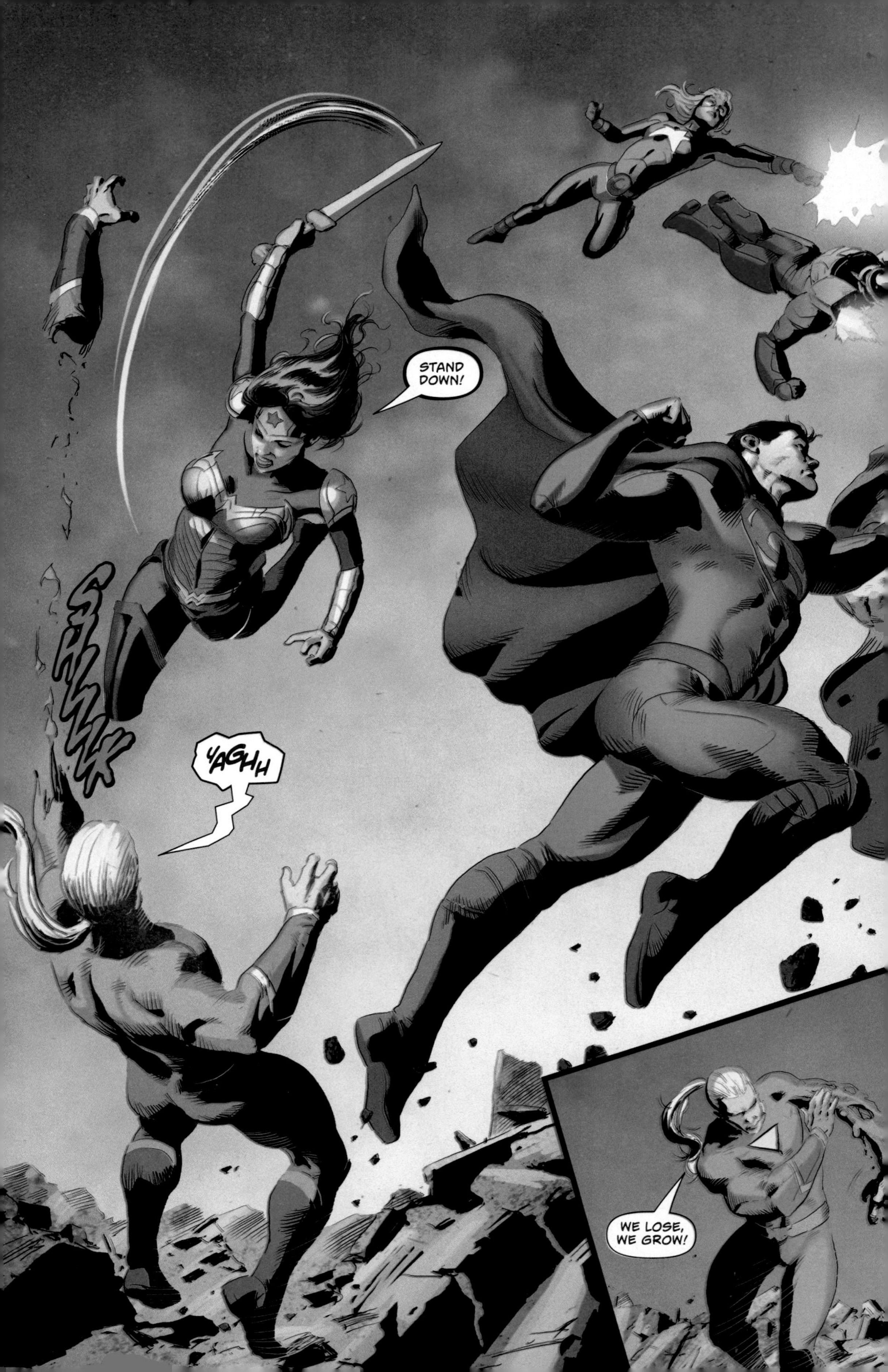
STAND DOWN!
SHHNNK
YAGHH
WE LOSE, WE GROW!

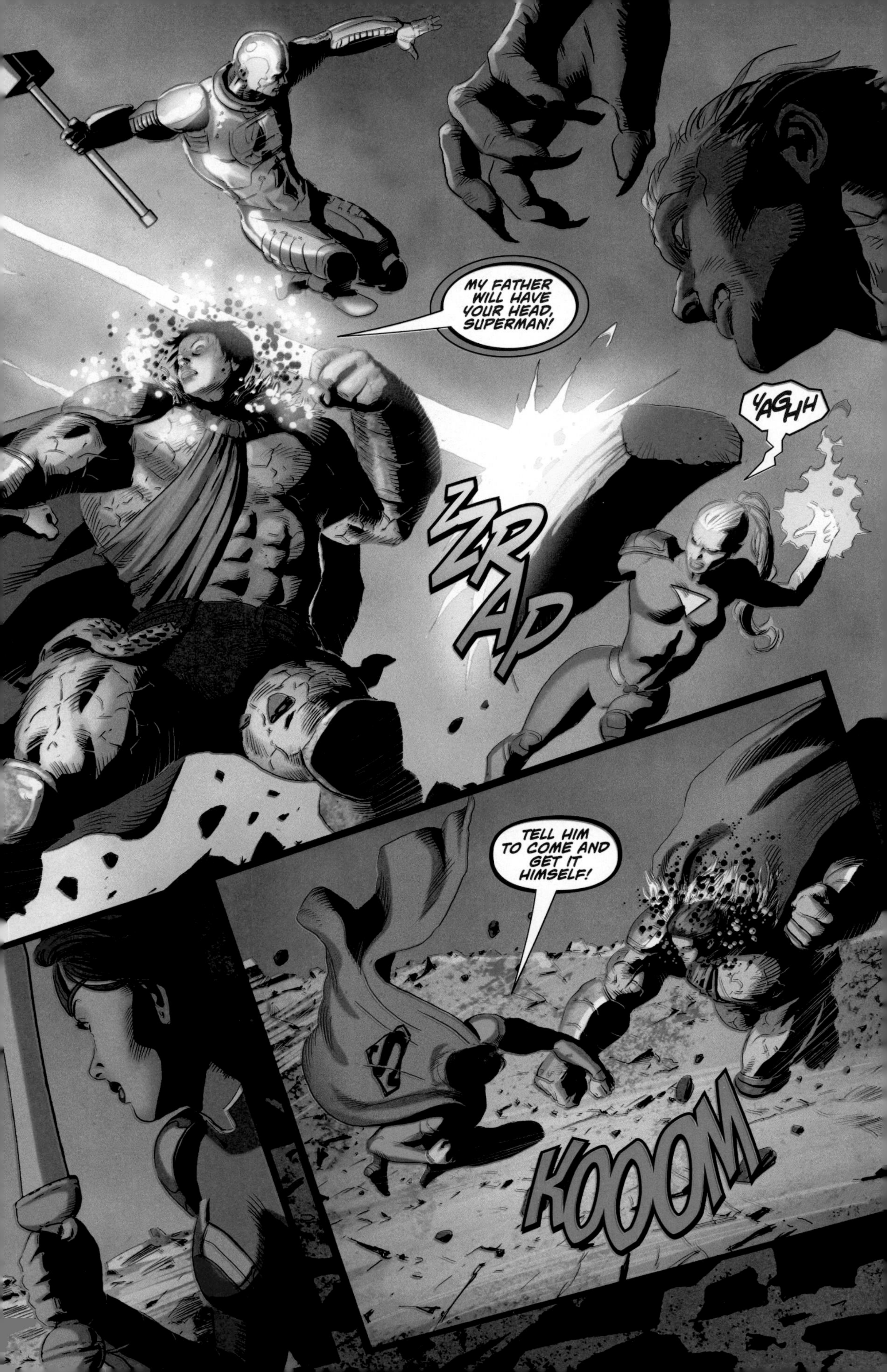
MY FATHER WILL HAVE YOUR HEAD, SUPERMAN!
YAGHH
ZZRAP
TELL HIM TO COME AND GET IT HIMSELF!
KOOOM

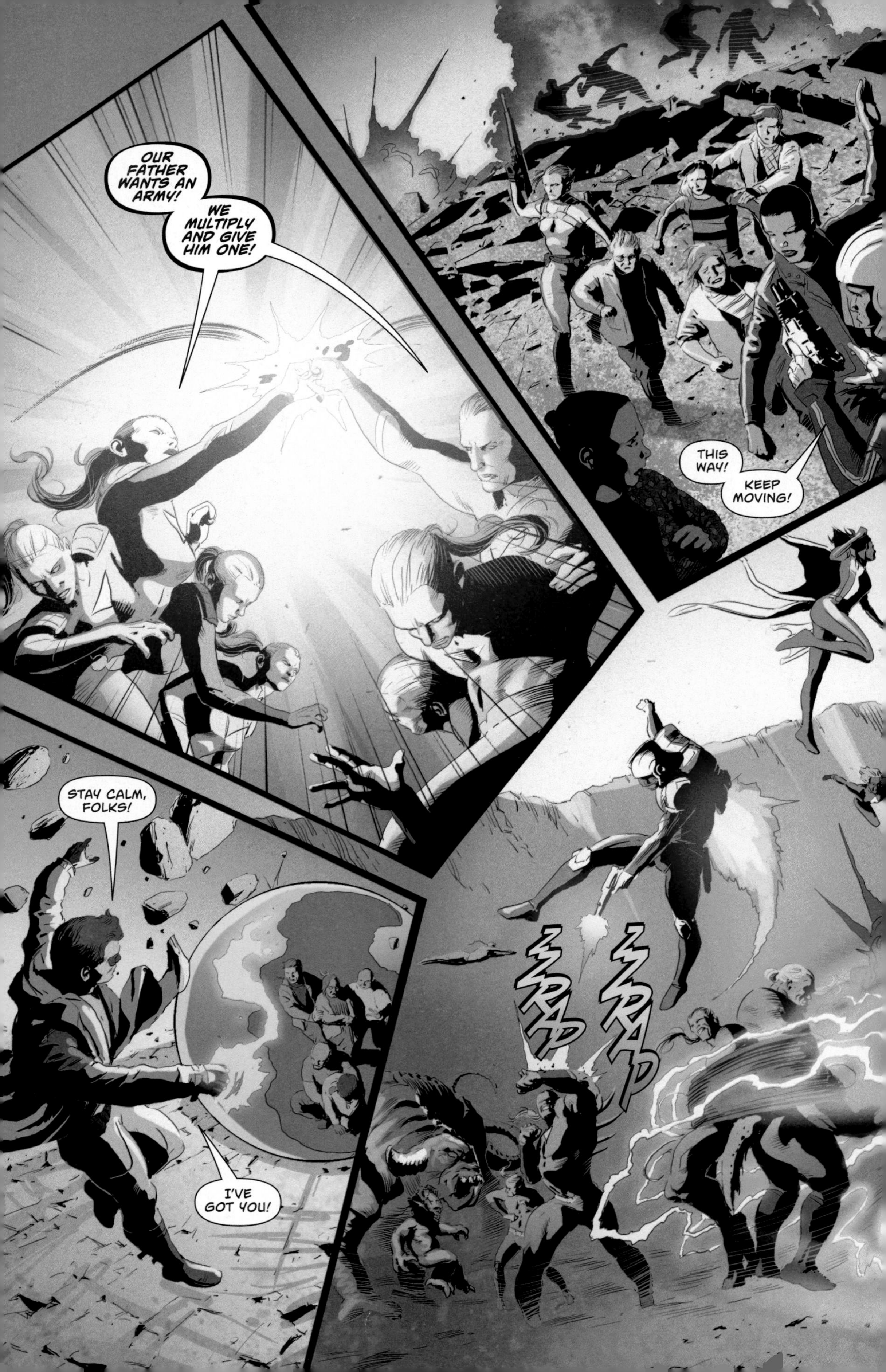
OUR FATHER WANTS AN ARMY!
WE MULTIPLY AND GIVE HIM ONE!
THIS WAY!
KEEP MOVING!
STAY CALM, FOLKS!
I'VE GOT YOU!
ZRAP
ZRAP

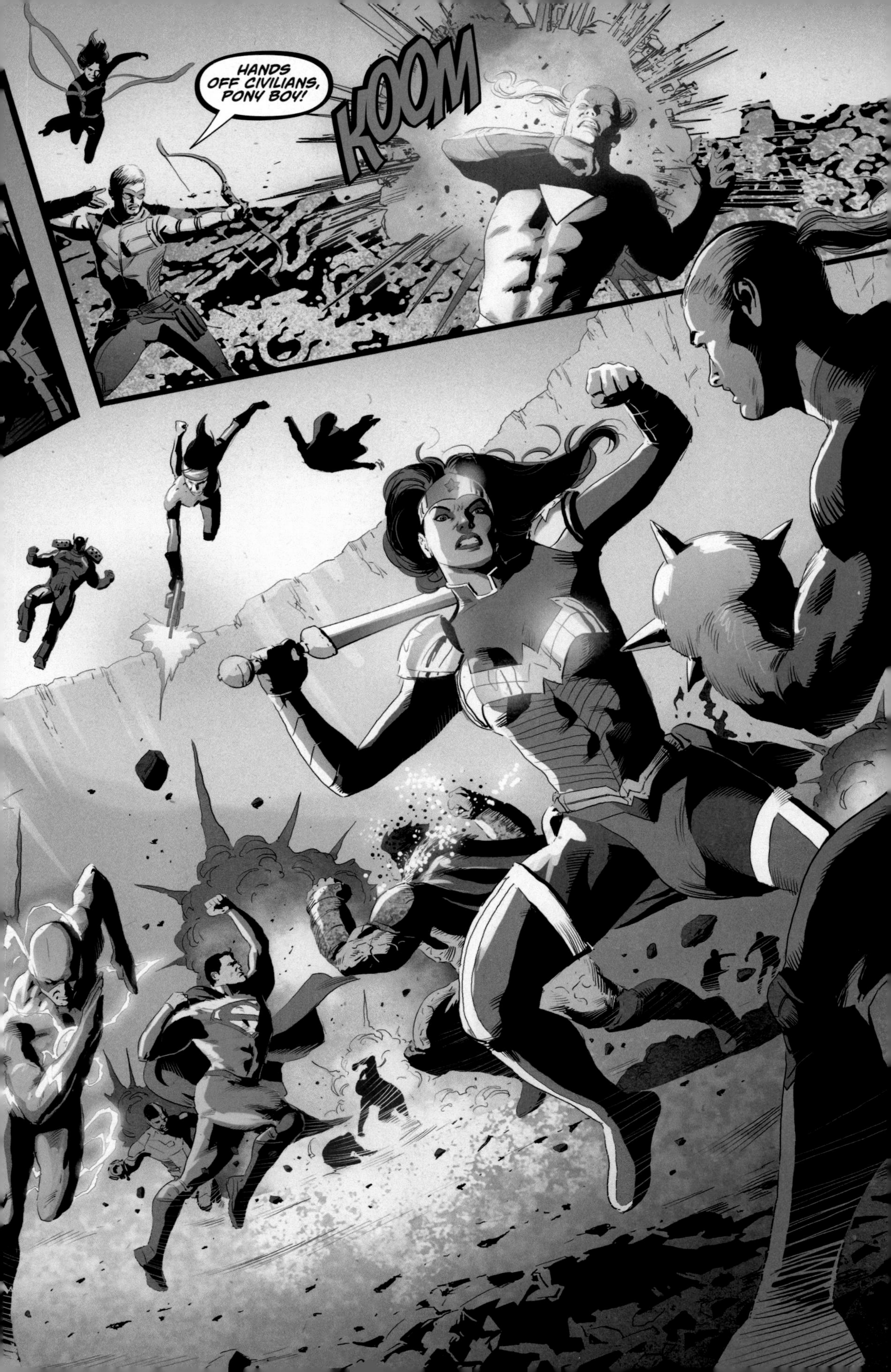
HANDS OFF CIVILIANS, PONY BOY!
KOOM

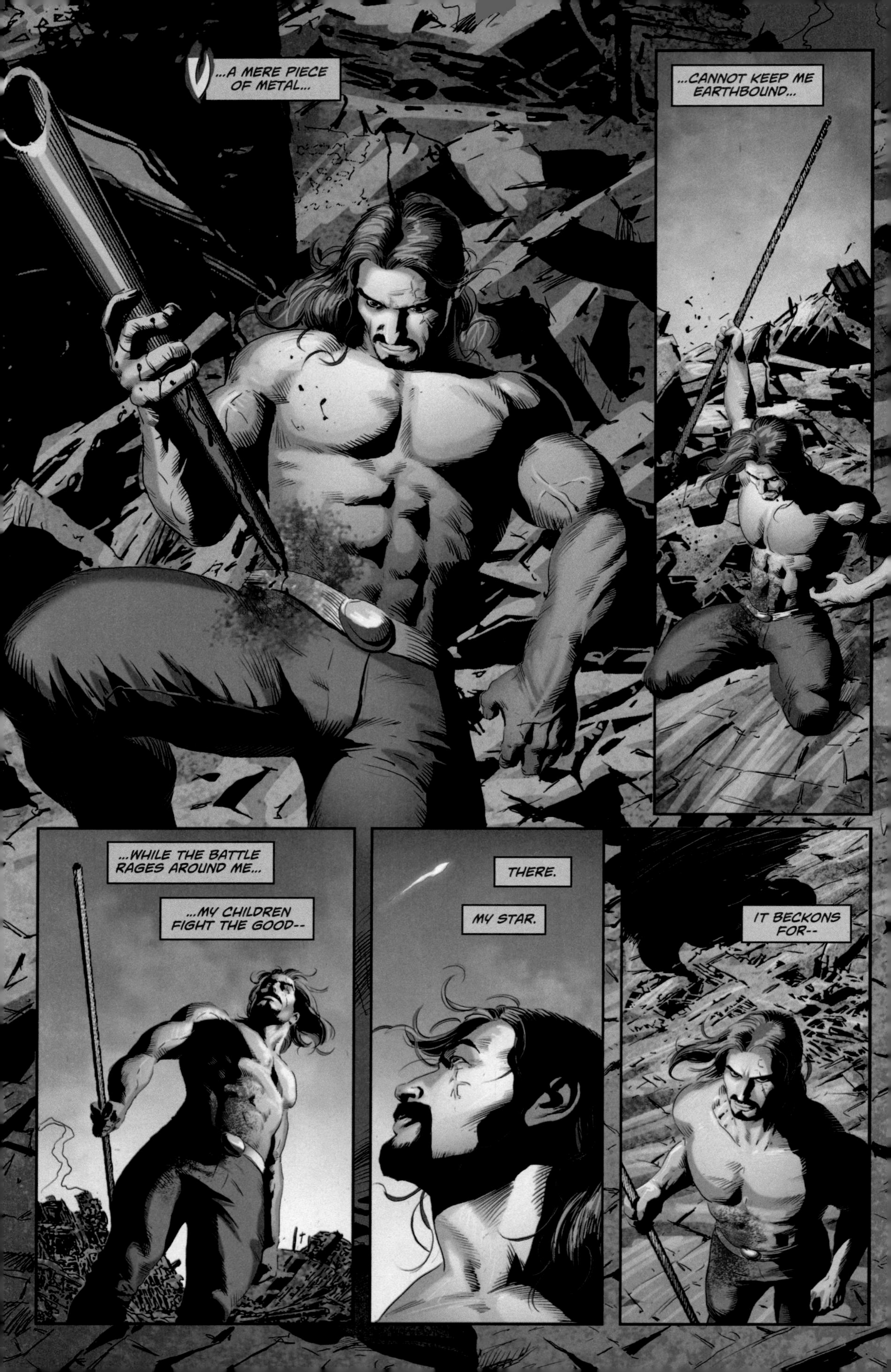
...A MERE PIECE OF METAL...
...CANNOT KEEP ME EARTHBOUND...
...WHILE THE BATTLE RAGES AROUND ME...
...MY CHILDREN FIGHT THE GOOD--
THERE.
MY STAR.
IT BECKONS FOR--

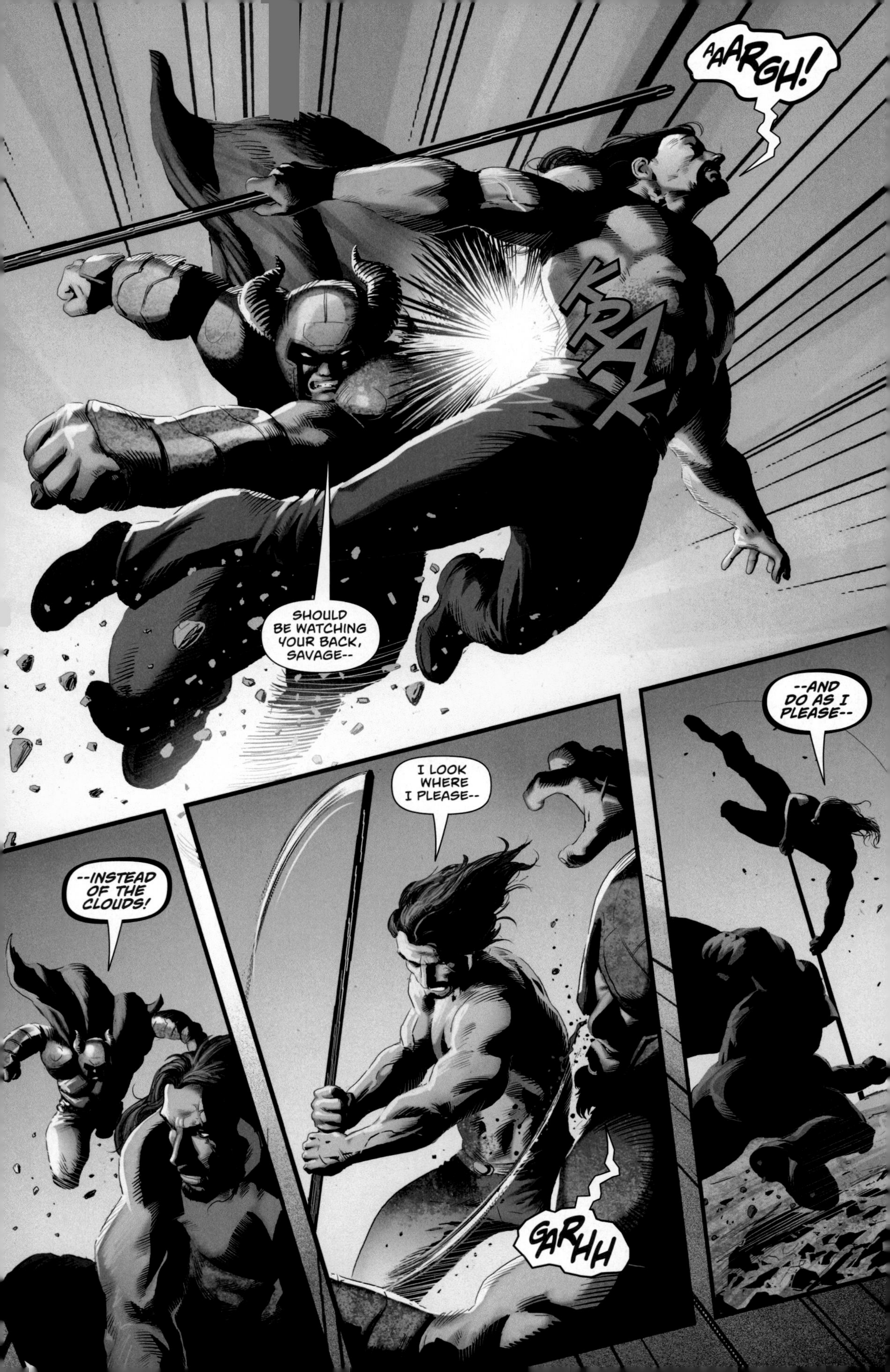
AAARGH!
KRAK
SHOULD BE WATCHING YOUR BACK, SAVAGE--
I LOOK WHERE I PLEASE--
--AND DO AS I PLEASE--
--INSTEAD OF THE CLOUDS!
GARHH

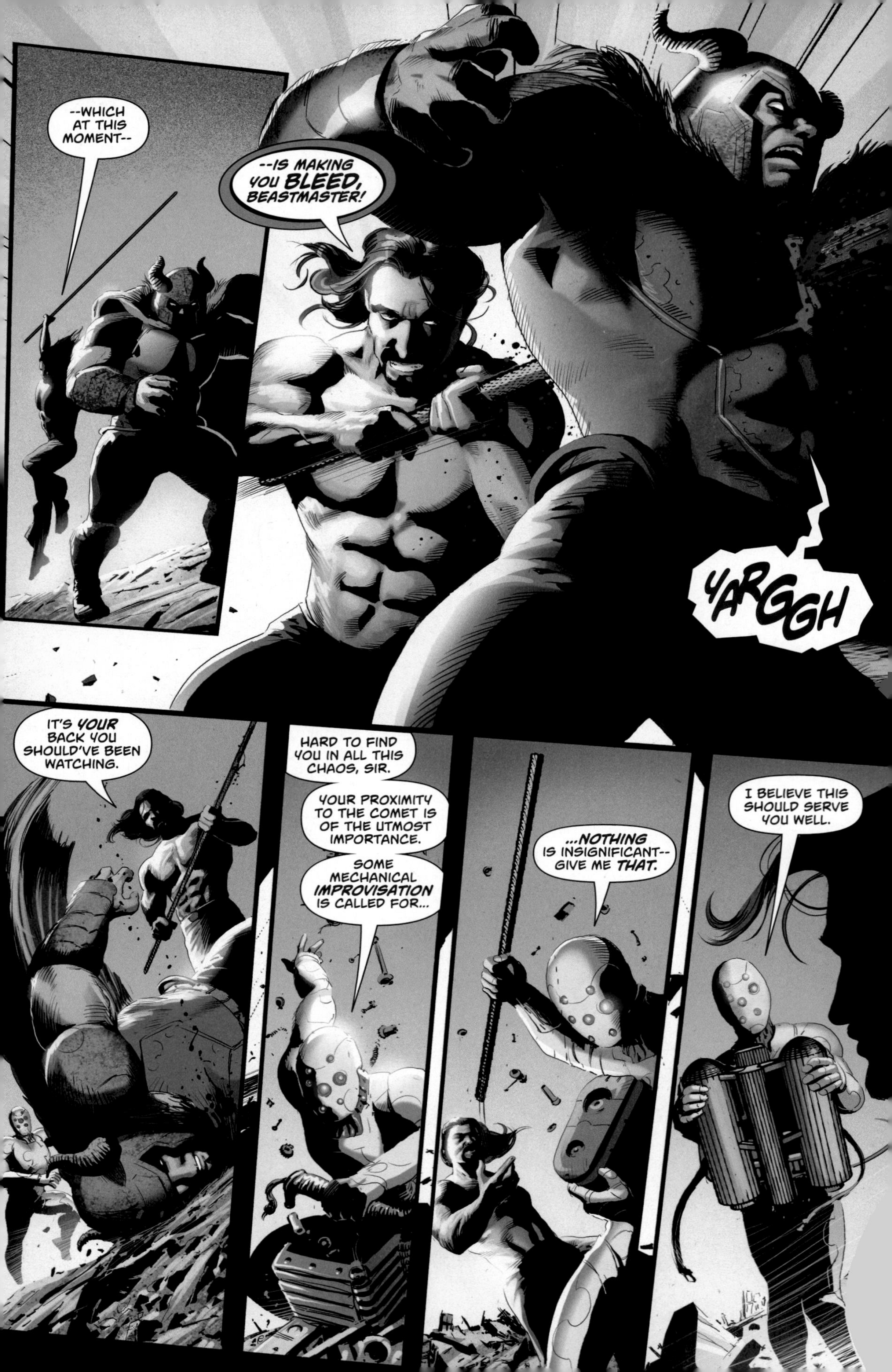
--WHICH AT THIS MOMENT--
--IS MAKING YOU BLEED, BEASTMASTER!
YARGGH
IT'S YOUR BACK YOU SHOULD'VE BEEN WATCHING.
HARD TO FIND YOU IN ALL THIS CHAOS, SIR.
YOUR PROXIMITY TO THE COMET IS OF THE UTMOST IMPORTANCE.
SOME MECHANICAL IMPROVISATION IS CALLED FOR...
...NOTHING IS INSIGNIFICANT--GIVE ME THAT.
I BELIEVE THIS SHOULD SERVE YOU WELL.

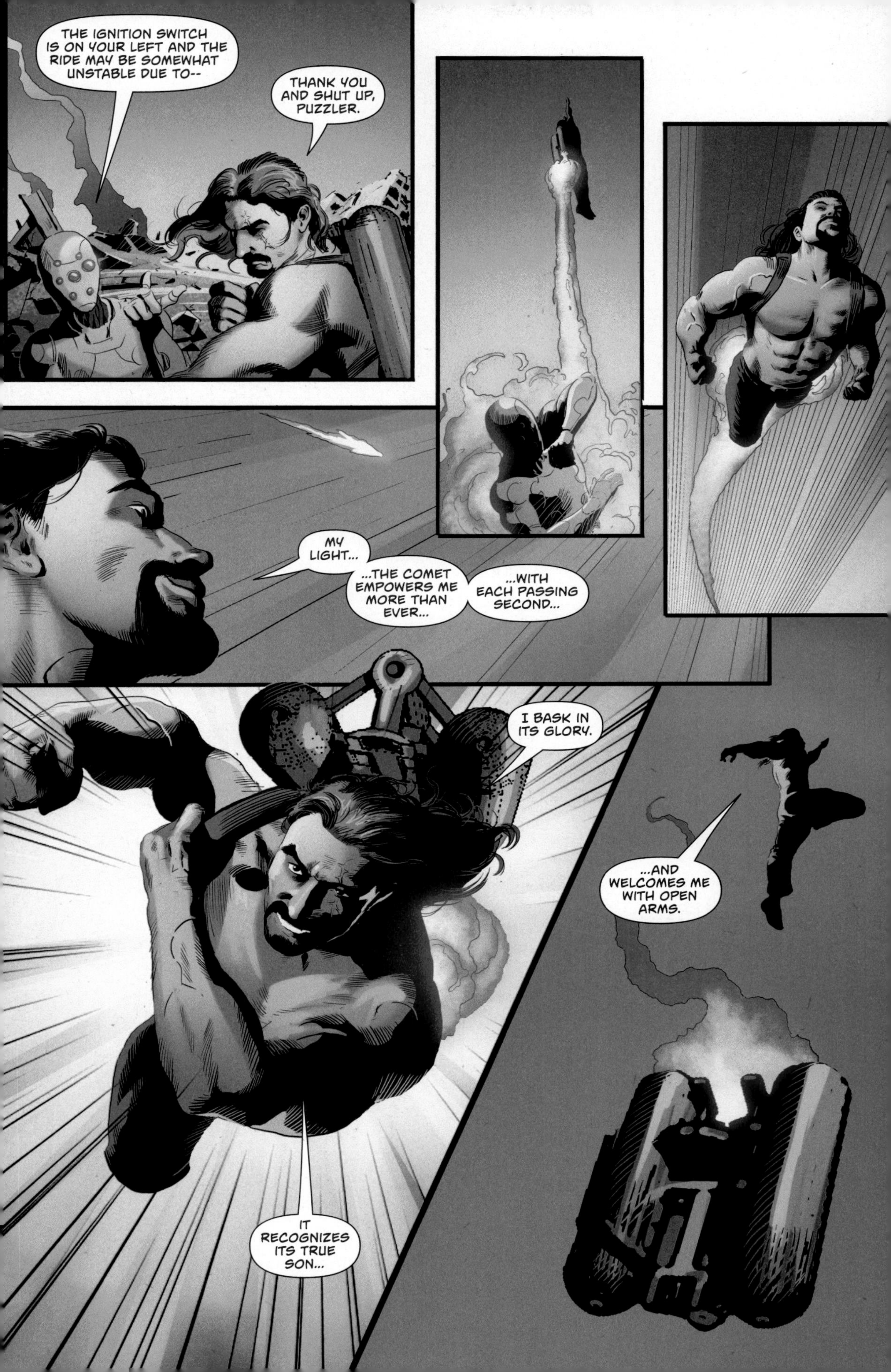
THE IGNITION SWITCH IS ON YOUR LEFT AND THE RIDE MAY BE SOMEWHAT UNSTABLE DUE TO--
THANK YOU AND SHUT UP, PUZZLER.
MY LIGHT...
...THE COMET EMPOWERS ME MORE THAN EVER...
...WITH EACH PASSING SECOND...
I BASK IN ITS GLORY.
IT RECOGNIZES ITS TRUE SON...
...AND WELCOMES ME WITH OPEN ARMS.

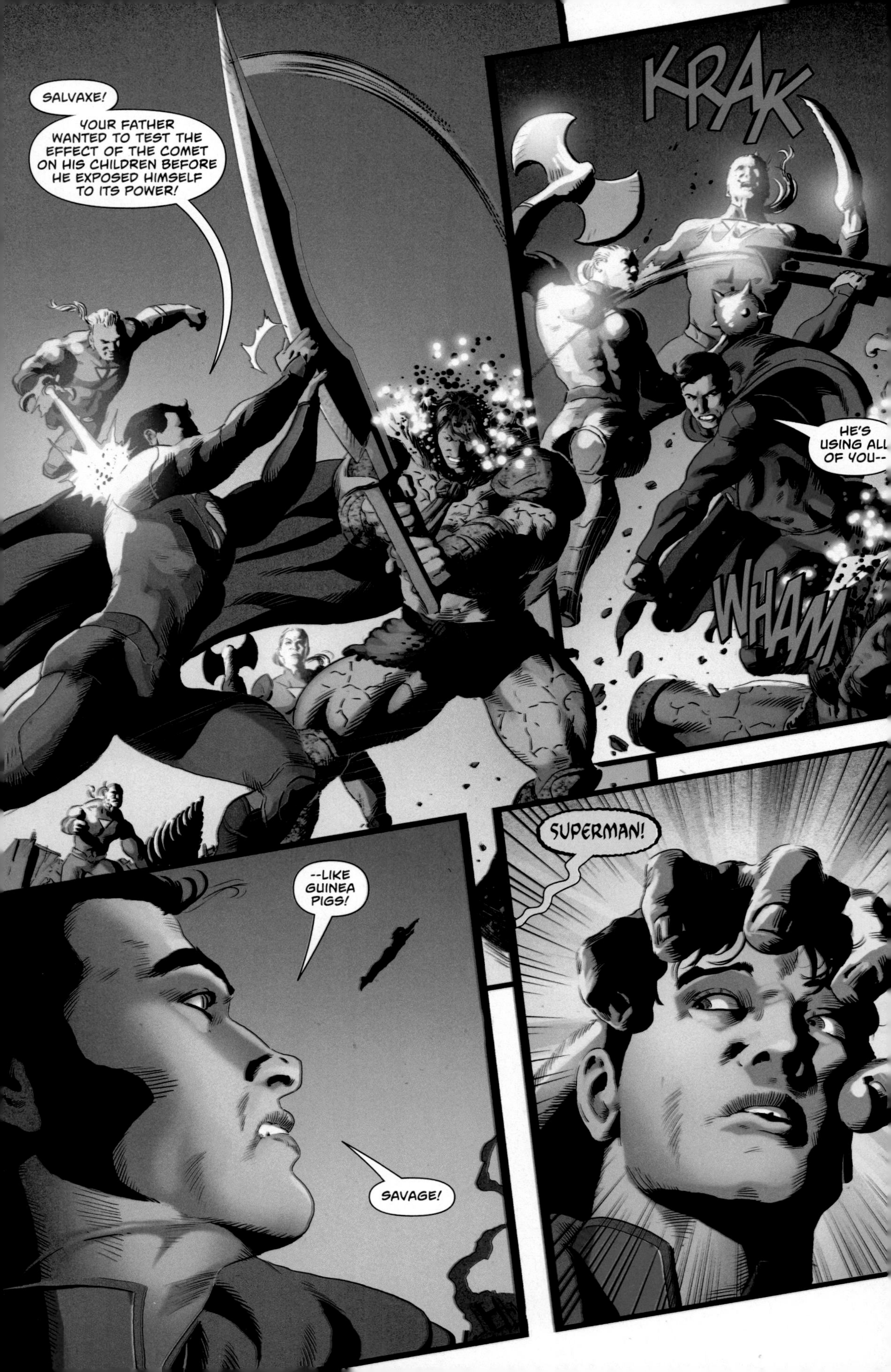
SALVAXE!
YOUR FATHER WANTED TO TEST THE EFFECT OF THE COMET ON HIS CHILDREN BEFORE HE EXPOSED HIMSELF TO ITS POWER!
KRAK
HE'S USING ALL OF YOU--
WHAM
--LIKE GUINEA PIGS!
SAVAGE!
SUPERMAN!

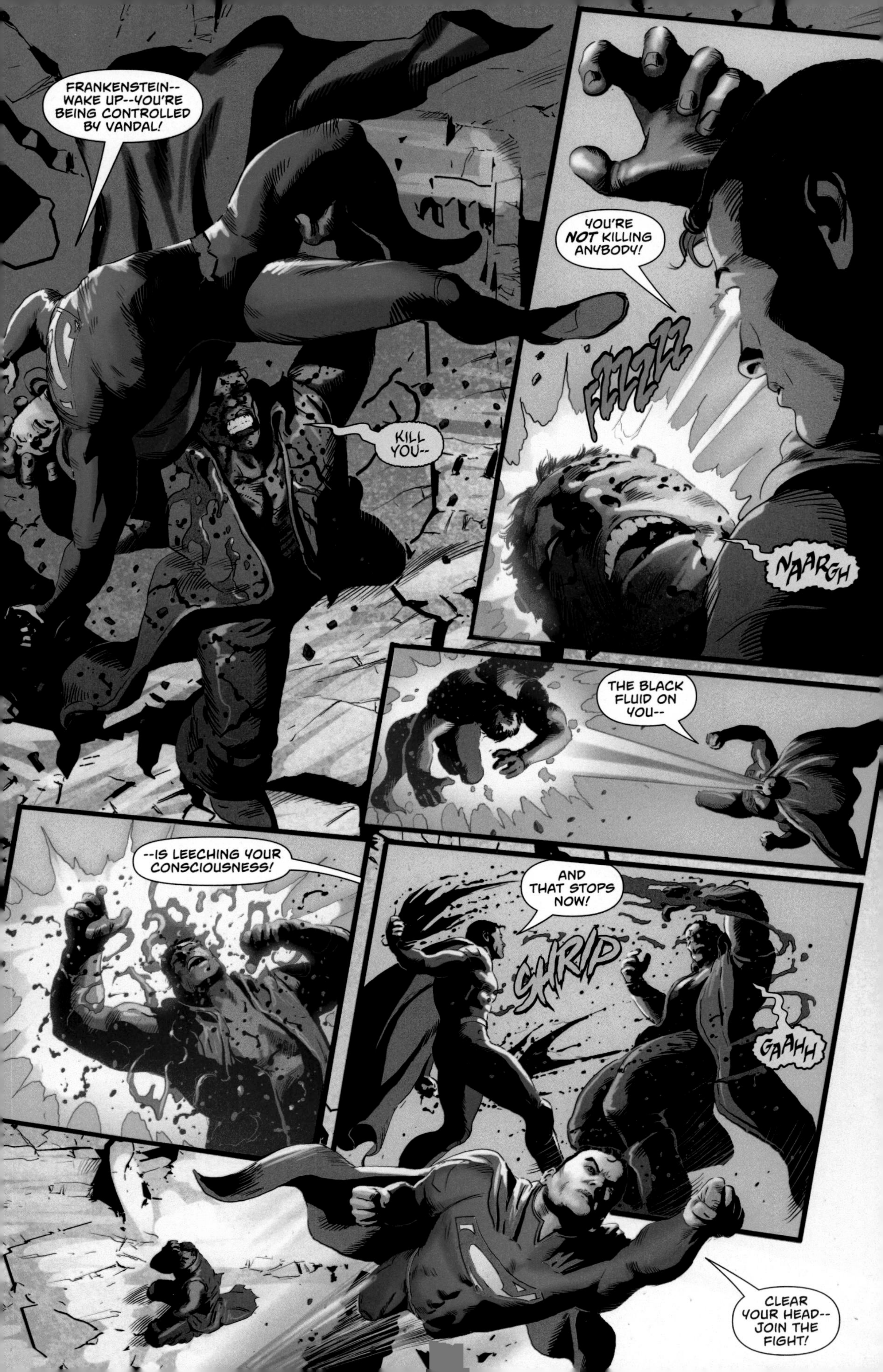
FRANKENSTEIN--
WAKE UP--YOU'RE
BEING CONTROLLED
BY VANDAL!
KILL YOU--
YOU'RE NOT KILLING ANYBODY!
FZZZZZ
NAARGH
THE BLACK FLUID ON YOU--
--IS LEECHING YOUR CONSCIOUSNESS!
AND THAT STOPS NOW!
SHRIP
GAAHH
CLEAR YOUR HEAD--
JOIN THE FIGHT!

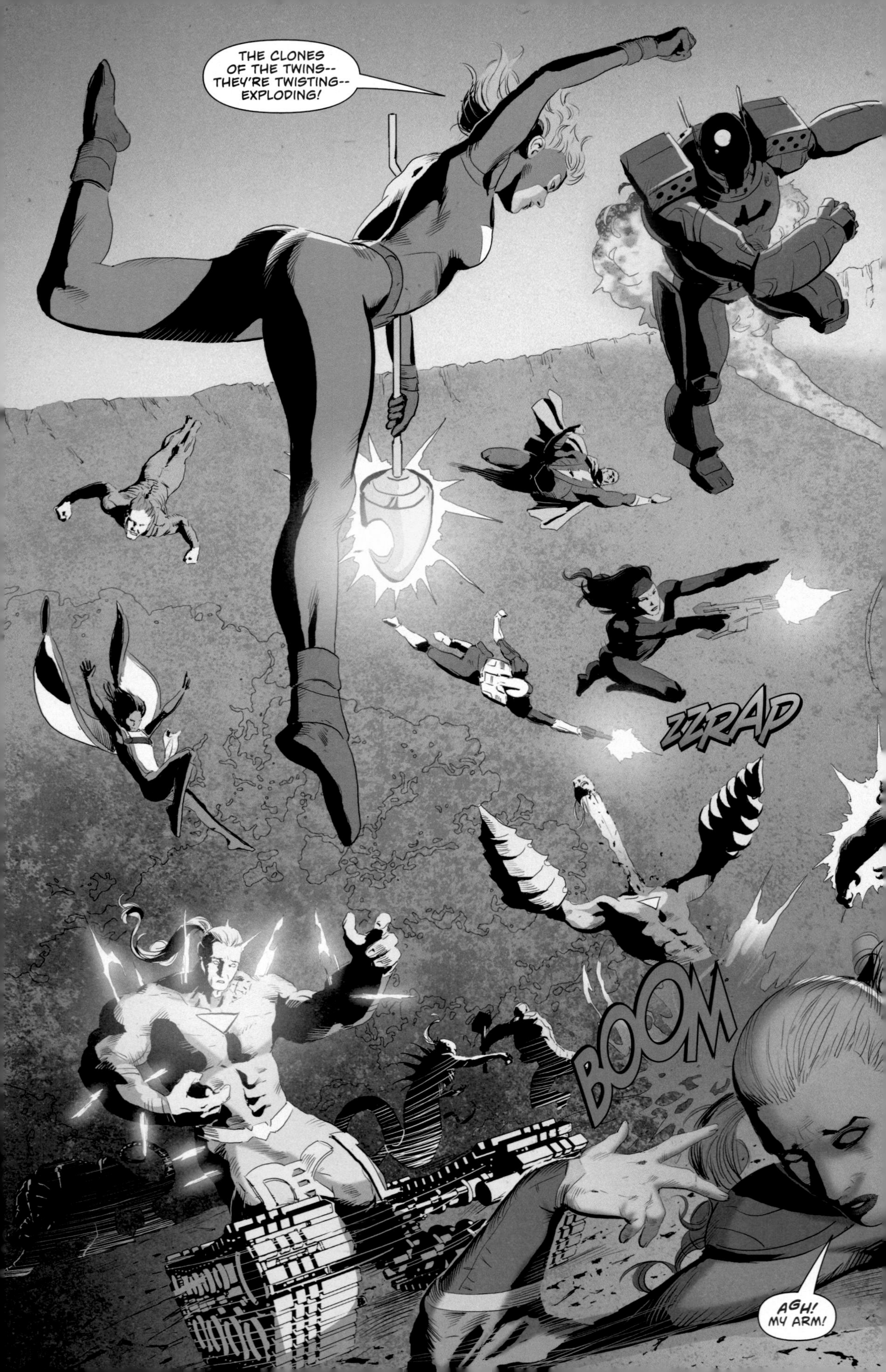
THE CLONES OF THE TWINS-- THEY'RE TWISTING-- EXPLODING!
ZZRAP
BOOM
AGH! MY ARM!

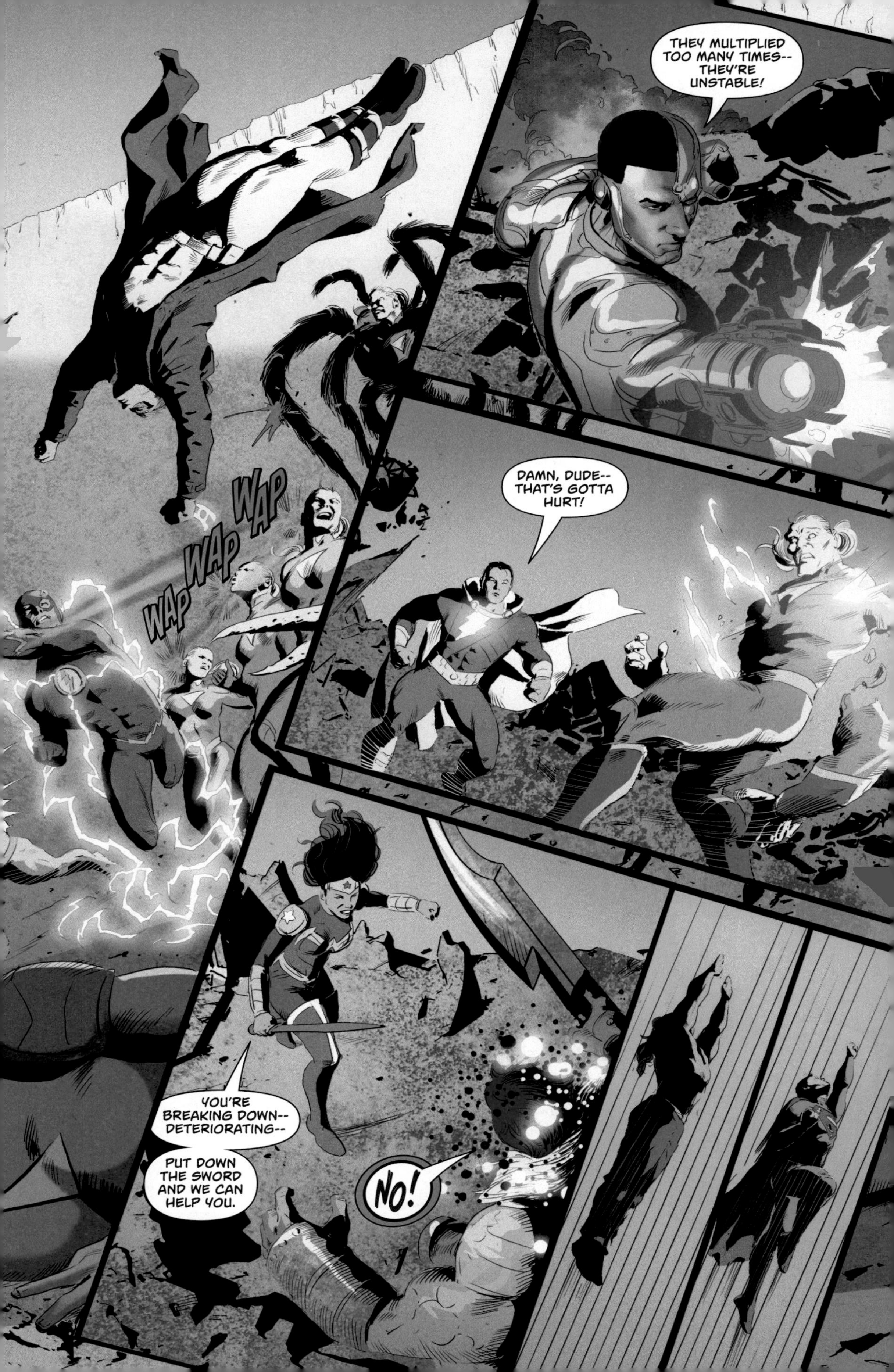
THEY MULTIPLIED TOO MANY TIMES-- THEY'RE UNSTABLE!
WAP
WAP
WAP
DAMN, DUDE-- THAT'S GOTTA HURT!
YOU'RE BREAKING DOWN-- DETERIORATING--
PUT DOWN THE SWORD AND WE CAN HELP YOU.
NO!

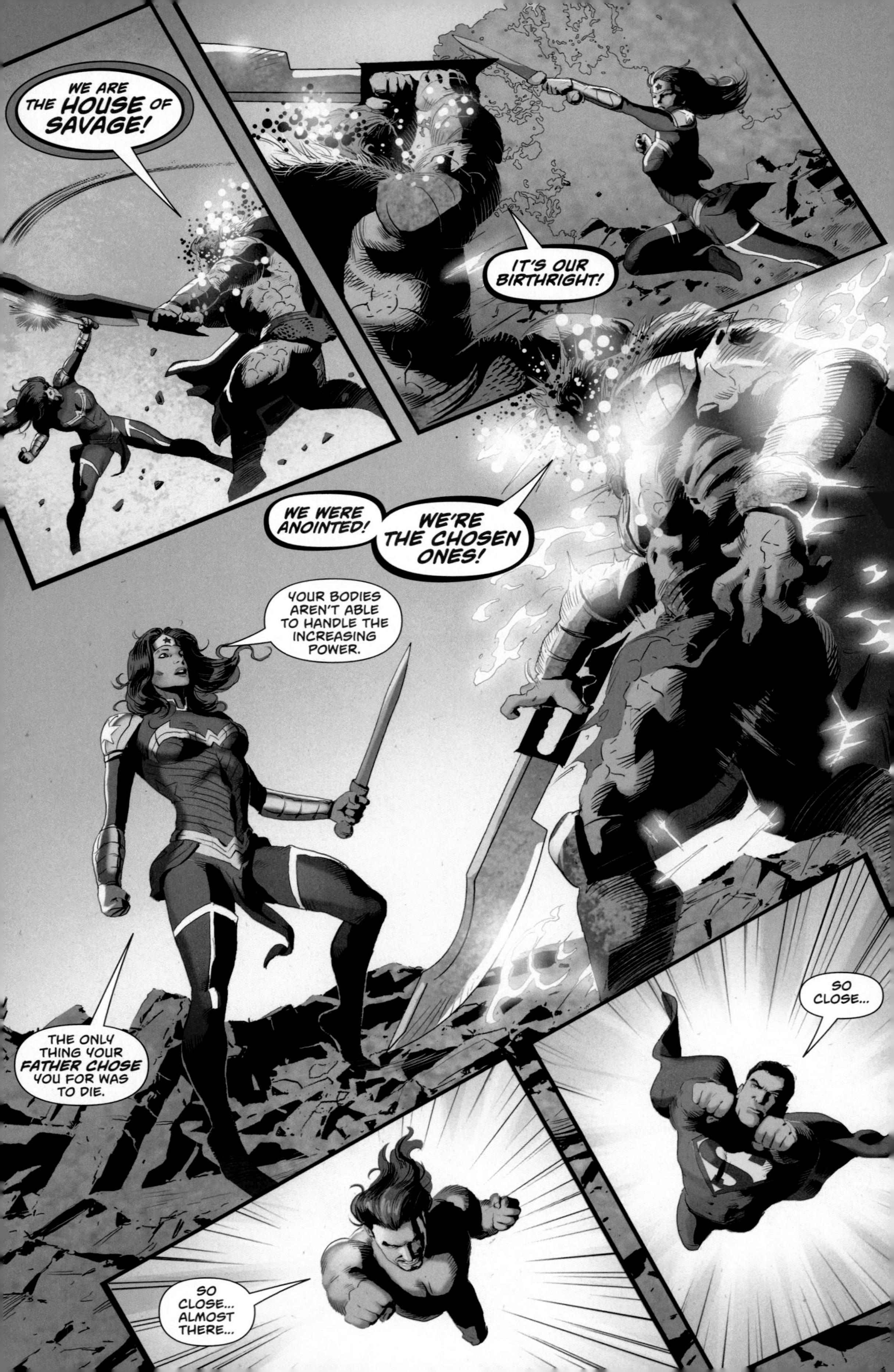
WE ARE THE HOUSE OF SAVAGE!
IT'S OUR BIRTHRIGHT!
WE WERE ANOINTED!
WE'RE THE CHOSEN ONES!
YOUR BODIES AREN'T ABLE TO HANDLE THE INCREASING POWER.
THE ONLY THING YOUR FATHER CHOSE YOU FOR WAS TO DIE.
SO CLOSE...
SO CLOSE... ALMOST THERE...

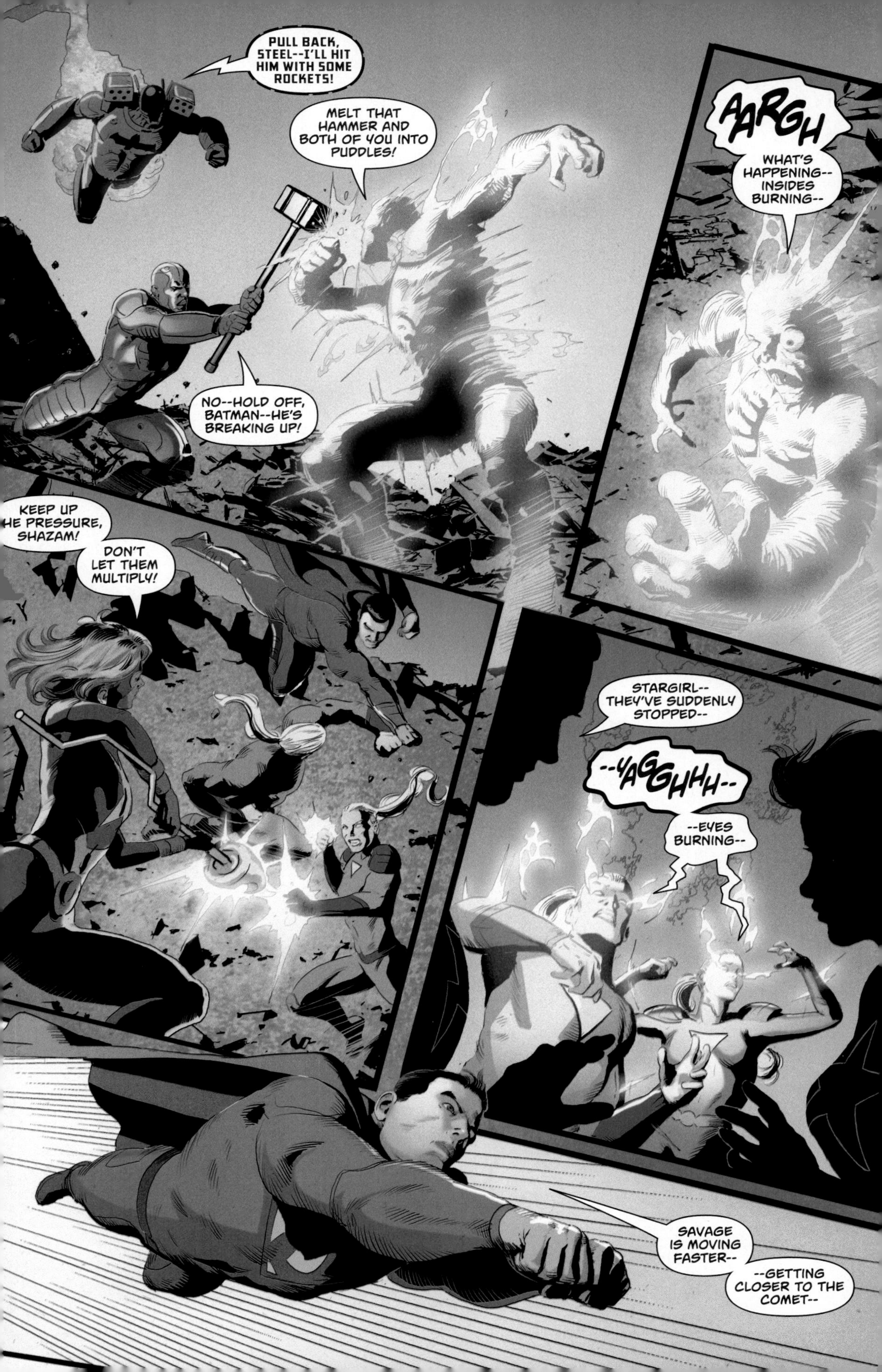
PULL BACK, STEEL--I'LL HIT HIM WITH SOME ROCKETS!
MELT THAT HAMMER AND BOTH OF YOU INTO PUDDLES!
NO--HOLD OFF, BATMAN--HE'S BREAKING UP!
AARGH
WHAT'S HAPPENING-- INSIDES BURNING--
KEEP UP HE PRESSURE, SHAZAM!
DON'T LET THEM MULTIPLY!
STARGIRL-- THEY'VE SUDDENLY STOPPED--
--YAGGHHH--
--EYES BURNING--
SAVAGE IS MOVING FASTER--
--GETTING CLOSER TO THE COMET--

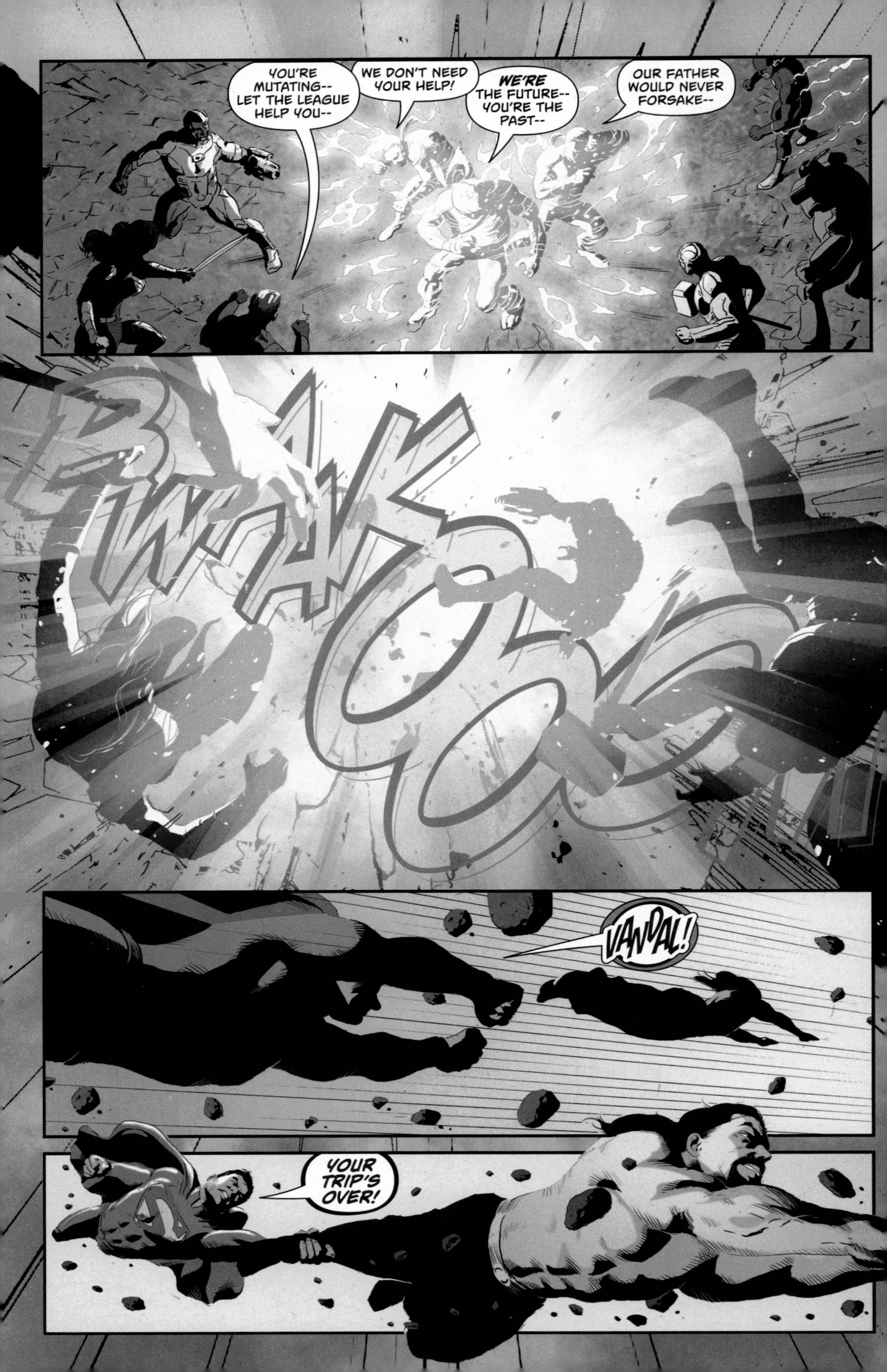

YOU'RE MUTATING-- LET THE LEAGUE HELP YOU--
WE DON'T NEED YOUR HELP!
WE'RE THE FUTURE-- YOU'RE THE PAST--
OUR FATHER WOULD NEVER FORSAKE--
BWAKOOM
VANDAL!
YOUR TRIP'S OVER!

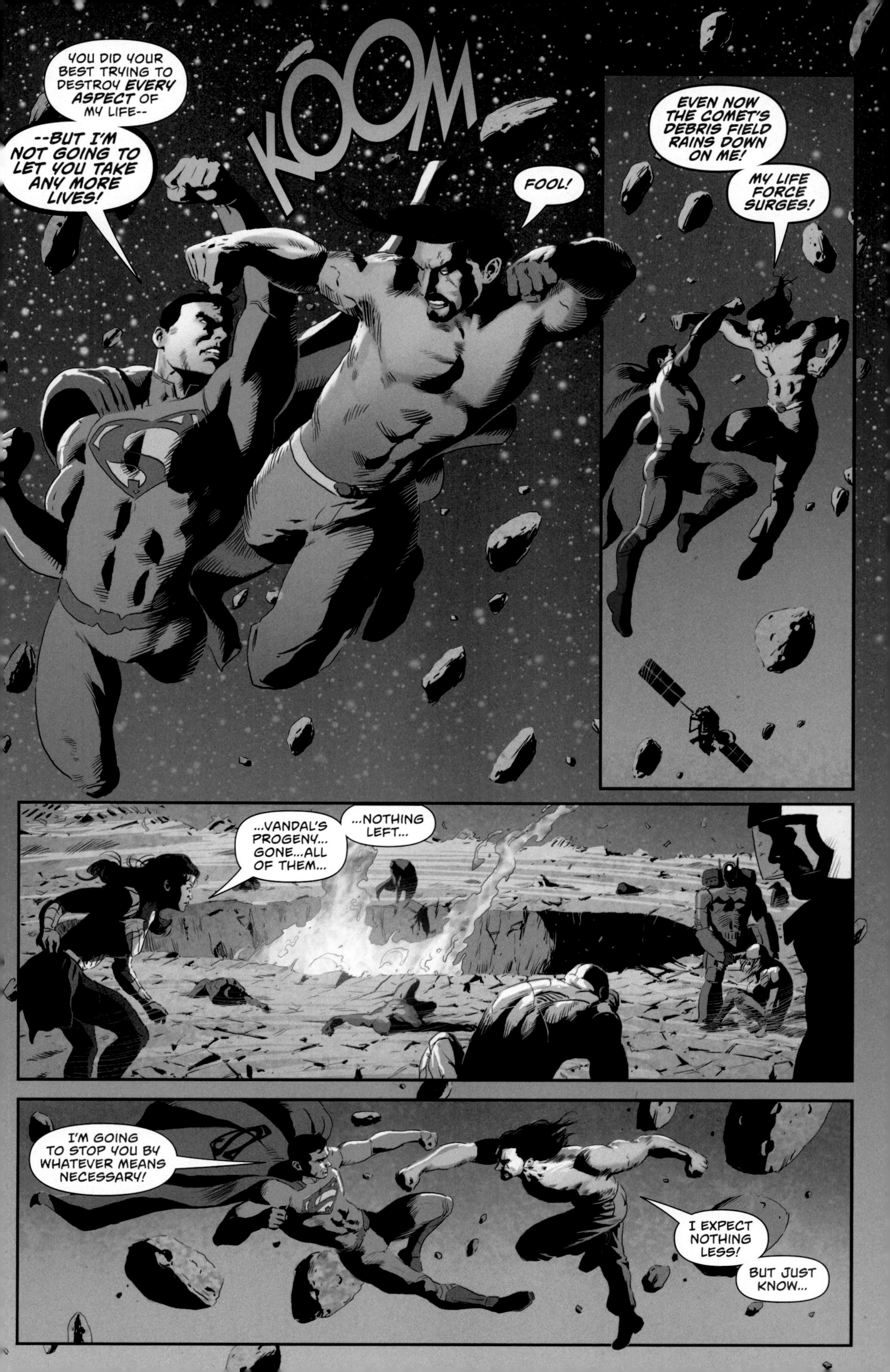
YOU DID YOUR BEST TRYING TO DESTROY EVERY ASPECT OF MY LIFE--
--BUT I'M NOT GOING TO LET YOU TAKE ANY MORE LIVES!
KOOM
FOOL!
EVEN NOW THE COMET'S DEBRIS FIELD RAINS DOWN ON ME!
MY LIFE FORCE SURGES!
...VANDAL'S PROGENY... GONE...ALL OF THEM...
...NOTHING LEFT...
I'M GOING TO STOP YOU BY WHATEVER MEANS NECESSARY!
I EXPECT NOTHING LESS!
BUT JUST KNOW...

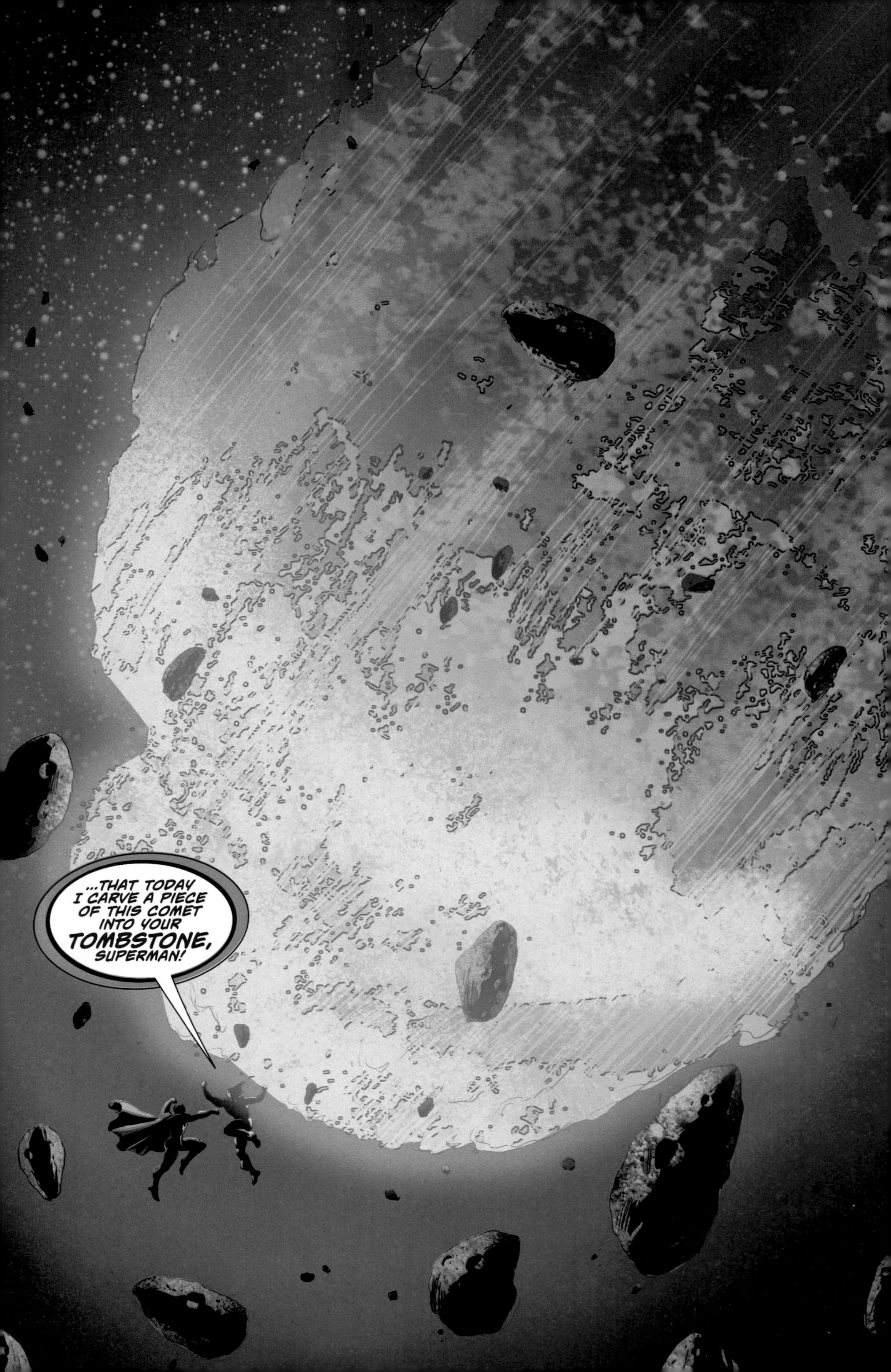
...THAT TODAY I CARVE A PIECE OF THIS COMET INTO YOUR TOMBSTONE, SUPERMAN!

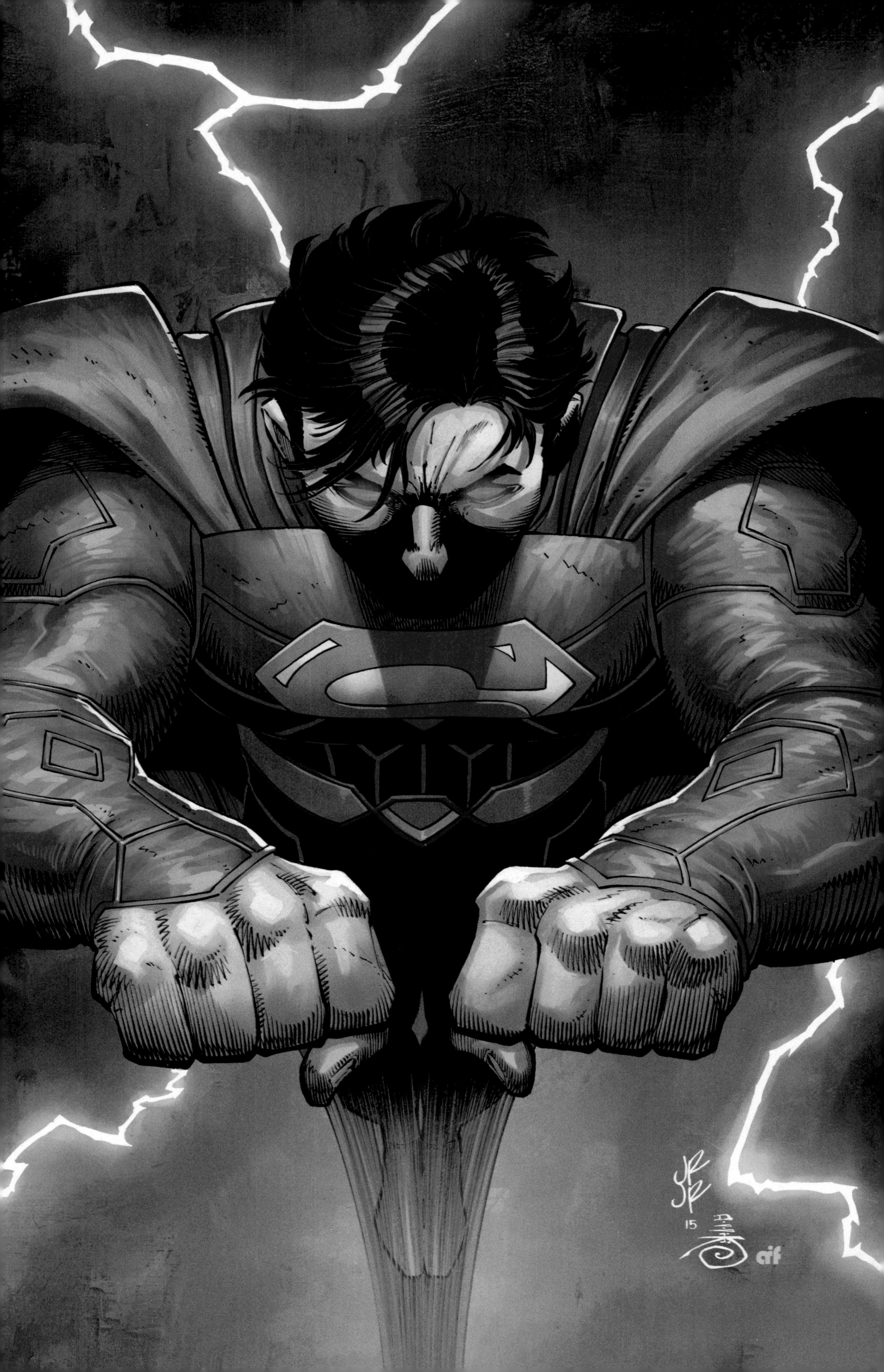

WHAT COULD HAVE BEEN, WHAT CAN STILL BE, AND WHAT IS

GENE LUEN YANG writer HOWARD PORTER ARDIAN SYAF PATRICK ZIRCHER JON BOGDANOVE pencillers HI-FI colorist ROB LEIGH letterer HOWARD PORTER HI-FI cover

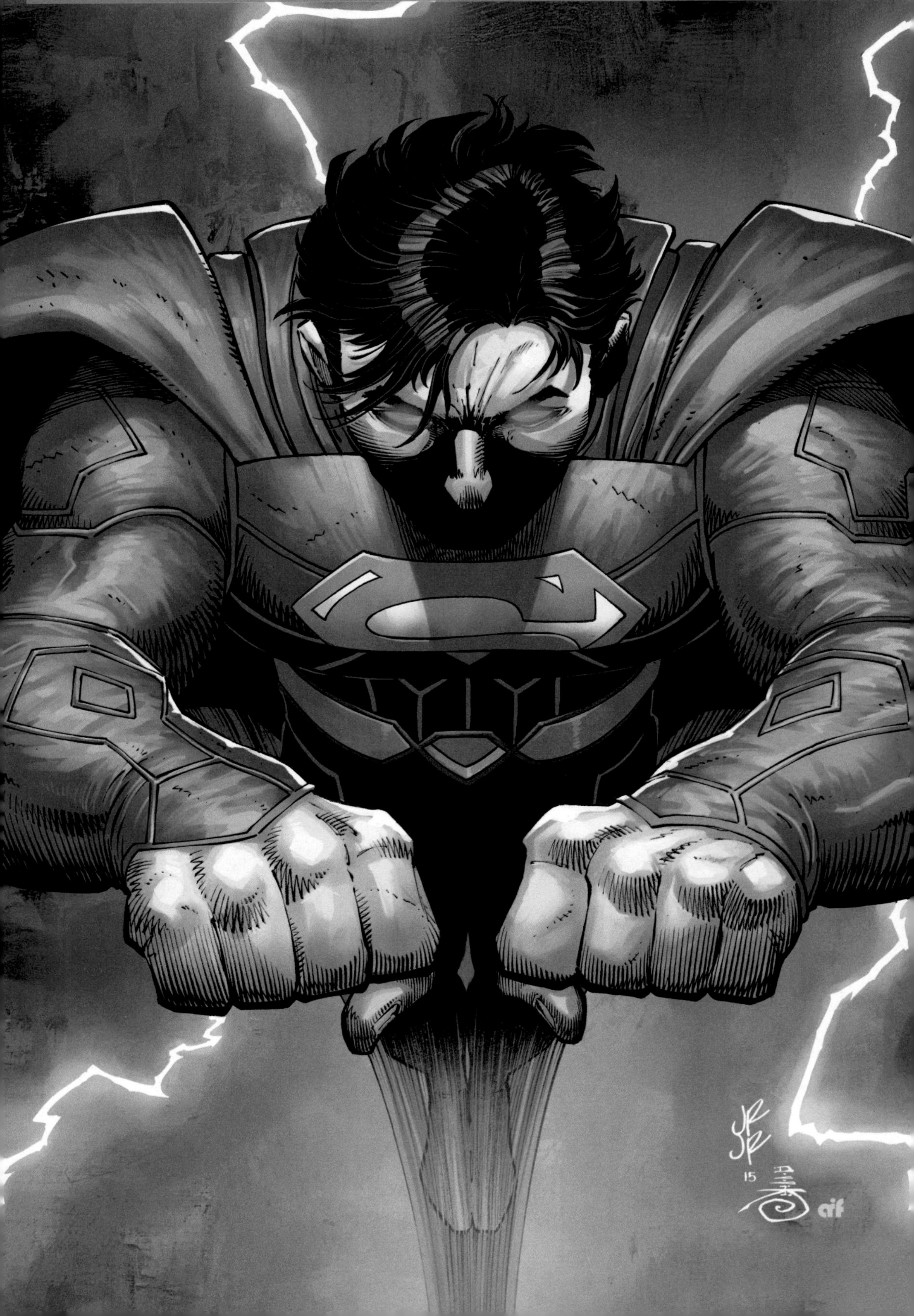

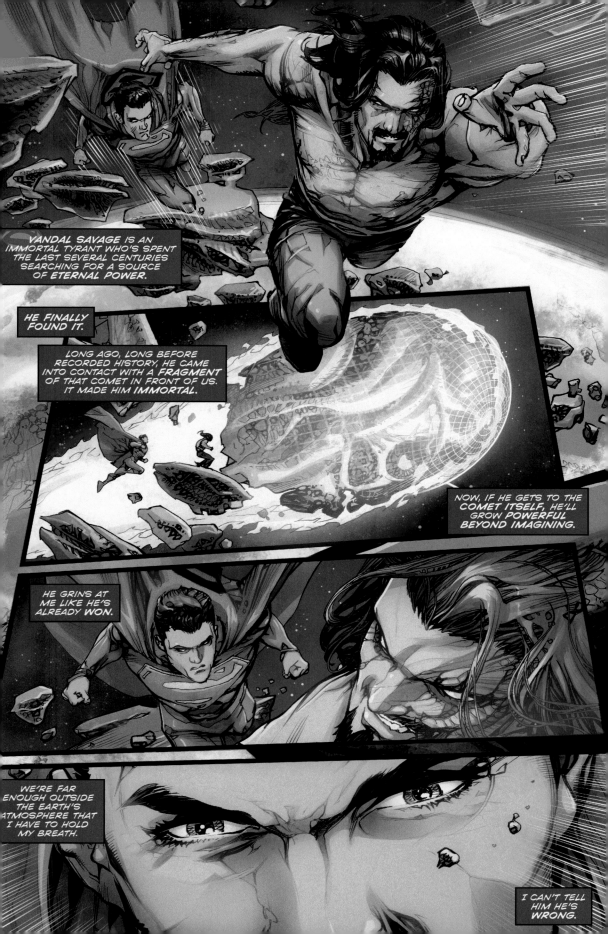

VANDAL SAVAGE IS AN IMMORTAL TYRANT WHO'S SPENT THE LAST SEVERAL CENTURIES SEARCHING FOR A SOURCE OF ETERNAL POWER.

HE FINALLY FOUND IT.

LONG AGO, LONG BEFORE RECORDED HISTORY, HE CAME INTO CONTACT WITH A FRAGMENT OF THAT COMET IN FRONT OF US. IT MADE HIM IMMORTAL.

NOW, IF HE GETS TO THE COMET ITSELF, HE'LL GROW POWERFUL BEYOND IMAGINING.

HE GRINS AT ME LIKE HE'S ALREADY WON.

WE'RE FAR ENOUGH OUTSIDE THE EARTH'S ATMOSPHERE THAT I HAVE TO HOLD MY BREATH.

I CAN'T TELL HIM HE'S WRONG.

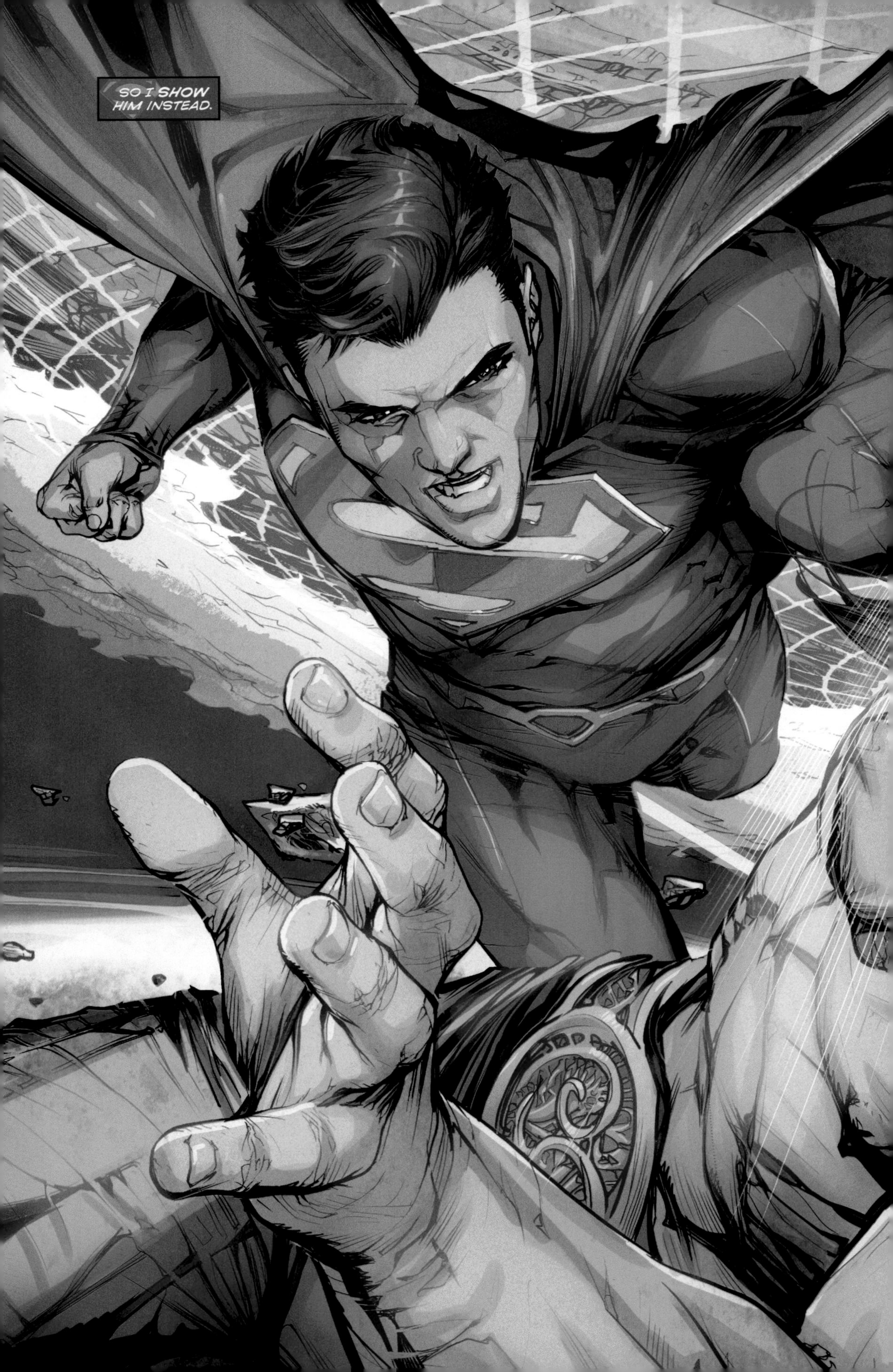
SO I SHOW HIM INSTEAD.

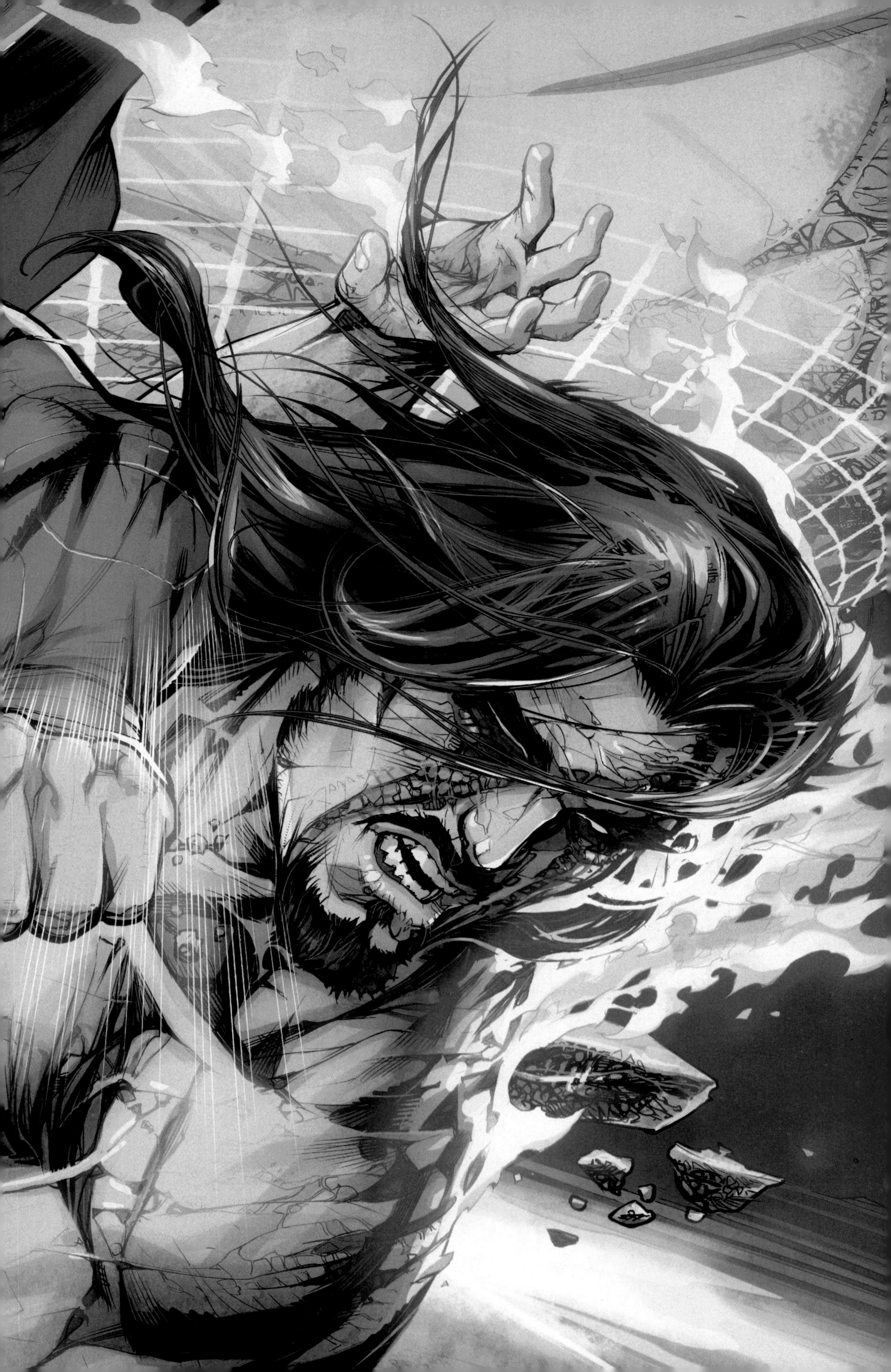

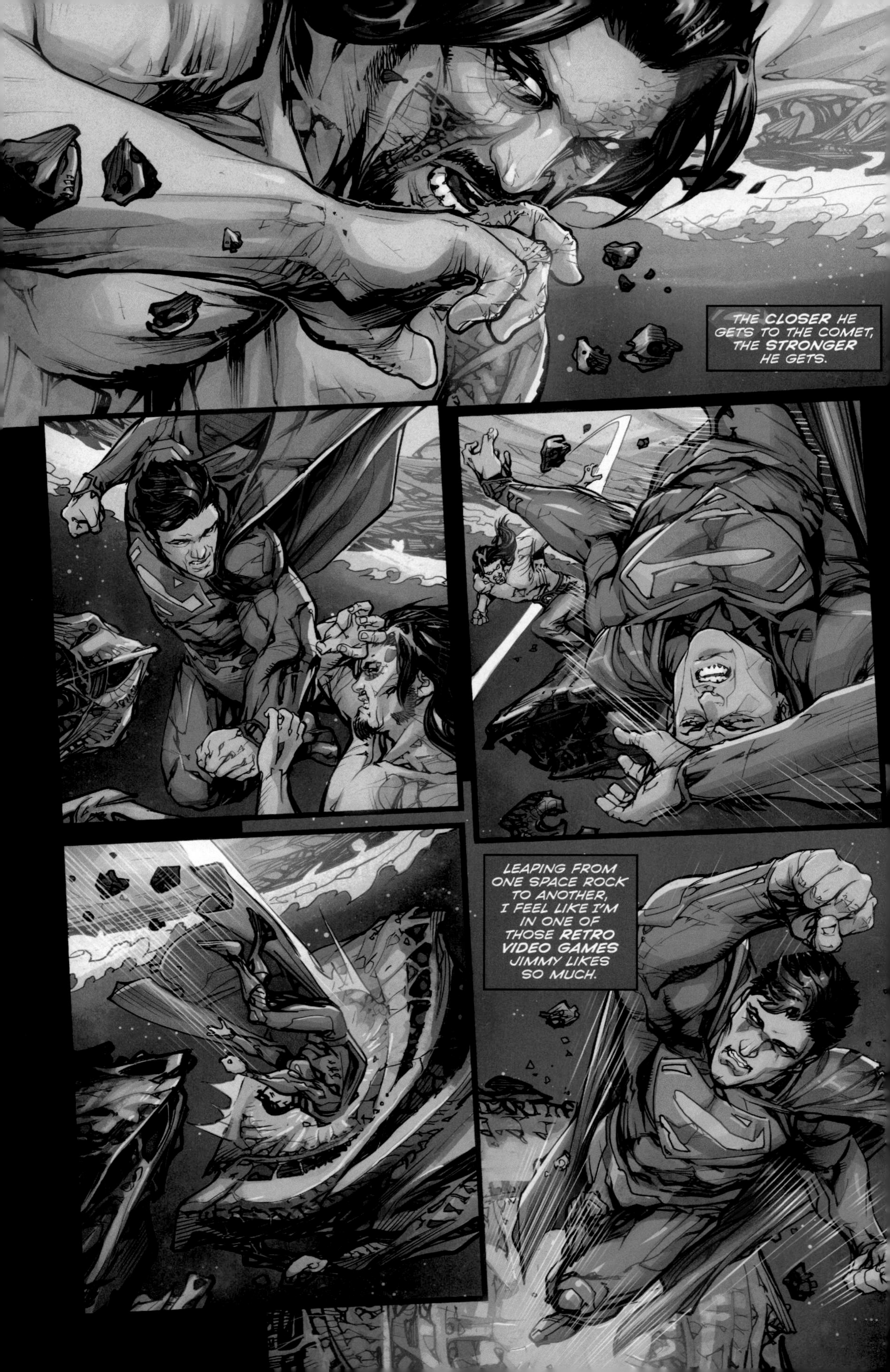
THE CLOSER HE GETS TO THE COMET, THE STRONGER HE GETS.
LEAPING FROM ONE SPACE ROCK TO ANOTHER, I FEEL LIKE I'M IN ONE OF THOSE RETRO VIDEO GAMES JIMMY LIKES SO MUCH.

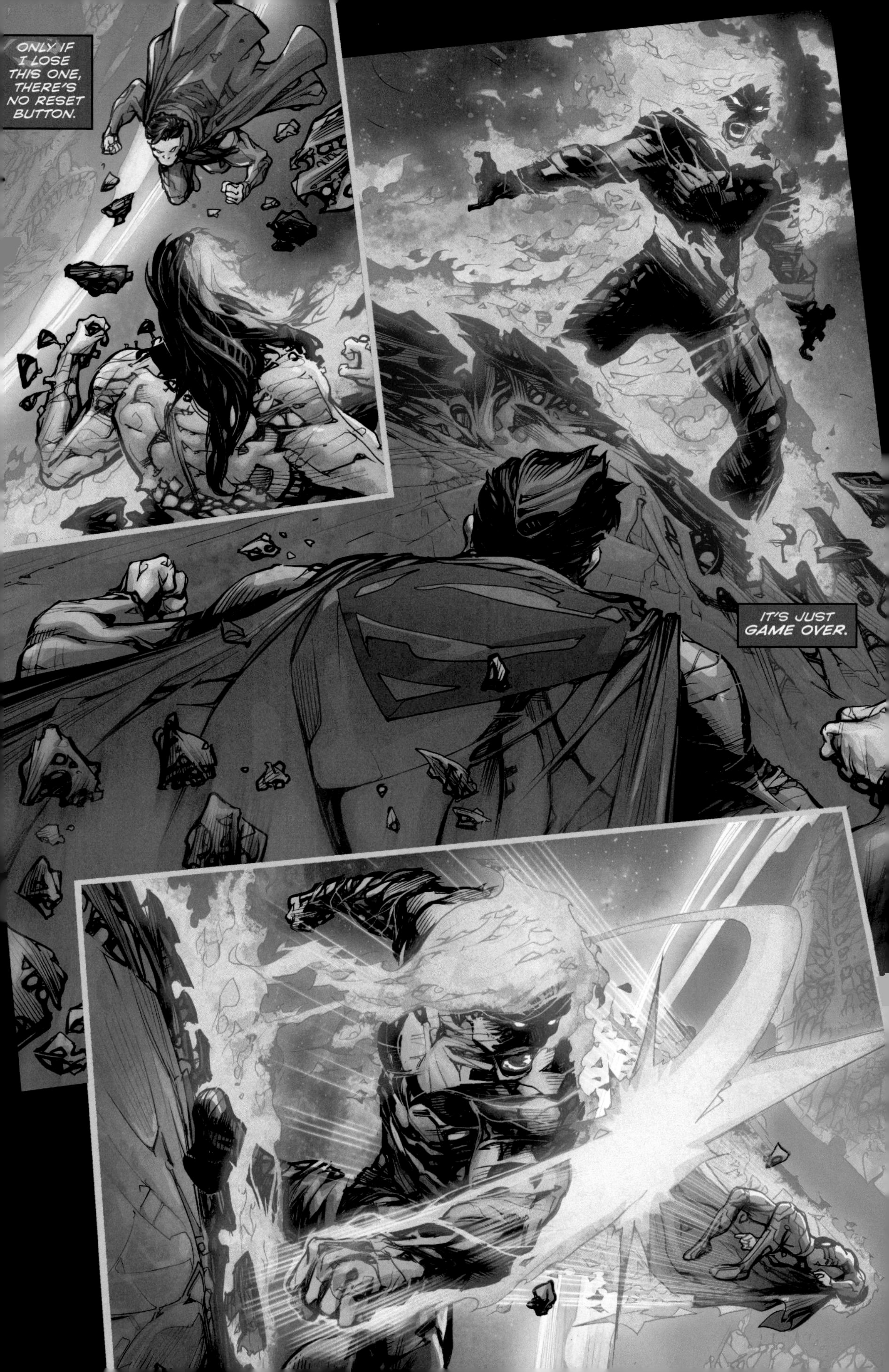
ONLY IF I LOSE THIS ONE, THERE'S NO RESET BUTTON.
IT'S JUST GAME OVER.

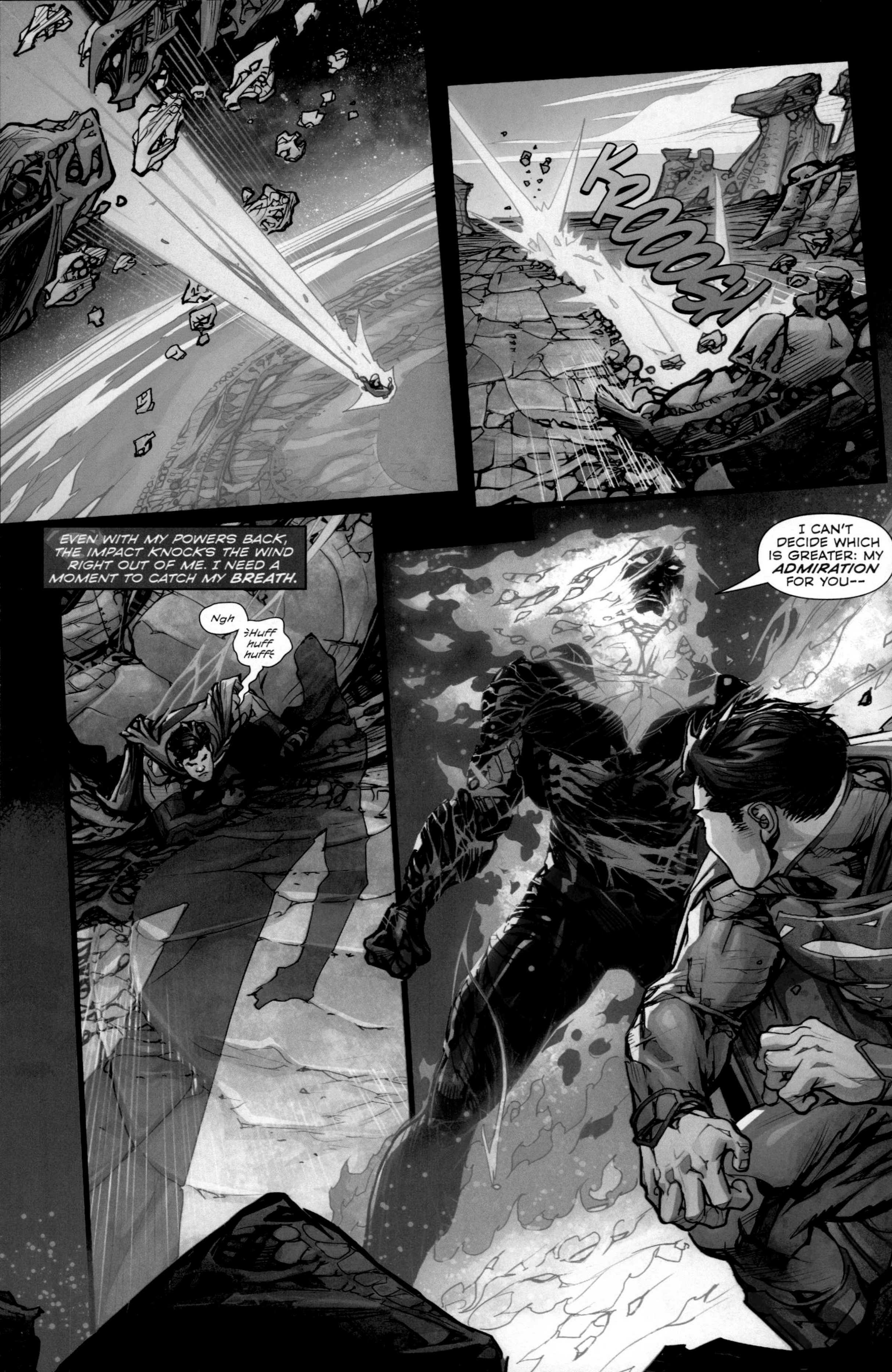
KROOOSH
EVEN WITH MY POWERS BACK, THE IMPACT KNOCKS THE WIND RIGHT OUT OF ME. I NEED A MOMENT TO CATCH MY BREATH.
Ngh
Huff huff huff
I CAN'T DECIDE WHICH IS GREATER: MY ADMIRATION FOR YOU--

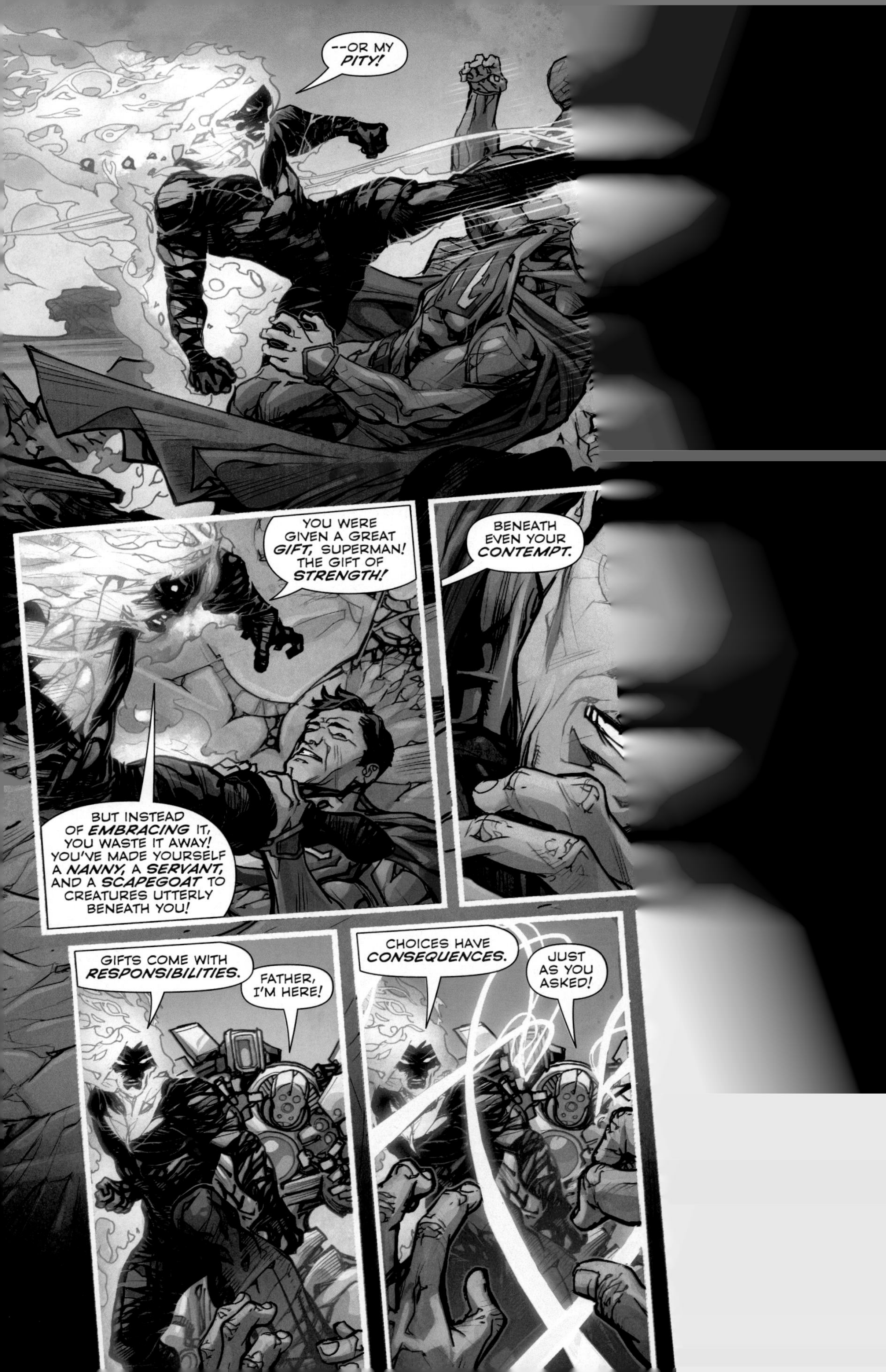
--OR MY PITY!
YOU WERE GIVEN A GREAT GIFT, SUPERMAN! THE GIFT OF STRENGTH!
BUT INSTEAD OF EMBRACING IT, YOU WASTE IT AWAY! YOU'VE MADE YOURSELF A NANNY, A SERVANT, AND A SCAPEGOAT TO CREATURES UTTERLY BENEATH YOU!
BENEATH EVEN YOUR CONTEMPT.
GIFTS COME WITH RESPONSIBILITIES.
FATHER, I'M HERE!
CHOICES HAVE CONSEQUENCES.
JUST AS YOU ASKED!

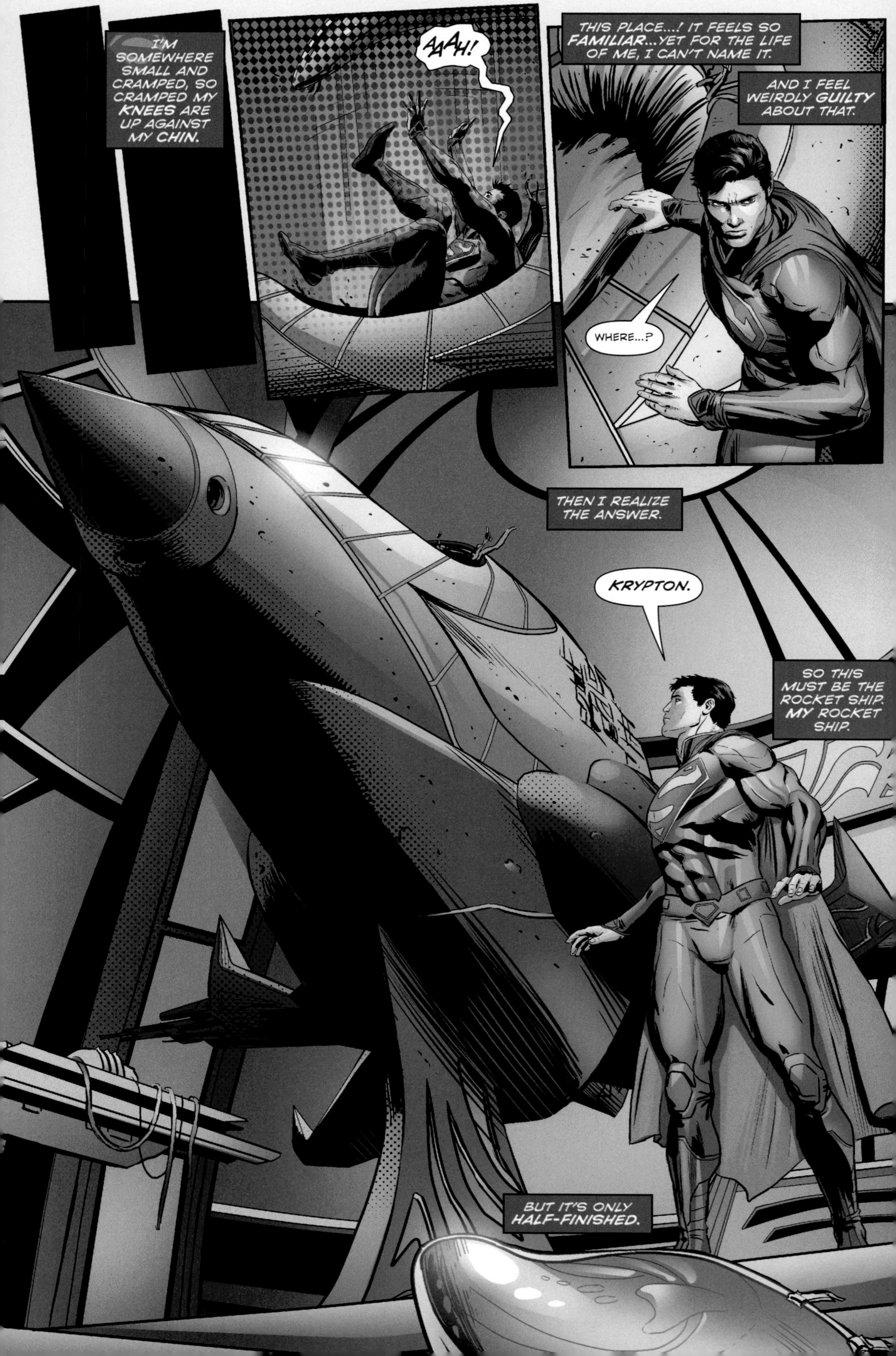
I'M SOMEWHERE SMALL AND CRAMPED, SO CRAMPED MY KNEES ARE UP AGAINST MY CHIN.
AAAH!
THIS PLACE...! IT FEELS SO FAMILIAR...YET FOR THE LIFE OF ME, I CAN'T NAME IT.
AND I FEEL WEIRDLY GUILTY ABOUT THAT.
WHERE...?
THEN I REALIZE THE ANSWER.
KRYPTON.
SO THIS MUST BE THE ROCKET SHIP. MY ROCKET SHIP.
BUT IT'S ONLY HALF-FINISHED.

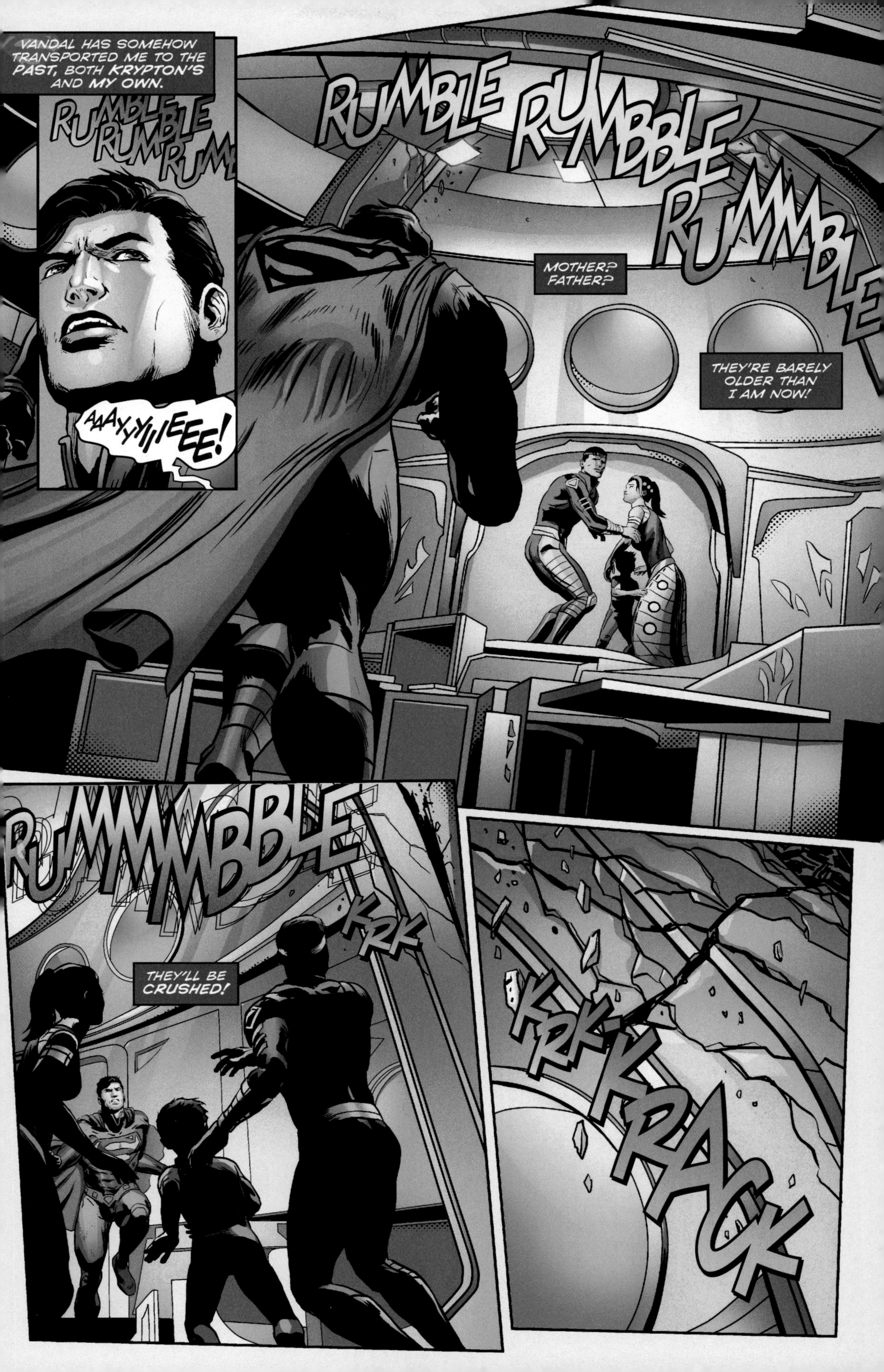
VANDAL HAS SOMEHOW TRANSPORTED ME TO THE PAST, BOTH KRYPTON'S AND MY OWN.
RUMBLE RUMBLE RUMBLE
AAAYYIIIEEE!
RUMBLE RUMBBLE RUMMBLE
MOTHER? FATHER?
THEY'RE BARELY OLDER THAN I AM NOW!
RUMMMBBLE
KRK
THEY'LL BE CRUSHED!
KRK KRACK

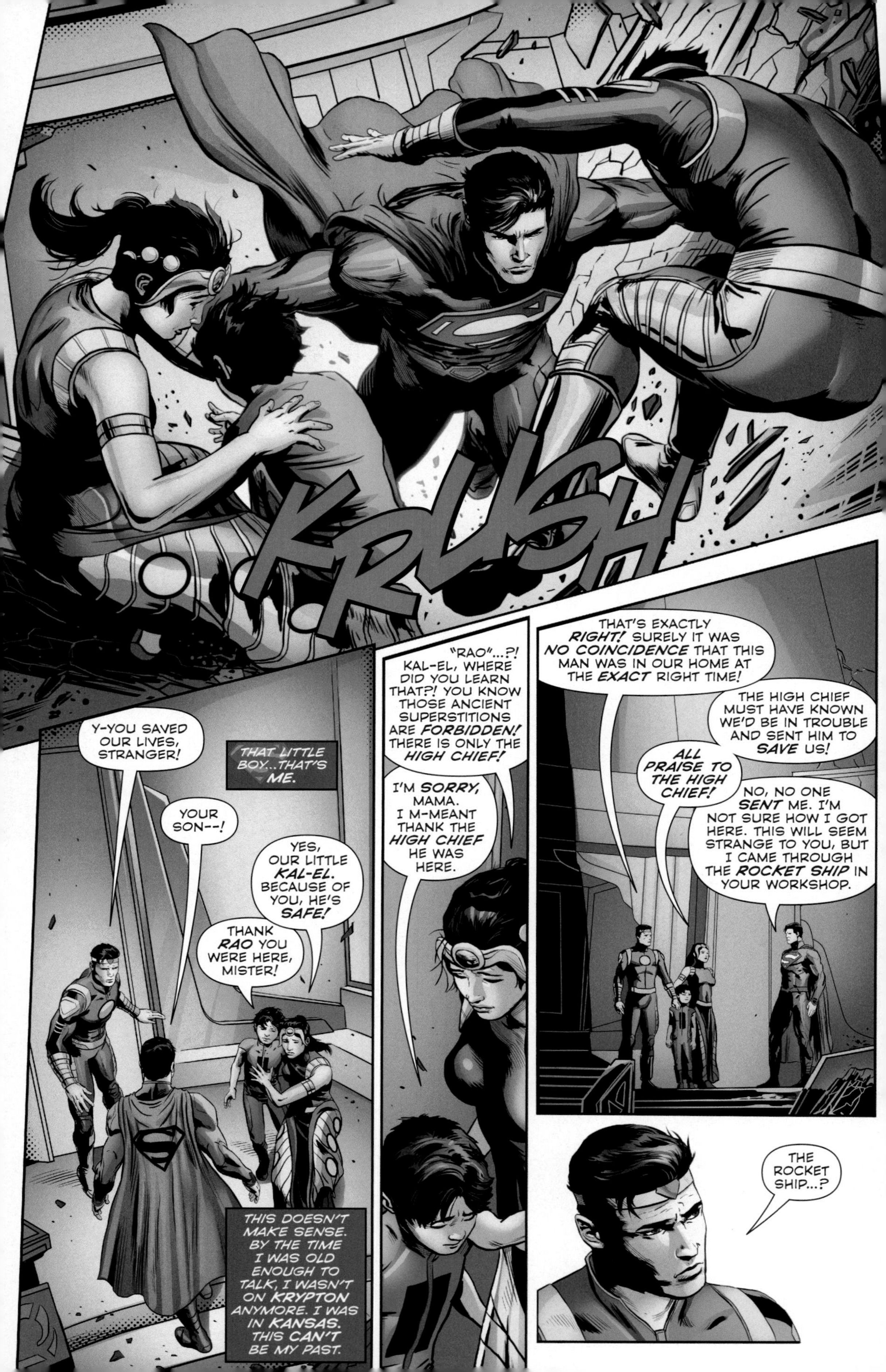
KRUSH
Y-YOU SAVED OUR LIVES, STRANGER!
THAT LITTLE BOY...THAT'S ME.
YOUR SON--!
YES, OUR LITTLE KAL-EL. BECAUSE OF YOU, HE'S SAFE!
THANK RAO YOU WERE HERE, MISTER!
THIS DOESN'T MAKE SENSE. BY THE TIME I WAS OLD ENOUGH TO TALK, I WASN'T ON KRYPTON ANYMORE. I WAS IN KANSAS. THIS CAN'T BE MY PAST.
"RAO"...?! KAL-EL, WHERE DID YOU LEARN THAT?! YOU KNOW THOSE ANCIENT SUPERSTITIONS ARE FORBIDDEN! THERE IS ONLY THE HIGH CHIEF!
I'M SORRY, MAMA. I M-MEANT THANK THE HIGH CHIEF HE WAS HERE.
THAT'S EXACTLY RIGHT! SURELY IT WAS NO COINCIDENCE THAT THIS MAN WAS IN OUR HOME AT THE EXACT RIGHT TIME!
THE HIGH CHIEF MUST HAVE KNOWN WE'D BE IN TROUBLE AND SENT HIM TO SAVE US!
ALL PRAISE TO THE HIGH CHIEF!
NO, NO ONE SENT ME. I'M NOT SURE HOW I GOT HERE. THIS WILL SEEM STRANGE TO YOU, BUT I CAME THROUGH THE ROCKET SHIP IN YOUR WORKSHOP.
THE ROCKET SHIP...?

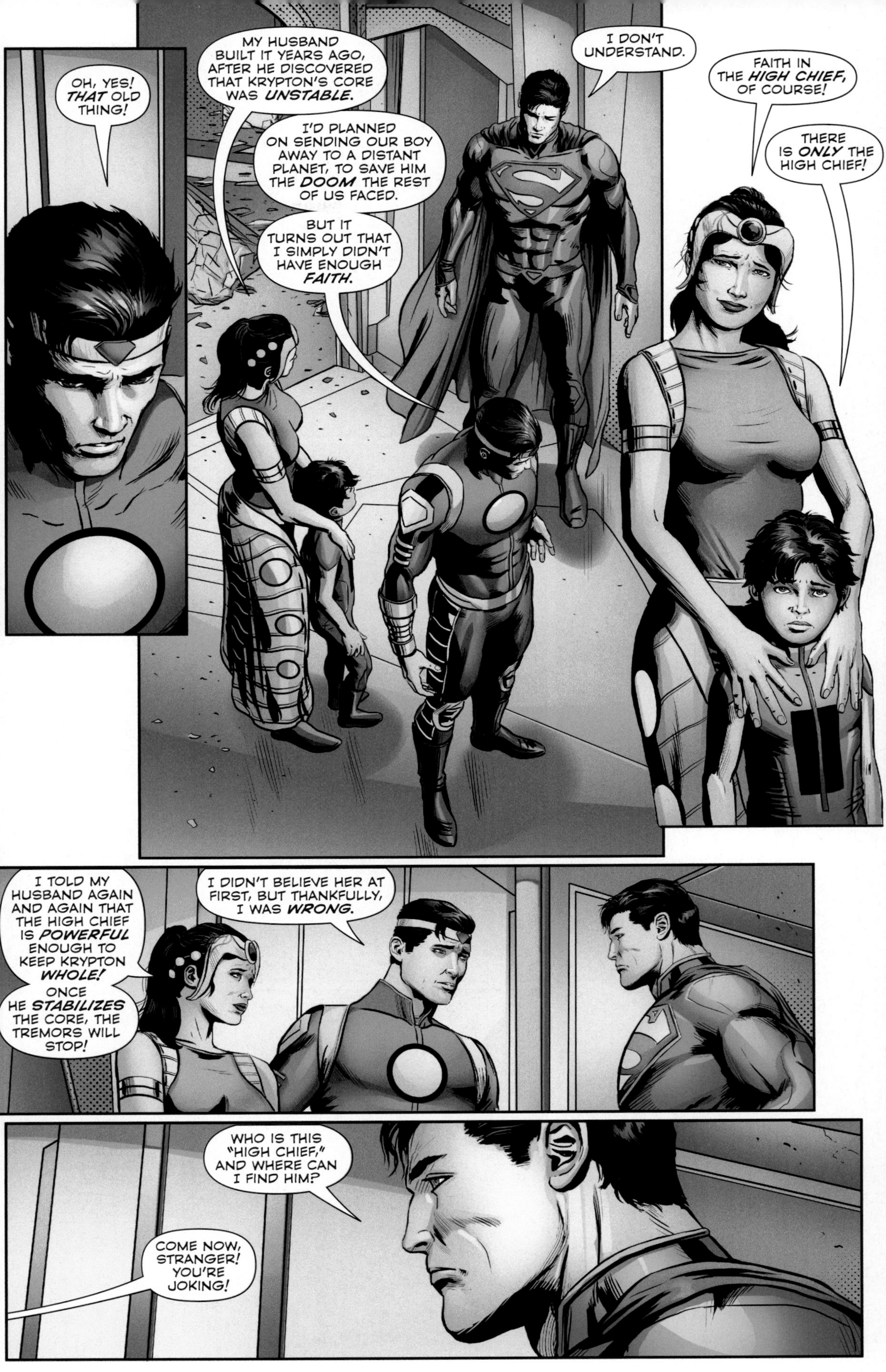
OH, YES! THAT OLD THING!
MY HUSBAND BUILT IT YEARS AGO, AFTER HE DISCOVERED THAT KRYPTON'S CORE WAS UNSTABLE.
I'D PLANNED ON SENDING OUR BOY AWAY TO A DISTANT PLANET, TO SAVE HIM THE DOOM THE REST OF US FACED.
BUT IT TURNS OUT THAT I SIMPLY DIDN'T HAVE ENOUGH FAITH.
I DON'T UNDERSTAND.
FAITH IN THE HIGH CHIEF, OF COURSE!
THERE IS ONLY THE HIGH CHIEF!
I TOLD MY HUSBAND AGAIN AND AGAIN THAT THE HIGH CHIEF IS POWERFUL ENOUGH TO KEEP KRYPTON WHOLE!
ONCE HE STABILIZES THE CORE, THE TREMORS WILL STOP!
I DIDN'T BELIEVE HER AT FIRST, BUT THANKFULLY, I WAS WRONG.
WHO IS THIS "HIGH CHIEF," AND WHERE CAN I FIND HIM?
COME NOW, STRANGER! YOU'RE JOKING!

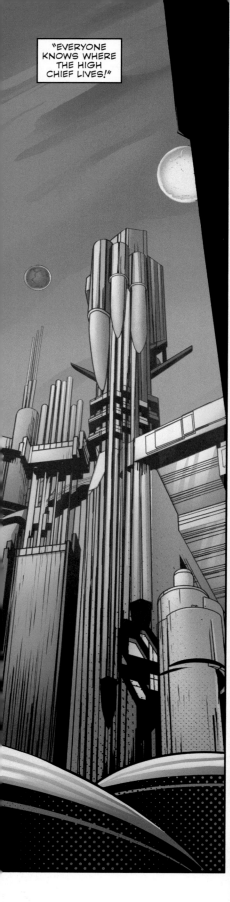

"EVERYONE KNOWS WHERE THE HIGH CHIEF LIVES!"

KRYPTON'S RED SUN DOESN'T ALLOW MY POWERS TO RECHARGE.

HALT WHERE YOU ARE, INTRUDER! HALT!

BZRAKT

BZRAKT

WHAM

NOT REALLY A PROBLEM FOR ME, GIVEN RECENT EVENTS.

IS THE HIGH CHIEF THROUGH THOSE DOORS?

Y-YES, BUT DON'T YOU DARE GO IN THERE!

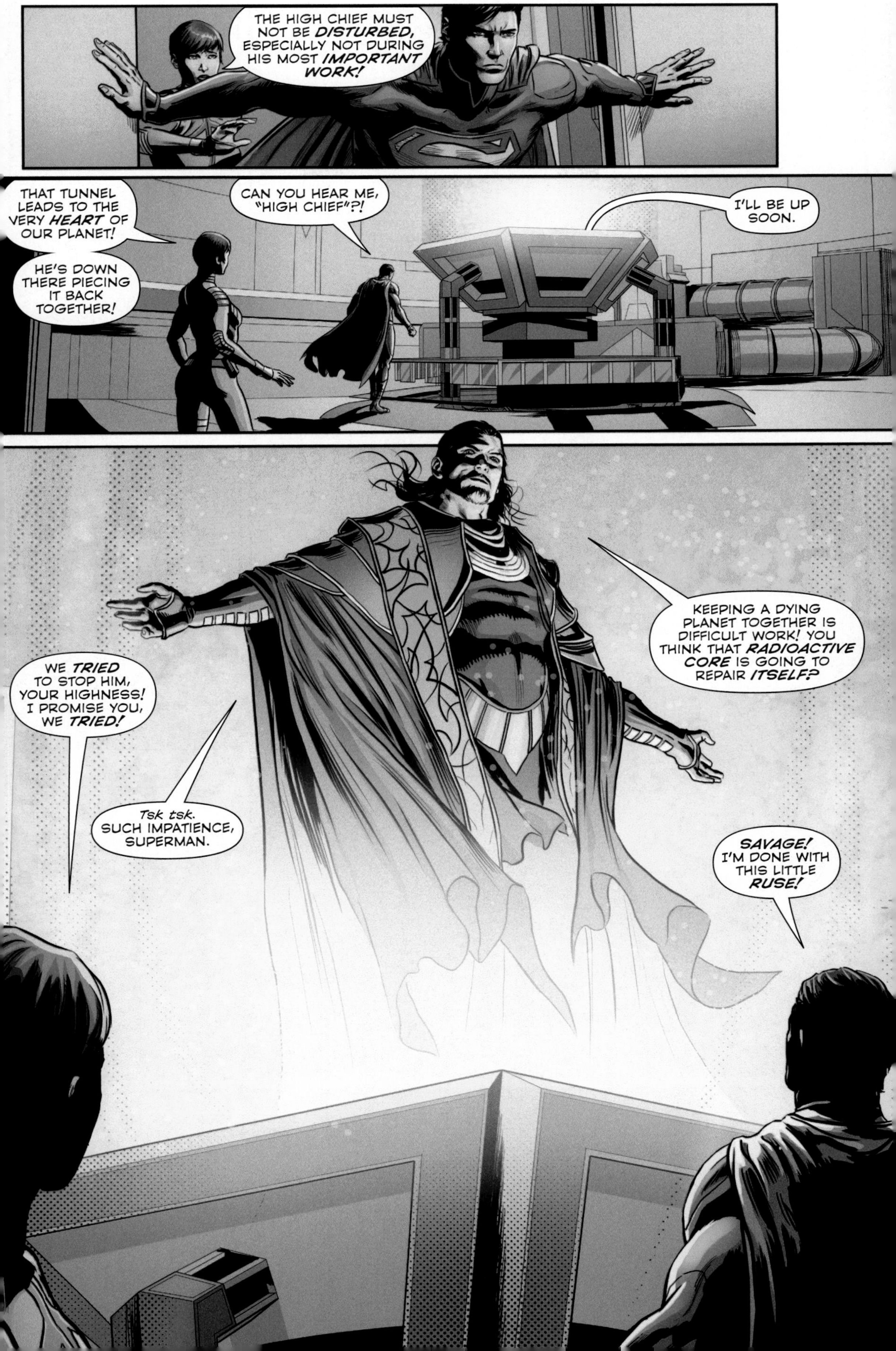
THE HIGH CHIEF MUST NOT BE DISTURBED, ESPECIALLY NOT DURING HIS MOST IMPORTANT WORK!
THAT TUNNEL LEADS TO THE VERY HEART OF OUR PLANET!
HE'S DOWN THERE PIECING IT BACK TOGETHER!
CAN YOU HEAR ME, "HIGH CHIEF"?!
I'LL BE UP SOON.
KEEPING A DYING PLANET TOGETHER IS DIFFICULT WORK! YOU THINK THAT RADIOACTIVE CORE IS GOING TO REPAIR ITSELF?
WE TRIED TO STOP HIM, YOUR HIGHNESS! I PROMISE YOU, WE TRIED!
Tsk tsk. SUCH IMPATIENCE, SUPERMAN.
SAVAGE! I'M DONE WITH THIS LITTLE RUSE!

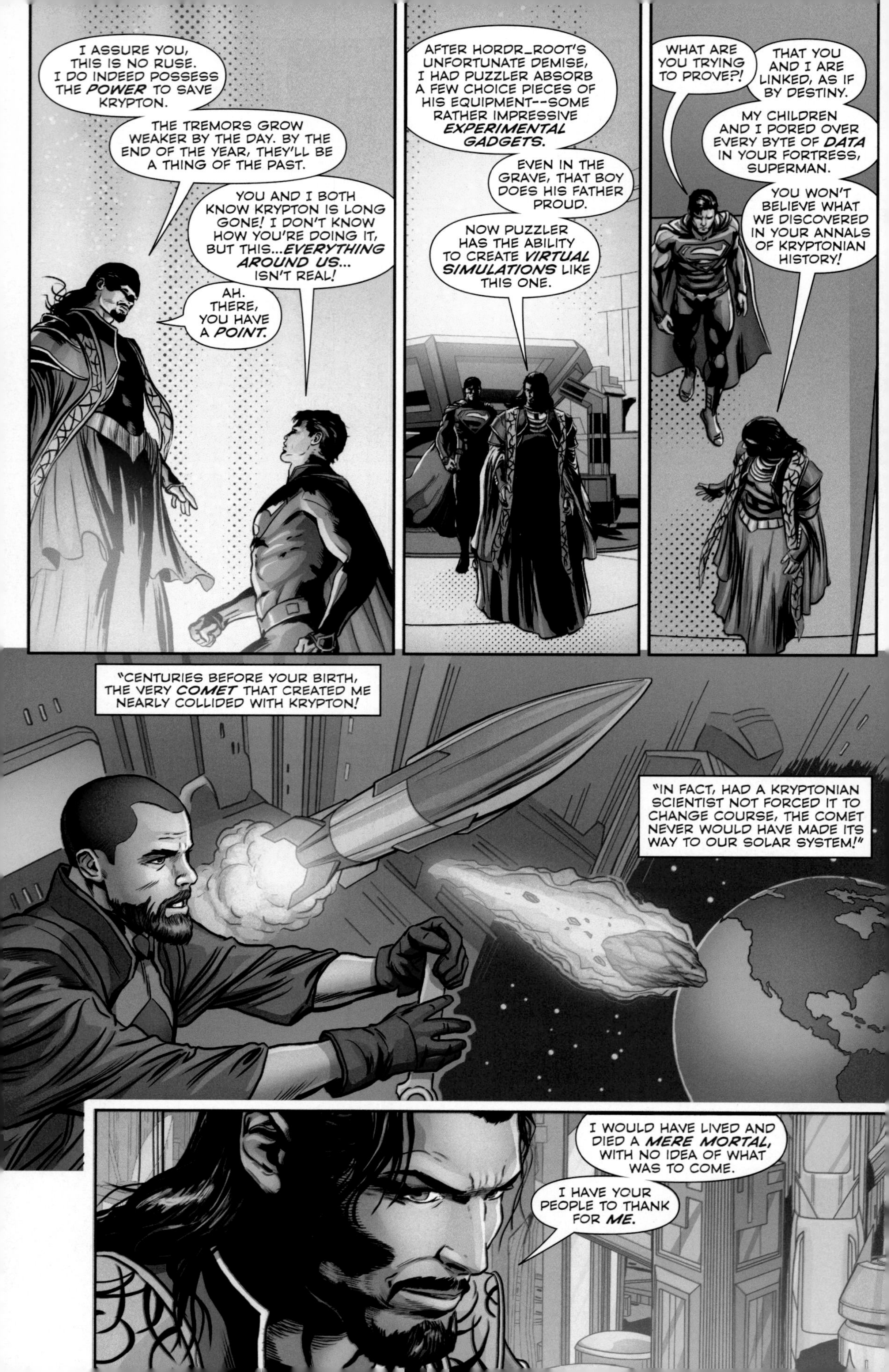
I ASSURE YOU, THIS IS NO RUSE. I DO INDEED POSSESS THE *POWER* TO SAVE KRYPTON.
THE TREMORS GROW WEAKER BY THE DAY. BY THE END OF THE YEAR, THEY'LL BE A THING OF THE PAST.
YOU AND I BOTH KNOW KRYPTON IS LONG GONE! I DON'T KNOW HOW YOU'RE DOING IT, BUT THIS...*EVERYTHING AROUND US*... ISN'T REAL!
AH. THERE, YOU HAVE A *POINT.*
AFTER HORDR_ROOT'S UNFORTUNATE DEMISE, I HAD PUZZLER ABSORB A FEW CHOICE PIECES OF HIS EQUIPMENT--SOME RATHER IMPRESSIVE *EXPERIMENTAL GADGETS.*
EVEN IN THE GRAVE, THAT BOY DOES HIS FATHER PROUD.
NOW PUZZLER HAS THE ABILITY TO CREATE *VIRTUAL SIMULATIONS* LIKE THIS ONE.
WHAT ARE YOU TRYING TO PROVE?!
THAT YOU AND I ARE LINKED, AS IF BY DESTINY.
MY CHILDREN AND I PORED OVER EVERY BYTE OF *DATA* IN YOUR FORTRESS, SUPERMAN.
YOU WON'T BELIEVE WHAT WE DISCOVERED IN YOUR ANNALS OF KRYPTONIAN HISTORY!
"CENTURIES BEFORE YOUR BIRTH, THE VERY *COMET* THAT CREATED ME NEARLY COLLIDED WITH KRYPTON!
"IN FACT, HAD A KRYPTONIAN SCIENTIST NOT FORCED IT TO CHANGE COURSE, THE COMET NEVER WOULD HAVE MADE ITS WAY TO OUR SOLAR SYSTEM!"
I WOULD HAVE LIVED AND DIED A *MERE MORTAL,* WITH NO IDEA OF WHAT WAS TO COME.
I HAVE YOUR PEOPLE TO THANK FOR *ME.*

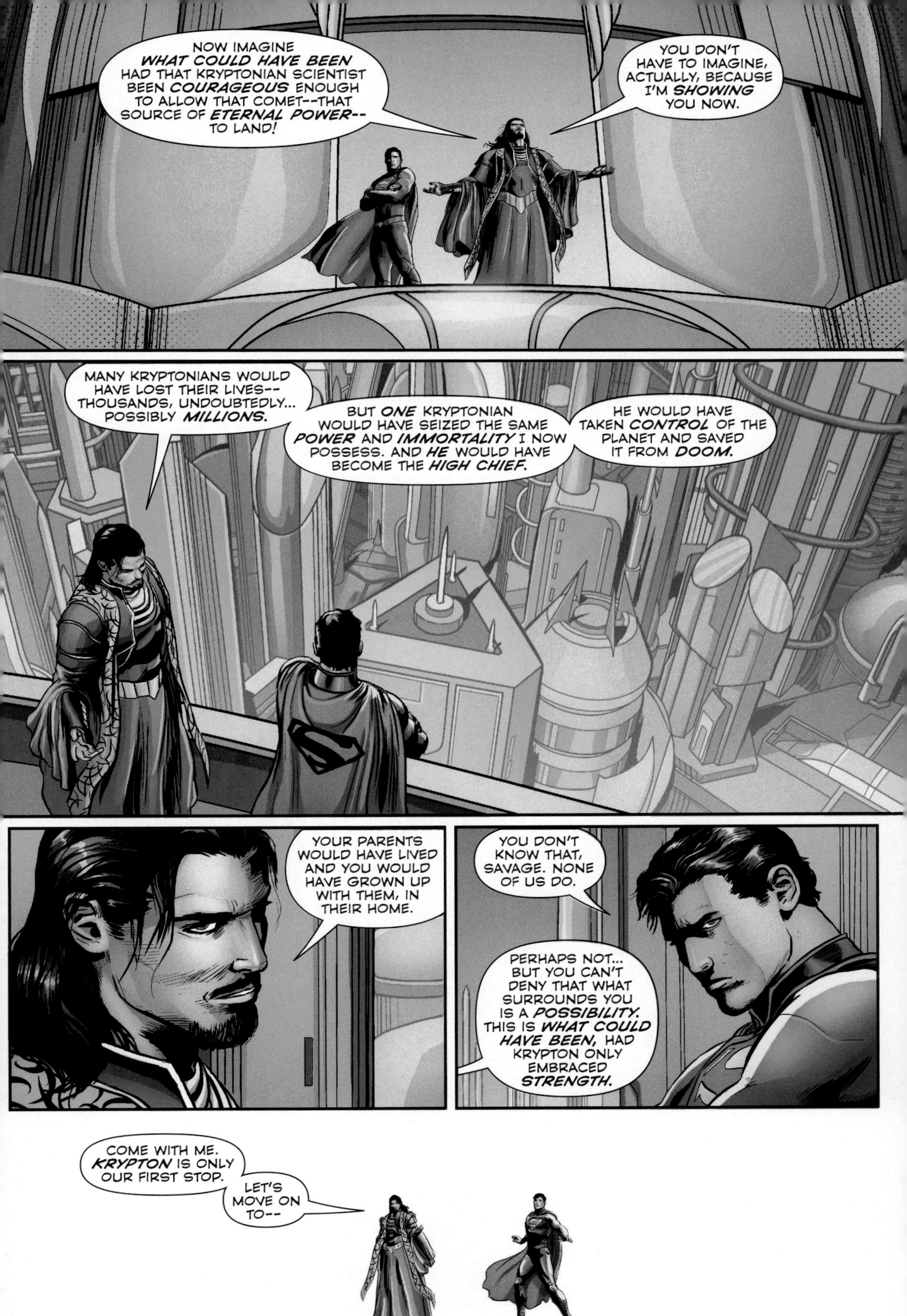
NOW IMAGINE WHAT COULD HAVE BEEN HAD THAT KRYPTONIAN SCIENTIST BEEN COURAGEOUS ENOUGH TO ALLOW THAT COMET--THAT SOURCE OF ETERNAL POWER--TO LAND!
YOU DON'T HAVE TO IMAGINE, ACTUALLY, BECAUSE I'M SHOWING YOU NOW.
MANY KRYPTONIANS WOULD HAVE LOST THEIR LIVES--THOUSANDS, UNDOUBTEDLY... POSSIBLY MILLIONS.
BUT ONE KRYPTONIAN WOULD HAVE SEIZED THE SAME POWER AND IMMORTALITY I NOW POSSESS. AND HE WOULD HAVE BECOME THE HIGH CHIEF.
HE WOULD HAVE TAKEN CONTROL OF THE PLANET AND SAVED IT FROM DOOM.
YOUR PARENTS WOULD HAVE LIVED AND YOU WOULD HAVE GROWN UP WITH THEM, IN THEIR HOME.
YOU DON'T KNOW THAT, SAVAGE. NONE OF US DO.
PERHAPS NOT... BUT YOU CAN'T DENY THAT WHAT SURROUNDS YOU IS A POSSIBILITY. THIS IS WHAT COULD HAVE BEEN, HAD KRYPTON ONLY EMBRACED STRENGTH.
COME WITH ME. KRYPTON IS ONLY OUR FIRST STOP.
LET'S MOVE ON TO--

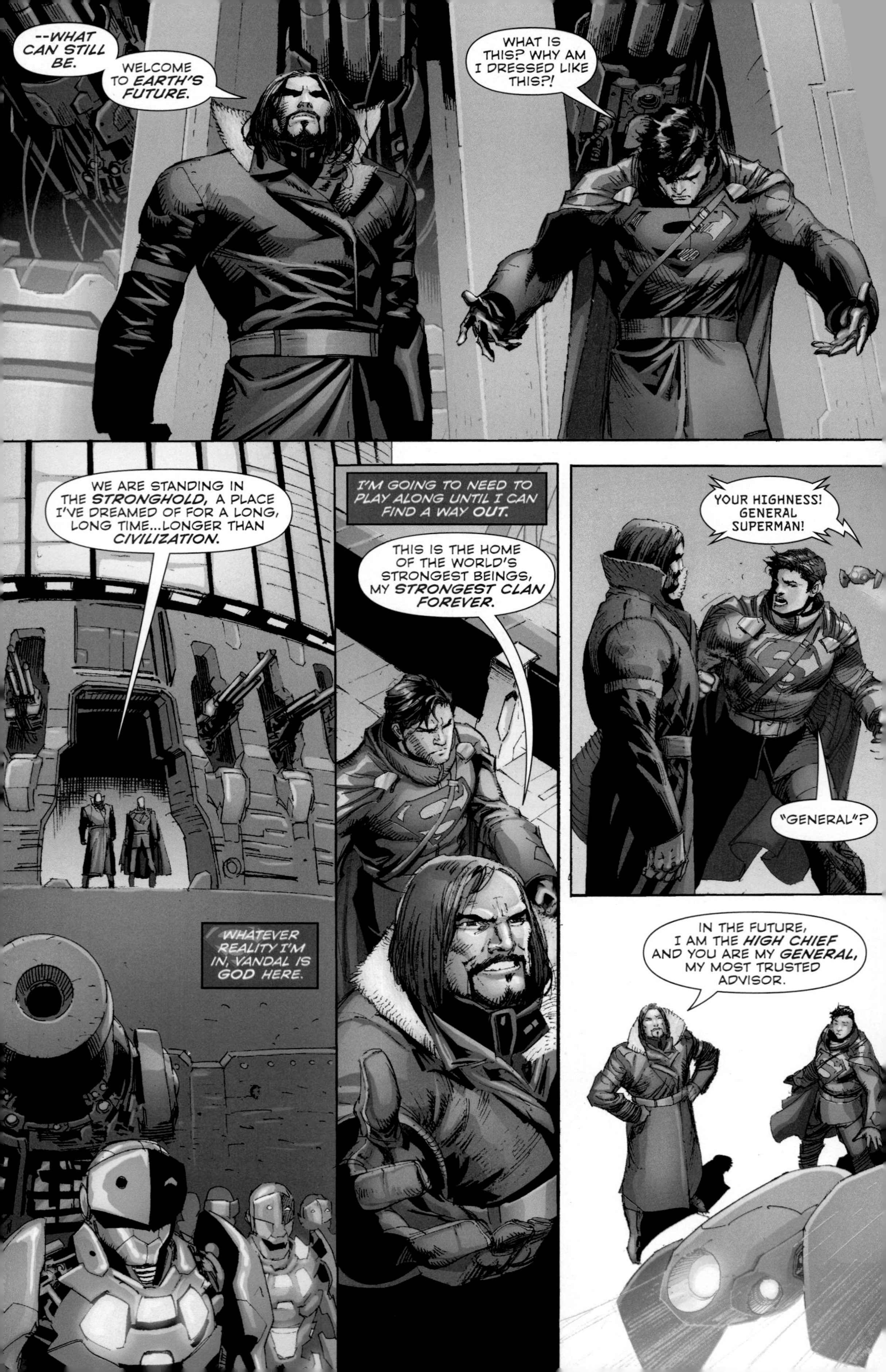
--WHAT CAN STILL BE.
WELCOME TO EARTH'S FUTURE.
WHAT IS THIS? WHY AM I DRESSED LIKE THIS?!
WE ARE STANDING IN THE STRONGHOLD, A PLACE I'VE DREAMED OF FOR A LONG, LONG TIME...LONGER THAN CIVILIZATION.
I'M GOING TO NEED TO PLAY ALONG UNTIL I CAN FIND A WAY OUT.
THIS IS THE HOME OF THE WORLD'S STRONGEST BEINGS, MY STRONGEST CLAN FOREVER.
YOUR HIGHNESS! GENERAL SUPERMAN!
"GENERAL"?
WHATEVER REALITY I'M IN, VANDAL IS GOD HERE.
IN THE FUTURE, I AM THE HIGH CHIEF AND YOU ARE MY GENERAL, MY MOST TRUSTED ADVISOR.

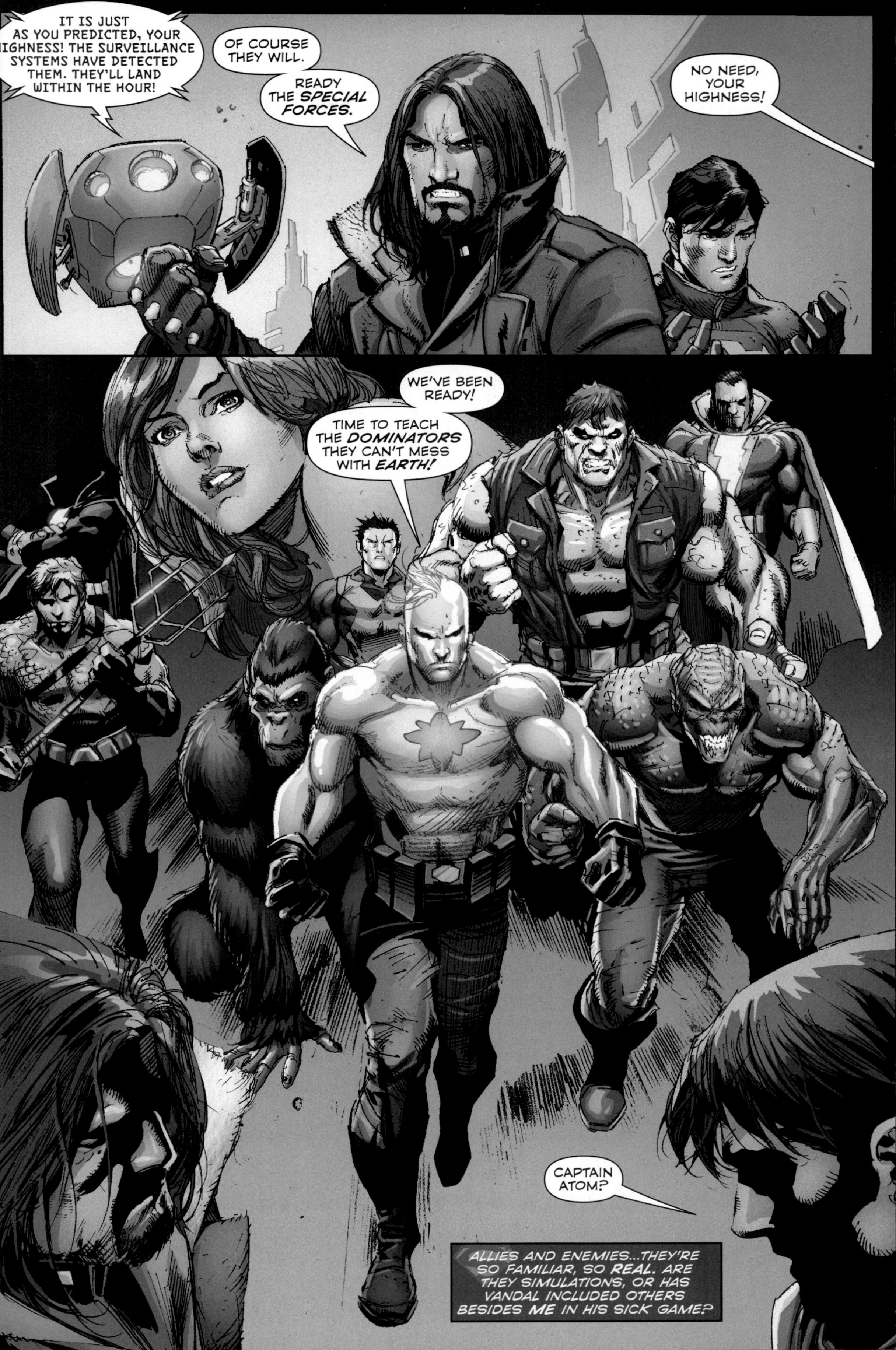
IT IS JUST AS YOU PREDICTED, YOUR HIGHNESS! THE SURVEILLANCE SYSTEMS HAVE DETECTED THEM. THEY'LL LAND WITHIN THE HOUR!
OF COURSE THEY WILL.
READY THE *SPECIAL FORCES.*
NO NEED, YOUR HIGHNESS!
WE'VE BEEN READY!
TIME TO TEACH THE *DOMINATORS* THEY CAN'T MESS WITH *EARTH!*
CAPTAIN ATOM?
ALLIES AND ENEMIES...THEY'RE SO FAMILIAR, SO *REAL*. ARE THEY SIMULATIONS, OR HAS VANDAL INCLUDED OTHERS BESIDES *ME* IN HIS SICK GAME?

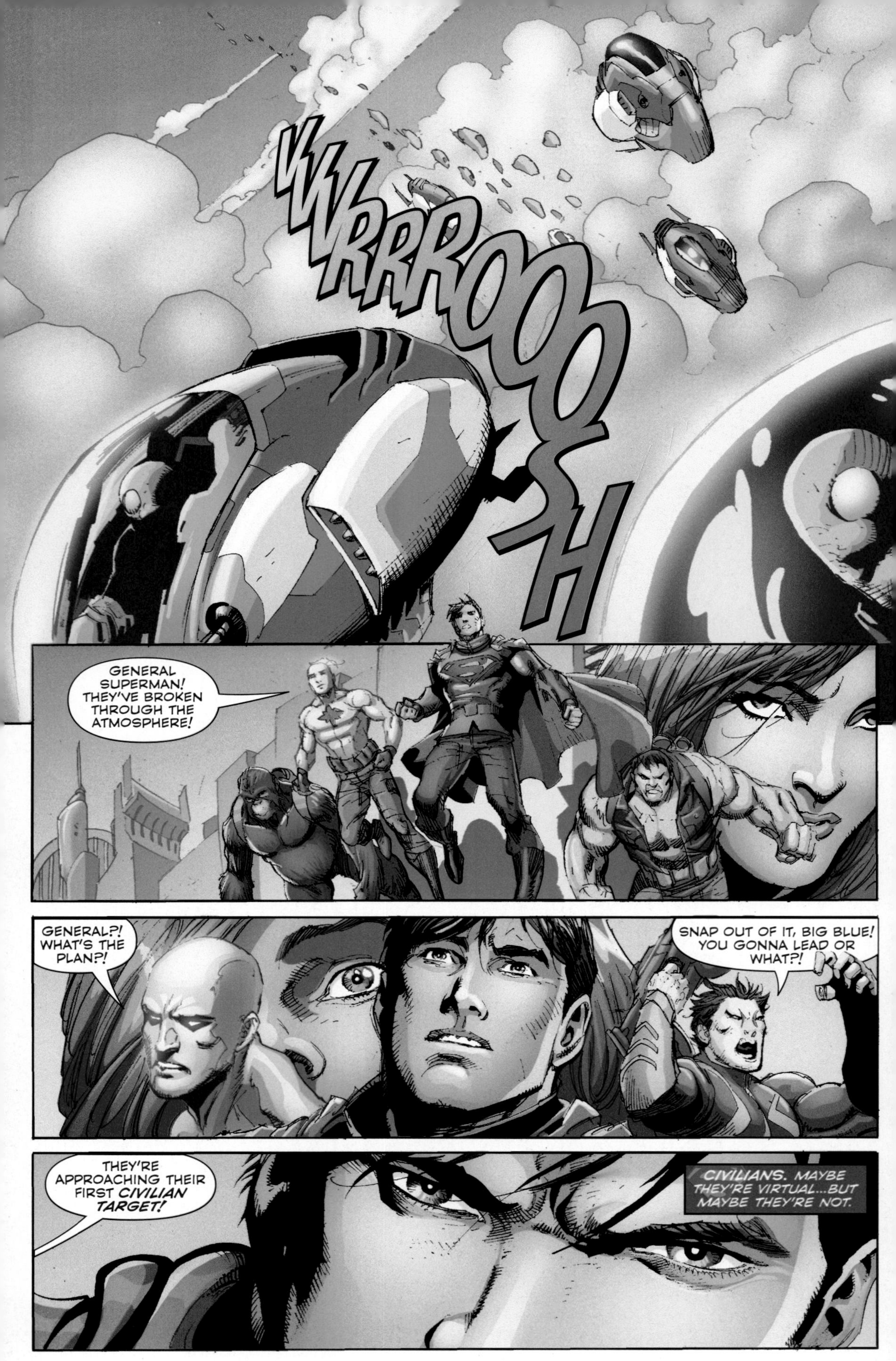
VVVRRROOOOSHH
GENERAL SUPERMAN! THEY'VE BROKEN THROUGH THE ATMOSPHERE!
GENERAL?! WHAT'S THE PLAN?!
SNAP OUT OF IT, BIG BLUE! YOU GONNA LEAD OR WHAT?!
THEY'RE APPROACHING THEIR FIRST *CIVILIAN TARGET!*
CIVILIANS. MAYBE THEY'RE VIRTUAL...BUT MAYBE THEY'RE NOT.

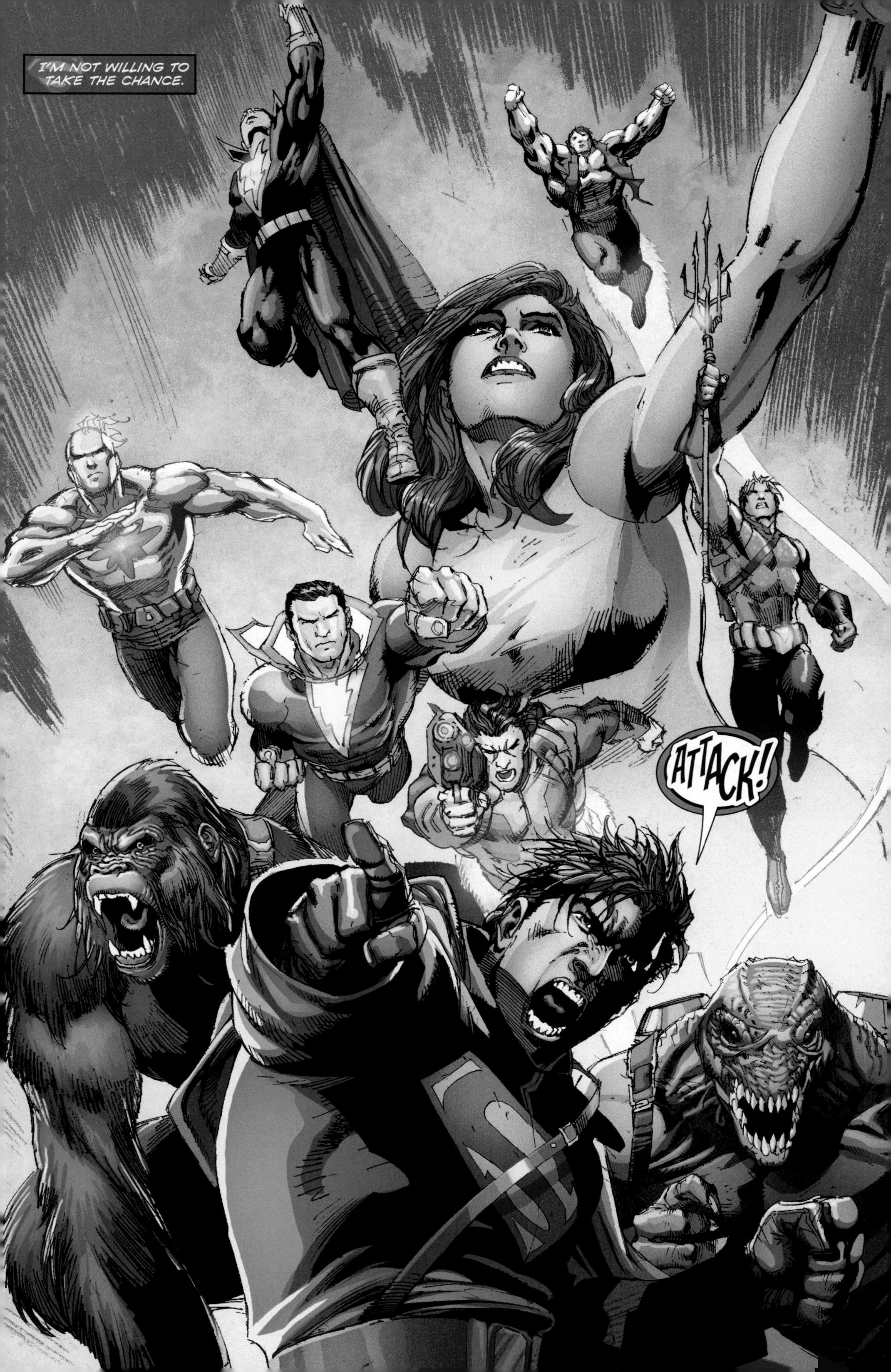
I'M NOT WILLING TO TAKE THE CHANCE.
ATTACK!

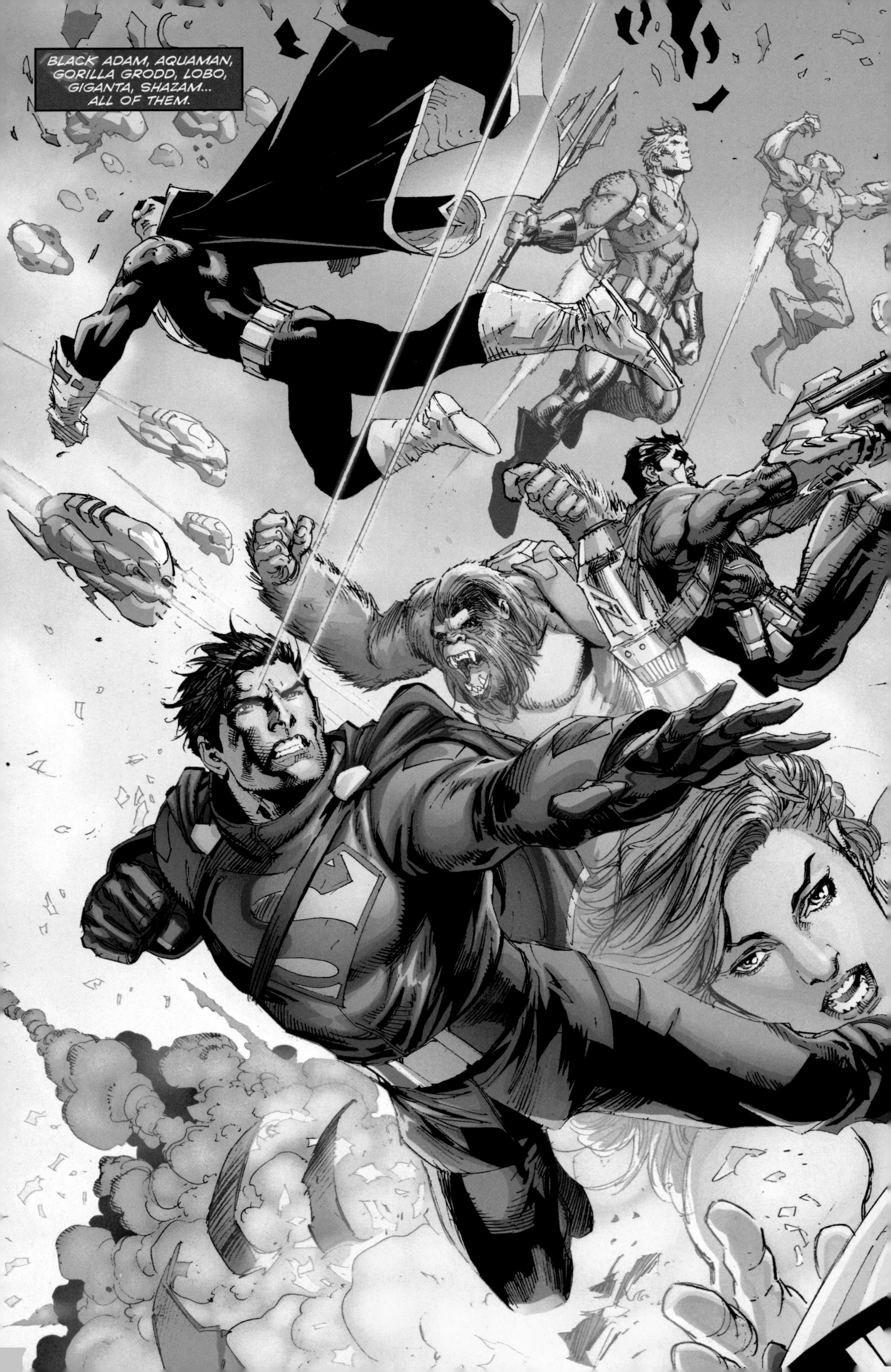
BLACK ADAM, AQUAMAN, GORILLA GRODD, LOBO, GIGANTA, SHAZAM... ALL OF THEM.

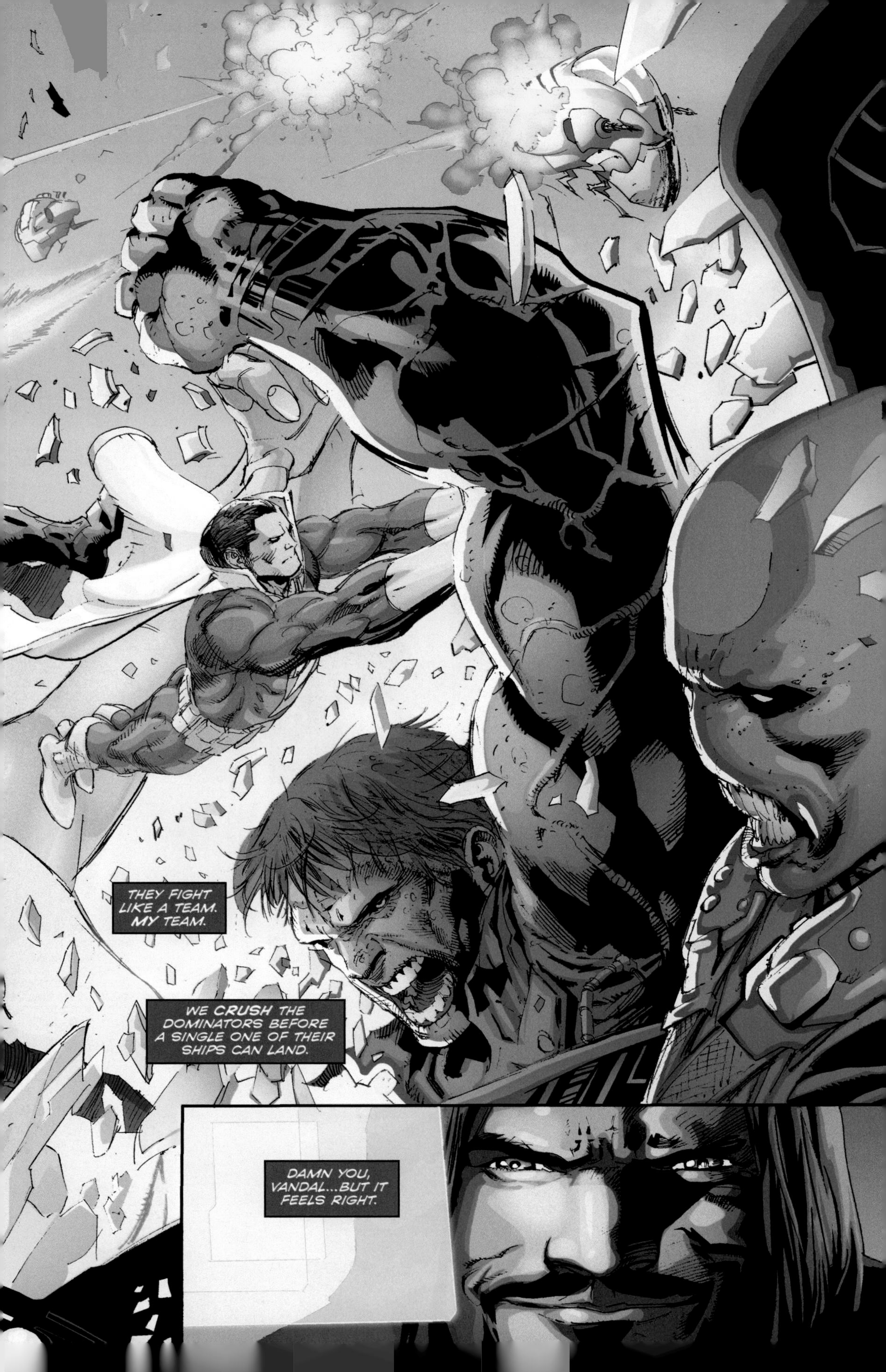
THEY FIGHT LIKE A TEAM. MY TEAM.
WE CRUSH THE DOMINATORS BEFORE A SINGLE ONE OF THEIR SHIPS CAN LAND.
DAMN YOU, VANDAL...BUT IT FEELS RIGHT.

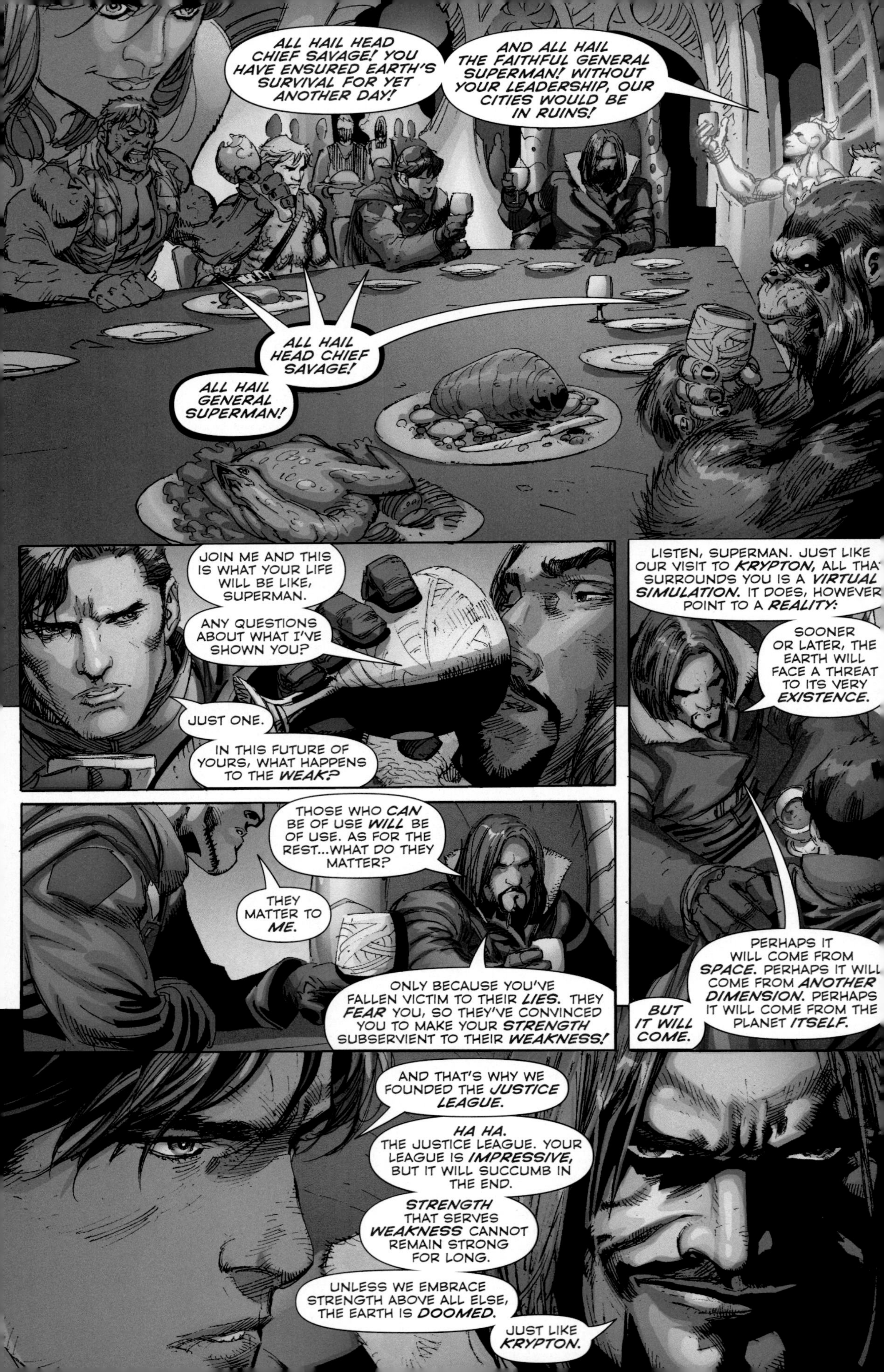

ALL HAIL HEAD CHIEF SAVAGE! YOU HAVE ENSURED EARTH'S SURVIVAL FOR YET ANOTHER DAY!
AND ALL HAIL THE FAITHFUL GENERAL SUPERMAN! WITHOUT YOUR LEADERSHIP, OUR CITIES WOULD BE IN RUINS!
ALL HAIL HEAD CHIEF SAVAGE!
ALL HAIL GENERAL SUPERMAN!
JOIN ME AND THIS IS WHAT YOUR LIFE WILL BE LIKE, SUPERMAN.
ANY QUESTIONS ABOUT WHAT I'VE SHOWN YOU?
JUST ONE.
IN THIS FUTURE OF YOURS, WHAT HAPPENS TO THE WEAK?
THOSE WHO CAN BE OF USE WILL BE OF USE. AS FOR THE REST...WHAT DO THEY MATTER?
THEY MATTER TO ME.
ONLY BECAUSE YOU'VE FALLEN VICTIM TO THEIR LIES. THEY FEAR YOU, SO THEY'VE CONVINCED YOU TO MAKE YOUR STRENGTH SUBSERVIENT TO THEIR WEAKNESS!
LISTEN, SUPERMAN. JUST LIKE OUR VISIT TO KRYPTON, ALL THA SURROUNDS YOU IS A VIRTUAL SIMULATION. IT DOES, HOWEVER POINT TO A REALITY:
SOONER OR LATER, THE EARTH WILL FACE A THREAT TO ITS VERY EXISTENCE.
PERHAPS IT WILL COME FROM SPACE. PERHAPS IT WILL COME FROM ANOTHER DIMENSION. PERHAPS IT WILL COME FROM THE PLANET ITSELF.
BUT IT WILL COME.
AND THAT'S WHY WE FOUNDED THE JUSTICE LEAGUE.
HA HA. THE JUSTICE LEAGUE. YOUR LEAGUE IS IMPRESSIVE, BUT IT WILL SUCCUMB IN THE END.
STRENGTH THAT SERVES WEAKNESS CANNOT REMAIN STRONG FOR LONG.
UNLESS WE EMBRACE STRENGTH ABOVE ALL ELSE, THE EARTH IS DOOMED.
JUST LIKE KRYPTON.

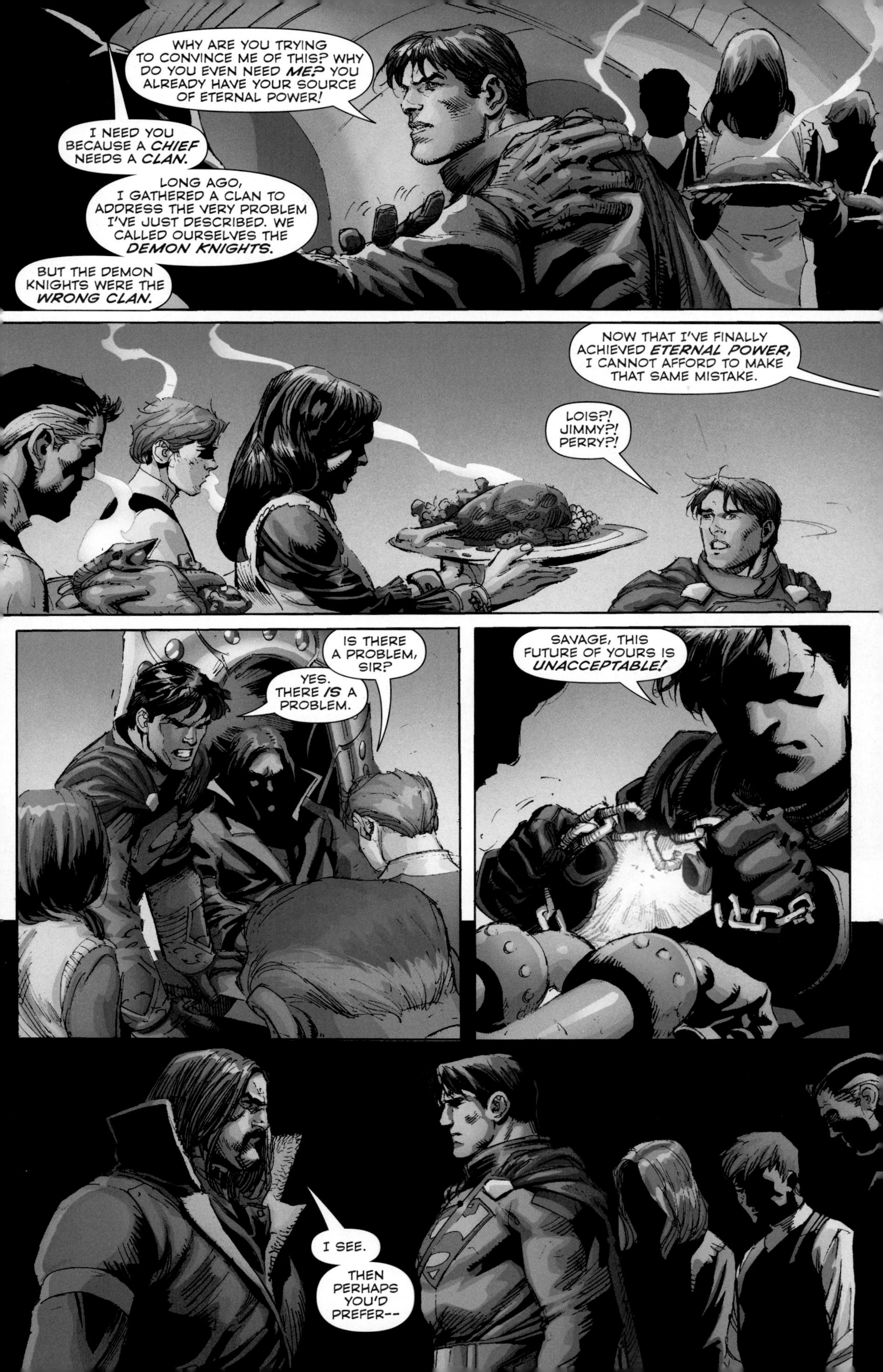
WHY ARE YOU TRYING TO CONVINCE ME OF THIS? WHY DO YOU EVEN NEED *ME?* YOU ALREADY HAVE YOUR SOURCE OF ETERNAL POWER!
I NEED YOU BECAUSE A *CHIEF* NEEDS A *CLAN.*
LONG AGO, I GATHERED A CLAN TO ADDRESS THE VERY PROBLEM I'VE JUST DESCRIBED. WE CALLED OURSELVES THE *DEMON KNIGHTS.*
BUT THE DEMON KNIGHTS WERE THE *WRONG CLAN.*
NOW THAT I'VE FINALLY ACHIEVED *ETERNAL POWER,* I CANNOT AFFORD TO MAKE THAT SAME MISTAKE.
LOIS?! JIMMY?! PERRY?!
IS THERE A PROBLEM, SIR?
YES. THERE *IS* A PROBLEM.
SAVAGE, THIS FUTURE OF YOURS IS *UNACCEPTABLE!*
I SEE.
THEN PERHAPS YOU'D PREFER--

--THIS ONE, WHERE EARTH'S DEFENSES *FAIL* AND EVERY LIVING THING ON THE PLANET IS BURNED TO *ASH*.

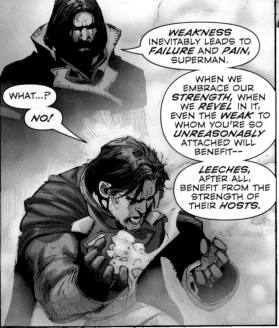

WEAKNESS INEVITABLY LEADS TO *FAILURE* AND *PAIN,* SUPERMAN.

WHAT...?

NO!

WHEN WE EMBRACE OUR *STRENGTH,* WHEN WE *REVEL* IN IT, EVEN THE *WEAK* TO WHOM YOU'RE SO *UNREASONABLY* ATTACHED WILL BENEFIT--

LEECHES, AFTER ALL, BENEFIT FROM THE STRENGTH OF THEIR *HOSTS.*

JOIN ME AND OTHERS WILL FOLLOW. WE WILL BE THE CLAN THE EARTH NEEDS, THE *STRONGEST CLAN FOREVER.*

I HAVE SHOWN YOU *WHAT COULD HAVE BEEN* AND *WHAT CAN STILL BE.*

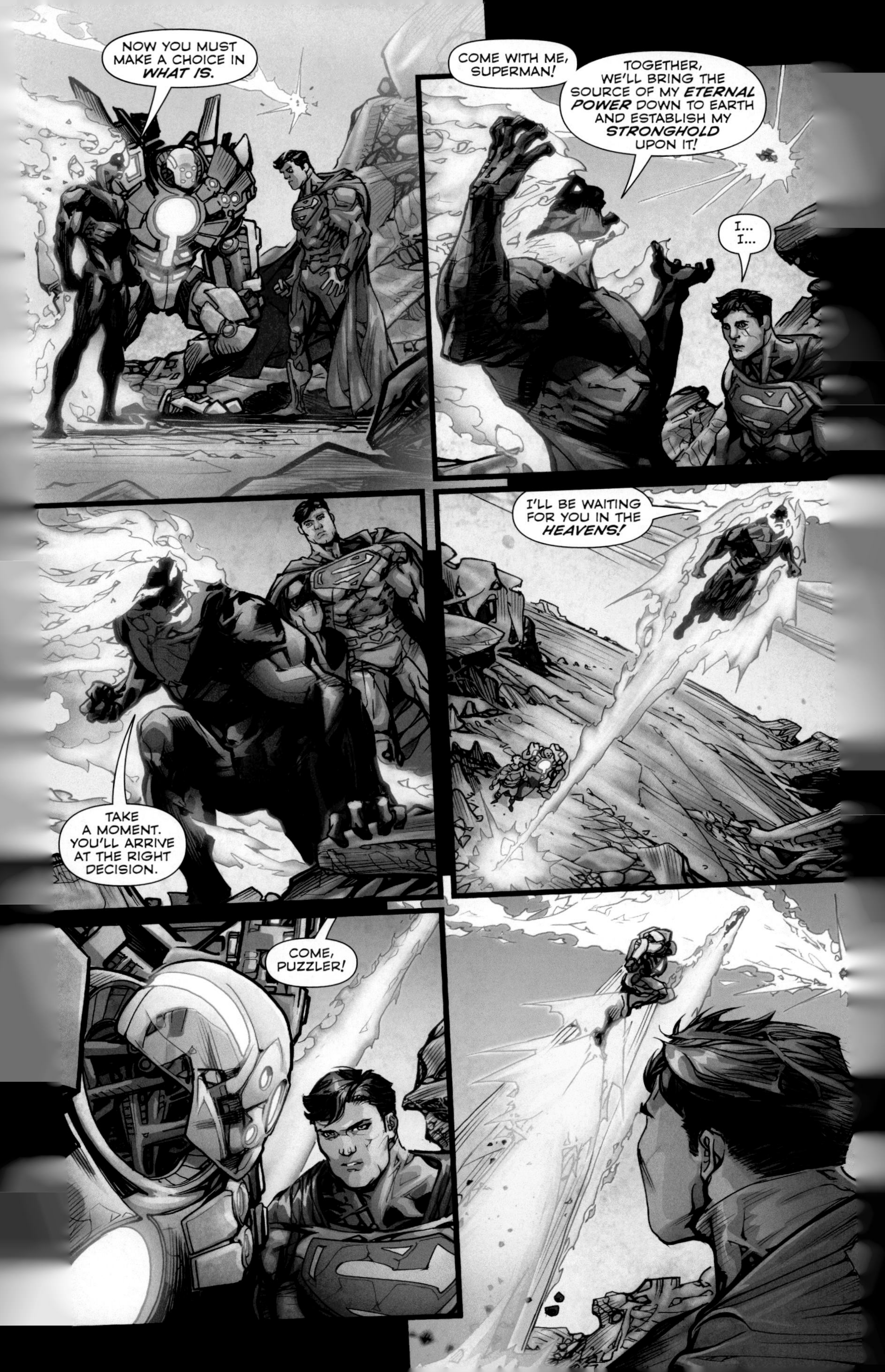
NOW YOU MUST MAKE A CHOICE IN WHAT IS.
COME WITH ME, SUPERMAN!
TOGETHER, WE'LL BRING THE SOURCE OF MY ETERNAL POWER DOWN TO EARTH AND ESTABLISH MY STRONGHOLD UPON IT!
I... I...
TAKE A MOMENT. YOU'LL ARRIVE AT THE RIGHT DECISION.
I'LL BE WAITING FOR YOU IN THE HEAVENS!
COME, PUZZLER!

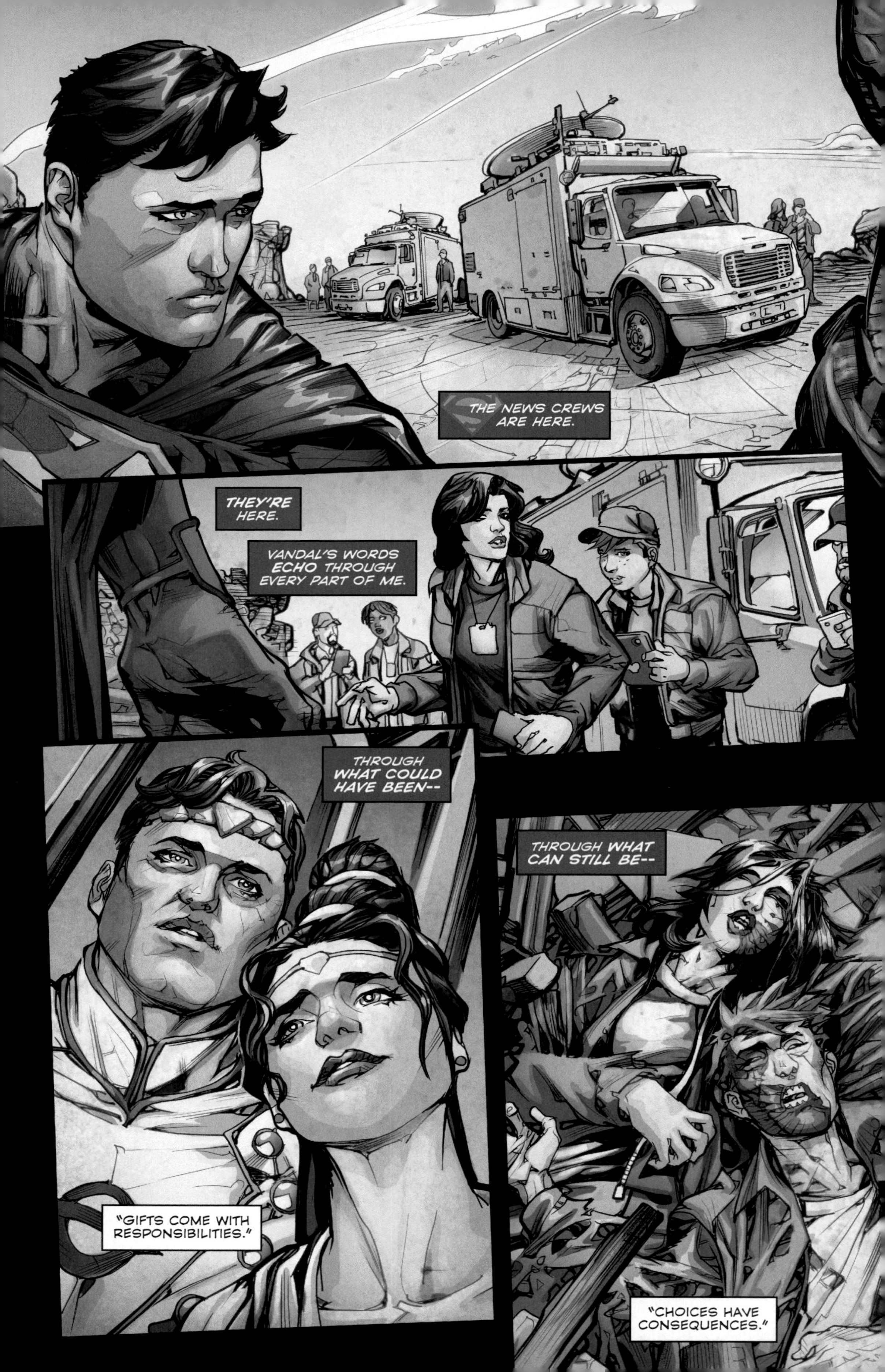
THE NEWS CREWS ARE HERE.
THEY'RE HERE.
VANDAL'S WORDS ECHO THROUGH EVERY PART OF ME.
THROUGH WHAT COULD HAVE BEEN--
"GIFTS COME WITH RESPONSIBILITIES."
THROUGH WHAT CAN STILL BE--
"CHOICES HAVE CONSEQUENCES."

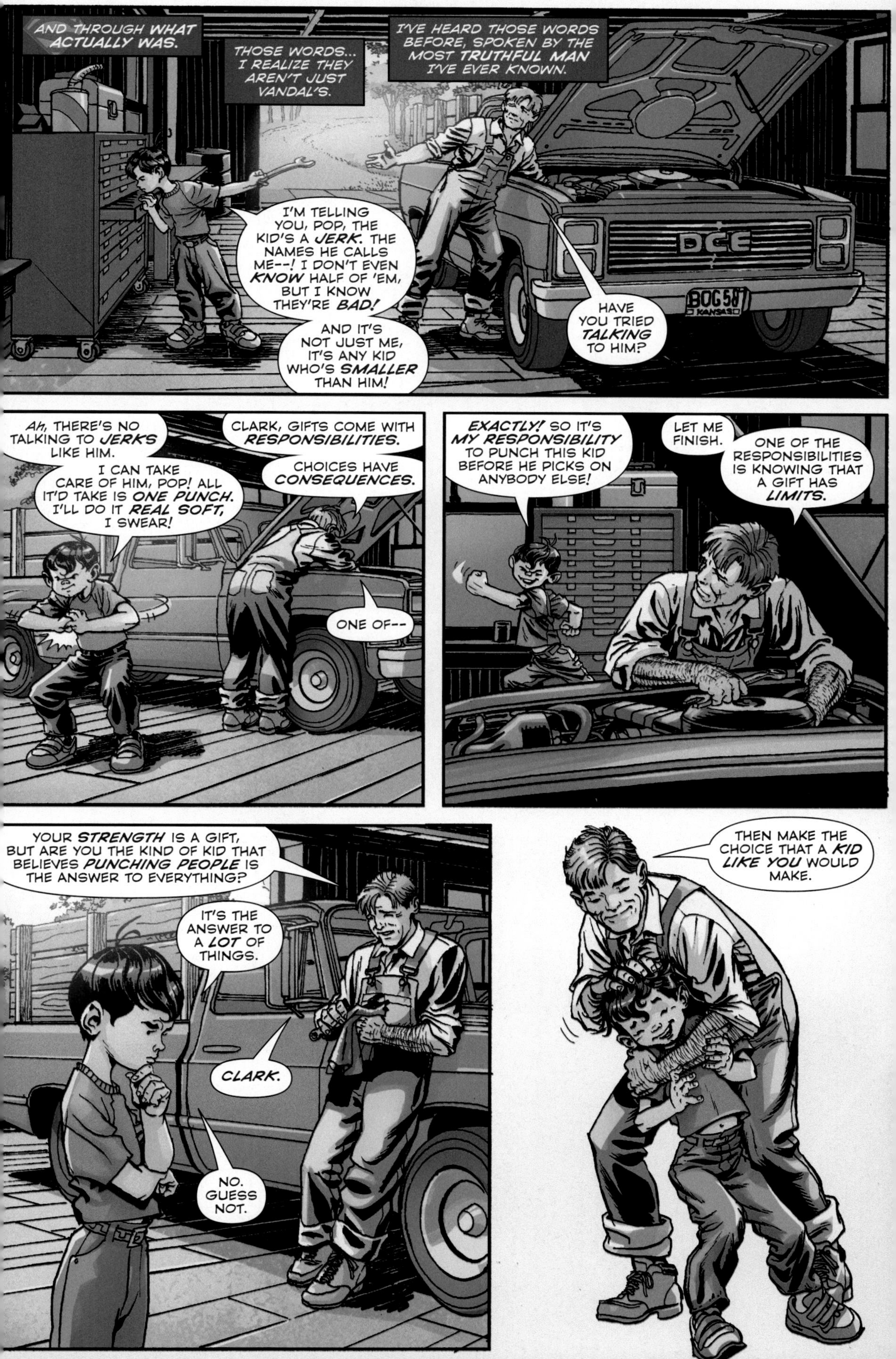
AND THROUGH WHAT ACTUALLY WAS.
THOSE WORDS... I REALIZE THEY AREN'T JUST VANDAL'S.
I'VE HEARD THOSE WORDS BEFORE, SPOKEN BY THE MOST TRUTHFUL MAN I'VE EVER KNOWN.
I'M TELLING YOU, POP, THE KID'S A JERK. THE NAMES HE CALLS ME--! I DON'T EVEN KNOW HALF OF 'EM, BUT I KNOW THEY'RE BAD!
AND IT'S NOT JUST ME, IT'S ANY KID WHO'S SMALLER THAN HIM!
HAVE YOU TRIED TALKING TO HIM?
BOG 58
KANSAS
Ah, THERE'S NO TALKING TO JERKS LIKE HIM.
I CAN TAKE CARE OF HIM, POP! ALL IT'D TAKE IS ONE PUNCH. I'LL DO IT REAL SOFT, I SWEAR!
CLARK, GIFTS COME WITH RESPONSIBILITIES.
CHOICES HAVE CONSEQUENCES.
ONE OF--
EXACTLY! SO IT'S MY RESPONSIBILITY TO PUNCH THIS KID BEFORE HE PICKS ON ANYBODY ELSE!
LET ME FINISH.
ONE OF THE RESPONSIBILITIES IS KNOWING THAT A GIFT HAS LIMITS.
YOUR STRENGTH IS A GIFT, BUT ARE YOU THE KIND OF KID THAT BELIEVES PUNCHING PEOPLE IS THE ANSWER TO EVERYTHING?
IT'S THE ANSWER TO A LOT OF THINGS.
CLARK.
NO. GUESS NOT.
THEN MAKE THE CHOICE THAT A KID LIKE YOU WOULD MAKE.

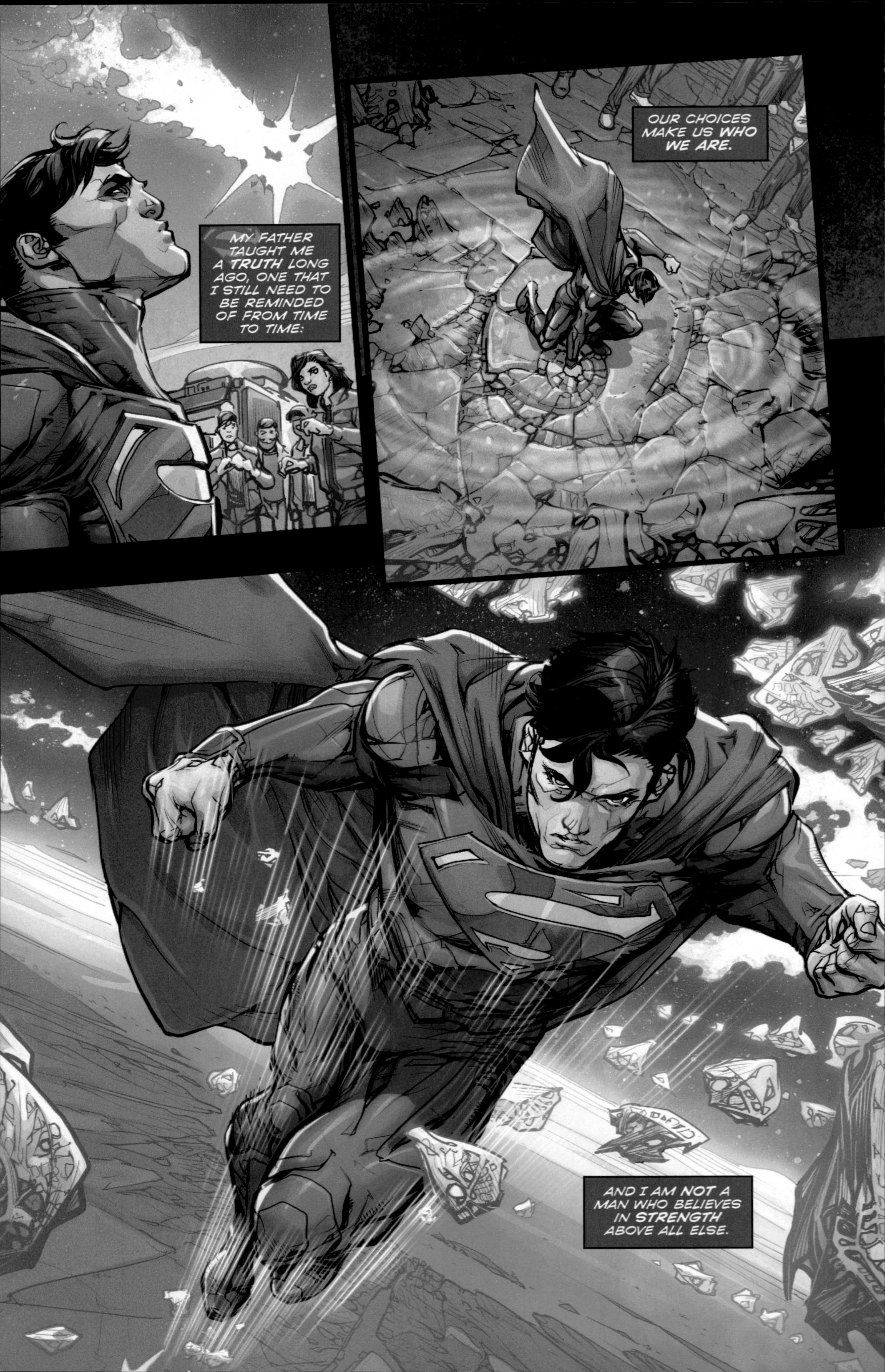

MY FATHER TAUGHT ME A TRUTH LONG AGO, ONE THAT I STILL NEED TO BE REMINDED OF FROM TIME TO TIME:
OUR CHOICES MAKE US WHO WE ARE.
AND I AM NOT A MAN WHO BELIEVES IN STRENGTH ABOVE ALL ELSE.

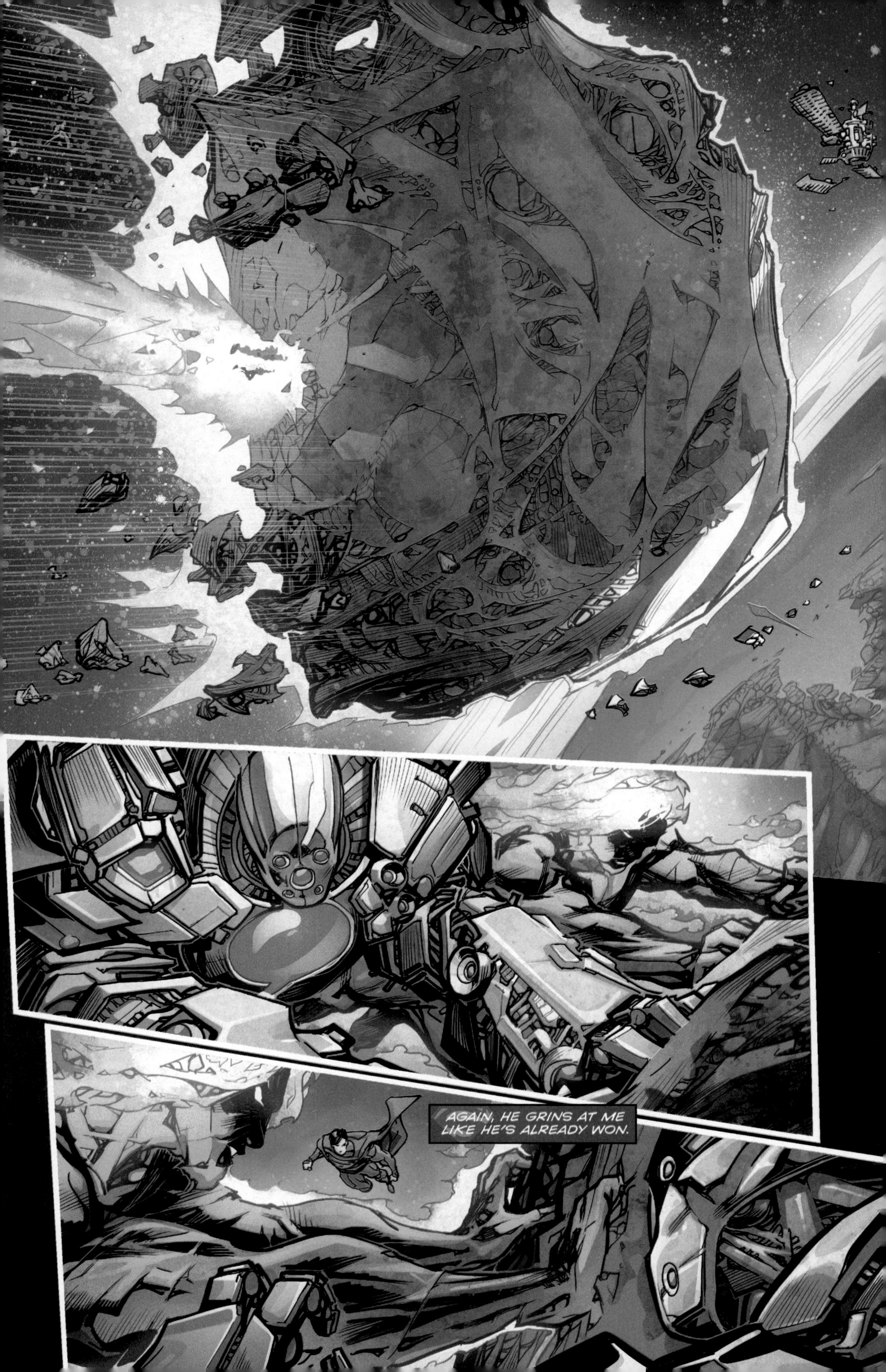
AGAIN, HE GRINS AT ME
LIKE HE'S ALREADY WON.

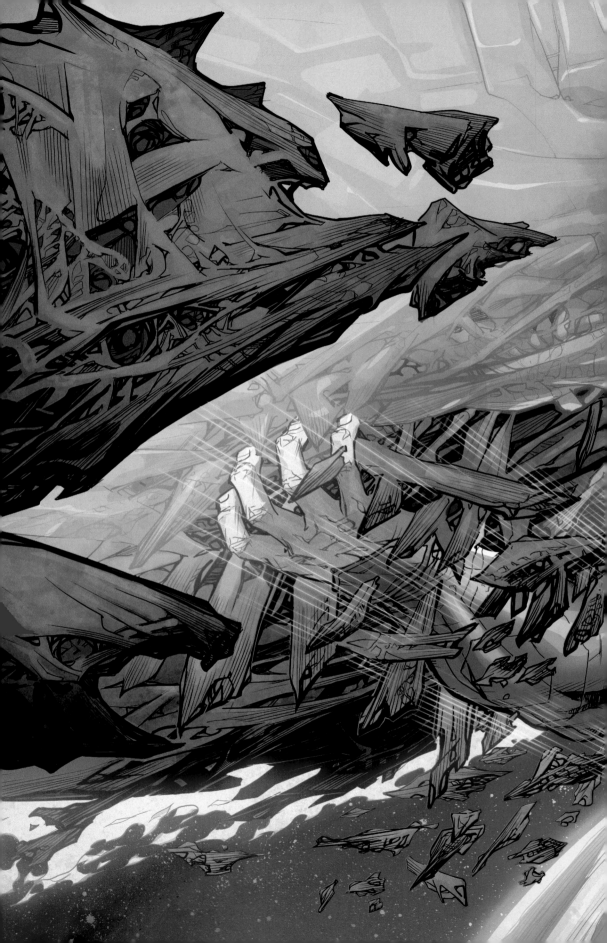

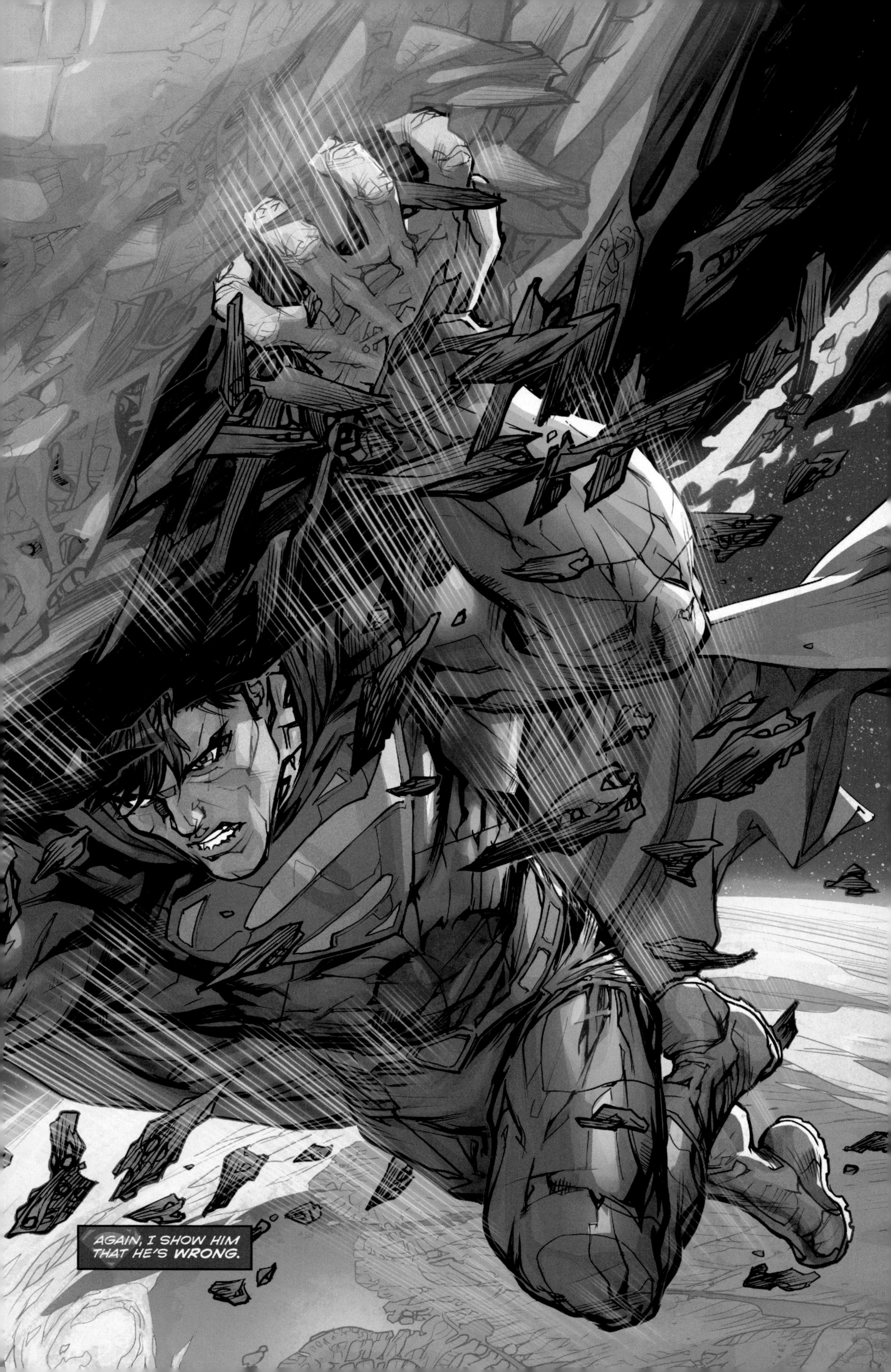
AGAIN, I SHOW HIM THAT HE'S **WRONG.**

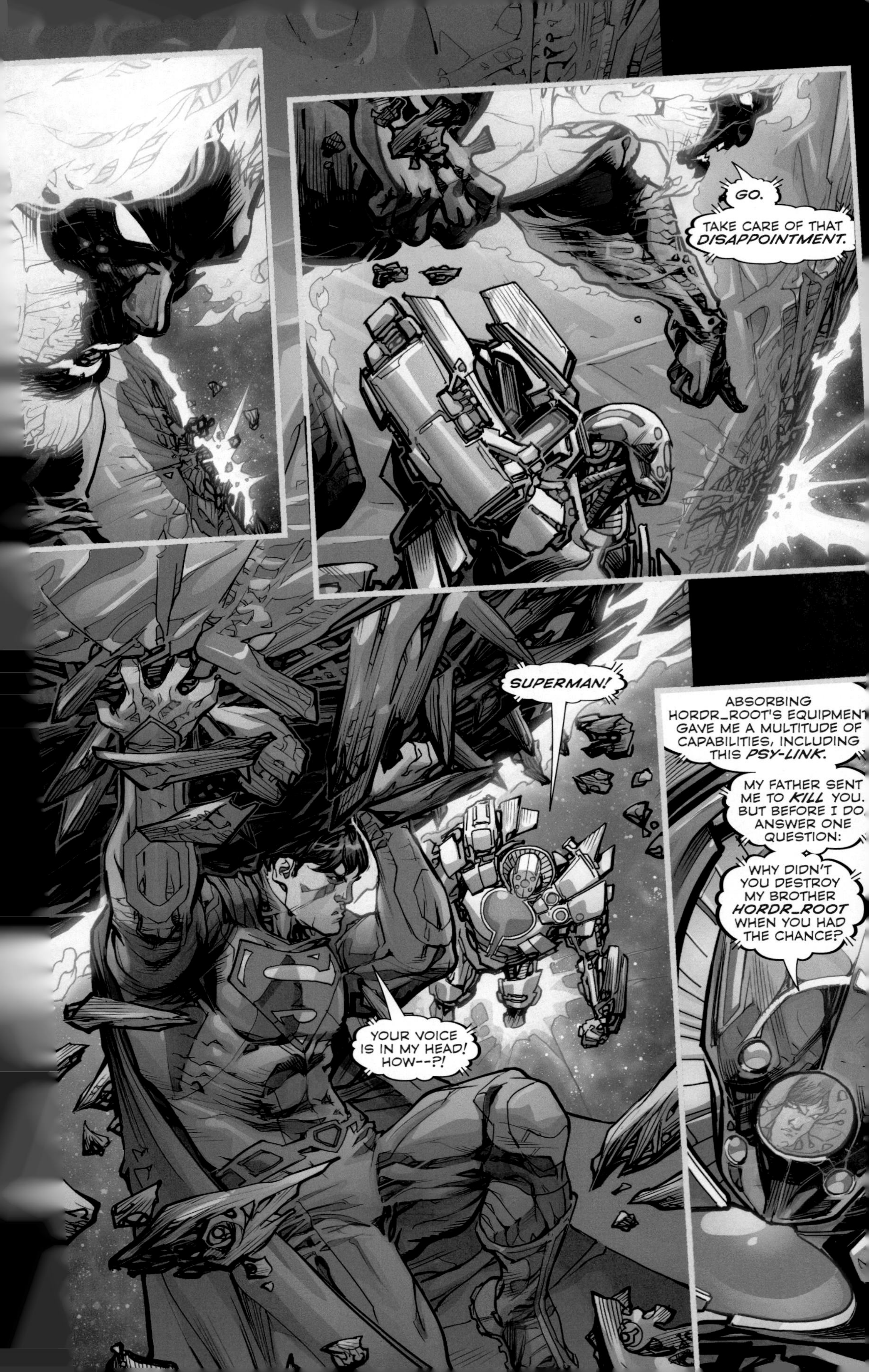
GO.
TAKE CARE OF THAT DISAPPOINTMENT.
SUPERMAN!
ABSORBING HORDR_ROOT'S EQUIPMENT GAVE ME A MULTITUDE OF CAPABILITIES, INCLUDING THIS PSY-LINK.
MY FATHER SENT ME TO KILL YOU. BUT BEFORE I DO, ANSWER ONE QUESTION:
WHY DIDN'T YOU DESTROY MY BROTHER HORDR_ROOT WHEN YOU HAD THE CHANCE?
YOUR VOICE IS IN MY HEAD! HOW--?!

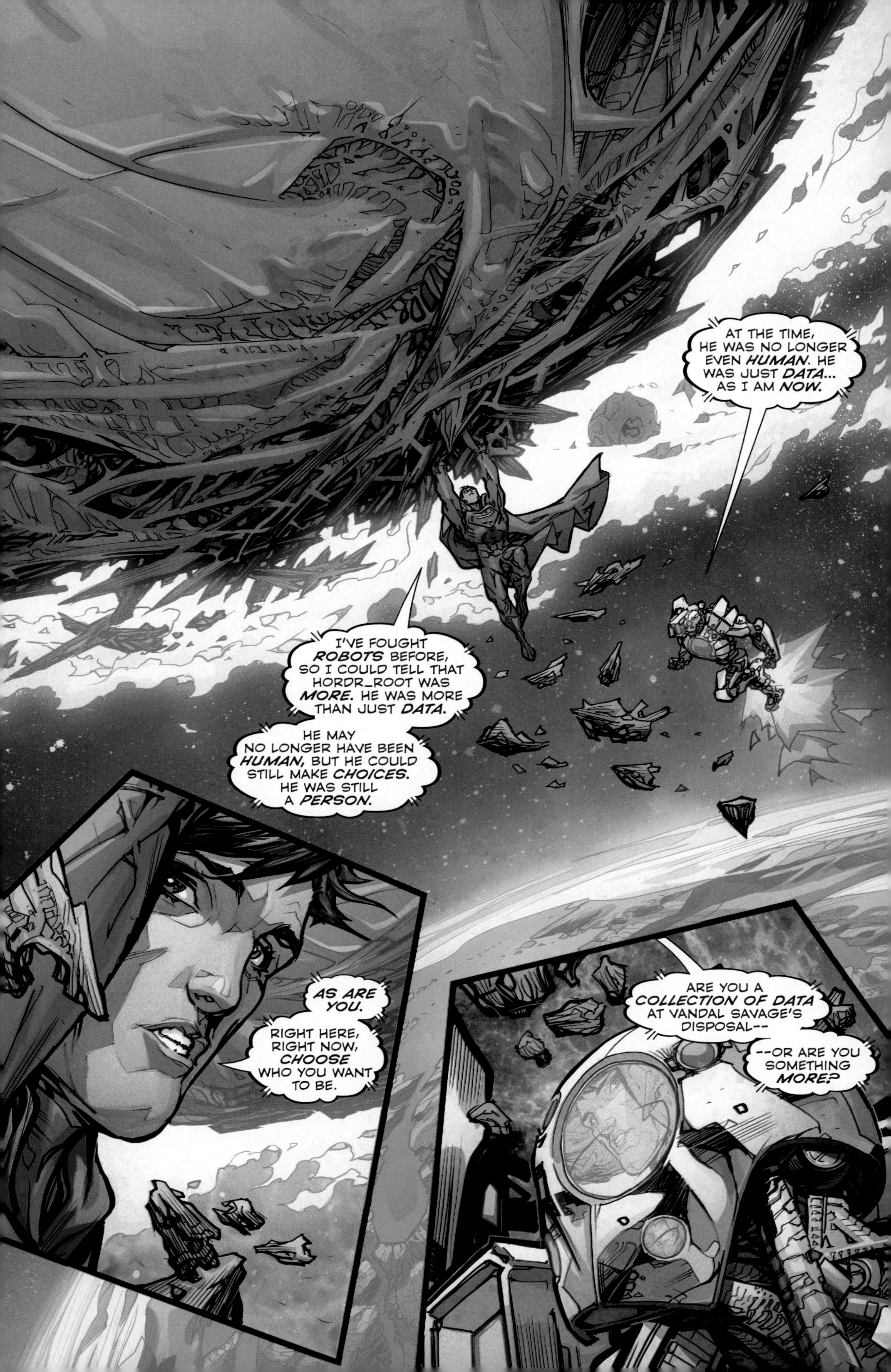
AT THE TIME, HE WAS NO LONGER EVEN HUMAN. HE WAS JUST DATA... AS I AM NOW.
I'VE FOUGHT ROBOTS BEFORE, SO I COULD TELL THAT HORDR_ROOT WAS MORE. HE WAS MORE THAN JUST DATA.
HE MAY NO LONGER HAVE BEEN HUMAN, BUT HE COULD STILL MAKE CHOICES. HE WAS STILL A PERSON.
AS ARE YOU.
RIGHT HERE, RIGHT NOW, CHOOSE WHO YOU WANT TO BE.
ARE YOU A COLLECTION OF DATA AT VANDAL SAVAGE'S DISPOSAL--
--OR ARE YOU SOMETHING MORE?

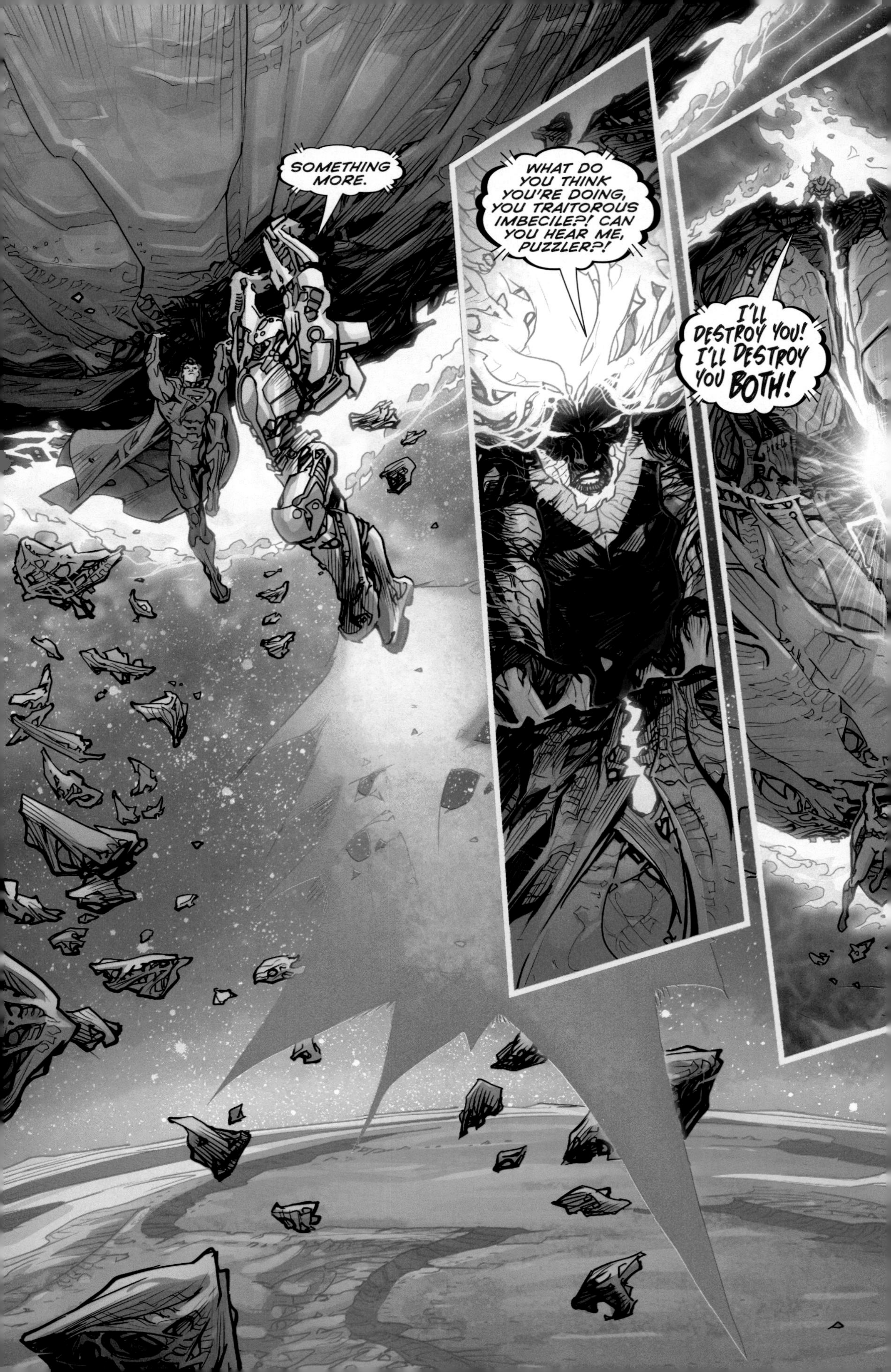
SOMETHING MORE.
WHAT DO YOU THINK YOU'RE DOING, YOU TRAITOROUS IMBECILE?! CAN YOU HEAR ME, PUZZLER?!
I'LL DESTROY YOU! I'LL DESTROY YOU BOTH!

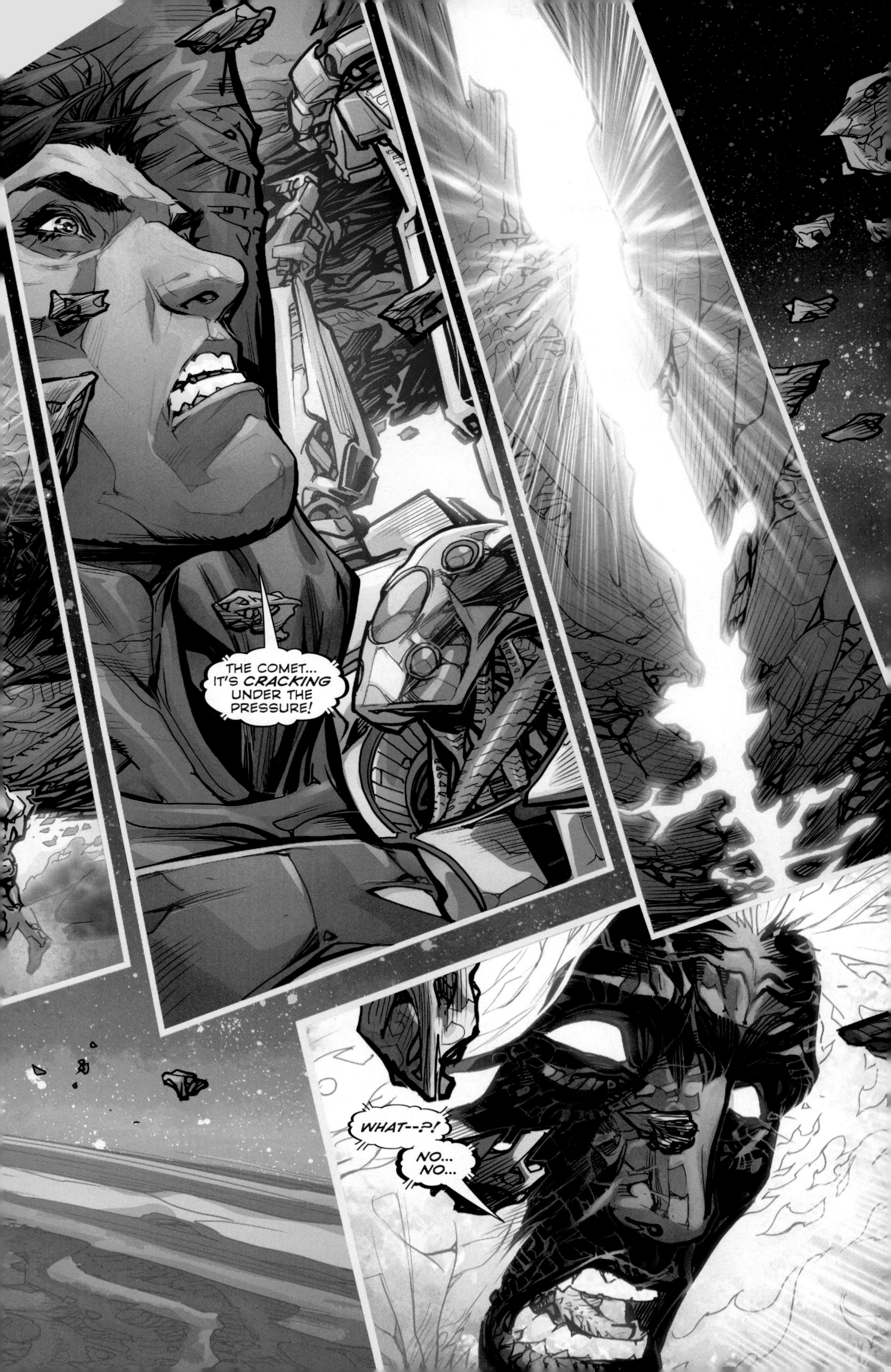
THE COMET... IT'S CRACKING UNDER THE PRESSURE!
WHAT--?!
NO... NO...

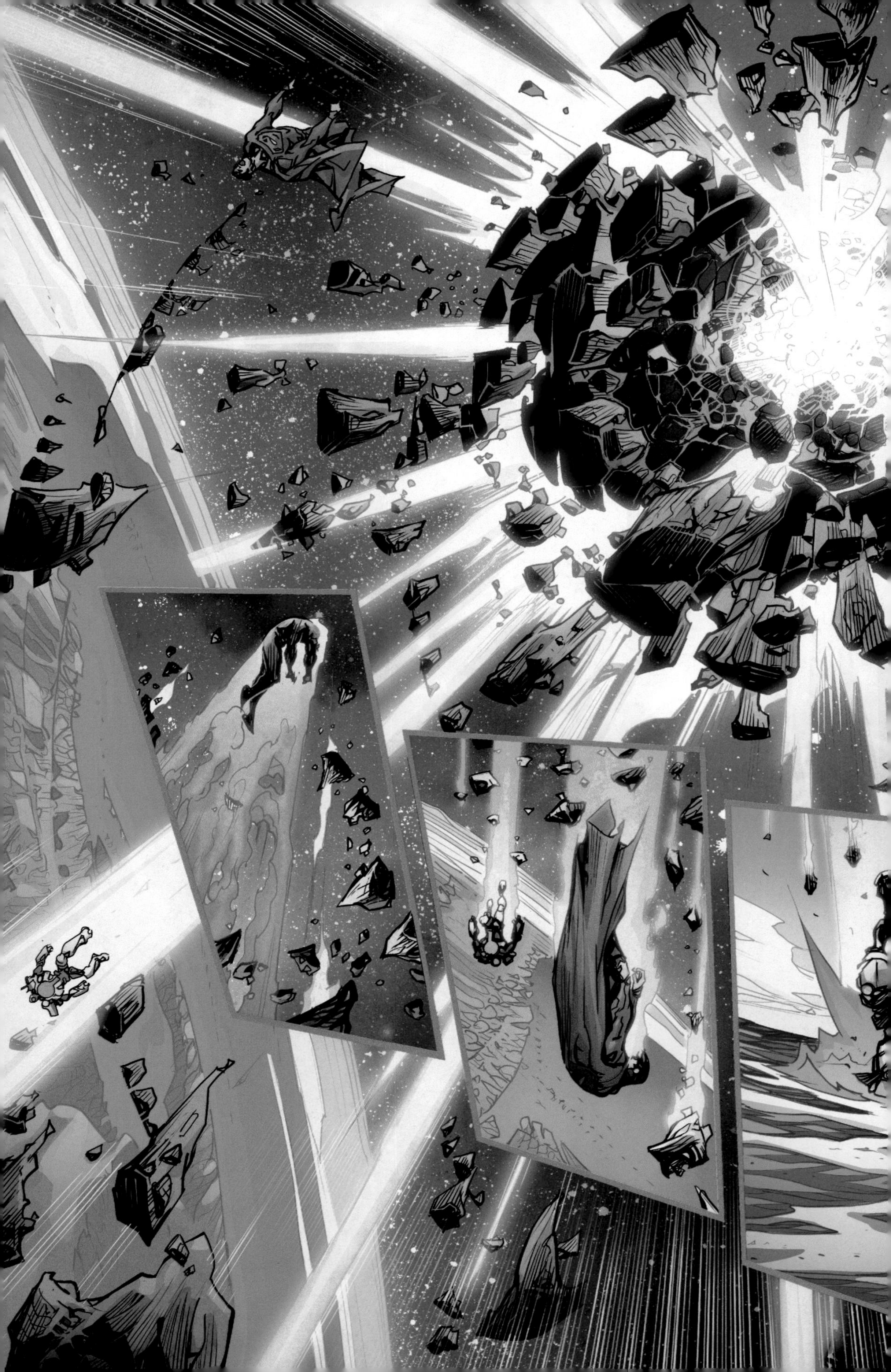

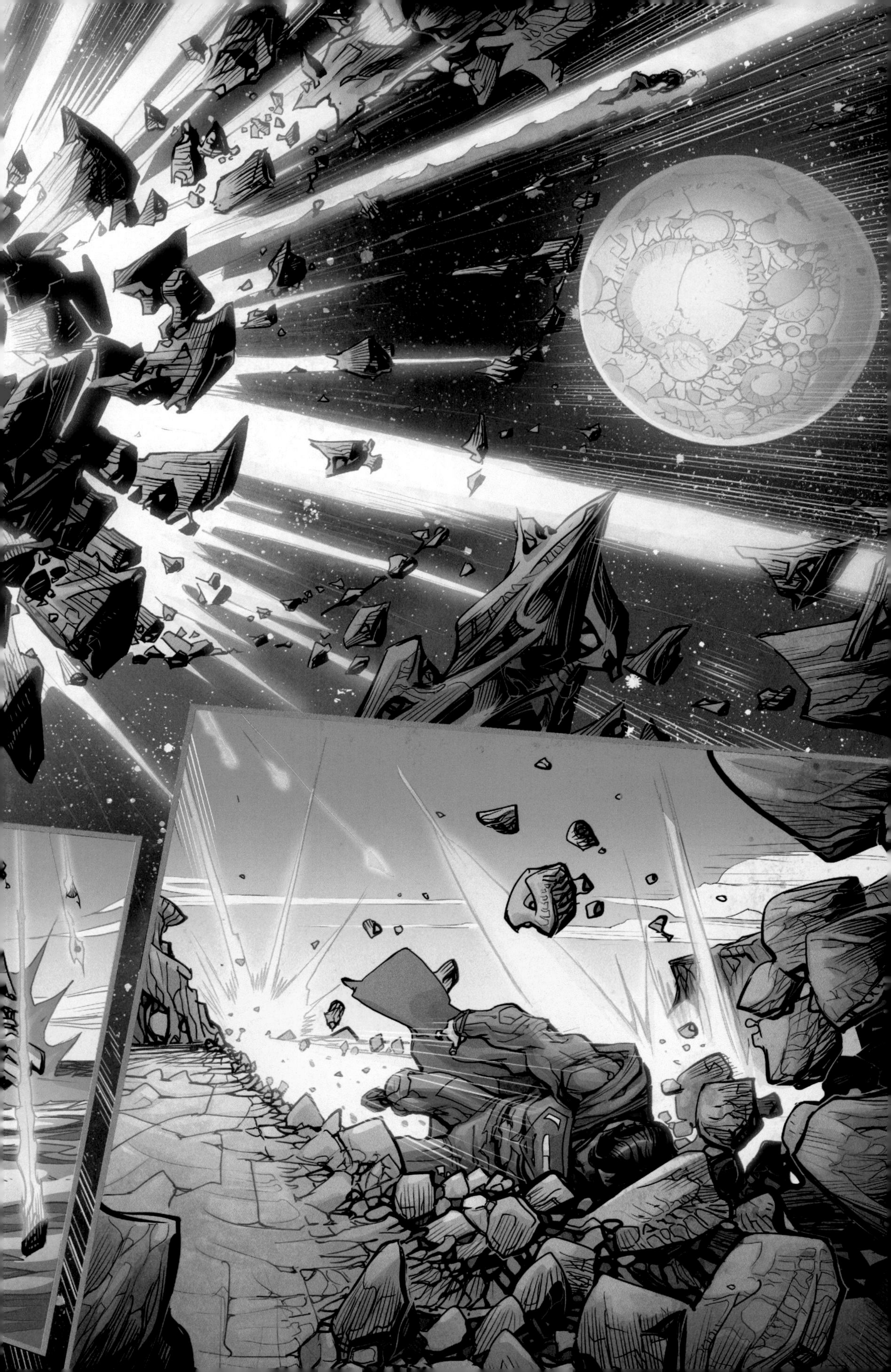

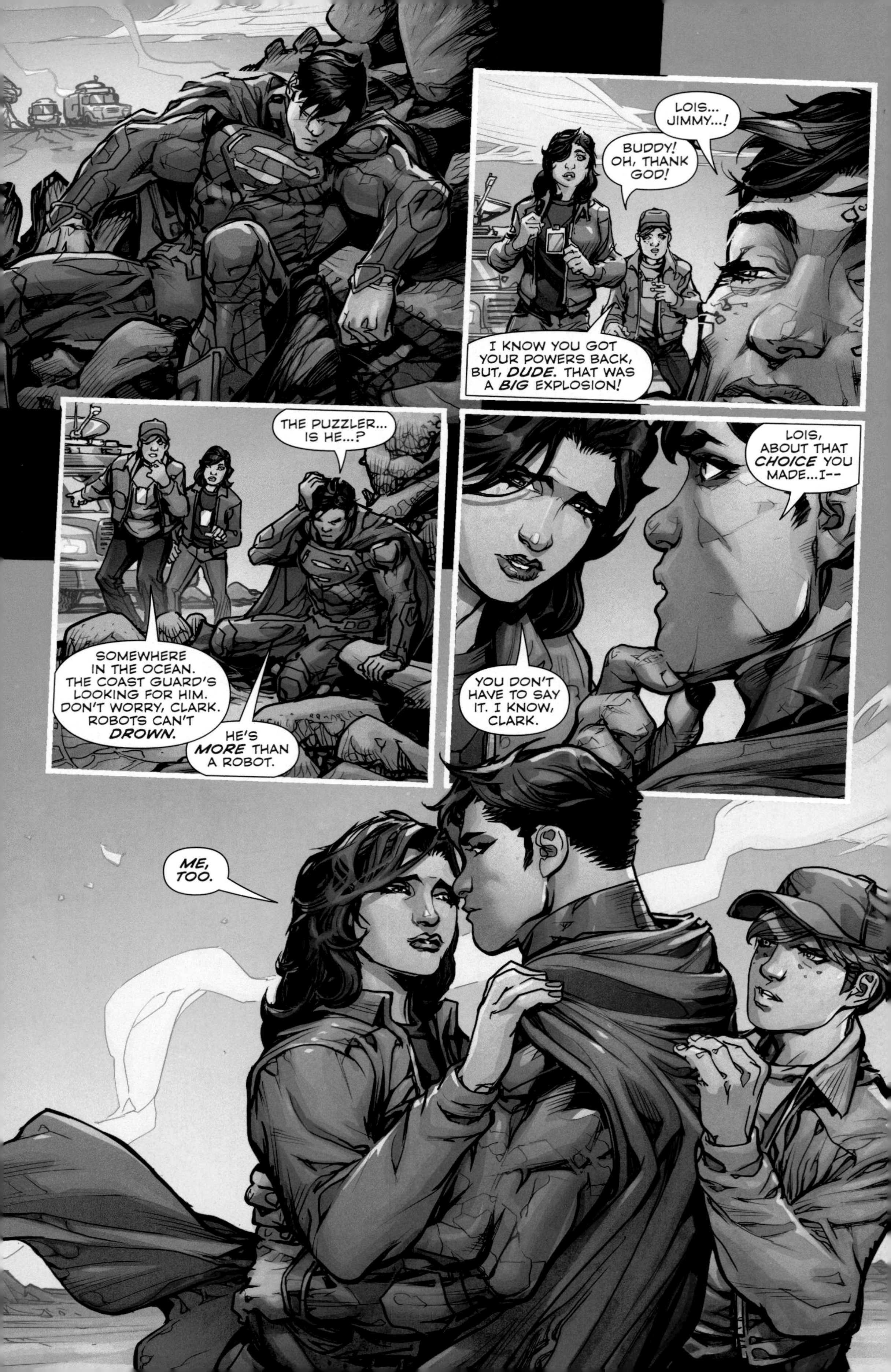
LOIS... JIMMY...!
BUDDY! OH, THANK GOD!
I KNOW YOU GOT YOUR POWERS BACK, BUT, DUDE. THAT WAS A BIG EXPLOSION!
THE PUZZLER... IS HE...?
SOMEWHERE IN THE OCEAN. THE COAST GUARD'S LOOKING FOR HIM. DON'T WORRY, CLARK. ROBOTS CAN'T DROWN.
HE'S MORE THAN A ROBOT.
LOIS, ABOUT THAT CHOICE YOU MADE...I--
YOU DON'T HAVE TO SAY IT. I KNOW, CLARK.
ME, TOO.

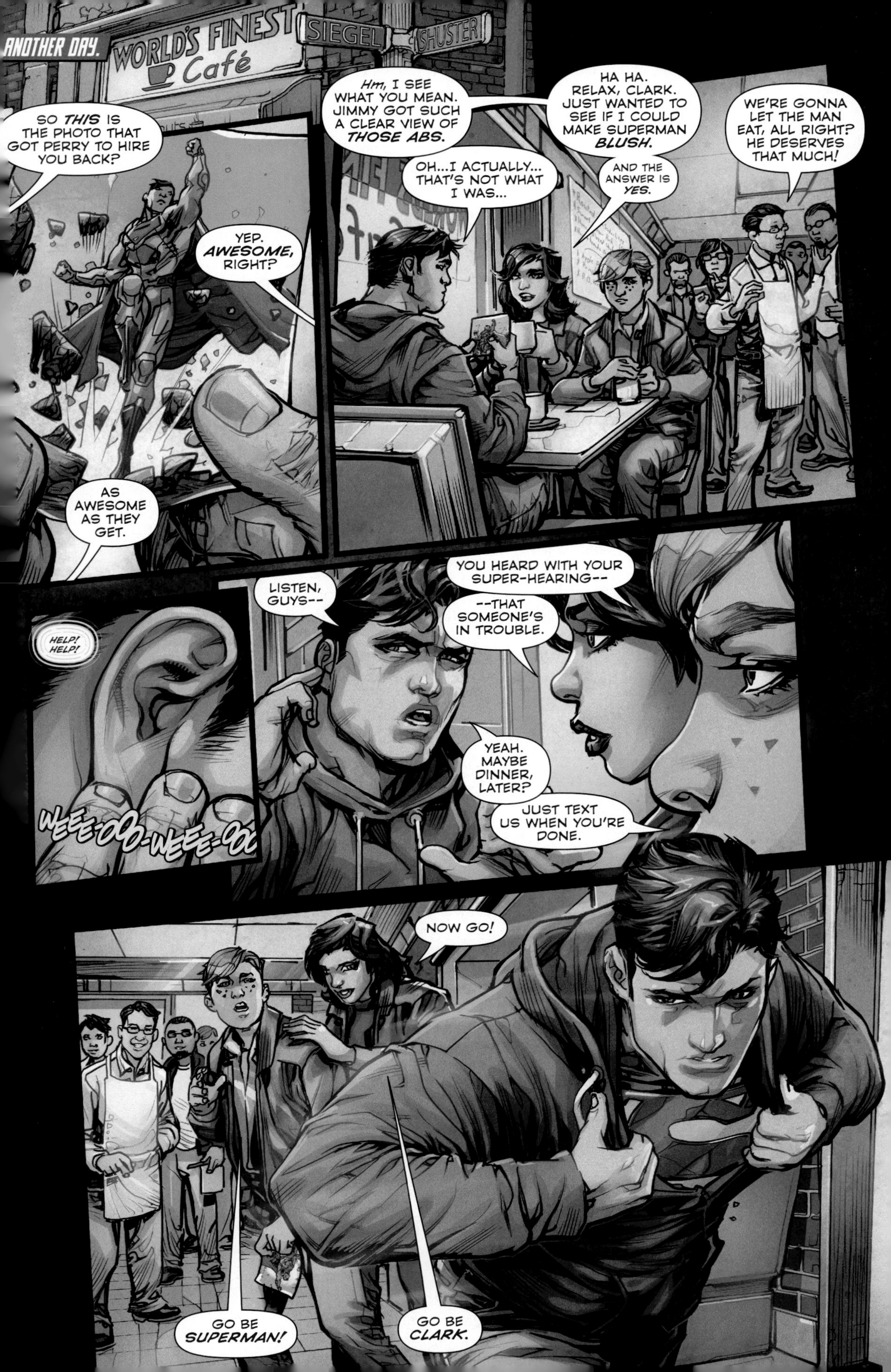
ANOTHER DAY.
WORLD'S FINEST Café
SIEGEL
SHUSTER
SO THIS IS THE PHOTO THAT GOT PERRY TO HIRE YOU BACK?
YEP. AWESOME, RIGHT?
AS AWESOME AS THEY GET.
Hm, I SEE WHAT YOU MEAN. JIMMY GOT SUCH A CLEAR VIEW OF THOSE ABS.
OH...I ACTUALLY... THAT'S NOT WHAT I WAS...
HA HA. RELAX, CLARK. JUST WANTED TO SEE IF I COULD MAKE SUPERMAN BLUSH.
AND THE ANSWER IS YES.
WE'RE GONNA LET THE MAN EAT, ALL RIGHT? HE DESERVES THAT MUCH!
HELP! HELP!
WEEE-OOO-WEEE-OOO
LISTEN, GUYS--
YOU HEARD WITH YOUR SUPER-HEARING--
--THAT SOMEONE'S IN TROUBLE.
YEAH. MAYBE DINNER, LATER?
JUST TEXT US WHEN YOU'RE DONE.
NOW GO!
GO BE SUPERMAN!
GO BE CLARK.

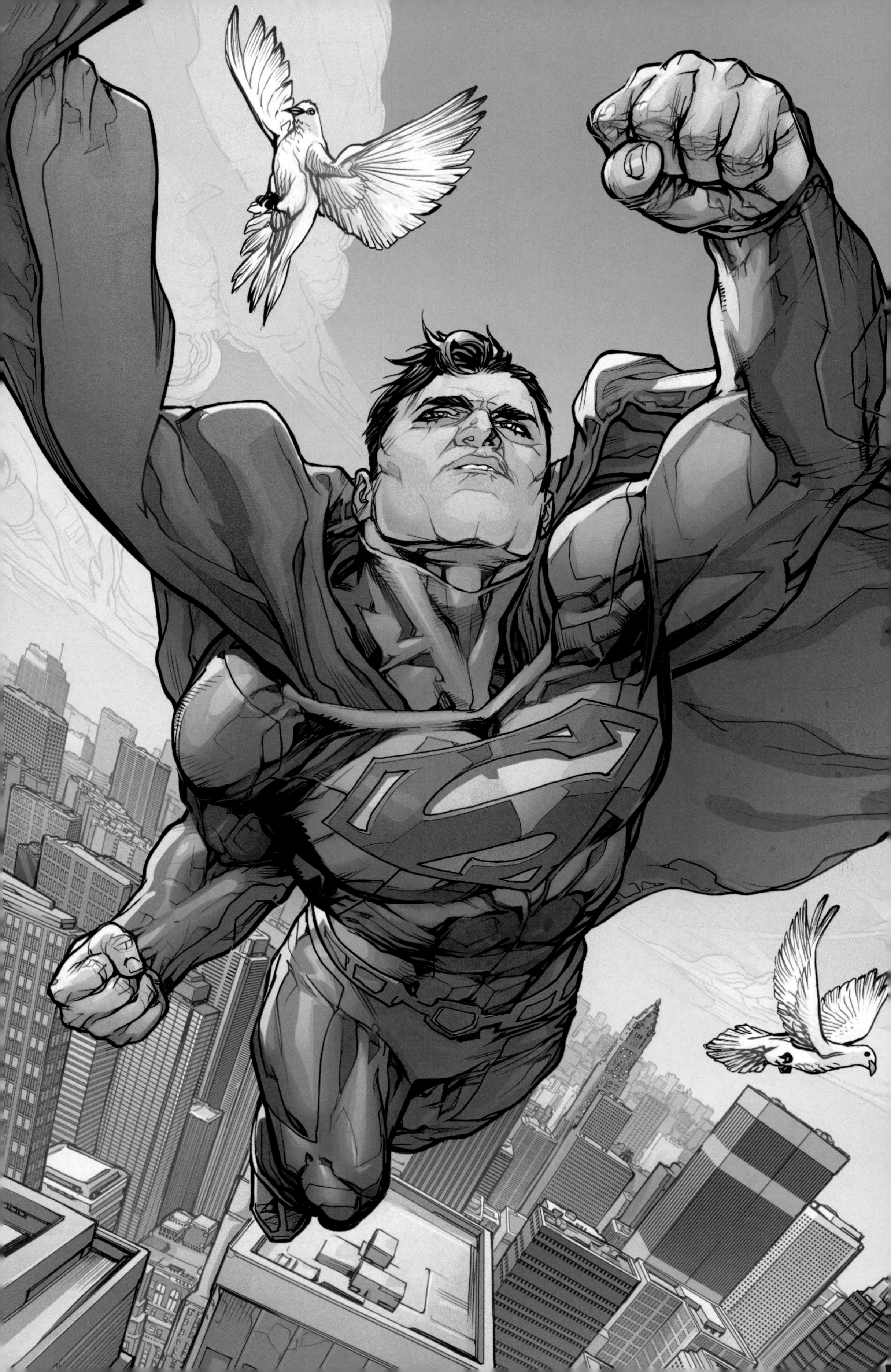

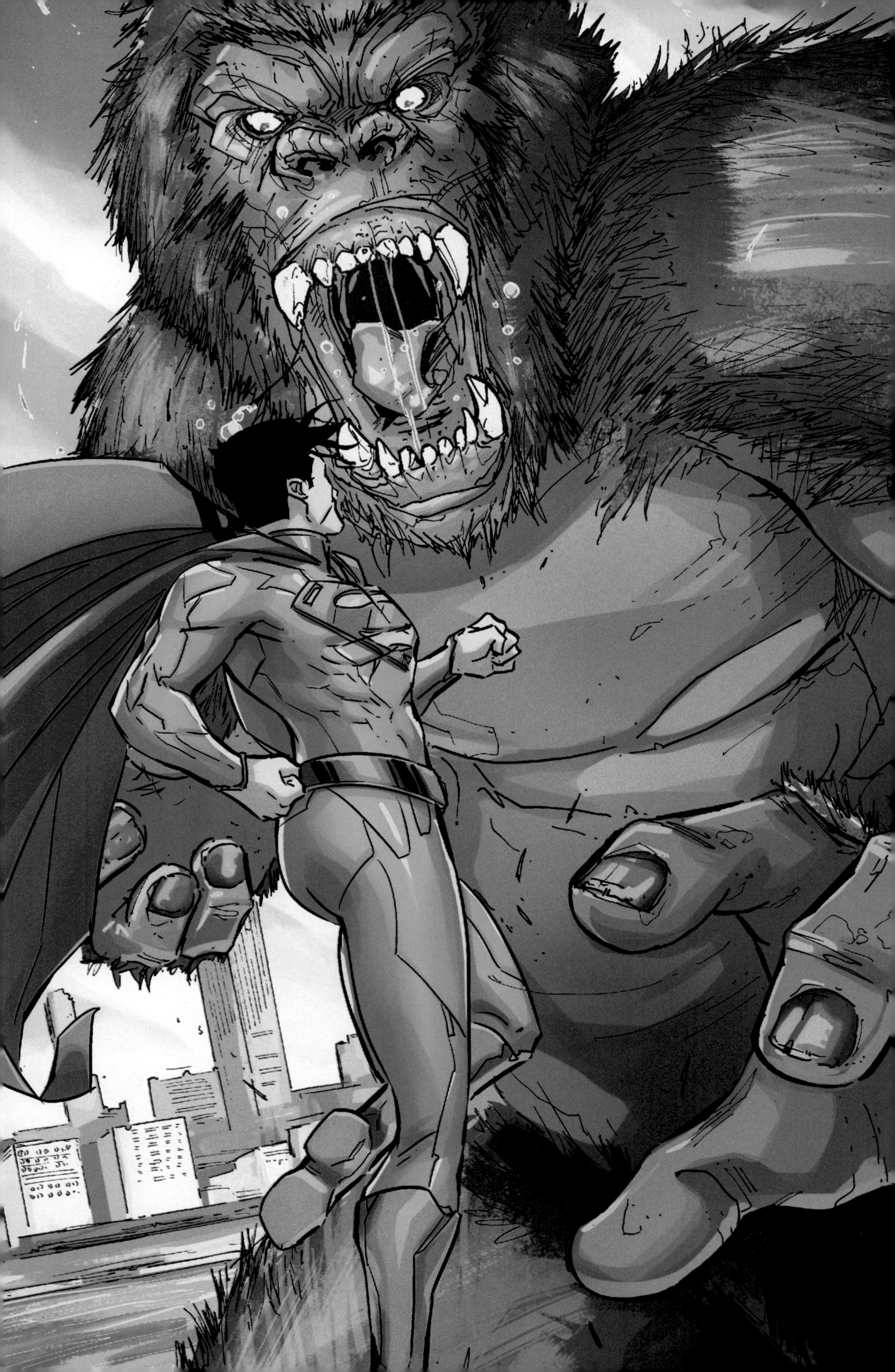

GRIEF

BRIAN BUCCELLATO writer **GIUSEPPE CAFARO** artist **HI FI** colorist **TRAVIS LANHAM** letterer

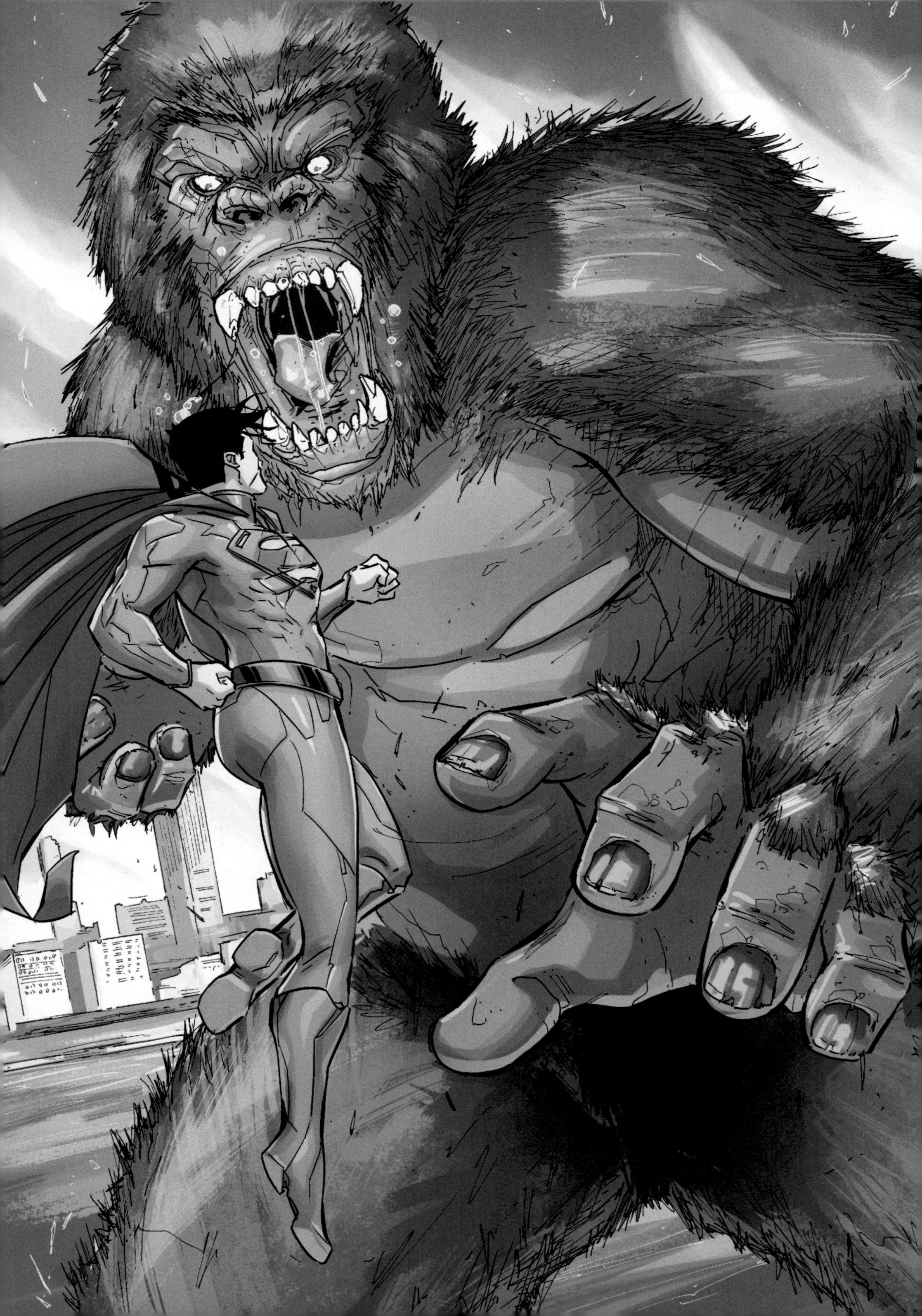

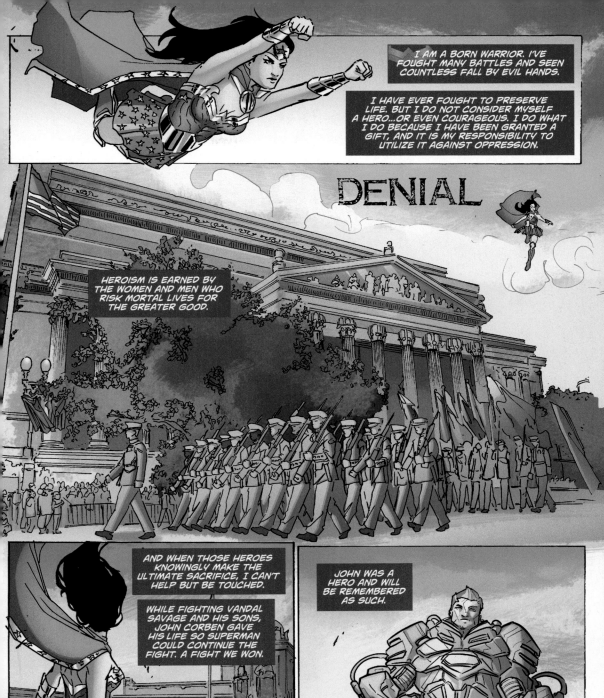

I AM A BORN WARRIOR. I'VE FOUGHT MANY BATTLES AND SEEN COUNTLESS FALL BY EVIL HANDS.

I HAVE EVER FOUGHT TO PRESERVE LIFE. BUT I DO NOT CONSIDER MYSELF A HERO...OR EVEN COURAGEOUS. I DO WHAT I DO BECAUSE I HAVE BEEN GRANTED A GIFT, AND IT IS MY RESPONSIBILITY TO UTILIZE IT AGAINST OPPRESSION.

DENIAL

HEROISM IS EARNED BY THE WOMEN AND MEN WHO RISK MORTAL LIVES FOR THE GREATER GOOD.

AND WHEN THOSE HEROES KNOWINGLY MAKE THE ULTIMATE SACRIFICE, I CAN'T HELP BUT BE TOUCHED.

WHILE FIGHTING VANDAL SAVAGE AND HIS SONS, JOHN CORBEN GAVE HIS LIFE SO SUPERMAN COULD CONTINUE THE FIGHT. A FIGHT WE WON.

JOHN WAS A HERO AND WILL BE REMEMBERED AS SUCH.

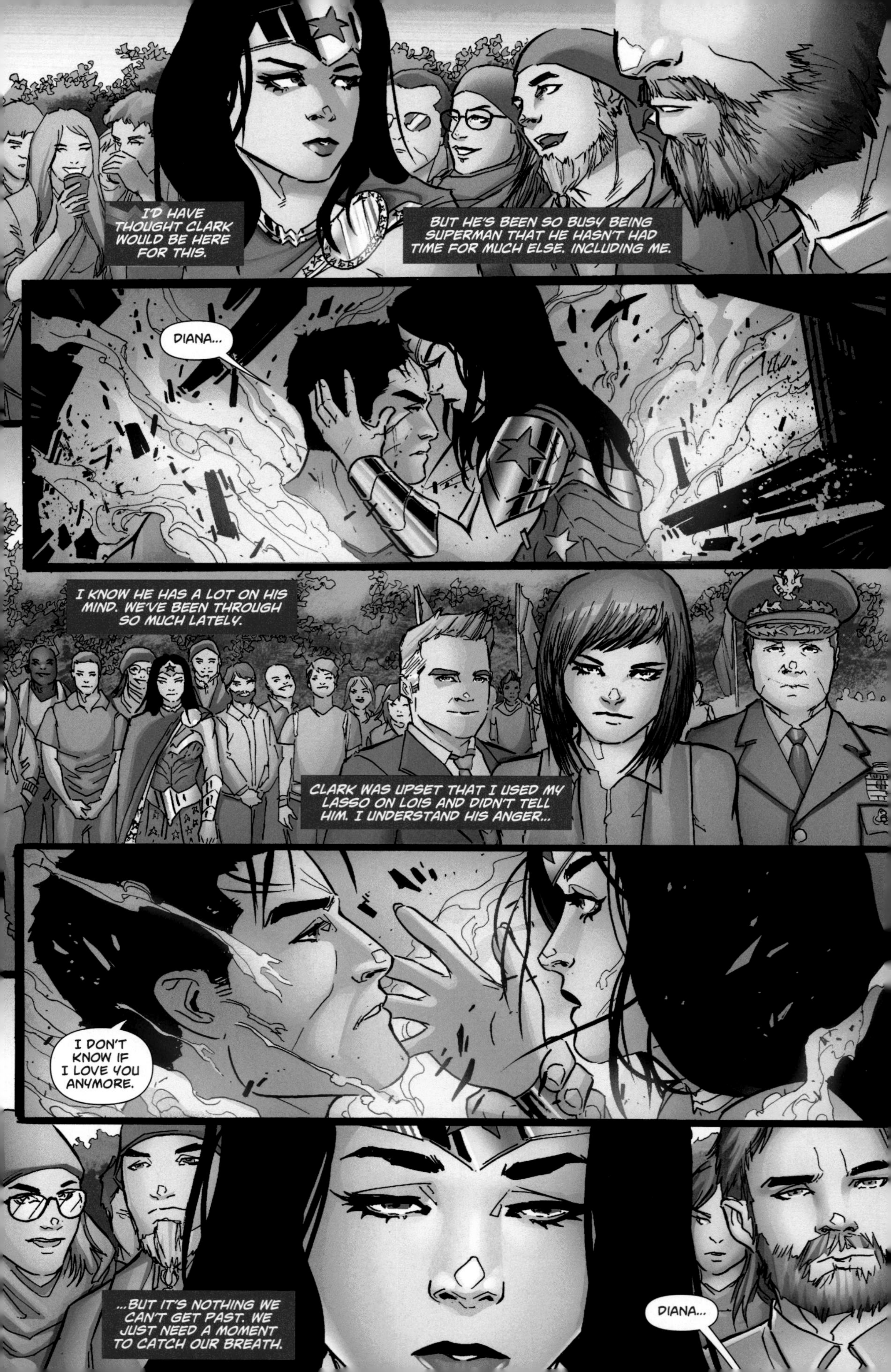

I'D HAVE THOUGHT CLARK WOULD BE HERE FOR THIS.
BUT HE'S BEEN SO BUSY BEING SUPERMAN THAT HE HASN'T HAD TIME FOR MUCH ELSE. INCLUDING ME.
DIANA...
I KNOW HE HAS A LOT ON HIS MIND. WE'VE BEEN THROUGH SO MUCH LATELY.
CLARK WAS UPSET THAT I USED MY LASSO ON LOIS AND DIDN'T TELL HIM. I UNDERSTAND HIS ANGER...
I DON'T KNOW IF I LOVE YOU ANYMORE.
...BUT IT'S NOTHING WE CAN'T GET PAST. WE JUST NEED A MOMENT TO CATCH OUR BREATH.
DIANA...

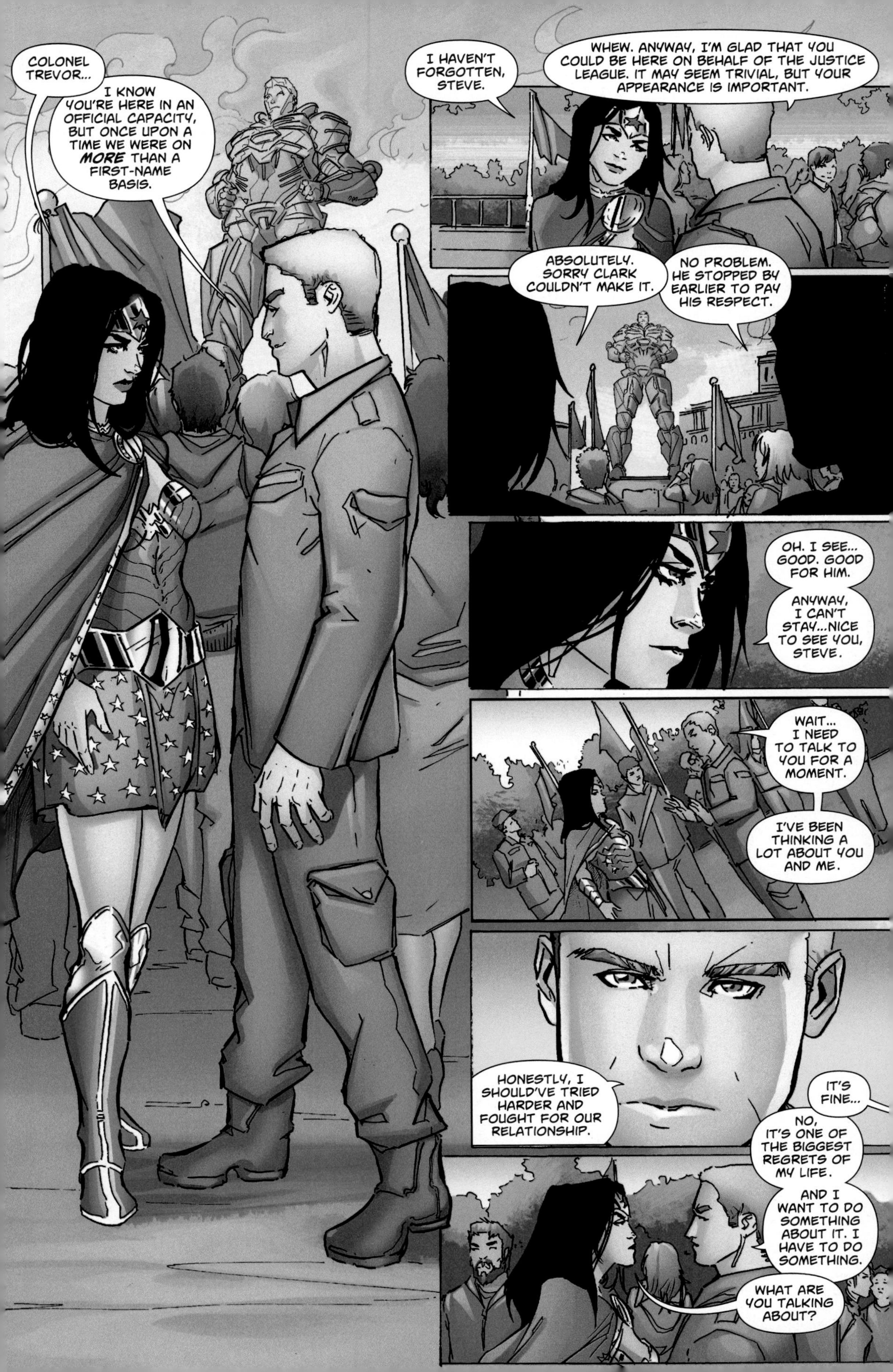
COLONEL TREVOR...
I KNOW YOU'RE HERE IN AN OFFICIAL CAPACITY, BUT ONCE UPON A TIME WE WERE ON *MORE* THAN A FIRST-NAME BASIS.
I HAVEN'T FORGOTTEN, STEVE.
WHEW. ANYWAY, I'M GLAD THAT YOU COULD BE HERE ON BEHALF OF THE JUSTICE LEAGUE. IT MAY SEEM TRIVIAL, BUT YOUR APPEARANCE IS IMPORTANT.
ABSOLUTELY. SORRY CLARK COULDN'T MAKE IT.
NO PROBLEM. HE STOPPED BY EARLIER TO PAY HIS RESPECT.
OH. I SEE... GOOD. GOOD FOR HIM.
ANYWAY, I CAN'T STAY...NICE TO SEE YOU, STEVE.
WAIT... I NEED TO TALK TO YOU FOR A MOMENT.
I'VE BEEN THINKING A LOT ABOUT YOU AND ME.
HONESTLY, I SHOULD'VE TRIED HARDER AND FOUGHT FOR OUR RELATIONSHIP.
IT'S FINE...
NO, IT'S ONE OF THE BIGGEST REGRETS OF MY LIFE.
AND I WANT TO DO SOMETHING ABOUT IT. I HAVE TO DO SOMETHING.
WHAT ARE YOU TALKING ABOUT?

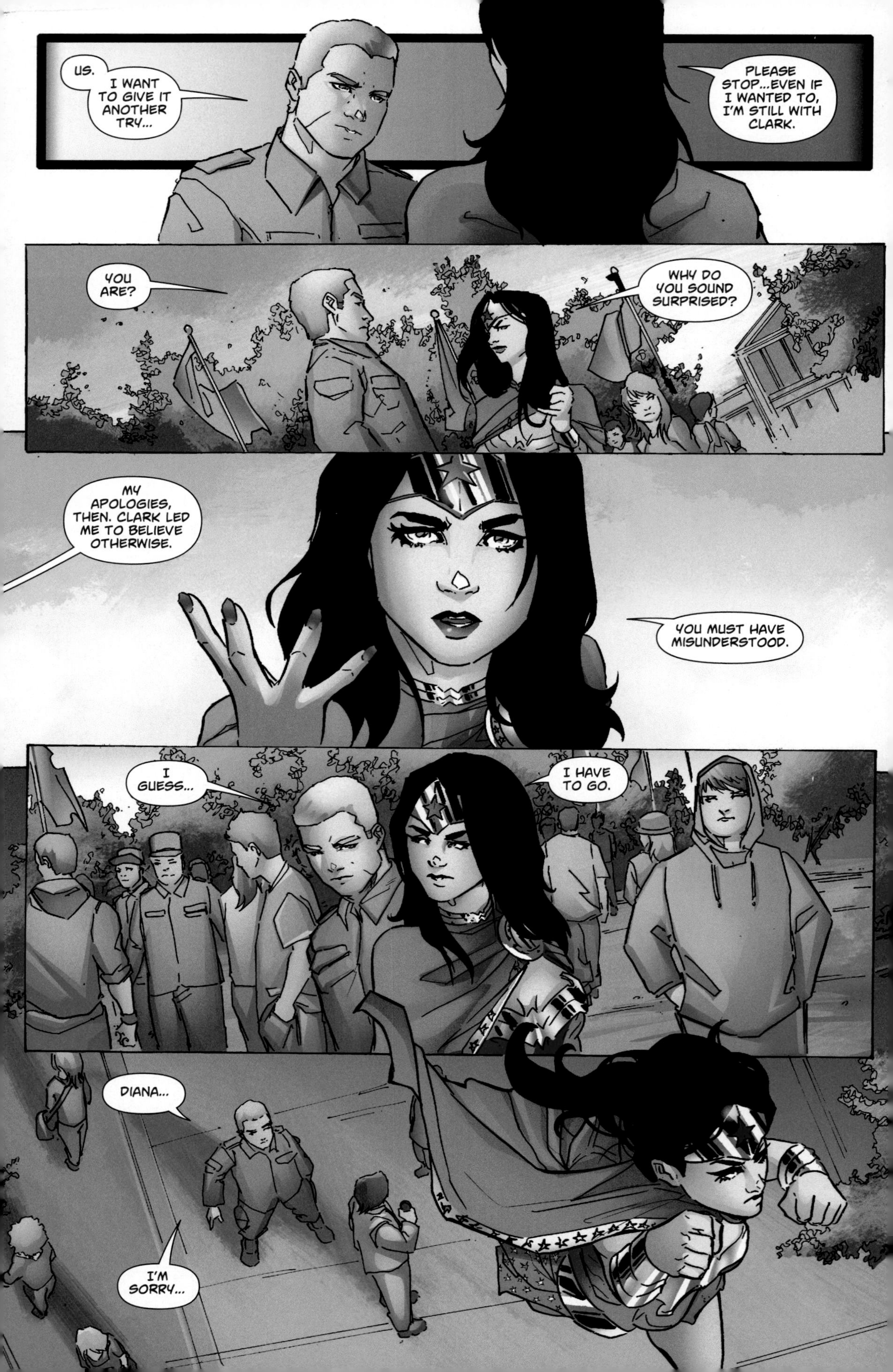
US. I WANT TO GIVE IT ANOTHER TRY...
PLEASE STOP...EVEN IF I WANTED TO, I'M STILL WITH CLARK.
YOU ARE?
WHY DO YOU SOUND SURPRISED?
MY APOLOGIES, THEN. CLARK LED ME TO BELIEVE OTHERWISE.
YOU MUST HAVE MISUNDERSTOOD.
I GUESS...
I HAVE TO GO.
DIANA...
I'M SORRY...

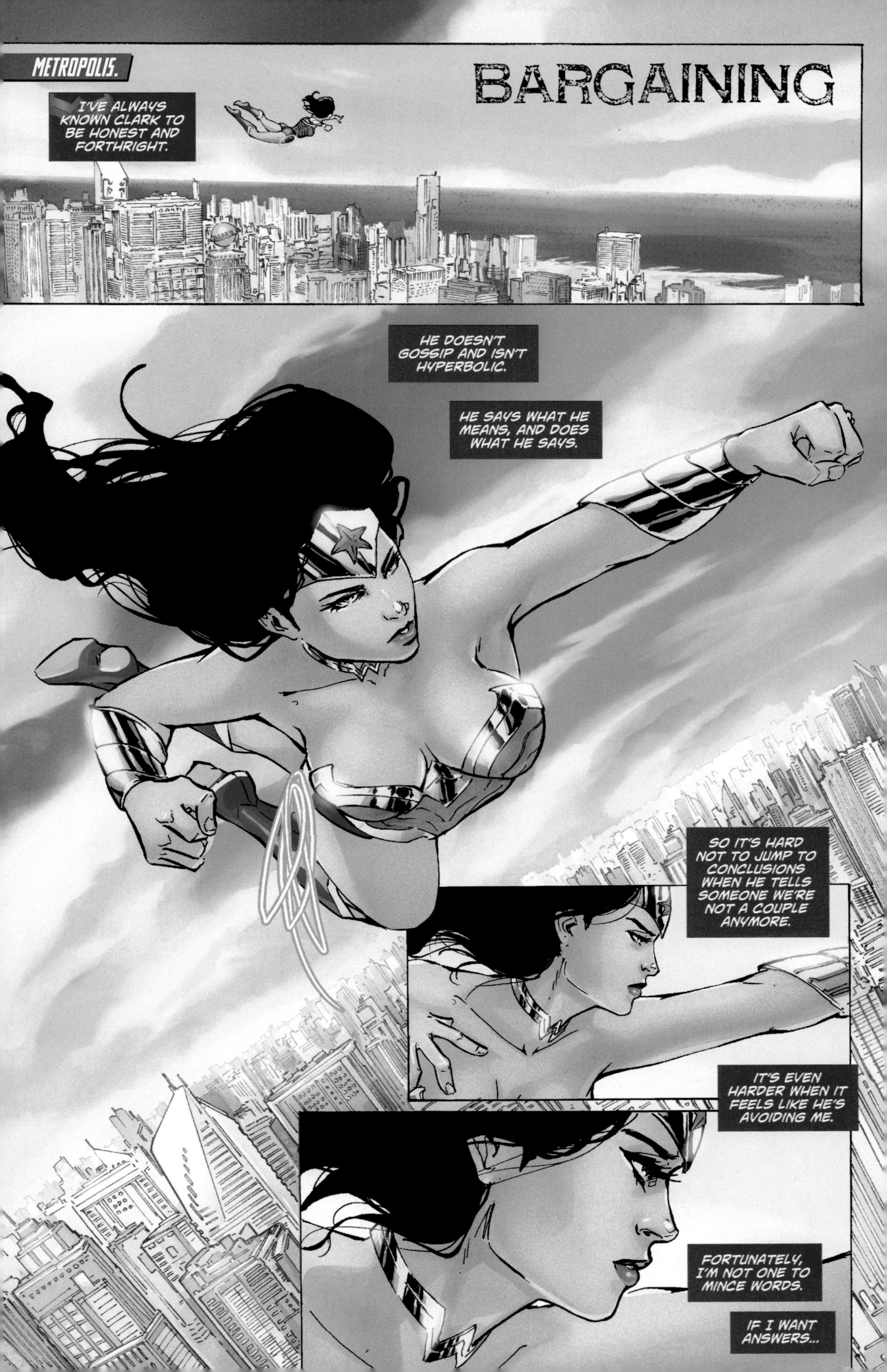
METROPOLIS.
BARGAINING
I'VE ALWAYS KNOWN CLARK TO BE HONEST AND FORTHRIGHT.
HE DOESN'T GOSSIP AND ISN'T HYPERBOLIC.
HE SAYS WHAT HE MEANS, AND DOES WHAT HE SAYS.
SO IT'S HARD NOT TO JUMP TO CONCLUSIONS WHEN HE TELLS SOMEONE WE'RE NOT A COUPLE ANYMORE.
IT'S EVEN HARDER WHEN IT FEELS LIKE HE'S AVOIDING ME.
FORTUNATELY, I'M NOT ONE TO MINCE WORDS.
IF I WANT ANSWERS...

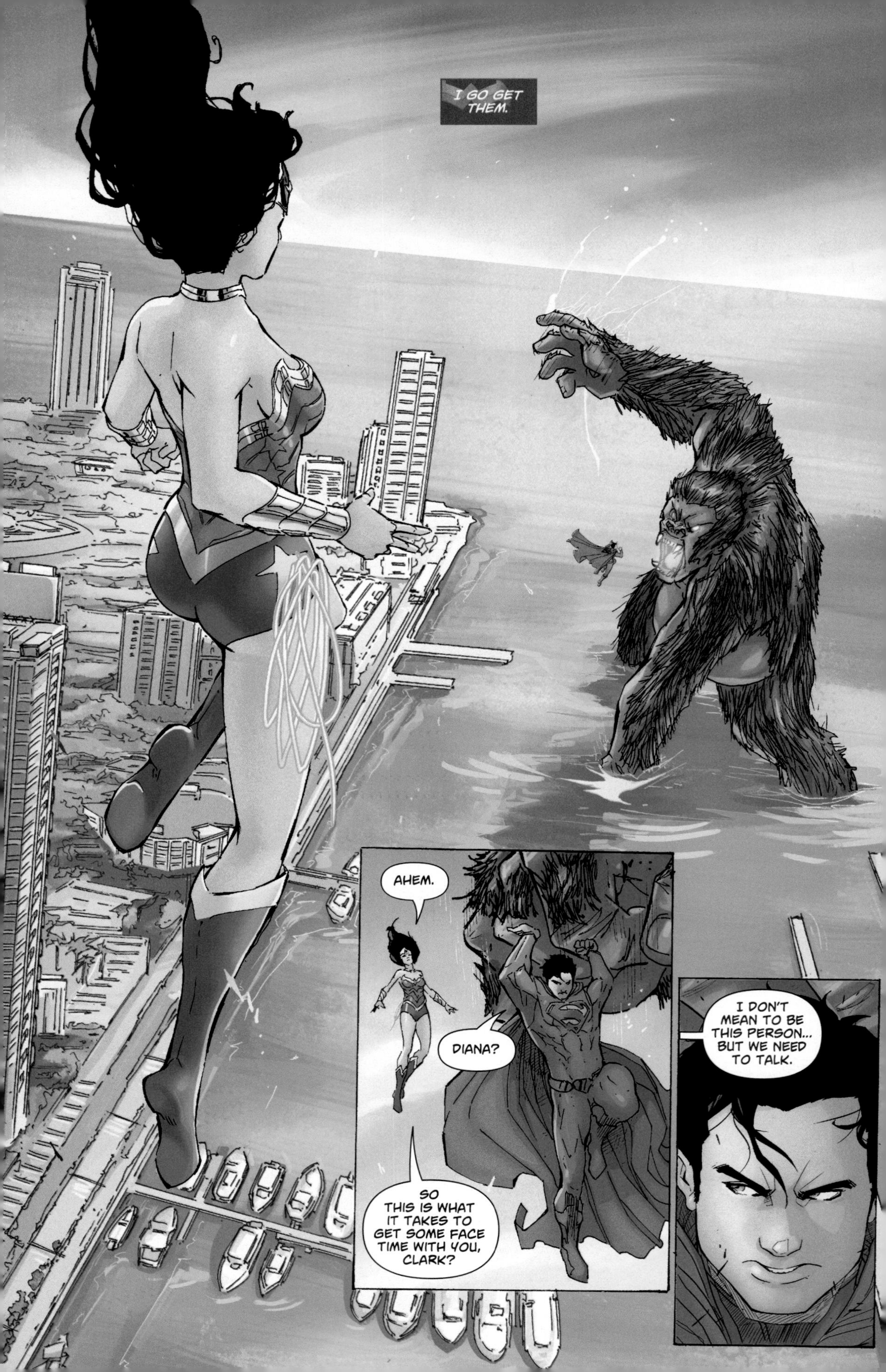
I GO GET THEM.
AHEM.
DIANA?
SO THIS IS WHAT IT TAKES TO GET SOME FACE TIME WITH YOU, CLARK?
I DON'T MEAN TO BE THIS PERSON... BUT WE NEED TO TALK.

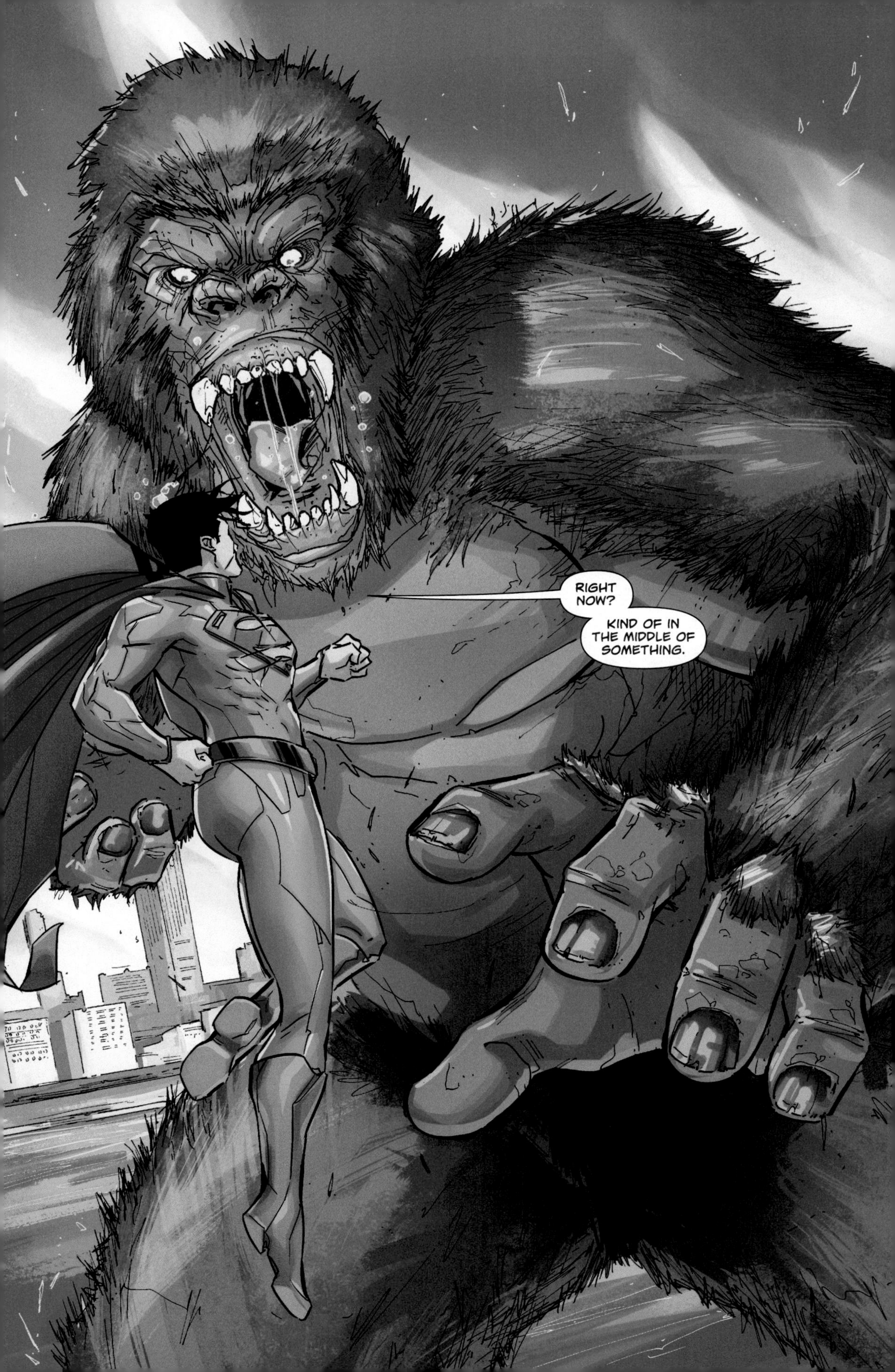
RIGHT NOW?
KIND OF IN THE MIDDLE OF SOMETHING.

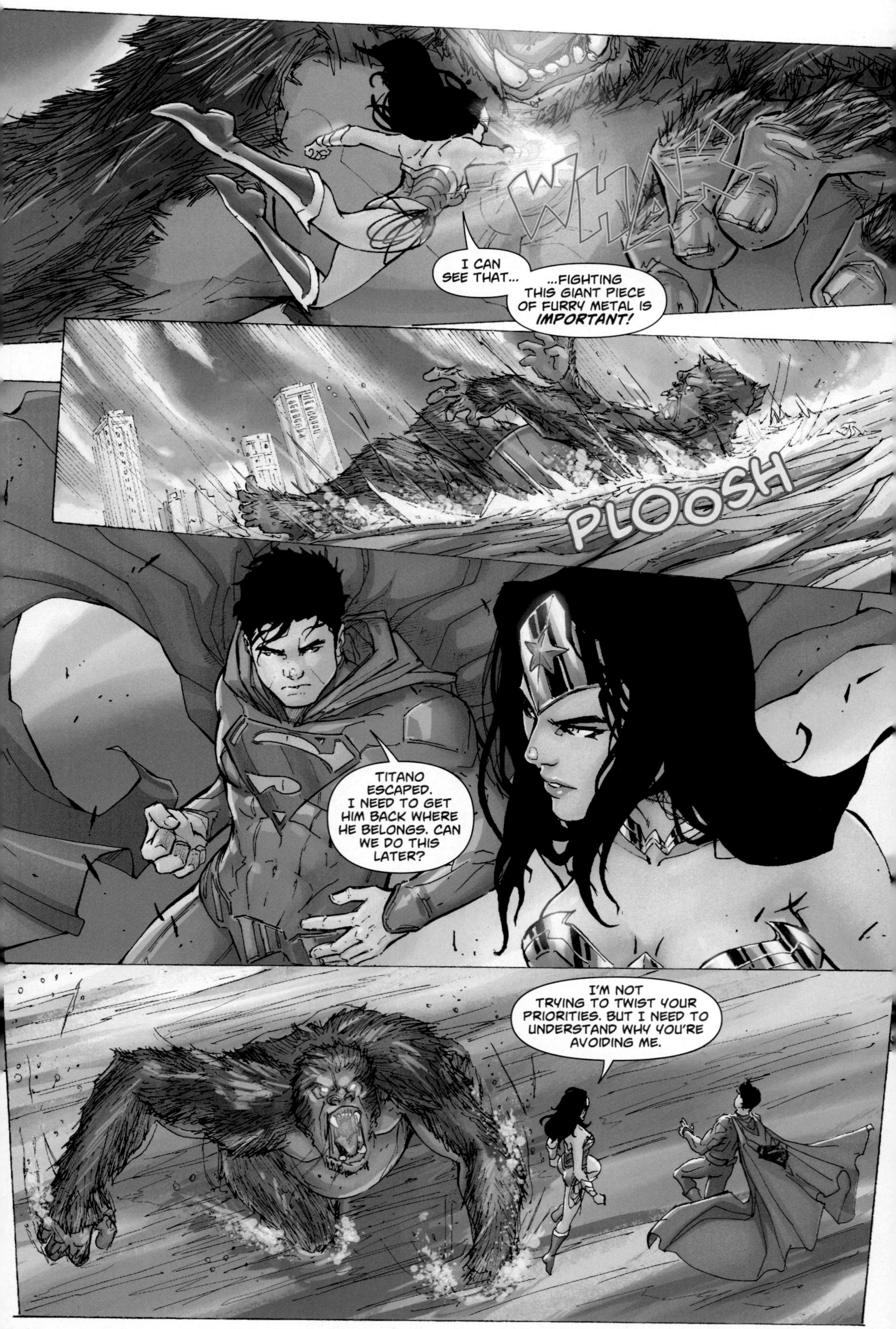
WHAK
I CAN SEE THAT...
...FIGHTING THIS GIANT PIECE OF FURRY METAL IS IMPORTANT!
PLOOSH
TITANO ESCAPED. I NEED TO GET HIM BACK WHERE HE BELONGS. CAN WE DO THIS LATER?
I'M NOT TRYING TO TWIST YOUR PRIORITIES. BUT I NEED TO UNDERSTAND WHY YOU'RE AVOIDING ME.

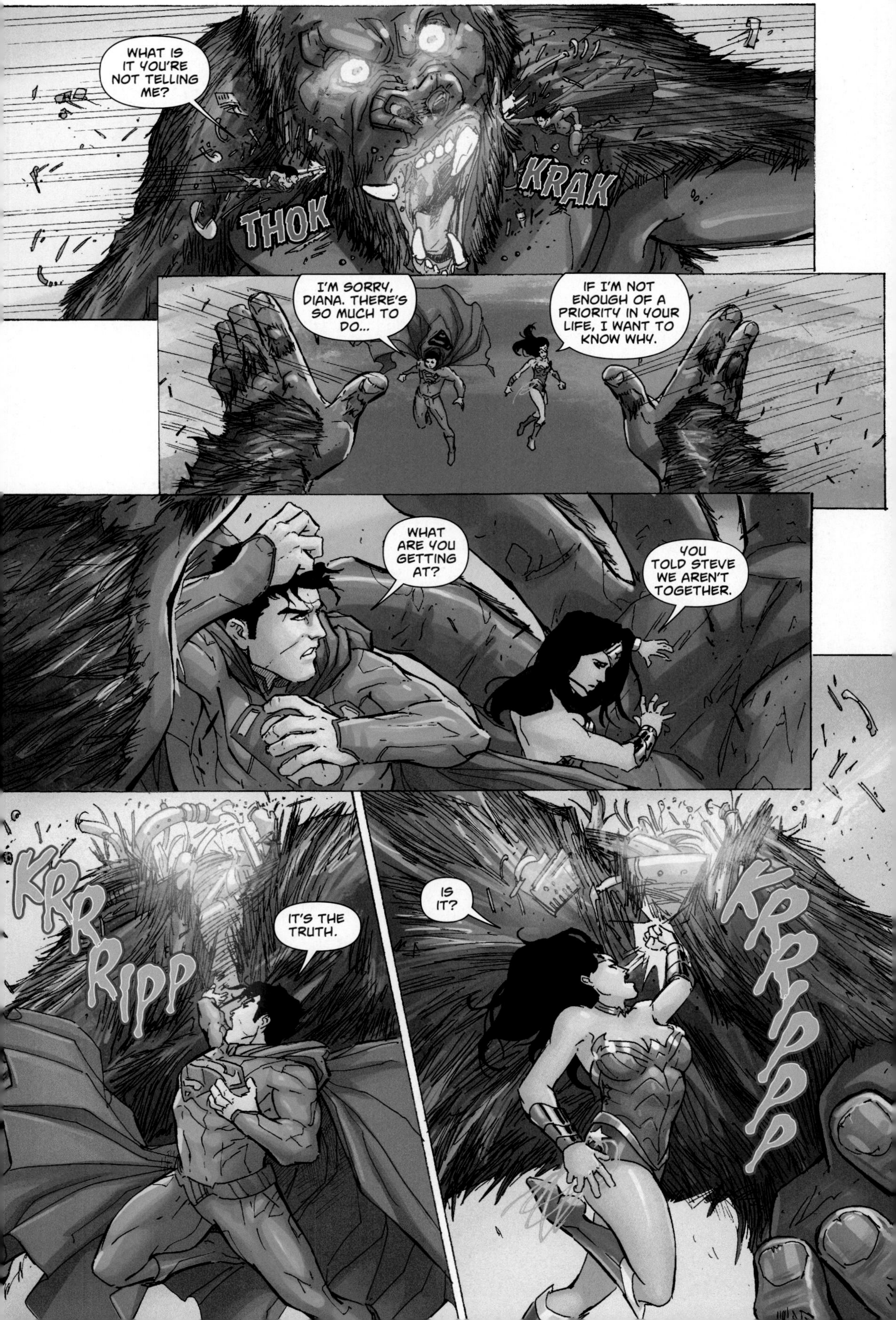
WHAT IS IT YOU'RE NOT TELLING ME?
KRAK
THOK
I'M SORRY, DIANA. THERE'S SO MUCH TO DO...
IF I'M NOT ENOUGH OF A PRIORITY IN YOUR LIFE, I WANT TO KNOW WHY.
WHAT ARE YOU GETTING AT?
YOU TOLD STEVE WE AREN'T TOGETHER.
KRRRIPP
IT'S THE TRUTH.
IS IT?
KRRIPPP

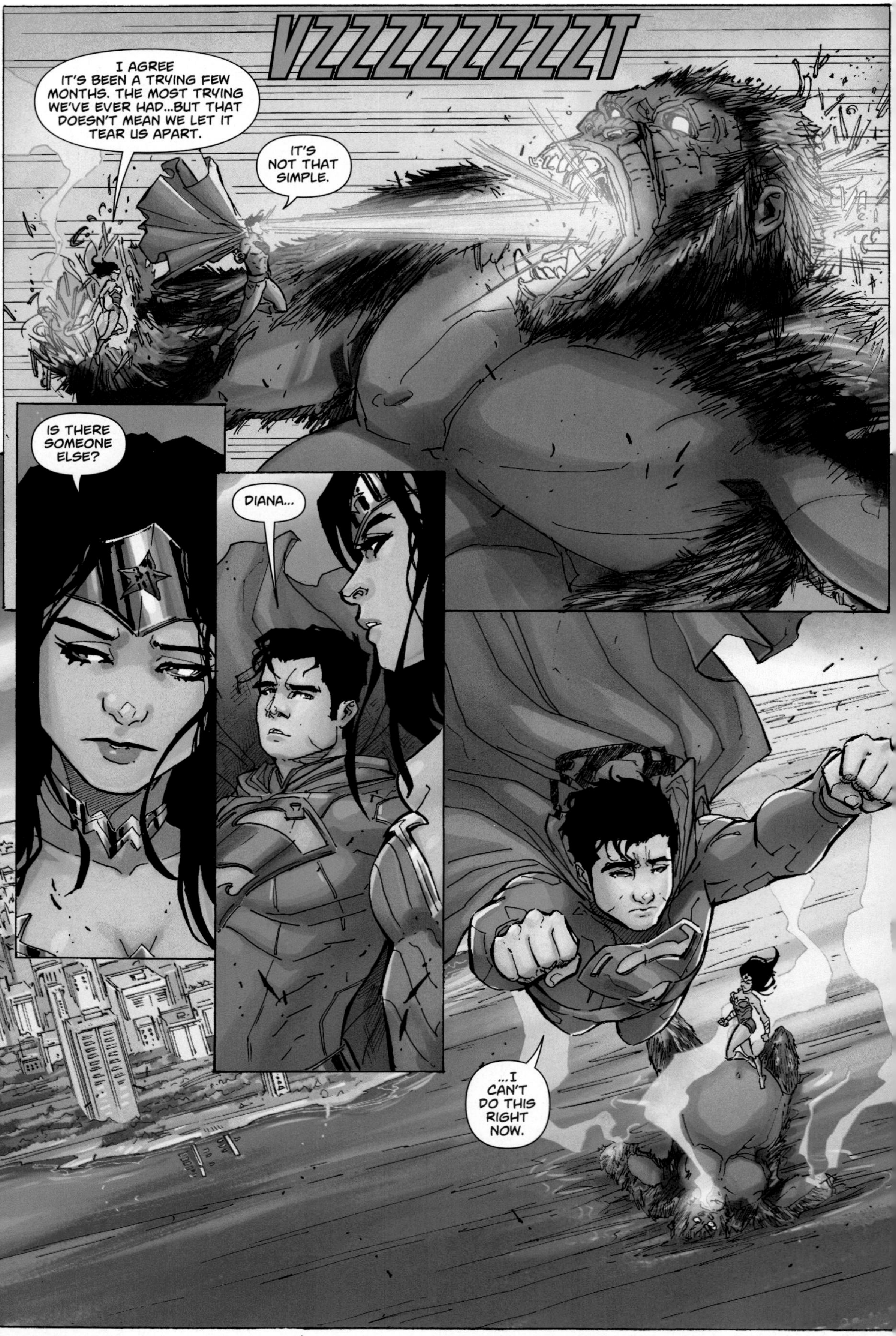
VZZZZZZZZZT
I AGREE IT'S BEEN A TRYING FEW MONTHS. THE MOST TRYING WE'VE EVER HAD...BUT THAT DOESN'T MEAN WE LET IT TEAR US APART.
IT'S NOT THAT SIMPLE.
IS THERE SOMEONE ELSE?
DIANA...
...I CAN'T DO THIS RIGHT NOW.

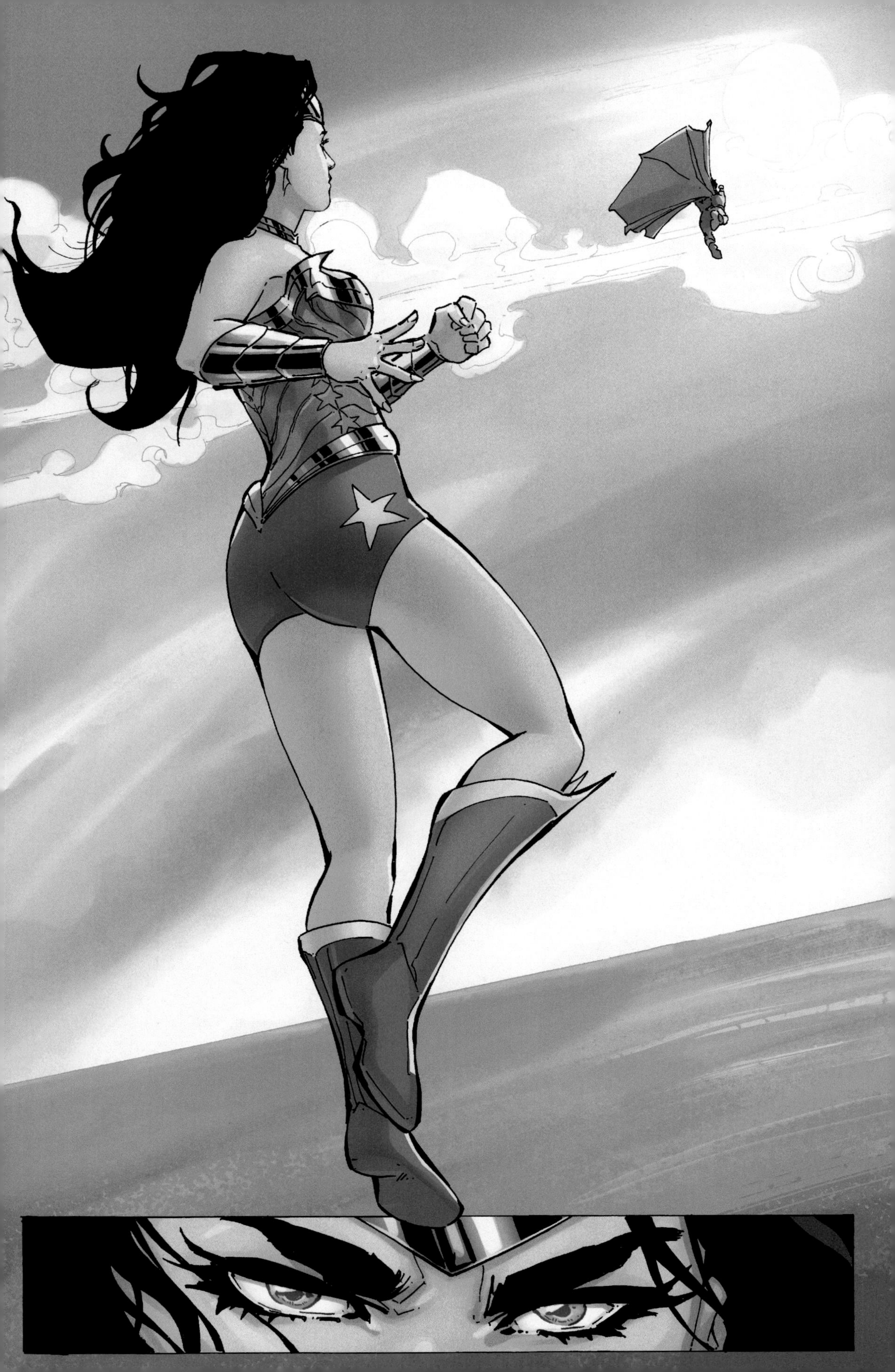

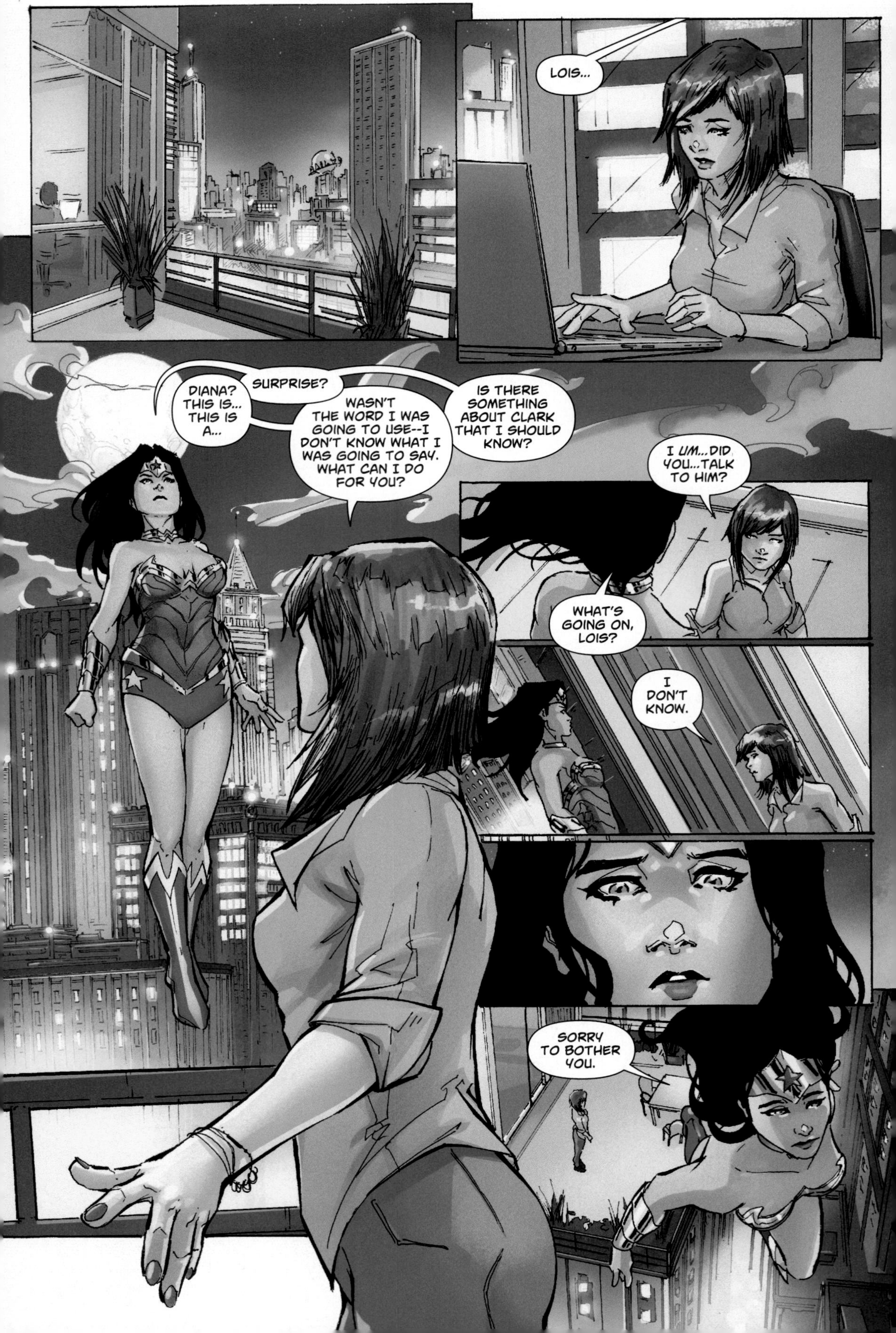
LOIS...
DIANA? THIS IS... THIS IS A...
SURPRISE?
WASN'T THE WORD I WAS GOING TO USE--I DON'T KNOW WHAT I WAS GOING TO SAY. WHAT CAN I DO FOR YOU?
IS THERE SOMETHING ABOUT CLARK THAT I SHOULD KNOW?
I UM...DID YOU...TALK TO HIM?
WHAT'S GOING ON, LOIS?
I DON'T KNOW.
SORRY TO BOTHER YOU.

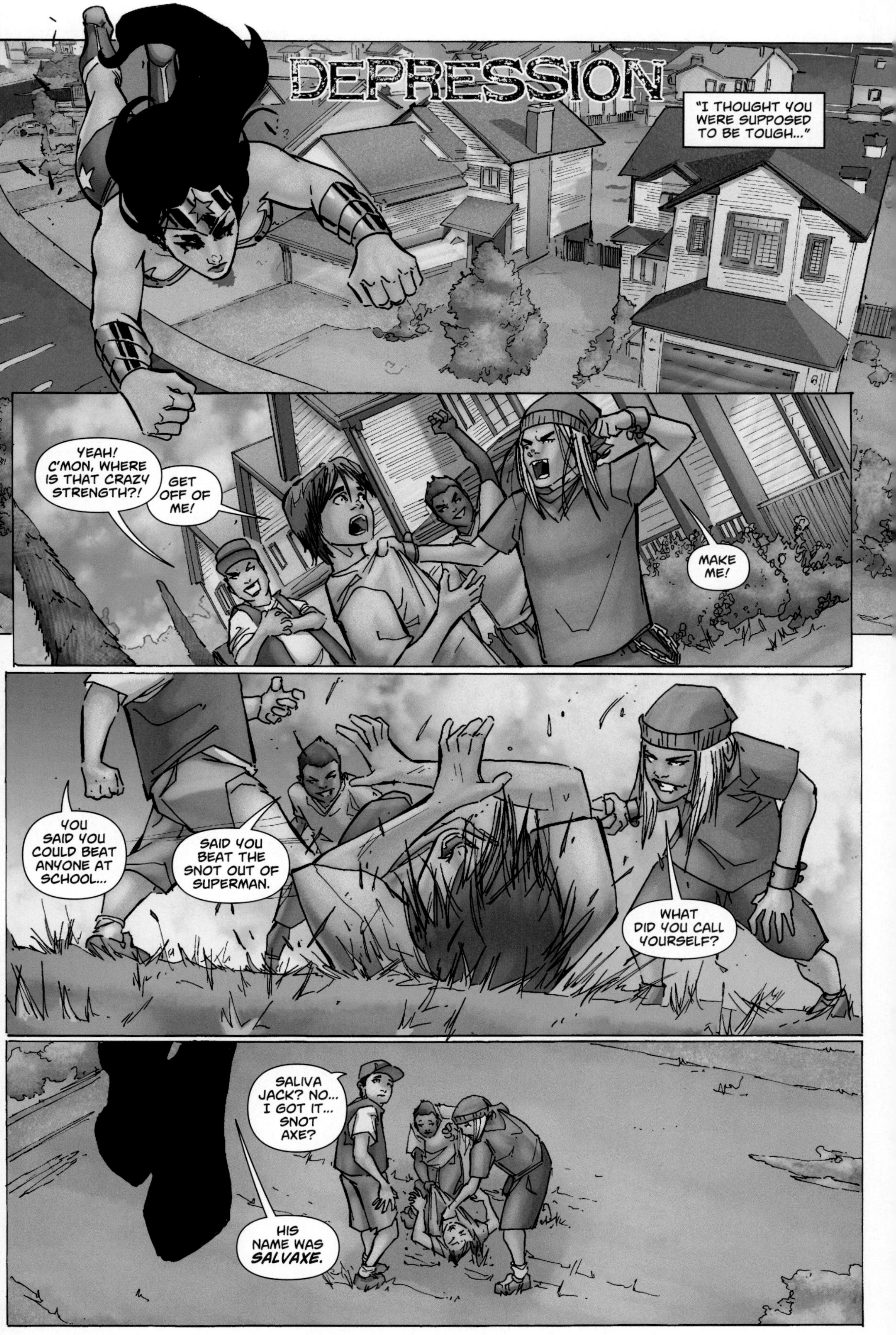
DEPRESSION
"I THOUGHT YOU WERE SUPPOSED TO BE TOUGH..."
YEAH! C'MON, WHERE IS THAT CRAZY STRENGTH?!
GET OFF OF ME!
MAKE ME!
YOU SAID YOU COULD BEAT ANYONE AT SCHOOL...
SAID YOU BEAT THE SNOT OUT OF SUPERMAN.
WHAT DID YOU CALL YOURSELF?
SALIVA JACK? NO... I GOT IT... SNOT AXE?
HIS NAME WAS SALVAXE.

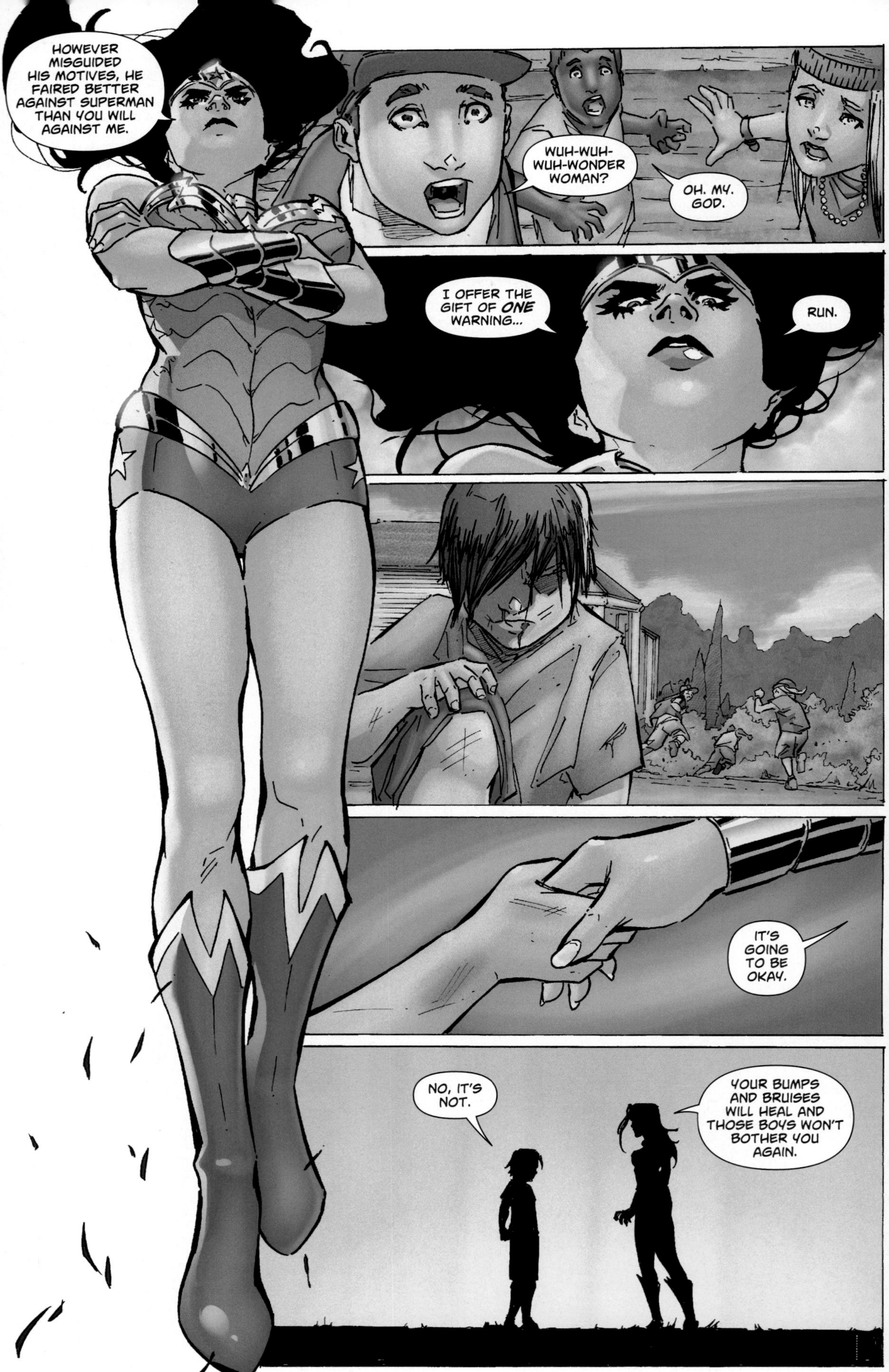
HOWEVER MISGUIDED HIS MOTIVES, HE FAIRED BETTER AGAINST SUPERMAN THAN YOU WILL AGAINST ME.
WUH-WUH-WUH-WONDER WOMAN?
OH. MY. GOD.
I OFFER THE GIFT OF ONE WARNING...
RUN.
IT'S GOING TO BE OKAY.
NO, IT'S NOT.
YOUR BUMPS AND BRUISES WILL HEAL AND THOSE BOYS WON'T BOTHER YOU AGAIN.

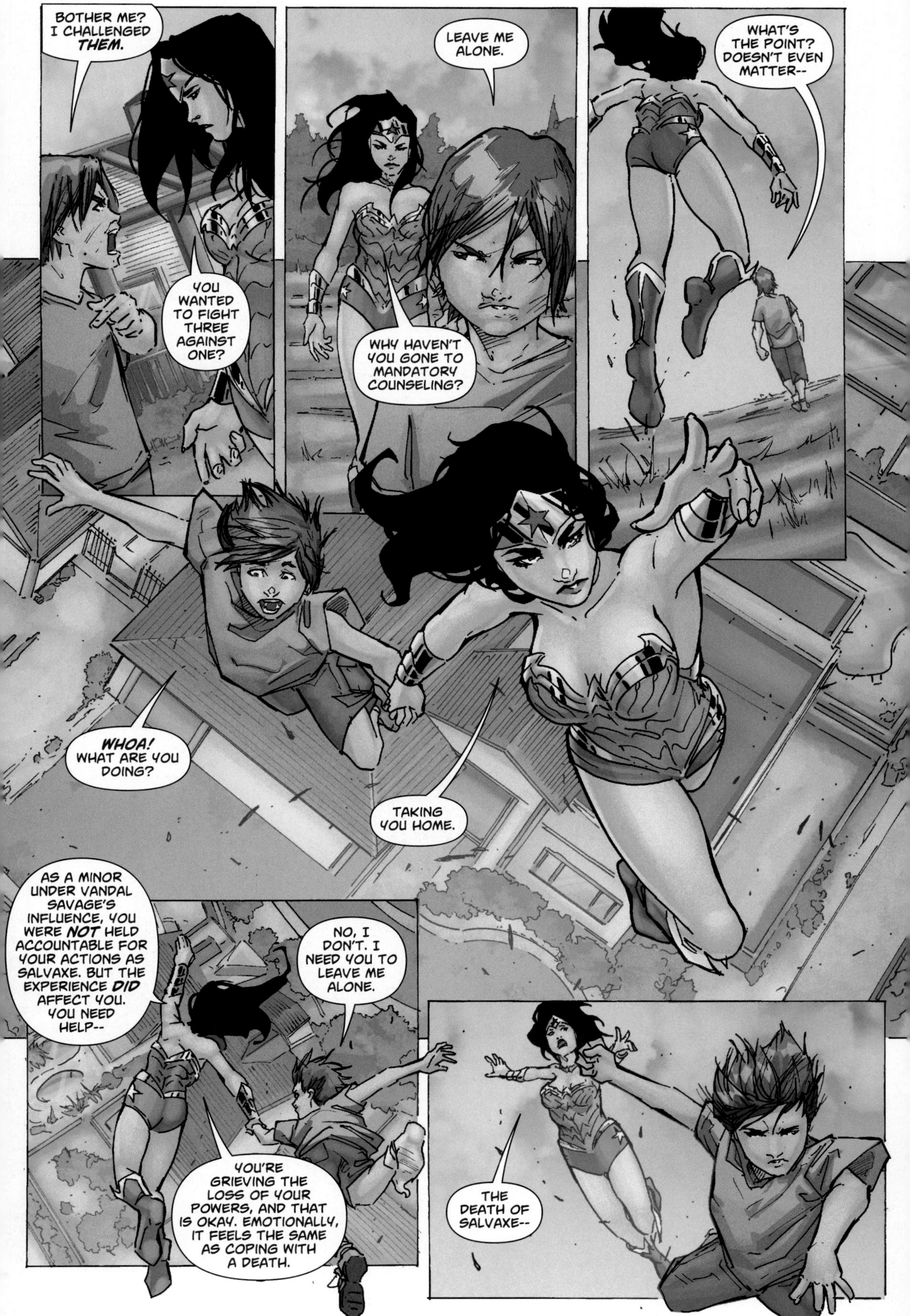
BOTHER ME? I CHALLENGED THEM.
YOU WANTED TO FIGHT THREE AGAINST ONE?
LEAVE ME ALONE.
WHY HAVEN'T YOU GONE TO MANDATORY COUNSELING?
WHAT'S THE POINT? DOESN'T EVEN MATTER--
WHOA! WHAT ARE YOU DOING?
TAKING YOU HOME.
AS A MINOR UNDER VANDAL SAVAGE'S INFLUENCE, YOU WERE NOT HELD ACCOUNTABLE FOR YOUR ACTIONS AS SALVAXE. BUT THE EXPERIENCE DID AFFECT YOU. YOU NEED HELP--
NO, I DON'T. I NEED YOU TO LEAVE ME ALONE.
YOU'RE GRIEVING THE LOSS OF YOUR POWERS, AND THAT IS OKAY. EMOTIONALLY, IT FEELS THE SAME AS COPING WITH A DEATH.
THE DEATH OF SALVAXE--

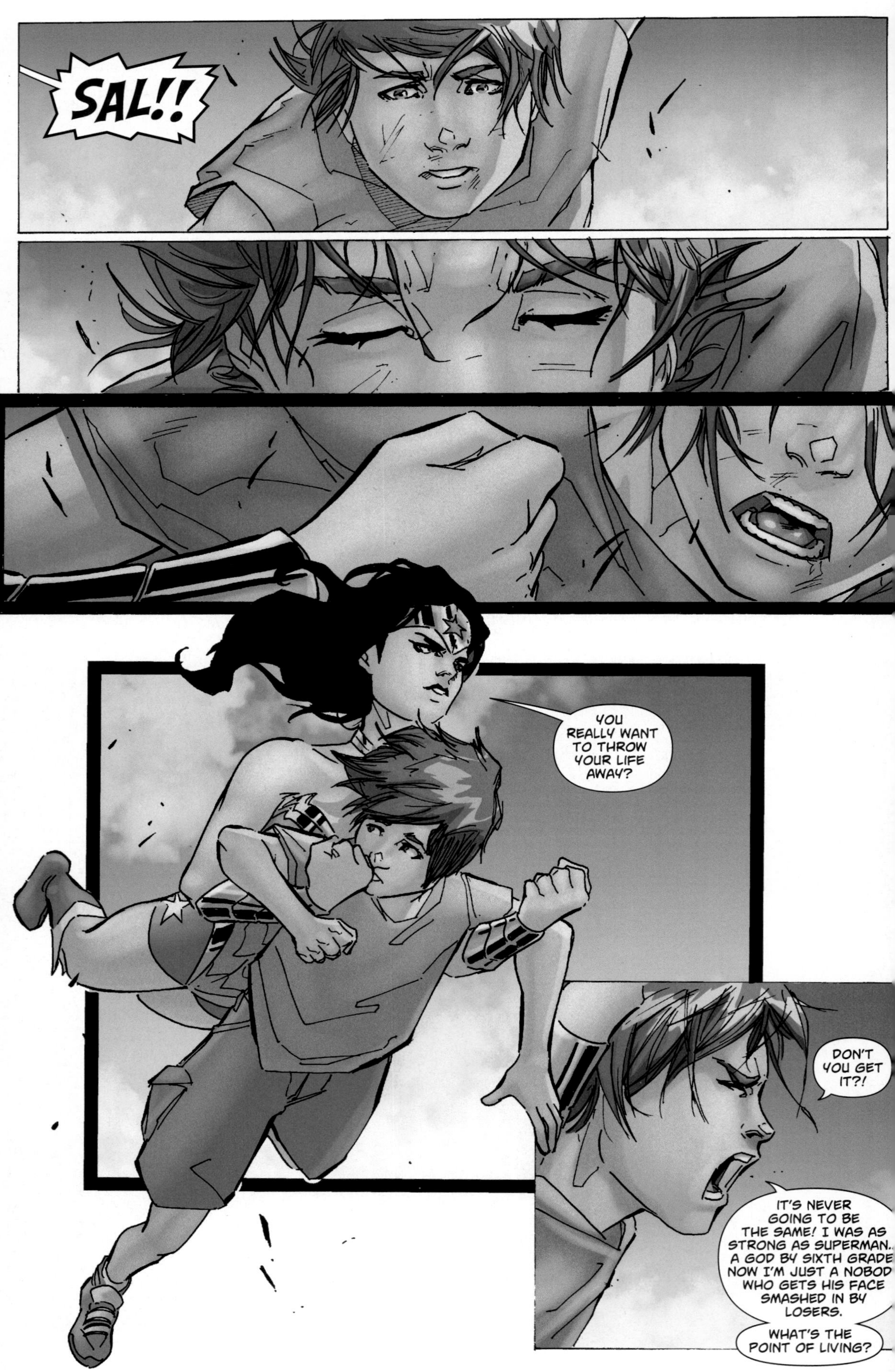
SAL!!
YOU REALLY WANT TO THROW YOUR LIFE AWAY?
DON'T YOU GET IT?!
IT'S NEVER GOING TO BE THE SAME! I WAS AS STRONG AS SUPERMAN. A GOD BY SIXTH GRADE NOW I'M JUST A NOBOD WHO GETS HIS FACE SMASHED IN BY LOSERS.
WHAT'S THE POINT OF LIVING?

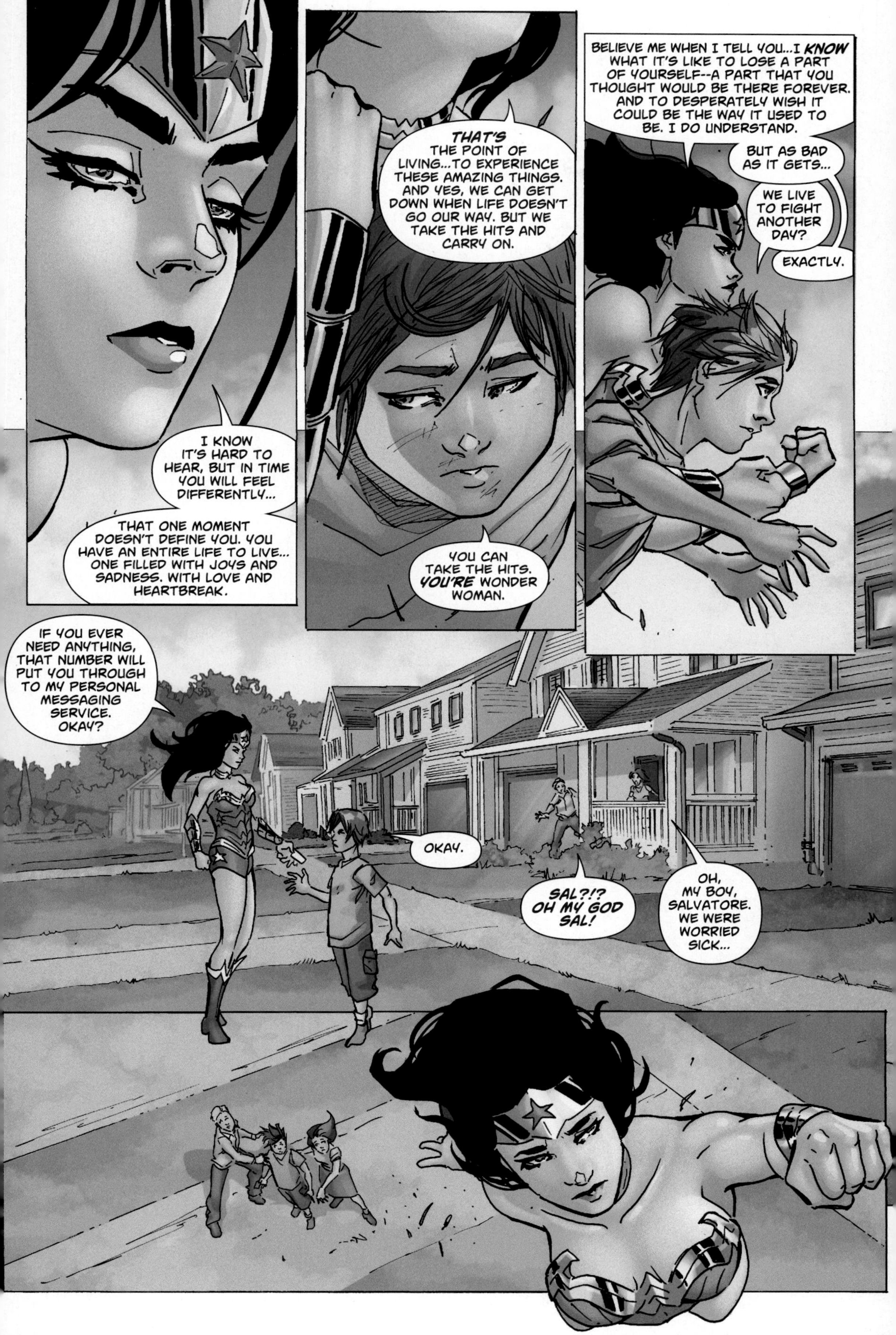
I KNOW IT'S HARD TO HEAR, BUT IN TIME YOU WILL FEEL DIFFERENTLY...
THAT ONE MOMENT DOESN'T DEFINE YOU. YOU HAVE AN ENTIRE LIFE TO LIVE... ONE FILLED WITH JOYS AND SADNESS. WITH LOVE AND HEARTBREAK.
THAT'S THE POINT OF LIVING...TO EXPERIENCE THESE AMAZING THINGS. AND YES, WE CAN GET DOWN WHEN LIFE DOESN'T GO OUR WAY. BUT WE TAKE THE HITS AND CARRY ON.
YOU CAN TAKE THE HITS. YOU'RE WONDER WOMAN.
BELIEVE ME WHEN I TELL YOU...I KNOW WHAT IT'S LIKE TO LOSE A PART OF YOURSELF--A PART THAT YOU THOUGHT WOULD BE THERE FOREVER. AND TO DESPERATELY WISH IT COULD BE THE WAY IT USED TO BE. I DO UNDERSTAND.
BUT AS BAD AS IT GETS...
WE LIVE TO FIGHT ANOTHER DAY?
EXACTLY.
IF YOU EVER NEED ANYTHING, THAT NUMBER WILL PUT YOU THROUGH TO MY PERSONAL MESSAGING SERVICE. OKAY?
OKAY.
SAL?!? OH MY GOD SAL!
OH, MY BOY, SALVATORE. WE WERE WORRIED SICK...

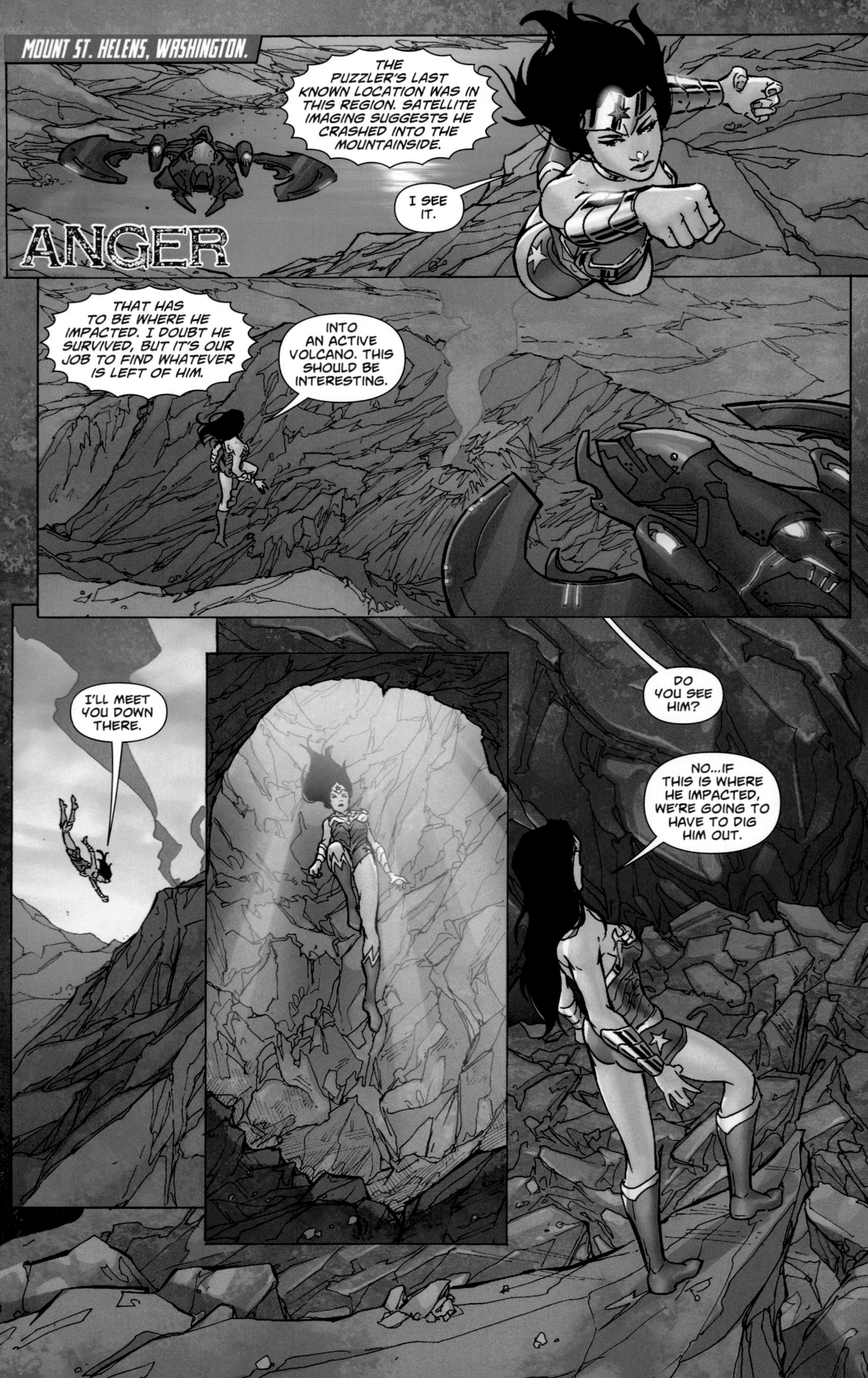
MOUNT ST. HELENS, WASHINGTON.
THE PUZZLER'S LAST KNOWN LOCATION WAS IN THIS REGION. SATELLITE IMAGING SUGGESTS HE CRASHED INTO THE MOUNTAINSIDE.
I SEE IT.
ANGER
THAT HAS TO BE WHERE HE IMPACTED. I DOUBT HE SURVIVED, BUT IT'S OUR JOB TO FIND WHATEVER IS LEFT OF HIM.
INTO AN ACTIVE VOLCANO. THIS SHOULD BE INTERESTING.
I'LL MEET YOU DOWN THERE.
DO YOU SEE HIM?
NO...IF THIS IS WHERE HE IMPACTED, WE'RE GOING TO HAVE TO DIG HIM OUT.

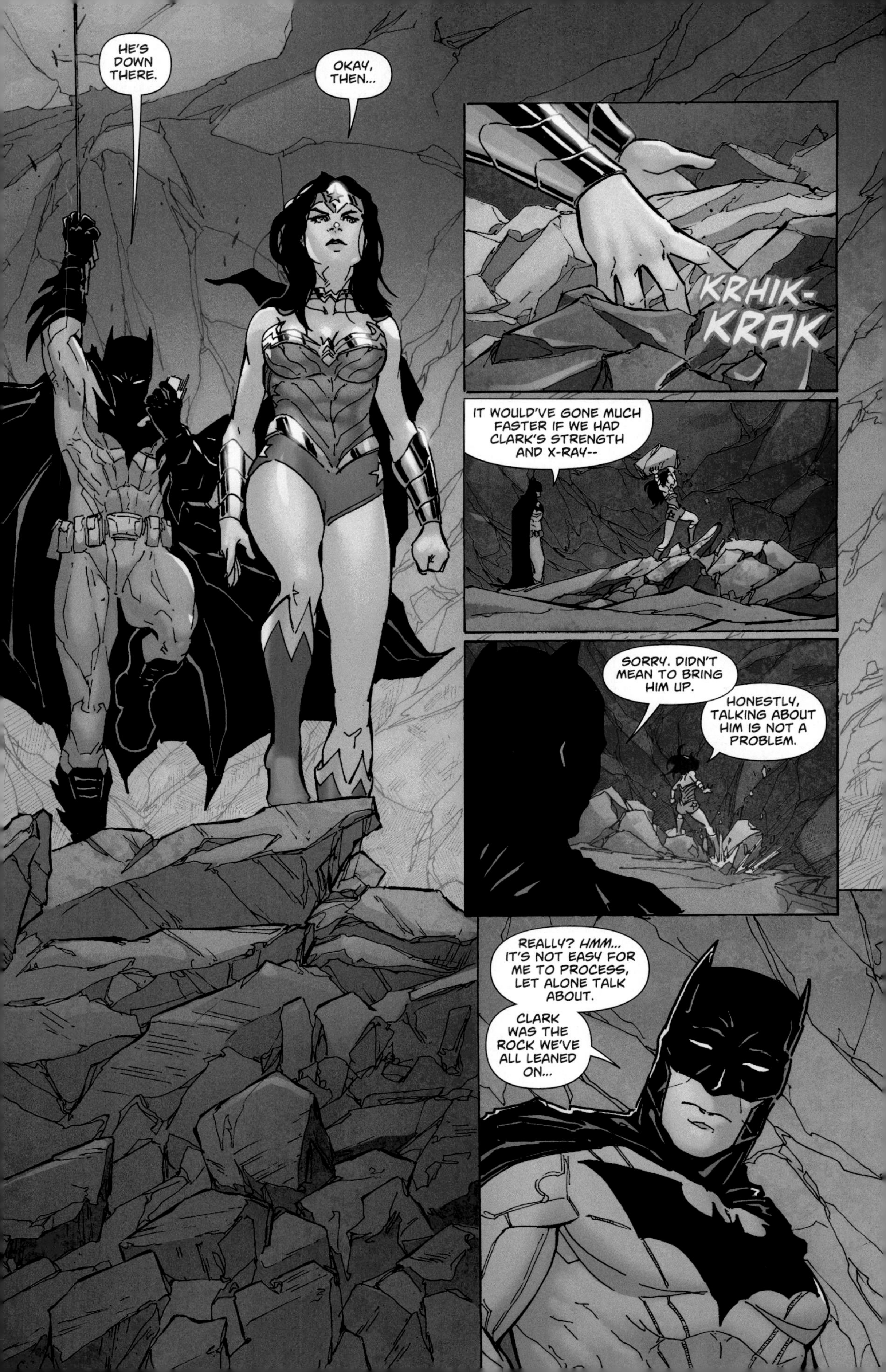
HE'S DOWN THERE.
OKAY, THEN...
KRHIK-KRAK
IT WOULD'VE GONE MUCH FASTER IF WE HAD CLARK'S STRENGTH AND X-RAY--
SORRY. DIDN'T MEAN TO BRING HIM UP.
HONESTLY, TALKING ABOUT HIM IS NOT A PROBLEM.
REALLY? HMM... IT'S NOT EASY FOR ME TO PROCESS, LET ALONE TALK ABOUT.
CLARK WAS THE ROCK WE'VE ALL LEANED ON...

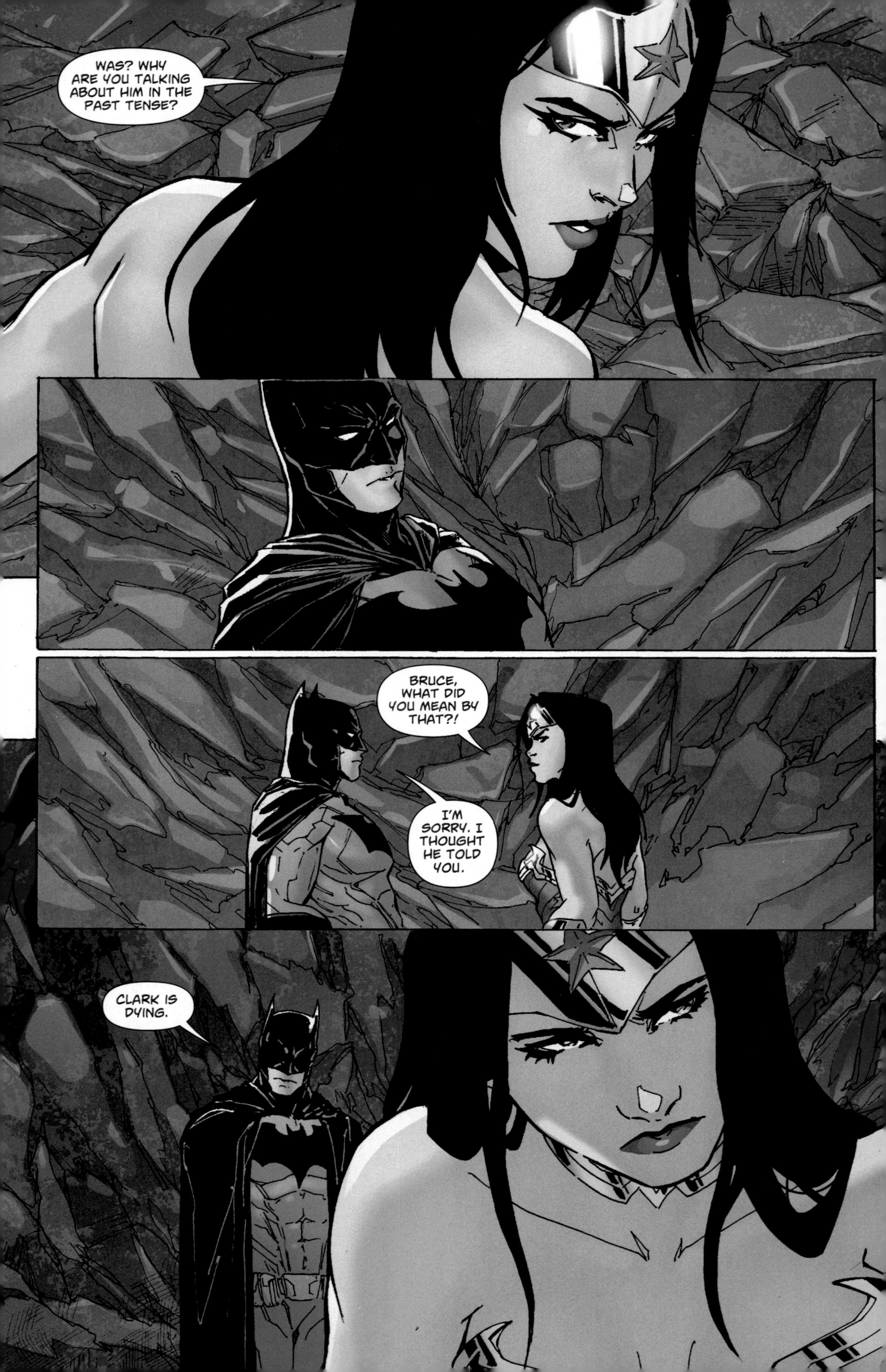
WAS? WHY ARE YOU TALKING ABOUT HIM IN THE PAST TENSE?
BRUCE, WHAT DID YOU MEAN BY THAT?!
I'M SORRY. I THOUGHT HE TOLD YOU.
CLARK IS DYING.

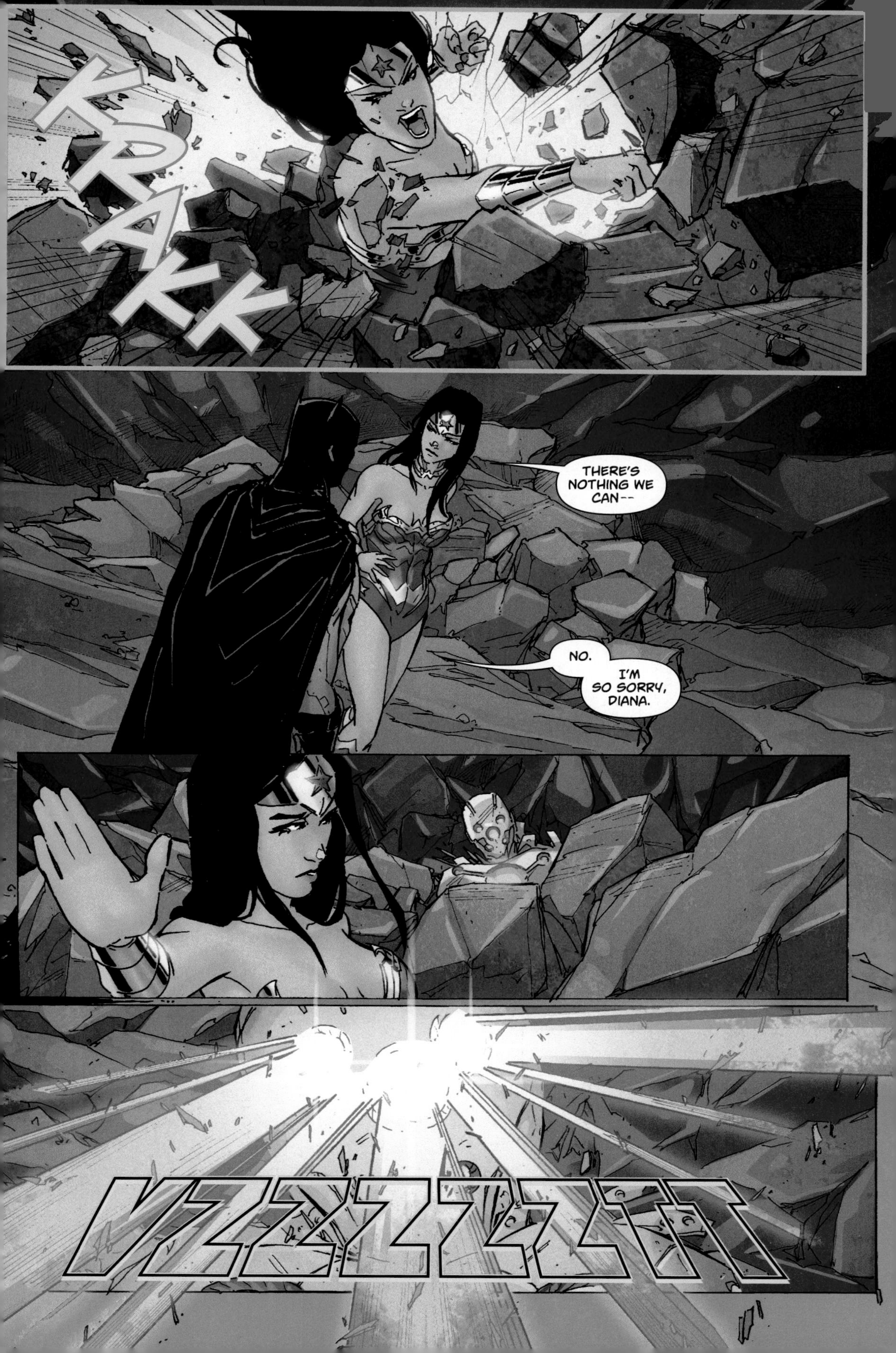
KRAKK
THERE'S NOTHING WE CAN--
NO.
I'M SO SORRY, DIANA.
VZZZZZIT

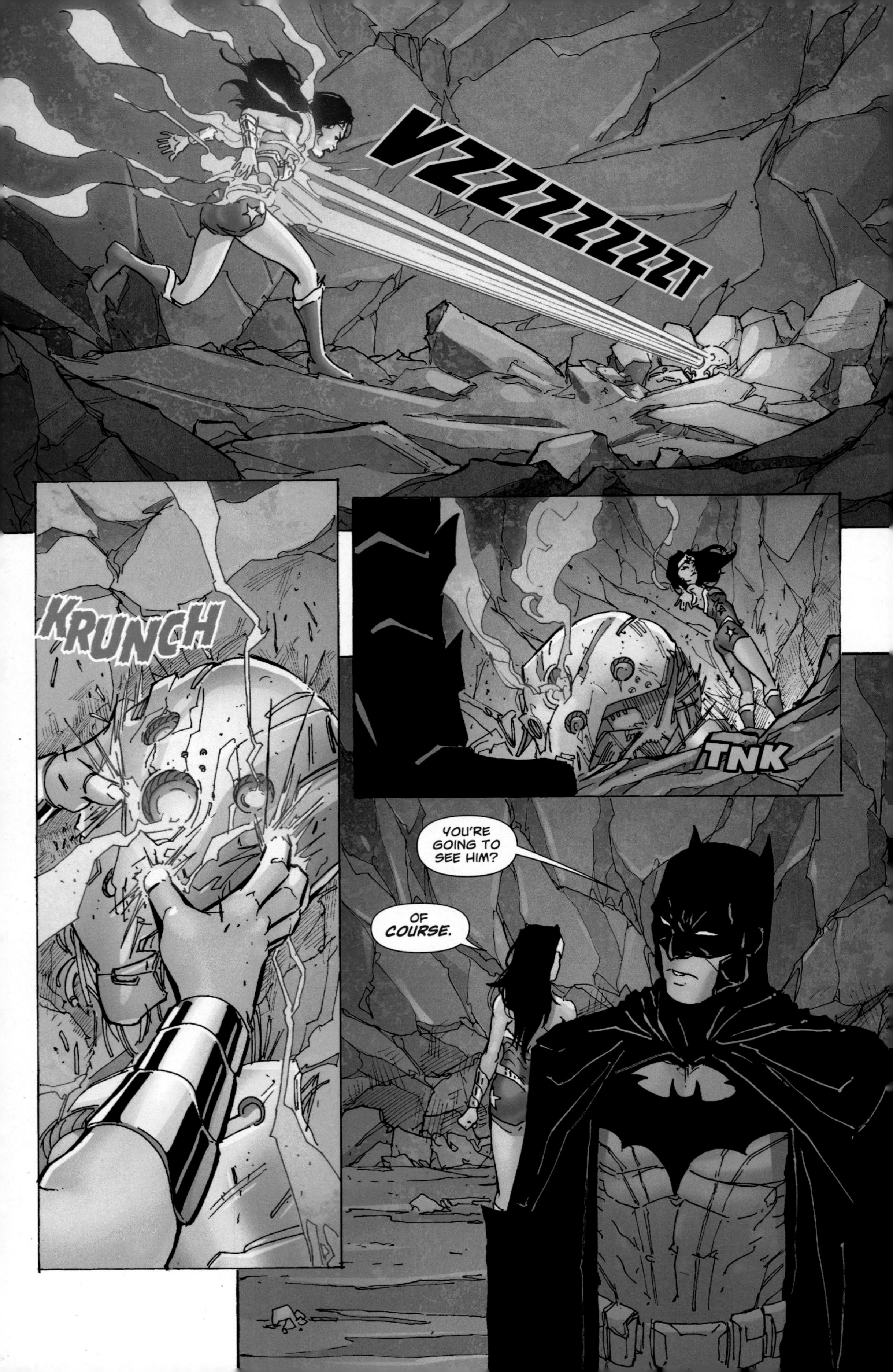
VZZZZZZZZT
KRUNCH
TNK
YOU'RE GOING TO SEE HIM?
OF COURSE.

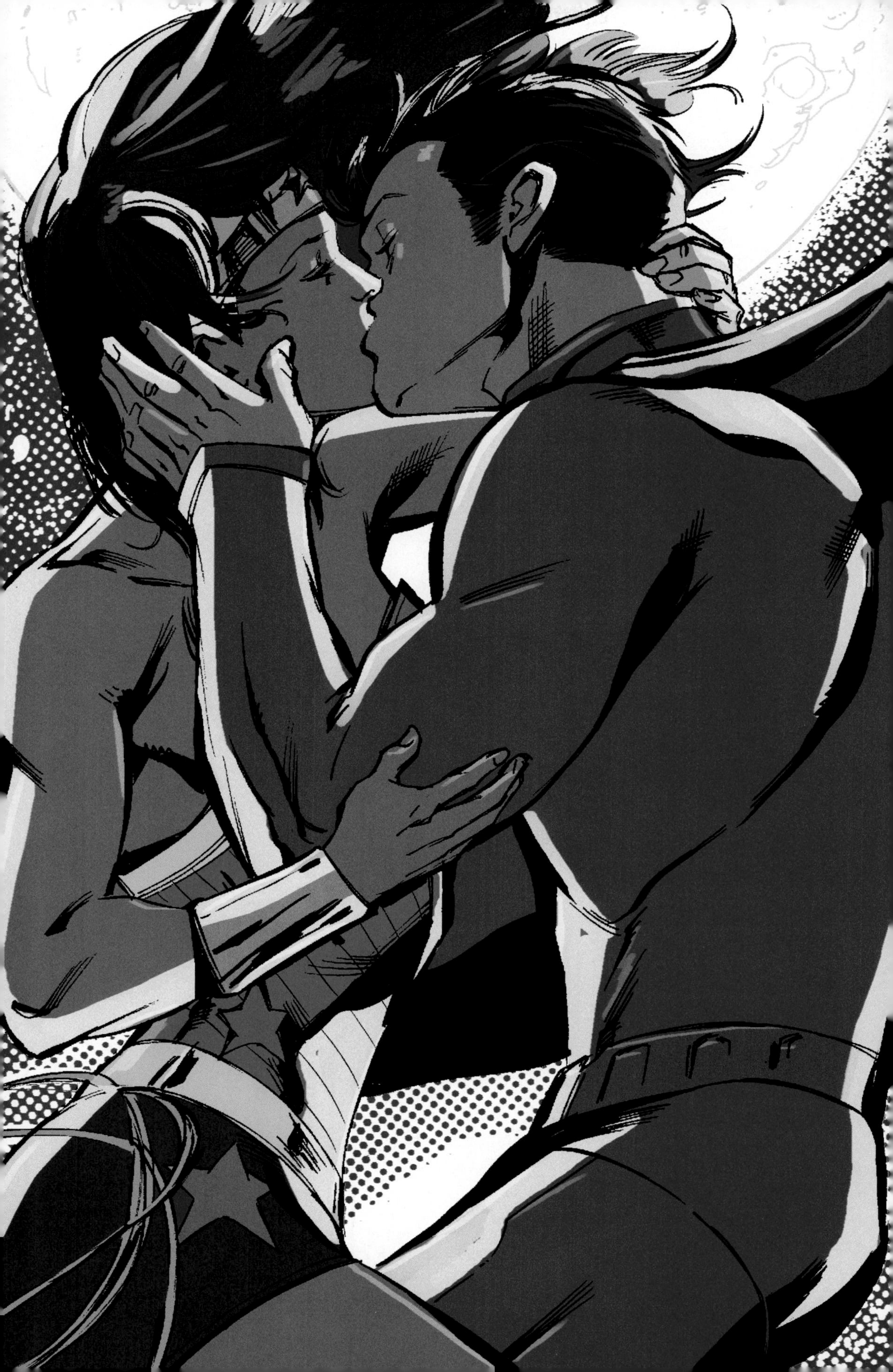

ACCEPTANCE

BRIAN BUCCELLATO writer GIUSEPPE CAFARO POP MHAN artists LEE LOUGHRIDGE colorist DAVID SHARPE letterer

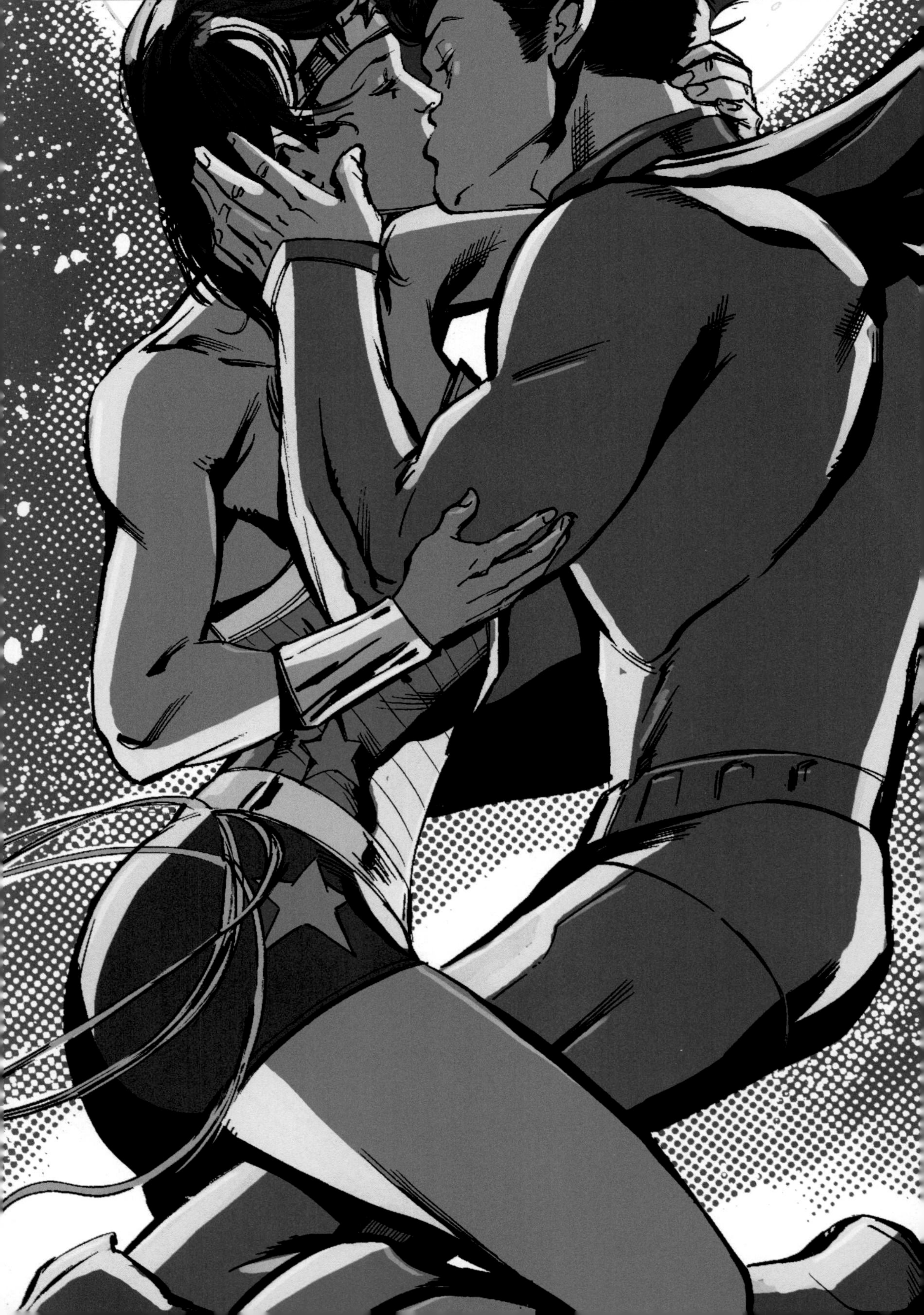

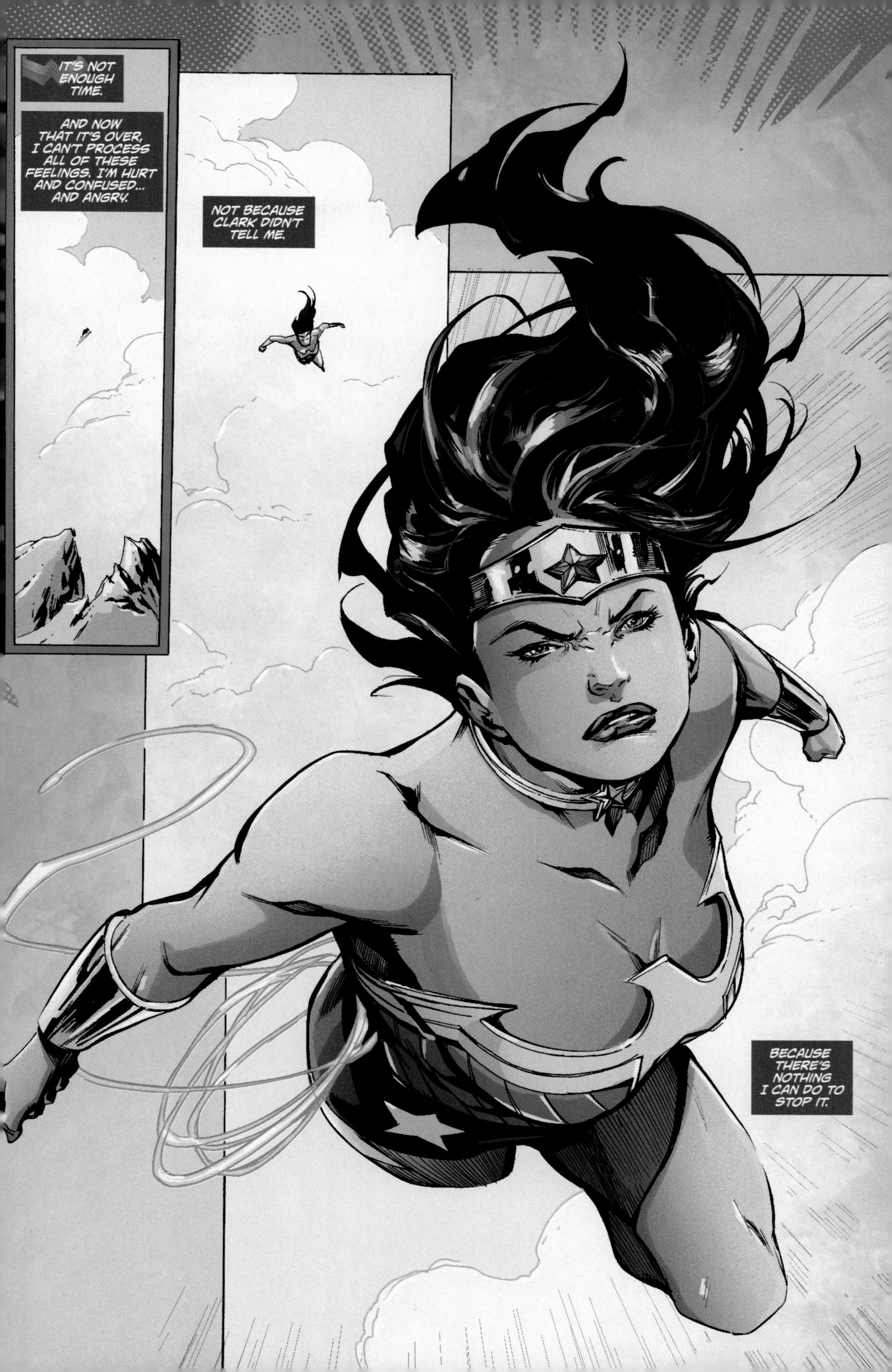
IT'S NOT ENOUGH TIME.
AND NOW THAT IT'S OVER, I CAN'T PROCESS ALL OF THESE FEELINGS. I'M HURT AND CONFUSED... AND ANGRY.
NOT BECAUSE CLARK DIDN'T TELL ME.
BECAUSE THERE'S NOTHING I CAN DO TO STOP IT.

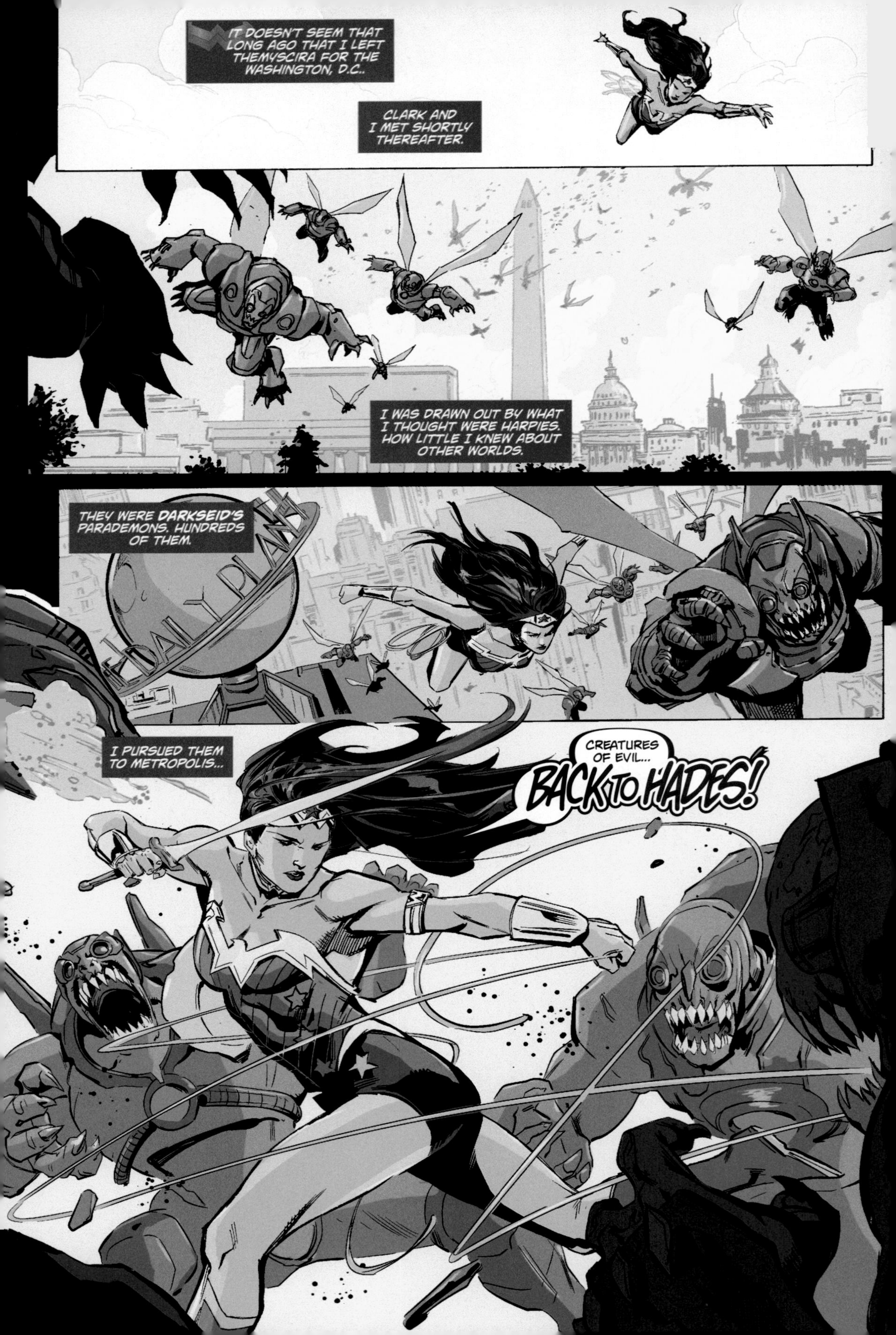

IT DOESN'T SEEM THAT LONG AGO THAT I LEFT THEMYSCIRA FOR THE WASHINGTON, D.C..
CLARK AND I MET SHORTLY THEREAFTER.
I WAS DRAWN OUT BY WHAT I THOUGHT WERE HARPIES. HOW LITTLE I KNEW ABOUT OTHER WORLDS.
THEY WERE DARKSEID'S PARADEMONS. HUNDREDS OF THEM.
DAILY PLANET
I PURSUED THEM TO METROPOLIS...
CREATURES OF EVIL...
BACK TO HADES!

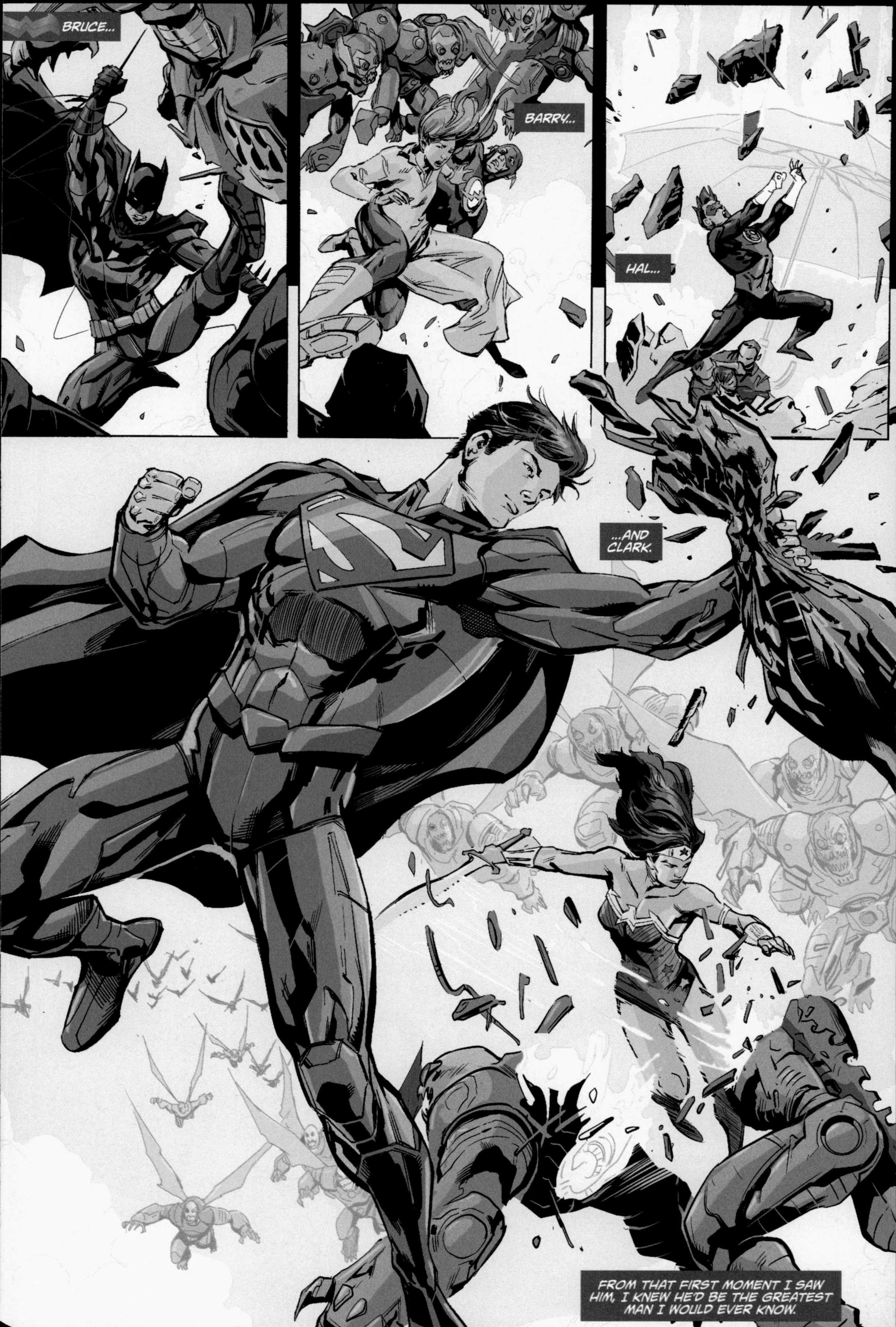
BRUCE...
BARRY...
HAL...
...AND CLARK.
FROM THAT FIRST MOMENT I SAW HIM, I KNEW HE'D BE THE GREATEST MAN I WOULD EVER KNOW.

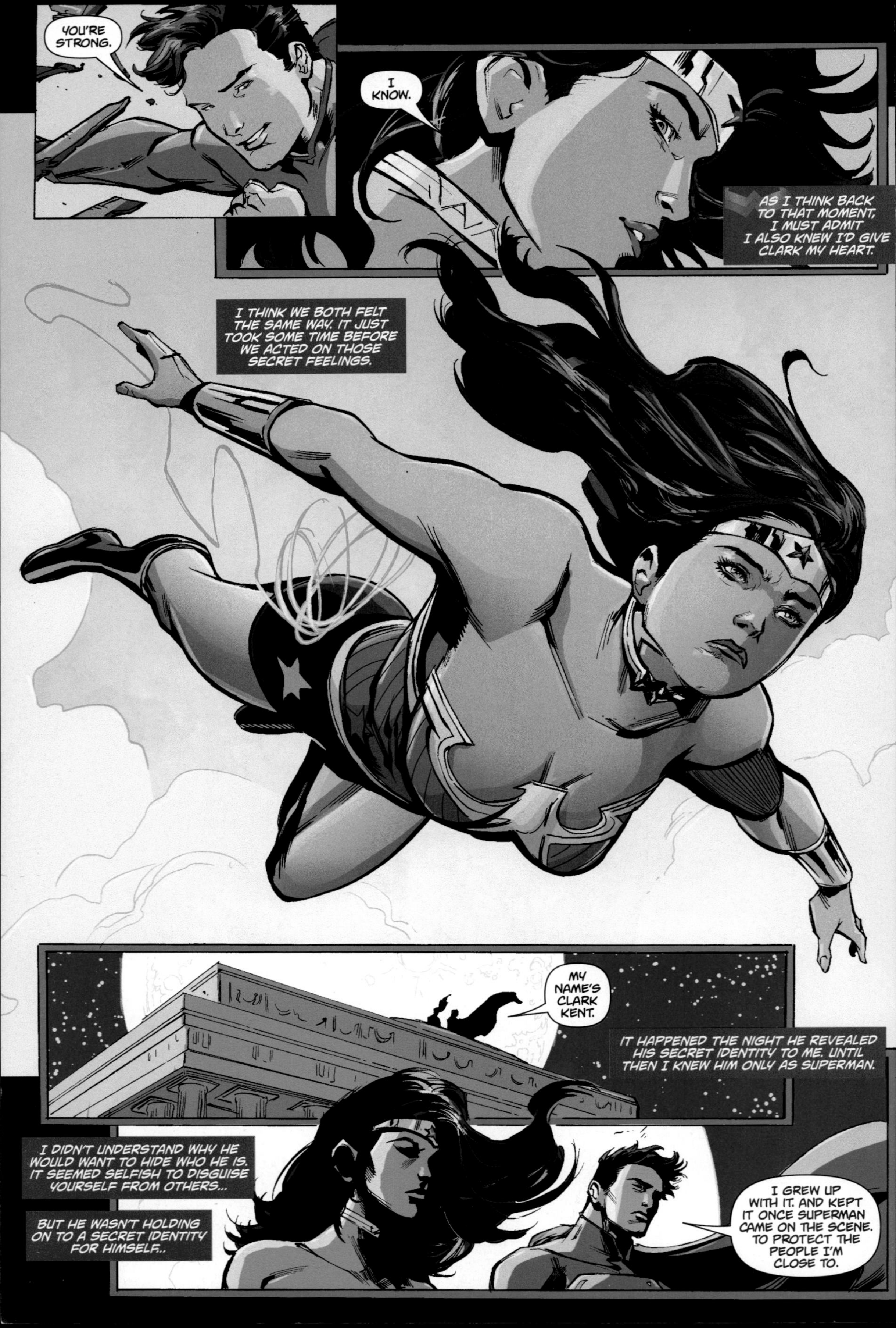
YOU'RE STRONG.
I KNOW.
AS I THINK BACK TO THAT MOMENT, I MUST ADMIT I ALSO KNEW I'D GIVE CLARK MY HEART.
I THINK WE BOTH FELT THE SAME WAY. IT JUST TOOK SOME TIME BEFORE WE ACTED ON THOSE SECRET FEELINGS.
MY NAME'S CLARK KENT.
IT HAPPENED THE NIGHT HE REVEALED HIS SECRET IDENTITY TO ME. UNTIL THEN I KNEW HIM ONLY AS SUPERMAN.
I DIDN'T UNDERSTAND WHY HE WOULD WANT TO HIDE WHO HE IS. IT SEEMED SELFISH TO DISGUISE YOURSELF FROM OTHERS...
BUT HE WASN'T HOLDING ON TO A SECRET IDENTITY FOR HIMSELF...
I GREW UP WITH IT. AND KEPT IT ONCE SUPERMAN CAME ON THE SCENE. TO PROTECT THE PEOPLE I'M CLOSE TO.

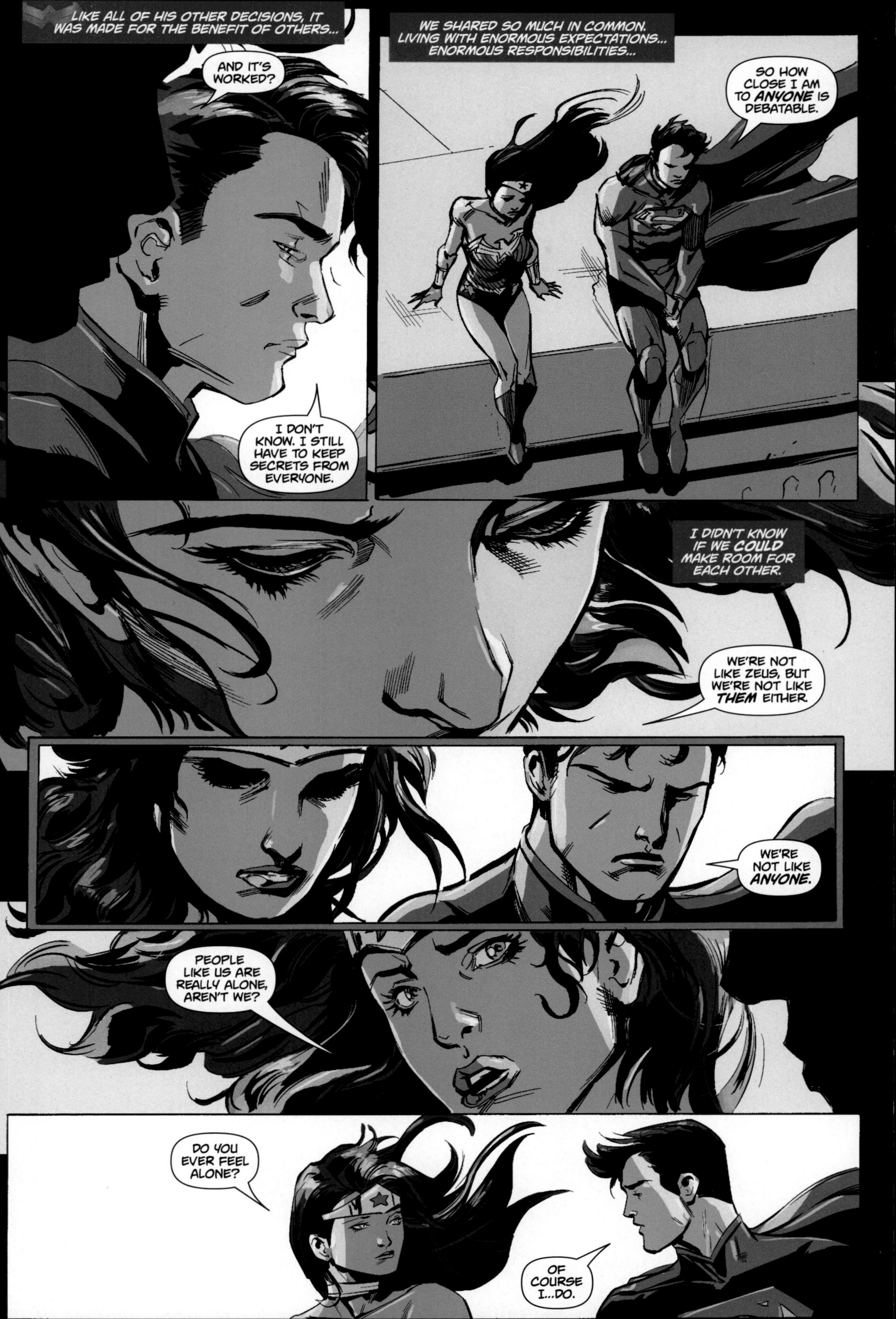
LIKE ALL OF HIS OTHER DECISIONS, IT WAS MADE FOR THE BENEFIT OF OTHERS...
AND IT'S WORKED?
I DON'T KNOW. I STILL HAVE TO KEEP SECRETS FROM EVERYONE.
WE SHARED SO MUCH IN COMMON. LIVING WITH ENORMOUS EXPECTATIONS... ENORMOUS RESPONSIBILITIES...
SO HOW CLOSE I AM TO ANYONE IS DEBATABLE.
I DIDN'T KNOW IF WE COULD MAKE ROOM FOR EACH OTHER.
WE'RE NOT LIKE ZEUS, BUT WE'RE NOT LIKE THEM EITHER.
WE'RE NOT LIKE ANYONE.
PEOPLE LIKE US ARE REALLY ALONE, AREN'T WE?
DO YOU EVER FEEL ALONE?
OF COURSE I...DO.

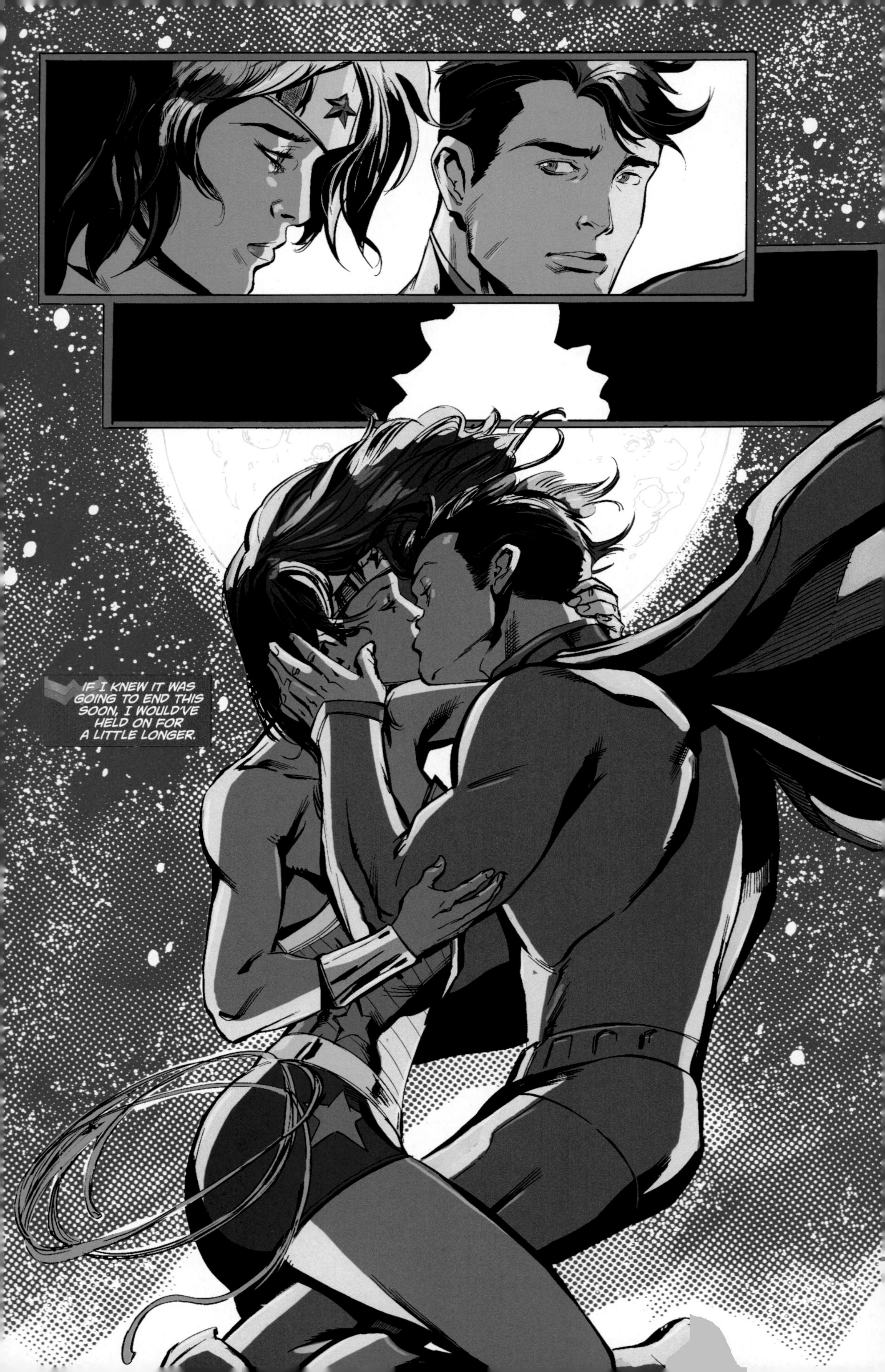
IF I KNEW IT WAS GOING TO END THIS SOON, I WOULD'VE HELD ON FOR A LITTLE LONGER.

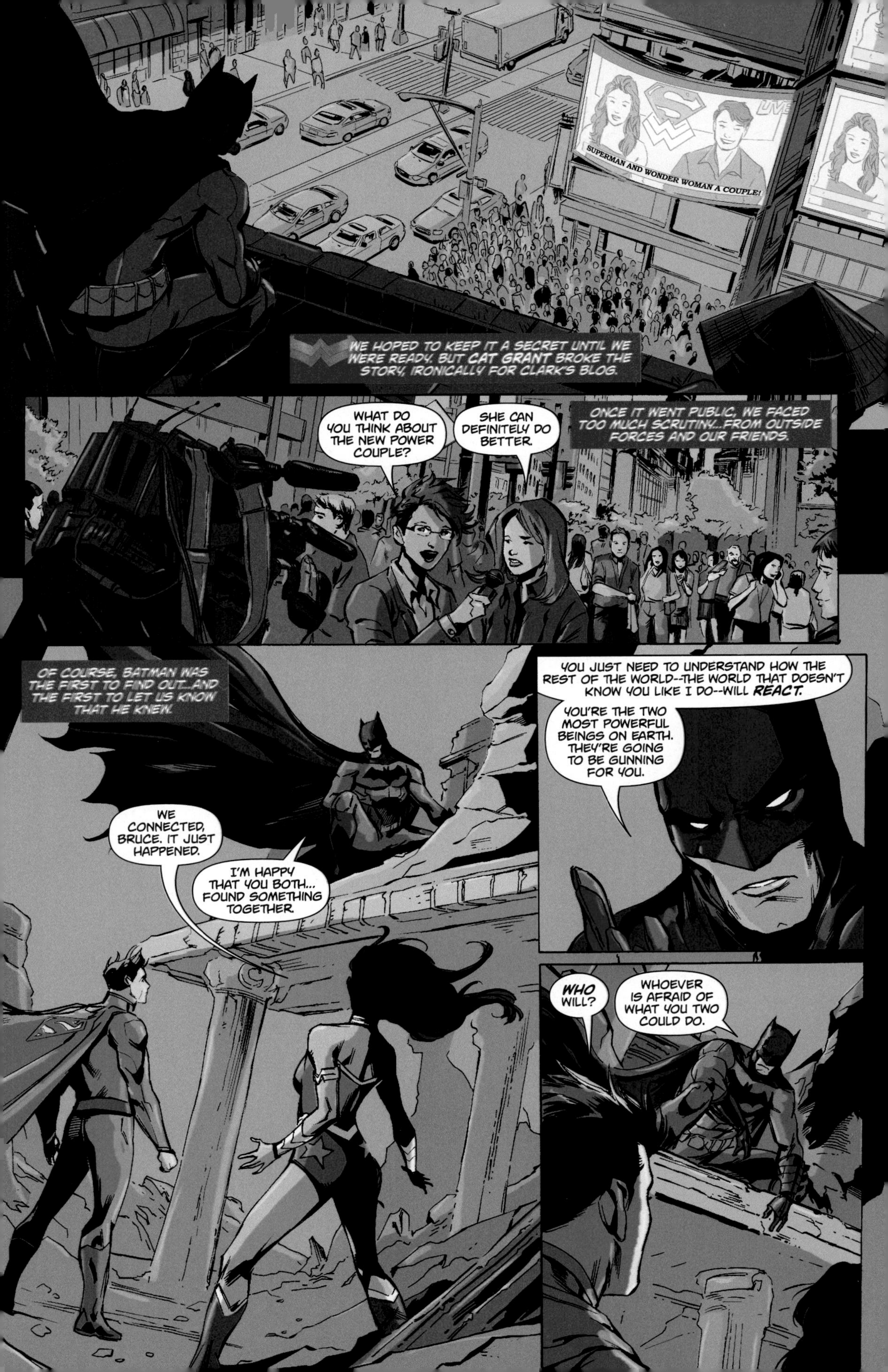
SUPERMAN AND WONDER WOMAN A COUPLE!
LIVE
WE HOPED TO KEEP IT A SECRET UNTIL WE WERE READY. BUT CAT GRANT BROKE THE STORY, IRONICALLY FOR CLARK'S BLOG.
WHAT DO YOU THINK ABOUT THE NEW POWER COUPLE?
SHE CAN DEFINITELY DO BETTER.
ONCE IT WENT PUBLIC, WE FACED TOO MUCH SCRUTINY...FROM OUTSIDE FORCES AND OUR FRIENDS.
OF COURSE, BATMAN WAS THE FIRST TO FIND OUT...AND THE FIRST TO LET US KNOW THAT HE KNEW.
WE CONNECTED, BRUCE. IT JUST HAPPENED.
I'M HAPPY THAT YOU BOTH... FOUND SOMETHING TOGETHER.
YOU JUST NEED TO UNDERSTAND HOW THE REST OF THE WORLD--THE WORLD THAT DOESN'T KNOW YOU LIKE I DO--WILL REACT.
YOU'RE THE TWO MOST POWERFUL BEINGS ON EARTH. THEY'RE GOING TO BE GUNNING FOR YOU.
WHO WILL?
WHOEVER IS AFRAID OF WHAT YOU TWO COULD DO.

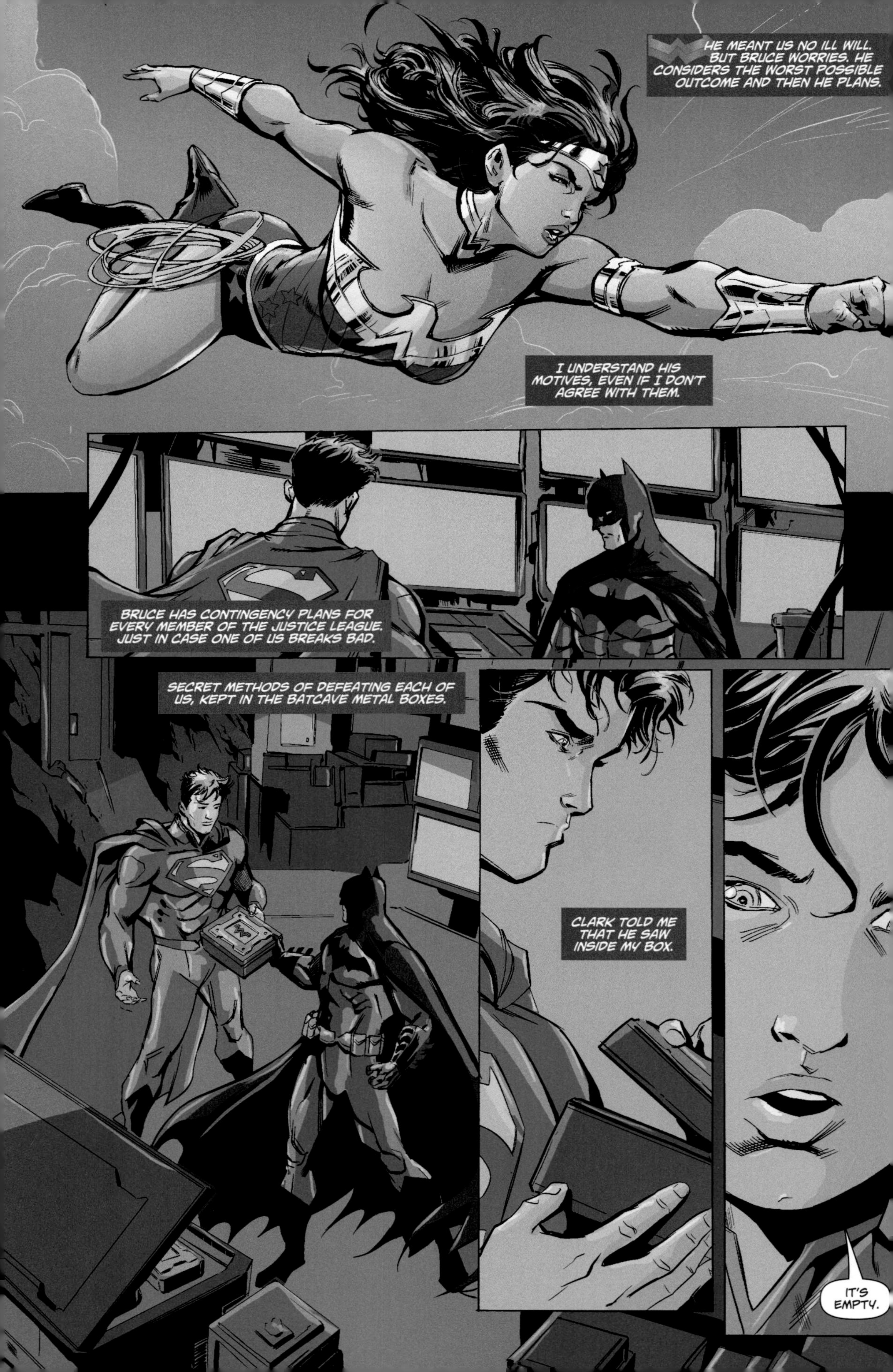
HE MEANT US NO ILL WILL. BUT BRUCE WORRIES. HE CONSIDERS THE WORST POSSIBLE OUTCOME AND THEN HE PLANS.
I UNDERSTAND HIS MOTIVES, EVEN IF I DON'T AGREE WITH THEM.
BRUCE HAS CONTINGENCY PLANS FOR EVERY MEMBER OF THE JUSTICE LEAGUE. JUST IN CASE ONE OF US BREAKS BAD.
SECRET METHODS OF DEFEATING EACH OF US, KEPT IN THE BATCAVE METAL BOXES.
CLARK TOLD ME THAT HE SAW INSIDE MY BOX.
IT'S EMPTY.

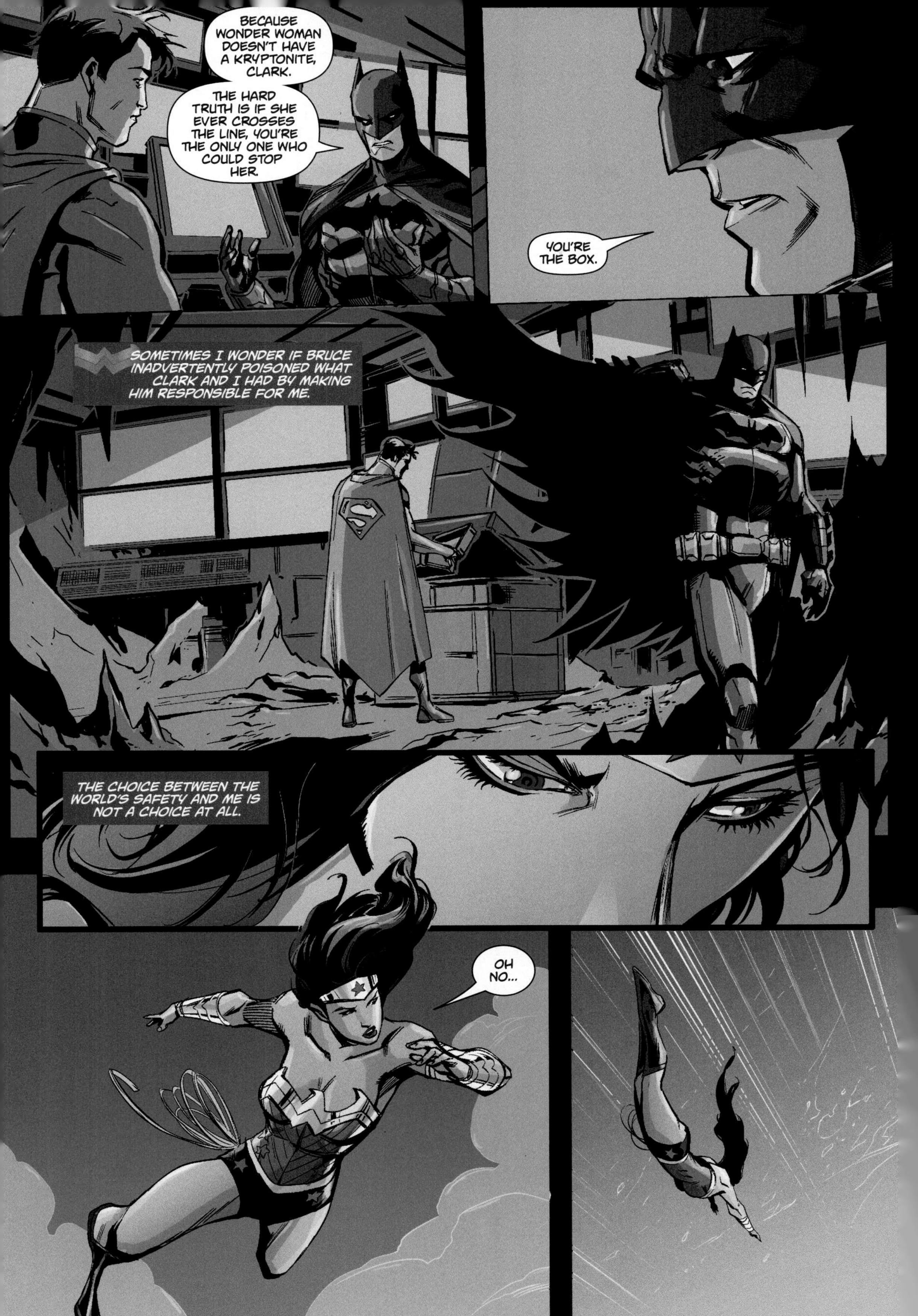
BECAUSE WONDER WOMAN DOESN'T HAVE A KRYPTONITE, CLARK.
THE HARD TRUTH IS IF SHE EVER CROSSES THE LINE, YOU'RE THE ONLY ONE WHO COULD STOP HER.
YOU'RE THE BOX.
SOMETIMES I WONDER IF BRUCE INADVERTENTLY POISONED WHAT CLARK AND I HAD BY MAKING HIM RESPONSIBLE FOR ME.
THE CHOICE BETWEEN THE WORLD'S SAFETY AND ME IS NOT A CHOICE AT ALL.
OH NO...

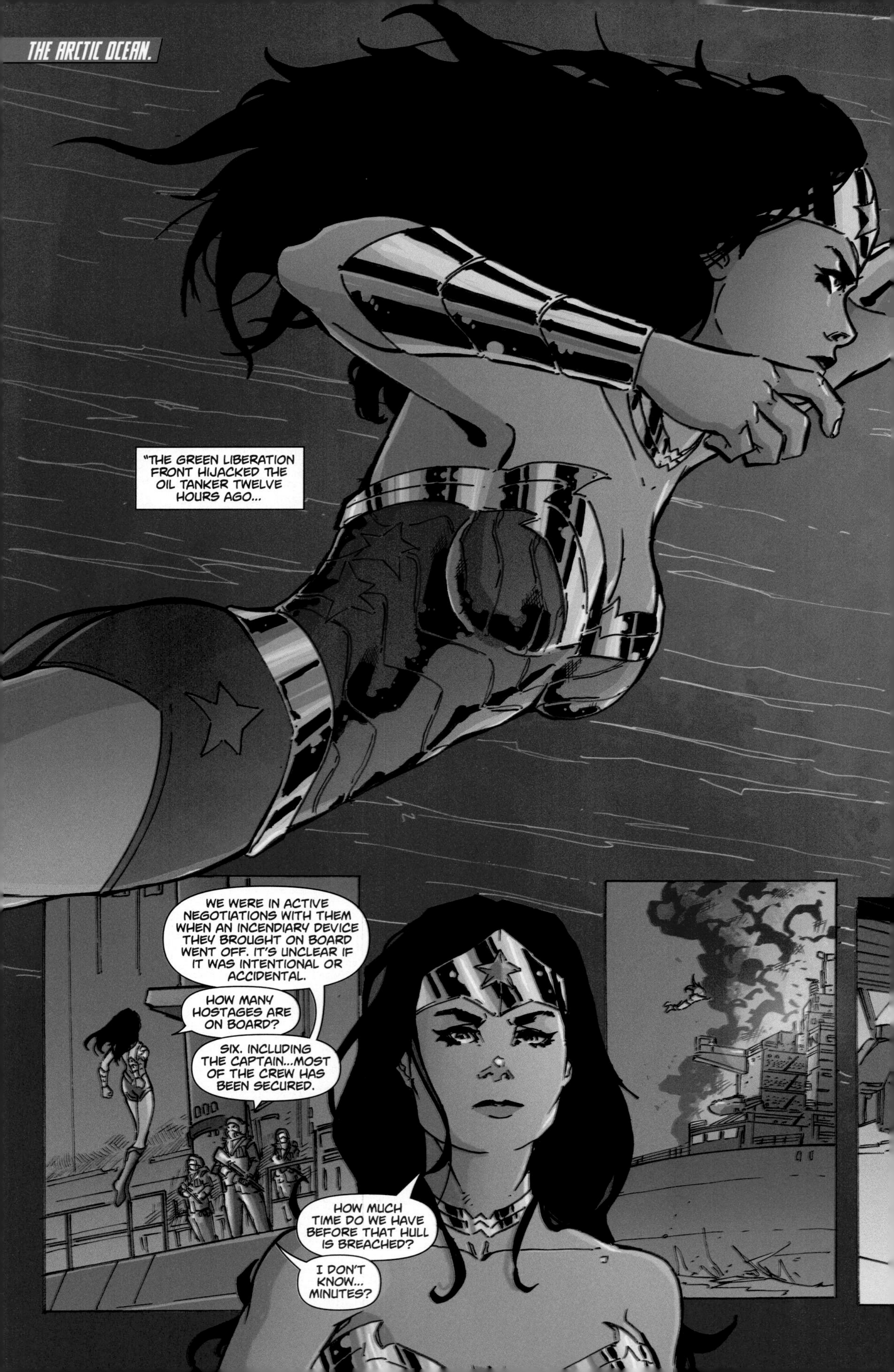
THE ARCTIC OCEAN.
"THE GREEN LIBERATION FRONT HIJACKED THE OIL TANKER TWELVE HOURS AGO...
WE WERE IN ACTIVE NEGOTIATIONS WITH THEM WHEN AN INCENDIARY DEVICE THEY BROUGHT ON BOARD WENT OFF. IT'S UNCLEAR IF IT WAS INTENTIONAL OR ACCIDENTAL.
HOW MANY HOSTAGES ARE ON BOARD?
SIX. INCLUDING THE CAPTAIN...MOST OF THE CREW HAS BEEN SECURED.
HOW MUCH TIME DO WE HAVE BEFORE THAT HULL IS BREACHED?
I DON'T KNOW... MINUTES?

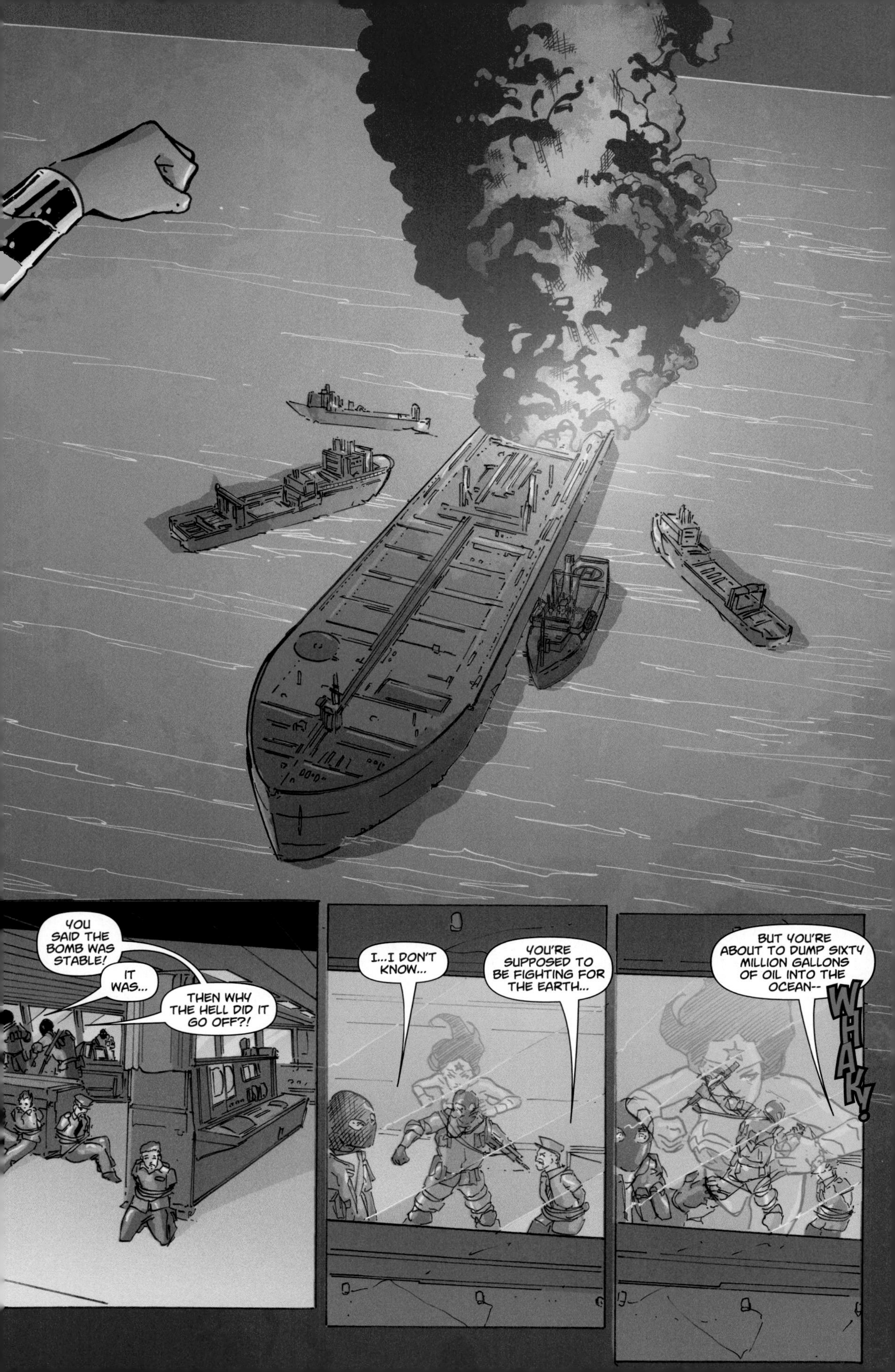
YOU SAID THE BOMB WAS STABLE!
IT WAS...
THEN WHY THE HELL DID IT GO OFF?!
I...I DON'T KNOW...
YOU'RE SUPPOSED TO BE FIGHTING FOR THE EARTH...
BUT YOU'RE ABOUT TO DUMP SIXTY MILLION GALLONS OF OIL INTO THE OCEAN--
WHAK!

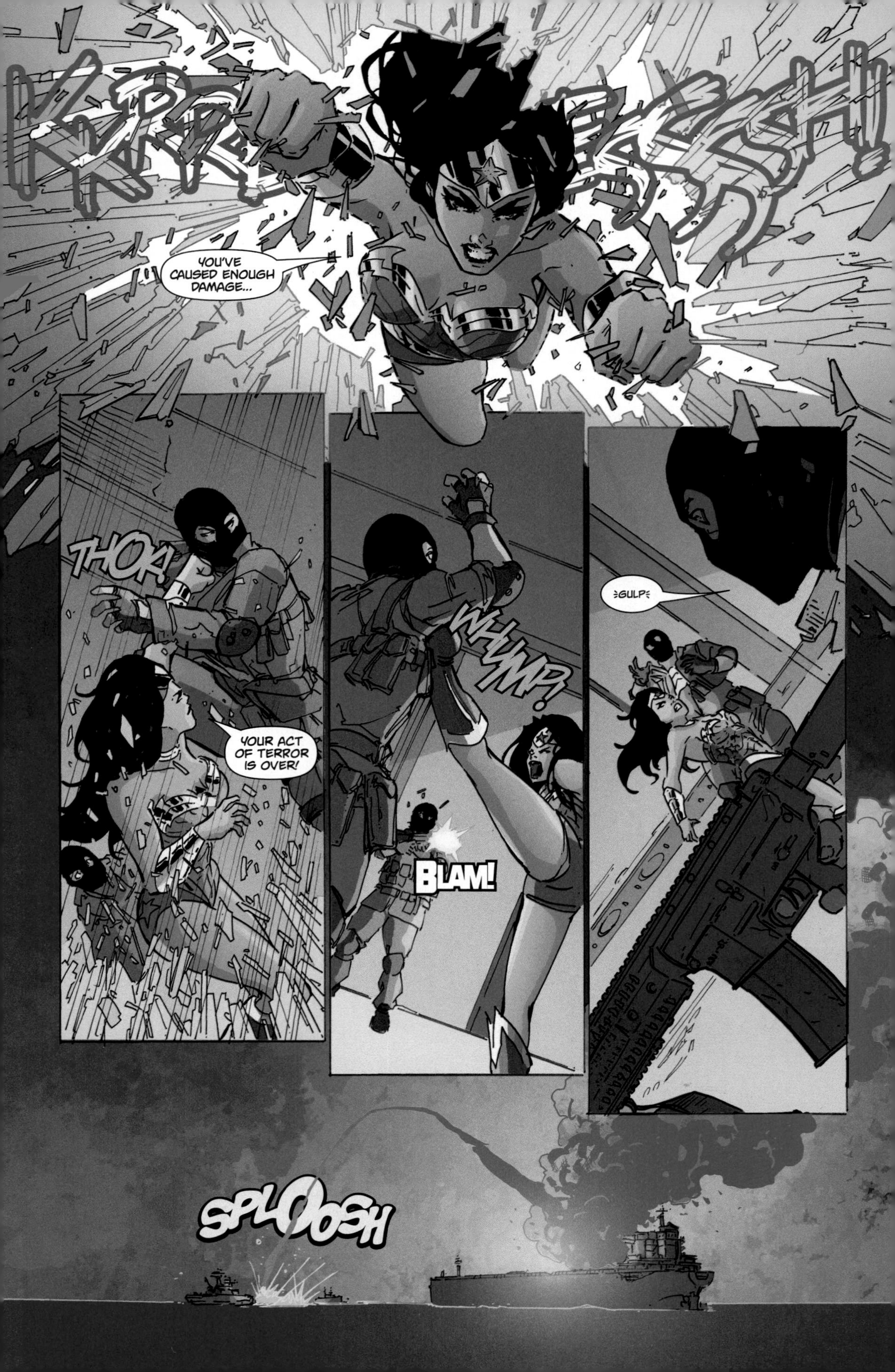
YOU'VE CAUSED ENOUGH DAMAGE...
THOK!
YOUR ACT OF TERROR IS OVER!
WHUMP!
BLAM!
GULP
SPLOOSH

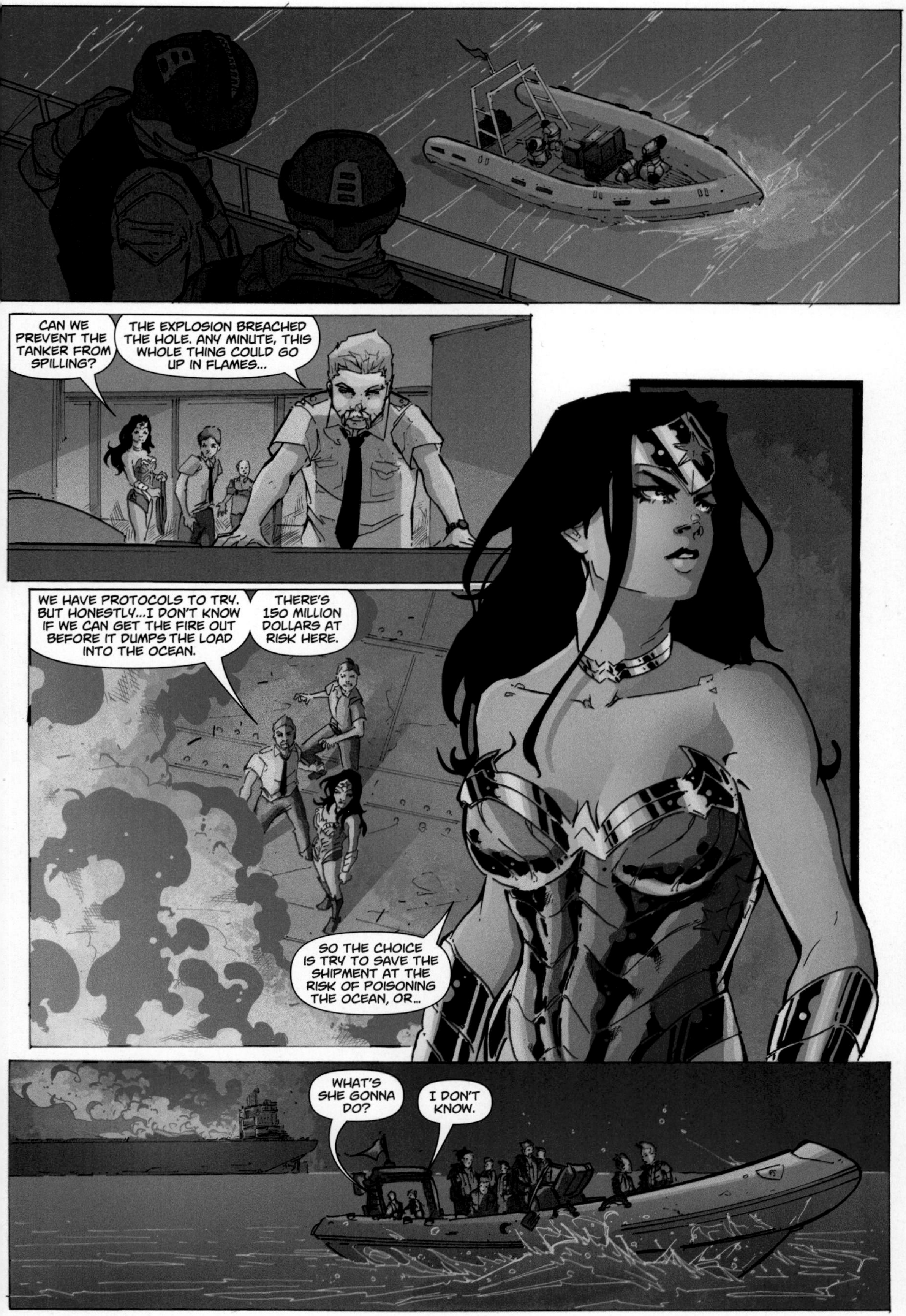
CAN WE PREVENT THE TANKER FROM SPILLING?
THE EXPLOSION BREACHED THE HOLE. ANY MINUTE, THIS WHOLE THING COULD GO UP IN FLAMES...
WE HAVE PROTOCOLS TO TRY. BUT HONESTLY...I DON'T KNOW IF WE CAN GET THE FIRE OUT BEFORE IT DUMPS THE LOAD INTO THE OCEAN.
THERE'S 150 MILLION DOLLARS AT RISK HERE.
SO THE CHOICE IS TRY TO SAVE THE SHIPMENT AT THE RISK OF POISONING THE OCEAN, OR...
WHAT'S SHE GONNA DO?
I DON'T KNOW.

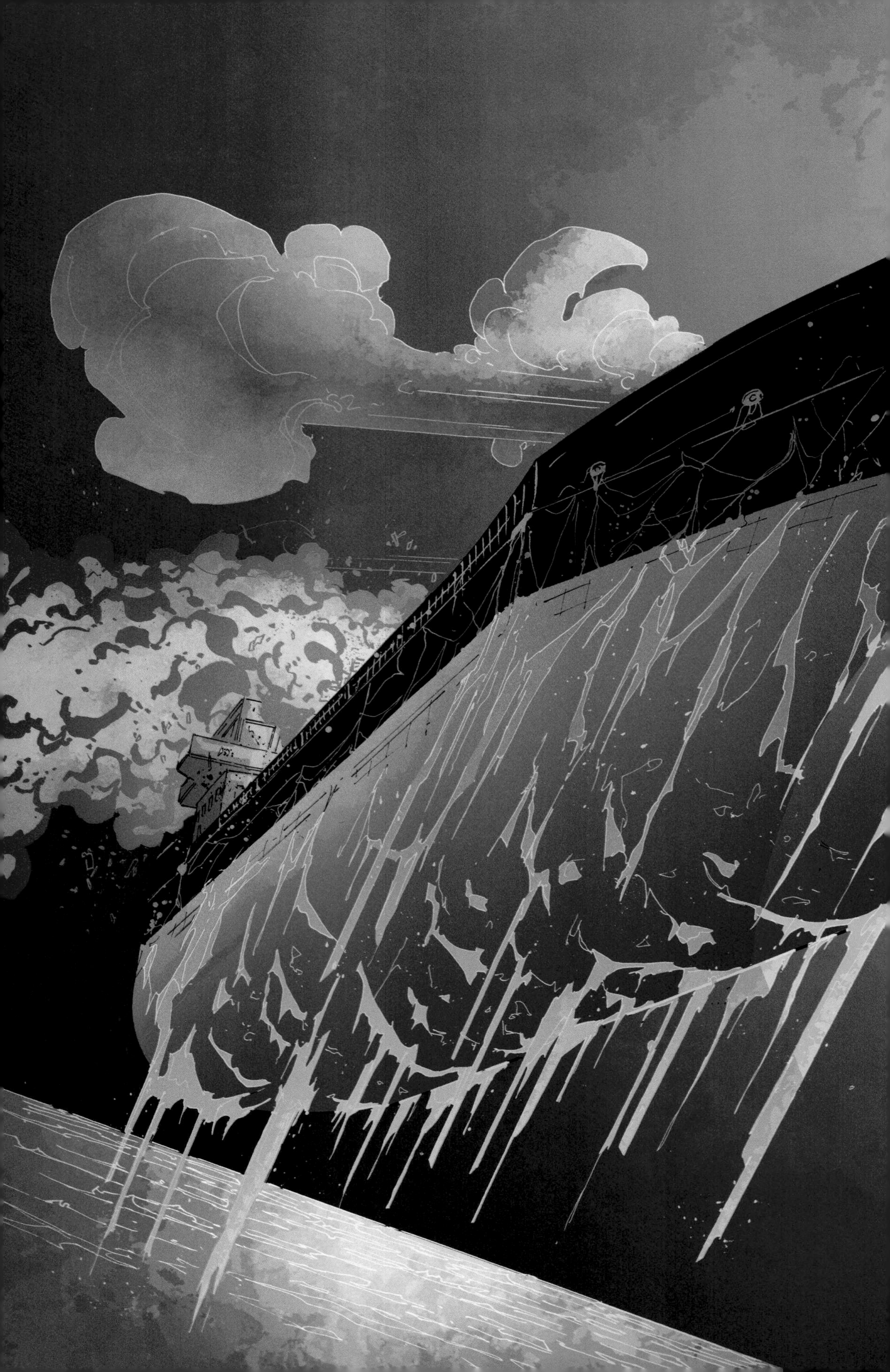

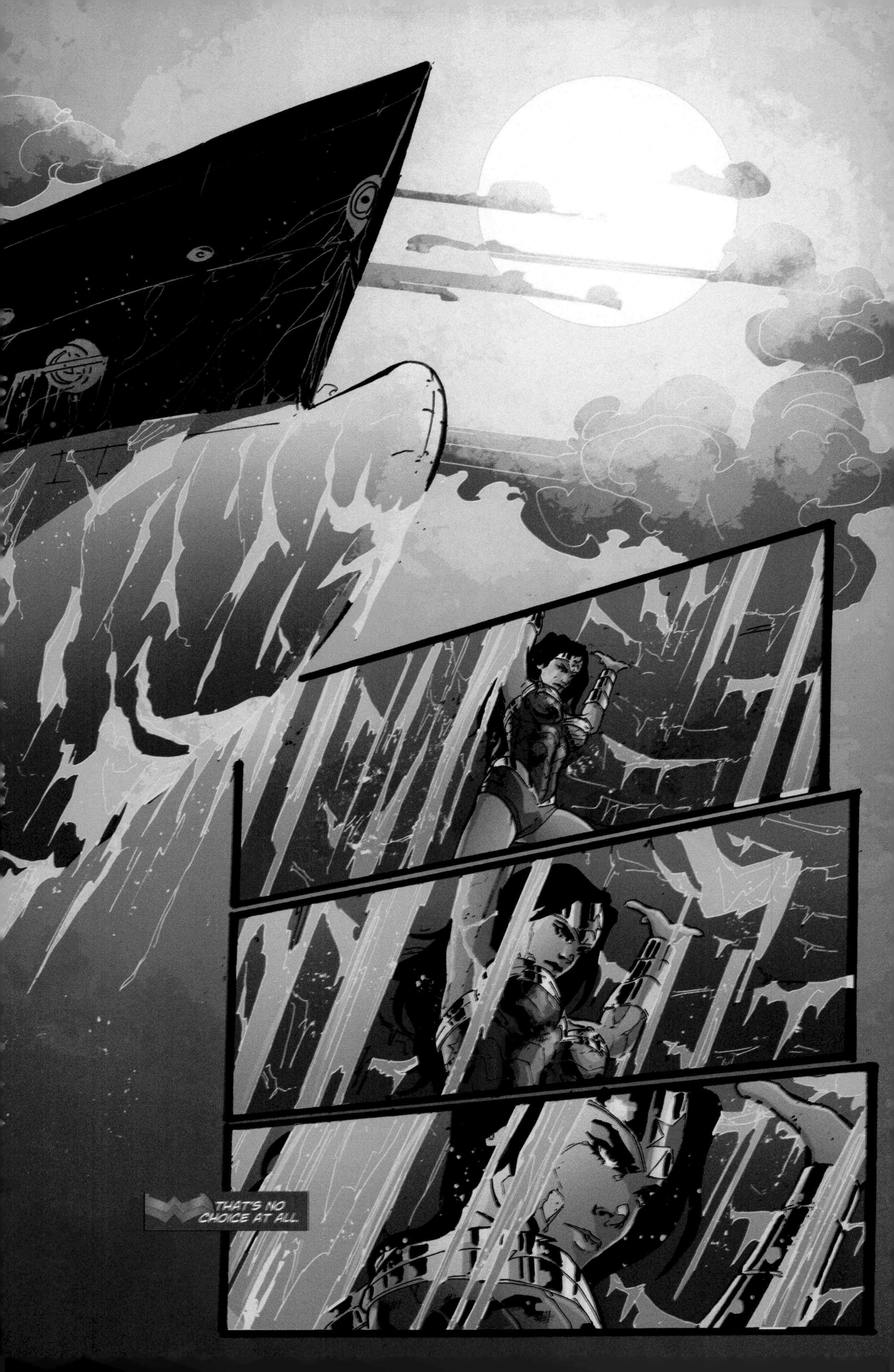
THAT'S NO CHOICE AT ALL.

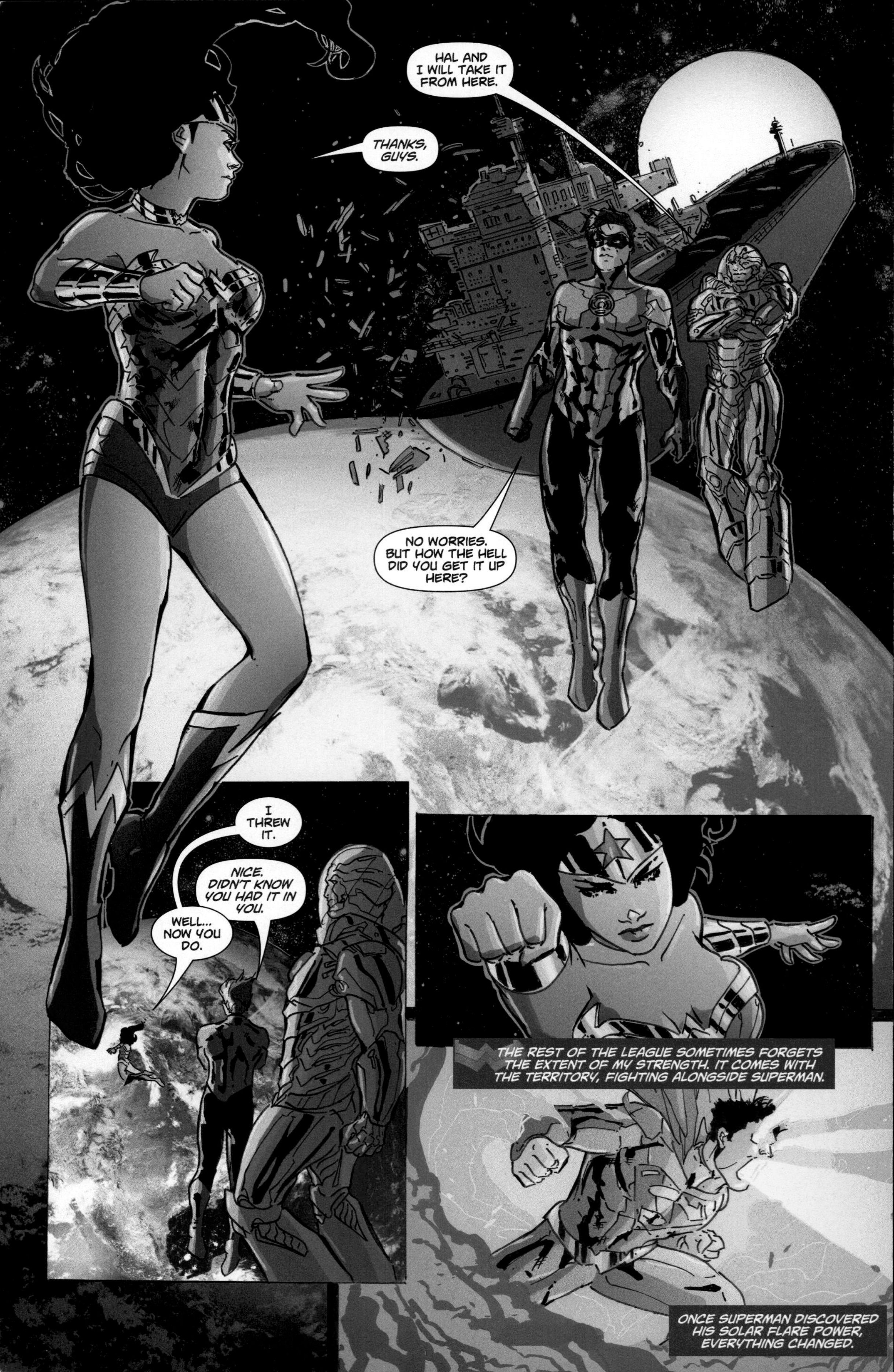
HAL AND I WILL TAKE IT FROM HERE.
THANKS, GUYS.
NO WORRIES. BUT HOW THE HELL DID YOU GET IT UP HERE?
I THREW IT.
NICE. DIDN'T KNOW YOU HAD IT IN YOU.
WELL... NOW YOU DO.
THE REST OF THE LEAGUE SOMETIMES FORGETS THE EXTENT OF MY STRENGTH. IT COMES WITH THE TERRITORY, FIGHTING ALONGSIDE SUPERMAN.
ONCE SUPERMAN DISCOVERED HIS SOLAR FLARE POWER, EVERYTHING CHANGED.

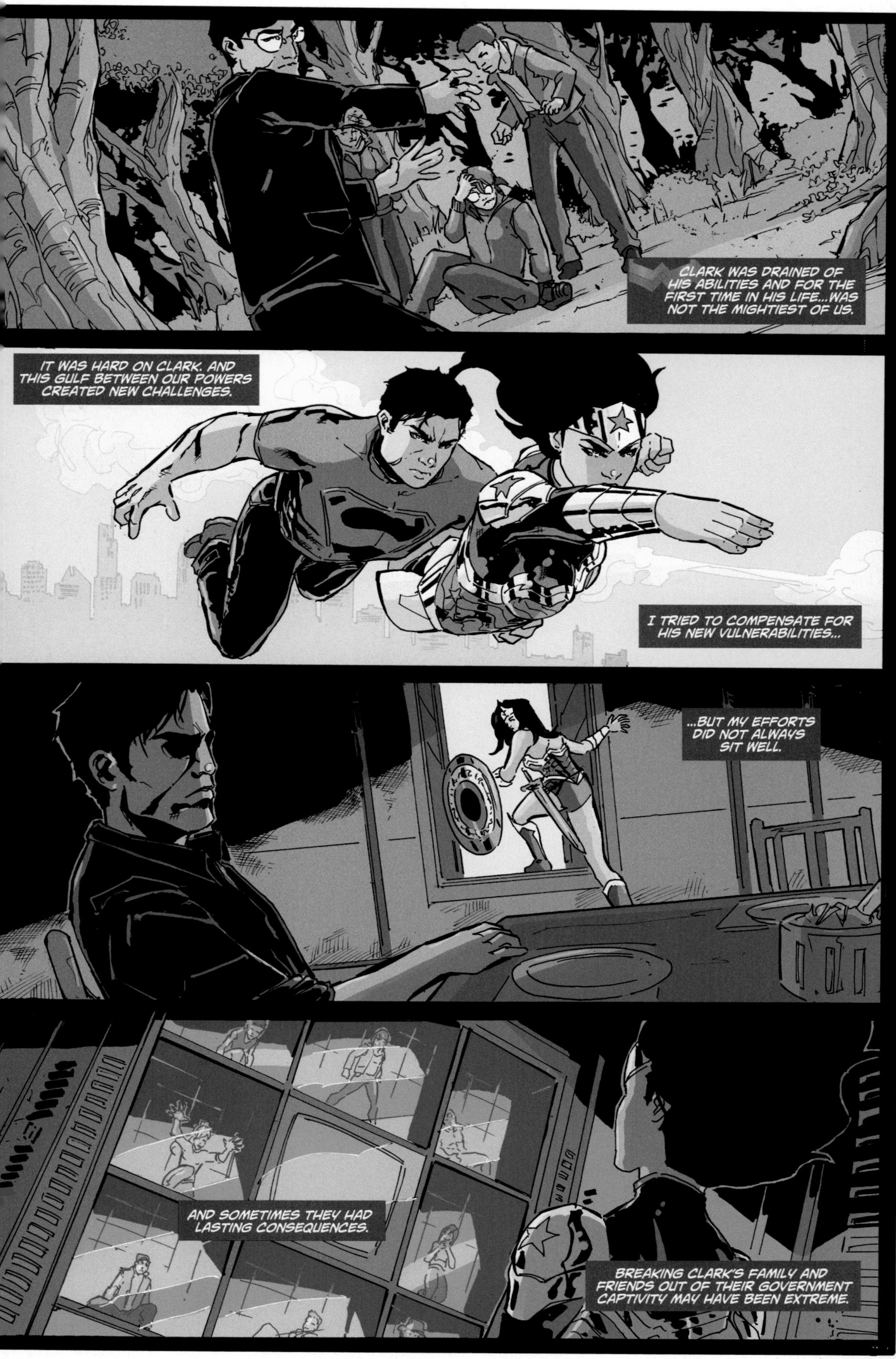
CLARK WAS DRAINED OF HIS ABILITIES AND FOR THE FIRST TIME IN HIS LIFE...WAS NOT THE MIGHTIEST OF US.
IT WAS HARD ON CLARK. AND THIS GULF BETWEEN OUR POWERS CREATED NEW CHALLENGES.
I TRIED TO COMPENSATE FOR HIS NEW VULNERABILITIES...
...BUT MY EFFORTS DID NOT ALWAYS SIT WELL.
AND SOMETIMES THEY HAD LASTING CONSEQUENCES.
BREAKING CLARK'S FAMILY AND FRIENDS OUT OF THEIR GOVERNMENT CAPTIVITY MAY HAVE BEEN EXTREME.

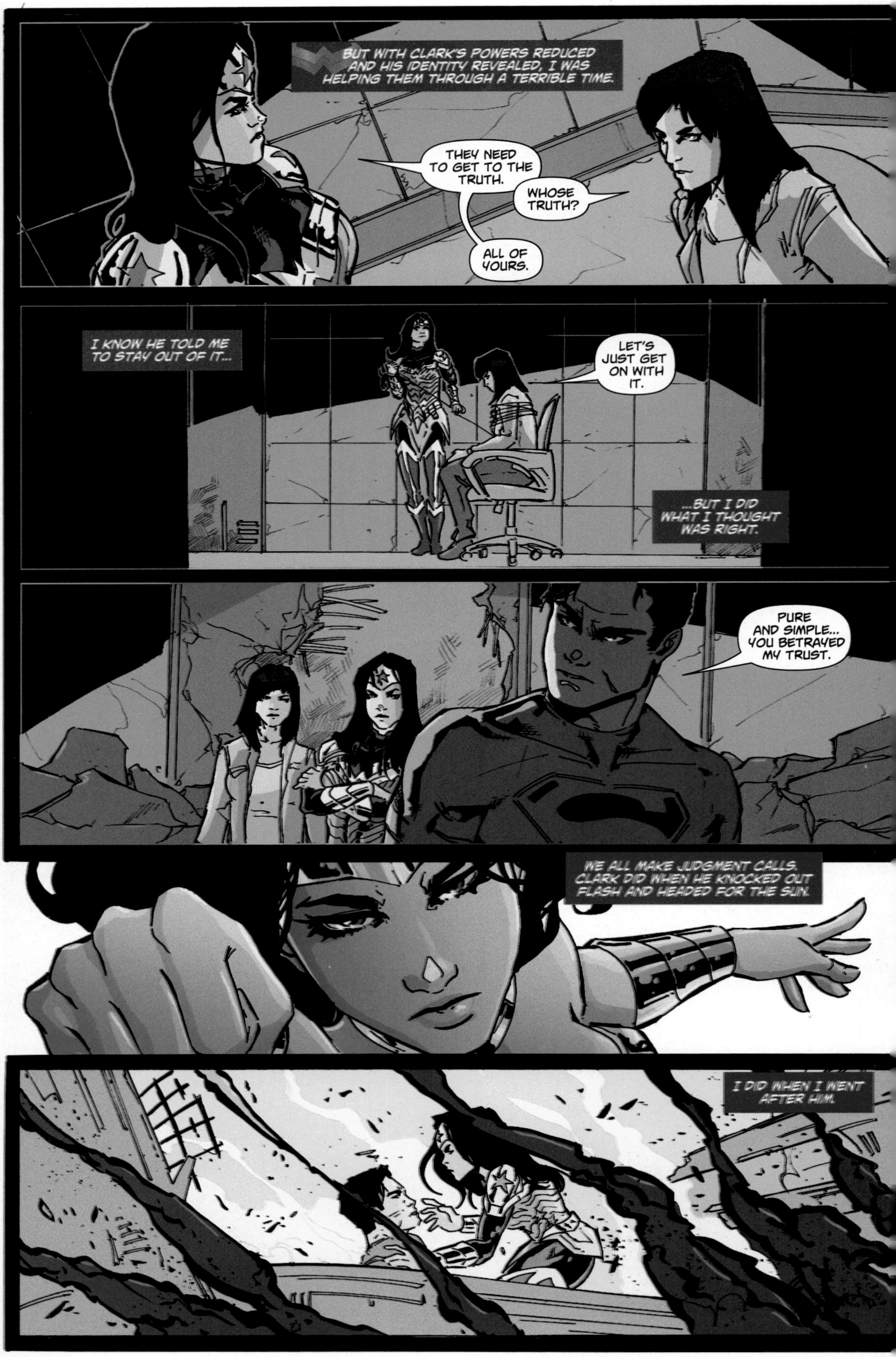
BUT WITH CLARK'S POWERS REDUCED AND HIS IDENTITY REVEALED, I WAS HELPING THEM THROUGH A TERRIBLE TIME.
THEY NEED TO GET TO THE TRUTH.
WHOSE TRUTH?
ALL OF YOURS.
I KNOW HE TOLD ME TO STAY OUT OF IT...
LET'S JUST GET ON WITH IT.
...BUT I DID WHAT I THOUGHT WAS RIGHT.
PURE AND SIMPLE... YOU BETRAYED MY TRUST.
WE ALL MAKE JUDGMENT CALLS. CLARK DID WHEN HE KNOCKED OUT FLASH AND HEADED FOR THE SUN.
I DID WHEN I WENT AFTER HIM.

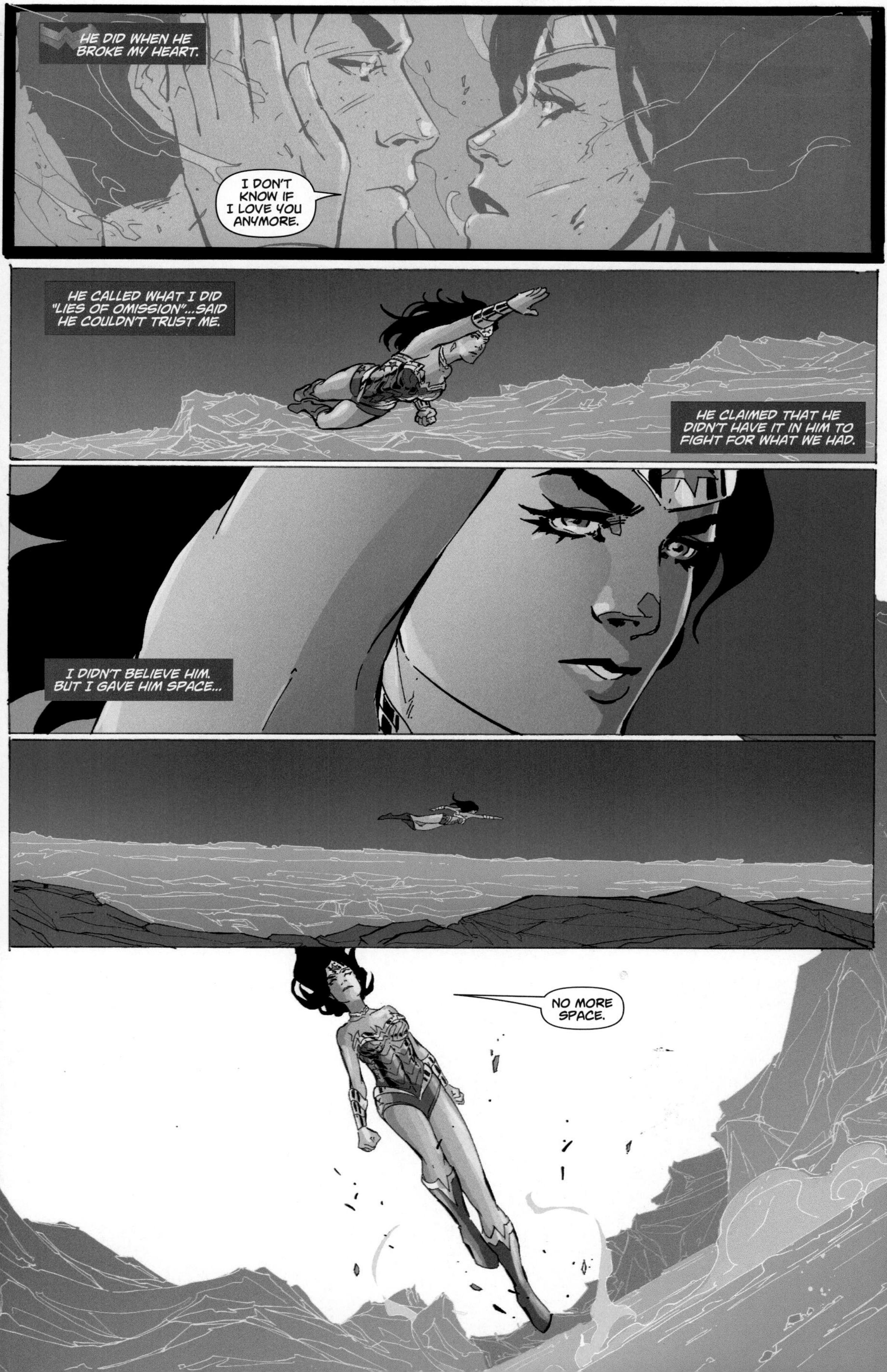
HE DID WHEN HE BROKE MY HEART.
I DON'T KNOW IF I LOVE YOU ANYMORE.
HE CALLED WHAT I DID "LIES OF OMISSION"...SAID HE COULDN'T TRUST ME.
HE CLAIMED THAT HE DIDN'T HAVE IT IN HIM TO FIGHT FOR WHAT WE HAD.
I DIDN'T BELIEVE HIM. BUT I GAVE HIM SPACE...
NO MORE SPACE.

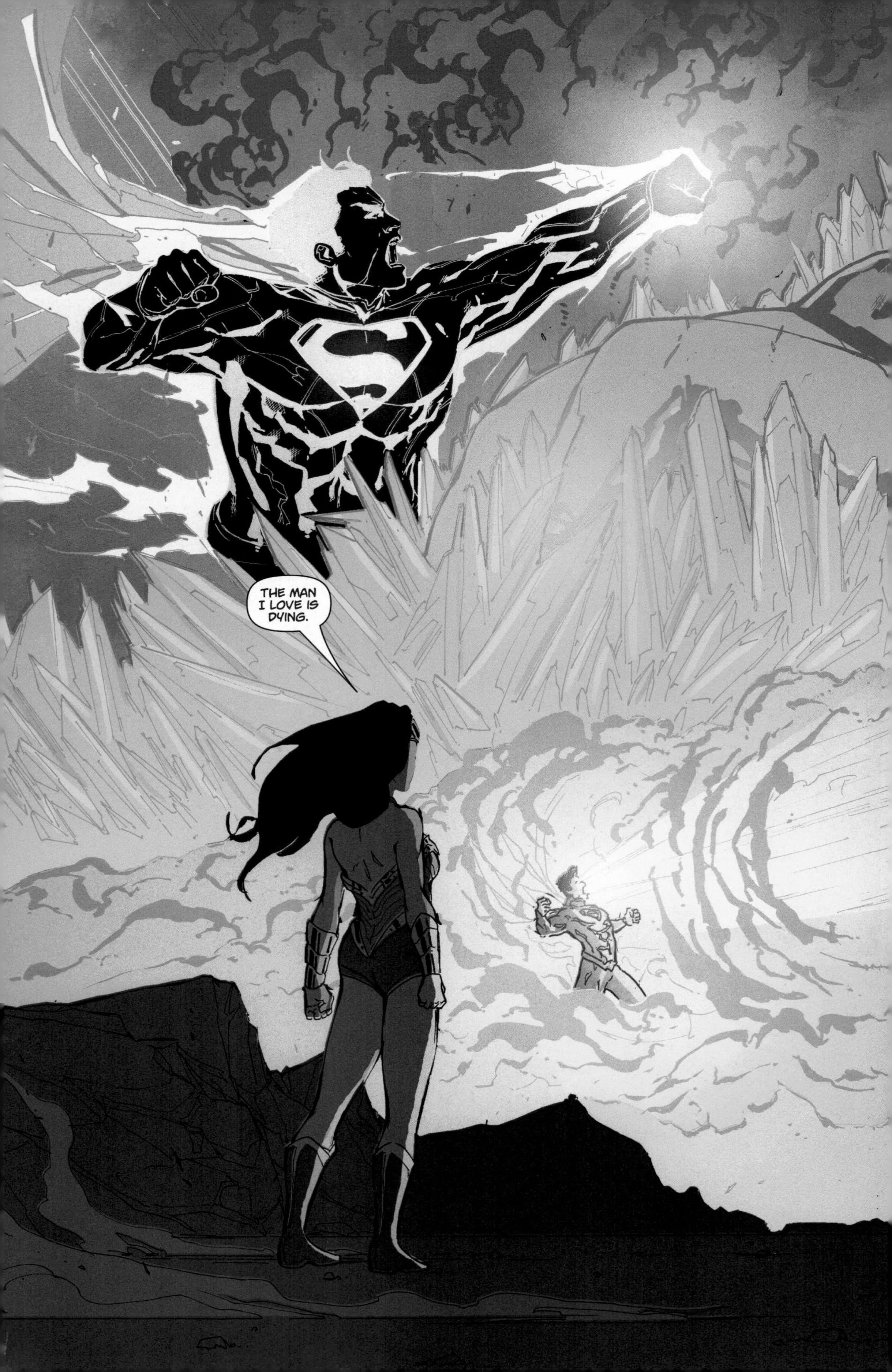
THE MAN I LOVE IS DYING.

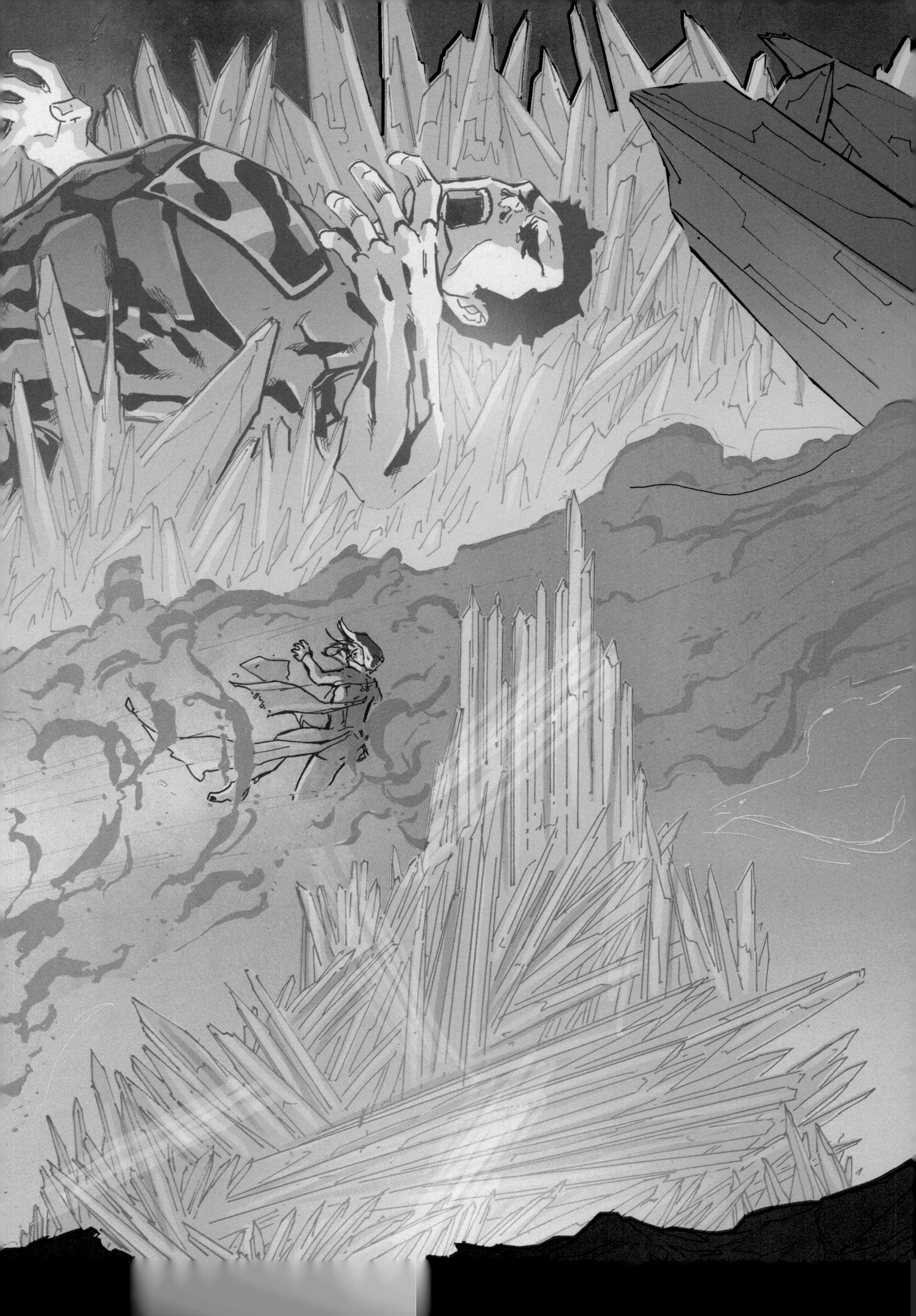

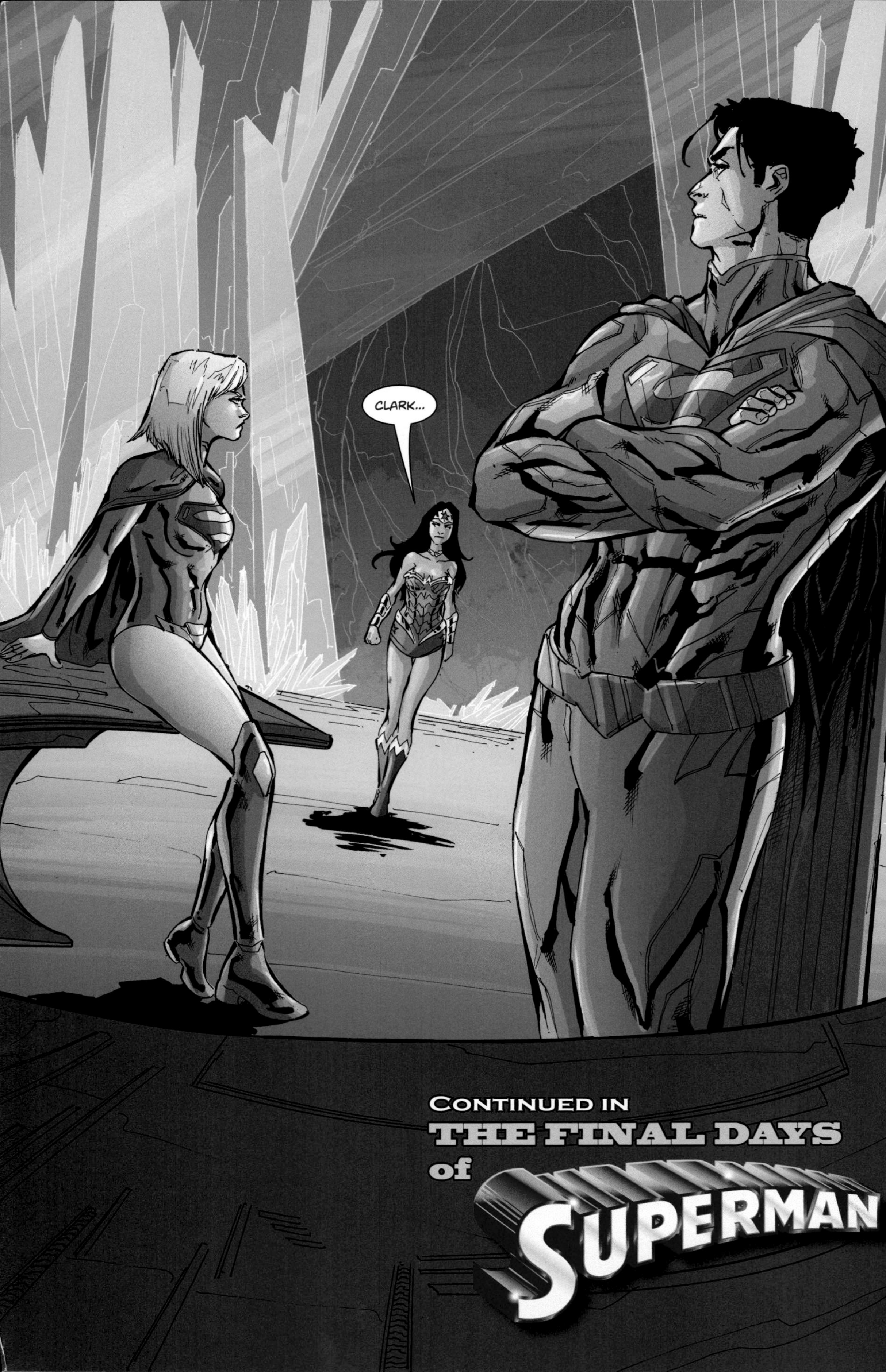
CLARK...
CONTINUED IN
THE FINAL DAYS
of
SUPERMAN

ART BY
DOUG MAHNKE
& JAIME MENDOZA

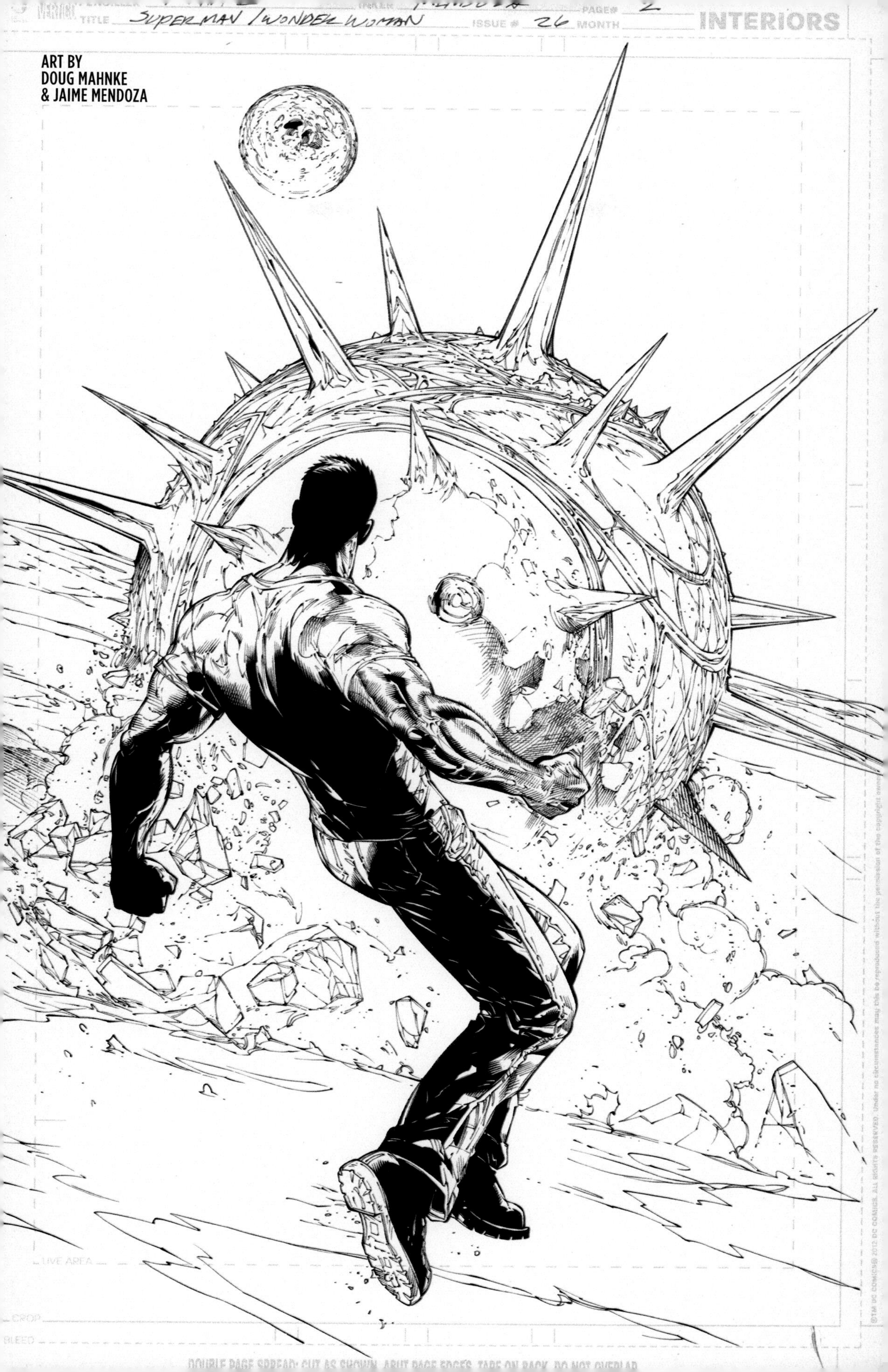
TITLE SUPERMAN / WONDER WOMAN
ISSUE # 26
PAGE# 2
INTERIORS
LIVE AREA
CROP
BLEED
DOUBLE PAGE SPREAD: CUT AS SHOWN, ABUT PAGE EDGES, TAPE ON BACK, DO NOT OVERLAP

PENCILLER INKER PAGE# INTERIORS
TITLE Superman Annual ISSUE # 2016 MONTH

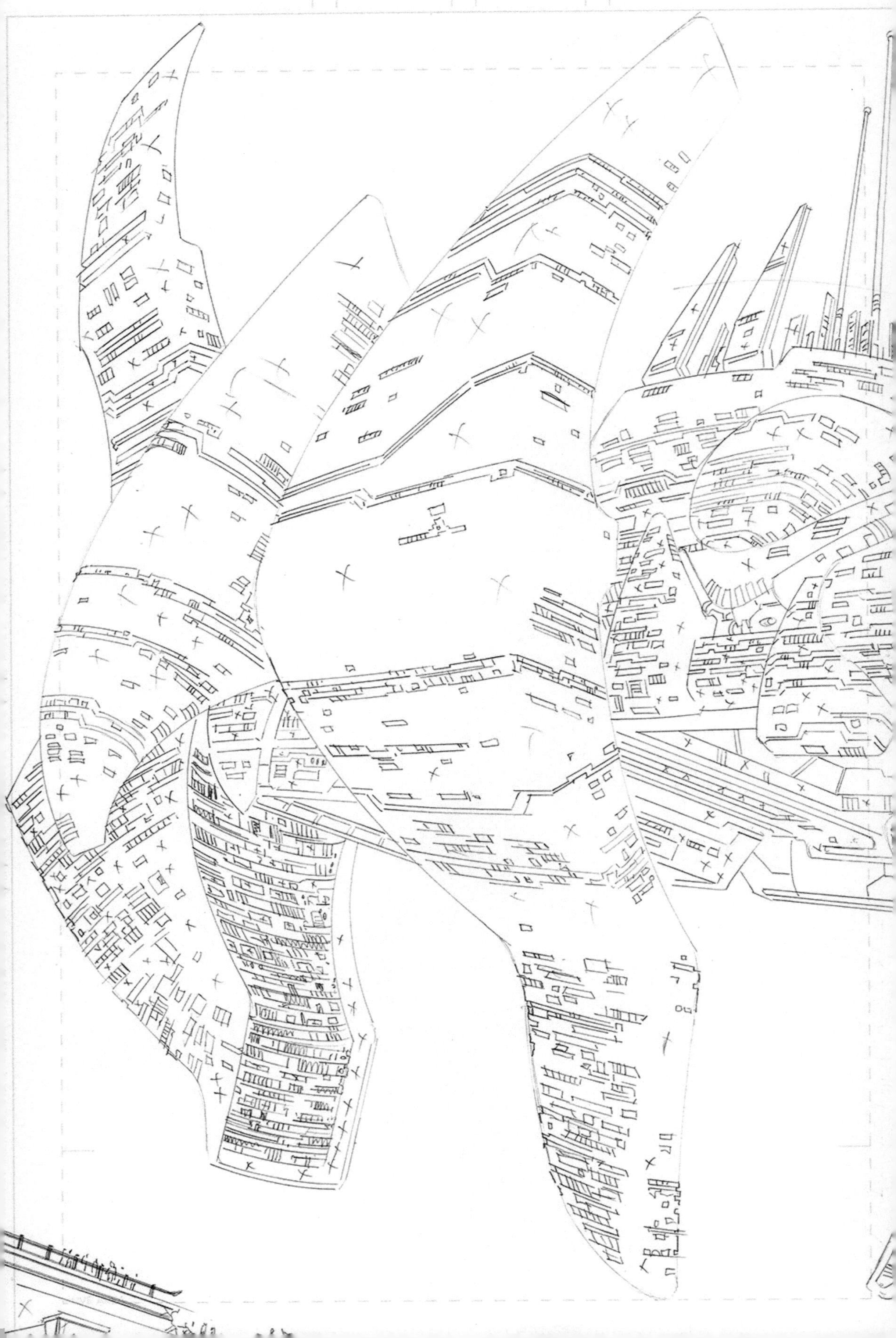

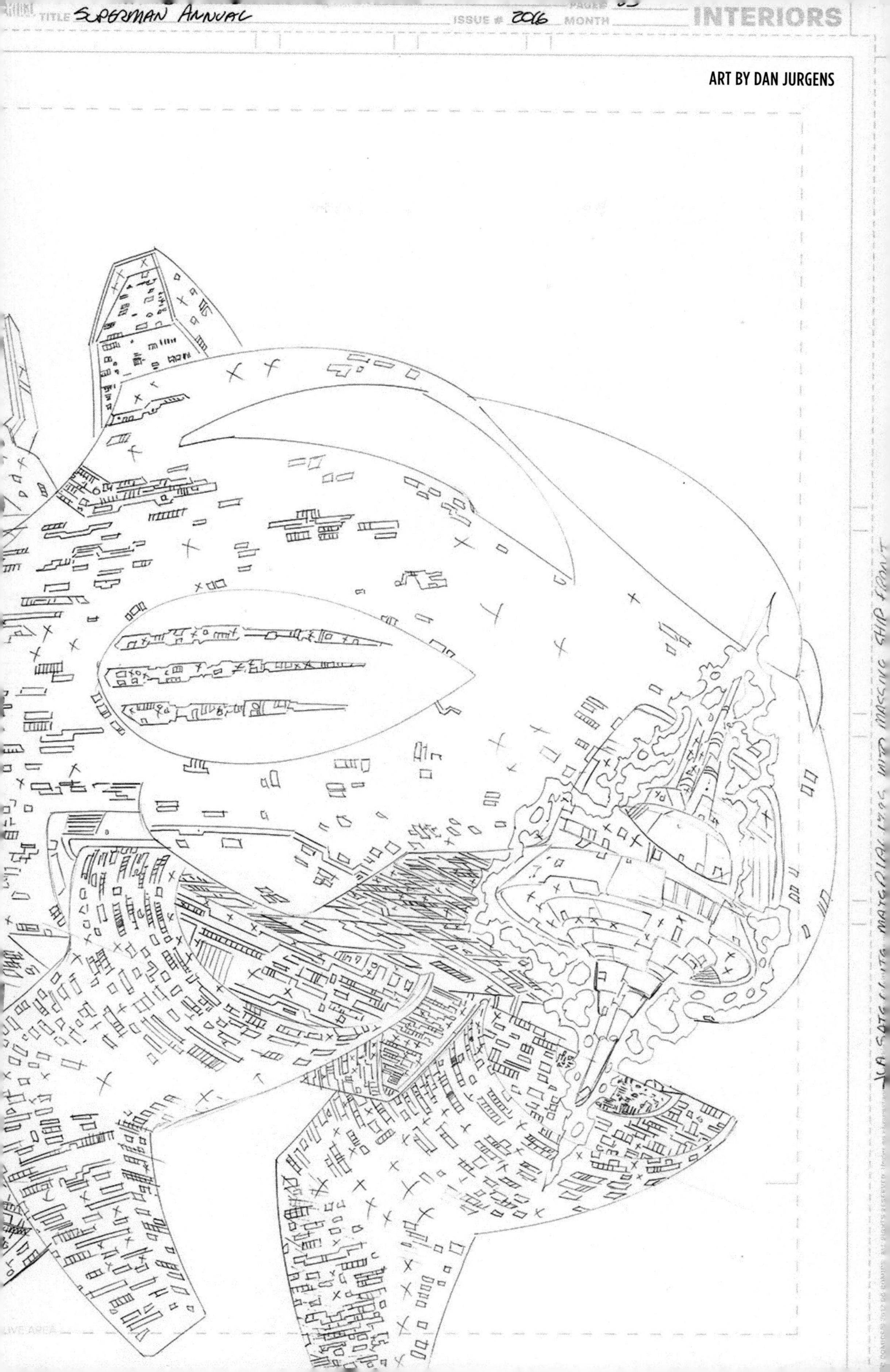
TITLE SUPERMAN ANNUAL
ISSUE # 2016
MONTH
INTERIORS
LIVE AREA
ART BY DAN JURGENS

ART BY ARDIAN SYAF

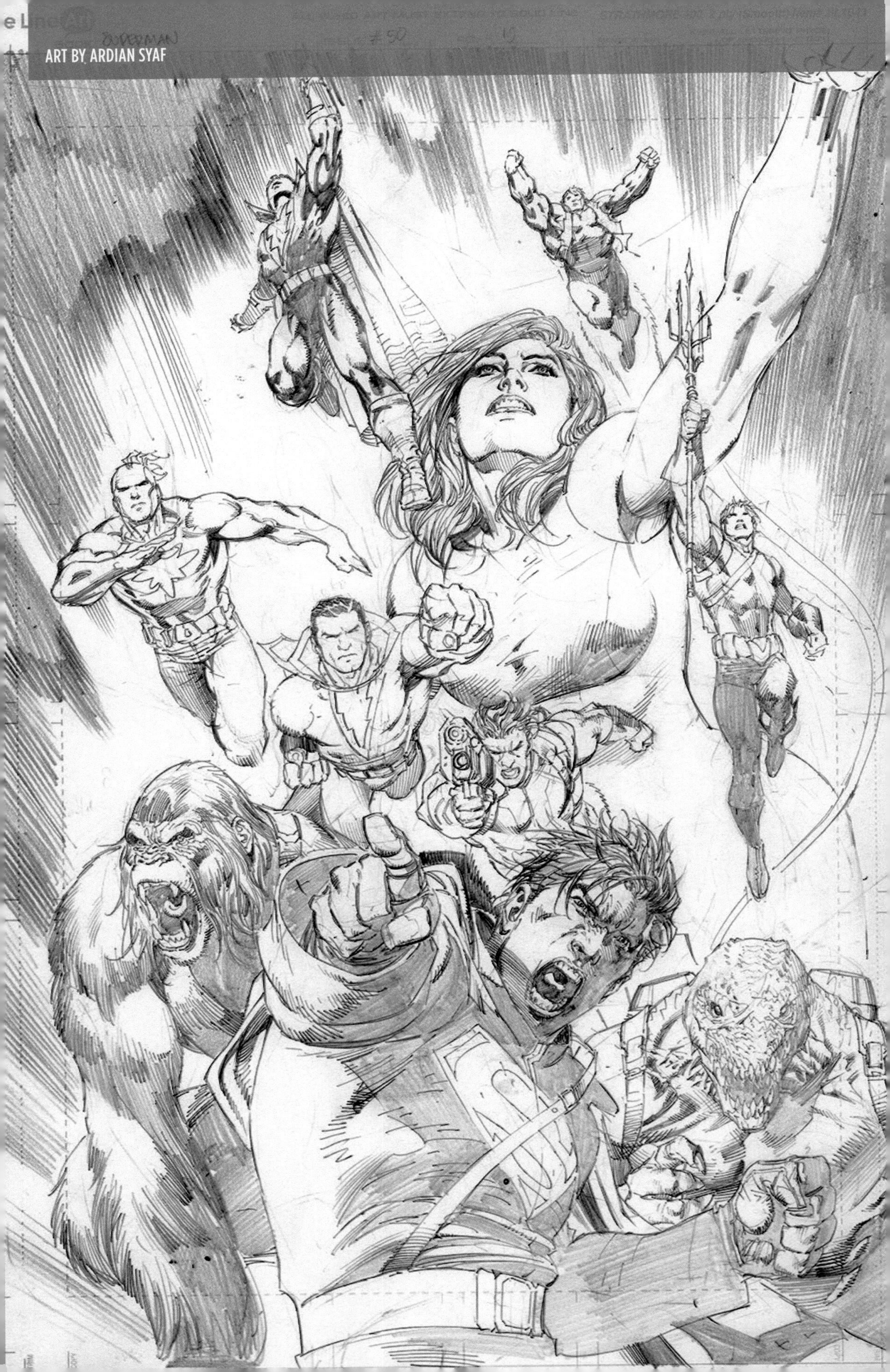

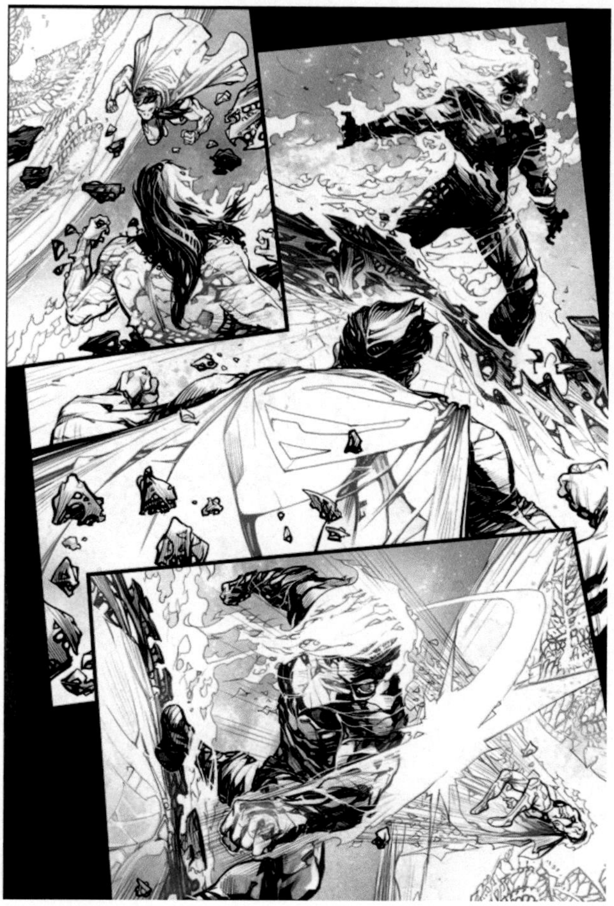

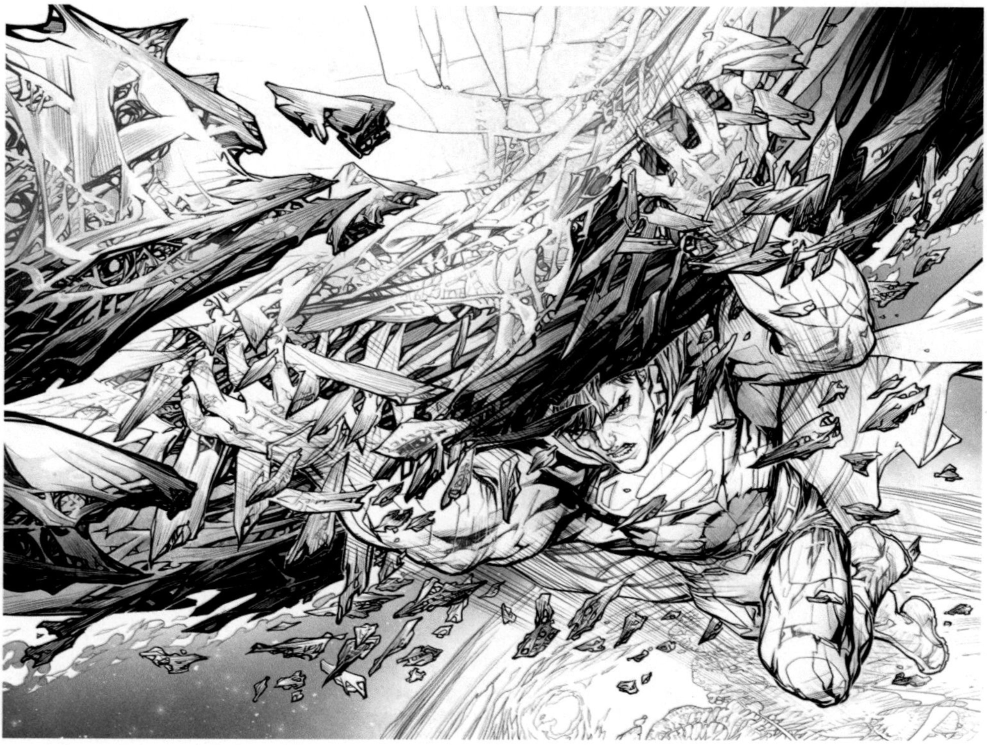

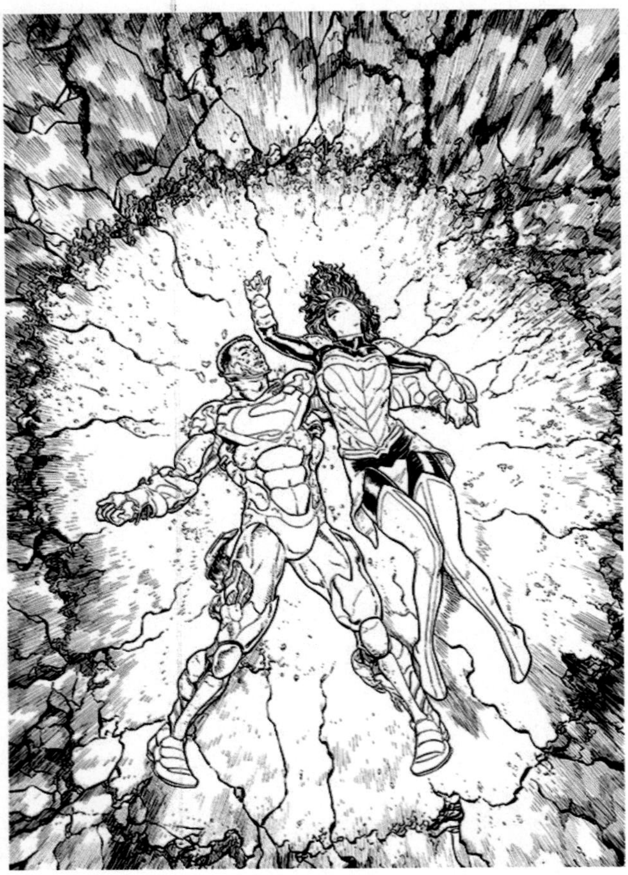

ART BY AARON KUDER

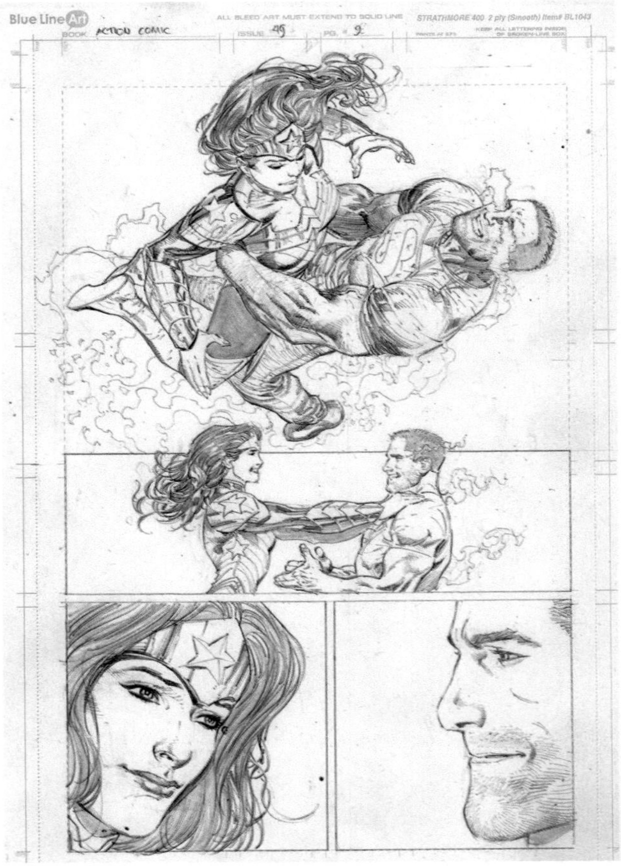
Blue Line Art
ALL BLEED ART MUST EXTEND TO SOLID LINE

ART BY ARDIAN SYAF